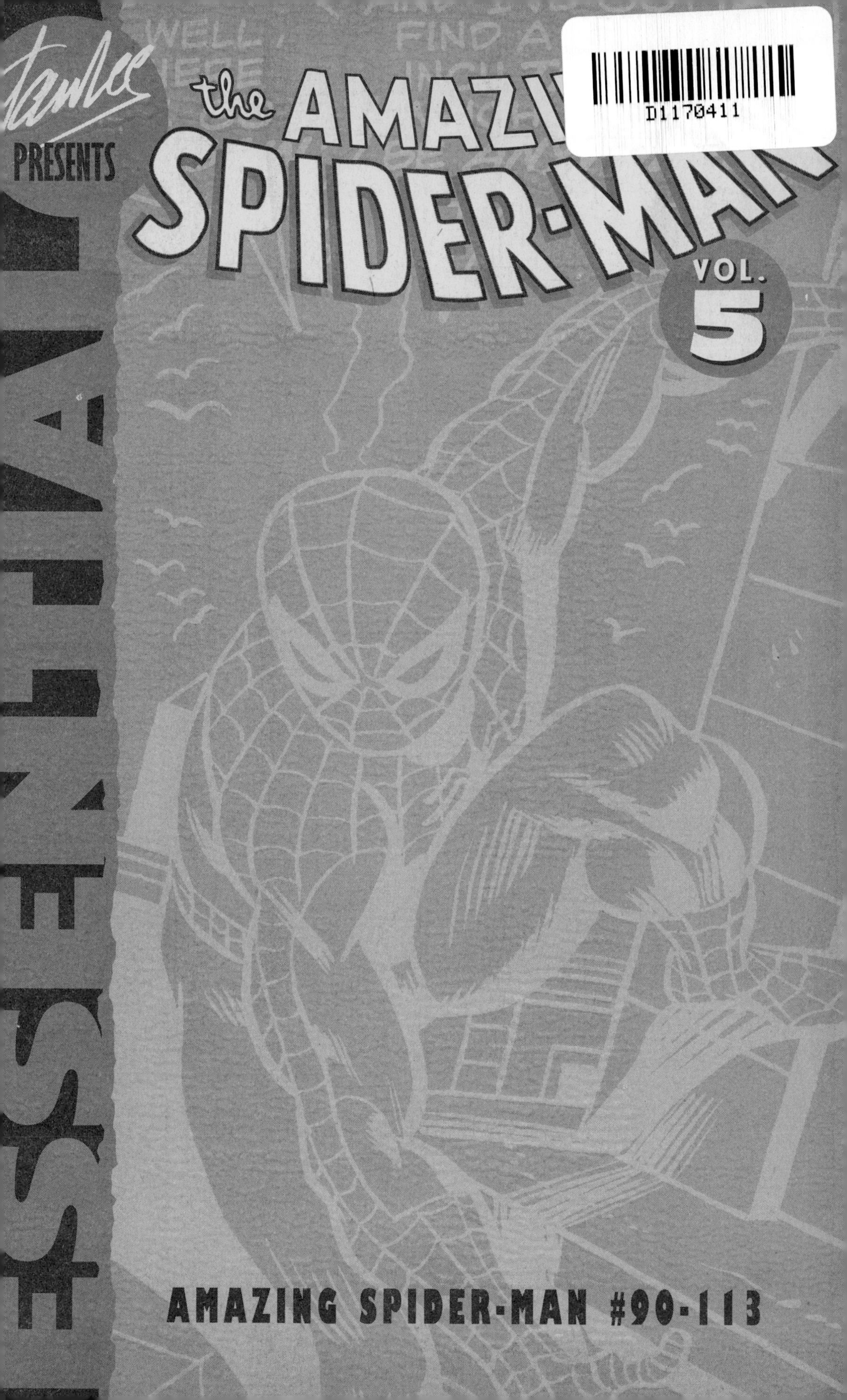
Stan Lee
PRESENTS
ESSENTIAL
the AMAZI
SPIDER-MAN
VOL. 5
AMAZING SPIDER-MAN #90-113

ESSENTIAL the AMAZING SPIDER-MAN VOL. 5

the AMAZING SPIDER-MAN #90

"AND DEATH SHALL COME"

WRITER: STAN LEE
PENCILER: GIL KANE
INKER: JOHN ROMITA
LETTERER: SAM ROSEN

the AMAZING SPIDER-MAN #91

"TO SMASH A SPIDER"

WRITER: STAN LEE
PENCILER: GIL KANE
INKER: JOHN ROMITA
LETTERER: SAM ROSEN

the AMAZING SPIDER-MAN #92

"WHEN ICEMAN ATTACKS"

WRITER: STAN LEE
PENCILER: GIL KANE
INKER: JOHN ROMITA
LETTERER: ART SIMEK

THE AMAZING SPIDER-MAN #93

"THE LADY AND THE PROWLER"

WRITER: STAN LEE
ILLUSTRATOR: JOHN ROMITA
LETTERER: ART SIMEK

THE AMAZING SPIDER-MAN #94

"ON WINGS OF DEATH"

WRITER: STAN LEE
PENCILER: JOHN ROMITA
INKER: SAL BUSCEMA
LETTERER: ART SIMEK

THE AMAZING SPIDER-MAN #95

"TRAP FOR A TERRORIST"

WRITER: STAN LEE
PENCILER: JOHN ROMITA
INKER: SAL BUSCEMA
LETTERER: ART SIMEK

THE AMAZING SPIDER-MAN #96

"AND NOW, THE GOBLIN"

WRITER: STAN LEE
PENCILER: GIL KANE
INKER: JOHN ROMITA
LETTERER: ART SIMEK

THE AMAZING SPIDER-MAN #97

"IN THE GRIP OF THE GOBLIN"

WRITER: STAN LEE
PENCILER: GIL KANE
INKER: FRANK GIACOIA
LETTERER: SAM ROSEN

THE AMAZING SPIDER-MAN #98

"THE GOBLIN'S LAST GASP'

WRITER: STAN LEE
PENCILER: GIL KANE
INKER: FRANK GIACOIA
LETTERER: ART SIMEK

THE AMAZING SPIDER-MAN #99

"A DAY IN THE LIFE OF..."

WRITER: STAN LEE
PENCILER: GIL KANE
INKER: FRANK GIACOIA
LETTERER: ART SIMEK

THE AMAZING SPIDER-MAN #100

"THE SPIDER OR THE MAN?"

WRITER: STAN LEE
PENCILER: GIL KANE
INKER: FRANK GIACOIA
LETTERER: ART SIMEK

THE AMAZING SPIDER-MAN #101

"A MONSTER CALLED MORBIUS"

WRITER: ROY THOMAS
PENCILER: GIL KANE
INKER: FRANK GIACOIA
LETTERER: ART SIMEK

the AMAZING SPIDER-MAN #107

"SPIDEY SMASHES THRU

WRITER: STAN LEE
PENCILER: JOHN ROMITA
INKER: FRANK GIACOIA
LETTERER: ART SIMEK

the AMAZING SPIDER-MAN #108

"VENGANCE FROM VIETNAM

WRITER: STAN LEE
ILLUSTRATOR: JOHN ROMITA
LETTERER: ART SIMEK

the AMAZING SPIDER-MAN #109

"ENTER: DR. STRANGE"

WRITER: STAN LEE
ILLUSTRATOR: JOHN ROMITA
LETTERER: ART SIMEK

the AMAZING SPIDER-MAN #110

"THE BIRTH OF THE GIBBON

WRITER: STAN LEE
ILLUSTRATOR: JOHN ROMITA
LETTERER: JOHN COSTANZA

SPECIAL THANKS TO: Tom Brevoort
Ralph Macchio
Darby McShain
Jared Osborn

ESSENTIAL SPIDER-MAN® VOL. 5. Contains material originally published in magazine form as AMAZING SPIDER-MAN (Vol. 1) #90-113. First printing, March 2002. ISBN# 0-7851-0881-5. Published by MARVEL COMICS, a division of MARVEL ENTERTAINMENT GROUP, INC. OFFICE OF PUBLICATION: 10 EAST 40th STREET, NEW YORK, NY 10016. Copyright © 1970, 1971, 1972 and 2002 Marvel Characters, Inc. All rights reserved. Price $14.95 in the U.S. and $23.95 in Canada (GST #R127032852). No similarity between any of the names, characters, persons, and/or institutions in this publication with those of any living or dead person or institutions is intended, and any such similarity which may exist is purely coincidental. This publication may not be sold except by authorized dealers and is sold subject to the conditions that it shall not be sold or distributed with any part of its cover or markings removed, nor in a mutilated condition. SPIDER-MAN (including prominent characters featured in this publication and the distinctive likenesses thereof) is a trademark of MARVEL CHARACTERS, INC. Printed in Canada. PETER CUNEO, Chief Executive Officer; AVI ARAD, Chief Creative Officer; GUI KARYO, Chief Information Officer; STAN LEE, Chairman Emeritus.

10 9 8 7 6 5 4 3 2 1

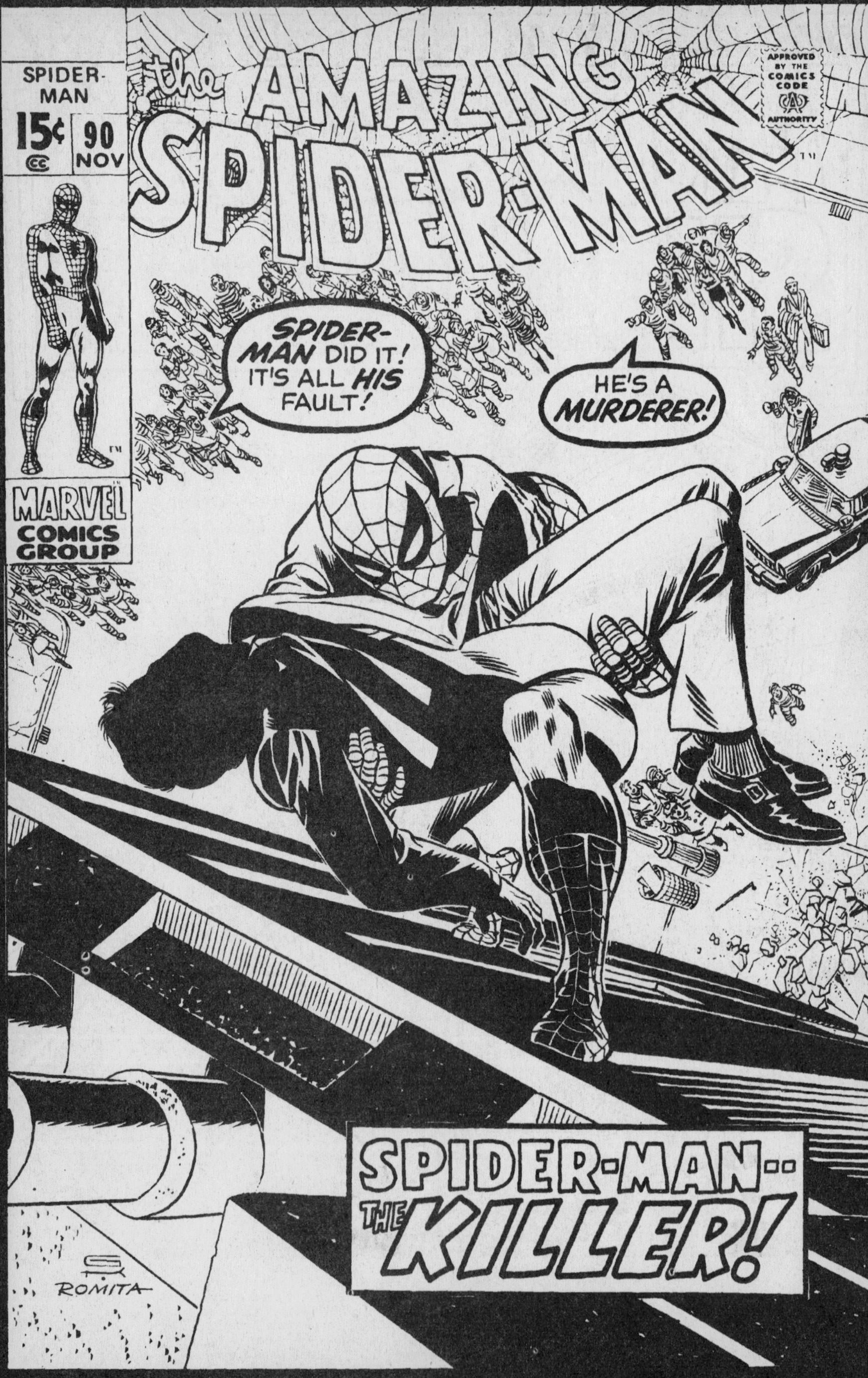
SPIDER-MAN
15¢
90
NOV
the AMAZING SPIDER-MAN
APPROVED BY THE COMICS CODE AUTHORITY
MARVEL COMICS GROUP
SPIDER-MAN DID IT! IT'S ALL HIS FAULT!
HE'S A MURDERER!
SPIDER-MAN.. THE KILLER!
ROMITA

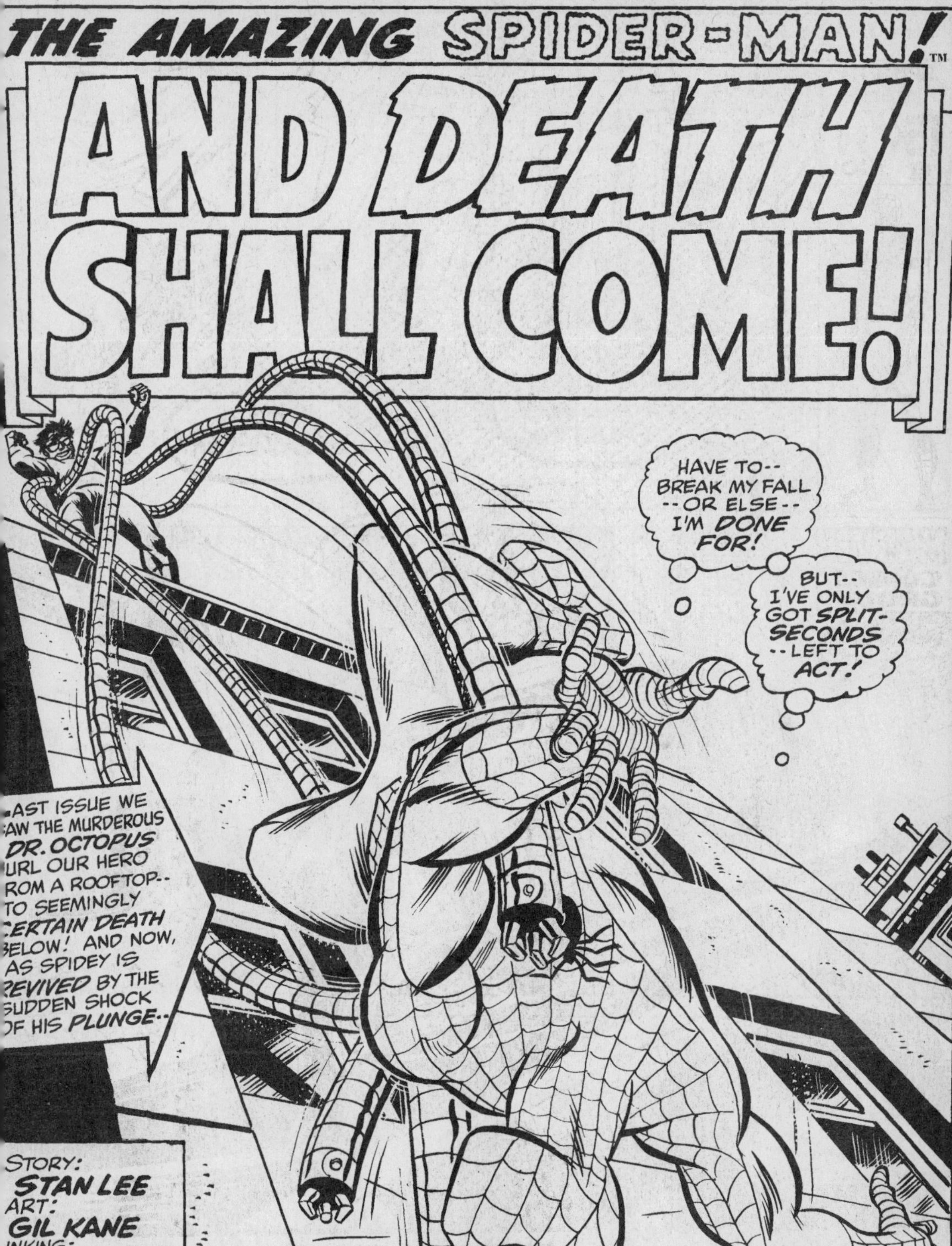

THE AMAZING SPIDER-MAN! TM
AND DEATH SHALL COME!
HAVE TO-- BREAK MY FALL --OR ELSE-- I'M DONE FOR!
BUT-- I'VE ONLY GOT SPLIT-SECONDS --LEFT TO ACT!
LAST ISSUE WE SAW THE MURDEROUS DR. OCTOPUS HURL OUR HERO FROM A ROOFTOP-- TO SEEMINGLY CERTAIN DEATH BELOW! AND NOW, AS SPIDEY IS REVIVED BY THE SUDDEN SHOCK OF HIS PLUNGE--
STORY: STAN LEE
ART: GIL KANE
INKING: JOHN ROMITA
LETTERING: SAM ROSEN

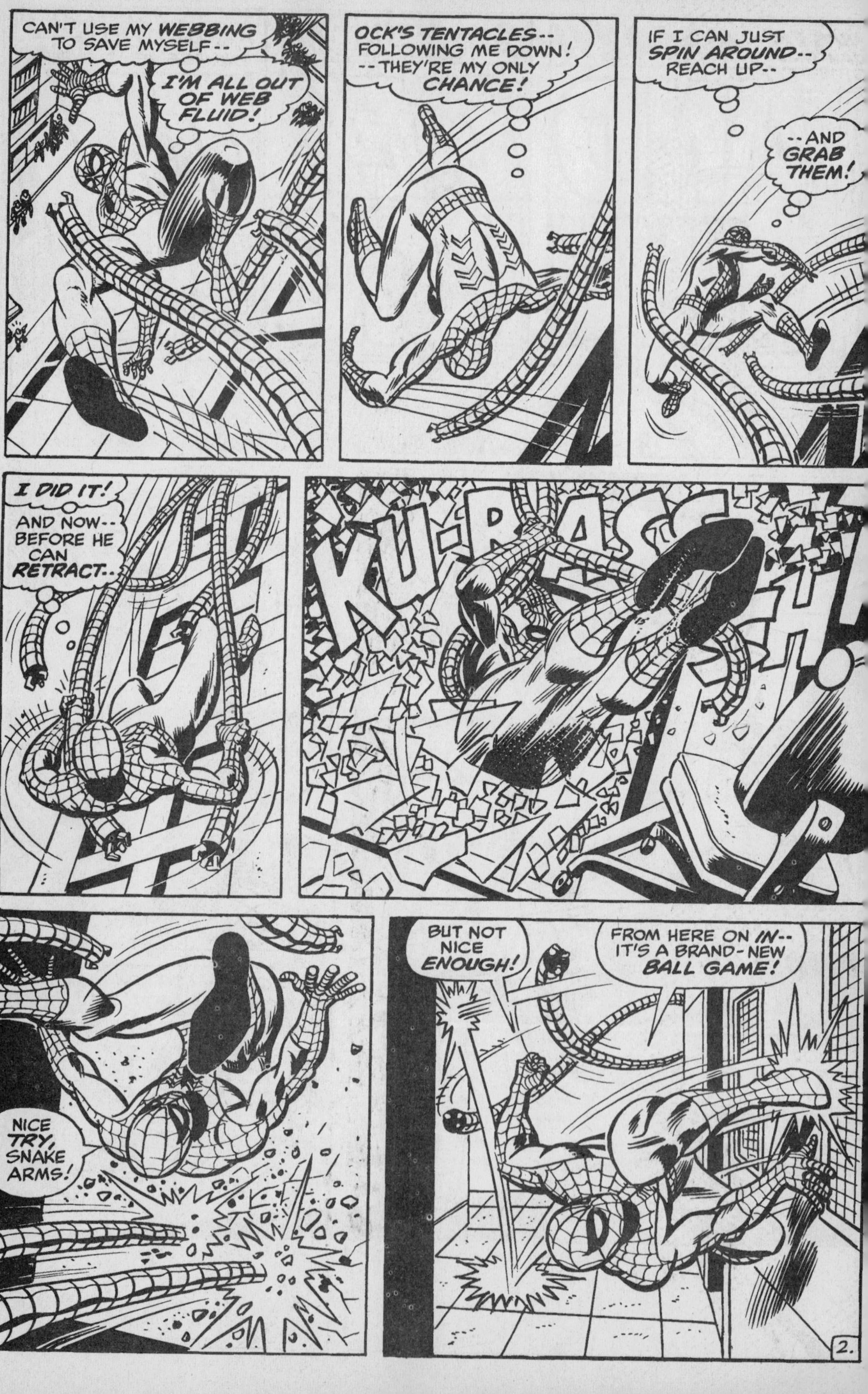
CAN'T USE MY WEBBING TO SAVE MYSELF--
I'M ALL OUT OF WEB FLUID!
OCK'S TENTACLES-- FOLLOWING ME DOWN! --THEY'RE MY ONLY CHANCE!
IF I CAN JUST SPIN AROUND-- REACH UP--
--AND GRAB THEM!
I DID IT!
AND NOW-- BEFORE HE CAN RETRACT--
KU-RASSH!
NICE TRY, SNAKE ARMS!
BUT NOT NICE ENOUGH!
FROM HERE ON IN-- IT'S A BRAND-NEW BALL GAME!
2.

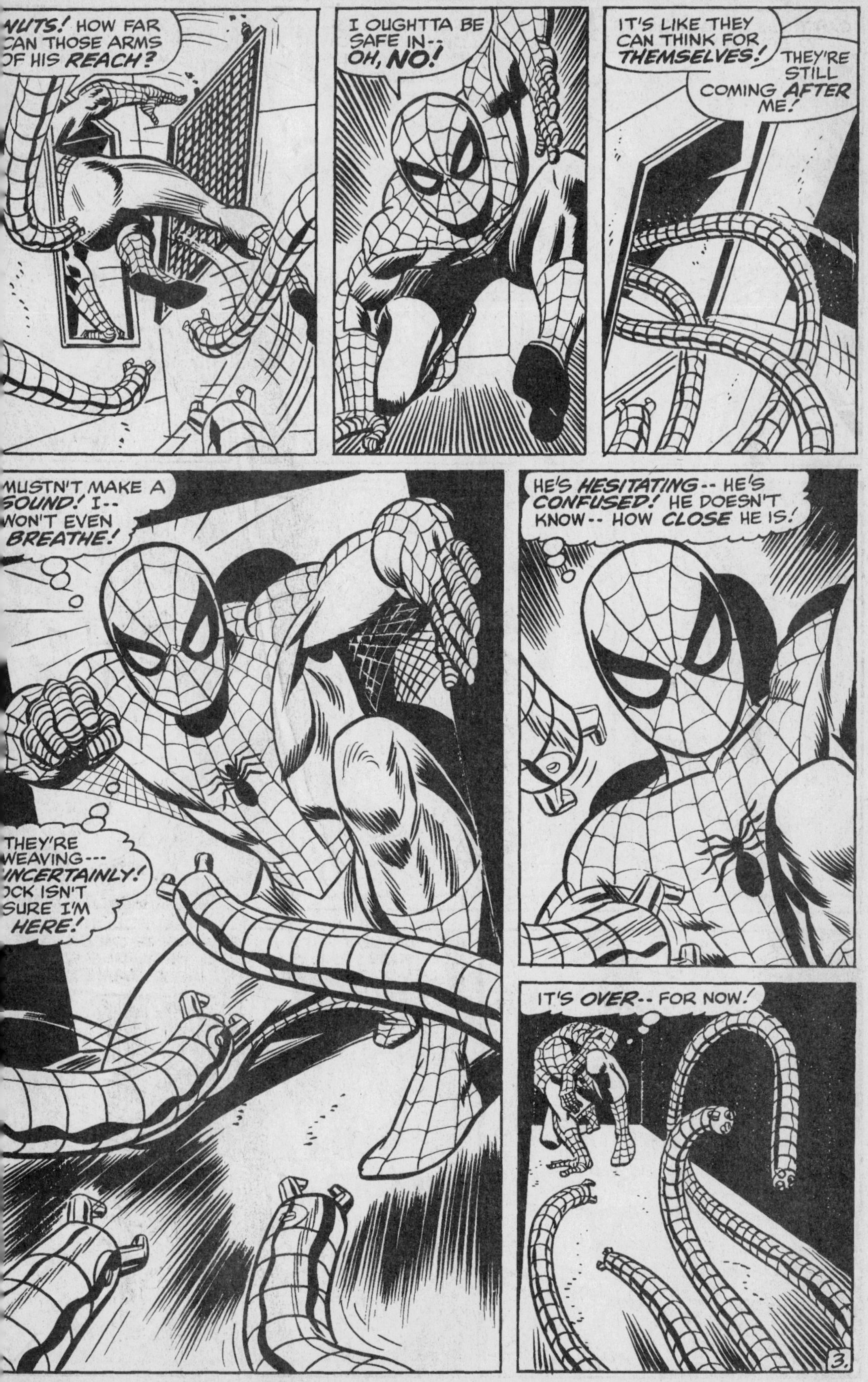

NUTS! HOW FAR CAN THOSE ARMS OF HIS REACH?
I OUGHTTA BE SAFE IN-- OH, NO!
IT'S LIKE THEY CAN THINK FOR THEMSELVES!
THEY'RE STILL COMING AFTER ME!
MUSTN'T MAKE A SOUND! I-- WON'T EVEN BREATHE!
THEY'RE WEAVING--- UNCERTAINLY! OCK ISN'T SURE I'M HERE!
HE'S HESITATING-- HE'S CONFUSED! HE DOESN'T KNOW-- HOW CLOSE HE IS!
IT'S OVER-- FOR NOW!
3.

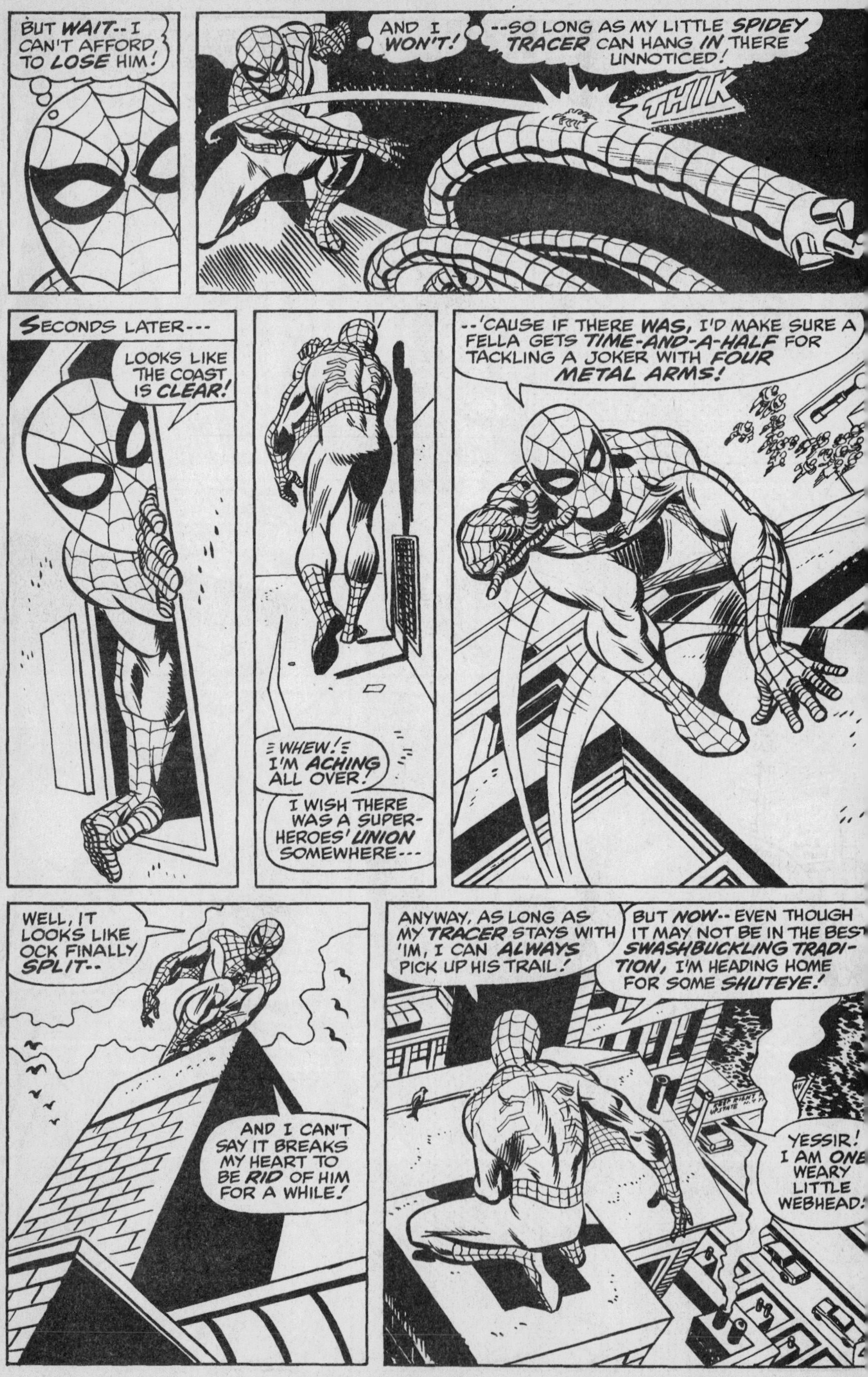

BUT WAIT-- I CAN'T AFFORD TO LOSE HIM!
AND I WON'T!
--SO LONG AS MY LITTLE SPIDEY TRACER CAN HANG IN THERE UNNOTICED!
THIK
SECONDS LATER---
LOOKS LIKE THE COAST IS CLEAR!
WHEW! I'M ACHING ALL OVER!
I WISH THERE WAS A SUPER-HEROES' UNION SOMEWHERE---
--'CAUSE IF THERE WAS, I'D MAKE SURE A FELLA GETS TIME-AND-A-HALF FOR TACKLING A JOKER WITH FOUR METAL ARMS!
WELL, IT LOOKS LIKE OCK FINALLY SPLIT--
AND I CAN'T SAY IT BREAKS MY HEART TO BE RID OF HIM FOR A WHILE!
ANYWAY, AS LONG AS MY TRACER STAYS WITH 'IM, I CAN ALWAYS PICK UP HIS TRAIL!
BUT NOW-- EVEN THOUGH IT MAY NOT BE IN THE BEST SWASHBUCKLING TRADITION, I'M HEADING HOME FOR SOME SHUTEYE!
YESSIR! I AM ONE WEARY LITTLE WEBHEAD!

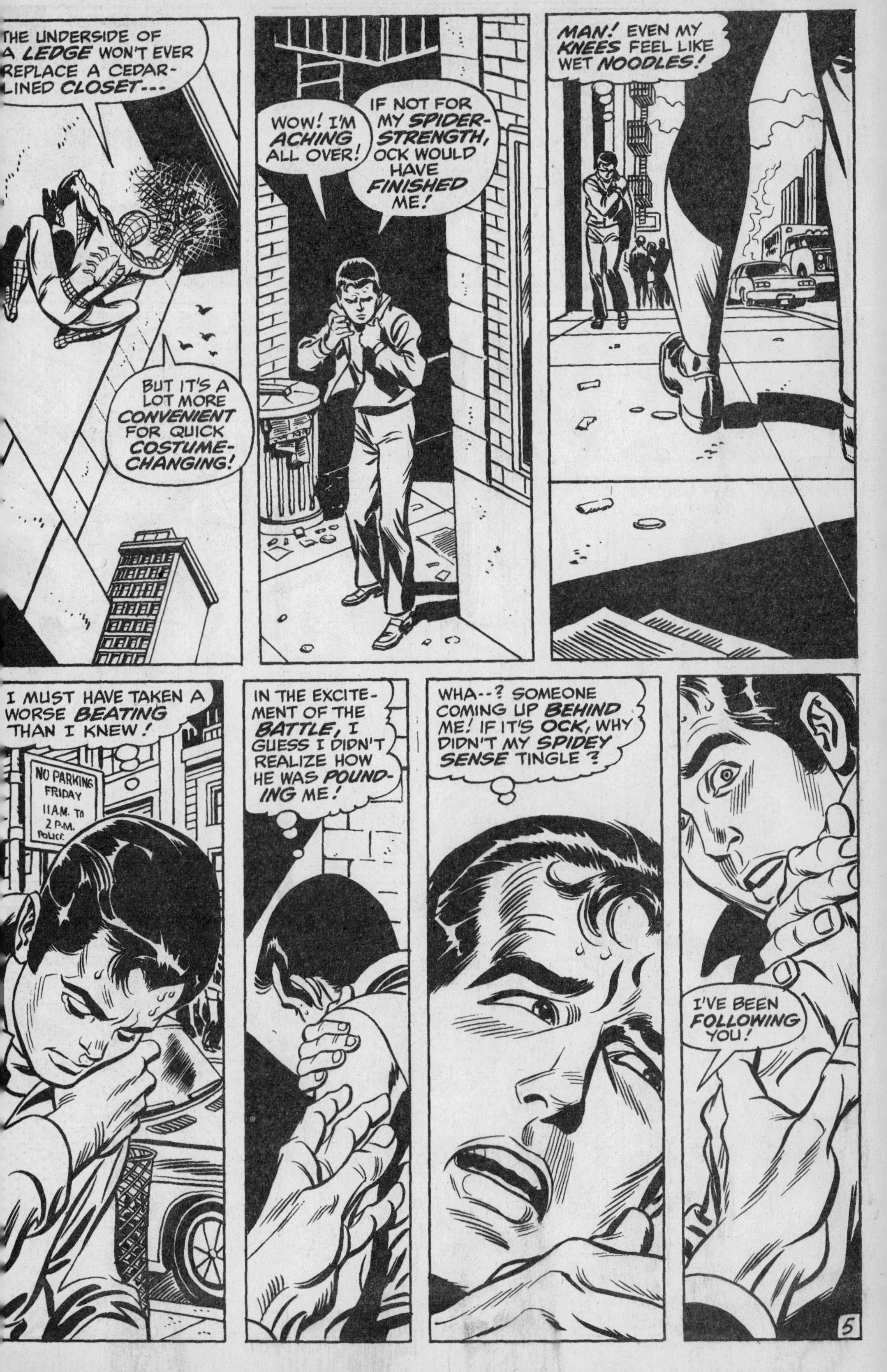
THE UNDERSIDE OF A LEDGE WON'T EVER REPLACE A CEDAR-LINED CLOSET---
BUT IT'S A LOT MORE CONVENIENT FOR QUICK COSTUME-CHANGING!
WOW! I'M ACHING ALL OVER!
IF NOT FOR MY SPIDER-STRENGTH, OCK WOULD HAVE FINISHED ME!
MAN! EVEN MY KNEES FEEL LIKE WET NOODLES!
I MUST HAVE TAKEN A WORSE BEATING THAN I KNEW!
NO PARKING FRIDAY 11 A.M. TO 2 P.M.
IN THE EXCITEMENT OF THE BATTLE, I GUESS I DIDN'T REALIZE HOW HE WAS POUNDING ME!
WHA--? SOMEONE COMING UP BEHIND ME! IF IT'S OCK, WHY DIDN'T MY SPIDEY SENSE TINGLE?
I'VE BEEN FOLLOWING YOU!
5

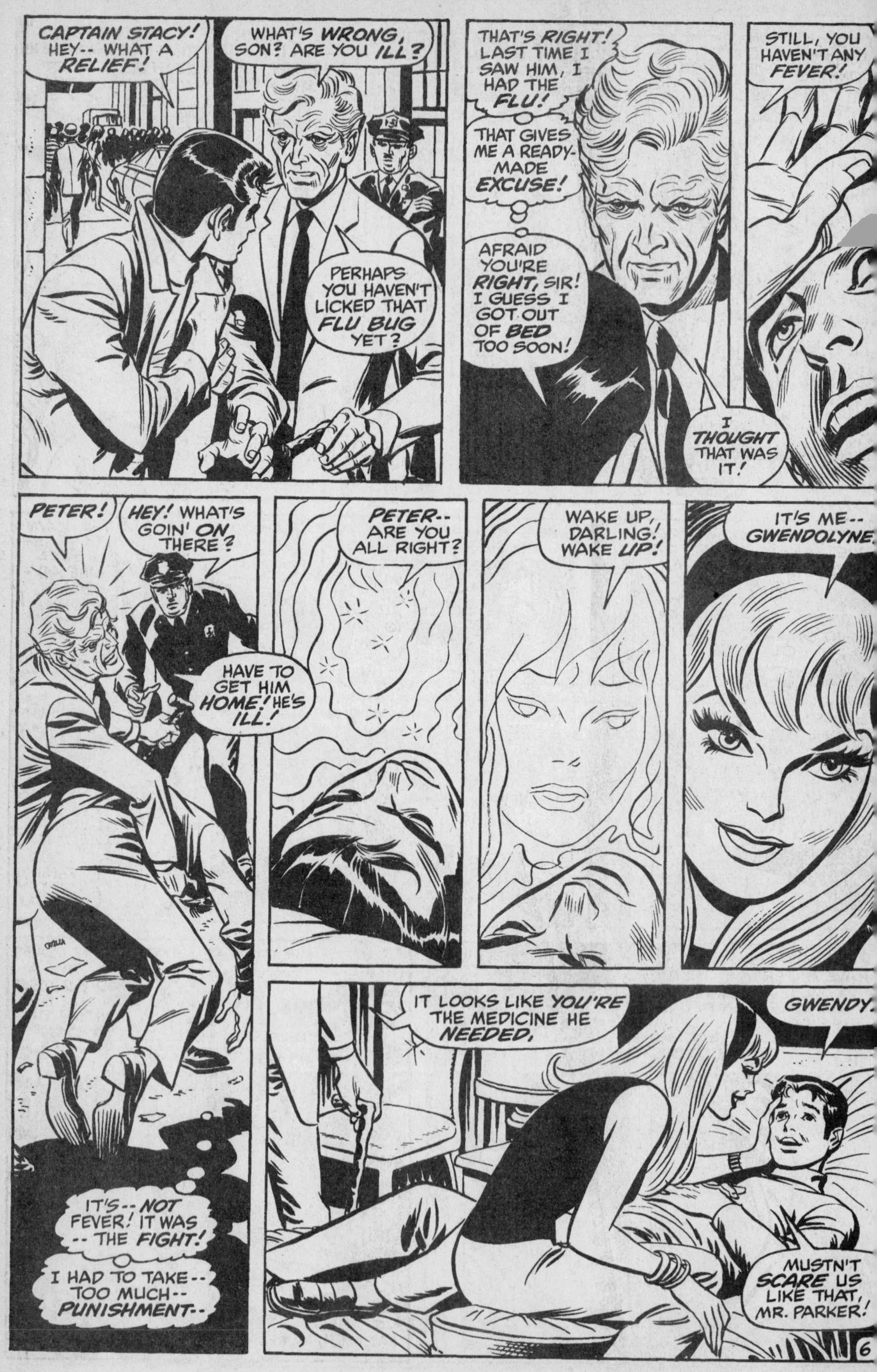
CAPTAIN STACY! HEY-- WHAT A RELIEF!
WHAT'S WRONG, SON? ARE YOU ILL?
PERHAPS YOU HAVEN'T LICKED THAT FLU BUG YET?
THAT'S RIGHT! LAST TIME I SAW HIM, I HAD THE FLU!
THAT GIVES ME A READY-MADE EXCUSE!
AFRAID YOU'RE RIGHT, SIR! I GUESS I GOT OUT OF BED TOO SOON!
STILL, YOU HAVEN'T ANY FEVER!
I THOUGHT THAT WAS IT!
PETER!
HEY! WHAT'S GOIN' ON THERE?
HAVE TO GET HIM HOME! HE'S ILL!
IT'S--NOT FEVER! IT WAS -- THE FIGHT!
I HAD TO TAKE-- TOO MUCH-- PUNISHMENT--
PETER-- ARE YOU ALL RIGHT?
WAKE UP, DARLING! WAKE UP!
IT'S ME-- GWENDOLYNE.
IT LOOKS LIKE YOU'RE THE MEDICINE HE NEEDED.
GWENDY.
MUSTN'T SCARE US LIKE THAT, MR. PARKER!
6

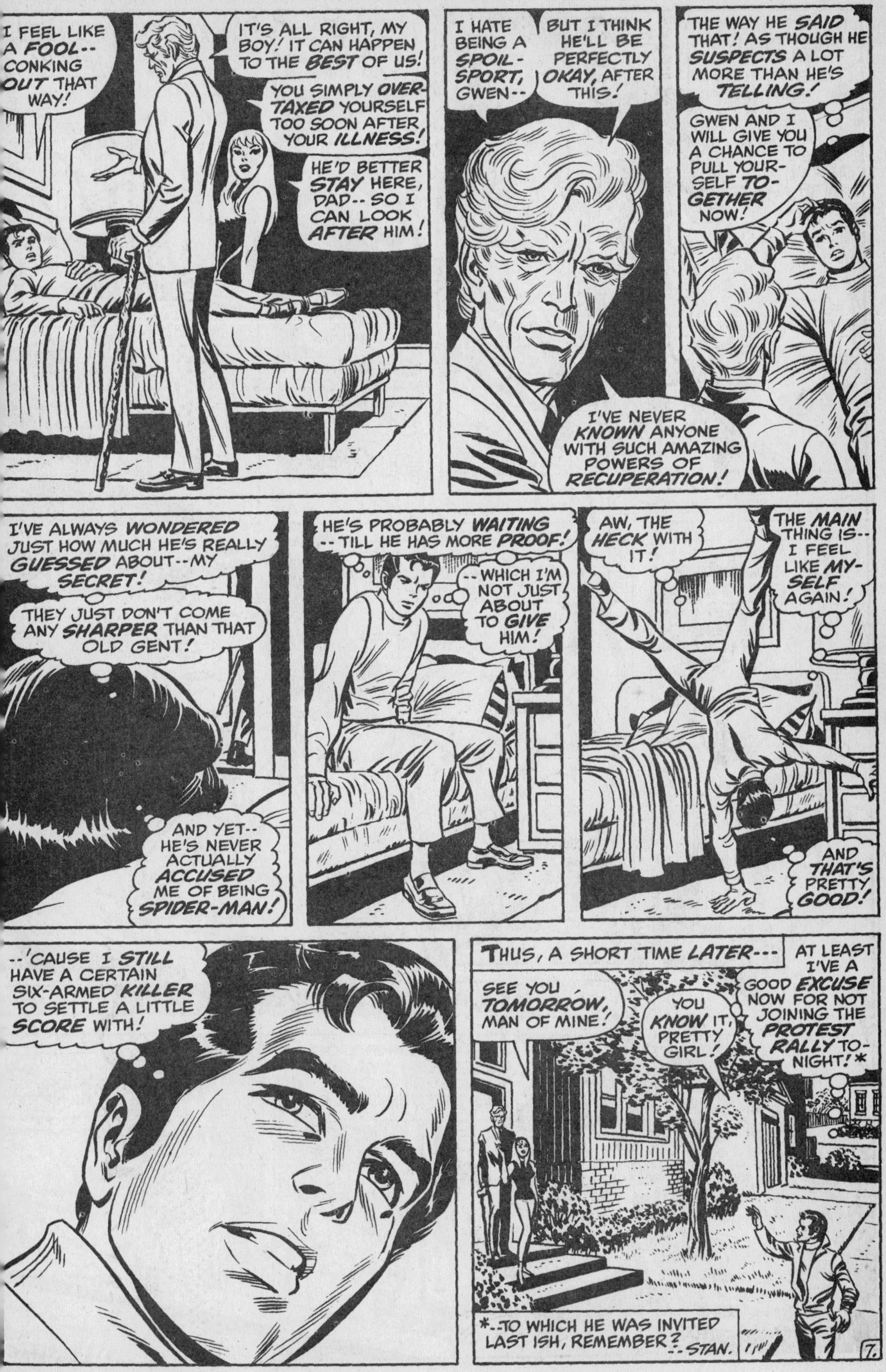

I FEEL LIKE A FOOL-- CONKING OUT THAT WAY!
IT'S ALL RIGHT, MY BOY! IT CAN HAPPEN TO THE BEST OF US!
YOU SIMPLY OVER-TAXED YOURSELF TOO SOON AFTER YOUR ILLNESS!
HE'D BETTER STAY HERE, DAD-- SO I CAN LOOK AFTER HIM!
I HATE BEING A SPOIL-SPORT, GWEN--
BUT I THINK HE'LL BE PERFECTLY OKAY, AFTER THIS!
I'VE NEVER KNOWN ANYONE WITH SUCH AMAZING POWERS OF RECUPERATION!
THE WAY HE SAID THAT! AS THOUGH HE SUSPECTS A LOT MORE THAN HE'S TELLING!
GWEN AND I WILL GIVE YOU A CHANCE TO PULL YOUR-SELF TO-GETHER NOW!
I'VE ALWAYS WONDERED JUST HOW MUCH HE'S REALLY GUESSED ABOUT--MY SECRET!
THEY JUST DON'T COME ANY SHARPER THAN THAT OLD GENT!
AND YET-- HE'S NEVER ACTUALLY ACCUSED ME OF BEING SPIDER-MAN!
HE'S PROBABLY WAITING -- TILL HE HAS MORE PROOF!
--WHICH I'M NOT JUST ABOUT TO GIVE HIM!
AW, THE HECK WITH IT!
THE MAIN THING IS-- I FEEL LIKE MY-SELF AGAIN!
AND THAT'S PRETTY GOOD!
--'CAUSE I STILL HAVE A CERTAIN SIX-ARMED KILLER TO SETTLE A LITTLE SCORE WITH!
THUS, A SHORT TIME LATER---
SEE YOU TOMORROW, MAN OF MINE!
YOU KNOW IT, PRETTY GIRL!
AT LEAST I'VE A GOOD EXCUSE NOW FOR NOT JOINING THE PROTEST RALLY TO-NIGHT!*
*--TO WHICH HE WAS INVITED LAST ISH, REMEMBER? --STAN.
7.

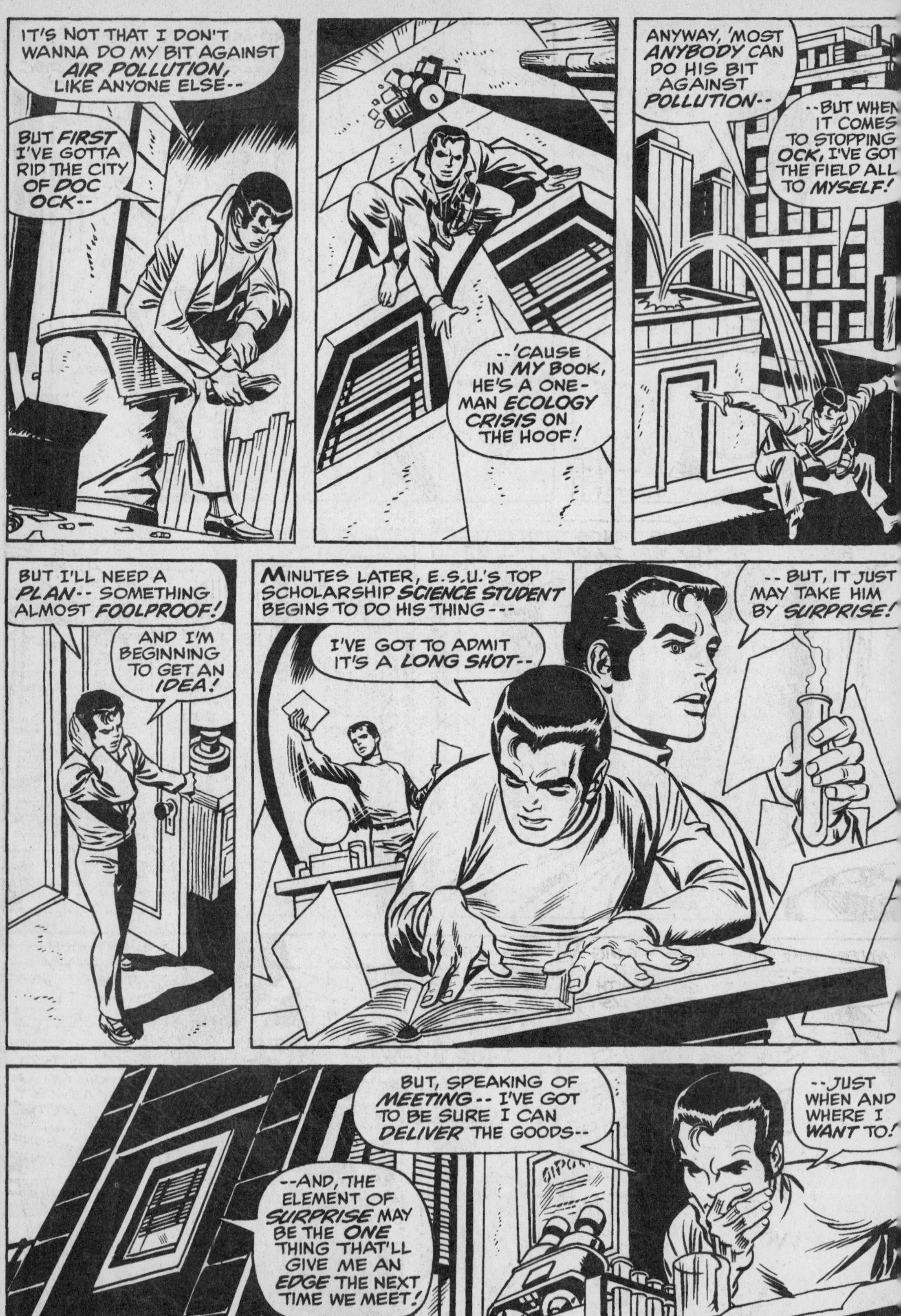
IT'S NOT THAT I DON'T WANNA DO MY BIT AGAINST AIR POLLUTION, LIKE ANYONE ELSE--
BUT FIRST I'VE GOTTA RID THE CITY OF DOC OCK--
--'CAUSE IN MY BOOK, HE'S A ONE-MAN ECOLOGY CRISIS ON THE HOOF!
ANYWAY, 'MOST ANYBODY CAN DO HIS BIT AGAINST POLLUTION--
--BUT WHEN IT COMES TO STOPPING OCK, I'VE GOT THE FIELD ALL TO MYSELF!
BUT I'LL NEED A PLAN-- SOMETHING ALMOST FOOLPROOF!
AND I'M BEGINNING TO GET AN IDEA!
MINUTES LATER, E.S.U.'S TOP SCHOLARSHIP SCIENCE STUDENT BEGINS TO DO HIS THING---
I'VE GOT TO ADMIT IT'S A LONG SHOT--
-- BUT, IT JUST MAY TAKE HIM BY SURPRISE!
BUT, SPEAKING OF MEETING-- I'VE GOT TO BE SURE I CAN DELIVER THE GOODS--
--JUST WHEN AND WHERE I WANT TO!
--AND, THE ELEMENT OF SURPRISE MAY BE THE ONE THING THAT'LL GIVE ME AN EDGE THE NEXT TIME WE MEET!
8

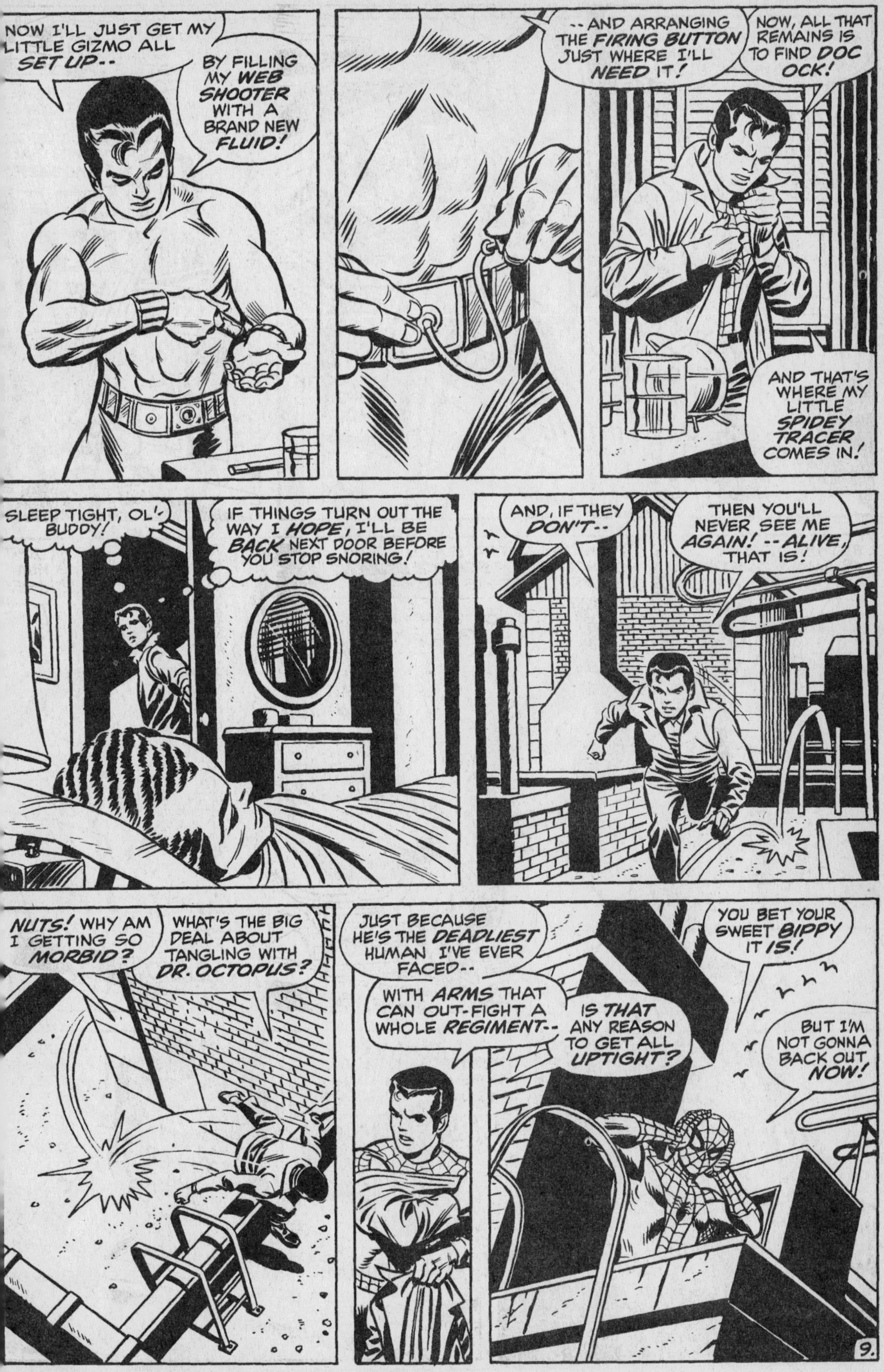

NOW I'LL JUST GET MY LITTLE GIZMO ALL SET UP--
BY FILLING MY WEB SHOOTER WITH A BRAND NEW FLUID!
--AND ARRANGING THE FIRING BUTTON JUST WHERE I'LL NEED IT!
NOW, ALL THAT REMAINS IS TO FIND DOC OCK!
AND THAT'S WHERE MY LITTLE SPIDEY TRACER COMES IN!
SLEEP TIGHT, OL' BUDDY!
IF THINGS TURN OUT THE WAY I HOPE, I'LL BE BACK NEXT DOOR BEFORE YOU STOP SNORING!
AND, IF THEY DON'T--
THEN YOU'LL NEVER SEE ME AGAIN! --ALIVE, THAT IS!
NUTS! WHY AM I GETTING SO MORBID?
WHAT'S THE BIG DEAL ABOUT TANGLING WITH DR. OCTOPUS?
JUST BECAUSE HE'S THE DEADLIEST HUMAN I'VE EVER FACED--
WITH ARMS THAT CAN OUT-FIGHT A WHOLE REGIMENT--
IS THAT ANY REASON TO GET ALL UPTIGHT?
YOU BET YOUR SWEET BIPPY IT IS!
BUT I'M NOT GONNA BACK OUT NOW!
9.

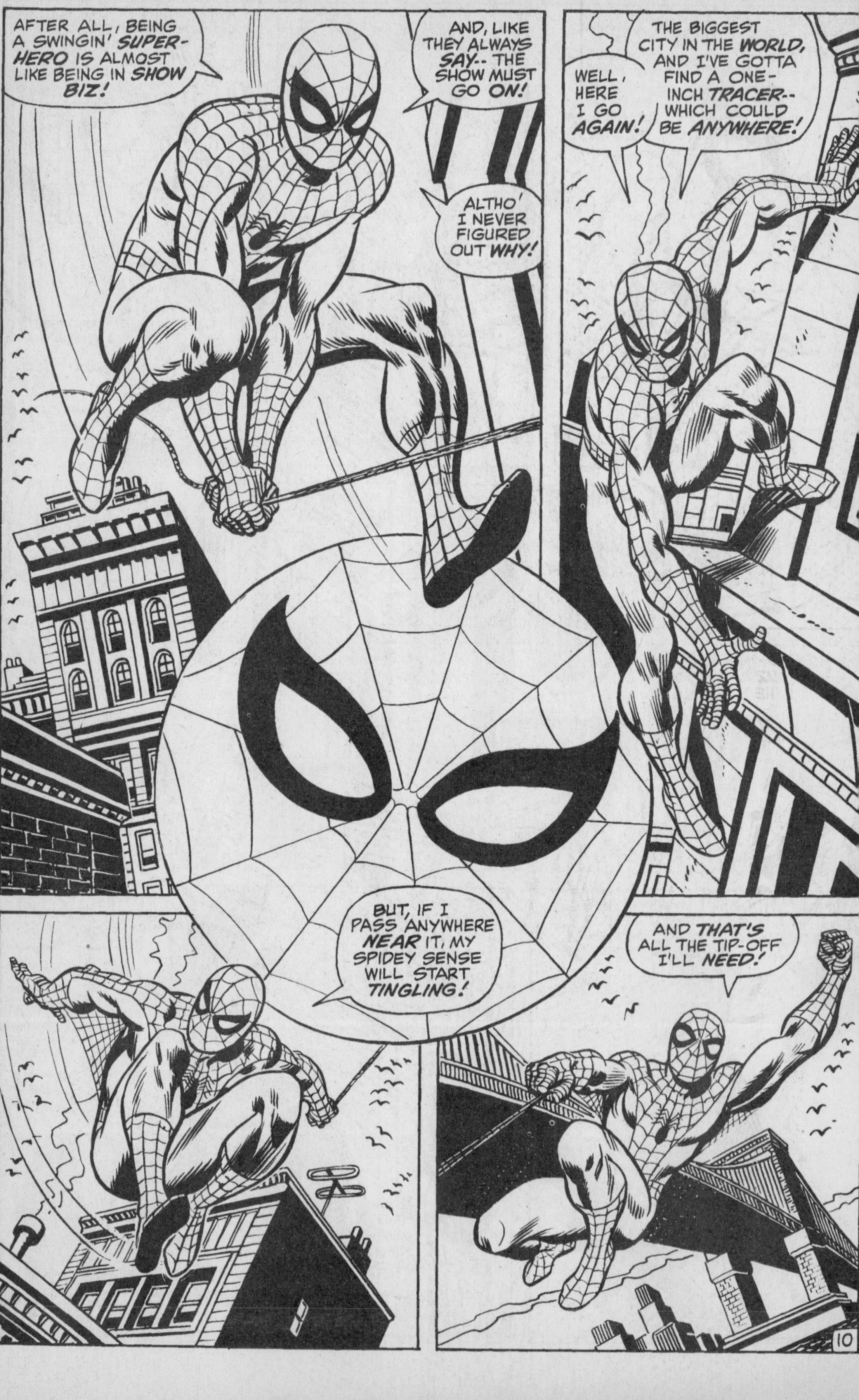
AFTER ALL, BEING A SWINGIN' SUPER-HERO IS ALMOST LIKE BEING IN SHOW BIZ!
AND, LIKE THEY ALWAYS SAY-- THE SHOW MUST GO ON!
ALTHO' I NEVER FIGURED OUT WHY!
WELL, HERE I GO AGAIN!
THE BIGGEST CITY IN THE WORLD, AND I'VE GOTTA FIND A ONE-INCH TRACER-- WHICH COULD BE ANYWHERE!
BUT, IF I PASS ANYWHERE NEAR IT, MY SPIDEY SENSE WILL START TINGLING!
AND THAT'S ALL THE TIP-OFF I'LL NEED!

THEN, ABOUT 82½ MINUTES LATER-- (FOR THE *STATISTI-CIANS* AMONG YOU) --

HE'S SOMEWHERE IN THE AREA!

ALL I HAVE TO DO IS *ZERO IN!*

THE TINGLING GETS *STRONGER* WHEN I CIRCLE THIS *BUILDING!*

THAT MEANS-- HE'S GOT TO BE *INSIDE!*

I'M HOMING-IN LIKE A *BUZZ BOMB!* THERE'S NO DOUBT ABOUT IT!

THAT *WINDOW* IS WHAT I'M AFTER!

I DON'T *GET IT!* THE ROOM'S *EMPTY!*

BUT-- THE *TINGLING* IS STRONGER THAN *EVER!*

OCK! HE WAS *WAITING* FOR ME!

THOD

I WAS A *FOOL!* I PUT TOO MUCH *FAITH* IN MY SPIDEY TRACER!

NOW PLAYING HIGH S: HUMI

BRAK!

ZROK!

DID YOU FORGET THAT I AM A *SCIENTIST?*

DID YOU *THINK,* WHEN I *FOUND* THE PRIMITIVE LITTLE GADGET YOU PLACED UPON MY TENTACLE, THAT I WOULDN'T FATHOM ITS *PURPOSE?*

SO, I MERELY PLACED IT IN THAT *ROOM* -- ONLY USING IT AS A *TRAP* IN WHICH TO CATCH *YOU* -- WHILE I SECRETLY *WAITED* UPON THIS ROOF ABOVE!

YOU CAN *NEVER* BE A MATCH FOR *ME!*

FOR NOT ONLY AM I YOUR MASTER IN *STRENGTH* --

-- BUT IN *CUNNING,* AND *GUILE,* AND *INTELLIGENCE* AS WELL!

13

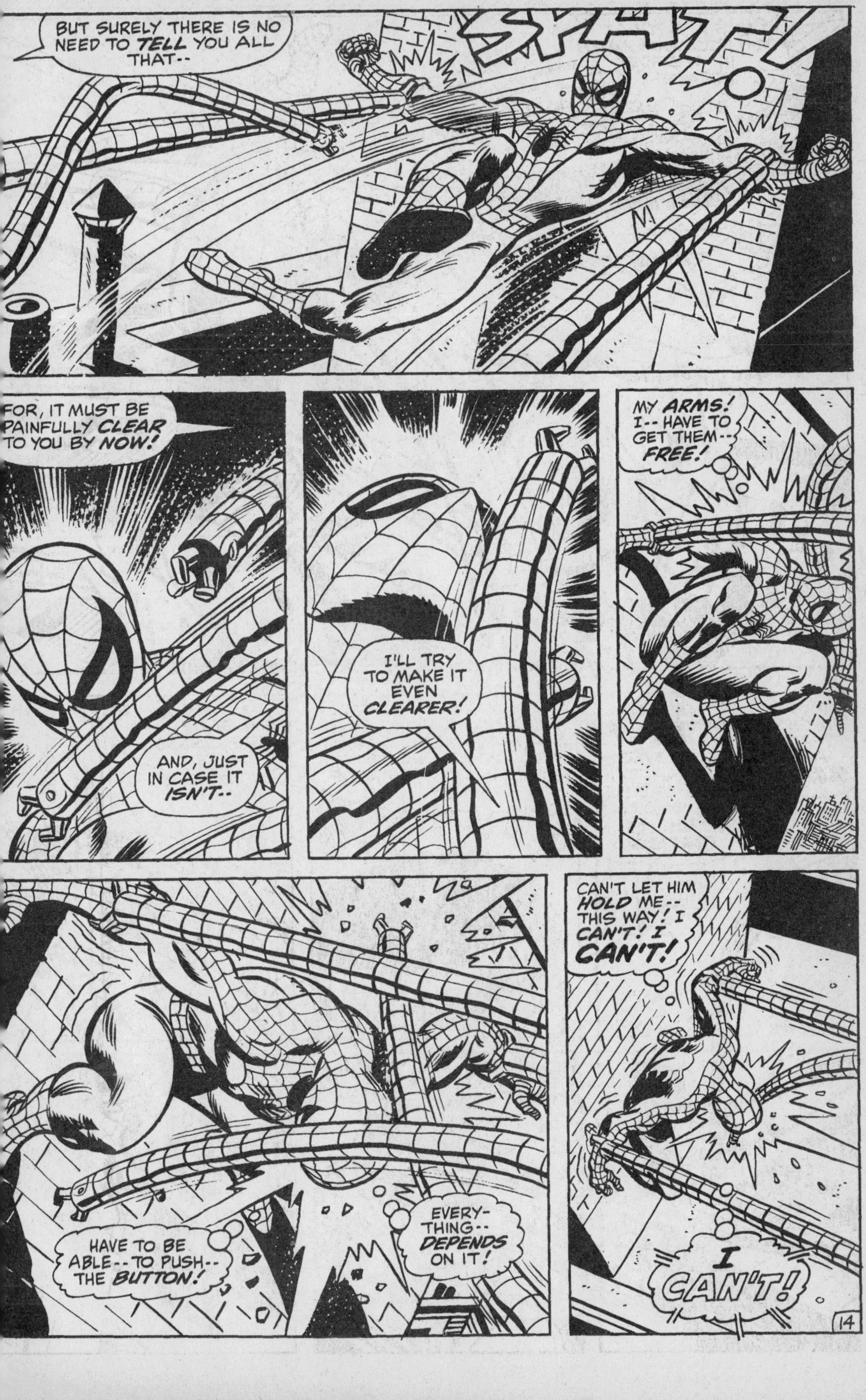

BUT SURELY THERE IS NO NEED TO TELL YOU ALL THAT--
SPAT!
FOR, IT MUST BE PAINFULLY CLEAR TO YOU BY NOW!
AND, JUST IN CASE IT ISN'T--
I'LL TRY TO MAKE IT EVEN CLEARER!
MY ARMS! I-- HAVE TO GET THEM-- FREE!
HAVE TO BE ABLE-- TO PUSH-- THE BUTTON!
EVERY-THING-- DEPENDS ON IT!
CAN'T LET HIM HOLD ME-- THIS WAY! I CAN'T! I CAN'T!
I CAN'T!
14

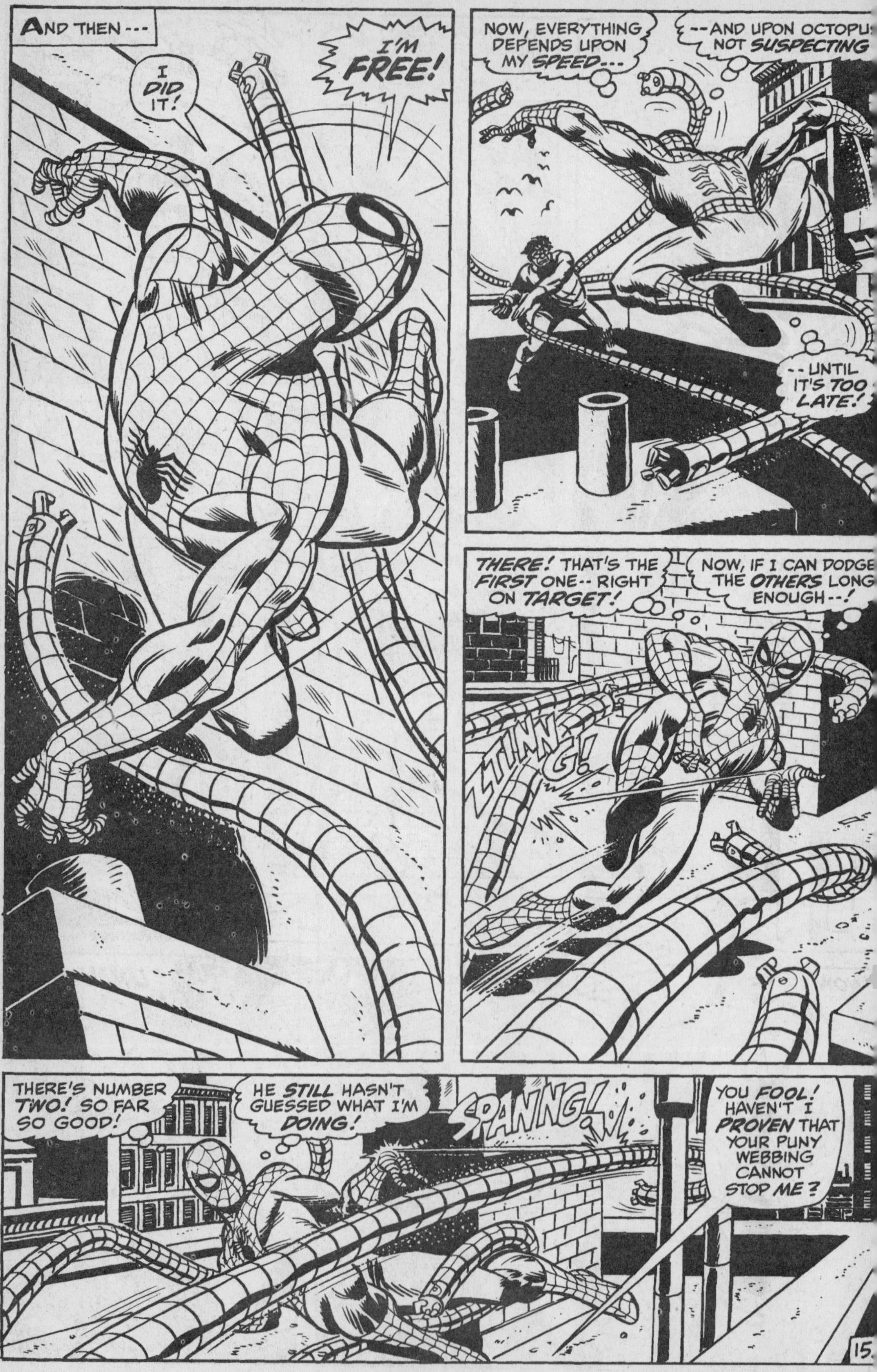
AND THEN ---
I DID IT!
I'M FREE!
NOW, EVERYTHING DEPENDS UPON MY SPEED...
--AND UPON OCTOPUS NOT SUSPECTING
--UNTIL IT'S TOO LATE!
THERE! THAT'S THE FIRST ONE-- RIGHT ON TARGET!
NOW, IF I CAN DODGE THE OTHERS LONG ENOUGH--!
ZTINNG!
THERE'S NUMBER TWO! SO FAR SO GOOD!
HE STILL HASN'T GUESSED WHAT I'M DOING!
SPANNG!
YOU FOOL! HAVEN'T I PROVEN THAT YOUR PUNY WEBBING CANNOT STOP ME?
15

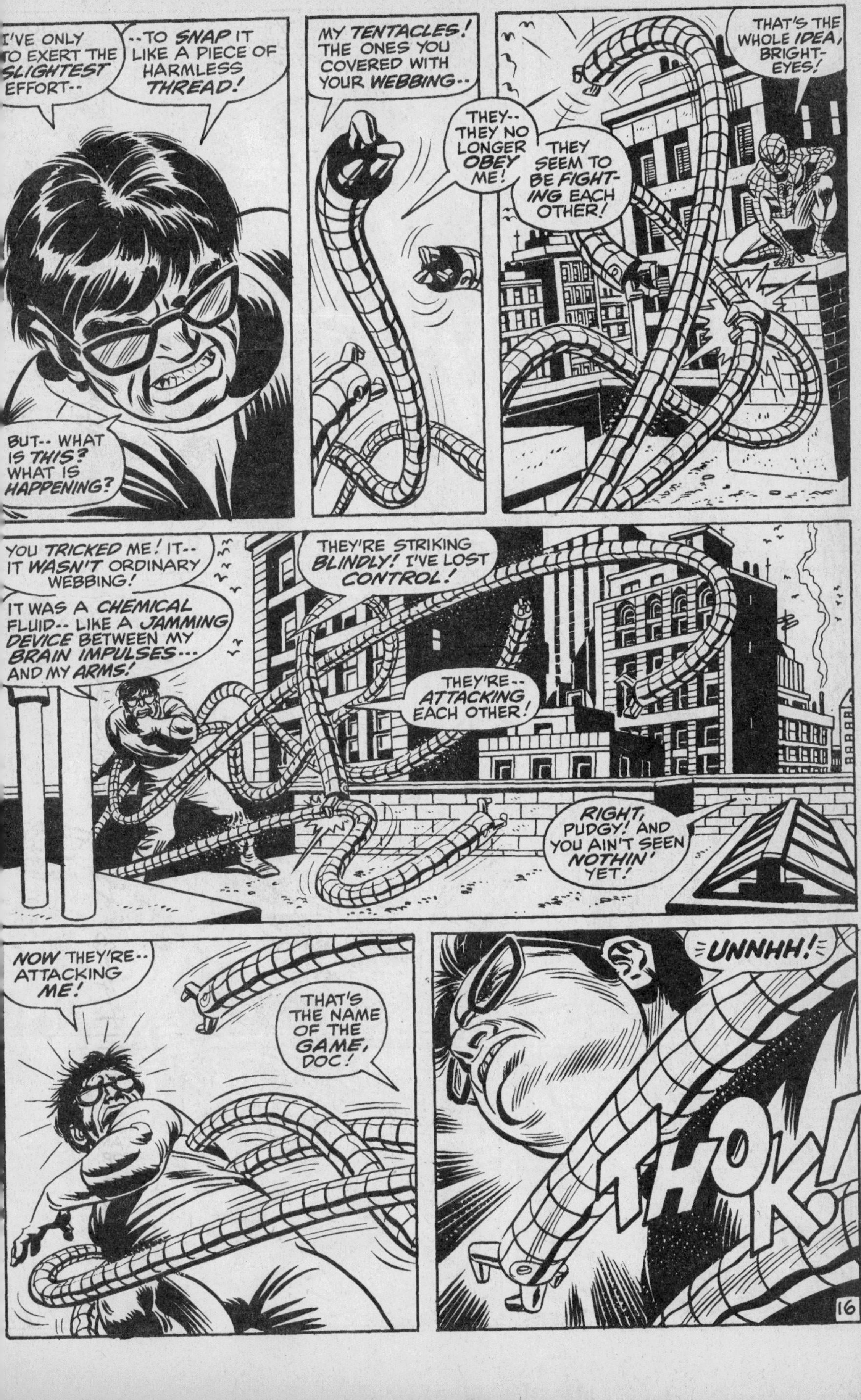
I'VE ONLY TO EXERT THE SLIGHTEST EFFORT--
--TO SNAP IT LIKE A PIECE OF HARMLESS THREAD!
BUT-- WHAT IS THIS? WHAT IS HAPPENING?
MY TENTACLES! THE ONES YOU COVERED WITH YOUR WEBBING--
THEY-- THEY NO LONGER OBEY ME!
THEY SEEM TO BE FIGHTING EACH OTHER!
THAT'S THE WHOLE IDEA, BRIGHT-EYES!
YOU TRICKED ME! IT-- IT WASN'T ORDINARY WEBBING!
IT WAS A CHEMICAL FLUID-- LIKE A JAMMING DEVICE BETWEEN MY BRAIN IMPULSES... AND MY ARMS!
THEY'RE STRIKING BLINDLY! I'VE LOST CONTROL!
THEY'RE-- ATTACKING EACH OTHER!
RIGHT, PUDGY! AND YOU AIN'T SEEN NOTHIN' YET!
NOW THEY'RE-- ATTACKING ME!
THAT'S THE NAME OF THE GAME, DOC!
UNNHH!
THOK!

IT WON'T **WORK!** I'LL BEAT YOU **YET!**

MY **OTHER** ARMS WILL SAVE ME!

IT'S **DOCTOR OCTOPUS**--- FIGHTING **SPIDER-MAN** UP THERE!

THE **BEST** THING THAT COULD HAPPEN FOR THIS TOWN WOULD BE IF THEY **BOTH** FINISH EACH OTHER OFF!

I REACHED HERE JUST IN **TIME!**

THEY'RE STILL **BATTLING**--- UP ON THAT **ROOF!**

BUT THE CROWD BELOW-- DOESN'T REALIZE THE **DANGER!**

THEY MUST **CLEAR** THE AREA!

I'D BETTER **GET** HIM-- BEFORE HE'S KILLED BY HIS OWN **ARMS!**

SPROK!

OH **BROTHER!** THERE'S JUST NO **STOPPING** THEM NOW!

HELP ME! HELP ME! I-- I CAN'T **HANDLE** THEM!

DON'T WORRY, MAN! THE **COPS** ARE ON THE WAY RIGHT **NOW!**

--THEY'LL HELP YOU TO A NICE COZY LITTLE **CELL** IN-- **HEY!**

THE CHIMNEY! YOU'VE **TOPPLED** IT!

K-O!

THEY'VE GONE **AMOK!** I-- I'M **DONE** FOR!

17

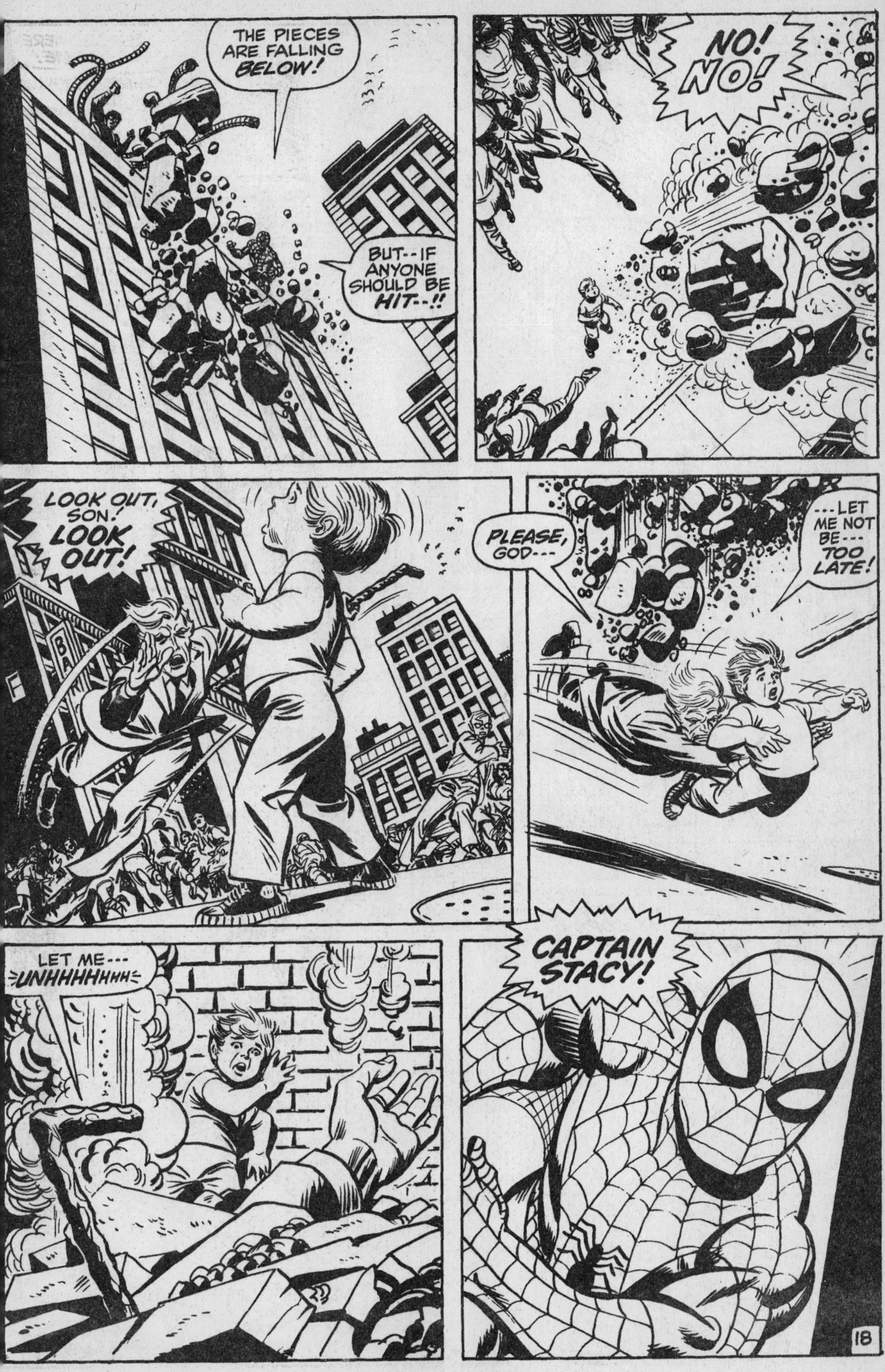
THE PIECES ARE FALLING BELOW!
BUT--IF ANYONE SHOULD BE HIT--!!
NO! NO!
LOOK OUT, SON! LOOK OUT!
PLEASE, GOD---
---LET ME NOT BE--- TOO LATE!
LET ME--- UNHHHHHHH
CAPTAIN STACY!
18

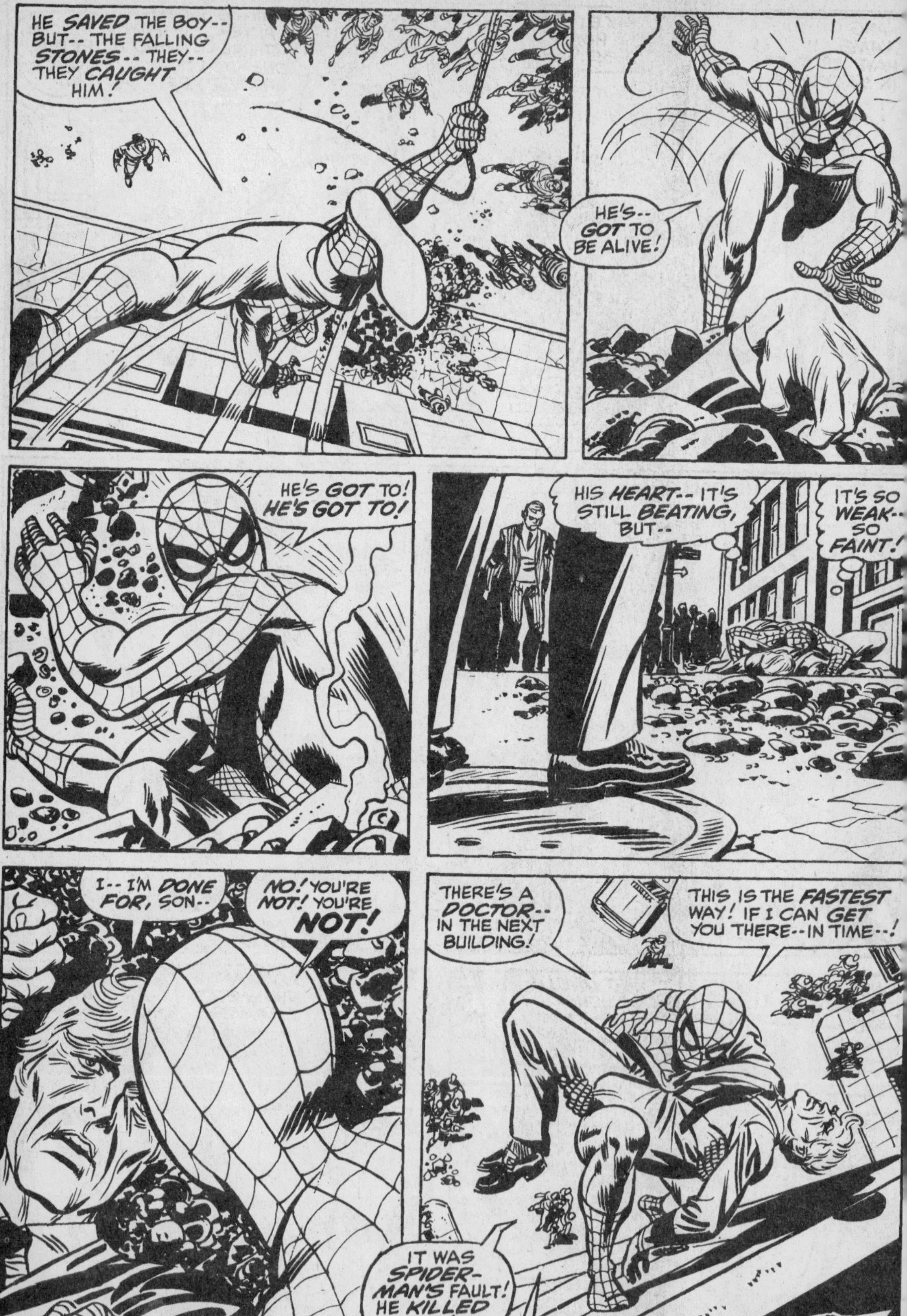

HE SAVED THE BOY-- BUT-- THE FALLING STONES-- THEY-- THEY CAUGHT HIM!
HE'S-- GOT TO BE ALIVE!
HE'S GOT TO! HE'S GOT TO!
HIS HEART-- IT'S STILL BEATING, BUT--
IT'S SO WEAK-- SO FAINT!
I-- I'M DONE FOR, SON--
NO! YOU'RE NOT! YOU'RE NOT!
THERE'S A DOCTOR-- IN THE NEXT BUILDING!
THIS IS THE FASTEST WAY! IF I CAN GET YOU THERE--IN TIME--!
IT WAS SPIDER-MAN'S FAULT! HE KILLED HIM!
AND NOW-- HE'S TAKING HIM AWAY!
19

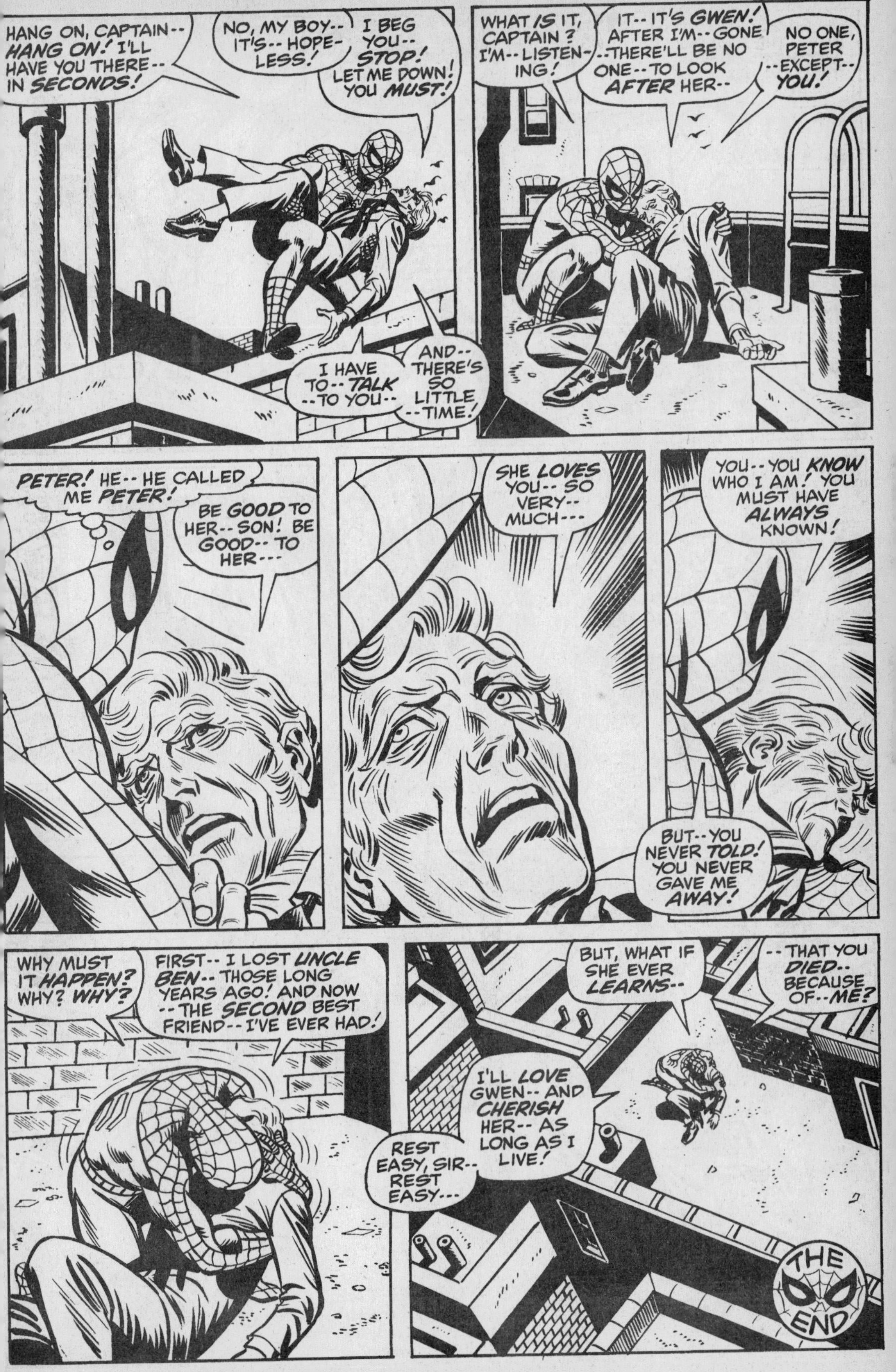
HANG ON, CAPTAIN-- HANG ON! I'LL HAVE YOU THERE-- IN SECONDS!
NO, MY BOY-- IT'S-- HOPE-LESS!
I BEG YOU-- STOP! LET ME DOWN! YOU MUST!
I HAVE TO-- TALK --TO YOU--
AND-- THERE'S SO LITTLE --TIME!
WHAT IS IT, CAPTAIN? I'M-- LISTEN-ING!
IT-- IT'S GWEN! AFTER I'M-- GONE --THERE'LL BE NO ONE-- TO LOOK AFTER HER--
NO ONE, PETER --EXCEPT-- YOU!
PETER! HE-- HE CALLED ME PETER!
BE GOOD TO HER-- SON! BE GOOD-- TO HER---
SHE LOVES YOU-- SO VERY-- MUCH---
YOU-- YOU KNOW WHO I AM! YOU MUST HAVE ALWAYS KNOWN!
BUT-- YOU NEVER TOLD! YOU NEVER GAVE ME AWAY!
WHY MUST IT HAPPEN? WHY? WHY?
FIRST-- I LOST UNCLE BEN-- THOSE LONG YEARS AGO! AND NOW --THE SECOND BEST FRIEND-- I'VE EVER HAD!
BUT, WHAT IF SHE EVER LEARNS--
--THAT YOU DIED-- BECAUSE OF--ME?
I'LL LOVE GWEN-- AND CHERISH HER-- AS LONG AS I LIVE!
REST EASY, SIR-- REST EASY...
THE END

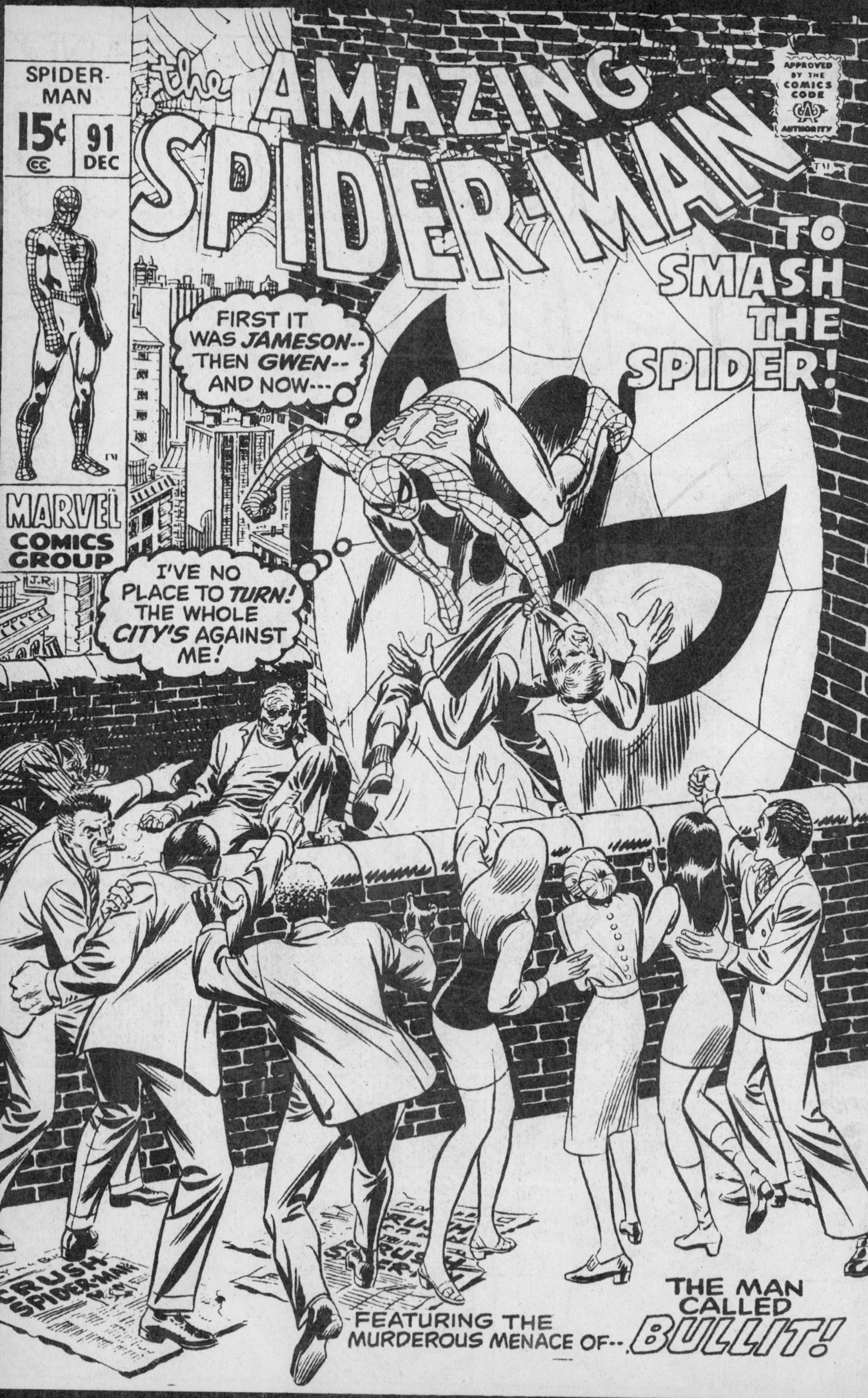
SPIDER-MAN
15¢
91
DEC
APPROVED BY THE COMICS CODE AUTHORITY
the AMAZING SPIDER-MAN
TO SMASH THE SPIDER!
MARVEL COMICS GROUP
FIRST IT WAS JAMESON-- THEN GWEN-- AND NOW---
I'VE NO PLACE TO TURN! THE WHOLE CITY'S AGAINST ME!
CRUSH SPIDER-MAN
-FEATURING THE MURDEROUS MENACE OF--.
THE MAN CALLED BULLIT!

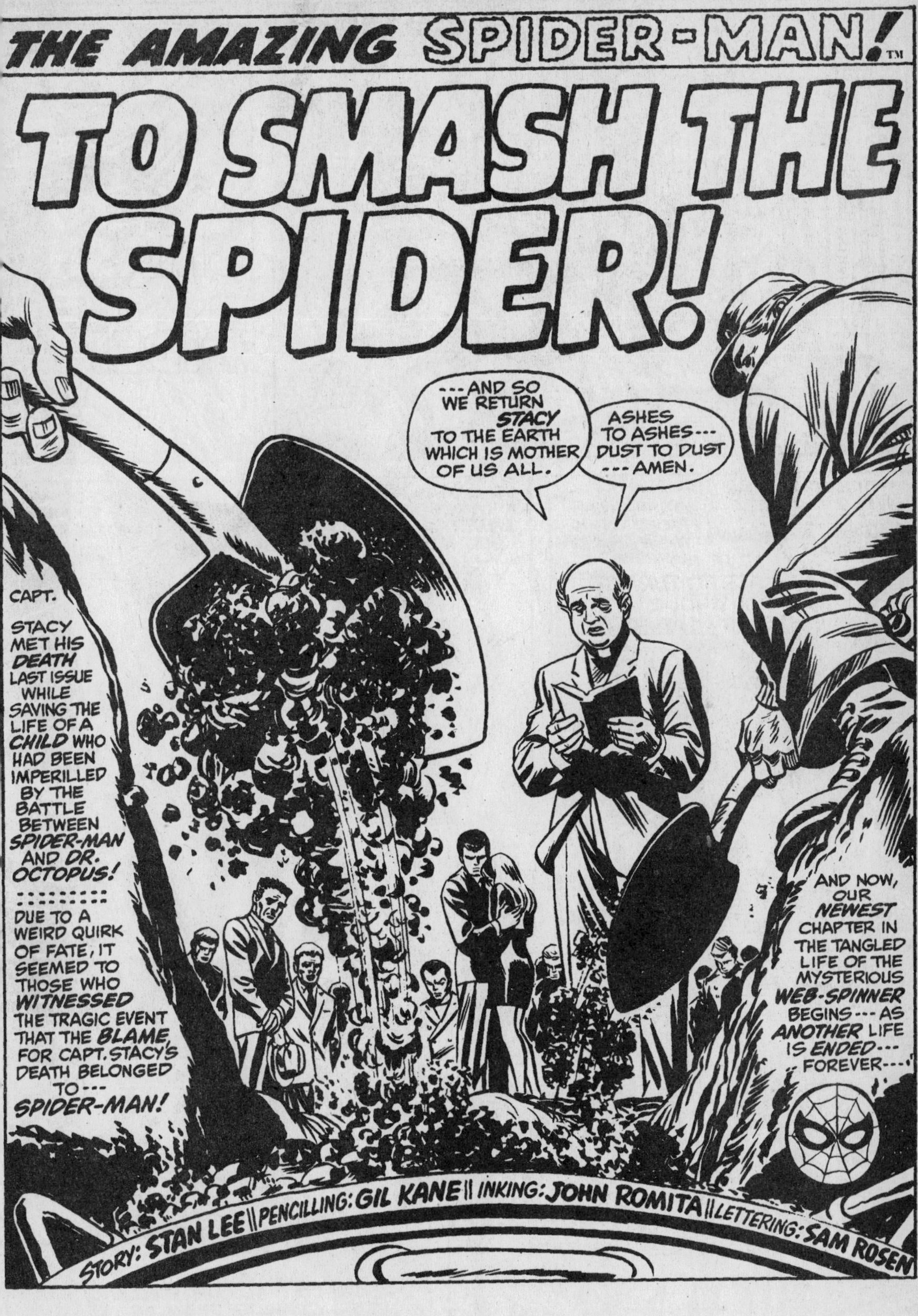
THE AMAZING SPIDER-MAN!™
TO SMASH THE SPIDER!
---AND SO WE RETURN STACY TO THE EARTH WHICH IS MOTHER OF US ALL.
ASHES TO ASHES--- DUST TO DUST ---AMEN.
CAPT. STACY MET HIS DEATH LAST ISSUE WHILE SAVING THE LIFE OF A CHILD WHO HAD BEEN IMPERILLED BY THE BATTLE BETWEEN SPIDER-MAN AND DR. OCTOPUS!
DUE TO A WEIRD QUIRK OF FATE, IT SEEMED TO THOSE WHO WITNESSED THE TRAGIC EVENT THAT THE BLAME FOR CAPT. STACY'S DEATH BELONGED TO--- SPIDER-MAN!
AND NOW, OUR NEWEST CHAPTER IN THE TANGLED LIFE OF THE MYSTERIOUS WEB-SPINNER BEGINS---AS ANOTHER LIFE IS ENDED--- FOREVER---
STORY: STAN LEE || PENCILLING: GIL KANE || INKING: JOHN ROMITA || LETTERING: SAM ROSEN

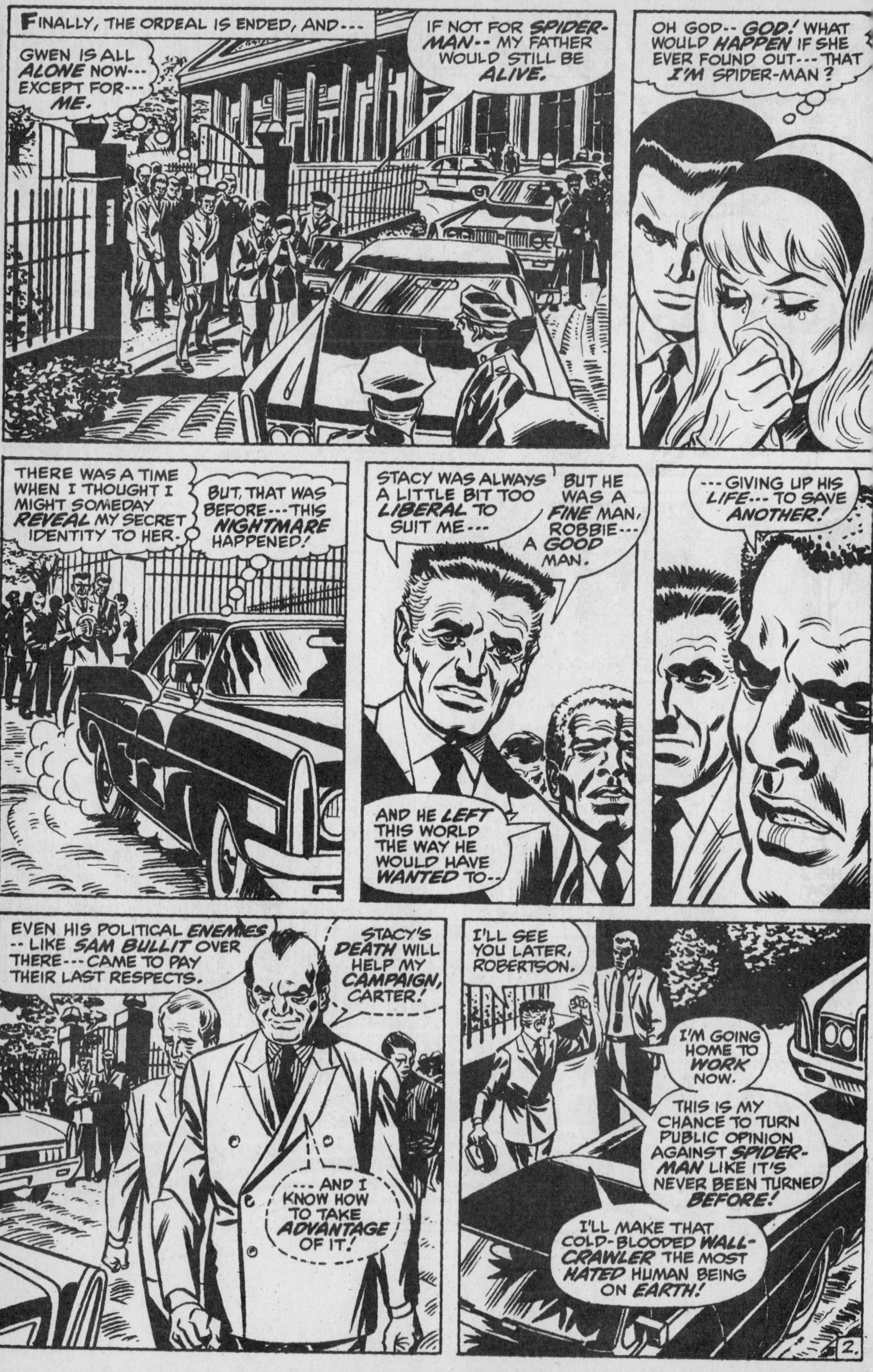
FINALLY, THE ORDEAL IS ENDED, AND---
GWEN IS ALL ALONE NOW--- EXCEPT FOR--- ME.
IF NOT FOR SPIDER-MAN-- MY FATHER WOULD STILL BE ALIVE.
OH GOD-- GOD! WHAT WOULD HAPPEN IF SHE EVER FOUND OUT---THAT I'M SPIDER-MAN?
THERE WAS A TIME WHEN I THOUGHT I MIGHT SOMEDAY REVEAL MY SECRET IDENTITY TO HER.
BUT, THAT WAS BEFORE---THIS NIGHTMARE HAPPENED!
STACY WAS ALWAYS A LITTLE BIT TOO LIBERAL TO SUIT ME---
BUT HE WAS A FINE MAN, ROBBIE--- A GOOD MAN.
AND HE LEFT THIS WORLD THE WAY HE WOULD HAVE WANTED TO--
---GIVING UP HIS LIFE--- TO SAVE ANOTHER!
EVEN HIS POLITICAL ENEMIES -- LIKE SAM BULLIT OVER THERE---CAME TO PAY THEIR LAST RESPECTS.
STACY'S DEATH WILL HELP MY CAMPAIGN, CARTER!
--- AND I KNOW HOW TO TAKE ADVANTAGE OF IT!
I'LL SEE YOU LATER, ROBERTSON.
I'M GOING HOME TO WORK NOW.
THIS IS MY CHANCE TO TURN PUBLIC OPINION AGAINST SPIDER-MAN LIKE IT'S NEVER BEEN TURNED BEFORE!
I'LL MAKE THAT COLD-BLOODED WALL-CRAWLER THE MOST HATED HUMAN BEING ON EARTH!
2.

THIS *PROVES* I WAS RIGHT! I WAS *ALWAYS* RIGHT!

NOBODY SHOULD BE ABLE TO SLINK AROUND TOWN, MASKED AND COSTUMED, TAKING THE *LAW* INTO HIS OWN *HANDS!*

AND, EVEN AS *JONAH JAMESON* PREPARES TO WRITE HIS NEXT EDITORIAL, *ANOTHER* CAR ALSO WENDS ITS WAY THRU THE CITY TRAFFIC...

WHAT CAN I *DO?* WHAT CAN I *SAY* TO *COMFORT* HER?

HOW CAN I EVER AGAIN *LOOK* AT HER-- *TOUCH* HER --WITHOUT BEING *TORTURED* BY PANGS OF GUILT?

BECAUSE, DEEP IN MY HEART I'LL ALWAYS *WONDER...*

IF NOT FOR *SPIDER-MAN,* WOULDN'T CAPT. STACY *STILL* BE ALIVE?

AND YET... *KNOWING* THAT I WAS SPIDER-MAN--

THE GIRL WHO WILL *ALWAYS* MEAN EVERY-THING -- TO ME.

I WAS A *FOOL,* PETE. I *SEE* IT NOW.

--HIS *DYING WISH* WAS THAT I *LOOK* AFTER GWEN---THE GIRL WHO MEANS *EVERYTHING* TO BOTH OF US.

WHY, GWEN? WHAT DO YOU *MEAN?*

I DIDN'T REALIZE HOW *OLD* MY DAD WAS -- AND HOW *TRUSTING.*

I DIDN'T TRY TO *WARN* HIM--- AGAINST *SPIDER-MAN*--- WHILE THERE STILL WAS *TIME.*

GWEN, DARLING-- *NO!* YOU CAN'T BLAME *YOURSELF,* YOU *MUSTN'T!*

SPIDER-MAN! SPIDER-MAN! I'LL *HATE* HIM ---FOREVER!

WHETHER HE *MEANT* TO OR NOT---HE KILLED MY *FATHER!* HE KILLED MY *FATHER!*

BUT, GWEN, YOU DON'T UNDERSTAND. HE-- HE--

IT'S NO USE. WHAT CAN I SAY? THERE JUST AREN'T ANY WORDS.

PETER, I--I'M NOT GOING TO WASTE TIME CRYING. I'M GOING TO WORK--

--TO DO WHAT I CAN TO RID THE CITY OF MENACES LIKE-- SPIDER-MAN!

HOW, GWEN? WHAT DO YOU MEAN?

IN THE COMING ELECTION-- ONE OF THE CANDIDATES, SAM BULLIT, IS RUNNING ON A LAW AND ORDER TICKET!

HE USED TO BE A COP-- JUST LIKE DAD. THEY KNEW EACH OTHER IN THE PAST.

I'M GOING TO VOLUNTEER TO HELP HIS CAMPAIGN!

AND SO, THE VERY NEXT DAY--

PERHAPS IT TAKES A HARD MAN LIKE SAM BULLIT TO BRING SOMEONE LIKE SPIDER-MAN TO JUSTICE!

AND IF IT DOES, I'M ALL FOR HIM.

MAY I HELP YOU YOUNG LADY?

WHAT AN OFFICE! I DIDN'T REALIZE HE WAS SO SUCCESSFUL!

I'D LIKE TO SEE MR. BULLIT, PLEASE.

I'M CAPTAIN STACY'S DAUGHTER, GWENDOLYN.

WHAT CAN THIS BE?

RRRINNG

STACY'S DAUGHTER TO SEE THE BIG MAN?

SURE, SEND HER RIGHT IN!

4

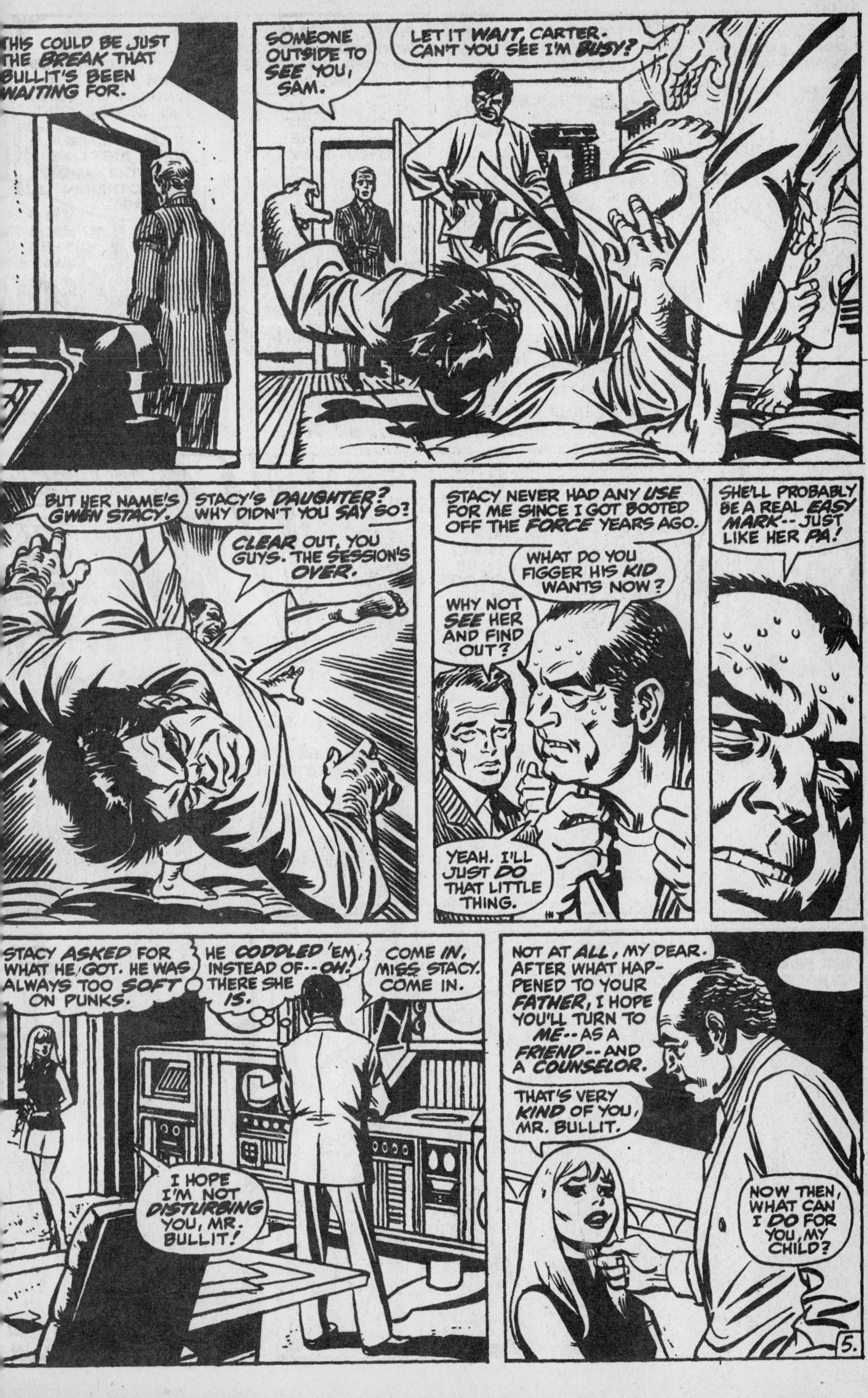
THIS COULD BE JUST THE BREAK THAT BULLIT'S BEEN WAITING FOR.
SOMEONE OUTSIDE TO SEE YOU, SAM.
LET IT WAIT, CARTER. CAN'T YOU SEE I'M BUSY?
BUT HER NAME'S GWEN STACY.
STACY'S DAUGHTER? WHY DIDN'T YOU SAY SO?
CLEAR OUT, YOU GUYS. THE SESSION'S OVER.
STACY NEVER HAD ANY USE FOR ME SINCE I GOT BOOTED OFF THE FORCE YEARS AGO.
WHAT DO YOU FIGGER HIS KID WANTS NOW?
WHY NOT SEE HER AND FIND OUT?
YEAH. I'LL JUST DO THAT LITTLE THING.
SHE'LL PROBABLY BE A REAL EASY MARK-- JUST LIKE HER PA!
STACY ASKED FOR WHAT HE GOT. HE WAS ALWAYS TOO SOFT ON PUNKS.
HE CODDLED 'EM, INSTEAD OF-- OH! THERE SHE IS.
COME IN, MISS STACY. COME IN.
I HOPE I'M NOT DISTURBING YOU, MR. BULLIT!
NOT AT ALL, MY DEAR. AFTER WHAT HAPPENED TO YOUR FATHER, I HOPE YOU'LL TURN TO ME-- AS A FRIEND-- AND A COUNSELOR.
THAT'S VERY KIND OF YOU, MR. BULLIT.
NOW THEN, WHAT CAN I DO FOR YOU, MY CHILD?
5.

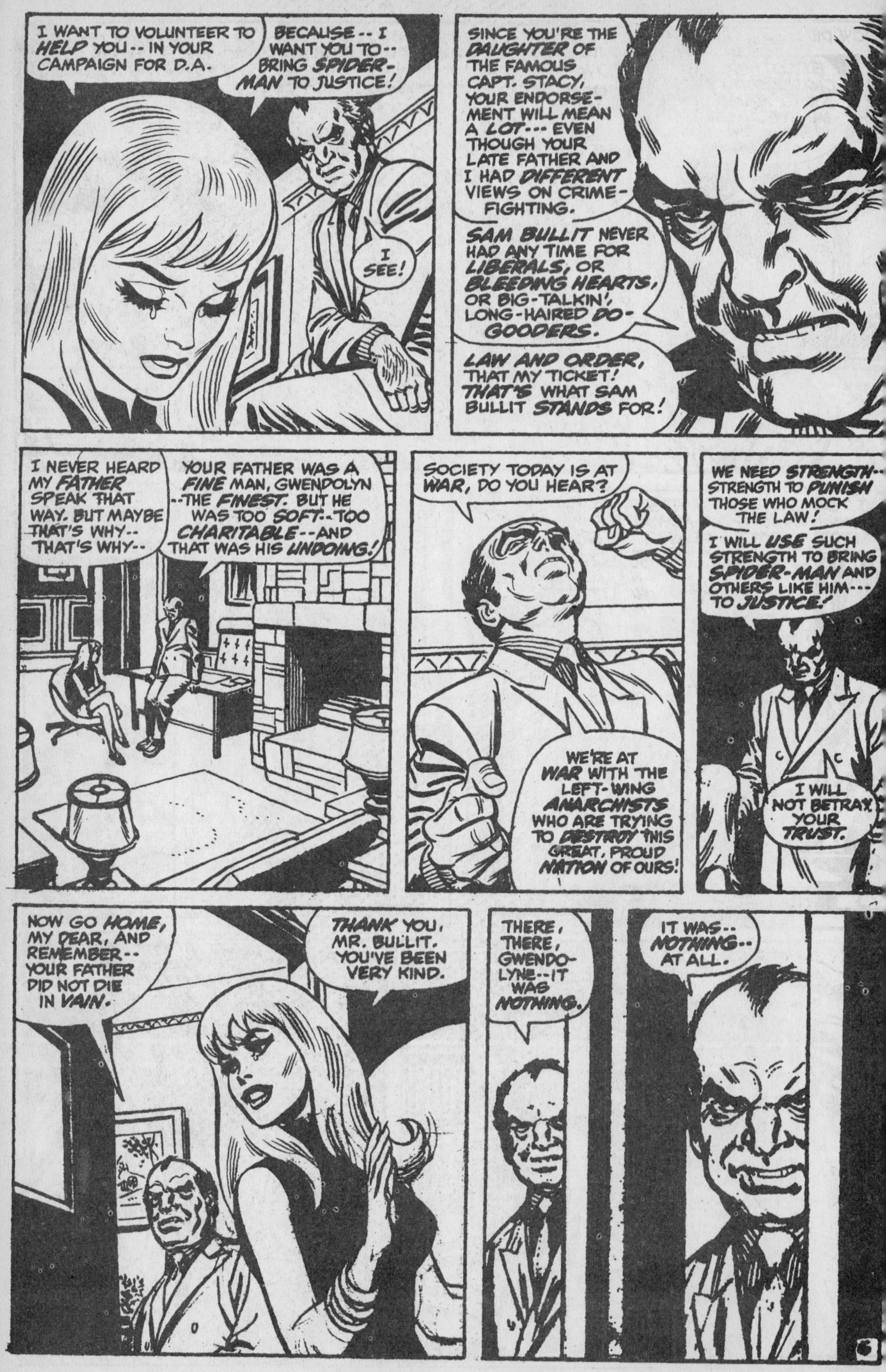
I WANT TO VOLUNTEER TO HELP YOU -- IN YOUR CAMPAIGN FOR D.A.
BECAUSE -- I WANT YOU TO -- BRING SPIDER-MAN TO JUSTICE!
I SEE!
SINCE YOU'RE THE DAUGHTER OF THE FAMOUS CAPT. STACY, YOUR ENDORSEMENT WILL MEAN A LOT --- EVEN THOUGH YOUR LATE FATHER AND I HAD DIFFERENT VIEWS ON CRIME-FIGHTING.
SAM BULLIT NEVER HAD ANY TIME FOR LIBERALS, OR BLEEDING HEARTS, OR BIG-TALKIN', LONG-HAIRED DO-GOODERS.
LAW AND ORDER, THAT MY TICKET! THAT'S WHAT SAM BULLIT STANDS FOR!
I NEVER HEARD MY FATHER SPEAK THAT WAY. BUT MAYBE THAT'S WHY-- THAT'S WHY--
YOUR FATHER WAS A FINE MAN, GWENDOLYN --THE FINEST. BUT HE WAS TOO SOFT--TOO CHARITABLE--AND THAT WAS HIS UNDOING!
SOCIETY TODAY IS AT WAR, DO YOU HEAR?
WE'RE AT WAR WITH THE LEFT-WING ANARCHISTS WHO ARE TRYING TO DESTROY THIS GREAT, PROUD NATION OF OURS!
WE NEED STRENGTH-- STRENGTH TO PUNISH THOSE WHO MOCK THE LAW!
I WILL USE SUCH STRENGTH TO BRING SPIDER-MAN AND OTHERS LIKE HIM--- TO JUSTICE!
I WILL NOT BETRAY YOUR TRUST.
NOW GO HOME, MY DEAR, AND REMEMBER-- YOUR FATHER DID NOT DIE IN VAIN.
THANK YOU, MR. BULLIT. YOU'VE BEEN VERY KIND.
THERE, THERE, GWENDOLYNE--IT WAS NOTHING.
IT WAS.. NOTHING.. AT ALL.
6

HOW DID IT GO, BOSS?

BEAUTIFUL, CARTER. WITH THE STACY NAME BEHIND ME, THE LIBERALS WON'T KNOW WHAT TO THINK.

NOW, I GOT ME A LITTLE CALL TO MAKE---

GET ME THE DAILY BUGLE.

SAM BULLIT! WHAT? YOU'LL MAKE A DEAL WITH ME?

CAREFUL, J.J. HE'S A SLIPPERY ONE!

YOU WANT THE BUGLE'S SUPPORT, EH?

AND IN RETURN YOU PROMISE TO DELIVER SPIDER-MAN?

MISTER, FROM THIS MINUTE ON, SAM BULLIT IS MY CANDIDATE!

YES SIR, ROBBIE-- THAT'S WHAT THIS OL' TOWN NEEDS-- A NO-NONSENSE DISTRICT ATTORNEY WHO'LL DELIVER THE GOODS!

YOU CAN'T MEAN BULLIT, MR. J.!

THAT FLEDGLING FASCIST'S STILL LIVING IN THE 1930's!

MAYBE THEY WERE BETTER DAYS THAN NOW!

AT LEAST WE HAD LAW AND ORDER THEN!

YEAH! AND LYNCH MOBS, AND BREAD-LINES, AND UNCLE TOMS--

COME OFF IT, ROBBIE! WHAT'S WRONG WITH A MAN STANDING FOR LAW AND ORDER, ANYWAY?

MAYBE IT JUST DEPENDS ON WHOSE LAW-- AND WHAT KIND OF ORDER YOU'RE TALKIN' ABOUT, MAN!

OKAY-- TO BE CONTINUED! WE STILL HAVE A PAPER TO PUT OUT!

IF I'M GONNA HAVE TO GET MY PAY CHECK FROM A PAPER THAT'S SUPPORTING SAM BULLIT, I'LL--

UH OH! LOOKS LIKE SOMETHING JUST HIT THE FAN.

SLAM

NEVER SAW JOE ROBERTSON SO ANGRY BEFORE!

7.

AND IF *ROBBIE'S* THAT MAD-- I CAN JUST IMAGINE *JAMESON'S* MOOD!

I'D BETTER *SPLIT!* I'LL ASK HIM ABOUT SOME PHOTO ASSIGNMENTS SOME *OTHER* TIME!

LATER--

ONE THING'S FOR SURE--- I CAN'T HANG AROUND *HERE!*

I'VE GOTTA DO *SOMETHING* TO TAKE MY MIND OFF *GWEN*---

--AND THE WAY SHE FEELS ABOUT *SPIDER-MAN!*

I'VE GOTTA KEEP *BUSY* TAKING *PICTURES* WALL-CRAWLING-- *ANY-THING!*

MAYBE THERE'S SOMETHING ON THE *BOOB TUBE* THAT'LL---

HEY! WHAT'S *THIS?*

IS IT *TRUE* THAT YOU'VE PROMISED TO APPREHEND *SPIDER-MAN* IF ELECTED, MR. *BULLIT!*

YOU CAN *BET* ON IT, MISTER! I PLEDGED TO MAKE THE STREETS OF THIS CITY *SAFE* FOR DECENT FOLK!

AND THAT MEANS PUTTING AN *END* TO THAT WEB-SPINNING *KILLER!*

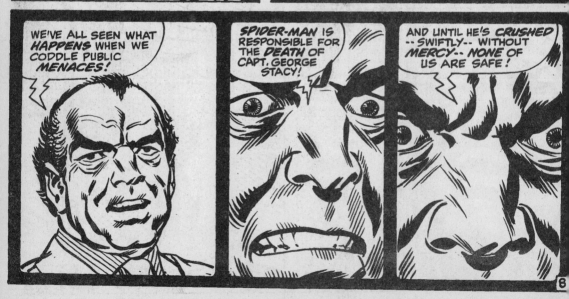

WE'VE ALL SEEN WHAT *HAPPENS* WHEN WE CODDLE PUBLIC *MENACES!*

SPIDER-MAN IS RESPONSIBLE FOR THE *DEATH* OF CAPT. GEORGE STACY!

AND UNTIL HE'S *CRUSHED* -- SWIFTLY-- WITHOUT *MERCY*-- NONE OF US ARE SAFE!

8

GREAT! THAT'S ALL I *NEED*-- SOME GUY WORKING UP A *LYNCH MOB* AGAINST ME!

CLICK

THE VERY NEXT DAY, AS THOUGH TO LEND *EMPHASIS* TO SPIDEY'S WORDS---

I'LL MAKE OUR CITY'S STREETS *SAFE* AGAIN!

I *SWEAR* THAT SPIDER-MAN'S DAYS ARE *NUMBERED!*

DAILY GLOBE — SPIDER-MAN MUST BE CRUSHED! SAYS SAM BULLIT

CRUSH SPIDER-MAN!

CRUSH SPIDER-MAN!

CRUSH SPIDER-MAN!

CRUSH SPIDER-MAN!

CRUSH SPIDER-MAN!

CRUSH SPIDER-MAN!

9.

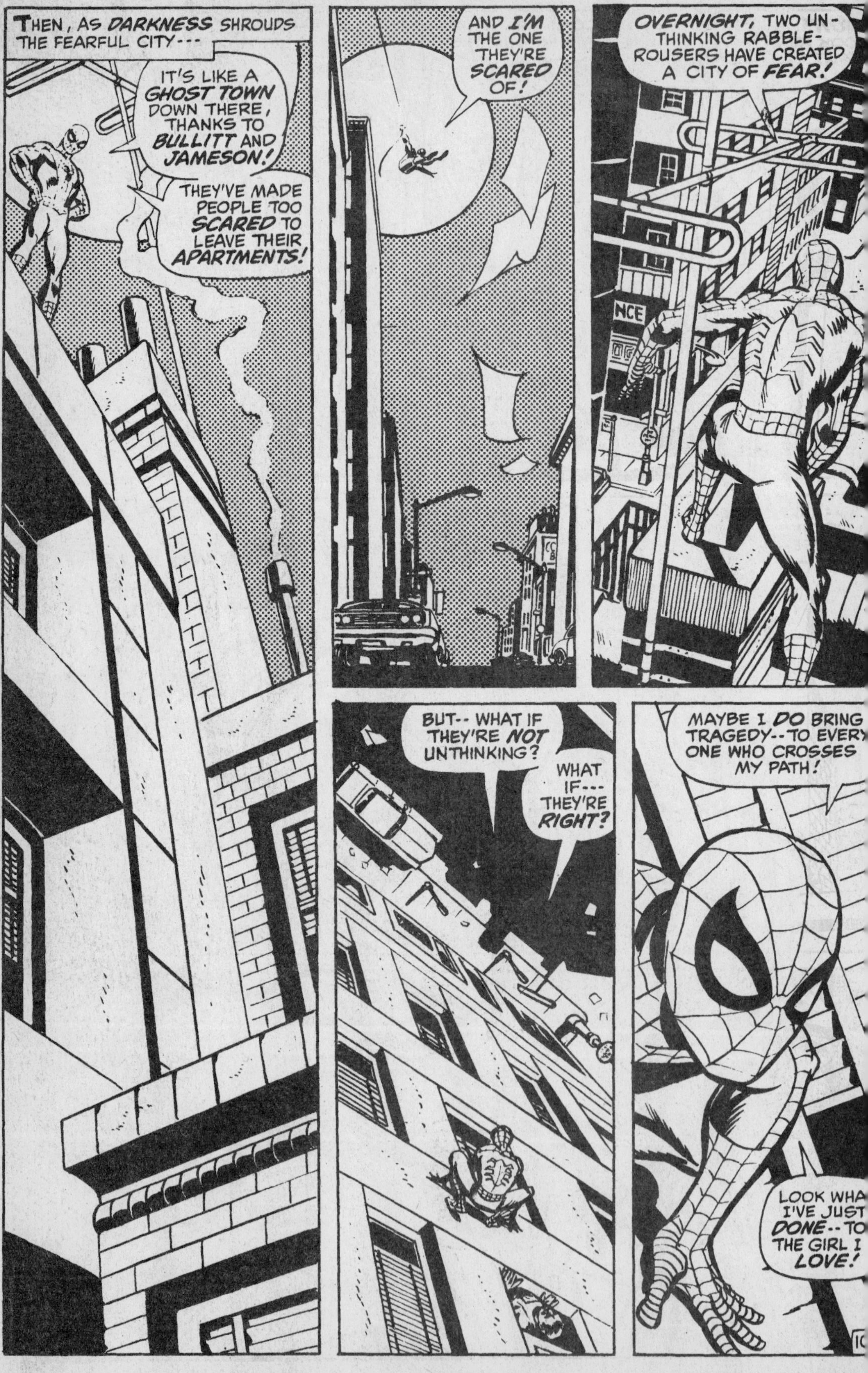
THEN, AS DARKNESS SHROUDS THE FEARFUL CITY---
IT'S LIKE A GHOST TOWN DOWN THERE, THANKS TO BULLITT AND JAMESON!
THEY'VE MADE PEOPLE TOO SCARED TO LEAVE THEIR APARTMENTS!
AND I'M THE ONE THEY'RE SCARED OF!
OVERNIGHT, TWO UN-THINKING RABBLE-ROUSERS HAVE CREATED A CITY OF FEAR!
BUT-- WHAT IF THEY'RE NOT UNTHINKING?
WHAT IF--- THEY'RE RIGHT?
MAYBE I DO BRING TRAGEDY--TO EVERY ONE WHO CROSSES MY PATH!
LOOK WHA I'VE JUST DONE--TO THE GIRL I LOVE!
10

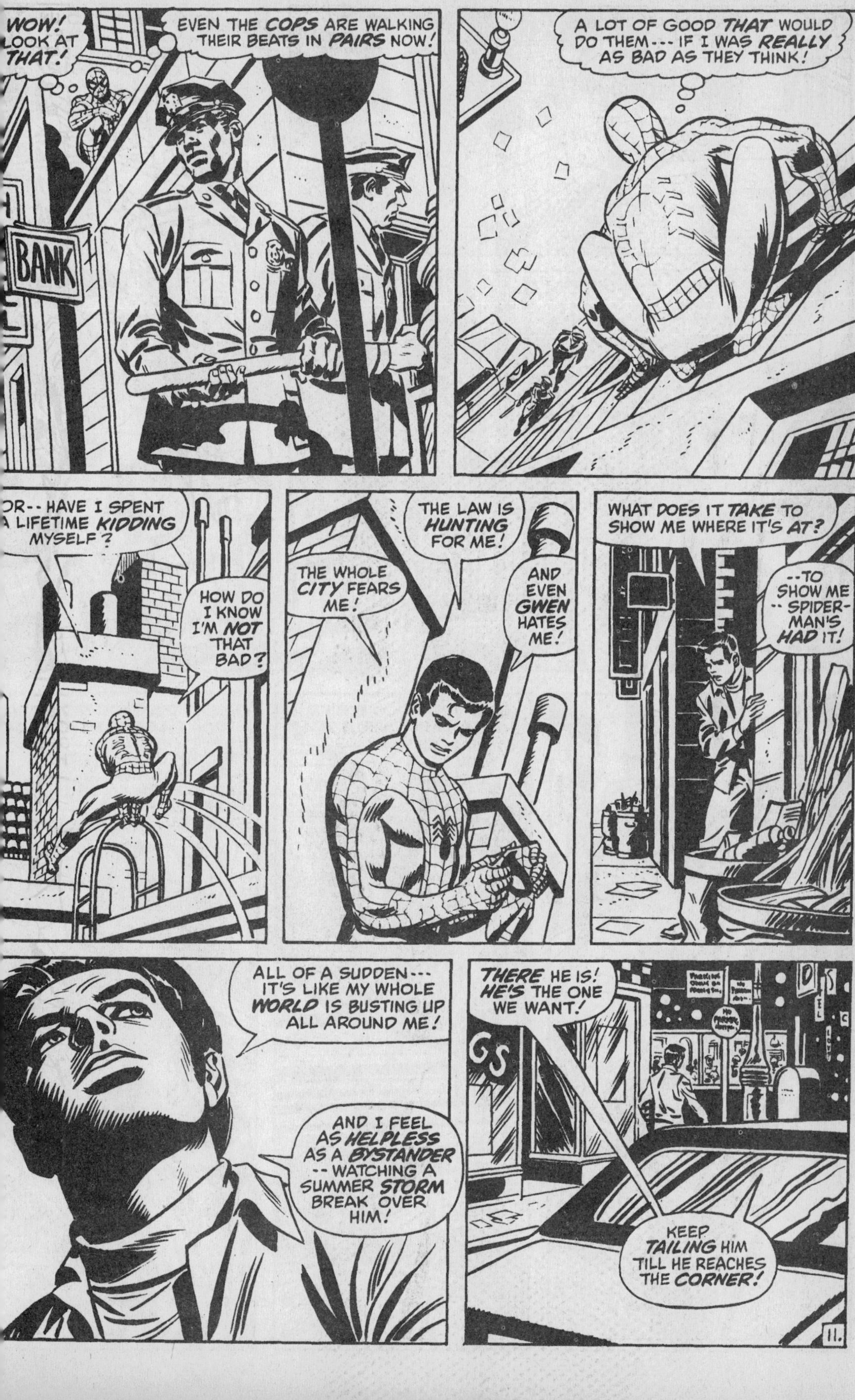
WOW! LOOK AT THAT!
EVEN THE COPS ARE WALKING THEIR BEATS IN PAIRS NOW!
BANK
A LOT OF GOOD THAT WOULD DO THEM--- IF I WAS REALLY AS BAD AS THEY THINK!
OR-- HAVE I SPENT A LIFETIME KIDDING MYSELF?
HOW DO I KNOW I'M NOT THAT BAD?
THE LAW IS HUNTING FOR ME!
THE WHOLE CITY FEARS ME!
AND EVEN GWEN HATES ME!
WHAT DOES IT TAKE TO SHOW ME WHERE IT'S AT?
--TO SHOW ME -- SPIDER-MAN'S HAD IT!
ALL OF A SUDDEN--- IT'S LIKE MY WHOLE WORLD IS BUSTING UP ALL AROUND ME!
AND I FEEL AS HELPLESS AS A BYSTANDER -- WATCHING A SUMMER STORM BREAK OVER HIM!
THERE HE IS! HE'S THE ONE WE WANT!
KEEP TAILING HIM TILL HE REACHES THE CORNER!
11.

"HOW CAN YOU BE SURE HE CAN *HELP* US, BOSS?"

"*EASY!* HE SNAPPED MORE *NEWS PICTURES* OF THE WALL-CRAWLER THAN *ANYONE!*"

"HE'S *GOTTA* KNOW A LOT MORE *ABOUT* HIM THAN HE'S BEEN *TELLIN'!*"

"MY *SPIDEY-SENSE* IS BEGINNING TO *TINGLE!* SOMEONE'S *FOLLOWING* ME!"

"WELL, MORE *POWER* TO 'EM! WHAT DO *I* CARE?"

"*OKAY!* HE'S GONE FAR *ENOUGH!* LET'S *TAKE* 'IM NOW!"

"*THIS'LL* BE A *CINCH!*"

SK-R-E-E-E

"*HOLD IT, BOY!* I WANT TO *TALK* TO YOU!"

"DO YOU KNOW WHO I *AM?*"

"*SAM BULLIT!* I'VE SEEN YOU ON *TV!*"

"*OKAY!* THEN YOU KNOW I DON'T *MINCE WORDS!*"

"I'M OUT TO GET *SPIDER-MAN*-- AND YOU CAN *HELP* ME! SO START *TALKING!*"

"ALL *I* CAN DO I WISH YO *LUCK!* I NOT HIS *KEEPER*"

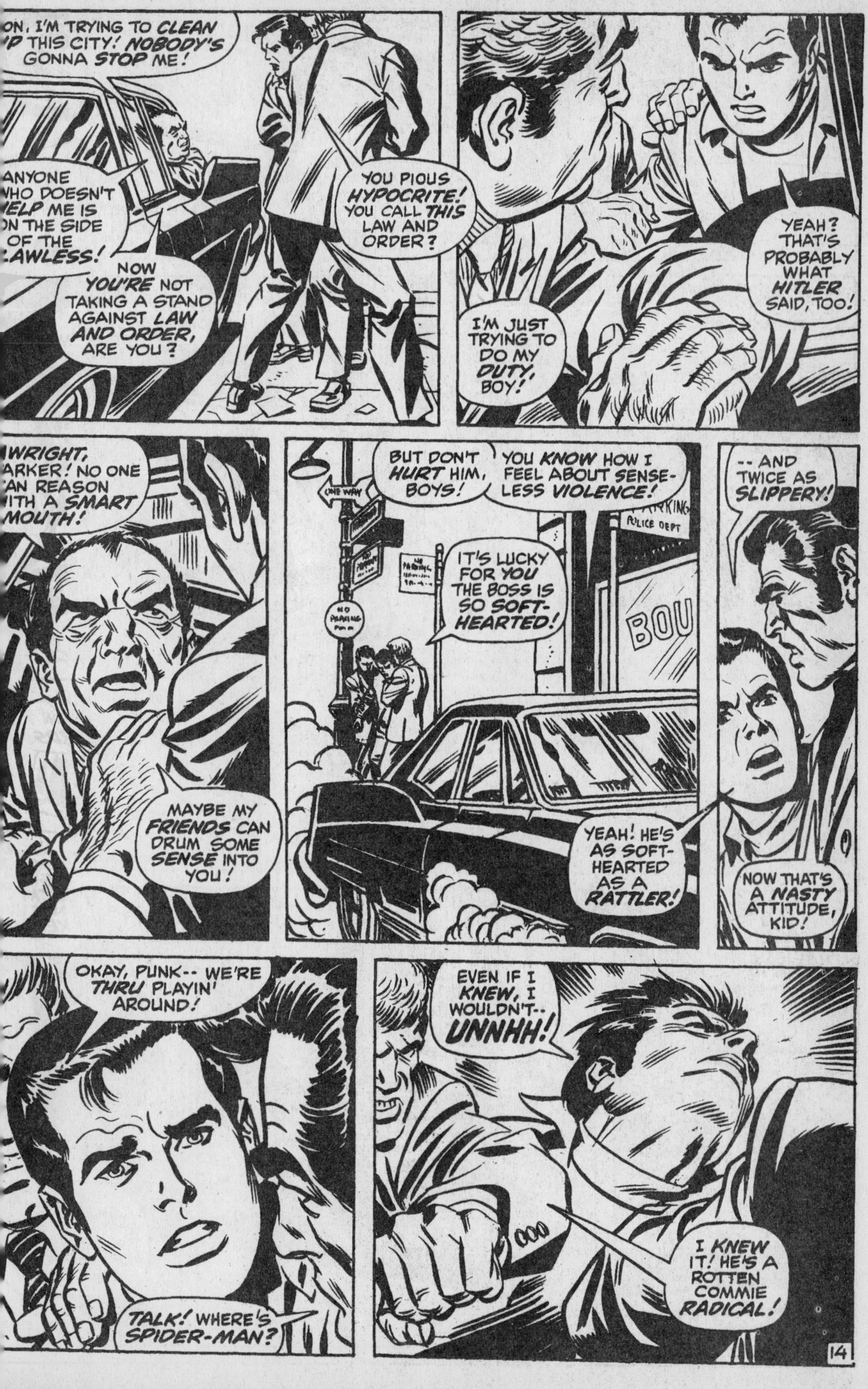

ON, I'M TRYING TO CLEAN
P THIS CITY! NOBODY'S GONNA STOP ME!
ANYONE WHO DOESN'T ELP ME IS ON THE SIDE OF THE AWLESS!
NOW YOU'RE NOT TAKING A STAND AGAINST LAW AND ORDER, ARE YOU?
YOU PIOUS HYPOCRITE! YOU CALL THIS LAW AND ORDER?
I'M JUST TRYING TO DO MY DUTY, BOY!
YEAH? THAT'S PROBABLY WHAT HITLER SAID, TOO!
WRIGHT, ARKER! NO ONE AN REASON ITH A SMART MOUTH!
MAYBE MY FRIENDS CAN DRUM SOME SENSE INTO YOU!
BUT DON'T HURT HIM, BOYS!
YOU KNOW HOW I FEEL ABOUT SENSELESS VIOLENCE!
ONE WAY
POLICE DEPT
IT'S LUCKY FOR YOU THE BOSS IS SO SOFT-HEARTED!
BOU
YEAH! HE'S AS SOFT-HEARTED AS A RATTLER!
-- AND TWICE AS SLIPPERY!
NOW THAT'S A NASTY ATTITUDE, KID!
OKAY, PUNK-- WE'RE THRU PLAYIN' AROUND!
TALK! WHERE'S SPIDER-MAN?
EVEN IF I KNEW, I WOULDN'T-- UNNHH!
I KNEW IT! HE'S A ROTTEN COMMIE RADICAL!

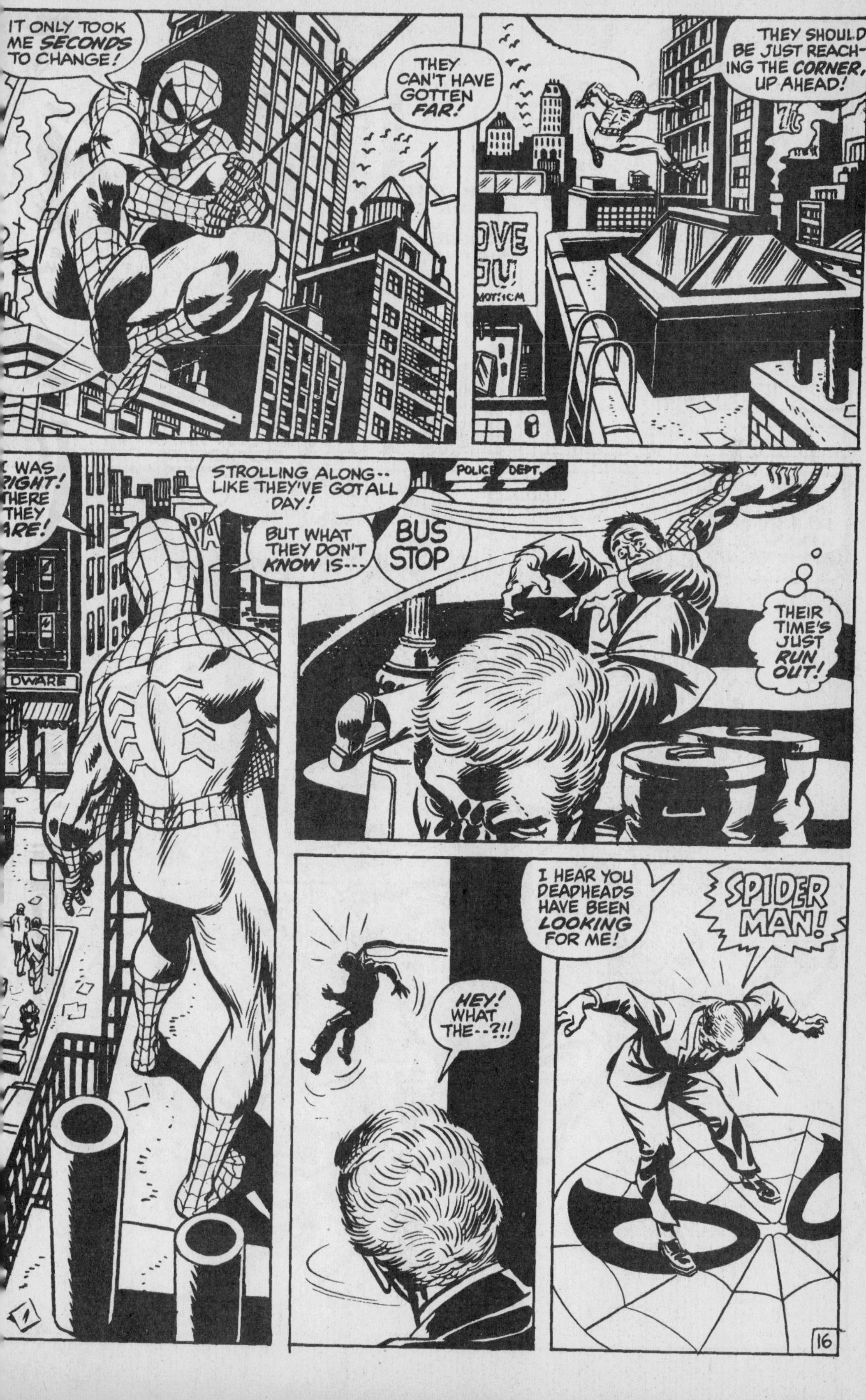
IT ONLY TOOK ME SECONDS TO CHANGE!
THEY CAN'T HAVE GOTTEN FAR!
THEY SHOULD BE JUST REACHING THE CORNER, UP AHEAD!
I WAS RIGHT! THERE THEY ARE!
STROLLING ALONG-- LIKE THEY'VE GOT ALL DAY!
BUT WHAT THEY DON'T KNOW IS---
POLICE DEPT.
BUS STOP
THEIR TIME'S JUST RUN OUT!
HEY! WHAT THE--?!!
I HEAR YOU DEADHEADS HAVE BEEN LOOKING FOR ME!
SPIDER MAN!
16

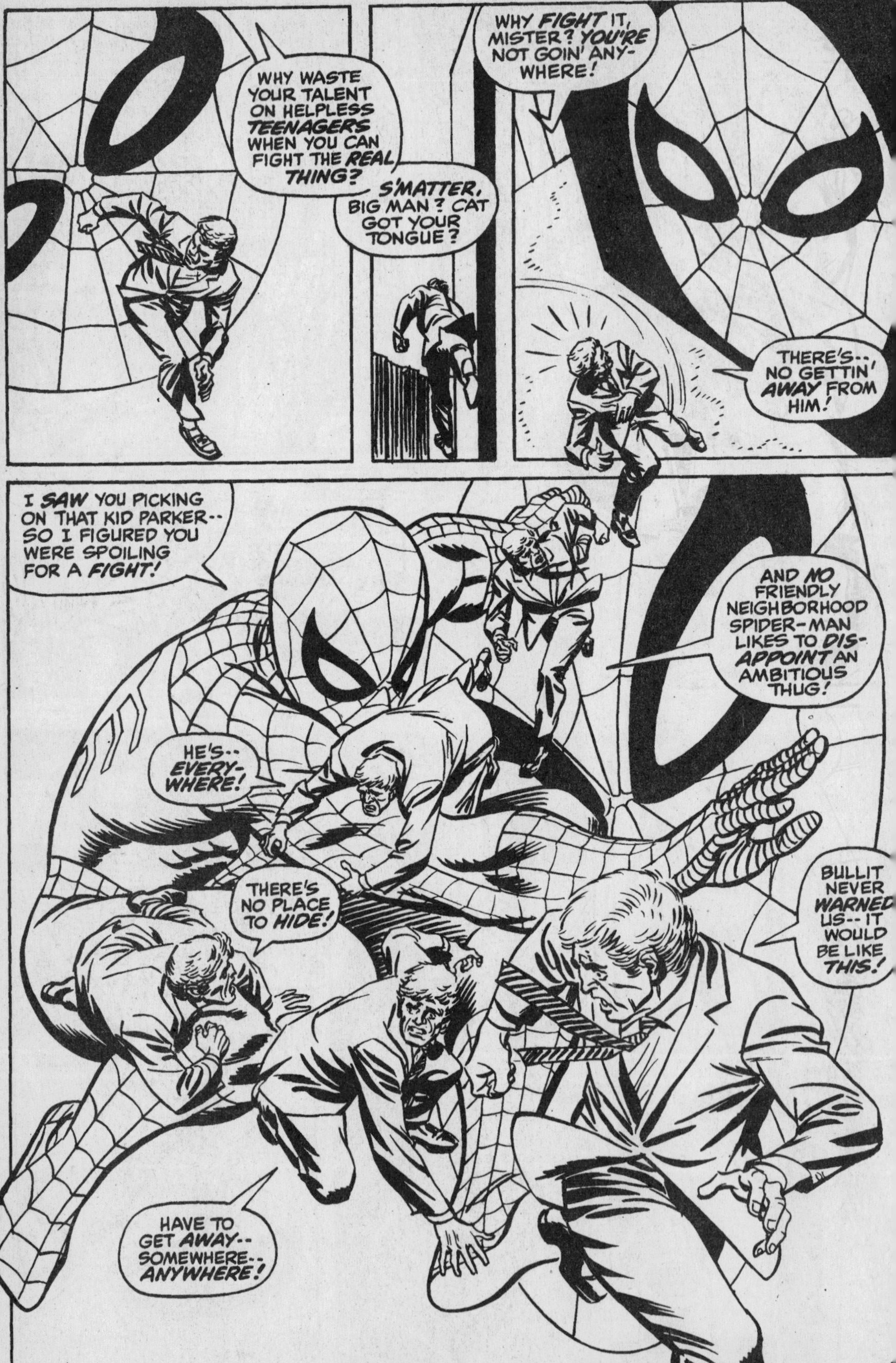
WHY WASTE YOUR TALENT ON HELPLESS TEENAGERS WHEN YOU CAN FIGHT THE REAL THING?
S'MATTER, BIG MAN? CAT GOT YOUR TONGUE?
WHY FIGHT IT, MISTER? YOU'RE NOT GOIN' ANY-WHERE!
THERE'S-- NO GETTIN' AWAY FROM HIM!
I SAW YOU PICKING ON THAT KID PARKER-- SO I FIGURED YOU WERE SPOILING FOR A FIGHT!
AND NO FRIENDLY NEIGHBORHOOD SPIDER-MAN LIKES TO DIS-APPOINT AN AMBITIOUS THUG!
HE'S-- EVERY-WHERE!
THERE'S NO PLACE TO HIDE!
BULLIT NEVER WARNED US-- IT WOULD BE LIKE THIS!
HAVE TO GET AWAY-- SOMEWHERE-- ANYWHERE!

I-- I *MADE* IT! I *LOST* 'IM!

I WOULDN'T *BET* ON IT, *BRIGHT BOY!*

I *SEE* YOU NOW! BUT-- YOU'RE *UNARMED!*

NO MATTER *HOW GOOD* YOU ARE-- --A *.45* CAN *STOP* YOU!

ONLY IF YOU *GET* A CHANCE TO *USE* IT, MAN!

NO!

ZIK!

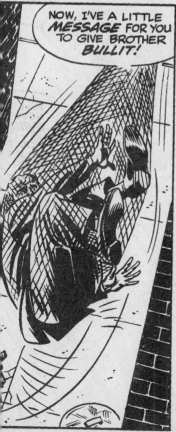

NOW, I'VE A LITTLE *MESSAGE* FOR YOU TO GIVE BROTHER *BULLIT!*

AND I WANNA MAKE SURE YOU GET IT *STRAIGHT*---

SO I'LL *PUNCTUATE* IT NICE AND *CAREFUL* FOR YOU!

18

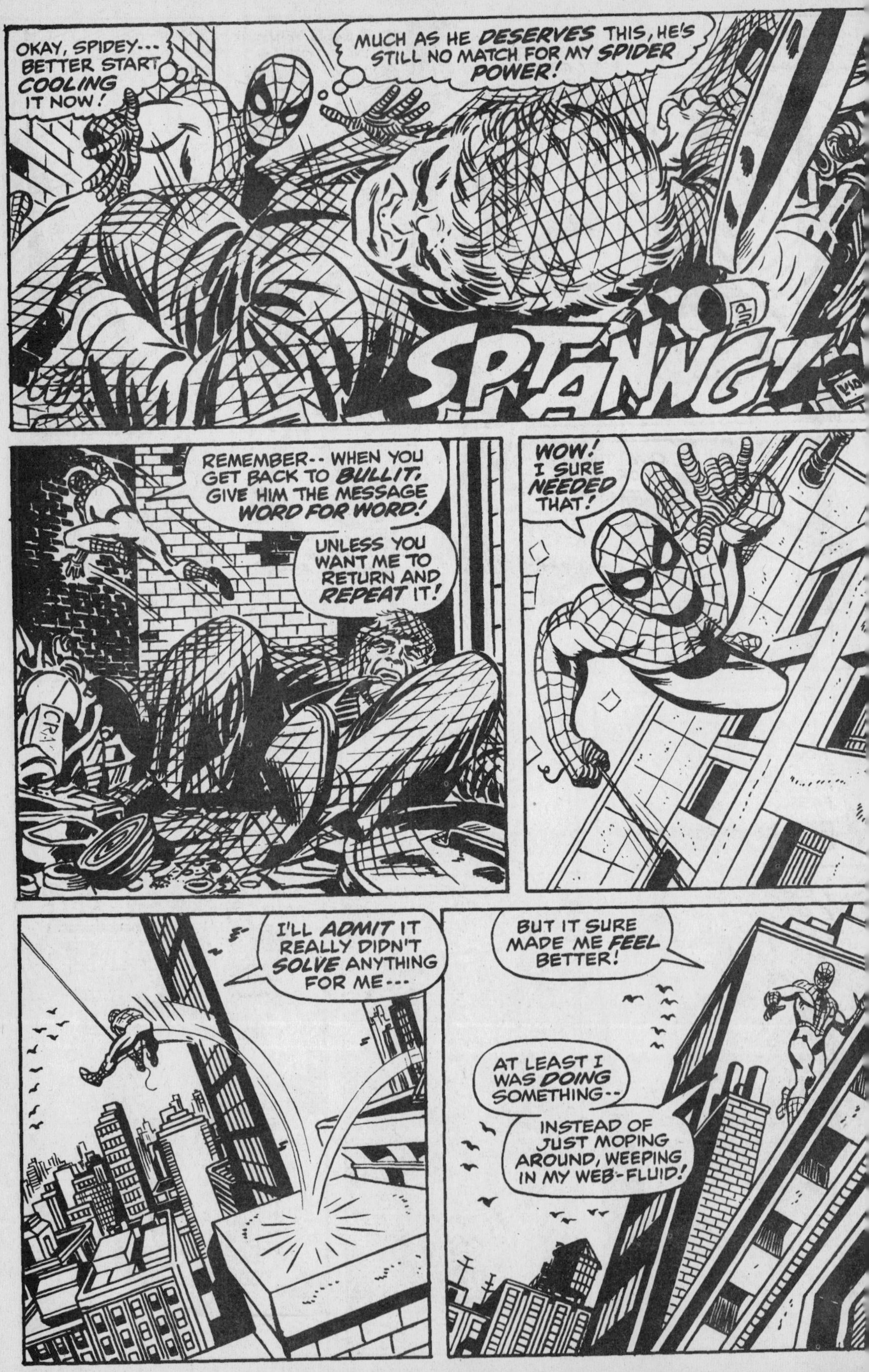

OKAY, SPIDEY--- BETTER START COOLING IT NOW!
MUCH AS HE DESERVES THIS, HE'S STILL NO MATCH FOR MY SPIDER POWER!
SPTANNG!
REMEMBER-- WHEN YOU GET BACK TO BULLIT, GIVE HIM THE MESSAGE WORD FOR WORD!
UNLESS YOU WANT ME TO RETURN AND REPEAT IT!
WOW! I SURE NEEDED THAT!
I'LL ADMIT IT REALLY DIDN'T SOLVE ANYTHING FOR ME---
BUT IT SURE MADE ME FEEL BETTER!
AT LEAST I WAS DOING SOMETHING--
INSTEAD OF JUST MOPING AROUND, WEEPING IN MY WEB-FLUID!

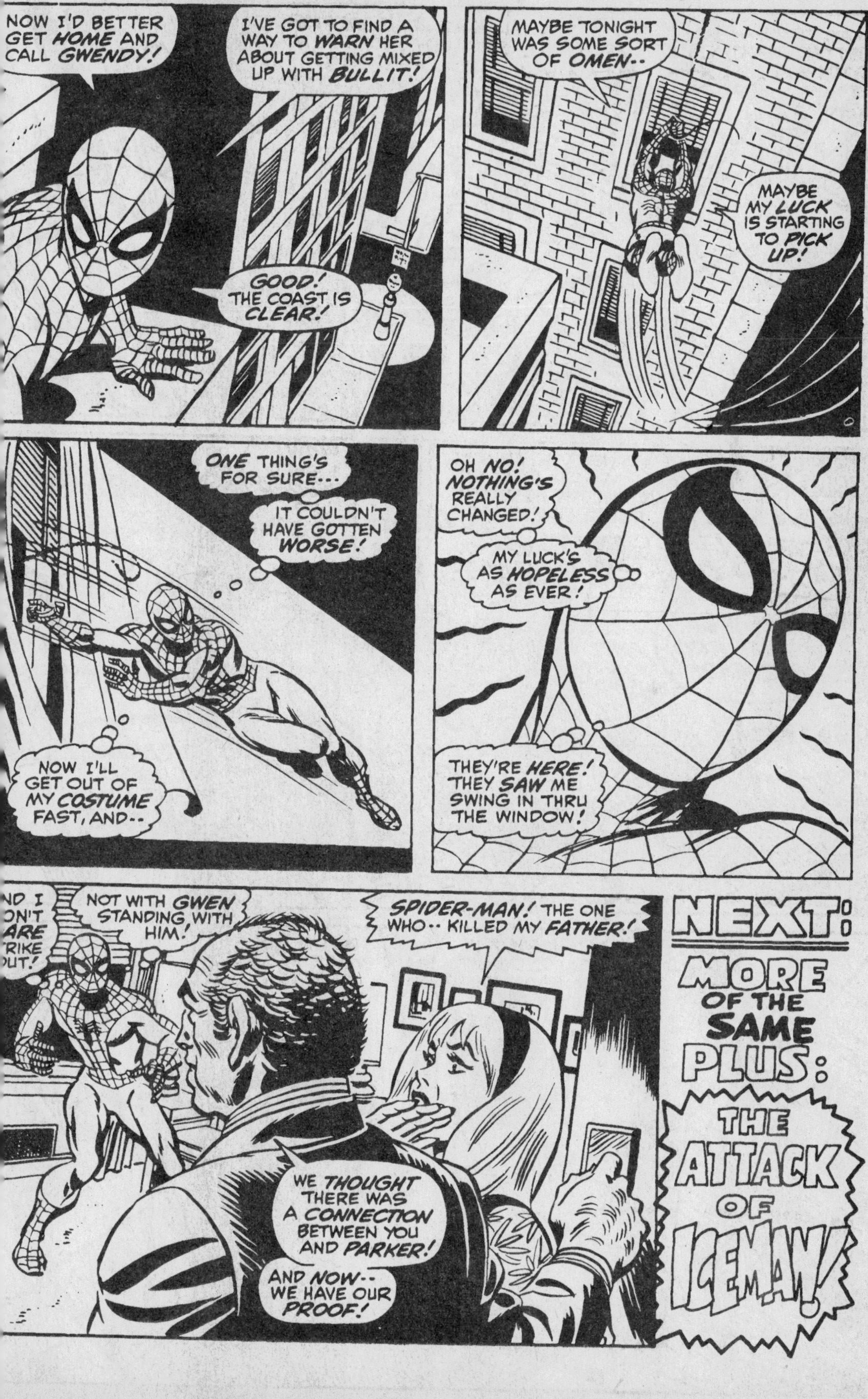

NOW I'D BETTER GET HOME AND CALL GWENDY!
I'VE GOT TO FIND A WAY TO WARN HER ABOUT GETTING MIXED UP WITH BULLIT!
GOOD! THE COAST IS CLEAR!
MAYBE TONIGHT WAS SOME SORT OF OMEN--
MAYBE MY LUCK IS STARTING TO PICK UP!
ONE THING'S FOR SURE...
IT COULDN'T HAVE GOTTEN WORSE!
NOW I'LL GET OUT OF MY COSTUME FAST, AND--
OH NO! NOTHING'S REALLY CHANGED!
MY LUCK'S AS HOPELESS AS EVER!
THEY'RE HERE! THEY SAW ME SWING IN THRU THE WINDOW!
NOT WITH GWEN STANDING WITH HIM!
SPIDER-MAN! THE ONE WHO-- KILLED MY FATHER!
WE THOUGHT THERE WAS A CONNECTION BETWEEN YOU AND PARKER!
AND NOW-- WE HAVE OUR PROOF!
NEXT:
MORE OF THE SAME PLUS:
THE ATTACK OF ICEMAN!

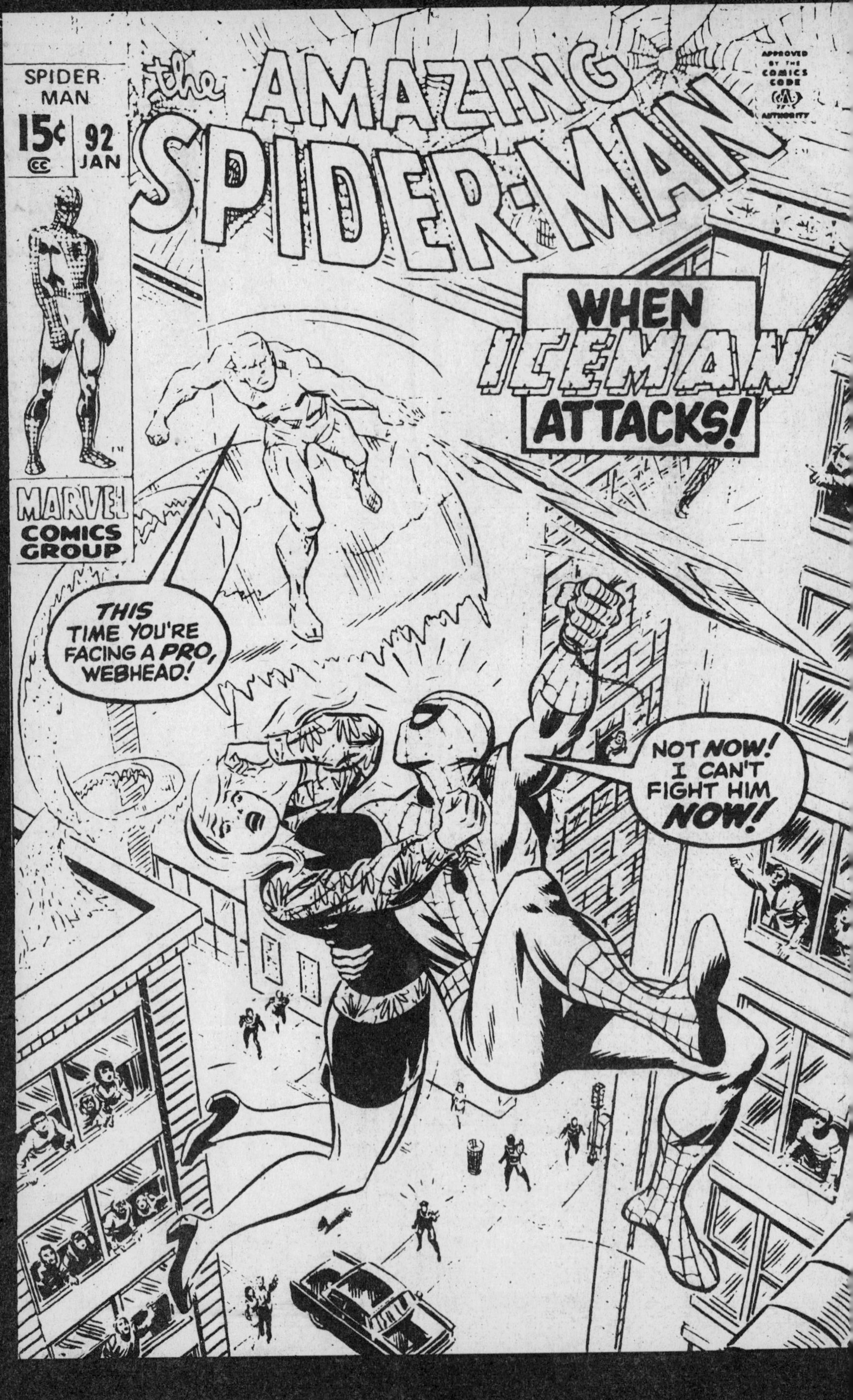
SPIDER MAN
15¢
92
JAN
CC
APPROVED BY THE COMICS CODE AUTHORITY
the AMAZING SPIDER-MAN
MARVEL COMICS GROUP
WHEN ICEMAN ATTACKS!
THIS TIME YOU'RE FACING A PRO, WEBHEAD!
NOT NOW! I CAN'T FIGHT HIM NOW!

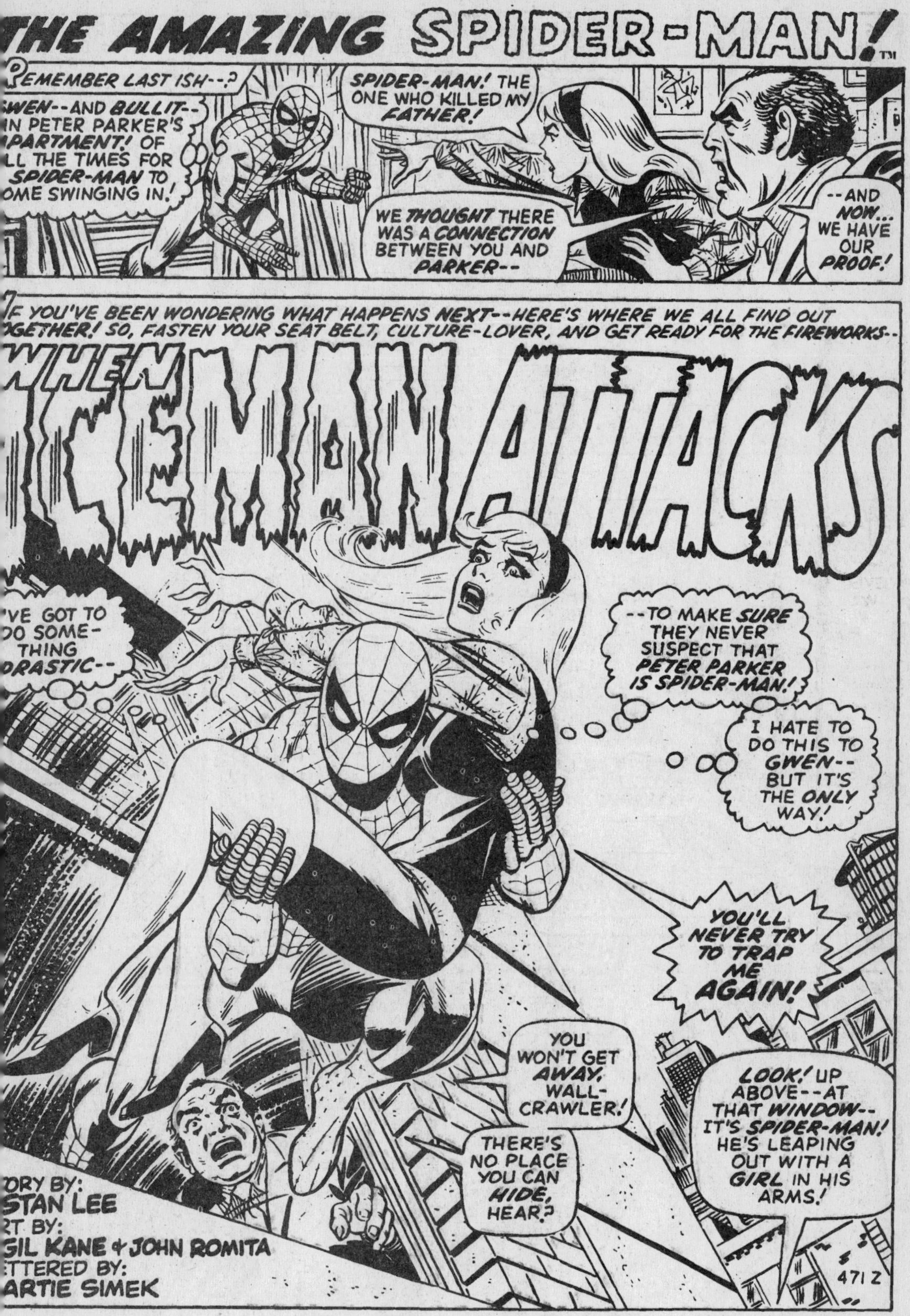

THE AMAZING SPIDER-MAN!
EMEMBER LAST ISH--?
WEN--AND BULLIT--IN PETER PARKER'S PARTMENT! OF LL THE TIMES FOR SPIDER-MAN TO OME SWINGING IN!
SPIDER-MAN! THE ONE WHO KILLED MY FATHER!
WE THOUGHT THERE WAS A CONNECTION BETWEEN YOU AND PARKER--
--AND NOW... WE HAVE OUR PROOF!
F YOU'VE BEEN WONDERING WHAT HAPPENS NEXT--HERE'S WHERE WE ALL FIND OUT OGETHER! SO, FASTEN YOUR SEAT BELT, CULTURE-LOVER, AND GET READY FOR THE FIREWORKS--
WHEN
CEMAN ATTACKS
'VE GOT TO DO SOME-THING DRASTIC--
--TO MAKE SURE THEY NEVER SUSPECT THAT PETER PARKER IS SPIDER-MAN!
I HATE TO DO THIS TO GWEN--BUT IT'S THE ONLY WAY!
YOU'LL NEVER TRY TO TRAP ME AGAIN!
YOU WON'T GET AWAY, WALL-CRAWLER!
THERE'S NO PLACE YOU CAN HIDE, HEAR?
LOOK! UP ABOVE--AT THAT WINDOW--IT'S SPIDER-MAN! HE'S LEAPING OUT WITH A GIRL IN HIS ARMS!
ORY BY: STAN LEE
RT BY: GIL KANE & JOHN ROMITA
ETTERED BY: ARTIE SIMEK
471 Z

Panel 1:
NY DOESN'T OMEBODY O SOMETHING?

AGAINST *SPIDER-MAN?* BITE YOUR *TONGUE*, BABY!

SHE'S *RIGHT!* BUT I HAVE TO GET *RID* OF HER FIRST!

Panel 2:
IT'S GETTING *LATE*, HONEY! I'LL CALL A *CAB* FOR YOU!

LATE? BUT--!

A GUY NEEDS HIS *BEAUTY* SLEEP!

TAXI!

Panel 3:
I *HATED* TO *DO* THAT!

--SPECIALLY AFTER IT TOOK ME *WEEKS* TO FINALLY GET A *DATE* WITH HER!

BUT THIS IS *MORE* IMPORTANT!

PARK 7AM TO 6PM

Panel 4:
VE BEEN OUT OF ACTION WITH THE MEN LONG ENOUGH, ANYWAY!*

BUT *THIS* TIME, I'LL HAVETA GO IT *ALONE!*

IT'LL ONLY TAKE *SECONDS* TO START *FREEZING* UP!

-MEN: A SECRET ROUP OF MUTANTS, CH WITH A STRANGE, PERHUMAN POWER -AS IF YOU DIDN'T KNOW! --STAN.

Panel 5:
OKAY, WEB-HEAD! YOU'RE A *BIG MAN* WITH A HELPLESS *FEMALE*--

BUT LET'S SEE HOW YOU DO *AGAINST*-- *ICEMAN!!*

A QUICK-FREEZE *ICE BRIDGE* WILL BE THE FASTEST WAY TO *REACH* HIM!

AND THEN-- IT'LL BE EVERY MAN FOR *HIMSELF!*

3

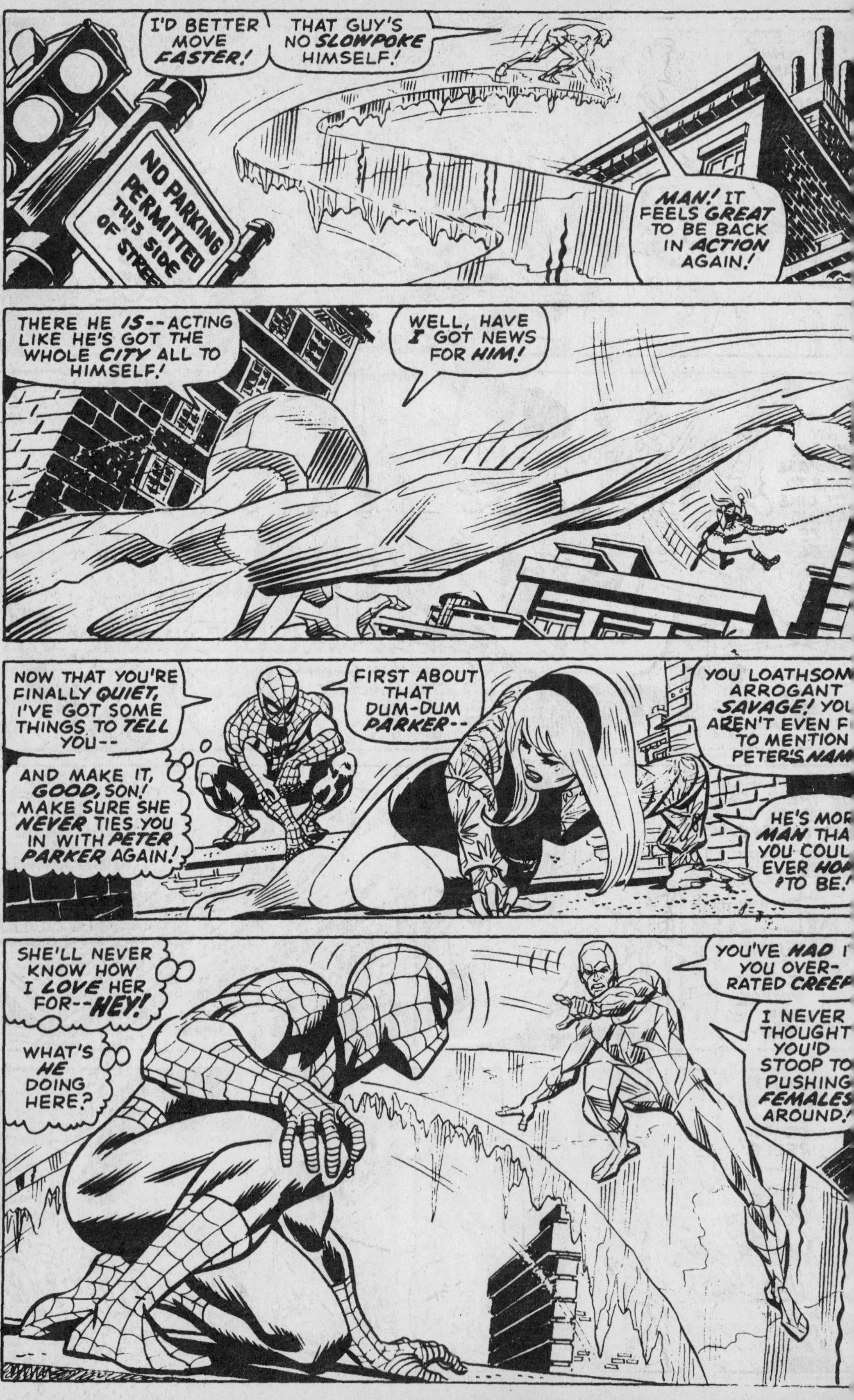
I'D BETTER MOVE FASTER!
THAT GUY'S NO SLOWPOKE HIMSELF!
NO PARKING PERMITTED THIS SIDE OF STREE
MAN! IT FEELS GREAT TO BE BACK IN ACTION AGAIN!
THERE HE IS--ACTING LIKE HE'S GOT THE WHOLE CITY ALL TO HIMSELF!
WELL, HAVE I GOT NEWS FOR HIM!
NOW THAT YOU'RE FINALLY QUIET, I'VE GOT SOME THINGS TO TELL YOU--
FIRST ABOUT THAT DUM-DUM PARKER--
AND MAKE IT, GOOD, SON! MAKE SURE SHE NEVER TIES YOU IN WITH PETER PARKER AGAIN!
YOU LOATHSOM ARROGANT SAVAGE! YOU AREN'T EVEN F TO MENTION PETER'S NAM
HE'S MOR MAN THA YOU COUL EVER HOP TO BE!
SHE'LL NEVER KNOW HOW I LOVE HER FOR--HEY!
WHAT'S HE DOING HERE?
YOU'VE HAD I YOU OVER-RATED CREEP
I NEVER THOUGHT YOU'D STOOP TO PUSHING FEMALES AROUND!

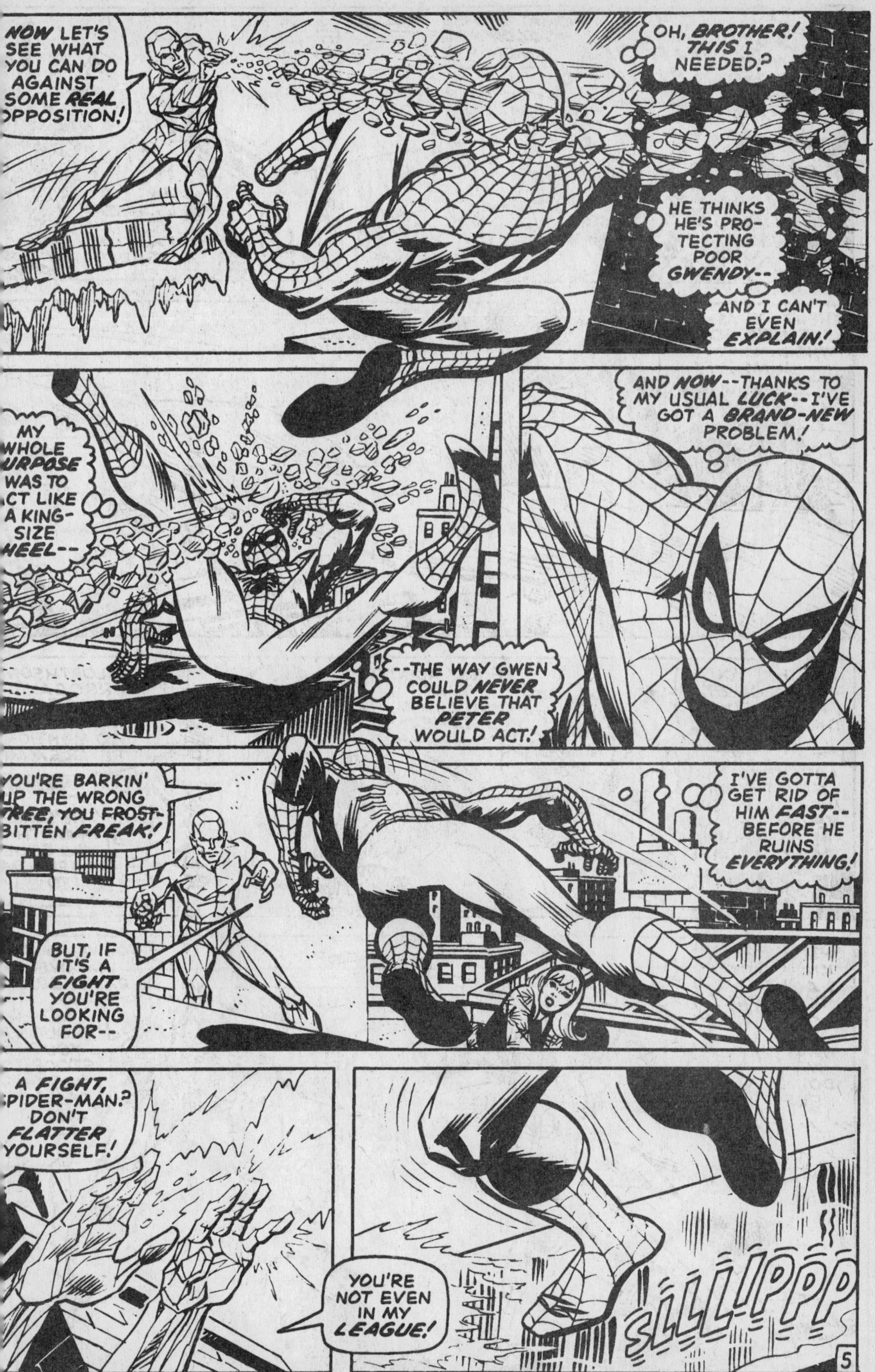

NOW LET'S SEE WHAT YOU CAN DO AGAINST SOME REAL OPPOSITION!
OH, BROTHER! THIS I NEEDED?
HE THINKS HE'S PROTECTING POOR GWENDY--
AND I CAN'T EVEN EXPLAIN!
MY WHOLE PURPOSE WAS TO ACT LIKE A KING-SIZE HEEL--
--THE WAY GWEN COULD NEVER BELIEVE THAT PETER WOULD ACT!
AND NOW--THANKS TO MY USUAL LUCK--I'VE GOT A BRAND-NEW PROBLEM!
YOU'RE BARKIN' UP THE WRONG TREE, YOU FROST-BITTEN FREAK!
BUT, IF IT'S A FIGHT YOU'RE LOOKING FOR--
I'VE GOTTA GET RID OF HIM FAST--BEFORE HE RUINS EVERYTHING!
A FIGHT, SPIDER-MAN? DON'T FLATTER YOURSELF!
YOU'RE NOT EVEN IN MY LEAGUE!
SLLLIPPP

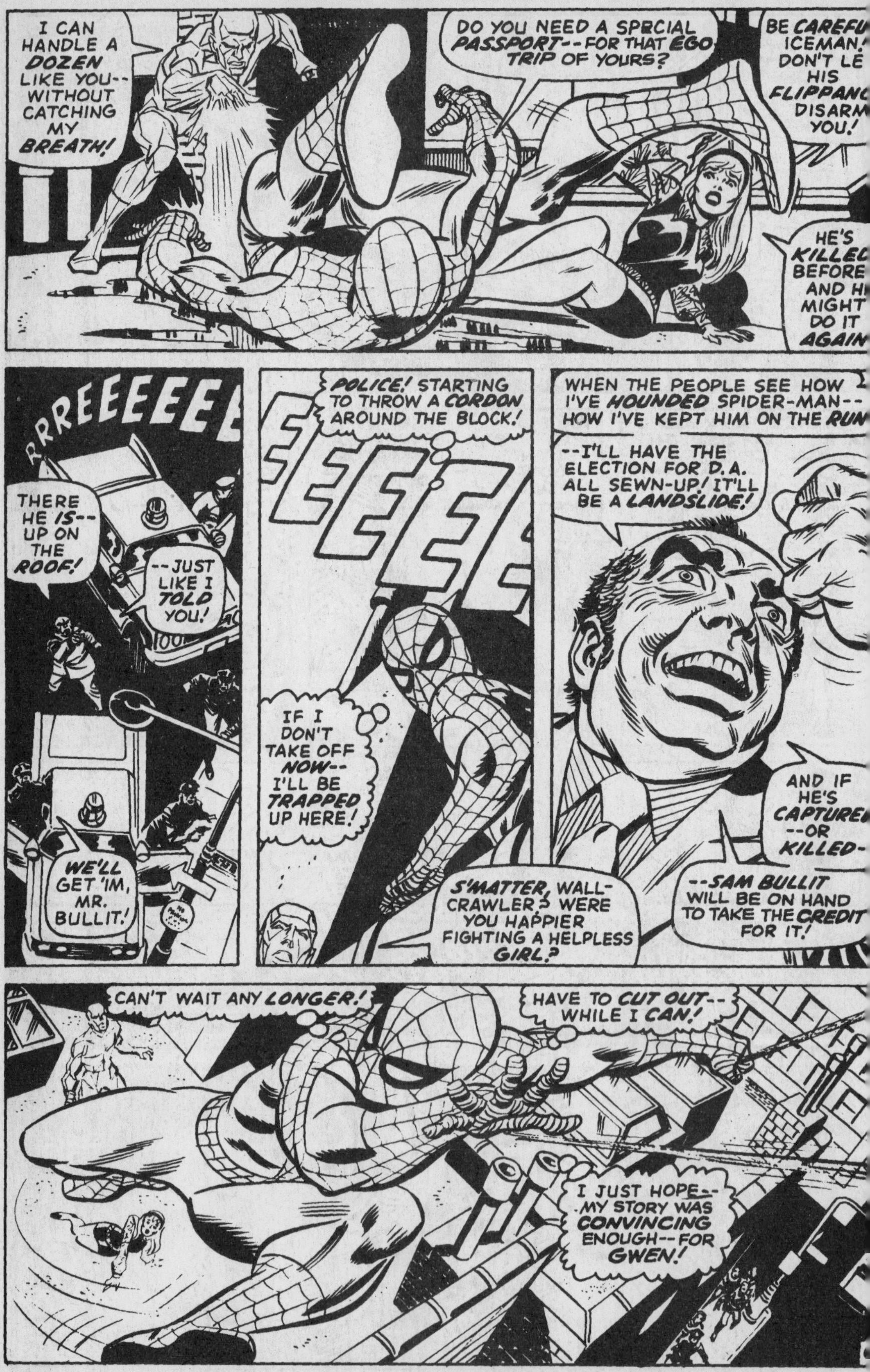

I CAN HANDLE A DOZEN LIKE YOU--WITHOUT CATCHING MY BREATH!
DO YOU NEED A SPECIAL PASSPORT--FOR THAT EGO TRIP OF YOURS?
BE CAREFU ICEMAN, DON'T LE HIS FLIPPAN DISARM YOU!
HE'S KILLE BEFORE AND H MIGHT DO IT AGAIN
RRREEEEEEE
THERE HE IS--UP ON THE ROOF!
--JUST LIKE I TOLD YOU!
WE'LL GET 'IM, MR. BULLIT!
POLICE! STARTING TO THROW A CORDON AROUND THE BLOCK!
EEEE
IF I DON'T TAKE OFF NOW--I'LL BE TRAPPED UP HERE!
S'MATTER, WALL-CRAWLER? WERE YOU HAPPIER FIGHTING A HELPLESS GIRL?
WHEN THE PEOPLE SEE HOW I'VE HOUNDED SPIDER-MAN--HOW I'VE KEPT HIM ON THE RUN
--I'LL HAVE THE ELECTION FOR D.A. ALL SEWN-UP! IT'LL BE A LANDSLIDE!
AND IF HE'S CAPTURE --OR KILLED-
--SAM BULLIT WILL BE ON HAND TO TAKE THE CREDIT FOR IT!
CAN'T WAIT ANY LONGER!
HAVE TO CUT OUT--WHILE I CAN!
I JUST HOPE--MY STORY WAS CONVINCING ENOUGH--FOR GWEN!

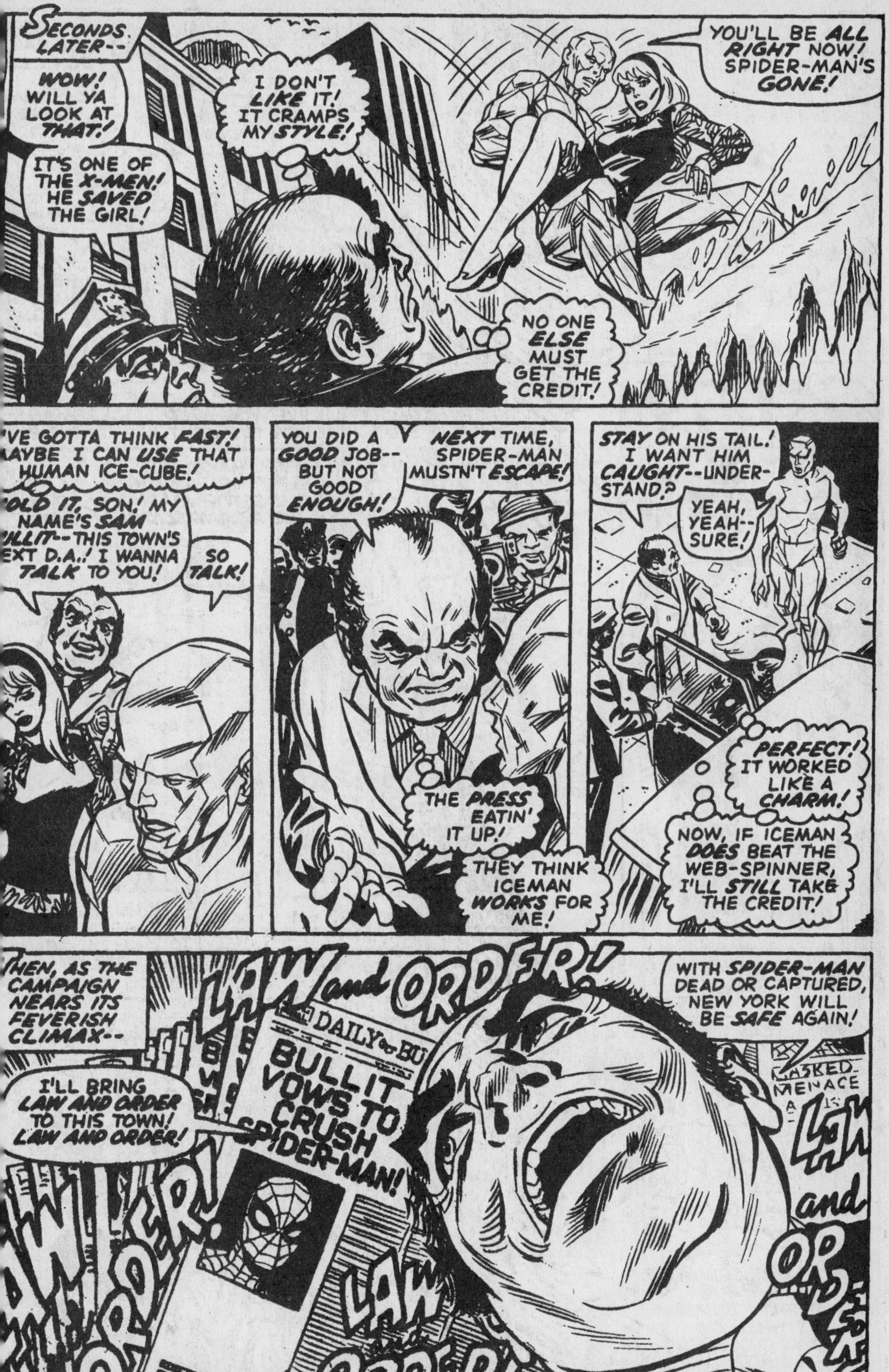

SECONDS LATER--
WOW! WILL YA LOOK AT THAT!
IT'S ONE OF THE X-MEN! HE SAVED THE GIRL!
I DON'T LIKE IT! IT CRAMPS MY STYLE!
YOU'LL BE ALL RIGHT NOW! SPIDER-MAN'S GONE!
NO ONE ELSE MUST GET THE CREDIT!
'VE GOTTA THINK FAST! AYBE I CAN USE THAT HUMAN ICE-CUBE!
OLD IT, SON! MY NAME'S SAM ULLIT--THIS TOWN'S EXT D.A.! I WANNA TALK TO YOU!
SO TALK!
YOU DID A GOOD JOB--BUT NOT GOOD ENOUGH!
NEXT TIME, SPIDER-MAN MUSTN'T ESCAPE!
THE PRESS EATIN' IT UP!
THEY THINK ICEMAN WORKS FOR ME!
STAY ON HIS TAIL! I WANT HIM CAUGHT--UNDERSTAND?
YEAH, YEAH--SURE!
PERFECT! IT WORKED LIKE A CHARM!
NOW, IF ICEMAN DOES BEAT THE WEB-SPINNER, I'LL STILL TAKE THE CREDIT!
THEN, AS THE CAMPAIGN NEARS ITS FEVERISH CLIMAX--
LAW and ORDER!
DAILY BU
BULLIT VOWS TO CRUSH SPIDER-MAN!
WITH SPIDER-MAN DEAD OR CAPTURED, NEW YORK WILL BE SAFE AGAIN!
I'LL BRING LAW AND ORDER TO THIS TOWN! LAW AND ORDER!
LAW and ORDER!
LAW ORDER!

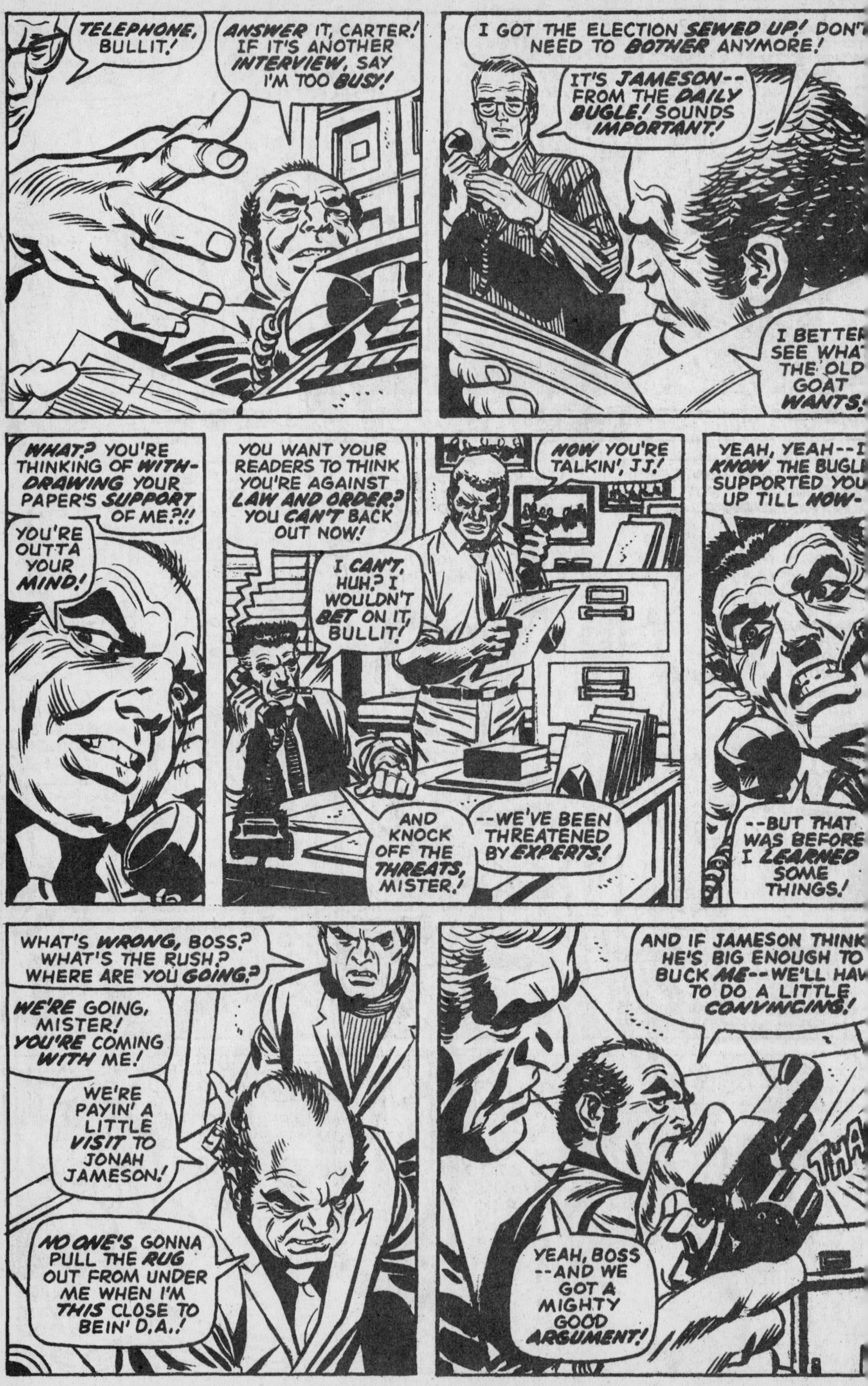
TELEPHONE, BULLIT!
ANSWER IT, CARTER! IF IT'S ANOTHER INTERVIEW, SAY I'M TOO BUSY!
I GOT THE ELECTION SEWED UP! DON'T NEED TO BOTHER ANYMORE!
IT'S JAMESON-- FROM THE DAILY BUGLE! SOUNDS IMPORTANT!
I BETTER SEE WHAT THE OLD GOAT WANTS!
WHAT? YOU'RE THINKING OF WITH-DRAWING YOUR PAPER'S SUPPORT OF ME?!!
YOU'RE OUTTA YOUR MIND!
YOU WANT YOUR READERS TO THINK YOU'RE AGAINST LAW AND ORDER? YOU CAN'T BACK OUT NOW!
I CAN'T, HUH? I WOULDN'T BET ON IT, BULLIT!
NOW YOU'RE TALKIN', JJ!
AND KNOCK OFF THE THREATS, MISTER!
--WE'VE BEEN THREATENED BY EXPERTS!
YEAH, YEAH--I KNOW THE BUGLE SUPPORTED YOU UP TILL NOW--
--BUT THAT WAS BEFORE I LEARNED SOME THINGS!
WHAT'S WRONG, BOSS? WHAT'S THE RUSH? WHERE ARE YOU GOING?
WE'RE GOING, MISTER! YOU'RE COMING WITH ME!
WE'RE PAYIN' A LITTLE VISIT TO JONAH JAMESON!
NO ONE'S GONNA PULL THE RUG OUT FROM UNDER ME WHEN I'M THIS CLOSE TO BEIN' D.A.!
AND IF JAMESON THINKS HE'S BIG ENOUGH TO BUCK ME--WE'LL HAVE TO DO A LITTLE CONVINCING!
YEAH, BOSS --AND WE GOT A MIGHTY GOOD ARGUMENT!

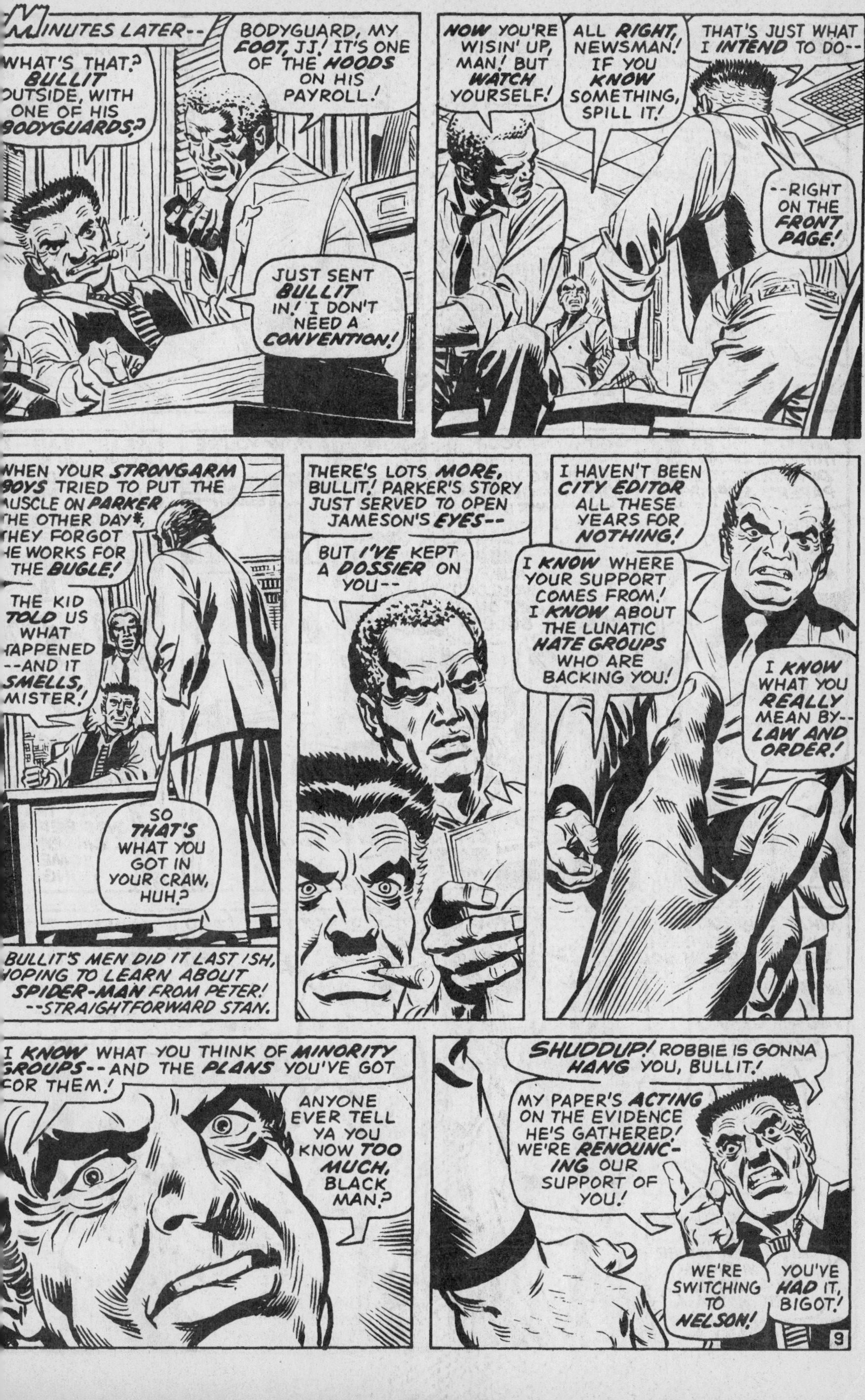
MINUTES LATER--
WHAT'S THAT? BULLIT OUTSIDE, WITH ONE OF HIS BODYGUARDS?
BODYGUARD, MY FOOT, J.J.! IT'S ONE OF THE HOODS ON HIS PAYROLL!
JUST SENT BULLIT IN! I DON'T NEED A CONVENTION!
NOW YOU'RE WISIN' UP, MAN! BUT WATCH YOURSELF!
ALL RIGHT, NEWSMAN! IF YOU KNOW SOMETHING, SPILL IT!
THAT'S JUST WHAT I INTEND TO DO--
--RIGHT ON THE FRONT PAGE!
WHEN YOUR STRONGARM BOYS TRIED TO PUT THE MUSCLE ON PARKER THE OTHER DAY*, THEY FORGOT HE WORKS FOR THE BUGLE!
THE KID TOLD US WHAT HAPPENED --AND IT SMELLS, MISTER!
SO THAT'S WHAT YOU GOT IN YOUR CRAW, HUH?
*BULLIT'S MEN DID IT LAST ISH, HOPING TO LEARN ABOUT SPIDER-MAN FROM PETER! --STRAIGHTFORWARD STAN.
THERE'S LOTS MORE, BULLIT! PARKER'S STORY JUST SERVED TO OPEN JAMESON'S EYES--
BUT I'VE KEPT A DOSSIER ON YOU--
I HAVEN'T BEEN CITY EDITOR ALL THESE YEARS FOR NOTHING!
I KNOW WHERE YOUR SUPPORT COMES FROM! I KNOW ABOUT THE LUNATIC HATE GROUPS WHO ARE BACKING YOU!
I KNOW WHAT YOU REALLY MEAN BY-- LAW AND ORDER!
I KNOW WHAT YOU THINK OF MINORITY GROUPS--AND THE PLANS YOU'VE GOT FOR THEM!
ANYONE EVER TELL YA YOU KNOW TOO MUCH, BLACK MAN?
SHUDDUP! ROBBIE IS GONNA HANG YOU, BULLIT!
MY PAPER'S ACTING ON THE EVIDENCE HE'S GATHERED! WE'RE RENOUNCING OUR SUPPORT OF YOU!
WE'RE SWITCHING TO NELSON!
YOU'VE HAD IT, BIGOT!
9

AND DON'T THINK WE'RE *BLUFFING*, MAN! I'VE GOT IT ALL *DOWN* HERE--NAMES, DATES AND PLACES!

AND *SAMBO* AINT *NEVER* GONNA USE IT!

I THINK HE JUST QUIT OUR *FAN CLUB*, JONAH!

TELL 'IM HE CAN *SHOVE* IT, JAMESON! EVIDENCE DON'T MEAN *NOTHING* UNLESS YA CAN *USE* IT!

GET *OUT*, BULLIT! YOU'RE TURNING MY *STOMACH!*

NOW AINT THAT A SHAME!

SLAM!

I'M GLAD YOU LISTENED TO *PARKER*, JJ! I *HOPED* IT WOULD OPEN YOUR EYES!

NUTS! I HAD BULLIT PEGGED ALL THE *TIME!*

BUT YOU BETTER *WATCH* YOURSELF, ROBBIE!

HE CAN BE *DANGEROUS!*

LATER, IN THE HALL OUTSIDE--

IT'S LUCKY I STAYED AROUND!

THOSE ARE THE SAME TWO *HOODS* WHO HASSLED ME *BEFORE!*

AND-- *NOW--* THEY'RE HEADING FOR *ROBBIE'S OFFICE!*

I *THOUGHT* SOMETHING LIKE THIS MIGHT HAPPEN!

I *THOUGHT* SO! HE'S *LEAVING* WITH THEM!

AND I'M BETTING THAT IT ISN'T 'CAUSE HE LIKES THEIR *COMPANY!*

YOU DON'T REALLY EXPECT TO GET *AWAY* WITH THIS?

JUST KEEP *WALKIN'*, SMART GUY!

I WAS *RIGHT!*

IT'S LIKE WATCHING AN OLD *HUMPHREY BOGART* MOVIE!

ONLY THIS IS FOR *REAL!*

ONE THING ABOUT BULLIT--HE SURE DOESN'T WASTE ANY *TIME!*

AND THE SAME BETTER GO FOR *SPIDER MAN!*

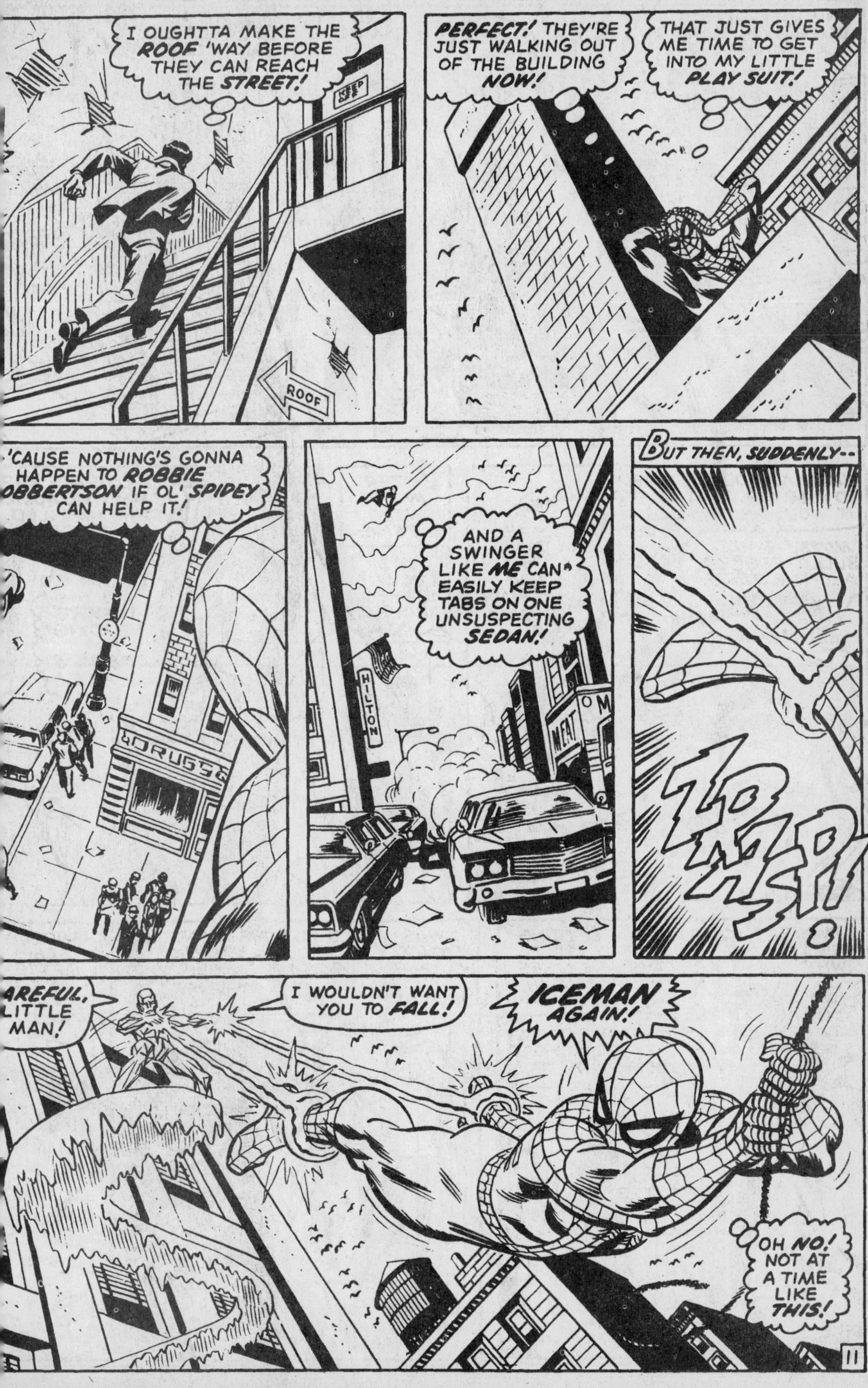
I OUGHTTA MAKE THE ROOF 'WAY BEFORE THEY CAN REACH THE STREET!
KEEP OFF
ROOF
PERFECT! THEY'RE JUST WALKING OUT OF THE BUILDING NOW!
THAT JUST GIVES ME TIME TO GET INTO MY LITTLE PLAY SUIT!
'CAUSE NOTHING'S GONNA HAPPEN TO ROBBIE OBBERTSON IF OL' SPIDEY CAN HELP IT!
DRUGS
AND A SWINGER LIKE ME CAN EASILY KEEP TABS ON ONE UNSUSPECTING SEDAN!
HILTON
MEAT
BUT THEN, SUDDENLY--
ZOWSP!
AREFUL, LITTLE MAN!
I WOULDN'T WANT YOU TO FALL!
ICEMAN AGAIN!
OH NO! NOT AT A TIME LIKE THIS!
11

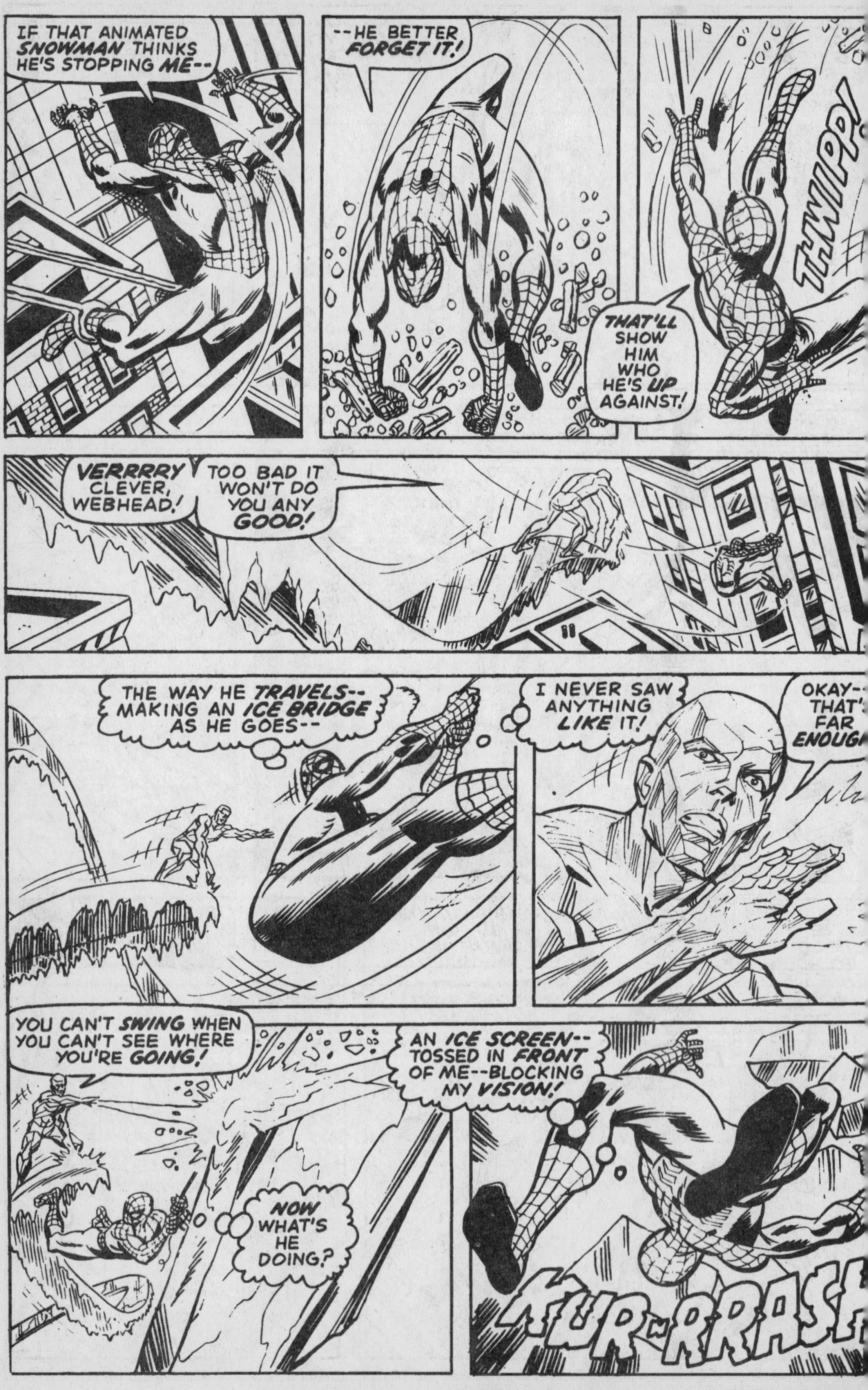

IF THAT ANIMATED SNOWMAN THINKS HE'S STOPPING ME--
--HE BETTER FORGET IT!
THAT'LL SHOW HIM WHO HE'S UP AGAINST!
THWIPP!
VERRRRY CLEVER, WEBHEAD!
TOO BAD IT WON'T DO YOU ANY GOOD!
THE WAY HE TRAVELS-- MAKING AN ICE BRIDGE AS HE GOES--
I NEVER SAW ANYTHING LIKE IT!
OKAY-- THAT'S FAR ENOUG
YOU CAN'T SWING WHEN YOU CAN'T SEE WHERE YOU'RE GOING!
NOW WHAT'S HE DOING?
AN ICE SCREEN-- TOSSED IN FRONT OF ME--BLOCKING MY VISION!
KUR-RRASH

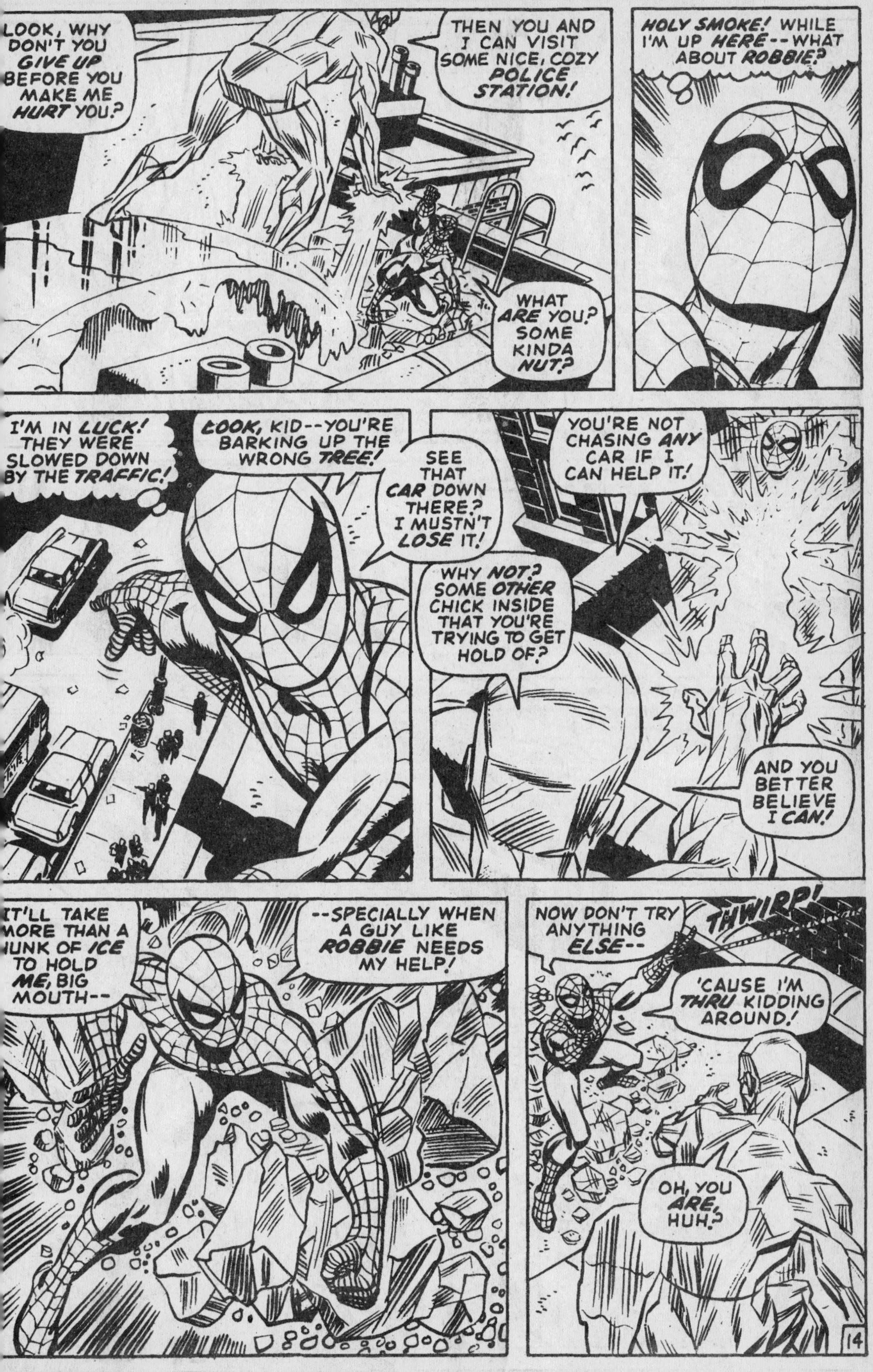
LOOK, WHY DON'T YOU GIVE UP BEFORE YOU MAKE ME HURT YOU?
THEN YOU AND I CAN VISIT SOME NICE, COZY POLICE STATION!
WHAT ARE YOU? SOME KINDA NUT?
HOLY SMOKE! WHILE I'M UP HERE--WHAT ABOUT ROBBIE?
I'M IN LUCK! THEY WERE SLOWED DOWN BY THE TRAFFIC!
LOOK, KID--YOU'RE BARKING UP THE WRONG TREE!
SEE THAT CAR DOWN THERE? I MUSTN'T LOSE IT!
WHY NOT? SOME OTHER CHICK INSIDE THAT YOU'RE TRYING TO GET HOLD OF?
YOU'RE NOT CHASING ANY CAR IF I CAN HELP IT!
AND YOU BETTER BELIEVE I CAN!
IT'LL TAKE MORE THAN A HUNK OF ICE TO HOLD ME, BIG MOUTH--
--SPECIALLY WHEN A GUY LIKE ROBBIE NEEDS MY HELP!
NOW DON'T TRY ANYTHING ELSE--
THWIRP!
'CAUSE I'M THRU KIDDING AROUND!
OH, YOU ARE, HUH?
14

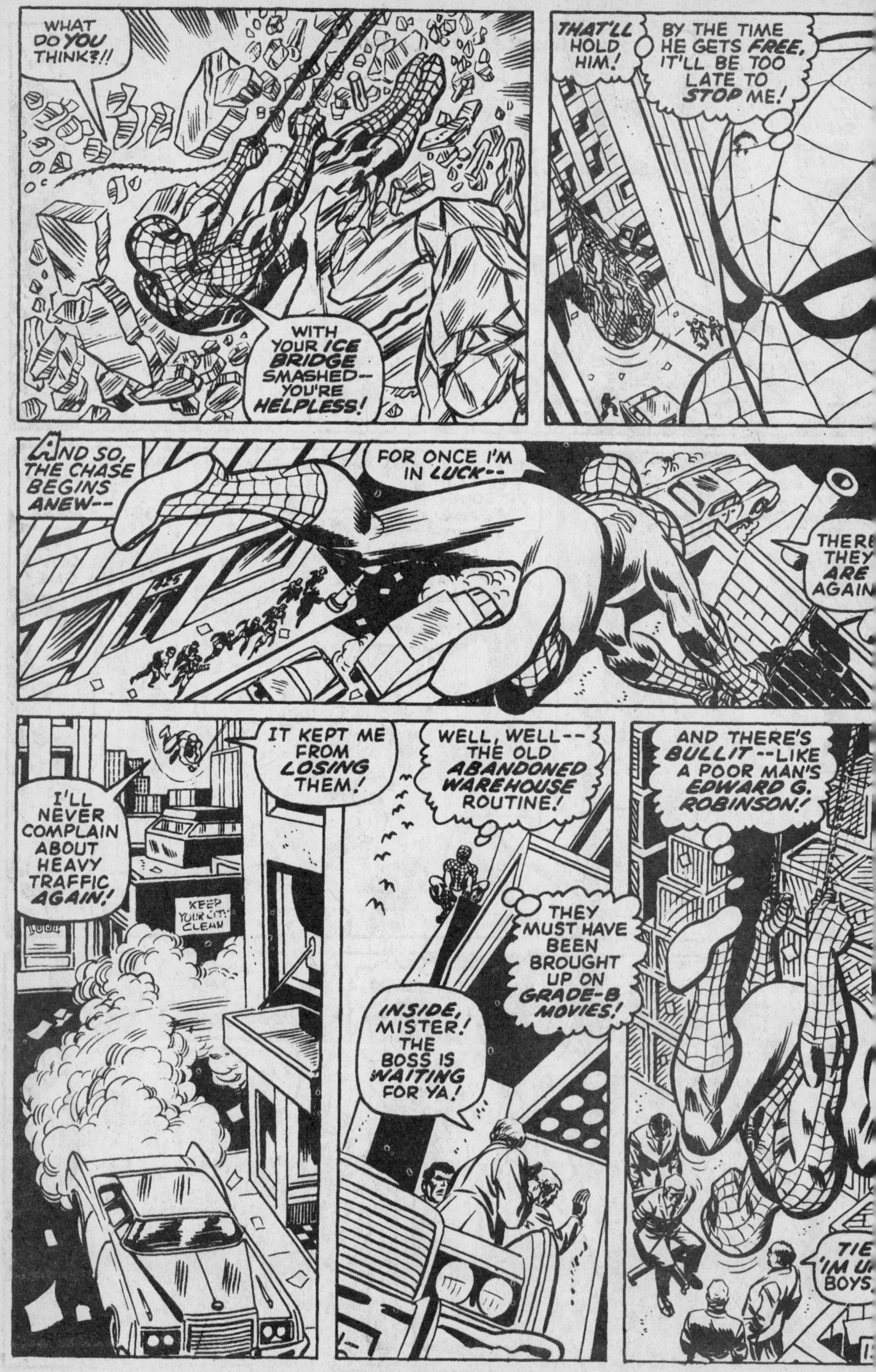

WHAT DO YOU THINK?!!
WITH YOUR ICE BRIDGE SMASHED--YOU'RE HELPLESS!
THAT'LL HOLD HIM!
BY THE TIME HE GETS FREE, IT'LL BE TOO LATE TO STOP ME!
AND SO, THE CHASE BEGINS ANEW--
FOR ONCE I'M IN LUCK--
IT KEPT ME FROM LOSING THEM!
I'LL NEVER COMPLAIN ABOUT HEAVY TRAFFIC AGAIN!
KEEP YOUR CITY CLEAN
WELL, WELL-- THE OLD ABANDONED WAREHOUSE ROUTINE!
THEY MUST HAVE BEEN BROUGHT UP ON GRADE-B MOVIES!
INSIDE, MISTER! THE BOSS IS WAITING FOR YA!
AND THERE'S BULLIT--LIKE A POOR MAN'S EDWARD G. ROBINSON!

SO--YOU'VE BEEN KEEPING A *FILE* ON ME, HUH?

NOT VERY *SMART*, BLACK MAN!

ROBBY'S IN *TROUBLE!* BULLIT MEANS *BUSINESS!*

MEANWHILE--

I *SAW* HIM SWING ONTO THIS ROOF--

THERE! THAT OPEN *SKYLIGHT* PANEL! I'VE *GOT* 'IM!

AND *THIS* TIME HE'S-- *HEY!* WHAT'S *GOIN' ON* DOWN THERE?

WITH *YOU* GONE, YOUR *FILE'S WORTH-LESS!*

YOU CAN'T KEEP ME PRISONER *FOREVER!*

WHO'S *TALKIN'* ABOUT KEEPING YOU A *PRISONER?*

THE WEB-SPINNER WAS TELLING THE *TRUTH!*

HE *WAS* CHASING THEIR CAR!

YOU WON'T BE THAT *LUCKY!*

THE BIG-MOUTH LOOKS *TIRED!* SEE THAT HE GETS A *REST,* CHARLIE--

--A *LONG* ONE!

I'M *LEAVING* --SO DO IT *NOW!*

IT'S *ICEMAN!* HE'S *SMILING!*

HE *HEARD* THEM! HE'S *WITH* ME NOW!

SO YOU WERE GONNA BLOW THE WHISTLE ON THE *BOSS,* HUH?

SKIP THE *TALK,* CHARLIE! LET'S *BLAST* 'IM!

GO *AHEAD!* IF YOU'RE WAITING FOR ME TO *CRAWL* --FORGET IT!

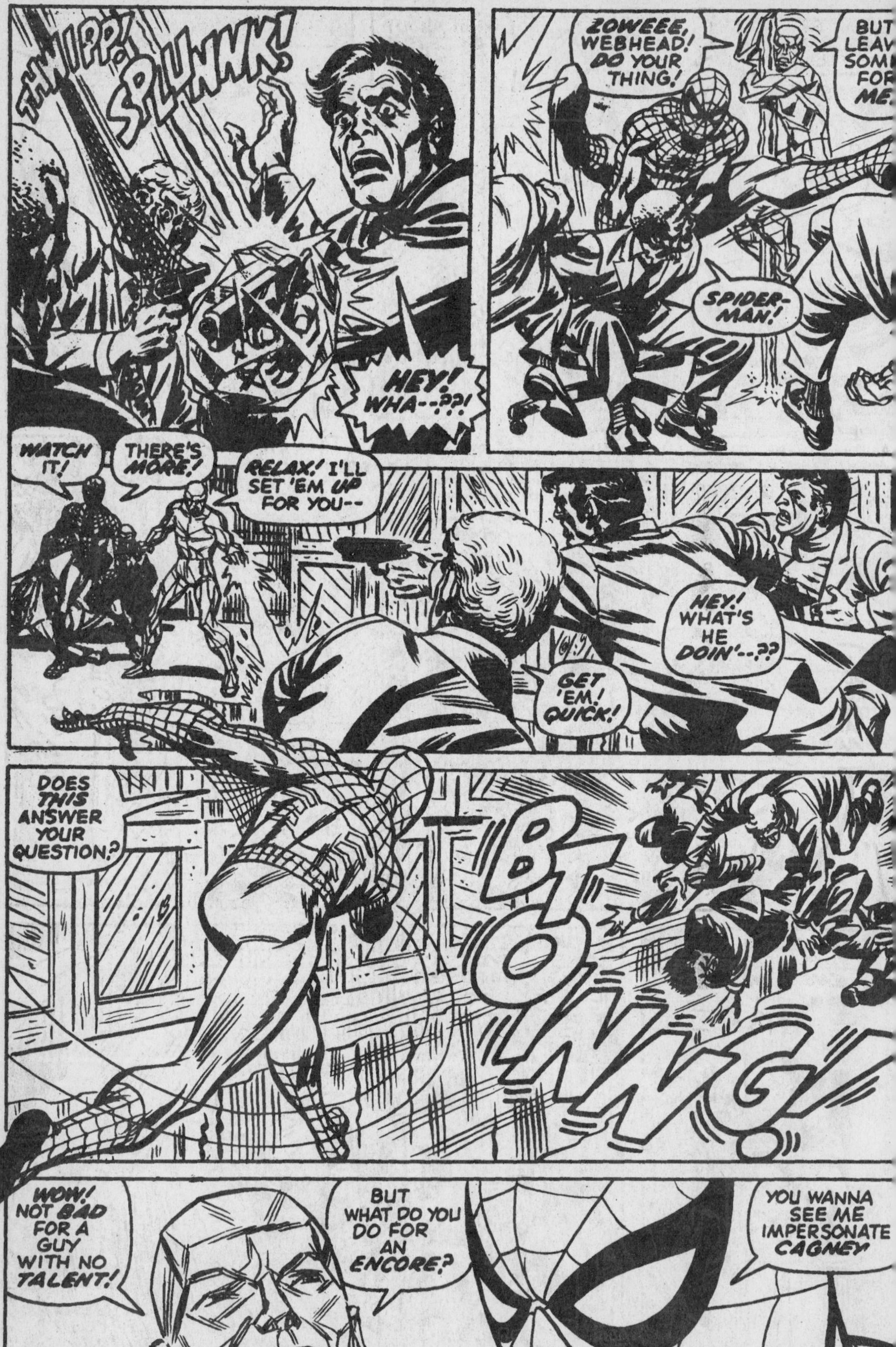
THWIPP!
SPLUNNK!
HEY! WHA--??!
ZOWEEE, WEBHEAD! DO YOUR THING!
BUT LEAV SOM FOR ME.
SPIDER-MAN!
WATCH IT!
THERE'S MORE!
RELAX! I'LL SET 'EM UP FOR YOU--
HEY! WHAT'S HE DOIN'--??
GET 'EM! QUICK!
DOES THIS ANSWER YOUR QUESTION?
BTOWNNG!
WOW! NOT BAD FOR A GUY WITH NO TALENT!
BUT WHAT DO YOU DO FOR AN ENCORE?
YOU WANNA SEE ME IMPERSONATE CAGNEY?

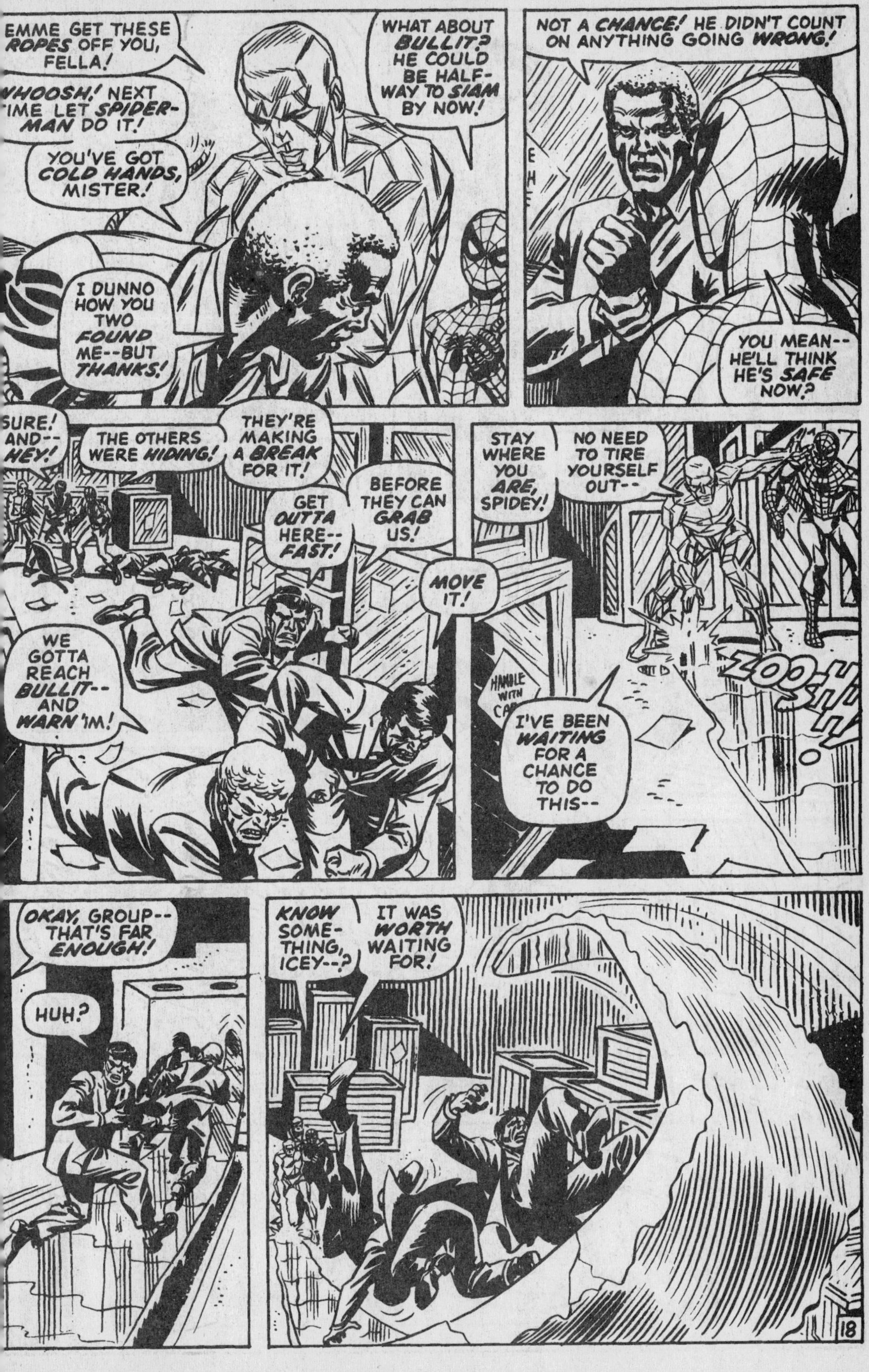

EMME GET THESE ROPES OFF YOU, FELLA!
WHOOSH! NEXT TIME LET SPIDER-MAN DO IT!
YOU'VE GOT COLD HANDS, MISTER!
I DUNNO HOW YOU TWO FOUND ME--BUT THANKS!
WHAT ABOUT BULLIT? HE COULD BE HALF-WAY TO SIAM BY NOW!
NOT A CHANCE! HE DIDN'T COUNT ON ANYTHING GOING WRONG!
YOU MEAN-- HE'LL THINK HE'S SAFE NOW?
SURE! AND-- HEY!
THE OTHERS WERE HIDING!
THEY'RE MAKING A BREAK FOR IT!
BEFORE THEY CAN GRAB US!
GET OUTTA HERE-- FAST!
MOVE IT!
WE GOTTA REACH BULLIT-- AND WARN 'IM!
STAY WHERE YOU ARE, SPIDEY!
NO NEED TO TIRE YOURSELF OUT--
I'VE BEEN WAITING FOR A CHANCE TO DO THIS--
ZOO-HH
OKAY, GROUP-- THAT'S FAR ENOUGH!
HUH?
KNOW SOME-THING, ICEY--?
IT WAS WORTH WAITING FOR!

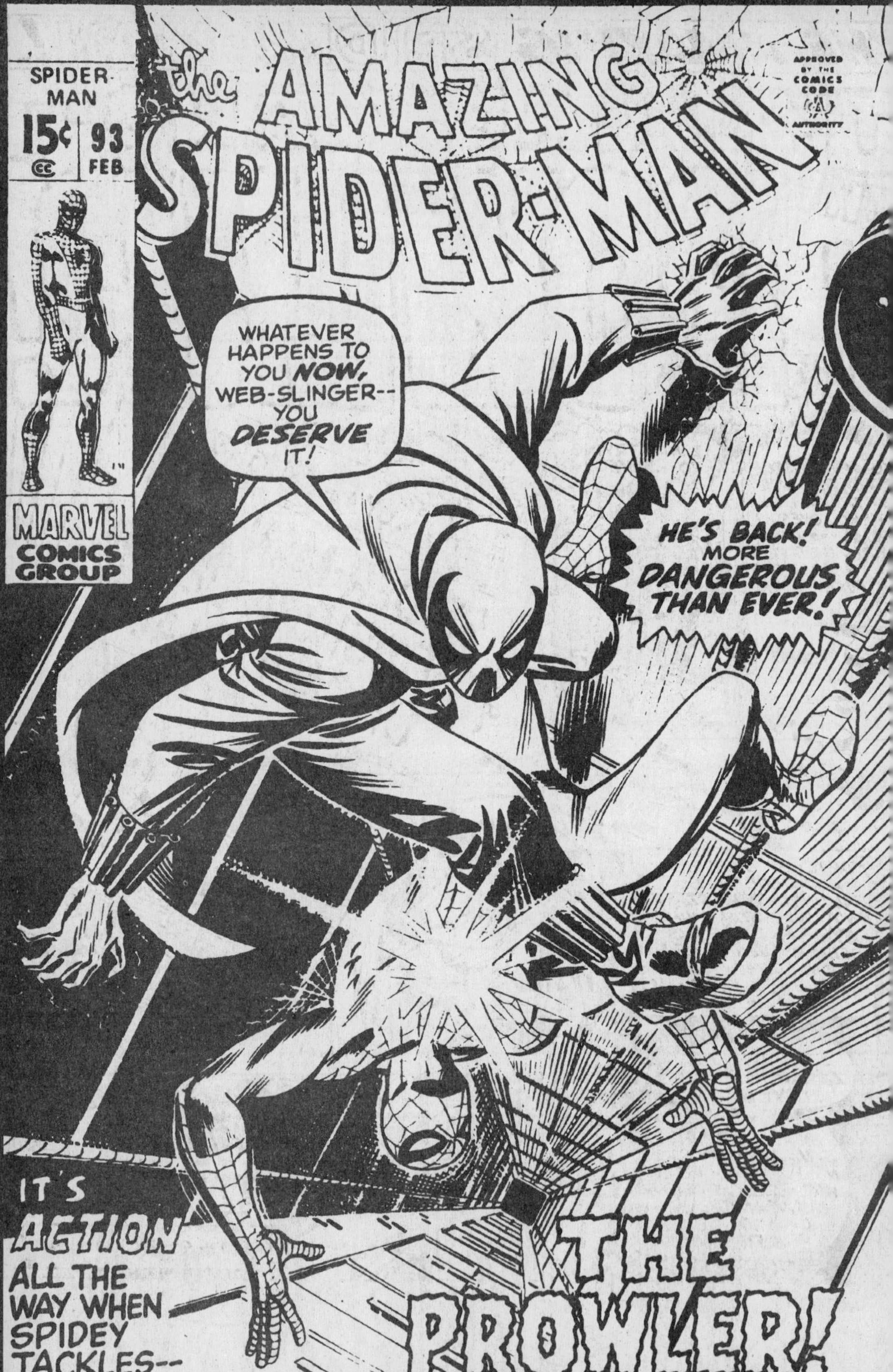

SPIDER-MAN
15¢
93
FEB
MARVEL COMICS GROUP
the AMAZING SPIDER-MAN
APPROVED BY THE COMICS CODE AUTHORITY
WHATEVER HAPPENS TO YOU NOW, WEB-SLINGER-- YOU DESERVE IT!
HE'S BACK! MORE DANGEROUS THAN EVER!
IT'S ACTION ALL THE WAY WHEN SPIDEY TACKLES--
THE PROWLER!

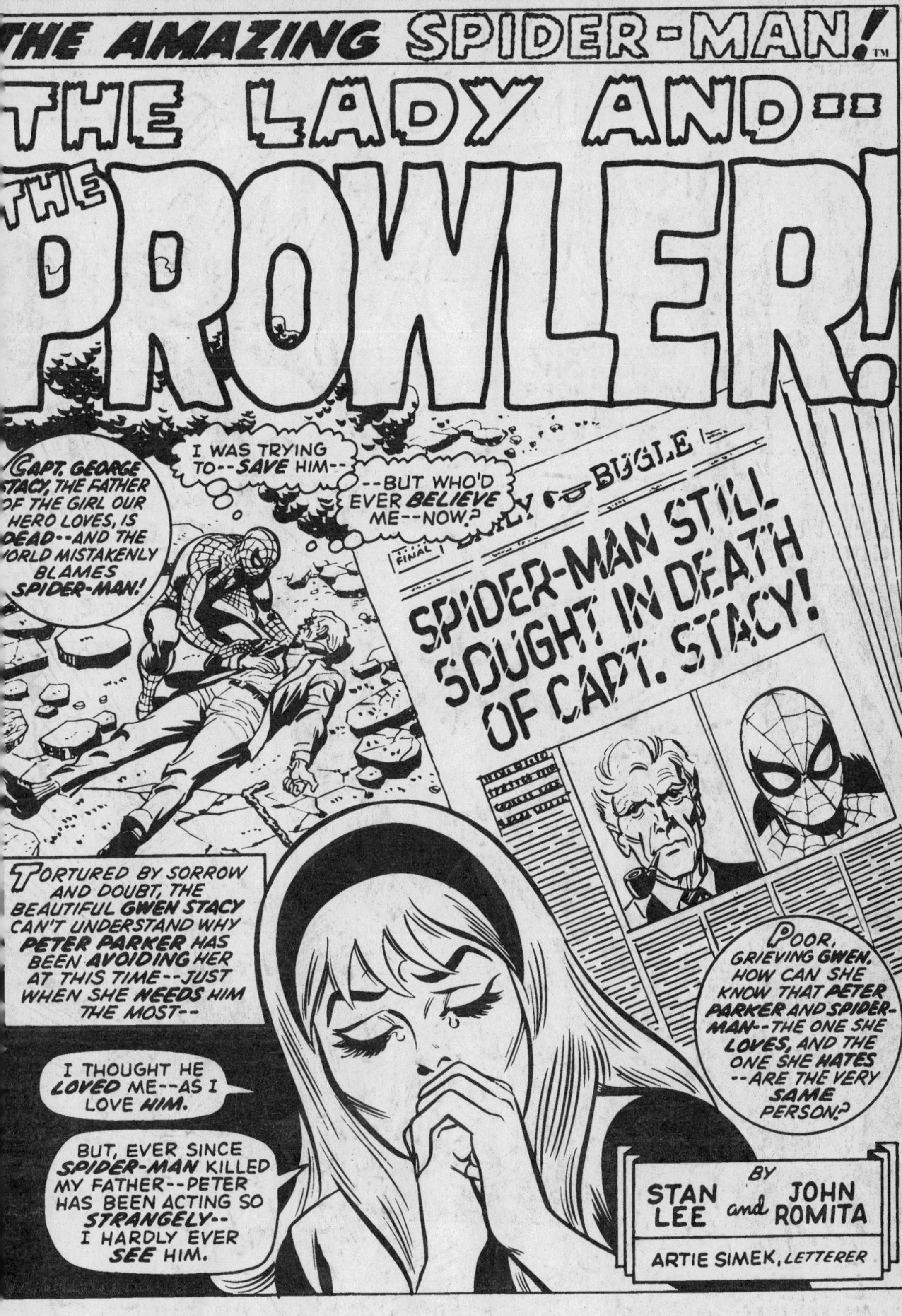
THE AMAZING SPIDER-MAN!
THE LADY AND-- THE PROWLER!
CAPT. GEORGE STACY, THE FATHER OF THE GIRL OUR HERO LOVES, IS DEAD--AND THE WORLD MISTAKENLY BLAMES SPIDER-MAN!
I WAS TRYING TO--SAVE HIM--
--BUT WHO'D EVER BELIEVE ME--NOW?
BUGLE
FINAL
SPIDER-MAN STILL SOUGHT IN DEATH OF CAPT. STACY!
TORTURED BY SORROW AND DOUBT, THE BEAUTIFUL GWEN STACY CAN'T UNDERSTAND WHY PETER PARKER HAS BEEN AVOIDING HER AT THIS TIME--JUST WHEN SHE NEEDS HIM THE MOST--
POOR, GRIEVING GWEN. HOW CAN SHE KNOW THAT PETER PARKER AND SPIDER-MAN--THE ONE SHE LOVES, AND THE ONE SHE HATES--ARE THE VERY SAME PERSON?
I THOUGHT HE LOVED ME--AS I LOVE HIM.
BUT, EVER SINCE SPIDER-MAN KILLED MY FATHER--PETER HAS BEEN ACTING SO STRANGELY--I HARDLY EVER SEE HIM.
BY STAN LEE and JOHN ROMITA
ARTIE SIMEK, LETTERER

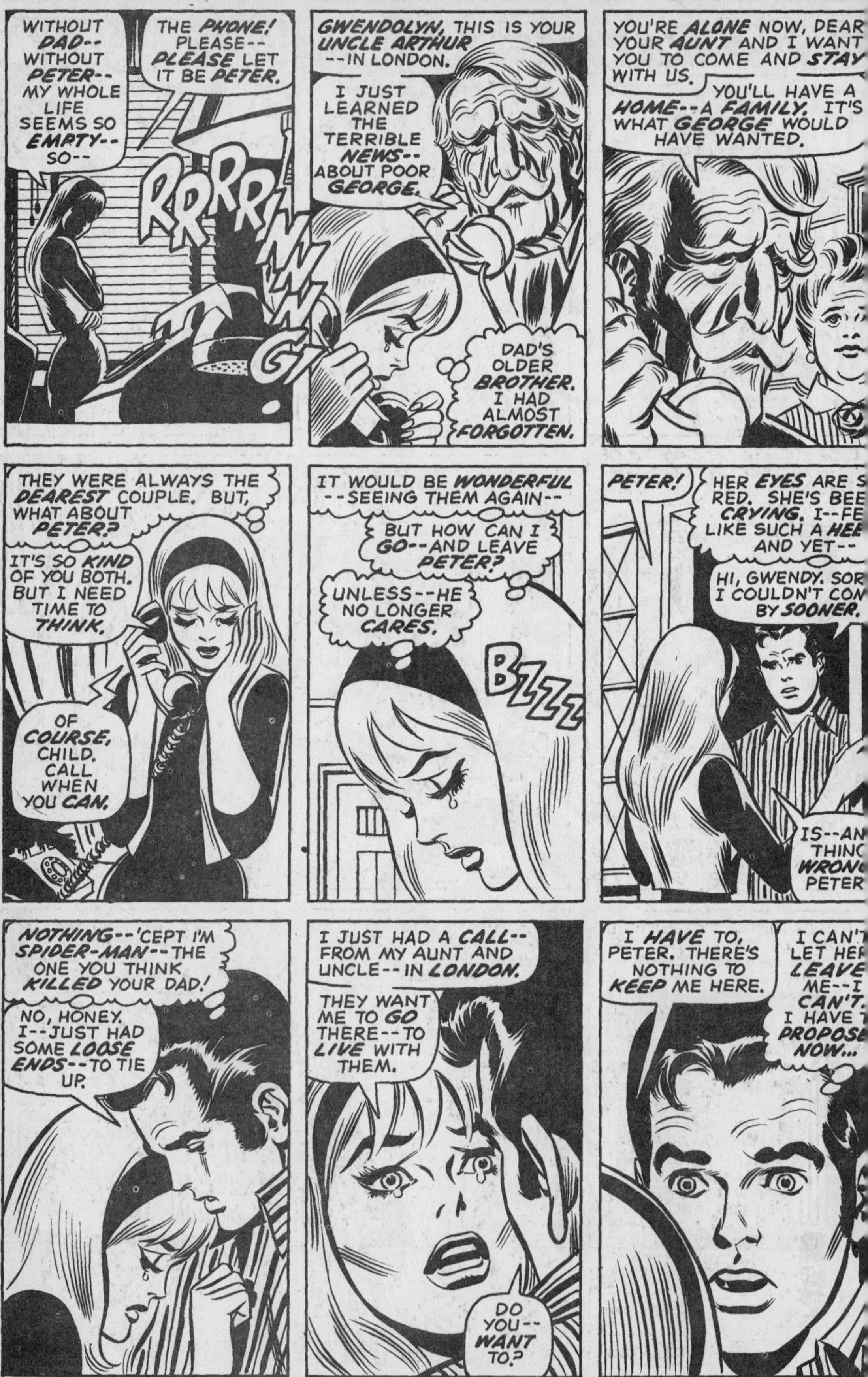

WITHOUT DAD-- WITHOUT PETER-- MY WHOLE LIFE SEEMS SO EMPTY-- SO--
THE PHONE! PLEASE-- PLEASE LET IT BE PETER.
RRRRINNNNGG
GWENDOLYN, THIS IS YOUR UNCLE ARTHUR --IN LONDON.
I JUST LEARNED THE TERRIBLE NEWS-- ABOUT POOR GEORGE.
DAD'S OLDER BROTHER. I HAD ALMOST FORGOTTEN.
YOU'RE ALONE NOW, DEAR YOUR AUNT AND I WANT YOU TO COME AND STAY WITH US.
YOU'LL HAVE A HOME--A FAMILY. IT'S WHAT GEORGE WOULD HAVE WANTED.
THEY WERE ALWAYS THE DEAREST COUPLE. BUT, WHAT ABOUT PETER?
IT'S SO KIND OF YOU BOTH. BUT I NEED TIME TO THINK.
OF COURSE, CHILD. CALL WHEN YOU CAN.
IT WOULD BE WONDERFUL --SEEING THEM AGAIN--
BUT HOW CAN I GO--AND LEAVE PETER?
UNLESS--HE NO LONGER CARES.
BZZZ
PETER!
HER EYES ARE S RED. SHE'S BEE CRYING. I--FE LIKE SUCH A HE AND YET--
HI, GWENDY. SOR I COULDN'T COM BY SOONER.
IS--AN THING WRON PETER
NOTHING--'CEPT I'M SPIDER-MAN--THE ONE YOU THINK KILLED YOUR DAD!
NO, HONEY. I--JUST HAD SOME LOOSE ENDS--TO TIE UP.
I JUST HAD A CALL-- FROM MY AUNT AND UNCLE--IN LONDON.
THEY WANT ME TO GO THERE--TO LIVE WITH THEM.
DO YOU-- WANT TO?
I HAVE TO, PETER. THERE'S NOTHING TO KEEP ME HERE.
I CAN'T LET HE LEAVE ME--I CAN'T. I HAVE T PROPOSE NOW...

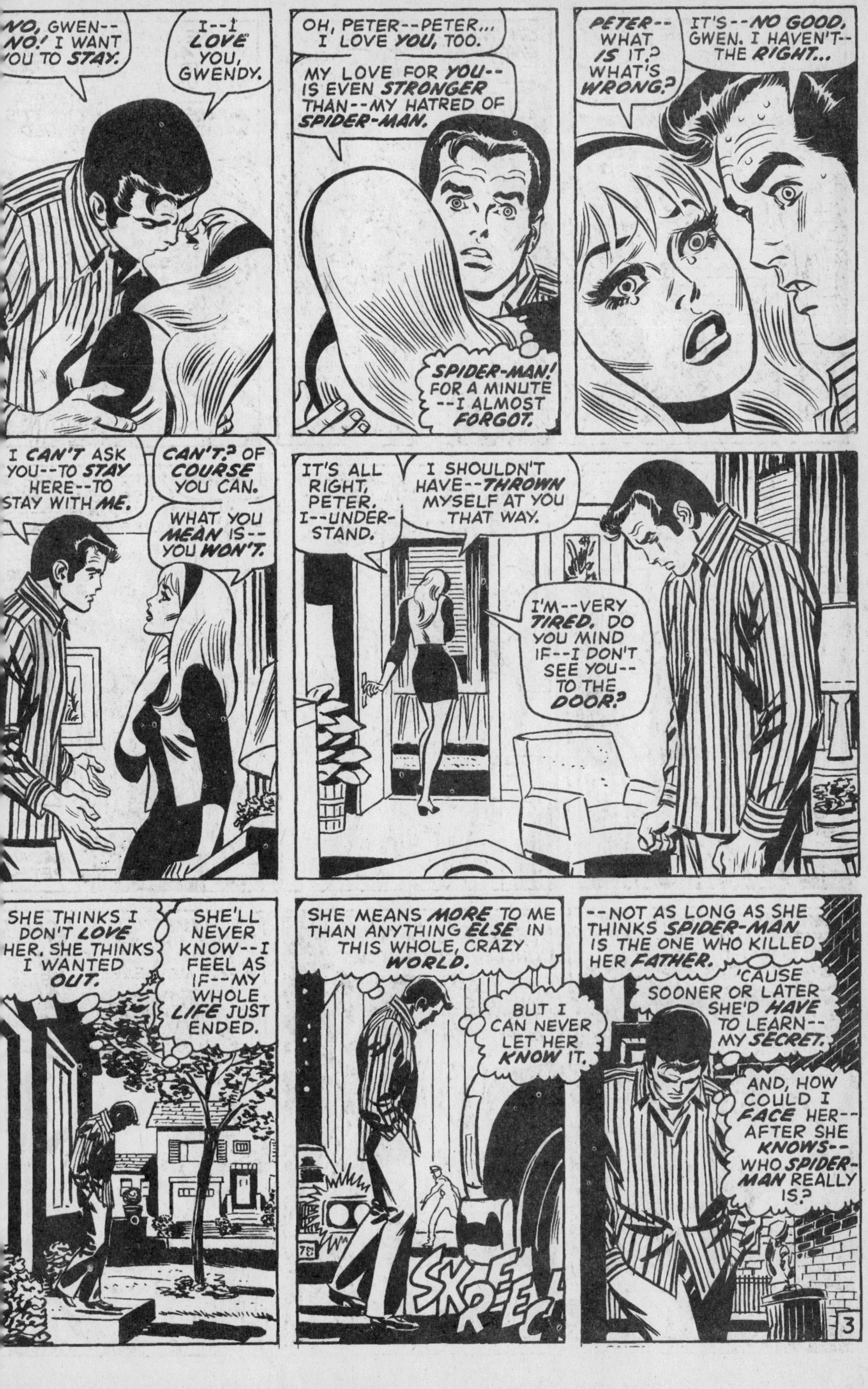
NO, GWEN-- NO! I WANT YOU TO STAY.
I--I LOVE YOU, GWENDY.
OH, PETER--PETER... I LOVE YOU, TOO.
MY LOVE FOR YOU-- IS EVEN STRONGER THAN--MY HATRED OF SPIDER-MAN.
SPIDER-MAN! FOR A MINUTE --I ALMOST FORGOT.
PETER-- WHAT IS IT? WHAT'S WRONG?
IT'S--NO GOOD, GWEN. I HAVEN'T-- THE RIGHT...
I CAN'T ASK YOU--TO STAY HERE--TO STAY WITH ME.
CAN'T? OF COURSE YOU CAN.
WHAT YOU MEAN IS-- YOU WON'T.
IT'S ALL RIGHT, PETER. I--UNDER-STAND.
I SHOULDN'T HAVE--THROWN MYSELF AT YOU THAT WAY.
I'M--VERY TIRED. DO YOU MIND IF--I DON'T SEE YOU-- TO THE DOOR?
SHE THINKS I DON'T LOVE HER. SHE THINKS I WANTED OUT.
SHE'LL NEVER KNOW--I FEEL AS IF--MY WHOLE LIFE JUST ENDED.
SHE MEANS MORE TO ME THAN ANYTHING ELSE IN THIS WHOLE, CRAZY WORLD.
BUT I CAN NEVER LET HER KNOW IT.
SKREEEECH
--NOT AS LONG AS SHE THINKS SPIDER-MAN IS THE ONE WHO KILLED HER FATHER.
'CAUSE SOONER OR LATER SHE'D HAVE TO LEARN-- MY SECRET.
AND, HOW COULD I FACE HER-- AFTER SHE KNOWS-- WHO SPIDER-MAN REALLY IS?
3

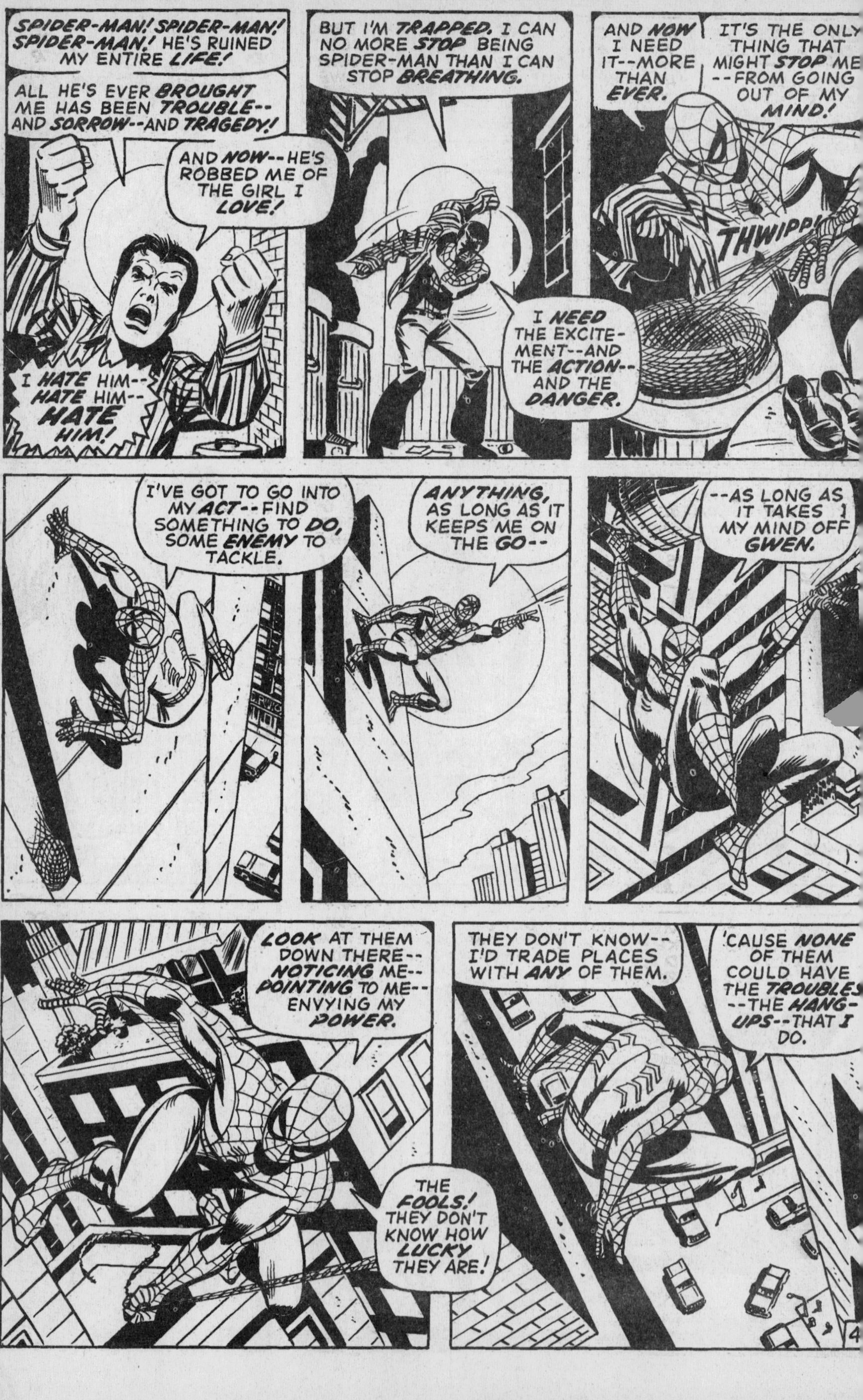

SPIDER-MAN! SPIDER-MAN! SPIDER-MAN! HE'S RUINED MY ENTIRE LIFE!
ALL HE'S EVER BROUGHT ME HAS BEEN TROUBLE-- AND SORROW--AND TRAGEDY!
AND NOW--HE'S ROBBED ME OF THE GIRL I LOVE!
I HATE HIM-- HATE HIM-- HATE HIM!
BUT I'M TRAPPED. I CAN NO MORE STOP BEING SPIDER-MAN THAN I CAN STOP BREATHING.
I NEED THE EXCITE-MENT--AND THE ACTION-- AND THE DANGER.
AND NOW I NEED IT--MORE THAN EVER.
IT'S THE ONLY THING THAT MIGHT STOP ME --FROM GOING OUT OF MY MIND!
THWIPP!
I'VE GOT TO GO INTO MY ACT--FIND SOMETHING TO DO, SOME ENEMY TO TACKLE.
ANYTHING, AS LONG AS IT KEEPS ME ON THE GO--
--AS LONG AS IT TAKES MY MIND OFF GWEN.
LOOK AT THEM DOWN THERE-- NOTICING ME-- POINTING TO ME-- ENVYING MY POWER.
THE FOOLS! THEY DON'T KNOW HOW LUCKY THEY ARE!
THEY DON'T KNOW-- I'D TRADE PLACES WITH ANY OF THEM.
'CAUSE NONE OF THEM COULD HAVE THE TROUBLES --THE HANG-UPS--THAT I DO.

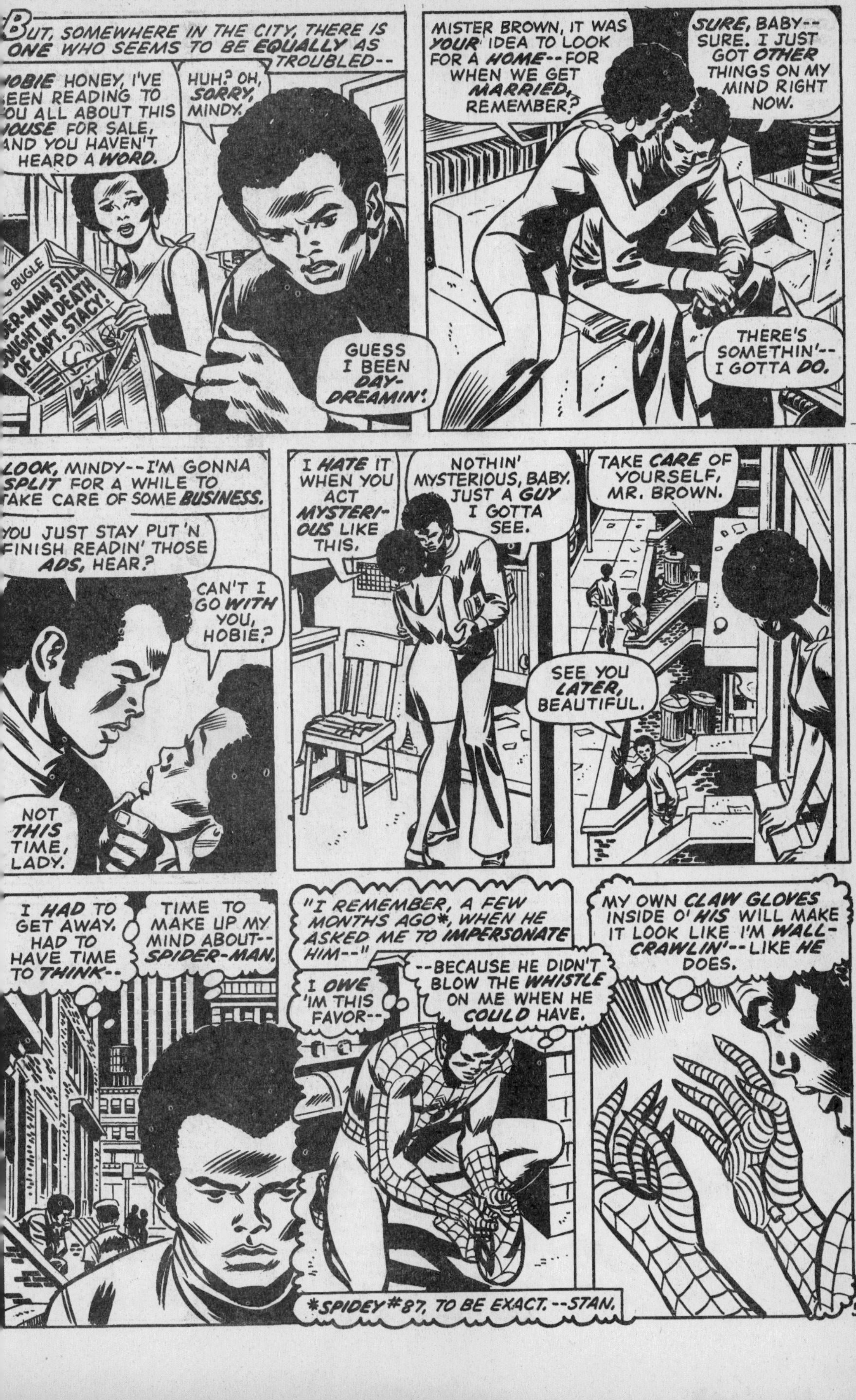
BUT, SOMEWHERE IN THE CITY, THERE IS ONE WHO SEEMS TO BE EQUALLY AS TROUBLED--
HOBIE HONEY, I'VE BEEN READING TO YOU ALL ABOUT THIS HOUSE FOR SALE, AND YOU HAVEN'T HEARD A WORD.
HUH? OH, SORRY, MINDY.
GUESS I BEEN DAY-DREAMIN'.
MISTER BROWN, IT WAS YOUR IDEA TO LOOK FOR A HOME--FOR WHEN WE GET MARRIED, REMEMBER?
SURE, BABY--SURE. I JUST GOT OTHER THINGS ON MY MIND RIGHT NOW.
THERE'S SOMETHIN'--I GOTTA DO.
LOOK, MINDY--I'M GONNA SPLIT FOR A WHILE TO TAKE CARE OF SOME BUSINESS.
YOU JUST STAY PUT 'N FINISH READIN' THOSE ADS, HEAR?
CAN'T I GO WITH YOU, HOBIE?
NOT THIS TIME, LADY.
I HATE IT WHEN YOU ACT MYSTERIOUS LIKE THIS.
NOTHIN' MYSTERIOUS, BABY. JUST A GUY I GOTTA SEE.
TAKE CARE OF YOURSELF, MR. BROWN.
SEE YOU LATER, BEAUTIFUL.
I HAD TO GET AWAY. HAD TO HAVE TIME TO THINK--
TIME TO MAKE UP MY MIND ABOUT--SPIDER-MAN.
"I REMEMBER, A FEW MONTHS AGO*, WHEN HE ASKED ME TO IMPERSONATE HIM--"
I OWE 'IM THIS FAVOR--
--BECAUSE HE DIDN'T BLOW THE WHISTLE ON ME WHEN HE COULD HAVE.
MY OWN CLAW GLOVES INSIDE O' HIS WILL MAKE IT LOOK LIKE I'M WALL-CRAWLIN'--LIKE HE DOES.
*SPIDEY #87, TO BE EXACT. --STAN.

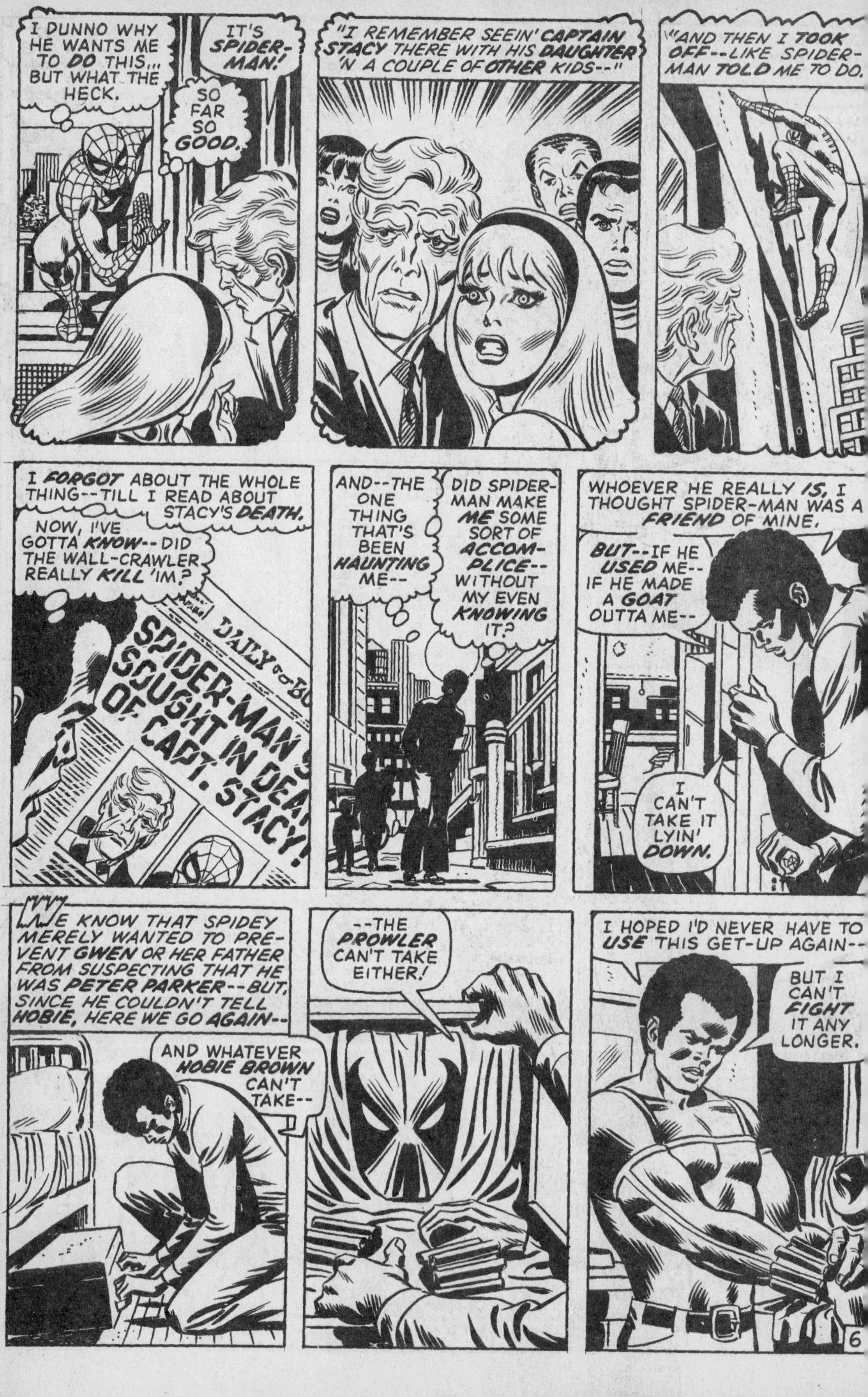

I DUNNO WHY HE WANTS ME TO DO THIS... BUT WHAT THE HECK.
IT'S SPIDER-MAN!
SO FAR SO GOOD.
"I REMEMBER SEEIN' CAPTAIN STACY THERE WITH HIS DAUGHTER 'N A COUPLE OF OTHER KIDS--"
"AND THEN I TOOK OFF--LIKE SPIDER-MAN TOLD ME TO DO.
I FORGOT ABOUT THE WHOLE THING--TILL I READ ABOUT STACY'S DEATH.
NOW, I'VE GOTTA KNOW--DID THE WALL-CRAWLER REALLY KILL 'IM?
DAILY BU
SPIDER-MAN SOUGHT IN DEA OF CAPT. STACY!
AND--THE ONE THING THAT'S BEEN HAUNTING ME--
DID SPIDER-MAN MAKE ME SOME SORT OF ACCOMPLICE--WITHOUT MY EVEN KNOWING IT?
WHOEVER HE REALLY IS, I THOUGHT SPIDER-MAN WAS A FRIEND OF MINE.
BUT--IF HE USED ME--IF HE MADE A GOAT OUTTA ME--
I CAN'T TAKE IT LYIN' DOWN.
WE KNOW THAT SPIDEY MERELY WANTED TO PREVENT GWEN OR HER FATHER FROM SUSPECTING THAT HE WAS PETER PARKER--BUT, SINCE HE COULDN'T TELL HOBIE, HERE WE GO AGAIN--
AND WHATEVER HOBIE BROWN CAN'T TAKE--
--THE PROWLER CAN'T TAKE EITHER!
I HOPED I'D NEVER HAVE TO USE THIS GET-UP AGAIN--
BUT I CAN'T FIGHT IT ANY LONGER.
6

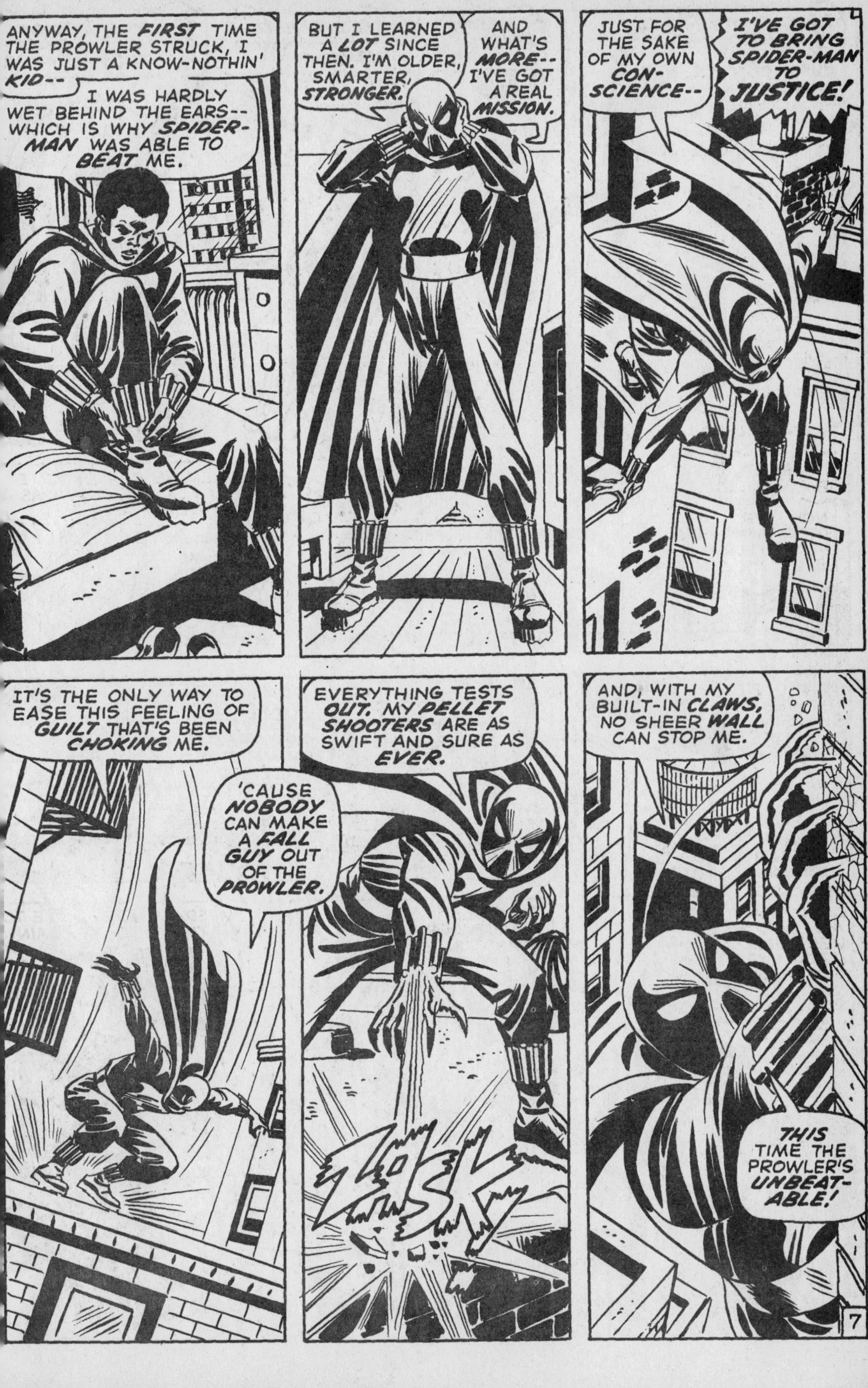
ANYWAY, THE FIRST TIME THE PROWLER STRUCK, I WAS JUST A KNOW-NOTHIN' KID--
I WAS HARDLY WET BEHIND THE EARS-- WHICH IS WHY SPIDER-MAN WAS ABLE TO BEAT ME.
BUT I LEARNED A LOT SINCE THEN. I'M OLDER, SMARTER, STRONGER.
AND WHAT'S MORE-- I'VE GOT A REAL MISSION.
JUST FOR THE SAKE OF MY OWN CON-SCIENCE--
I'VE GOT TO BRING SPIDER-MAN TO JUSTICE!
IT'S THE ONLY WAY TO EASE THIS FEELING OF GUILT THAT'S BEEN CHOKING ME.
'CAUSE NOBODY CAN MAKE A FALL GUY OUT OF THE PROWLER.
EVERYTHING TESTS OUT. MY PELLET SHOOTERS ARE AS SWIFT AND SURE AS EVER.
AND, WITH MY BUILT-IN CLAWS, NO SHEER WALL CAN STOP ME.
THIS TIME THE PROWLER'S UNBEAT-ABLE!

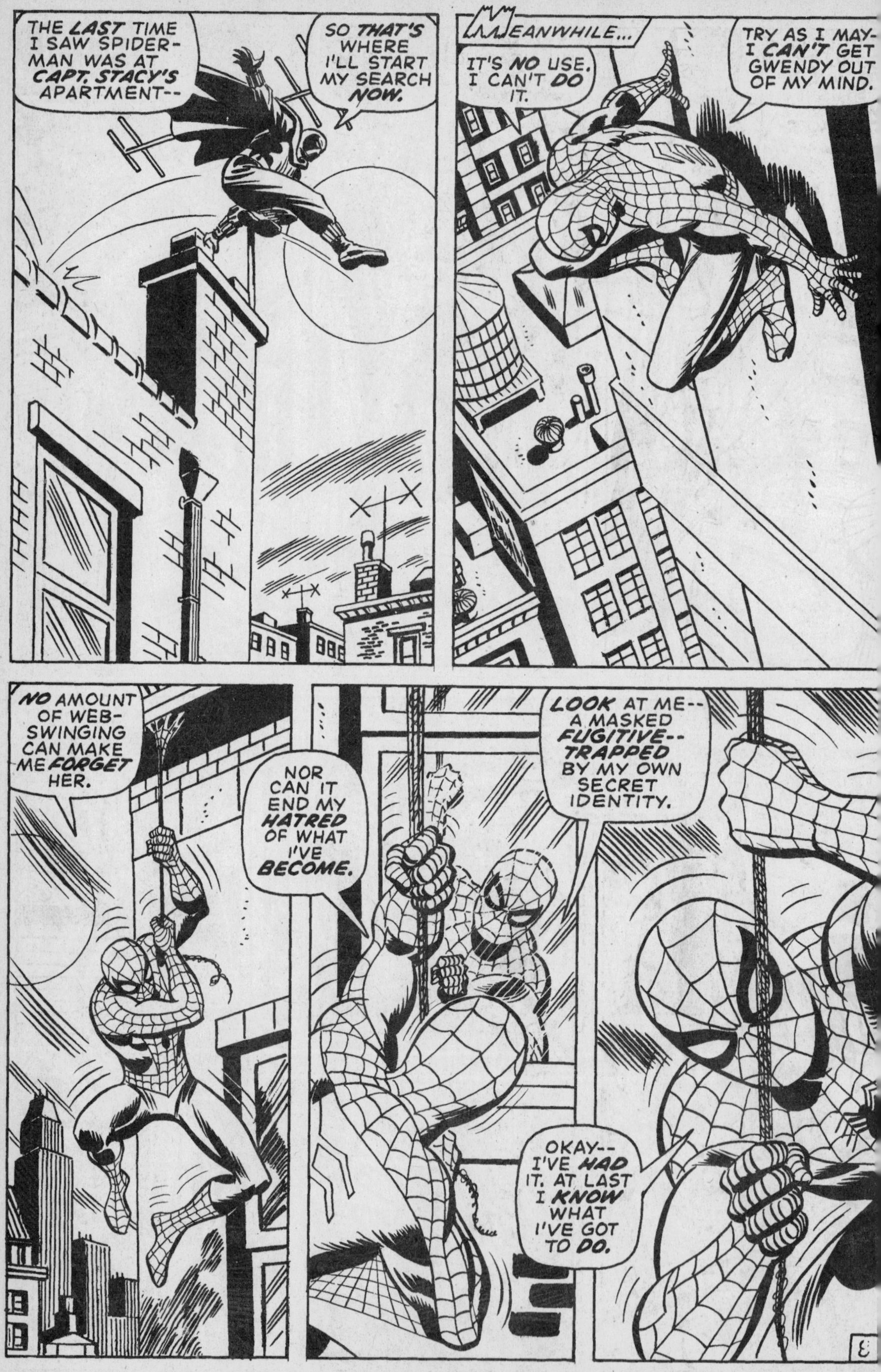
THE LAST TIME I SAW SPIDER-MAN WAS AT CAPT. STACY'S APARTMENT--
SO THAT'S WHERE I'LL START MY SEARCH NOW.
MEANWHILE...
IT'S NO USE. I CAN'T DO IT.
TRY AS I MAY-- I CAN'T GET GWENDY OUT OF MY MIND.
NO AMOUNT OF WEB-SWINGING CAN MAKE ME FORGET HER.
NOR CAN IT END MY HATRED OF WHAT I'VE BECOME.
LOOK AT ME-- A MASKED FUGITIVE-- TRAPPED BY MY OWN SECRET IDENTITY.
OKAY-- I'VE HAD IT. AT LAST I KNOW WHAT I'VE GOT TO DO.
8

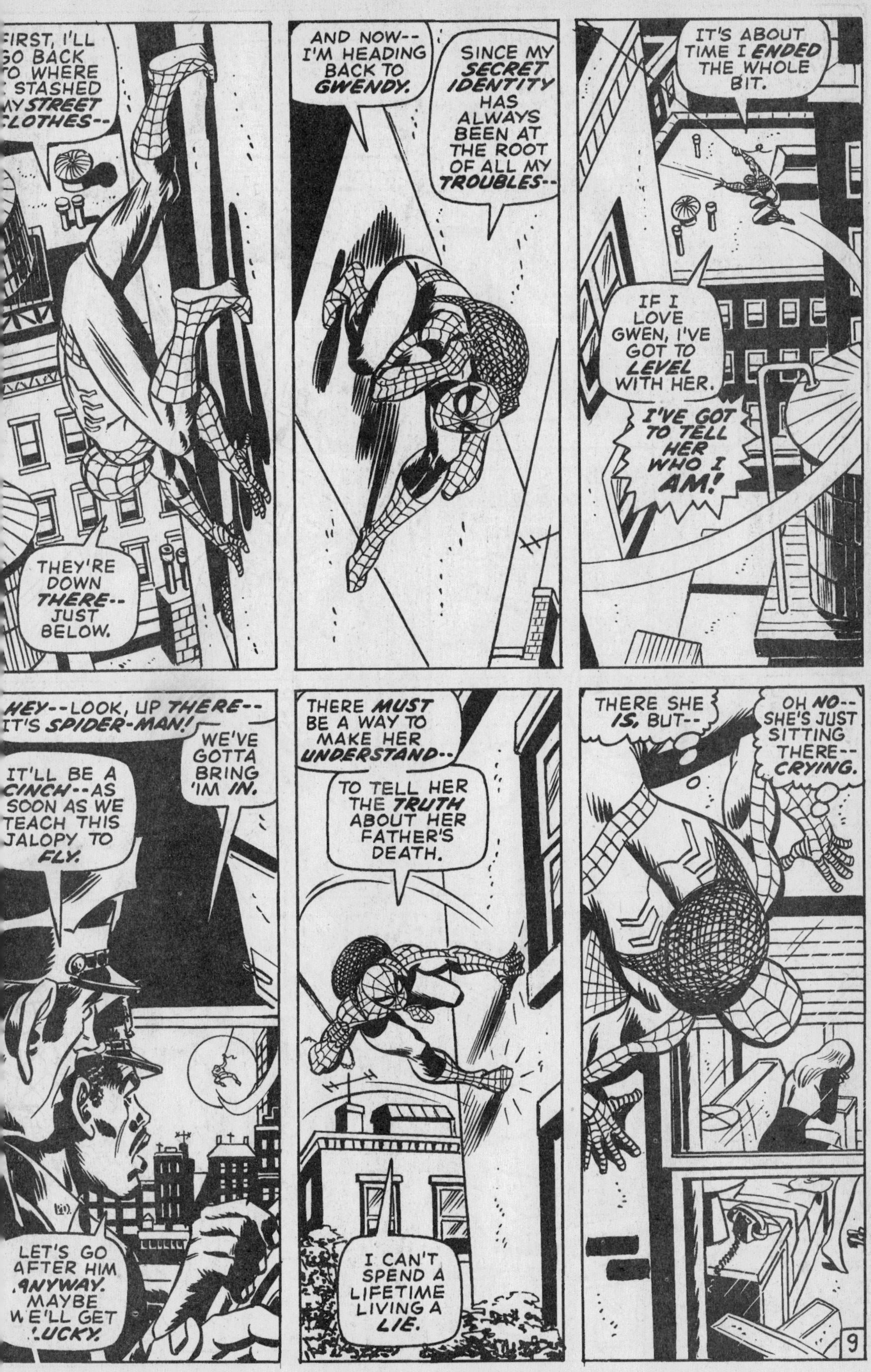
FIRST, I'LL GO BACK TO WHERE I STASHED MY STREET CLOTHES--
THEY'RE DOWN THERE-- JUST BELOW.
AND NOW-- I'M HEADING BACK TO GWENDY.
SINCE MY SECRET IDENTITY HAS ALWAYS BEEN AT THE ROOT OF ALL MY TROUBLES--
IT'S ABOUT TIME I ENDED THE WHOLE BIT.
IF I LOVE GWEN, I'VE GOT TO LEVEL WITH HER.
I'VE GOT TO TELL HER WHO I AM!
HEY--LOOK, UP THERE-- IT'S SPIDER-MAN!
WE'VE GOTTA BRING 'IM IN.
IT'LL BE A CINCH--AS SOON AS WE TEACH THIS JALOPY TO FLY.
LET'S GO AFTER HIM ANYWAY. MAYBE WE'LL GET LUCKY.
THERE MUST BE A WAY TO MAKE HER UNDERSTAND--
TO TELL HER THE TRUTH ABOUT HER FATHER'S DEATH.
I CAN'T SPEND A LIFETIME LIVING A LIE.
THERE SHE IS, BUT--
OH NO-- SHE'S JUST SITTING THERE-- CRYING.
9

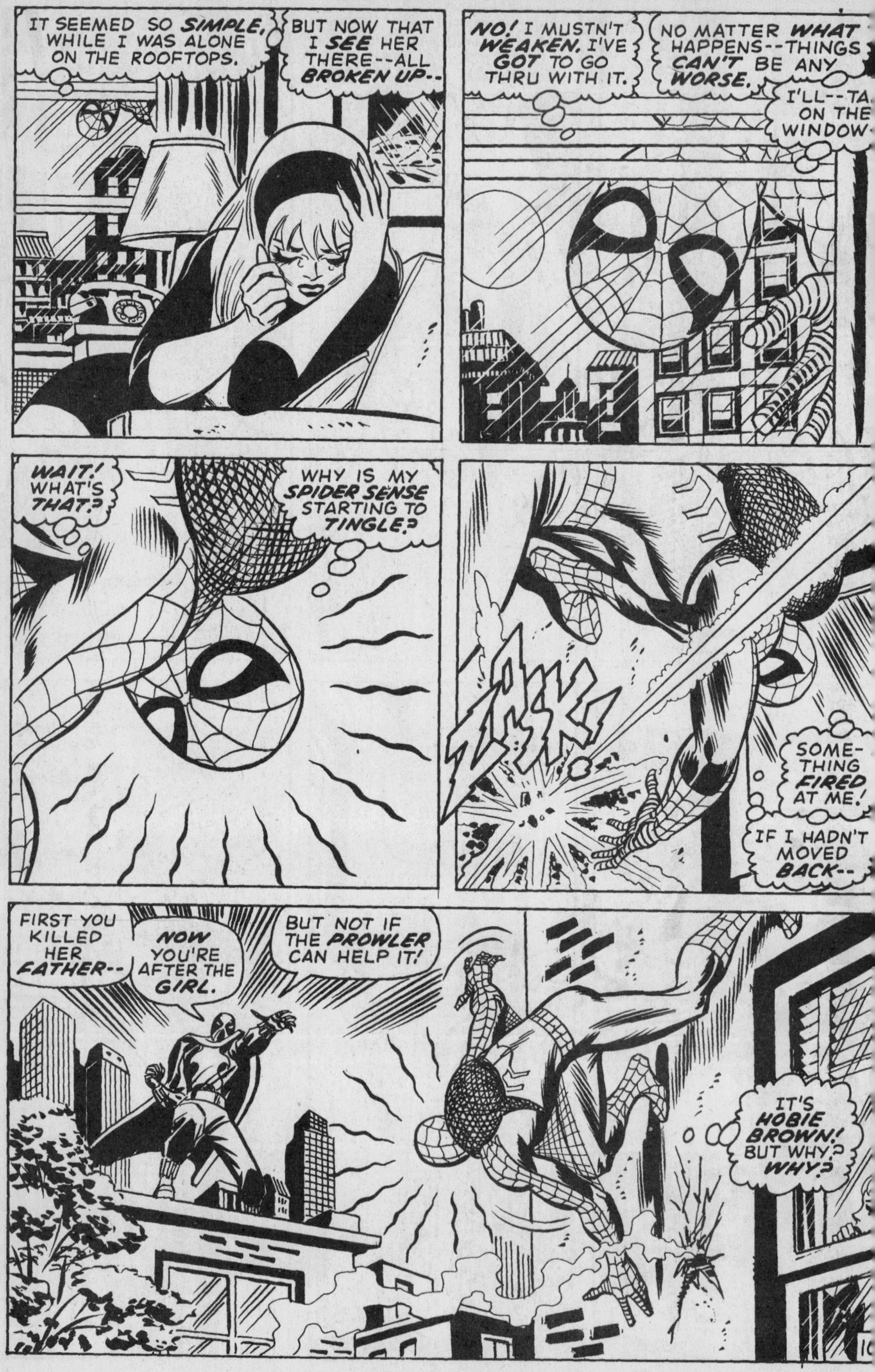
IT SEEMED SO SIMPLE, WHILE I WAS ALONE ON THE ROOFTOPS.
BUT NOW THAT I SEE HER THERE--ALL BROKEN UP--
NO! I MUSTN'T WEAKEN. I'VE GOT TO GO THRU WITH IT.
NO MATTER WHAT HAPPENS--THINGS CAN'T BE ANY WORSE.
I'LL--TA
ON THE
WINDOW-
WAIT! WHAT'S THAT?
WHY IS MY SPIDER SENSE STARTING TO TINGLE?
ZAK!
SOME-THING FIRED AT ME!
IF I HADN'T MOVED BACK--
FIRST YOU KILLED HER FATHER--
NOW YOU'RE AFTER THE GIRL.
BUT NOT IF THE PROWLER CAN HELP IT!
IT'S HOBIE BROWN! BUT WHY? WHY?

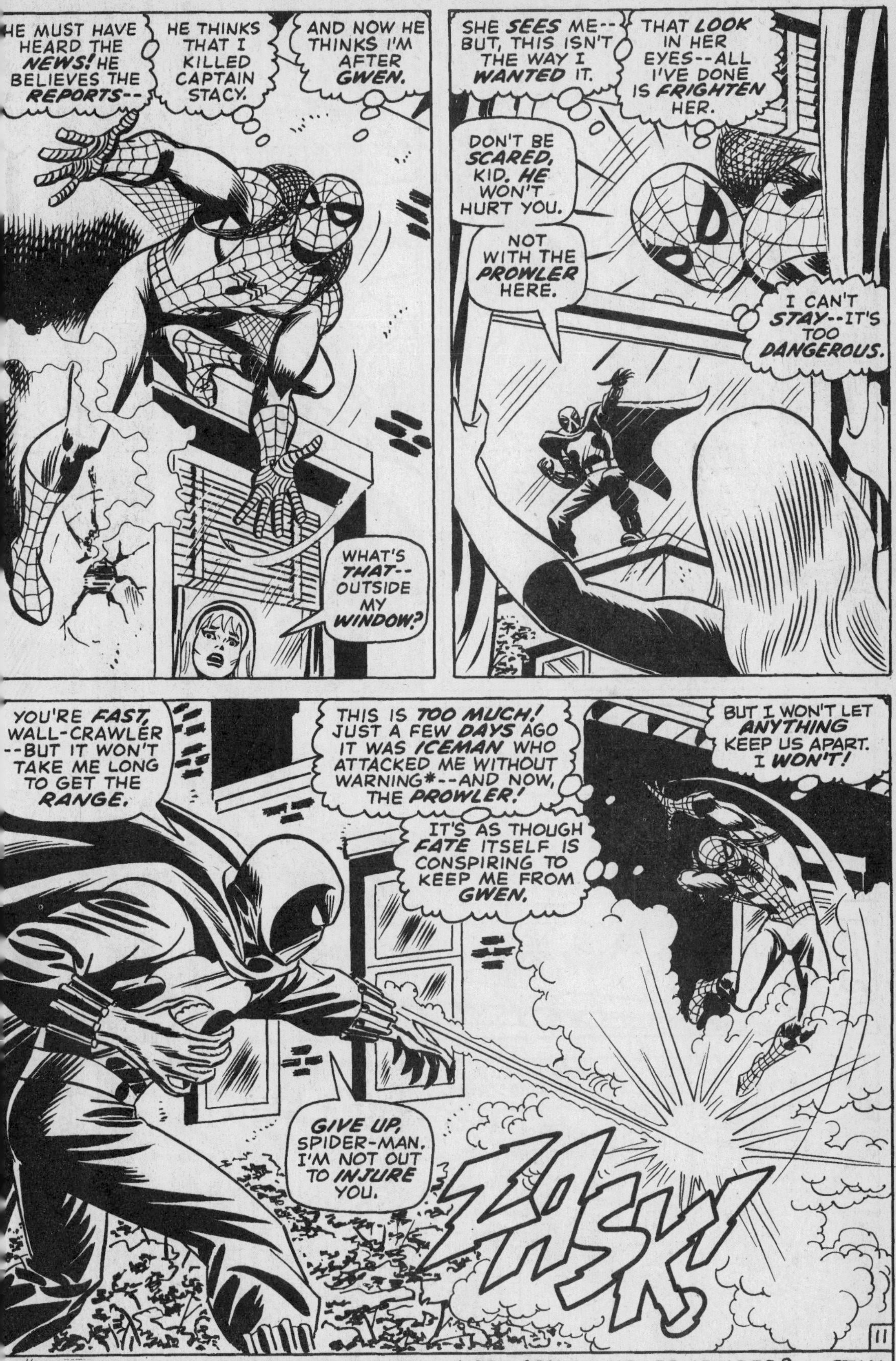
HE MUST HAVE HEARD THE NEWS! HE BELIEVES THE REPORTS--
HE THINKS THAT I KILLED CAPTAIN STACY.
AND NOW HE THINKS I'M AFTER GWEN.
WHAT'S THAT--OUTSIDE MY WINDOW?
SHE SEES ME--BUT, THIS ISN'T THE WAY I WANTED IT.
THAT LOOK IN HER EYES--ALL I'VE DONE IS FRIGHTEN HER.
DON'T BE SCARED, KID. HE WON'T HURT YOU.
NOT WITH THE PROWLER HERE.
I CAN'T STAY--IT'S TOO DANGEROUS.
YOU'RE FAST, WALL-CRAWLER--BUT IT WON'T TAKE ME LONG TO GET THE RANGE.
THIS IS TOO MUCH! JUST A FEW DAYS AGO IT WAS ICEMAN WHO ATTACKED ME WITHOUT WARNING*--AND NOW, THE PROWLER!
IT'S AS THOUGH FATE ITSELF IS CONSPIRING TO KEEP ME FROM GWEN.
BUT I WON'T LET ANYTHING KEEP US APART. I WON'T!
GIVE UP, SPIDER-MAN. I'M NOT OUT TO INJURE YOU.
ZASK!
11

*"A FEW DAYS" TO SPIDEY--BUT IT WAS LAST ISH TO US, REMEMBER? --STAN.

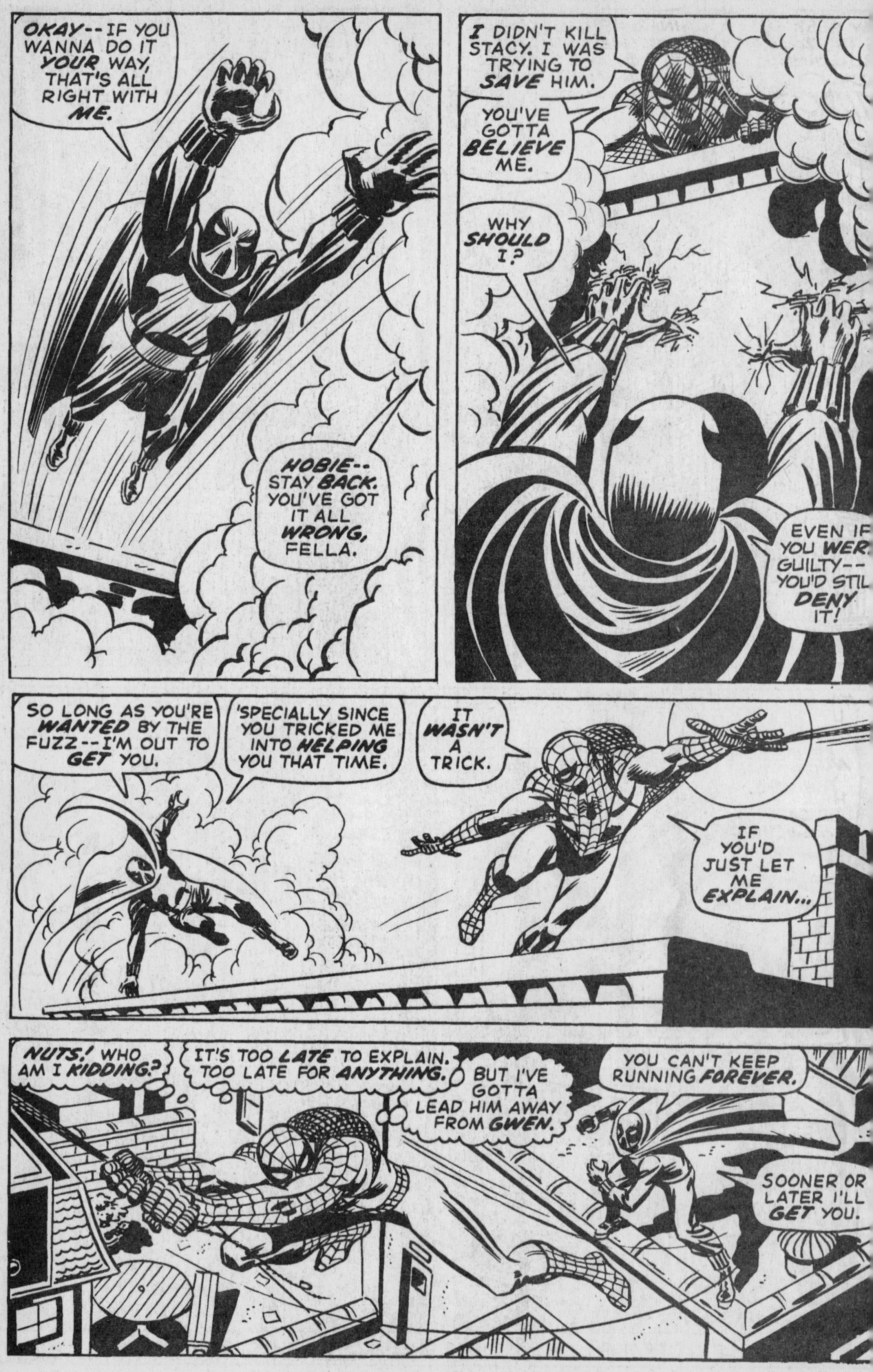
OKAY--IF YOU WANNA DO IT YOUR WAY, THAT'S ALL RIGHT WITH ME.
HOBIE--STAY BACK. YOU'VE GOT IT ALL WRONG, FELLA.
I DIDN'T KILL STACY. I WAS TRYING TO SAVE HIM.
YOU'VE GOTTA BELIEVE ME.
WHY SHOULD I?
EVEN IF YOU WER GUILTY--YOU'D STIL DENY IT!
SO LONG AS YOU'RE WANTED BY THE FUZZ--I'M OUT TO GET YOU.
'SPECIALLY SINCE YOU TRICKED ME INTO HELPING YOU THAT TIME.
IT WASN'T A TRICK.
IF YOU'D JUST LET ME EXPLAIN...
NUTS! WHO AM I KIDDING?
IT'S TOO LATE TO EXPLAIN. TOO LATE FOR ANYTHING.
BUT I'VE GOTTA LEAD HIM AWAY FROM GWEN.
YOU CAN'T KEEP RUNNING FOREVER.
SOONER OR LATER I'LL GET YOU.

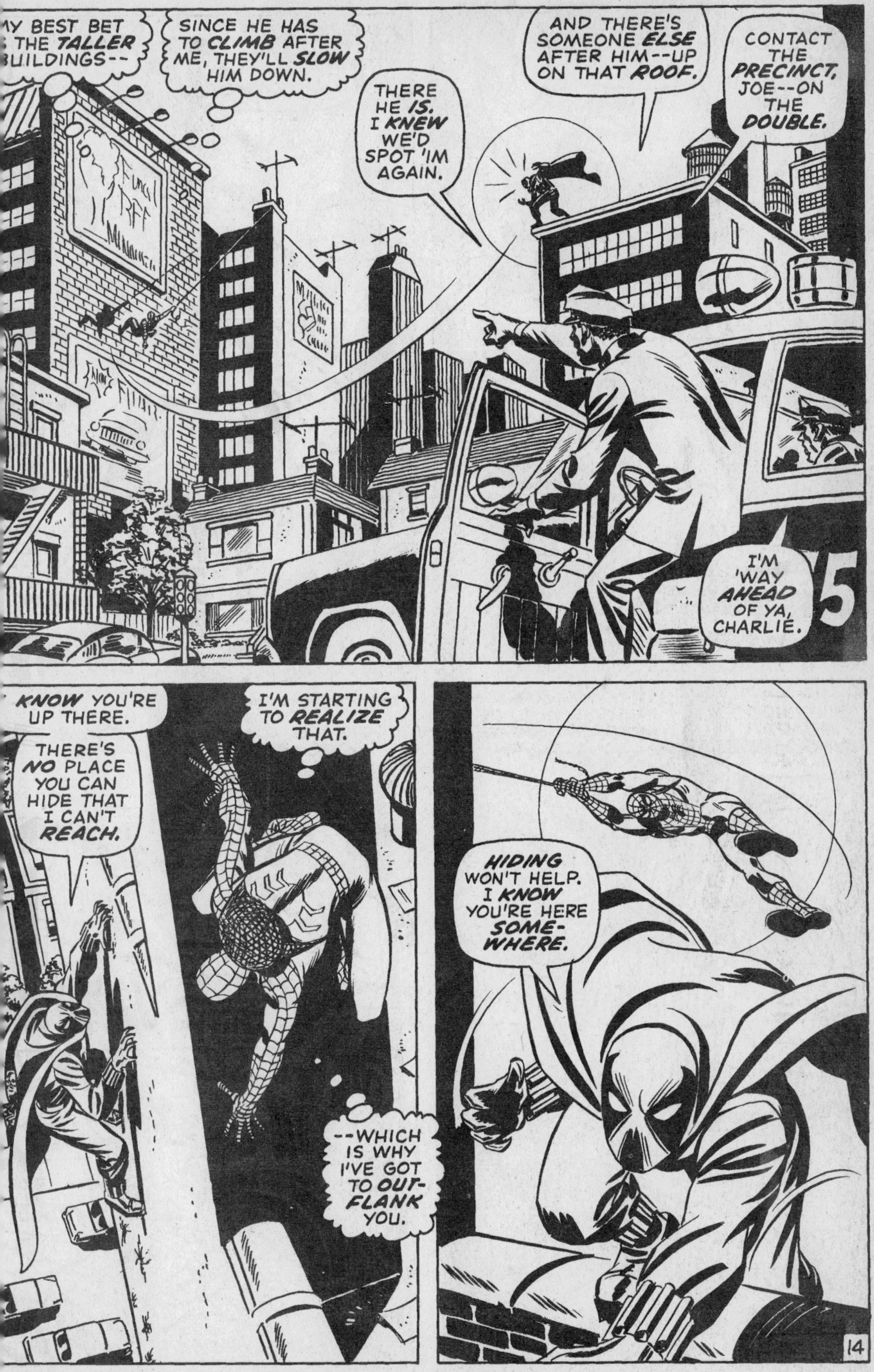

MY BEST BET THE TALLER BUILDINGS--
SINCE HE HAS TO CLIMB AFTER ME, THEY'LL SLOW HIM DOWN.
THERE HE IS. I KNEW WE'D SPOT 'IM AGAIN.
AND THERE'S SOMEONE ELSE AFTER HIM--UP ON THAT ROOF.
CONTACT THE PRECINCT, JOE--ON THE DOUBLE.
I'M 'WAY AHEAD OF YA, CHARLIE.
KNOW YOU'RE UP THERE.
THERE'S NO PLACE YOU CAN HIDE THAT I CAN'T REACH.
I'M STARTING TO REALIZE THAT.
--WHICH IS WHY I'VE GOT TO OUT-FLANK YOU.
HIDING WON'T HELP. I KNOW YOU'RE HERE SOME-WHERE.
14

Panel 1: GOT YOU! NOW YOU'LL HAVE TO LISTEN TO REASON.

OH NO-- YOU DON'T STOP ME THIS TIME.

Panel 2: --NOT WHEN I CAN THROW US BOTH DOWN THRU THE SKYLIGHT.

WHAT DO I DO? HE'S DETERMINED TO BEAT ME.

Panel 3: I'M NO BLEEDING HEART DO-GOODER, MAN--

BUT, IF YOU USED ME IN SOME KIND OF MURDER SCHEME--

I DIDN'T USE YOU...

I NEVER MURDERED ANYONE.

Panel 4: YOU'RE STALLING FOR TIME--TRYING TO FIGURE HOW TO ESCAPE ME.

BUT YOU CAN'T! THIS TIME I'M GONNA-- HEY!

I-- KICKED TOO HARD --LOOSENED MY CLAW HOLD--

HE'S FALLING!

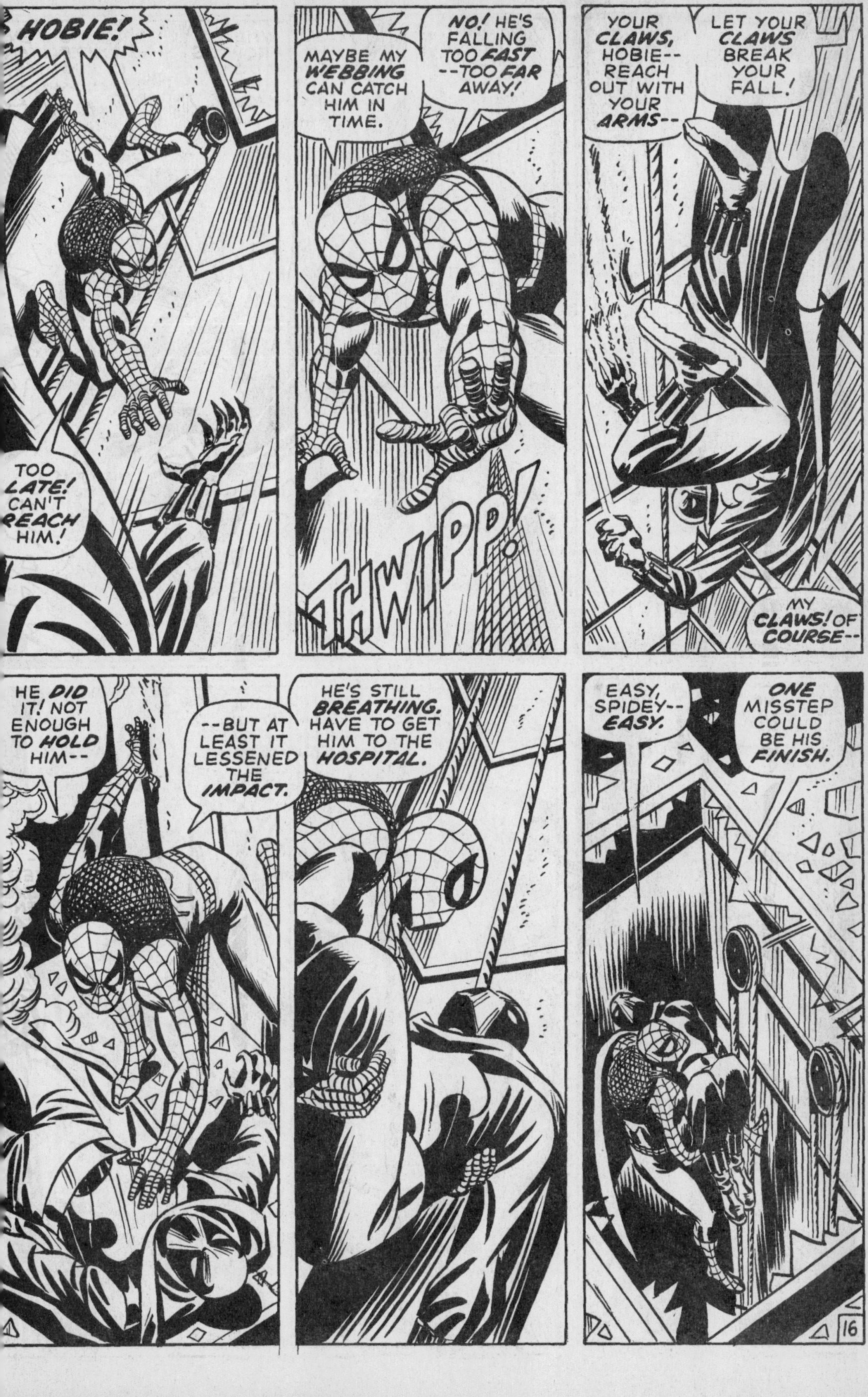
HOBIE!
TOO LATE! CAN'T REACH HIM!
MAYBE MY WEBBING CAN CATCH HIM IN TIME.
NO! HE'S FALLING TOO FAST --TOO FAR AWAY!
THWIPP!
YOUR CLAWS, HOBIE-- REACH OUT WITH YOUR ARMS--
LET YOUR CLAWS BREAK YOUR FALL!
MY CLAWS! OF COURSE--
HE DID IT! NOT ENOUGH TO HOLD HIM--
--BUT AT LEAST IT LESSENED THE IMPACT.
HE'S STILL BREATHING. HAVE TO GET HIM TO THE HOSPITAL.
EASY, SPIDEY-- EASY.
ONE MISSTEP COULD BE HIS FINISH.
16

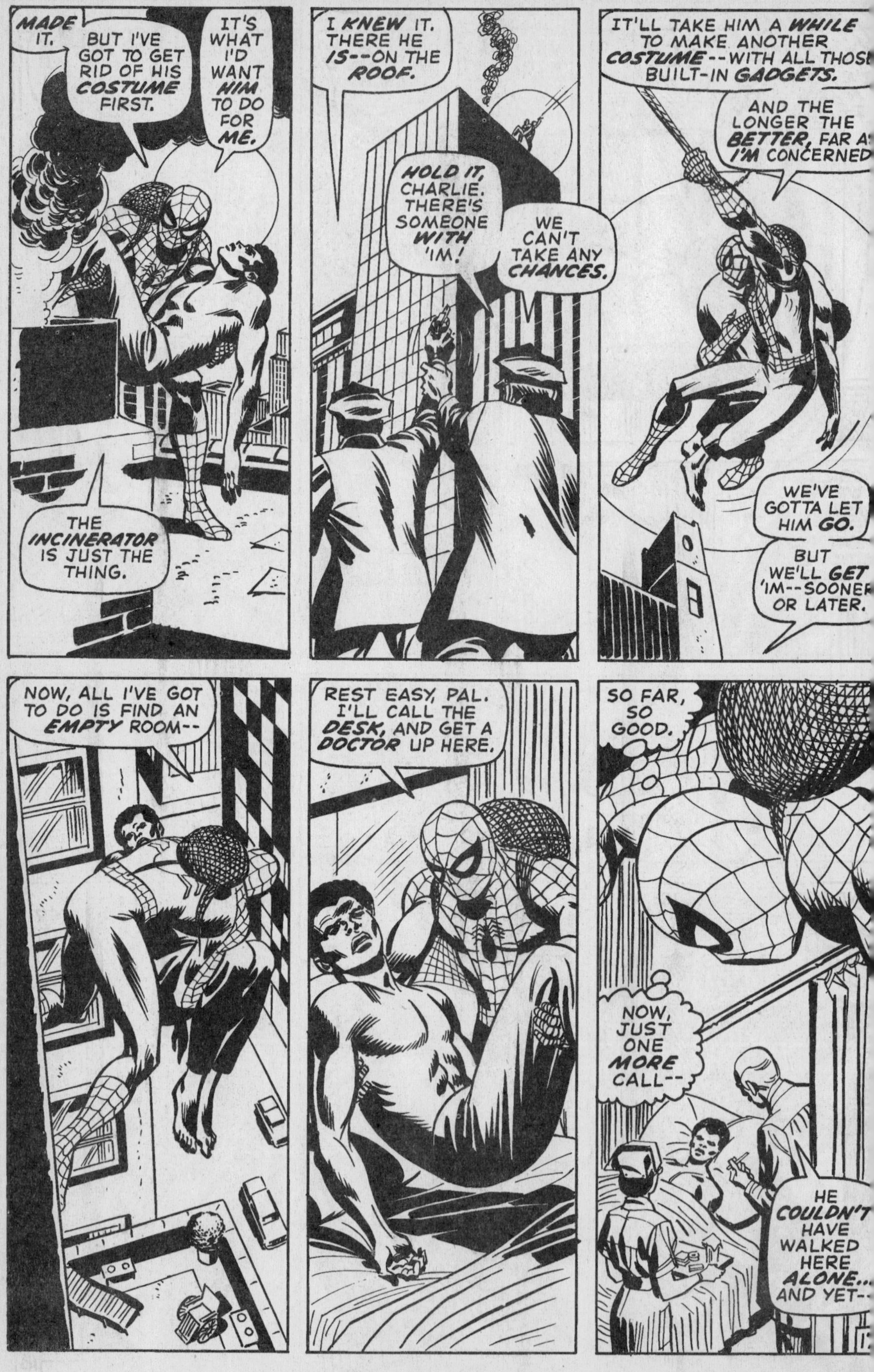

MADE IT.
BUT I'VE GOT TO GET RID OF HIS COSTUME FIRST.
IT'S WHAT I'D WANT HIM TO DO FOR ME.
THE INCINERATOR IS JUST THE THING.
I KNEW IT. THERE HE IS--ON THE ROOF.
HOLD IT, CHARLIE. THERE'S SOMEONE WITH 'IM!
WE CAN'T TAKE ANY CHANCES.
IT'LL TAKE HIM A WHILE TO MAKE ANOTHER COSTUME--WITH ALL THOS BUILT-IN GADGETS.
AND THE LONGER THE BETTER, FAR A I'M CONCERNED
WE'VE GOTTA LET HIM GO.
BUT WE'LL GET 'IM--SOONEF OR LATER.
NOW, ALL I'VE GOT TO DO IS FIND AN EMPTY ROOM--
REST EASY, PAL. I'LL CALL THE DESK, AND GET A DOCTOR UP HERE.
SO FAR, SO GOOD.
NOW, JUST ONE MORE CALL--
HE COULDN'T HAVE WALKED HERE ALONE... AND YET--

MINUTES LATER--

I'M LOOKING FOR *HOBIE BROWN.* I--RECEIVED A *CALL*--

OH YES. HE'S IN THE *FOURTH* ROOM --JUST DOWN THE HALL.

HOBIE! WHAT--OH, HE--HE'S *UNCONSCIOUS.* WHAT *IS* IT, DOCTOR? WHAT *HAPPENED?*

HE'S *SLEEPING* NOW, MISS. WE GAVE HIM A *SEDATIVE.*

HE'S BEEN BADLY *BRUISED,* BUT HE'LL PULL *THRU* ALL RIGHT.

HOBIE, HOBIE-- WHATEVER IS *WRONG*--WHATEVER'S THE *MATTER*--I'LL STICK *BY* YOU. I *SWEAR* IT.

I *GUESS* THAT'S MY *EXIT* LINE.

HOW LUCKY CAN YOU *BE*-- WITH A GAL LIKE *THAT?*

AND YET, *GWENDY* IS THE SAME TYPE--JUST AS *DEVOTED*--JUST AS *LOYAL.*

I CAN'T LET HER *GO*--I JUST *CANT.*

AND *THIS* TIME I *WON'T!*

HEY! WHAT *IS* THIS?

SOMEONE *ELSE* IN HER APARTMENT-- SOMEONE WHO'S *UNPACKING!*

IT--IT CAN'T *MEAN*--

18

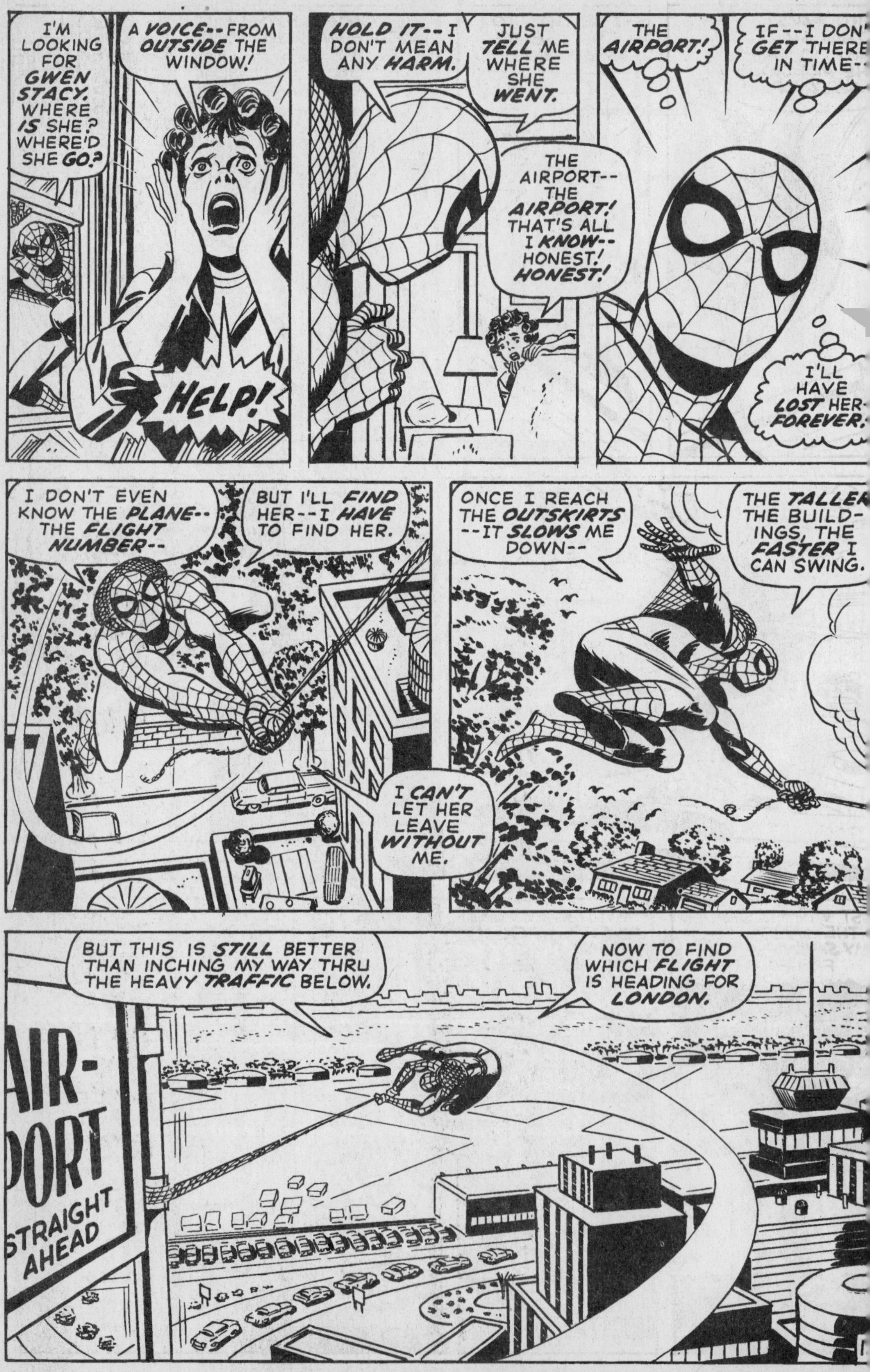

I'M LOOKING FOR GWEN STACY. WHERE IS SHE? WHERE'D SHE GO?
A VOICE--FROM OUTSIDE THE WINDOW!
HELP!
HOLD IT--I DON'T MEAN ANY HARM.
JUST TELL ME WHERE SHE WENT.
THE AIRPORT--THE AIRPORT! THAT'S ALL I KNOW--HONEST! HONEST!
THE AIRPORT!
IF--I DON' GET THERE IN TIME--
I'LL HAVE LOST HER FOREVER.
I DON'T EVEN KNOW THE PLANE--THE FLIGHT NUMBER--
BUT I'LL FIND HER--I HAVE TO FIND HER.
I CAN'T LET HER LEAVE WITHOUT ME.
ONCE I REACH THE OUTSKIRTS--IT SLOWS ME DOWN--
THE TALLER THE BUILD-INGS, THE FASTER I CAN SWING.
BUT THIS IS STILL BETTER THAN INCHING MY WAY THRU THE HEAVY TRAFFIC BELOW.
NOW TO FIND WHICH FLIGHT IS HEADING FOR LONDON.
AIR-
STRAIGHT AHEAD

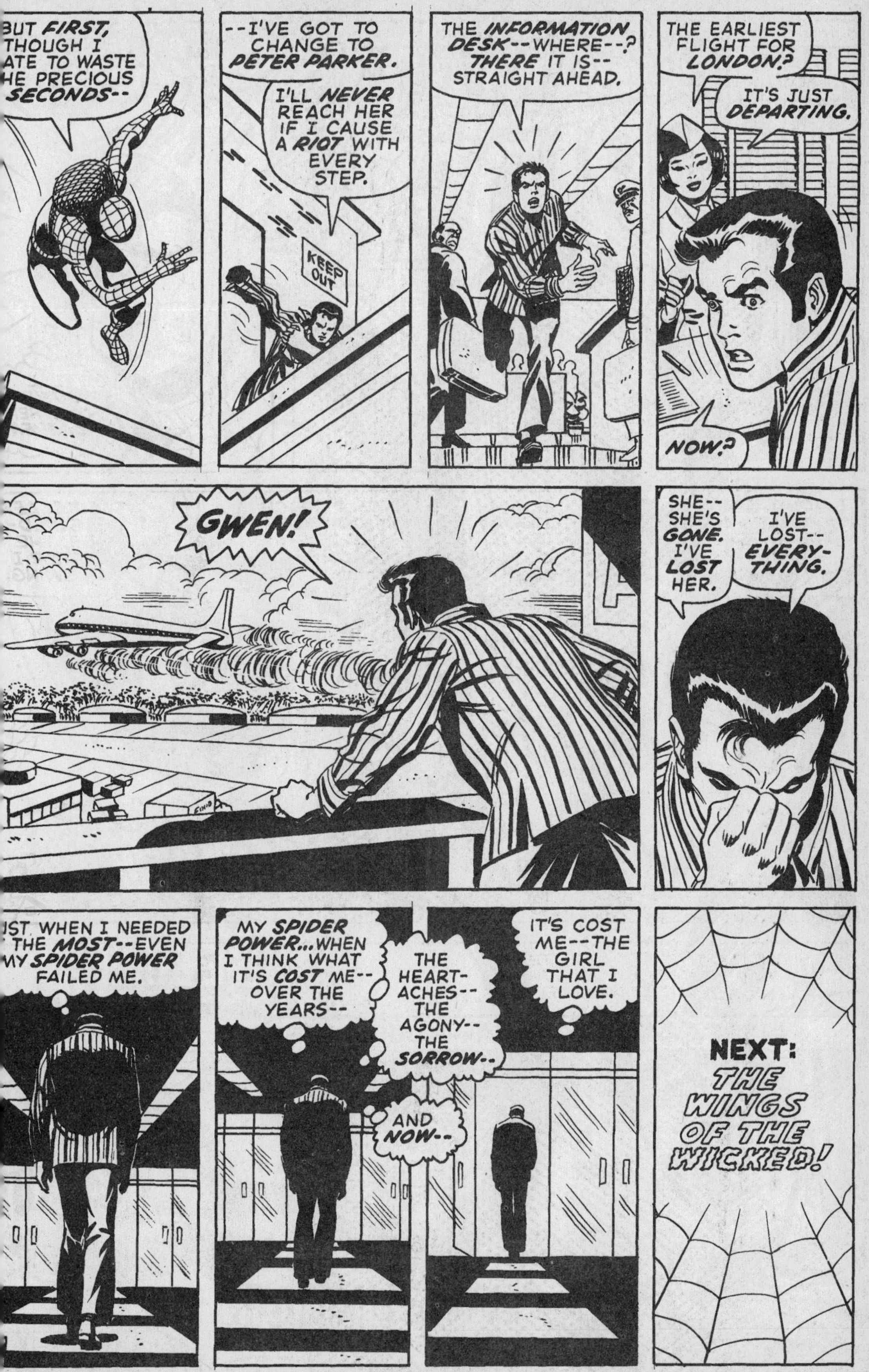
BUT FIRST, THOUGH I ATE TO WASTE HE PRECIOUS SECONDS--
--I'VE GOT TO CHANGE TO PETER PARKER.
I'LL NEVER REACH HER IF I CAUSE A RIOT WITH EVERY STEP.
KEEP OUT
THE INFORMATION DESK--WHERE--? THERE IT IS--STRAIGHT AHEAD.
THE EARLIEST FLIGHT FOR LONDON?
IT'S JUST DEPARTING.
NOW?
GWEN!
SHE--SHE'S GONE. I'VE LOST HER.
I'VE LOST--EVERY-THING.
UST WHEN I NEEDED THE MOST--EVEN MY SPIDER POWER FAILED ME.
MY SPIDER POWER...WHEN I THINK WHAT IT'S COST ME--OVER THE YEARS--
THE HEART-ACHES--THE AGONY--THE SORROW--
AND NOW--
IT'S COST ME--THE GIRL THAT I LOVE.
NEXT: THE WINGS OF THE WICKED!

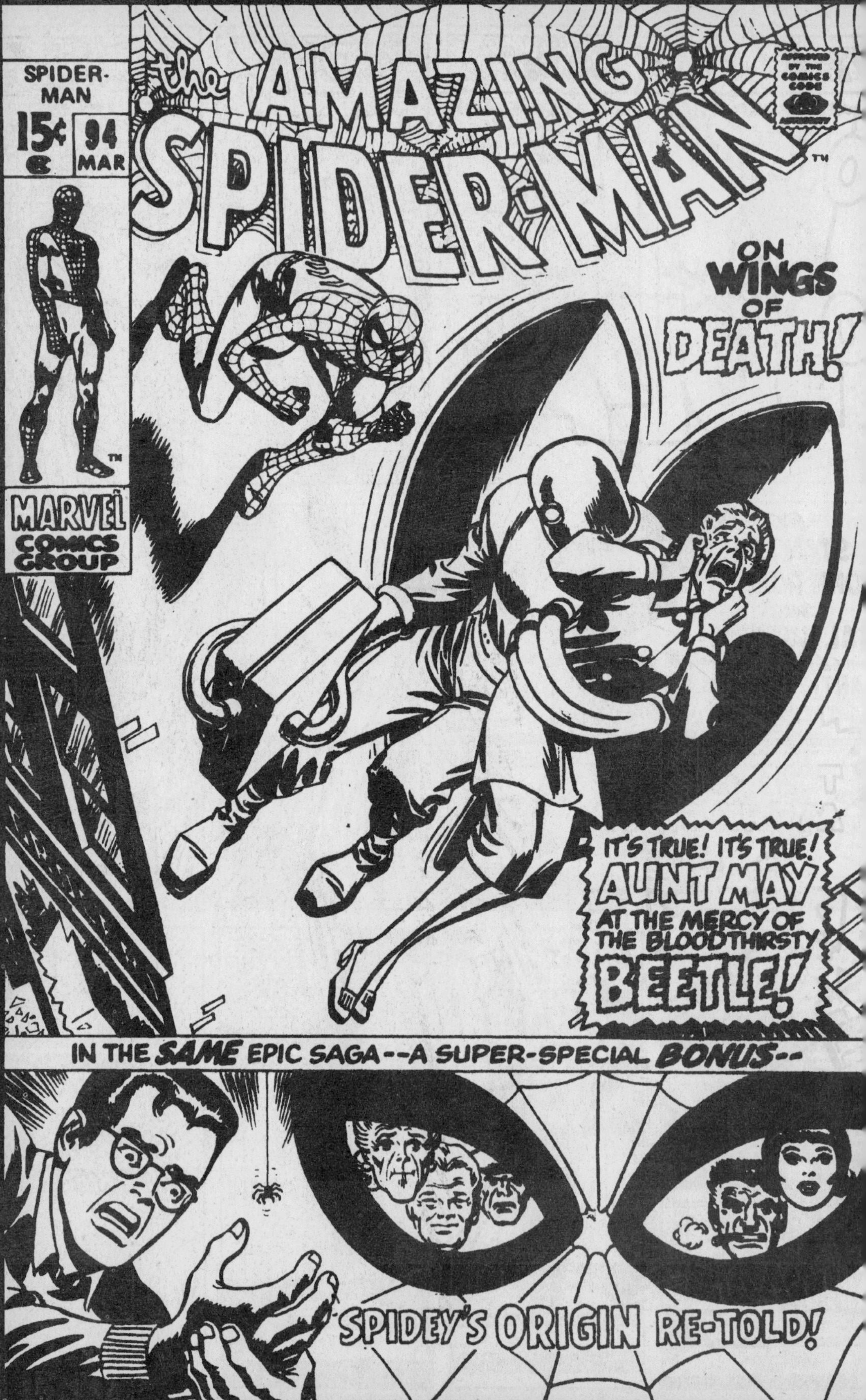
SPIDER-MAN
15¢
94
MAR
the AMAZING SPIDER-MAN
MARVEL COMICS GROUP
ON WINGS OF DEATH!
IT'S TRUE! IT'S TRUE! AUNT MAY AT THE MERCY OF THE BLOODTHIRSTY BEETLE!
IN THE SAME EPIC SAGA--A SUPER-SPECIAL BONUS--
SPIDEY'S ORIGIN RE-TOLD!

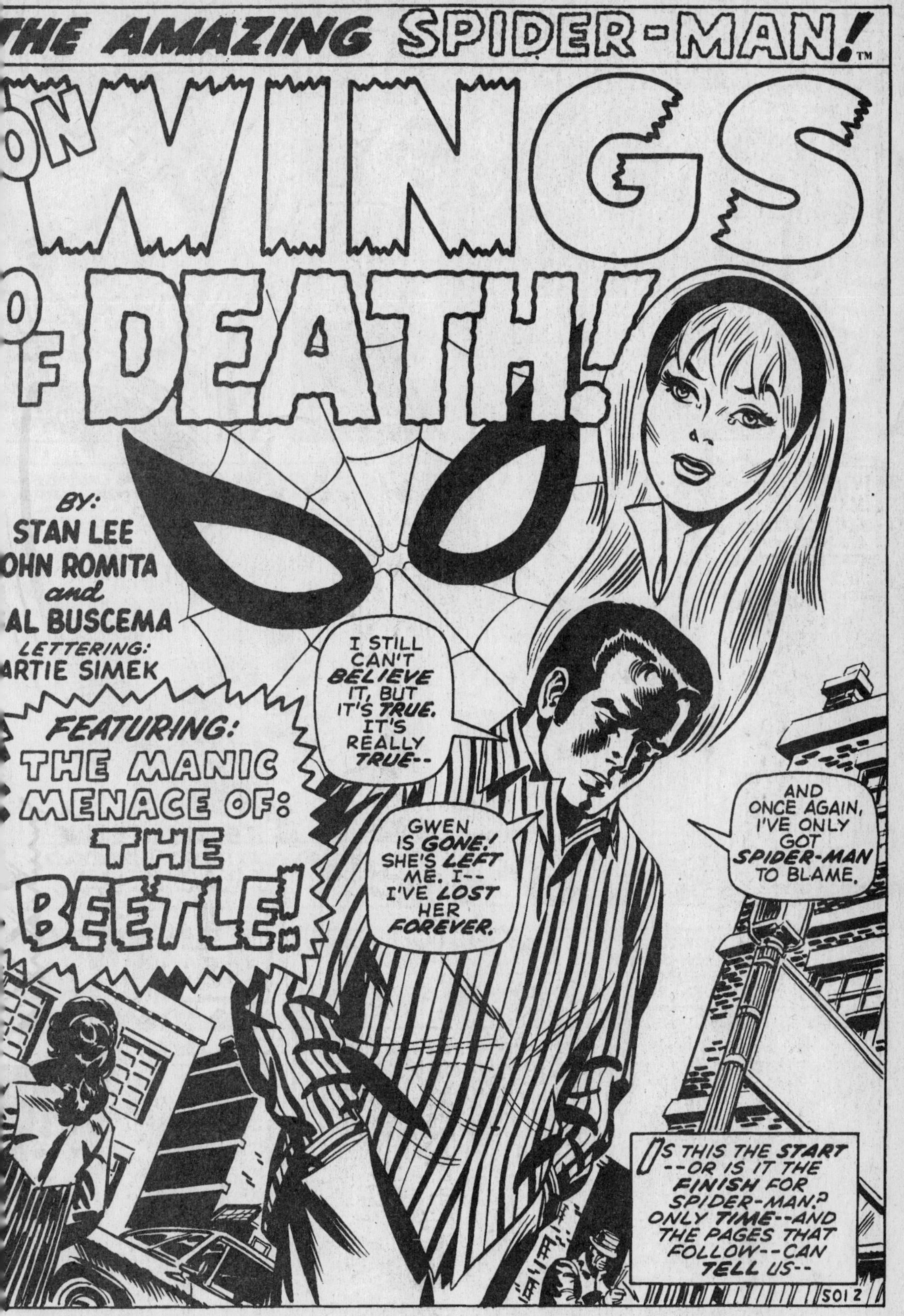
THE AMAZING SPIDER-MAN! TM
ON WINGS OF DEATH!
BY: STAN LEE JOHN ROMITA and AL BUSCEMA
LETTERING: ARTIE SIMEK
FEATURING: THE MANIC MENACE OF: THE BEETLE!
I STILL CAN'T BELIEVE IT, BUT IT'S TRUE. IT'S REALLY TRUE--
GWEN IS GONE! SHE'S LEFT ME. I-- I'VE LOST HER FOREVER.
AND ONCE AGAIN, I'VE ONLY GOT SPIDER-MAN TO BLAME.
IS THIS THE START --OR IS IT THE FINISH FOR SPIDER-MAN? ONLY TIME--AND THE PAGES THAT FOLLOW--CAN TELL US--
S01 2

EVERYTHING *BAD* THAT'S EVER HAPPENED TO ME--ALL OF MY *LIFE*--

WAS BECAUSE OF MY *SECRET IDENTITY*...

--BECAUSE OF-- *SPIDER-MAN*.

BUT, I WASN'T *BORN* WITH SPIDER POWERS --I WASN'T *BORN* WEARING AN ICKY *COSTUME*...

I DON'T *HAVE* TO STAY THIS WAY.

NOTHING'S *STOPPING* ME FROM GIVING IT ALL *UP*.

SOMETIMES--I ALMOST *HATE* TO THINK BACK--TO REMEMBER HOW IT *WAS*--WHEN IT ALL *STARTED*--

I NEVER DREAMED WHAT I WAS GETTING *INTO*...

"IT WAS A SCIENCE LECTURE--LIKE ANY OTHER--OR, SO I *THOUGHT*--"

RADIOACTIVITY... WHAT A *FASCINATING* SUBJECT.

NOW, IF YOU'LL ALL GIVE ME YOUR CLOSE ATTENTION--

WE KNOW SO *MUCH*, YET SO *LITTLE* ABOUT IT.

"IT WAS A ONE IN A *BILLION* CHANCE-- AN ACCIDENT THAT *COULDN'T* HAPPEN-- AND YET-- IT DID."

"A LONE *SPIDER*, SILENTLY DESCENDING, WAS UNWITTINGLY SUBJECTED TO A BLAST OF POWERFUL *RADIATION*--"

"AND, MINUTES LATER, AS IT KEPT SLOWLY *LOWERING* ITSELF ON A THIN STRAND OF *WEBBING*--"

"I FELT SOMETHING *BITE* ME--"

‡*OWW!*‡ WHAT THE--?

SOMETHING *BIT* ME.

IT WAS JUST A *SPIDER*.

BUT--WHY DO I FEEL SO-- *STRANGE*?

EVEN WALKING HOME, I COULDN'T SHAKE THE ODD, UNFAMILIAR *SENSATION* WHICH TINGLED THRU MY BODY. THEN, AS A COUPLE OF LOCAL CREEPS TRIED TO PICK A *FIGHT* WITH ME--"

HERE'S SOMETHIN' *FOR* YA, PUNY PARKER.

I--HARDLY *FELT* IT.

CAN'T BECOME A *PUNCHING* BAG. I'VE GOT TO FIGHT *BACK*-- SOMEHOW.

BT5K!

HEY--

TAKE *OFF*, MAN. NOBODY CAN PUNCH LIKE *THAT!*

I--SNAPPED A *LAMP-POST*--WITH MY BARE *FIST!*

BUT HOW? *HOW?*

WHAT'S *HAPPENING* TO ME?

"I WAS SO *SHAKEN* BY WHAT HAPPENED, THAT I DIDN'T HEAR AN APPROACHING *CAR* AS I STEPPED OFF THE CURB UNTIL--"

HE CAN'T *STOP* IN TIME!

HAVE TO *JUMP* FOR SAFETY!

I *MADE* IT.

BUT--HOW DID I JUMP SO *HIGH?*

AND HOW CAN I *CLING* TO THE SHEER WALL LIKE THIS?

I'M CLIMBING *UP*--EASY AS A *SPIDER!*

"*SPIDER!* THAT GAVE ME THE *CLUE.* I RACED BACK TO MY ROOM--"

IF THE SPIDER THAT *BIT* ME WAS *RADIO-ACTIVE*--

--IT AFFECTED MY *BLOOD.* I'VE GAINED HIS *POWERS!*

AND, THAT MEANS--

"IN THE DAYS THAT FOLLOWED, I DESIGNED MY *WEB-SHOOTER*--"

ALL I NEED DO IS HIT THE *BUTTON.*

IT WORKS. I CAN SNARE *ANY-THING.*

AND MY SPIDER POWER GIVES ME SUPERHUMAN *AIM* AND *CONTROL.*

"I CAN'T REMEMBER *WHAT* MADE ME DO IT--BUT, BEFORE LONG, I HAD DE-SIGNED MYSELF A *COSTUME,*"

THERE MUST BE *SOME* WAY TO MAKE SOME MONEY OUT OF THIS.

FLAK!

3

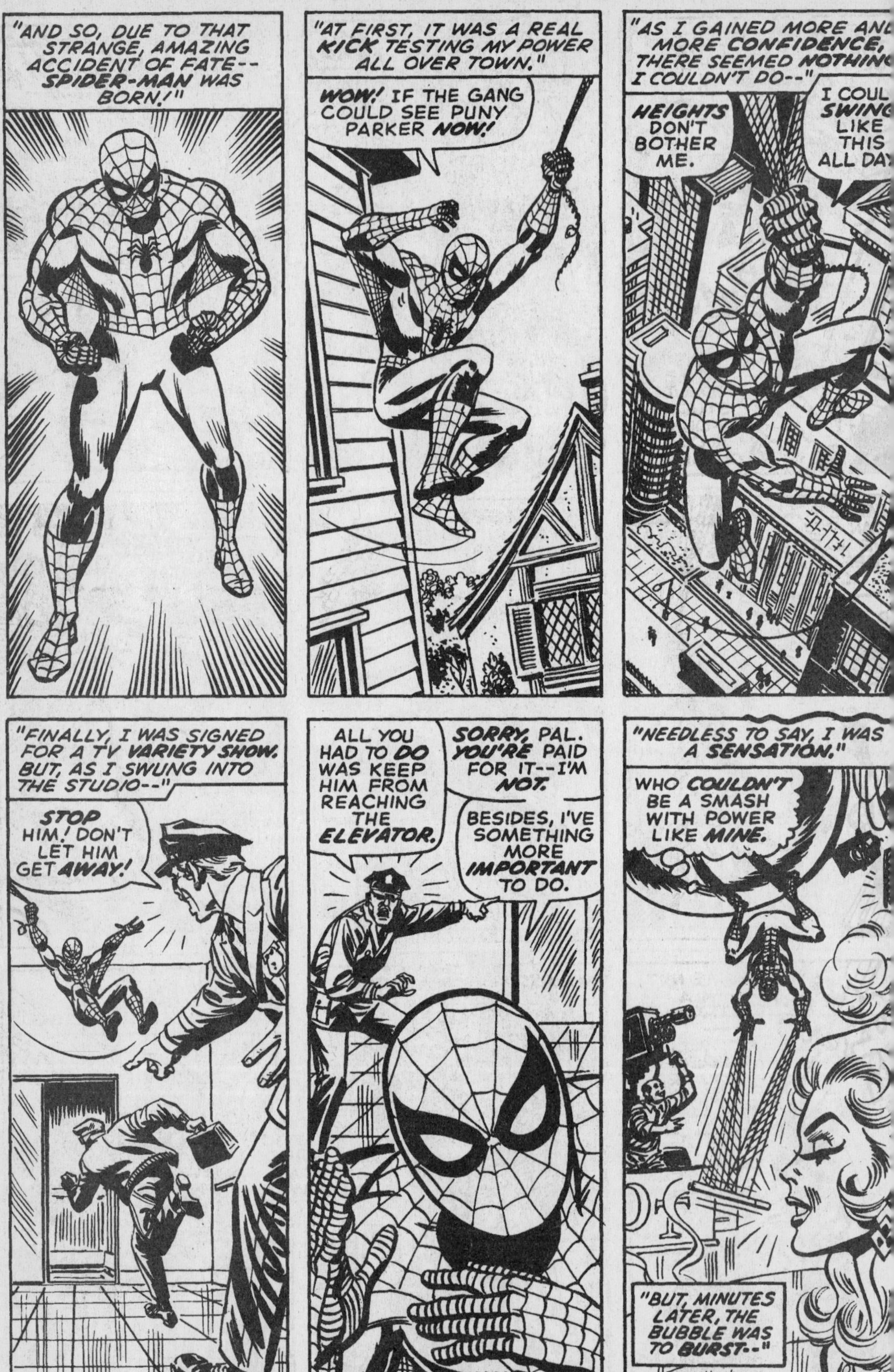
"AND SO, DUE TO THAT STRANGE, AMAZING ACCIDENT OF FATE-- SPIDER-MAN WAS BORN!"
"AT FIRST, IT WAS A REAL KICK TESTING MY POWER ALL OVER TOWN."
WOW! IF THE GANG COULD SEE PUNY PARKER NOW!
"AS I GAINED MORE AND MORE CONFIDENCE, THERE SEEMED NOTHIN I COULDN'T DO--"
HEIGHTS DON'T BOTHER ME.
I COUL SWING LIKE THIS ALL DA
"FINALLY, I WAS SIGNED FOR A TV VARIETY SHOW. BUT, AS I SWUNG INTO THE STUDIO--"
STOP HIM! DON'T LET HIM GET AWAY!
ALL YOU HAD TO DO WAS KEEP HIM FROM REACHING THE ELEVATOR.
SORRY, PAL. YOU'RE PAID FOR IT--I'M NOT.
BESIDES, I'VE SOMETHING MORE IMPORTANT TO DO.
"NEEDLESS TO SAY, I WAS A SENSATION."
WHO COULDN'T BE A SMASH WITH POWER LIKE MINE.
"BUT, MINUTES LATER, THE BUBBLE WAS TO BURST--"

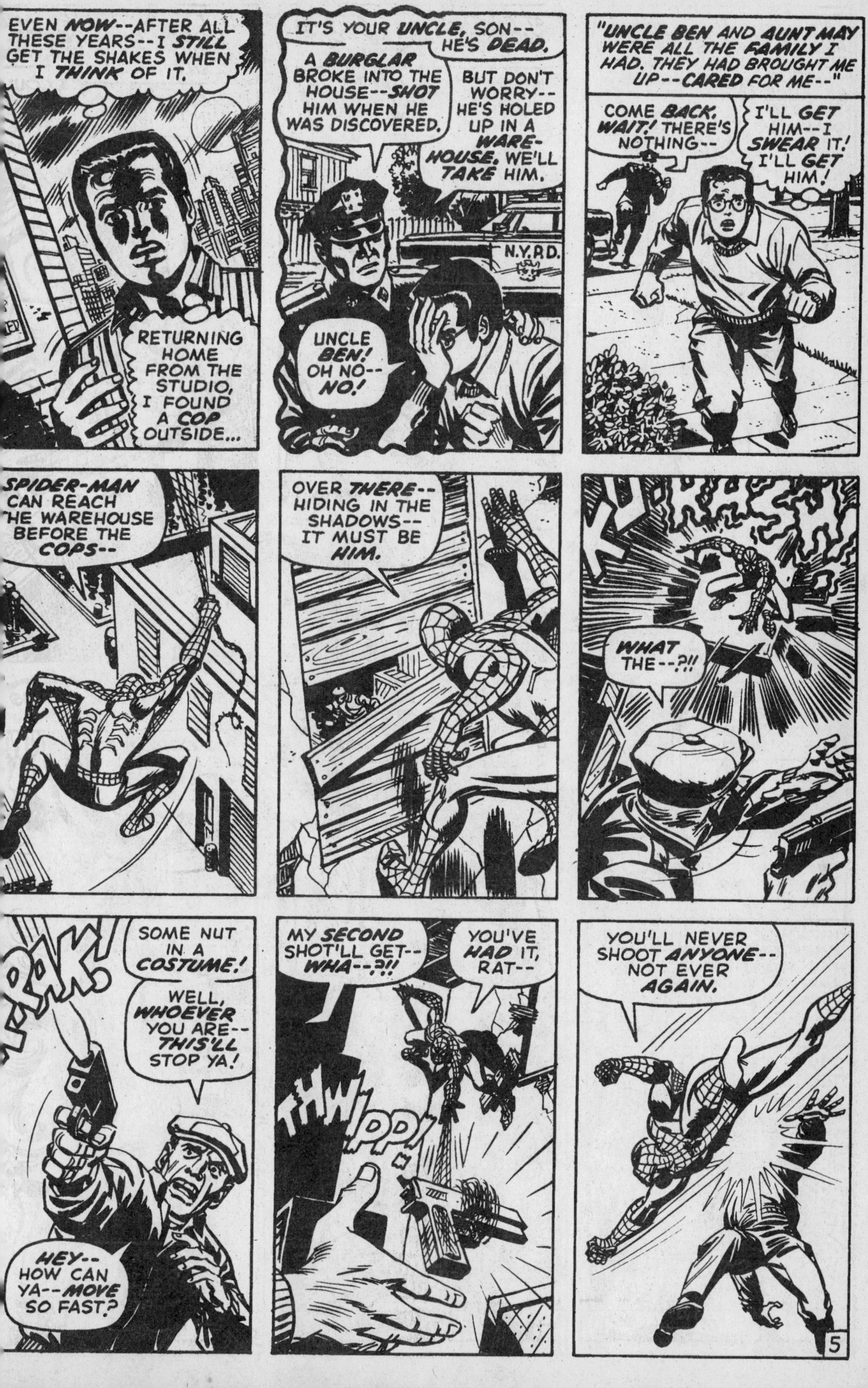
EVEN NOW--AFTER ALL THESE YEARS--I STILL GET THE SHAKES WHEN I THINK OF IT.
RETURNING HOME FROM THE STUDIO, I FOUND A COP OUTSIDE...
IT'S YOUR UNCLE, SON--HE'S DEAD.
A BURGLAR BROKE INTO THE HOUSE--SHOT HIM WHEN HE WAS DISCOVERED.
BUT DON'T WORRY--HE'S HOLED UP IN A WARE-HOUSE. WE'LL TAKE HIM.
N.Y.P.D.
UNCLE BEN! OH NO--NO!
"UNCLE BEN AND AUNT MAY WERE ALL THE FAMILY I HAD. THEY HAD BROUGHT ME UP--CARED FOR ME--"
COME BACK. WAIT! THERE'S NOTHING--
I'LL GET HIM--I SWEAR IT! I'LL GET HIM!
SPIDER-MAN CAN REACH THE WAREHOUSE BEFORE THE COPS--
OVER THERE--HIDING IN THE SHADOWS--IT MUST BE HIM.
WHAT THE--?!!
PAK!
SOME NUT IN A COSTUME!
WELL, WHOEVER YOU ARE--THIS'LL STOP YA!
HEY--HOW CAN YA--MOVE SO FAST?
MY SECOND SHOT'LL GET--WHA--?!!
YOU'VE HAD IT, RAT--
THWIPP!
YOU'LL NEVER SHOOT ANYONE--NOT EVER AGAIN.
5

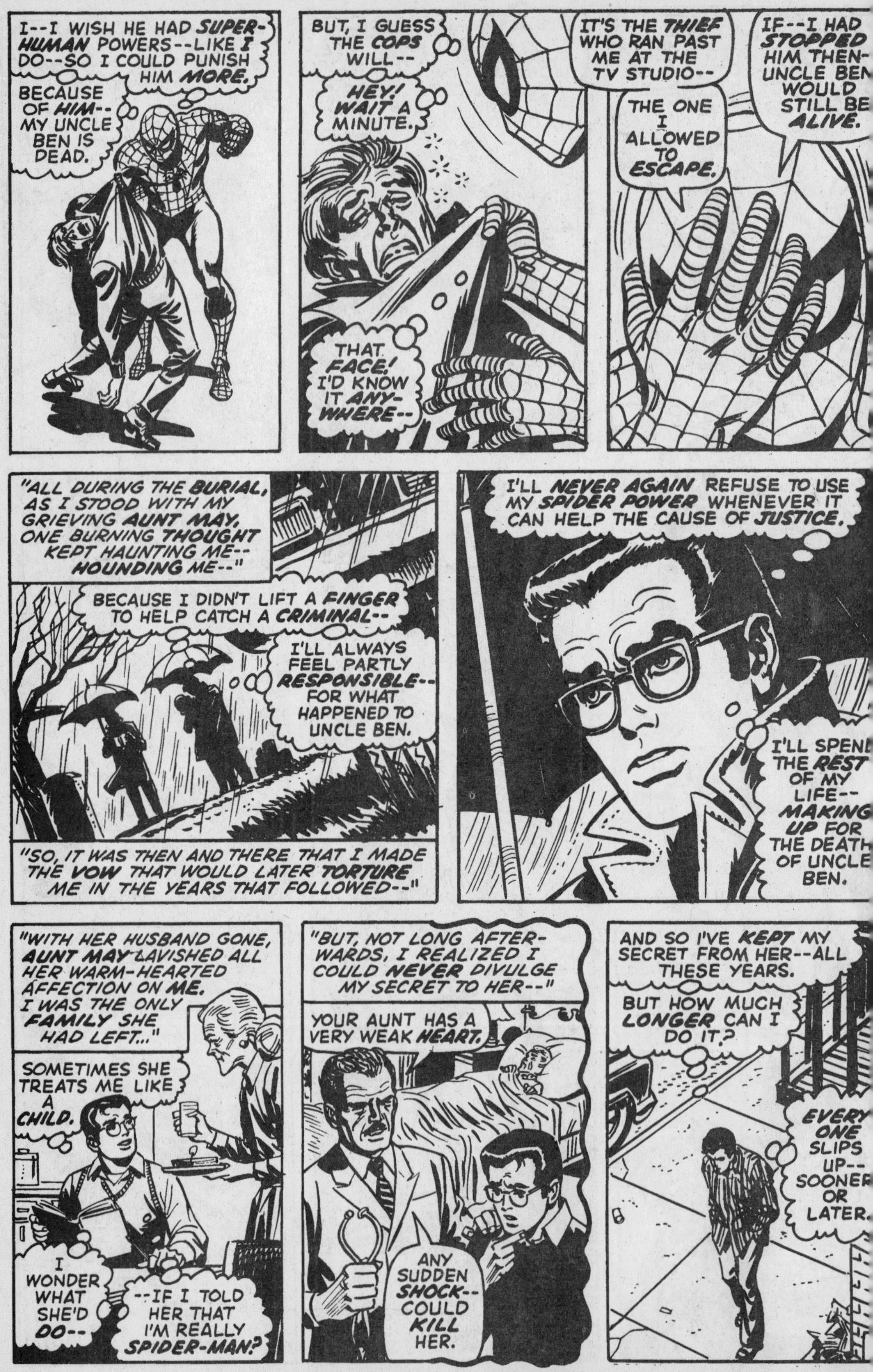
I--I WISH HE HAD SUPER-HUMAN POWERS--LIKE I DO--SO I COULD PUNISH HIM MORE.
BECAUSE OF HIM--MY UNCLE BEN IS DEAD.
BUT, I GUESS THE COPS WILL--
HEY! WAIT A MINUTE.
THAT FACE! I'D KNOW IT ANYWHERE--
IT'S THE THIEF WHO RAN PAST ME AT THE TV STUDIO--
THE ONE I ALLOWED TO ESCAPE.
IF--I HAD STOPPED HIM THEN--UNCLE BEN WOULD STILL BE ALIVE.
"ALL DURING THE BURIAL, AS I STOOD WITH MY GRIEVING AUNT MAY, ONE BURNING THOUGHT KEPT HAUNTING ME--HOUNDING ME--"
BECAUSE I DIDN'T LIFT A FINGER TO HELP CATCH A CRIMINAL--
I'LL ALWAYS FEEL PARTLY RESPONSIBLE--FOR WHAT HAPPENED TO UNCLE BEN.
"SO, IT WAS THEN AND THERE THAT I MADE THE VOW THAT WOULD LATER TORTURE ME IN THE YEARS THAT FOLLOWED--"
I'LL NEVER AGAIN REFUSE TO USE MY SPIDER POWER WHENEVER IT CAN HELP THE CAUSE OF JUSTICE.
I'LL SPEND THE REST OF MY LIFE--MAKING UP FOR THE DEATH OF UNCLE BEN.
"WITH HER HUSBAND GONE, AUNT MAY LAVISHED ALL HER WARM-HEARTED AFFECTION ON ME. I WAS THE ONLY FAMILY SHE HAD LEFT..."
SOMETIMES SHE TREATS ME LIKE A CHILD.
I WONDER WHAT SHE'D DO--
--IF I TOLD HER THAT I'M REALLY SPIDER-MAN?
"BUT, NOT LONG AFTERWARDS, I REALIZED I COULD NEVER DIVULGE MY SECRET TO HER--"
YOUR AUNT HAS A VERY WEAK HEART.
ANY SUDDEN SHOCK--COULD KILL HER.
AND SO I'VE KEPT MY SECRET FROM HER--ALL THESE YEARS.
BUT HOW MUCH LONGER CAN I DO IT?
EVERY ONE SLIPS UP--SOONER OR LATER.

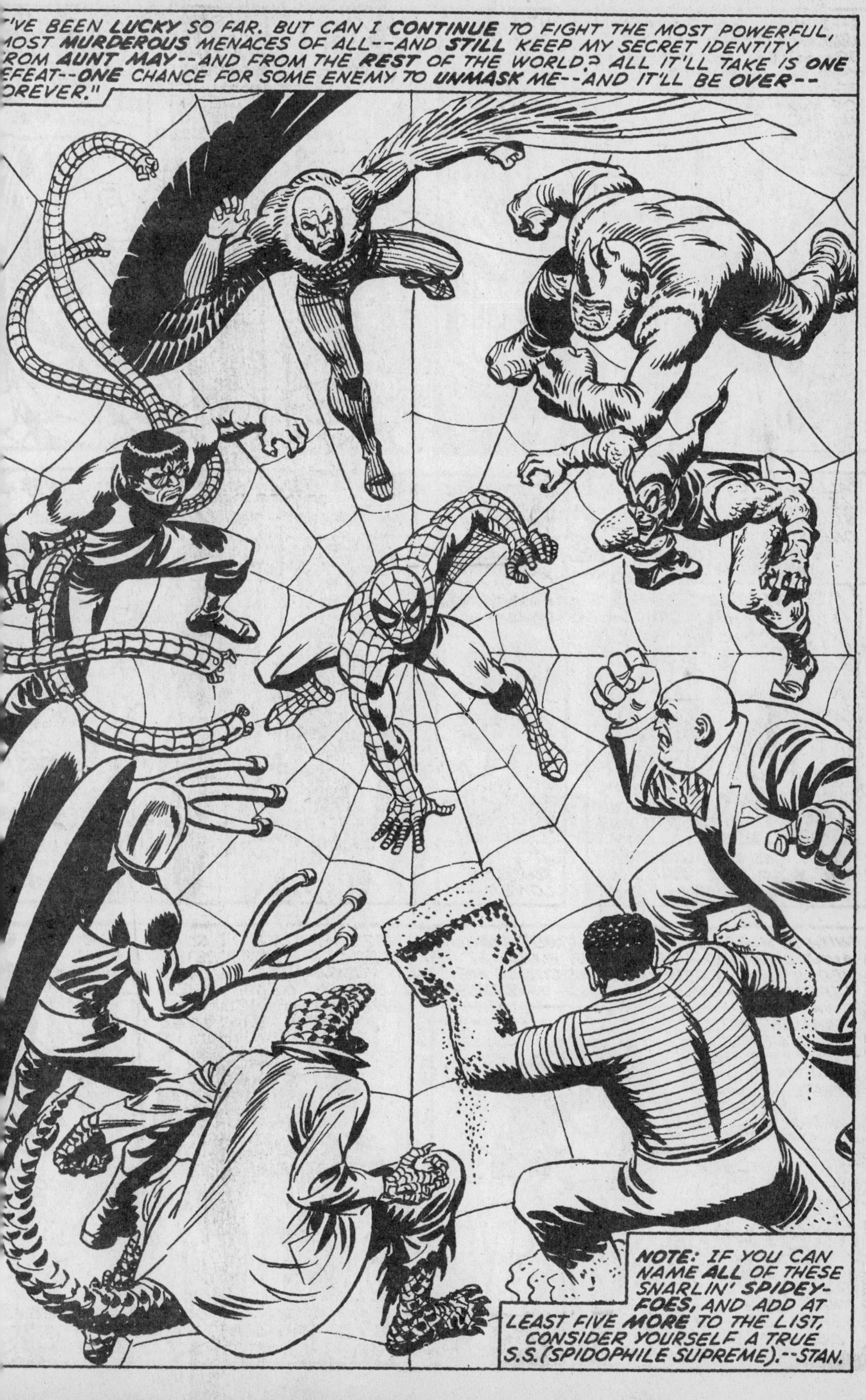
"I'VE BEEN LUCKY SO FAR. BUT CAN I CONTINUE TO FIGHT THE MOST POWERFUL, MOST MURDEROUS MENACES OF ALL--AND STILL KEEP MY SECRET IDENTITY FROM AUNT MAY--AND FROM THE REST OF THE WORLD? ALL IT'LL TAKE IS ONE DEFEAT--ONE CHANCE FOR SOME ENEMY TO UNMASK ME--AND IT'LL BE OVER--FOREVER."
NOTE: IF YOU CAN NAME ALL OF THESE SNARLIN' SPIDEY-FOES, AND ADD AT LEAST FIVE MORE TO THE LIST, CONSIDER YOURSELF A TRUE S.S. (SPIDOPHILE SUPREME).--STAN.

I'VE BEEN WALKING FOR *HOURS*-- *THINKING* FOR HOURS--AND I'M MORE *UNDECIDED* THAN EVER

THERE'S THE *BUGLE* BUILDING. DID MY *SUBCONSCIOUS* MAKE ME WALK HERE --OR IS IT JUST *COINCIDENCE?*

DAILY BUGLE

NUTS. EITHER WAY-- WHO *CARES?*

I'VE *MORE* ON MY MIND THAN SELLING A FEW CRUMMY PHOTOS TO THAT TIGHTWAD *JAMESON.*

AND THERE'S *NOTHING* IN THAT *RAG* OF HIS THAT COULD INTEREST ME *NOW.*

CRIME

BEETLE AT LARGE!

*D*ON'T BE TOO *SURE* OF THAT, PETE. FATE MAY HAVE A LITTLE *SURPRISE* IN STORE FOR YOU.

PETER *PARKER!* I HAVEN'T SEEN YOU IN *AGES.*

HUH? OH-- HI, BETTY.

IS ANYTHING *WRONG?* HAVE YOU GIVEN UP TAKING *NEWS PHOTOS?*

EVEN *MR. JAMESON* WAS WONDERING WHERE YOU'VE BEEN *KEEPING* YOURSELF.

S'MATTER? HE MISSES HIS *FAVORITE WHIPPING BOY?*

HOPE SHE'S NOT IN THE MOOD FOR A LONG *CONVER- SATION.*

I'VE-- JUST BEEN *BUSY*--THAT'S ALL.

IF HE GETS TOO *LONELY* WITHOUT ME, HE CAN ALWAYS GO TO THE *CEMETERY* AND CHUCKLE OVER THE *TOMBSTONES.*

SEE YOU AROUND, LADY.

NOW *WHY* DID I HAVE TO *SNAP* AT HER LIKE THAT?

"BETTY BRANT WAS THE FIRST GIRL I EVER *LOVED*--OR THOUGHT I DID. IT WAS ONLY A FEW YEARS AGO THAT WE *BROKE UP*--AGAIN, BECAUSE OF *SPIDER-MAN.*"

BECAUSE OF MY *SECRET*--IT'S *BETTER* THIS WAY--

FOR *BOTH* OF US.

"BUT, I MUSTN'T *THINK* OF BETTY --'CAUSE SHE REMINDS ME OF *GWEN*--AND THAT'S TOO MUCH TO BEAR."

"AND YET, EVERYTHING I THINK OF--REMINDS ME OF SOMETHING *ELSE*--"

"I REMEMBER HOW I TRIED TO *FORGET* BETTY--BY GOING INTO *ACTION*--JUST AS I'VE DONE LATELY--BECAUSE OF GWEN..."

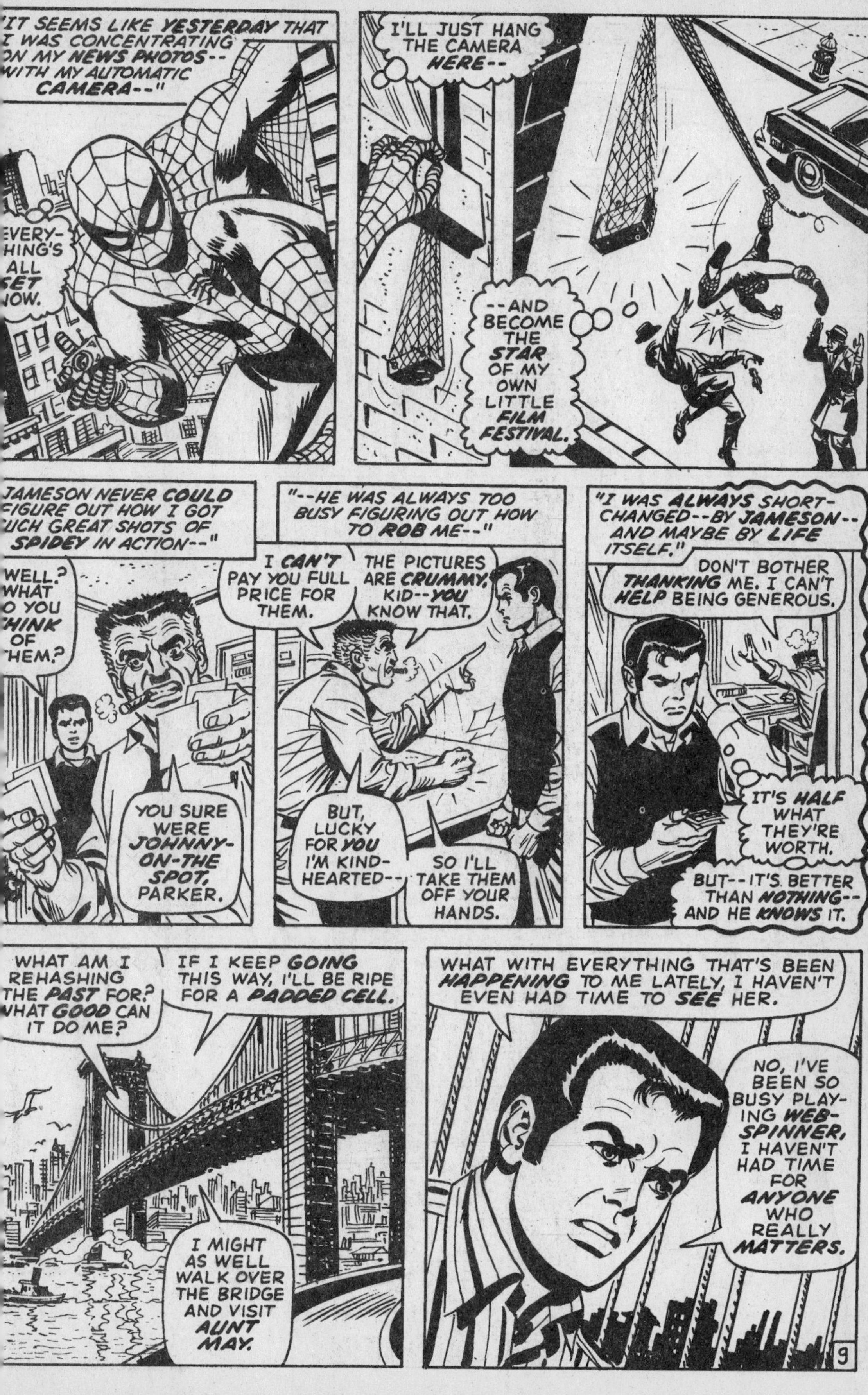
"IT SEEMS LIKE YESTERDAY THAT I WAS CONCENTRATING ON MY NEWS PHOTOS-- WITH MY AUTOMATIC CAMERA--"
EVERYTHING'S ALL SET NOW.
I'LL JUST HANG THE CAMERA HERE--
--AND BECOME THE STAR OF MY OWN LITTLE FILM FESTIVAL.
JAMESON NEVER COULD FIGURE OUT HOW I GOT SUCH GREAT SHOTS OF SPIDEY IN ACTION--"
WELL? WHAT DO YOU THINK OF THEM?
YOU SURE WERE JOHNNY-ON-THE-SPOT, PARKER.
"--HE WAS ALWAYS TOO BUSY FIGURING OUT HOW TO ROB ME--"
THE PICTURES ARE CRUMMY, KID--YOU KNOW THAT.
I CAN'T PAY YOU FULL PRICE FOR THEM.
BUT, LUCKY FOR YOU I'M KIND-HEARTED--
SO I'LL TAKE THEM OFF YOUR HANDS.
"I WAS ALWAYS SHORT-CHANGED--BY JAMESON--AND MAYBE BY LIFE ITSELF."
DON'T BOTHER THANKING ME. I CAN'T HELP BEING GENEROUS.
IT'S HALF WHAT THEY'RE WORTH.
BUT--IT'S BETTER THAN NOTHING--AND HE KNOWS IT.
WHAT AM I REHASHING THE PAST FOR? WHAT GOOD CAN IT DO ME?
IF I KEEP GOING THIS WAY, I'LL BE RIPE FOR A PADDED CELL.
I MIGHT AS WELL WALK OVER THE BRIDGE AND VISIT AUNT MAY.
WHAT WITH EVERYTHING THAT'S BEEN HAPPENING TO ME LATELY, I HAVEN'T EVEN HAD TIME TO SEE HER.
NO, I'VE BEEN SO BUSY PLAYING WEB-SPINNER, I HAVEN'T HAD TIME FOR ANYONE WHO REALLY MATTERS.
9

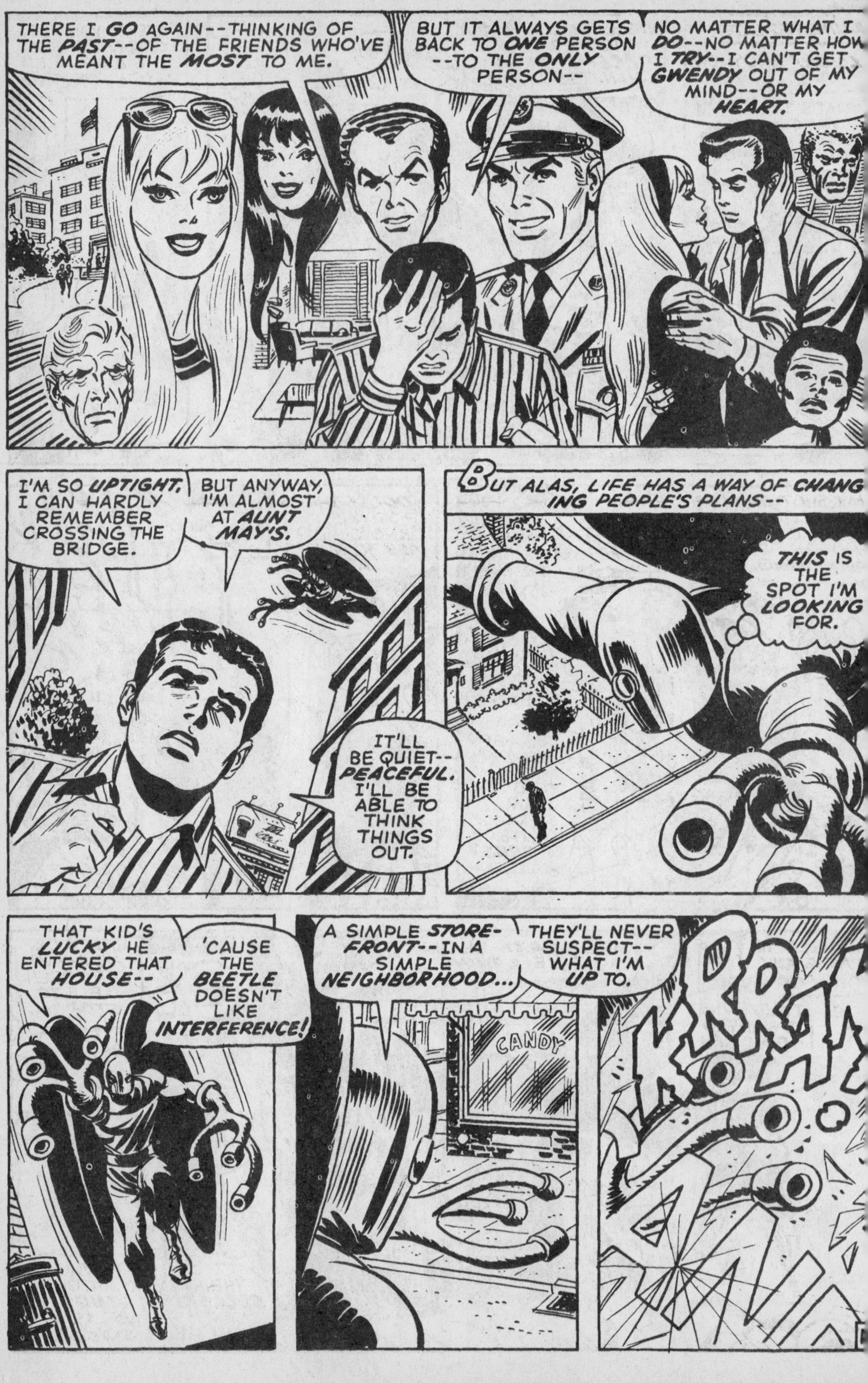
THERE I GO AGAIN--THINKING OF THE PAST--OF THE FRIENDS WHO'VE MEANT THE MOST TO ME.
BUT IT ALWAYS GETS BACK TO ONE PERSON --TO THE ONLY PERSON--
NO MATTER WHAT I DO--NO MATTER HOW I TRY--I CAN'T GET GWENDY OUT OF MY MIND--OR MY HEART.
I'M SO UPTIGHT, I CAN HARDLY REMEMBER CROSSING THE BRIDGE.
BUT ANYWAY, I'M ALMOST AT AUNT MAY'S.
IT'LL BE QUIET--PEACEFUL. I'LL BE ABLE TO THINK THINGS OUT.
BUT ALAS, LIFE HAS A WAY OF CHANGING PEOPLE'S PLANS--
THIS IS THE SPOT I'M LOOKING FOR.
THAT KID'S LUCKY HE ENTERED THAT HOUSE--
'CAUSE THE BEETLE DOESN'T LIKE INTERFERENCE!
A SIMPLE STORE-FRONT--IN A SIMPLE NEIGHBORHOOD...
THEY'LL NEVER SUSPECT--WHAT I'M UP TO.
CANDY
KRRA

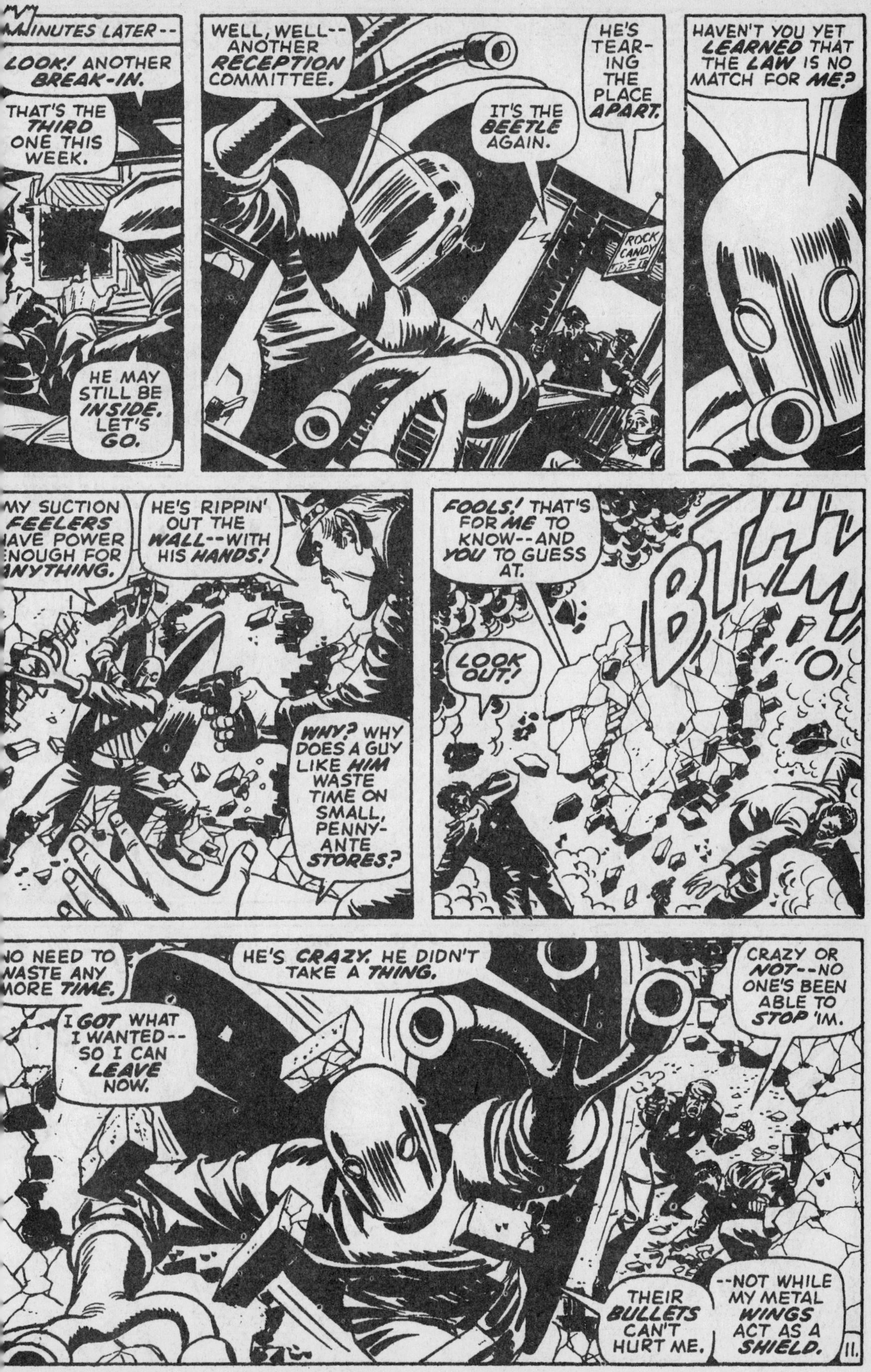
MINUTES LATER--
LOOK! ANOTHER BREAK-IN.
THAT'S THE THIRD ONE THIS WEEK.
HE MAY STILL BE INSIDE. LET'S GO.
WELL, WELL--ANOTHER RECEPTION COMMITTEE.
IT'S THE BEETLE AGAIN.
HE'S TEARING THE PLACE APART.
ROCK CANDY
HAVEN'T YOU YET LEARNED THAT THE LAW IS NO MATCH FOR ME?
MY SUCTION FEELERS HAVE POWER ENOUGH FOR ANYTHING.
HE'S RIPPIN' OUT THE WALL--WITH HIS HANDS!
WHY? WHY DOES A GUY LIKE HIM WASTE TIME ON SMALL, PENNY-ANTE STORES?
FOOLS! THAT'S FOR ME TO KNOW--AND YOU TO GUESS AT.
LOOK OUT!
NO NEED TO WASTE ANY MORE TIME.
I GOT WHAT I WANTED--SO I CAN LEAVE NOW.
HE'S CRAZY. HE DIDN'T TAKE A THING.
CRAZY OR NOT--NO ONE'S BEEN ABLE TO STOP 'IM.
THEIR BULLETS CAN'T HURT ME.
--NOT WHILE MY METAL WINGS ACT AS A SHIELD.

MEANWHILE--

I HEAR *VOICES*, SO I KNOW SHE'S *IN*.

IT SOUNDS LIKE *MRS. WATSON.*

SHE MUST BE *VISITING* AUNT MAY.

WHO'S *THERE?* WHAT DO YOU W--?

OH-- *PETER--* IT'S *YOU!*

SHE SOUNDS *FRIGHTENED.* WHAT CAN BE *WRONG?*

PETER, DEAR--YOU SHOULD HAVE *CALLED,* TO TELL US YOU WERE *COMING.*

WHY, AUNT MAY? WHY DO YOU SEEM SO *NERVOUS?*

YOU JUST GAVE US A *START,* DEAR-- THAT'S *ALL.*

OH, TELL HIM THE *TRUTH,* MAY.

IT'S THAT HORRIBLE *COSTUMED MENACE* WHO'S BEEN TERROR-IZING THE NEIGHBORHOOD.

IT'S *ALL HERE--* IN THE PAPER.

WHO CAN IT *BE?* I HAVEN'T EVEN *LOOKED* AT A PAPER IN DAYS.

MAY I *SEE* IT, MRS. WATSON?

THE BEETLE!

I DIDN'T EVEN KNOW HE WAS OUT OF *JAIL.* HE'S NO ONE TO KID *AROUND* WITH.

DAILY BUGLE
BEETLE STRIKES
SNIPERS MENACED

YOU SHOULDN'T HAVE *TOLD* HIM, ANNA. YOU *KNOW* HOW *SENSITIVE* PETER IS.

NOW HE'S ALL *UPSET.*

WHY WOULD *HE* WASTE TIME BREAKING INTO A *LAUNDRY*--A *BIKE SHOP*-- AND A *BAKERY*--

--AND NOT EVEN *TAKE* ANYTHING?

...CE PHOTOGRAPHED AT RECENT HOLD... ...P BELOW SHOWS LOCATION OF BREAK-INS

		BEETLE ATTACKS NUMBERED IN ORDER
1ST NATIONAL BANK		
SMITH IMPORTING CO. BUILDING	LAUNDRY	①
	BIKE SHOP	②
	BAKERY	③
MAP OF...		④
DRESS SHOP	GROCERY	CANDY STORE

...CE BAFFLED BY
...TTERN

YOU LOOK *TIRED,* PETER. WHY DON'T YOU TAKE A *NAP*--WHILE I FIX YOU A NICE *CHICKEN STEW?*

AND DON'T WORRY ABOUT THE *BEETLE,* DEAR. HE ONLY ATTACKS *STORES*-- NOT HOUSES.

SHE'LL *NEVER* STOP THINK-ING OF ME A FRAIL, *TIMID MILKSOP.*

BUT, MAYBE IT'S JUST AS *WELL.*

THAT'S A GOOD IDEA, AUNT MAY. I *AM* KIND OF TIRED.

...BUGLE...
STRIKES!

THE *BEETLE'S* THE *LEAST* OF MY *WORRIES* NOW.

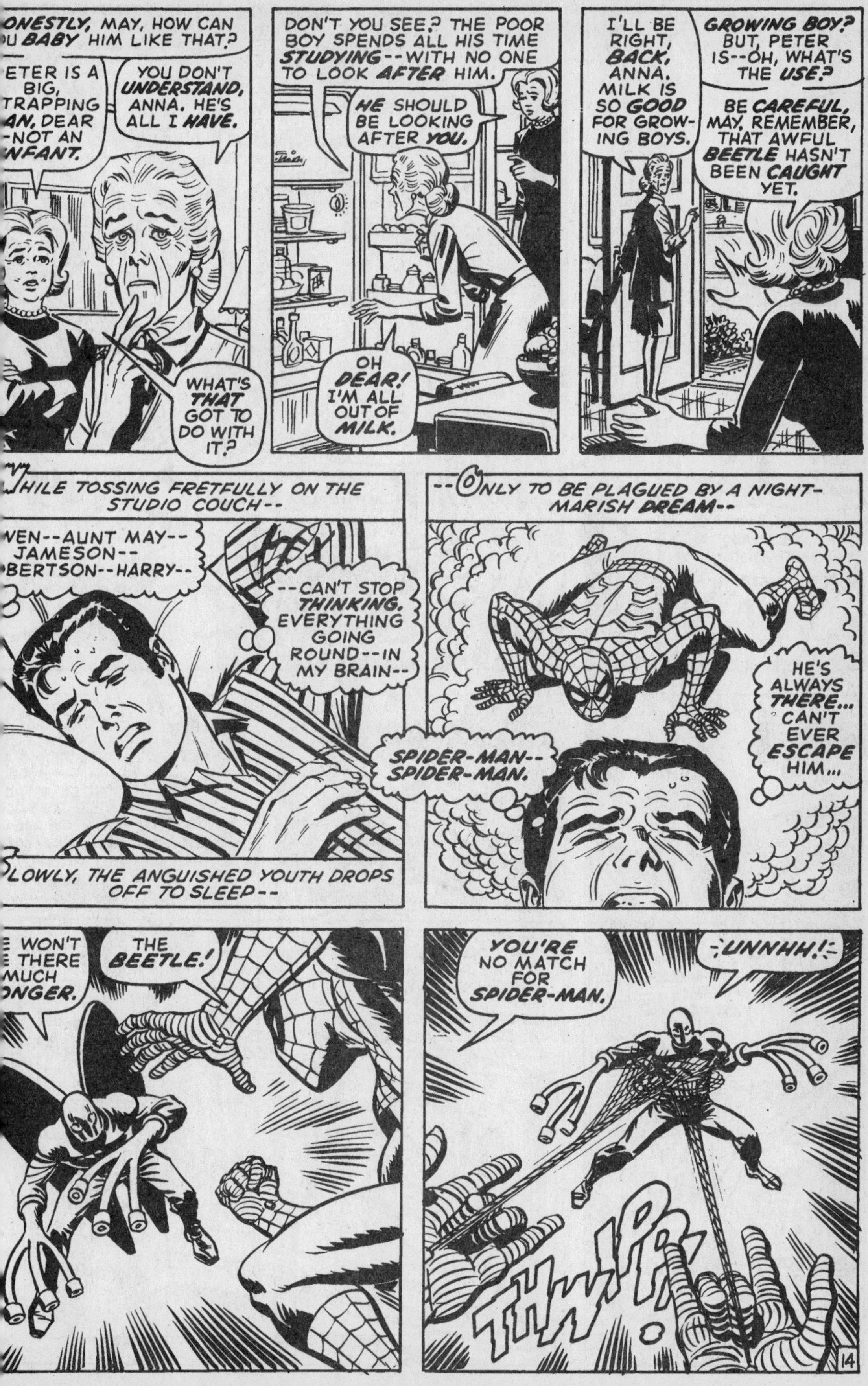
ONESTLY, MAY, HOW CAN U BABY HIM LIKE THAT?
ETER IS A BIG, TRAPPING AN, DEAR -NOT AN NFANT.
YOU DON'T UNDERSTAND, ANNA. HE'S ALL I HAVE.
WHAT'S THAT GOT TO DO WITH IT?
DON'T YOU SEE? THE POOR BOY SPENDS ALL HIS TIME STUDYING--WITH NO ONE TO LOOK AFTER HIM.
HE SHOULD BE LOOKING AFTER YOU.
OH DEAR! I'M ALL OUT OF MILK.
I'LL BE RIGHT BACK, ANNA. MILK IS SO GOOD FOR GROWING BOYS.
GROWING BOY? BUT, PETER IS--OH, WHAT'S THE USE?
BE CAREFUL, MAY. REMEMBER, THAT AWFUL BEETLE HASN'T BEEN CAUGHT YET.
WHILE TOSSING FRETFULLY ON THE STUDIO COUCH--
WEN--AUNT MAY--JAMESON--BERTSON--HARRY--
--CAN'T STOP THINKING. EVERYTHING GOING ROUND--IN MY BRAIN--
SLOWLY, THE ANGUISHED YOUTH DROPS OFF TO SLEEP--
--ONLY TO BE PLAGUED BY A NIGHTMARISH DREAM--
HE'S ALWAYS THERE... CAN'T EVER ESCAPE HIM...
SPIDER-MAN--SPIDER-MAN.
E WON'T E THERE MUCH ONGER.
THE BEETLE!
YOU'RE NO MATCH FOR SPIDER-MAN.
-UNNHH!-
THWIPP

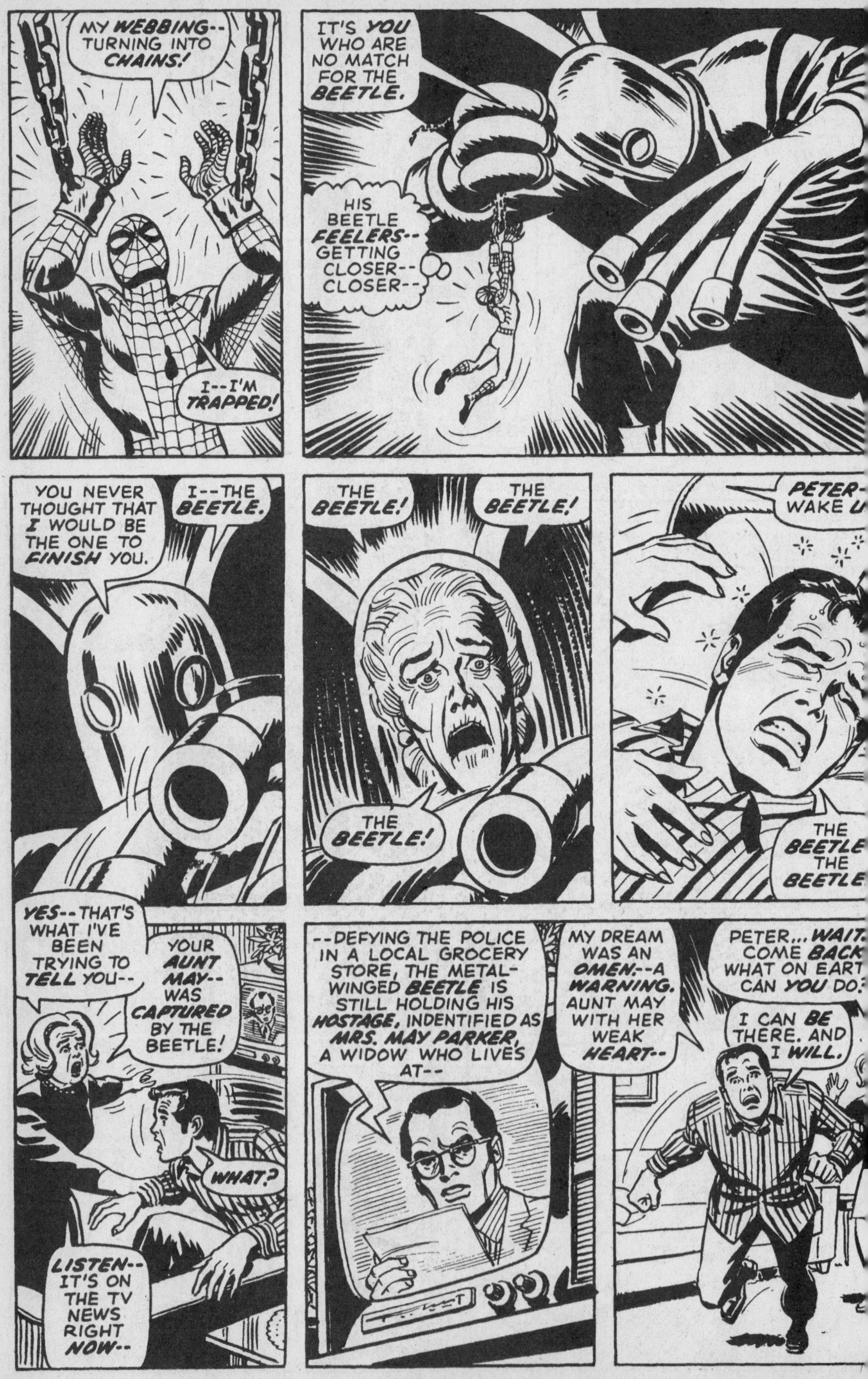

MY WEBBING-- TURNING INTO CHAINS!
I--I'M TRAPPED!
IT'S YOU WHO ARE NO MATCH FOR THE BEETLE.
HIS BEETLE FEELERS-- GETTING CLOSER-- CLOSER--
YOU NEVER THOUGHT THAT I WOULD BE THE ONE TO FINISH YOU.
I--THE BEETLE.
THE BEETLE!
THE BEETLE!
THE BEETLE!
PETER- WAKE U
THE BEETLE THE BEETLE
YES--THAT'S WHAT I'VE BEEN TRYING TO TELL YOU--
YOUR AUNT MAY-- WAS CAPTURED BY THE BEETLE!
WHAT?
LISTEN-- IT'S ON THE TV NEWS RIGHT NOW--
--DEFYING THE POLICE IN A LOCAL GROCERY STORE, THE METAL-WINGED BEETLE IS STILL HOLDING HIS HOSTAGE, INDENTIFIED AS MRS. MAY PARKER, A WIDOW WHO LIVES AT--
MY DREAM WAS AN OMEN--A WARNING. AUNT MAY WITH HER WEAK HEART--
PETER... WAIT. COME BACK WHAT ON EART CAN YOU DO?
I CAN BE THERE. AND I WILL.

I'LL HAVE TO HIDE MY CLOTHES BACK HERE--AND HOPE NOBODY STUMBLES OVER MY WEB-PACK.

AND IF THEY DO--WHO CARES?

ALL THAT MATTERS IS AUNT MAY.

PLEASE, GOD-- LET ME NOT BE --TOO LATE.

IF ONLY SHE HADN'T GONE FOR THAT MILK JUST THEN.

BUT--WHY WOULD THE BEETLE BREAK INTO A GROCERY?

THAT'S LIKE THE KINGPIN ROBBING A PENNY BANK.

BUT, INSIDE THE STORE, THE RIDDLE IS SOLVED--

I KNEW ONE OF THE STORES BACKED UP AGAINST THE IMPORTING COMPANY'S VAULT.

ONCE I FOUND IT, IT WAS SIMPLE FOR ME TO SMASH THE WALL--

BUT-- WHAT ABOUT ME?

YOU? YOU'RE MY TICKET OUT OF HERE.

IT'S SPIDER-MAN! HE MAY BE IN LEAGUE WITH THE BEETLE.

KEEP HIM FROM THE GROCERY-- AT ALL COSTS!

OH NO! THEY WON'T EVEN LET ME HELP THEM.

KRAK!

KRAK!

KEEP FIRING. YOU'VE GOT 'IM ON THE RUN.

HE'S HEADING FOR THE ROOF.

DON'T DROP ME. PLEASE-- DON'T DROP ME.

HOLD YOUR FIRE. HE'S GOT THE WOMAN.

IT WASN'T THE GROCERY HE WAS AFTER.

IT WAS THE VAULT BEHIND IT.

NOW HE'S MAKING HIS GETAWAY.

AUNT MAY WILL BE SAFE--'LONG AS HE NEEDS HER--

BUT, THE STRAIN ON HER HEART--

16

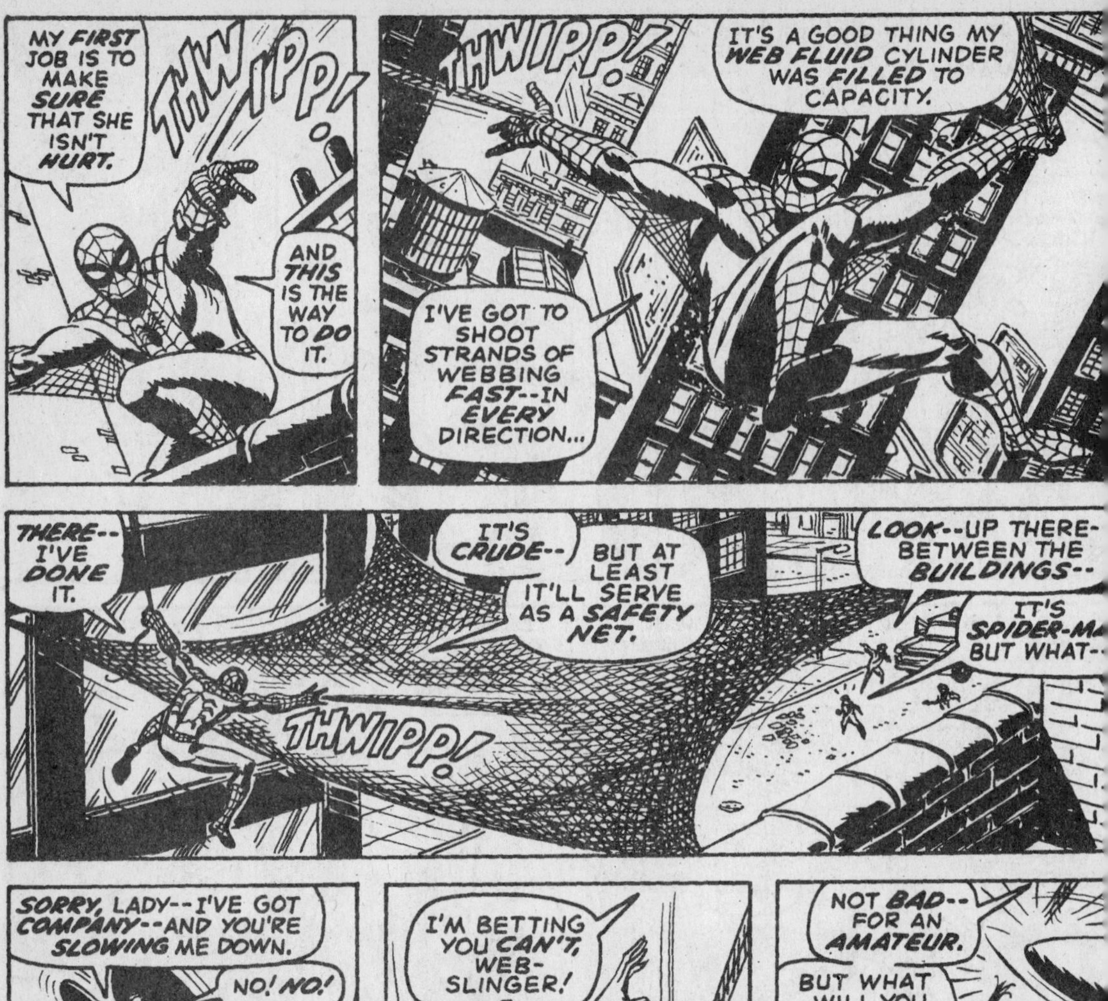

MY FIRST JOB IS TO MAKE SURE THAT SHE ISN'T HURT.
THWIPP!
AND THIS IS THE WAY TO DO IT.
THWIPP!
IT'S A GOOD THING MY WEB FLUID CYLINDER WAS FILLED TO CAPACITY.
I'VE GOT TO SHOOT STRANDS OF WEBBING FAST--IN EVERY DIRECTION...
THERE--I'VE DONE IT.
IT'S CRUDE--
BUT AT LEAST IT'LL SERVE AS A SAFETY NET.
THWIPP!
LOOK--UP THERE--BETWEEN THE BUILDINGS--
IT'S SPIDER-MA
BUT WHAT--
SORRY, LADY--I'VE GOT COMPANY--AND YOU'RE SLOWING ME DOWN.
NO! NO!
MRS. PARKER--LISTEN TO ME--
YOU WON'T BE HURT. I PROMISE YOU.
I'M BETTING YOU CAN'T, WEB-SLINGER!
HE DID IT!
IF YOU FALL--I'LL CATCH YOU!
NOT BAD--FOR AN AMATEUR.
BUT WHAT WILL YOU DO WITH HER--AFTER WING SLICES YOUR WEBBING?
JUST WHAT I THOUGHT HE'D DO.
TRUS ME--YOU'L BE SAFE

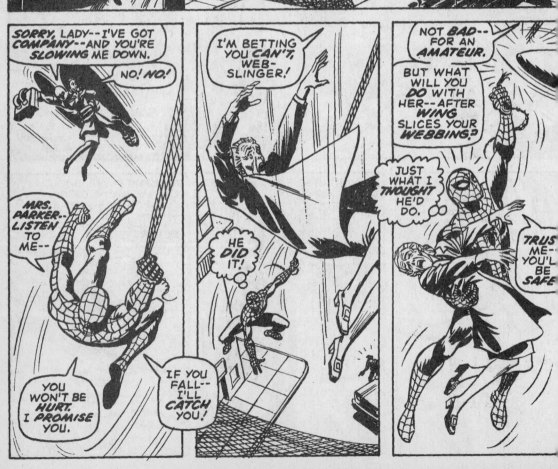

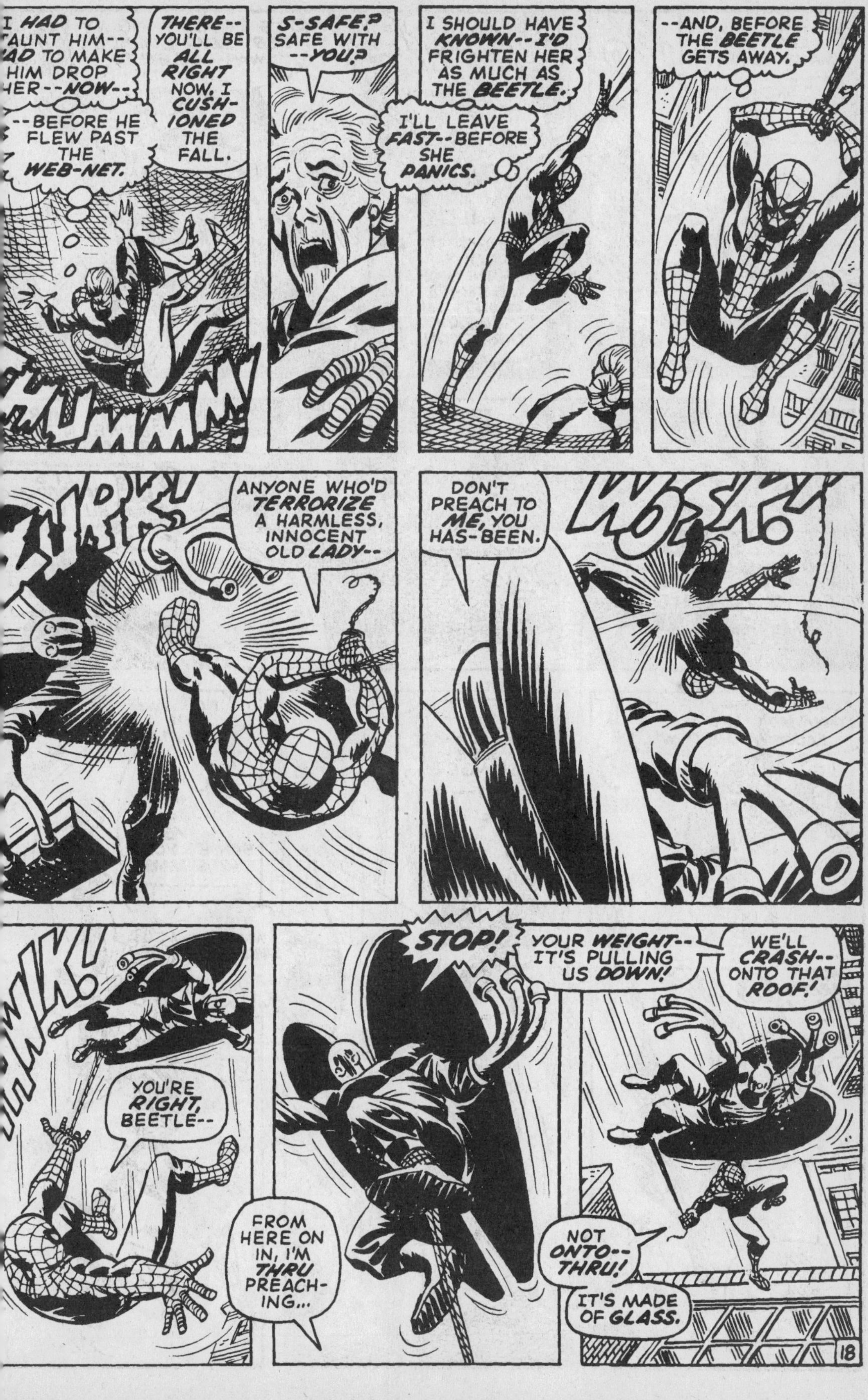

I HAD TO TAUNT HIM-- HAD TO MAKE HIM DROP HER--NOW--
--BEFORE HE FLEW PAST THE WEB-NET.
THERE-- YOU'LL BE ALL RIGHT NOW. I CUSHIONED THE FALL.
S-SAFE? SAFE WITH --YOU?
I SHOULD HAVE KNOWN--I'D FRIGHTEN HER AS MUCH AS THE BEETLE.
I'LL LEAVE FAST--BEFORE SHE PANICS.
--AND, BEFORE THE BEETLE GETS AWAY.
ANYONE WHO'D TERRORIZE A HARMLESS, INNOCENT OLD LADY--
DON'T PREACH TO ME, YOU HAS-BEEN.
YOU'RE RIGHT, BEETLE--
FROM HERE ON IN, I'M THRU PREACHING...
STOP!
YOUR WEIGHT-- IT'S PULLING US DOWN!
WE'LL CRASH-- ONTO THAT ROOF!
NOT ONTO-- THRU!
IT'S MADE OF GLASS.

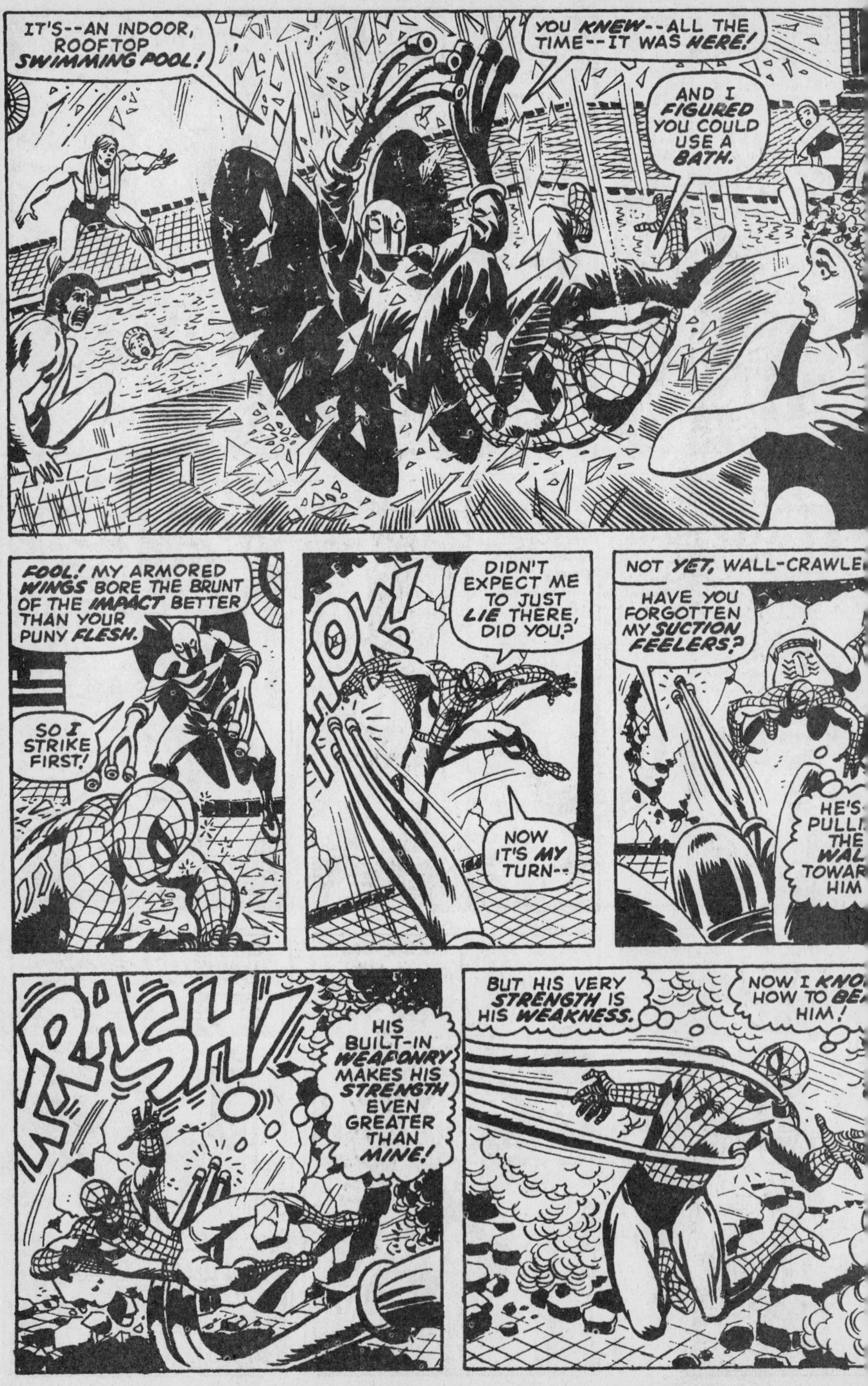
IT'S--AN INDOOR, ROOFTOP SWIMMING POOL!
YOU KNEW--ALL THE TIME--IT WAS HERE!
AND I FIGURED YOU COULD USE A BATH.
FOOL! MY ARMORED WINGS BORE THE BRUNT OF THE IMPACT BETTER THAN YOUR PUNY FLESH.
SO I STRIKE FIRST!
DIDN'T EXPECT ME TO JUST LIE THERE, DID YOU?
NOW IT'S MY TURN--
NOT YET, WALL-CRAWLE
HAVE YOU FORGOTTEN MY SUCTION FEELERS?
HE'S-- PULLI THE WAL TOWAR HIM
HIS BUILT-IN WEAPONRY MAKES HIS STRENGTH EVEN GREATER THAN MINE!
BUT HIS VERY STRENGTH IS HIS WEAKNESS.
NOW I KNO HOW TO BE HIM!

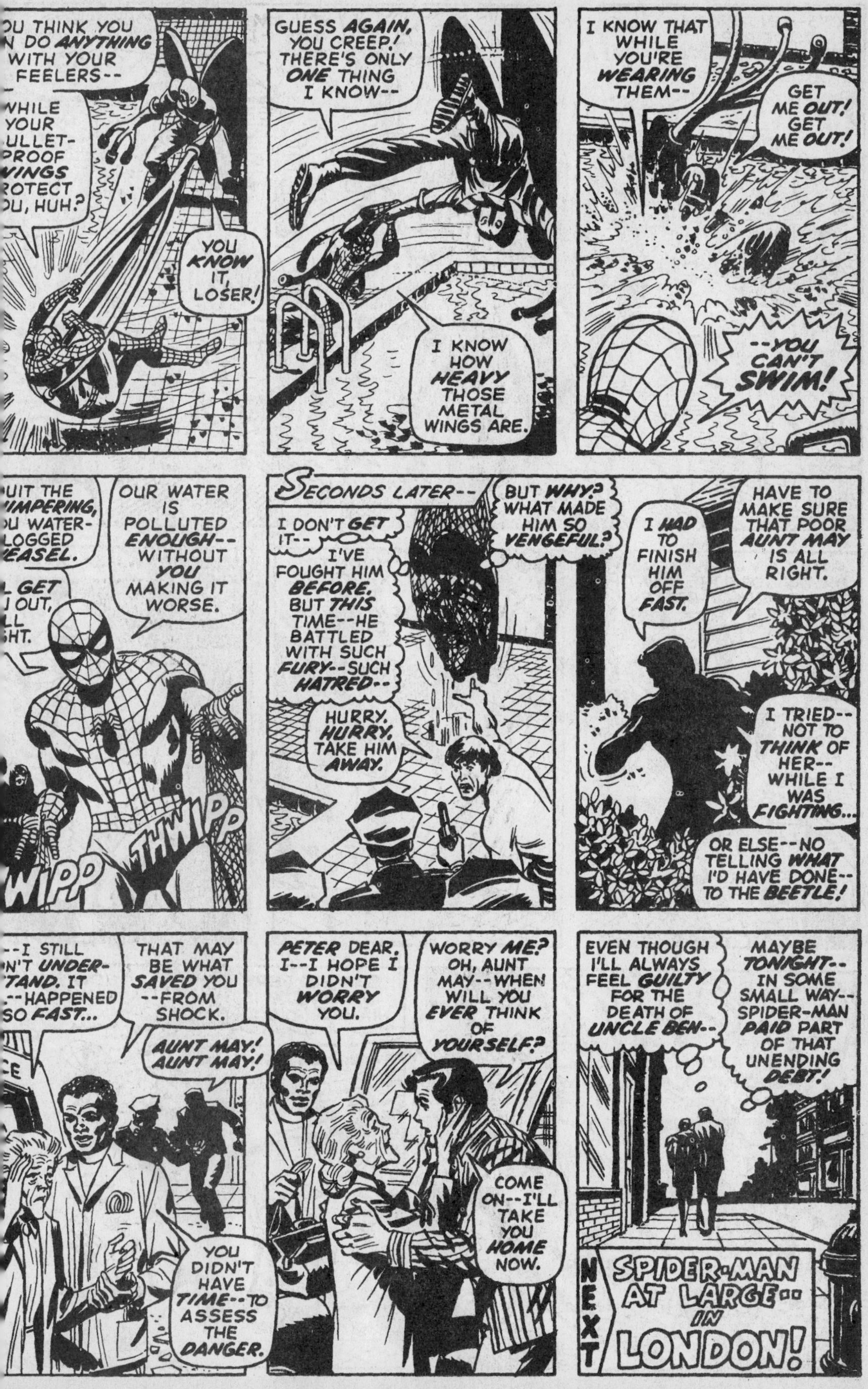
OU THINK YOU
N DO ANYTHING
WITH YOUR
FEELERS--
WHILE
YOUR
ULLET-
PROOF
WINGS
ROTECT
OU, HUH?
YOU
KNOW
IT,
LOSER!
GUESS AGAIN,
YOU CREEP!
THERE'S ONLY
ONE THING
I KNOW--
I KNOW
HOW
HEAVY
THOSE
METAL
WINGS ARE.
I KNOW THAT
WHILE
YOU'RE
WEARING
THEM--
GET
ME OUT!
GET
ME OUT!
--YOU
CAN'T
SWIM!
UIT THE
IMPERING,
OU WATER-
LOGGED
EASEL.
L GET
OUT,
LL
HT.
OUR WATER
IS
POLLUTED
ENOUGH--
WITHOUT
YOU
MAKING IT
WORSE.
THWIPP
WIPP
SECONDS LATER--
I DON'T GET
IT--
I'VE
FOUGHT HIM
BEFORE.
BUT THIS
TIME--HE
BATTLED
WITH SUCH
FURY--SUCH
HATRED--
BUT WHY?
WHAT MADE
HIM SO
VENGEFUL?
HURRY.
HURRY.
TAKE HIM
AWAY.
I HAD
TO
FINISH
HIM
OFF
FAST.
HAVE TO
MAKE SURE
THAT POOR
AUNT MAY
IS ALL
RIGHT.
I TRIED--
NOT TO
THINK OF
HER--
WHILE I
WAS
FIGHTING...
OR ELSE--NO
TELLING WHAT
I'D HAVE DONE--
TO THE BEETLE!
--I STILL
N'T UNDER-
TAND. IT
--HAPPENED
SO FAST...
THAT MAY
BE WHAT
SAVED YOU
--FROM
SHOCK.
AUNT MAY!
AUNT MAY!
YOU
DIDN'T
HAVE
TIME--TO
ASSESS
THE
DANGER.
PETER DEAR,
I--I HOPE I
DIDN'T
WORRY
YOU.
WORRY ME?
OH, AUNT
MAY--WHEN
WILL YOU
EVER THINK
OF
YOURSELF?
COME
ON--I'LL
TAKE
YOU
HOME
NOW.
EVEN THOUGH
I'LL ALWAYS
FEEL GUILTY
FOR THE
DEATH OF
UNCLE BEN--
MAYBE
TONIGHT--
IN SOME
SMALL WAY--
SPIDER-MAN
PAID PART
OF THAT
UNENDING
DEBT!
NEXT
SPIDER-MAN
AT LARGE--
IN
LONDON!

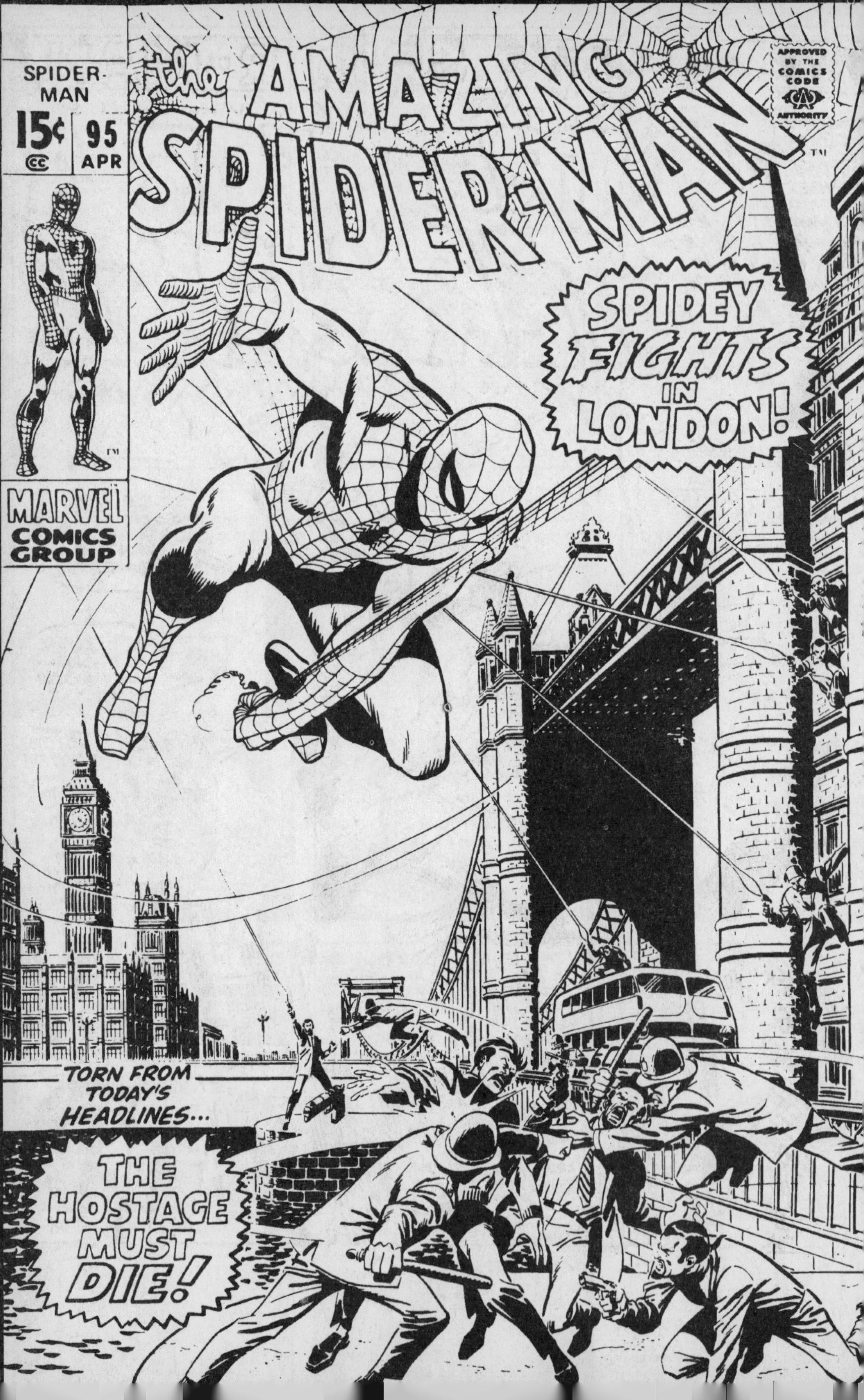
SPIDER-MAN
15¢
CC
95
APR
the AMAZING SPIDER-MAN
APPROVED BY THE COMICS CODE AUTHORITY
MARVEL COMICS GROUP
SPIDEY FIGHTS IN LONDON!
TORN FROM TODAY'S HEADLINES...
THE HOSTAGE MUST DIE!

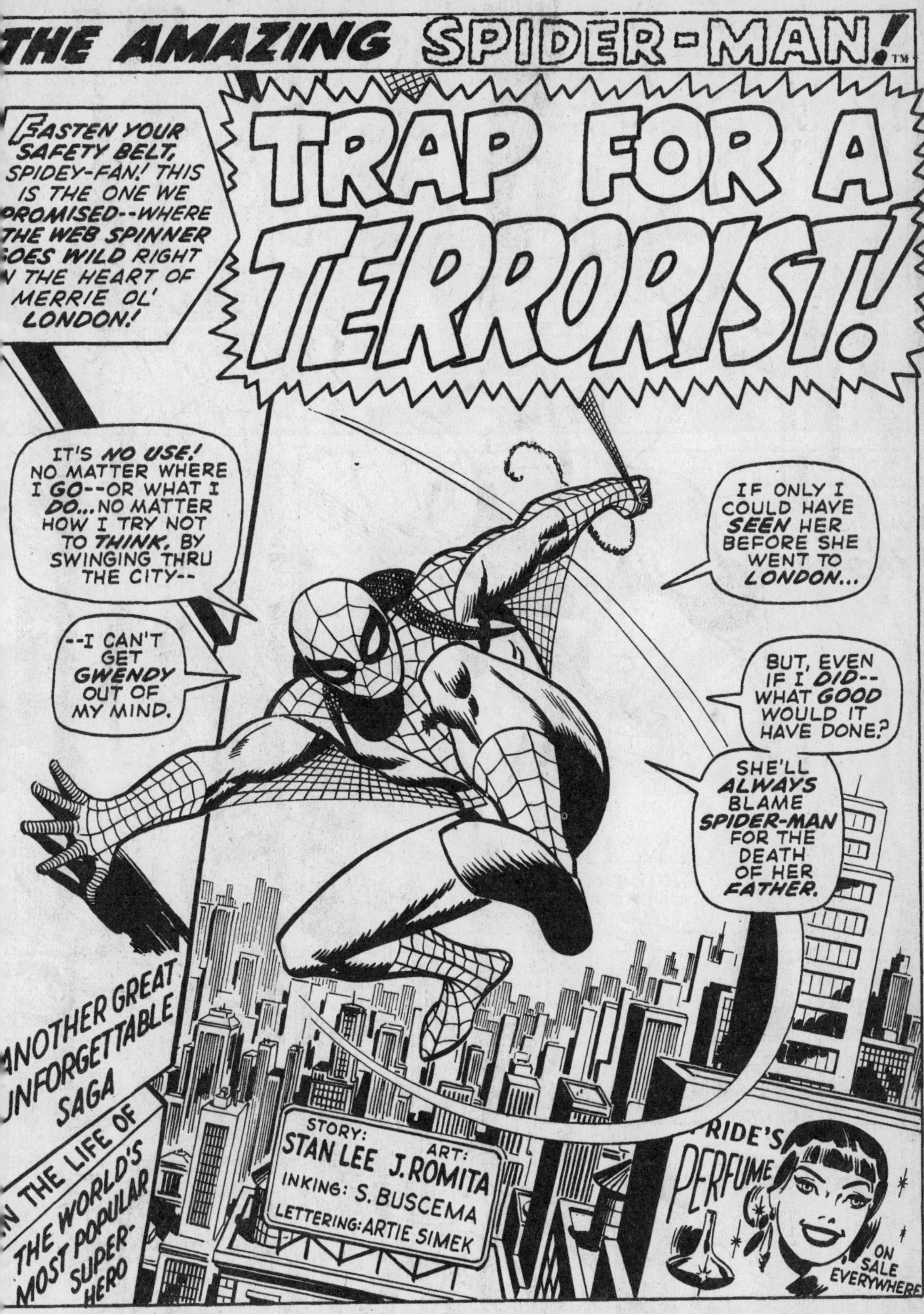
THE AMAZING SPIDER-MAN!
TM
FASTEN YOUR SAFETY BELT, SPIDEY-FAN! THIS IS THE ONE WE PROMISED--WHERE THE WEB SPINNER GOES WILD RIGHT IN THE HEART OF MERRIE OL' LONDON!
TRAP FOR A TERRORIST!
IT'S NO USE! NO MATTER WHERE I GO--OR WHAT I DO...NO MATTER HOW I TRY NOT TO THINK, BY SWINGING THRU THE CITY--
--I CAN'T GET GWENDY OUT OF MY MIND.
IF ONLY I COULD HAVE SEEN HER BEFORE SHE WENT TO LONDON...
BUT, EVEN IF I DID-- WHAT GOOD WOULD IT HAVE DONE?
SHE'LL ALWAYS BLAME SPIDER-MAN FOR THE DEATH OF HER FATHER.
ANOTHER GREAT UNFORGETTABLE SAGA
IN THE LIFE OF
THE WORLD'S MOST POPULAR SUPER-HERO
STORY: STAN LEE
ART: J. ROMITA
INKING: S. BUSCEMA
LETTERING: ARTIE SIMEK
RIDE'S PERFUME
ON SALE EVERYWHERE

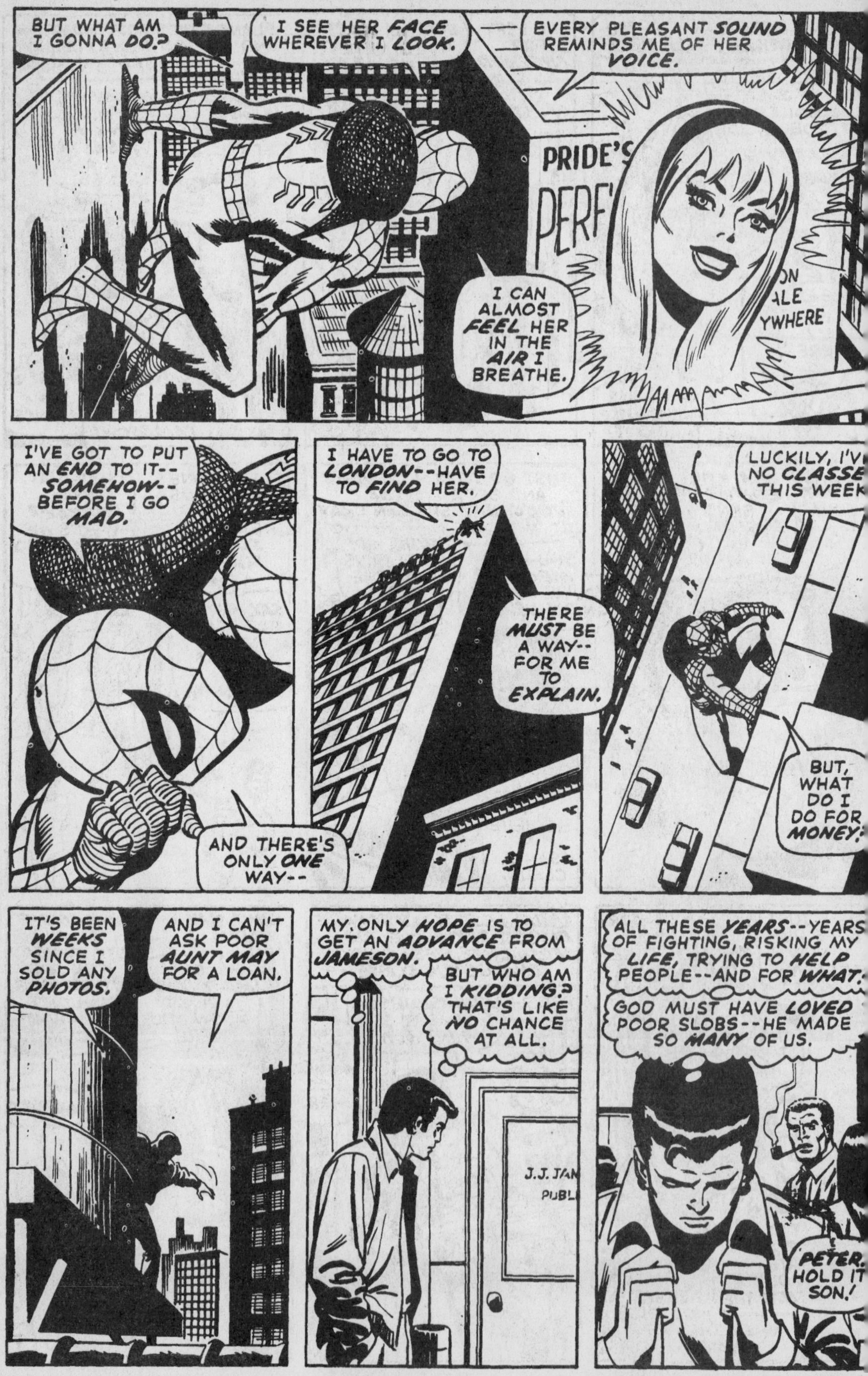
BUT WHAT AM I GONNA DO?
I SEE HER FACE WHEREVER I LOOK.
EVERY PLEASANT SOUND REMINDS ME OF HER VOICE.
PRIDE'S
PERF
ON
ALE
YWHERE
I CAN ALMOST FEEL HER IN THE AIR I BREATHE.
I'VE GOT TO PUT AN END TO IT--SOMEHOW--BEFORE I GO MAD.
AND THERE'S ONLY ONE WAY--
I HAVE TO GO TO LONDON--HAVE TO FIND HER.
THERE MUST BE A WAY--FOR ME TO EXPLAIN.
LUCKILY, I'V NO CLASSE THIS WEEK
BUT, WHAT DO I DO FOR MONEY?
IT'S BEEN WEEKS SINCE I SOLD ANY PHOTOS.
AND I CAN'T ASK POOR AUNT MAY FOR A LOAN.
MY ONLY HOPE IS TO GET AN ADVANCE FROM JAMESON.
BUT WHO AM I KIDDING? THAT'S LIKE NO CHANCE AT ALL.
J.J. JA
PUBL
ALL THESE YEARS--YEARS OF FIGHTING, RISKING MY LIFE, TRYING TO HELP PEOPLE--AND FOR WHAT?
GOD MUST HAVE LOVED POOR SLOBS--HE MADE SO MANY OF US.
PETER. HOLD IT SON!

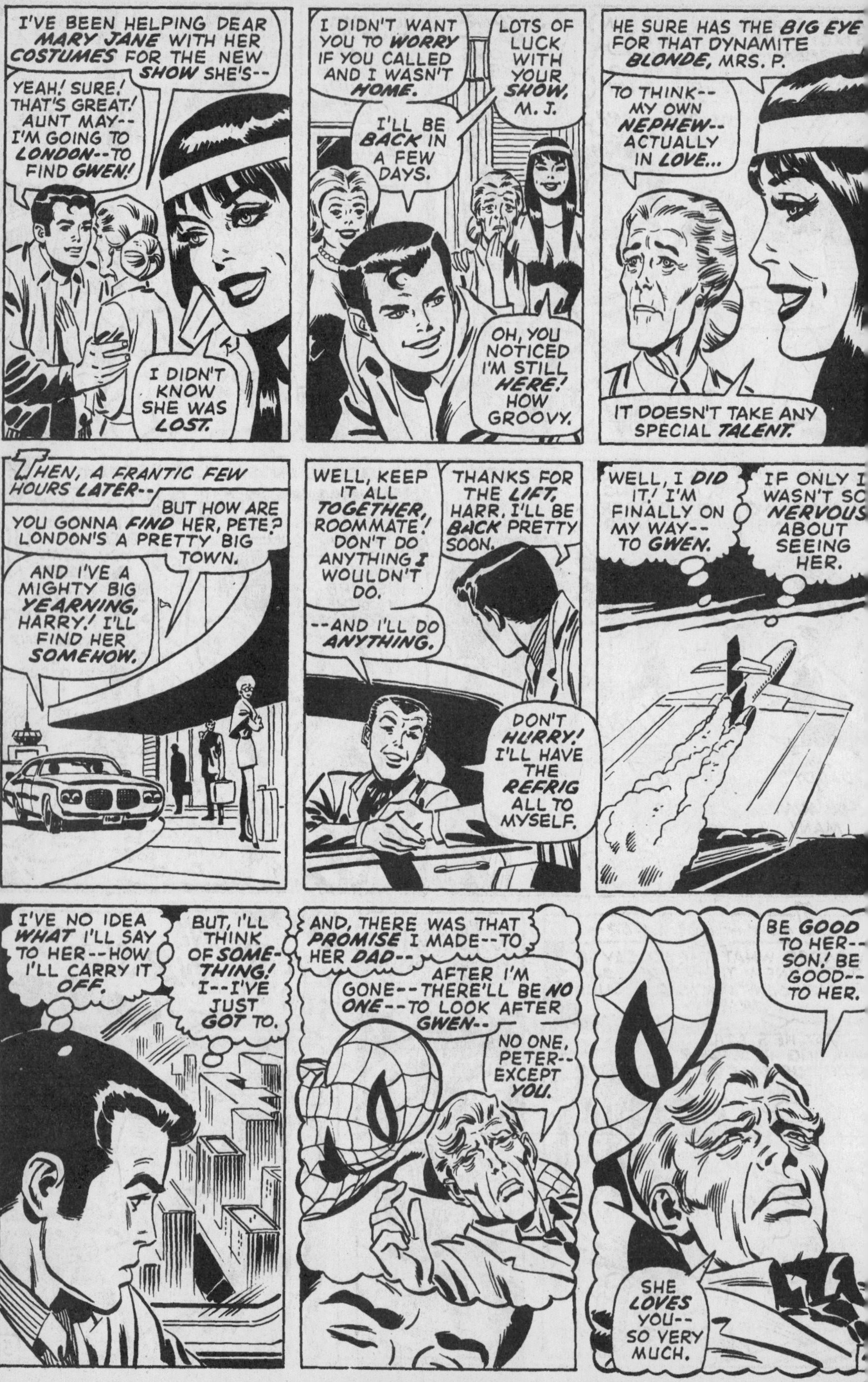

I'VE BEEN HELPING DEAR MARY JANE WITH HER COSTUMES FOR THE NEW SHOW SHE'S--
YEAH! SURE! THAT'S GREAT! AUNT MAY-- I'M GOING TO LONDON--TO FIND GWEN!
I DIDN'T KNOW SHE WAS LOST.
I DIDN'T WANT YOU TO WORRY IF YOU CALLED AND I WASN'T HOME.
LOTS OF LUCK WITH YOUR SHOW, M. J.
I'LL BE BACK IN A FEW DAYS.
OH, YOU NOTICED I'M STILL HERE! HOW GROOVY.
HE SURE HAS THE BIG EYE FOR THAT DYNAMITE BLONDE, MRS. P.
TO THINK-- MY OWN NEPHEW-- ACTUALLY IN LOVE...
IT DOESN'T TAKE ANY SPECIAL TALENT.
THEN, A FRANTIC FEW HOURS LATER--
BUT HOW ARE YOU GONNA FIND HER, PETE? LONDON'S A PRETTY BIG TOWN.
AND I'VE A MIGHTY BIG YEARNING, HARRY! I'LL FIND HER SOMEHOW.
WELL, KEEP IT ALL TOGETHER, ROOMMATE! DON'T DO ANYTHING I WOULDN'T DO.
THANKS FOR THE LIFT, HARR. I'LL BE BACK PRETTY SOON.
--AND I'LL DO ANYTHING.
DON'T HURRY! I'LL HAVE THE REFRIG ALL TO MYSELF.
WELL, I DID IT! I'M FINALLY ON MY WAY-- TO GWEN.
IF ONLY I WASN'T SO NERVOUS ABOUT SEEING HER.
I'VE NO IDEA WHAT I'LL SAY TO HER--HOW I'LL CARRY IT OFF.
BUT, I'LL THINK OF SOME-THING! I--I'VE JUST GOT TO.
AND, THERE WAS THAT PROMISE I MADE--TO HER DAD--
AFTER I'M GONE--THERE'LL BE NO ONE--TO LOOK AFTER GWEN--
NO ONE, PETER-- EXCEPT YOU.
BE GOOD TO HER-- SON! BE GOOD-- TO HER.
SHE LOVES YOU-- SO VERY MUCH.

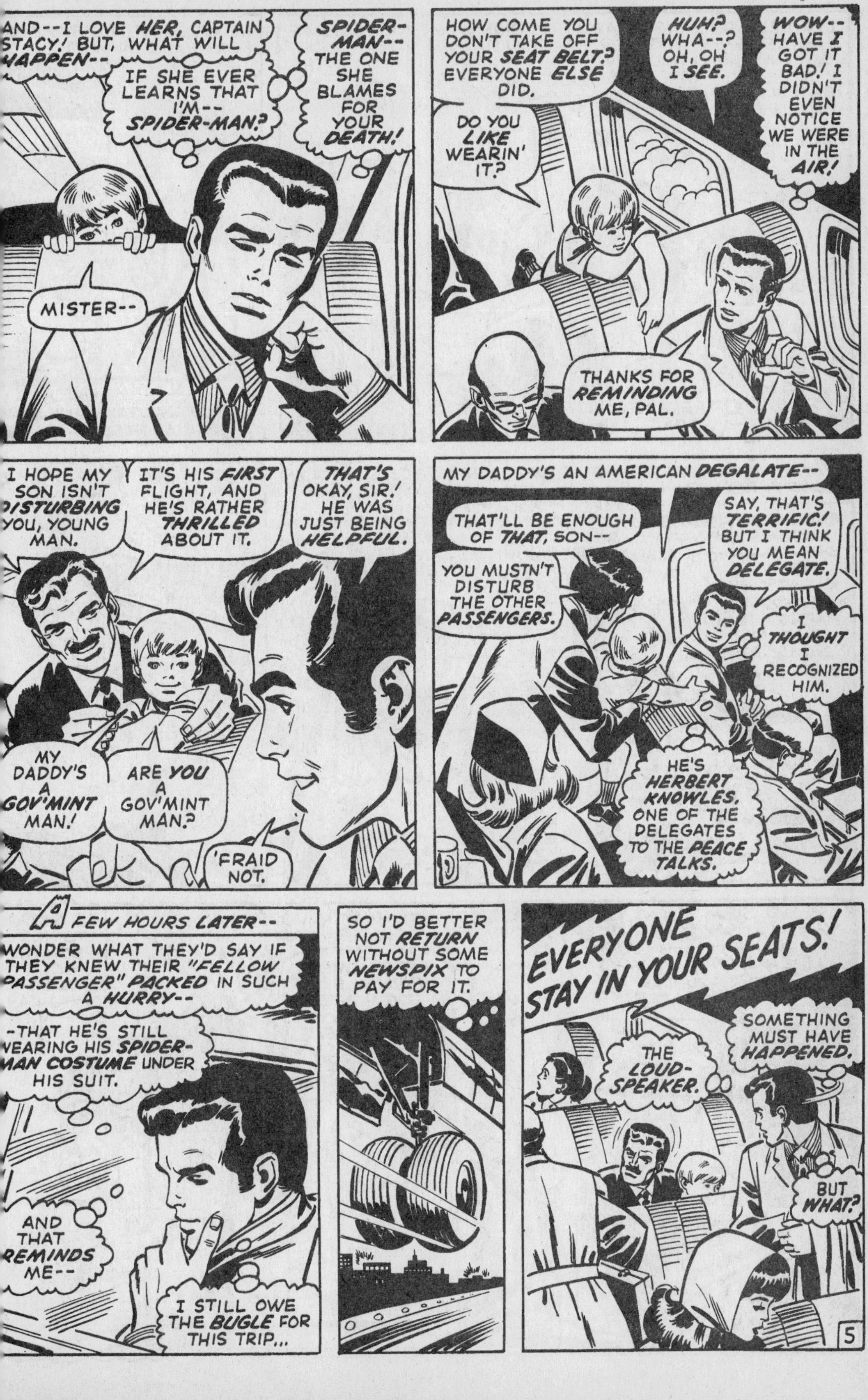

AND--I LOVE HER, CAPTAIN STACY! BUT, WHAT WILL HAPPEN--
IF SHE EVER LEARNS THAT I'M--SPIDER-MAN?
SPIDER-MAN--THE ONE SHE BLAMES FOR YOUR DEATH!
MISTER--
HOW COME YOU DON'T TAKE OFF YOUR SEAT BELT? EVERYONE ELSE DID.
DO YOU LIKE WEARIN' IT?
HUH? WHA--? OH, OH I SEE.
WOW--HAVE I GOT IT BAD! I DIDN'T EVEN NOTICE WE WERE IN THE AIR!
THANKS FOR REMINDING ME, PAL.
I HOPE MY SON ISN'T DISTURBING YOU, YOUNG MAN.
IT'S HIS FIRST FLIGHT, AND HE'S RATHER THRILLED ABOUT IT.
THAT'S OKAY, SIR! HE WAS JUST BEING HELPFUL.
MY DADDY'S A GOV'MINT MAN!
ARE YOU A GOV'MINT MAN?
'FRAID NOT.
MY DADDY'S AN AMERICAN DEGALATE--
THAT'LL BE ENOUGH OF THAT, SON--
YOU MUSTN'T DISTURB THE OTHER PASSENGERS.
SAY, THAT'S TERRIFIC! BUT I THINK YOU MEAN DELEGATE.
I THOUGHT I RECOGNIZED HIM.
HE'S HERBERT KNOWLES, ONE OF THE DELEGATES TO THE PEACE TALKS.
A FEW HOURS LATER--
WONDER WHAT THEY'D SAY IF THEY KNEW THEIR "FELLOW PASSENGER" PACKED IN SUCH A HURRY--
-THAT HE'S STILL WEARING HIS SPIDER-MAN COSTUME UNDER HIS SUIT.
AND THAT REMINDS ME--
I STILL OWE THE BUGLE FOR THIS TRIP...
SO I'D BETTER NOT RETURN WITHOUT SOME NEWSPIX TO PAY FOR IT.
EVERYONE STAY IN YOUR SEATS!
THE LOUD-SPEAKER.
SOMETHING MUST HAVE HAPPENED.
BUT WHAT?

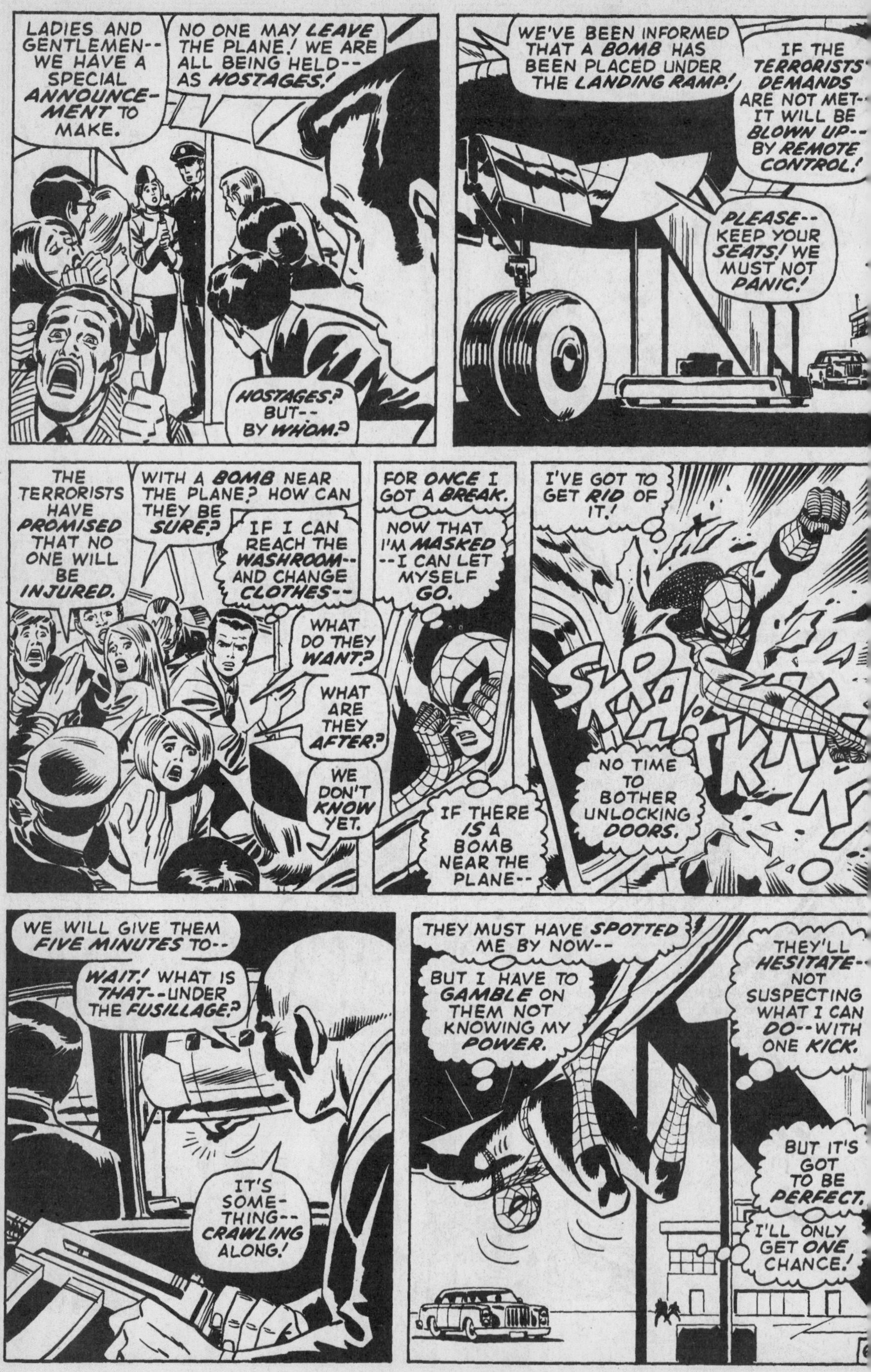

LADIES AND GENTLEMEN-- WE HAVE A SPECIAL ANNOUNCEMENT TO MAKE.
NO ONE MAY LEAVE THE PLANE! WE ARE ALL BEING HELD-- AS HOSTAGES!
HOSTAGES? BUT-- BY WHOM?
WE'VE BEEN INFORMED THAT A BOMB HAS BEEN PLACED UNDER THE LANDING RAMP!
IF THE TERRORISTS' DEMANDS ARE NOT MET-- IT WILL BE BLOWN UP-- BY REMOTE CONTROL!
PLEASE-- KEEP YOUR SEATS! WE MUST NOT PANIC!
THE TERRORISTS HAVE PROMISED THAT NO ONE WILL BE INJURED.
WITH A BOMB NEAR THE PLANE? HOW CAN THEY BE SURE?
IF I CAN REACH THE WASHROOM-- AND CHANGE CLOTHES--
WHAT DO THEY WANT?
WHAT ARE THEY AFTER?
WE DON'T KNOW YET.
FOR ONCE I GOT A BREAK.
NOW THAT I'M MASKED --I CAN LET MYSELF GO.
IF THERE IS A BOMB NEAR THE PLANE--
I'VE GOT TO GET RID OF IT!
SKPATKK
NO TIME TO BOTHER UNLOCKING DOORS.
WE WILL GIVE THEM FIVE MINUTES TO--
WAIT! WHAT IS THAT--UNDER THE FUSILLAGE?
IT'S SOME-THING-- CRAWLING ALONG!
THEY MUST HAVE SPOTTED ME BY NOW--
BUT I HAVE TO GAMBLE ON THEM NOT KNOWING MY POWER.
THEY'LL HESITATE-- NOT SUSPECTING WHAT I CAN DO--WITH ONE KICK.
BUT IT'S GOT TO BE PERFECT.
I'LL ONLY GET ONE CHANCE!

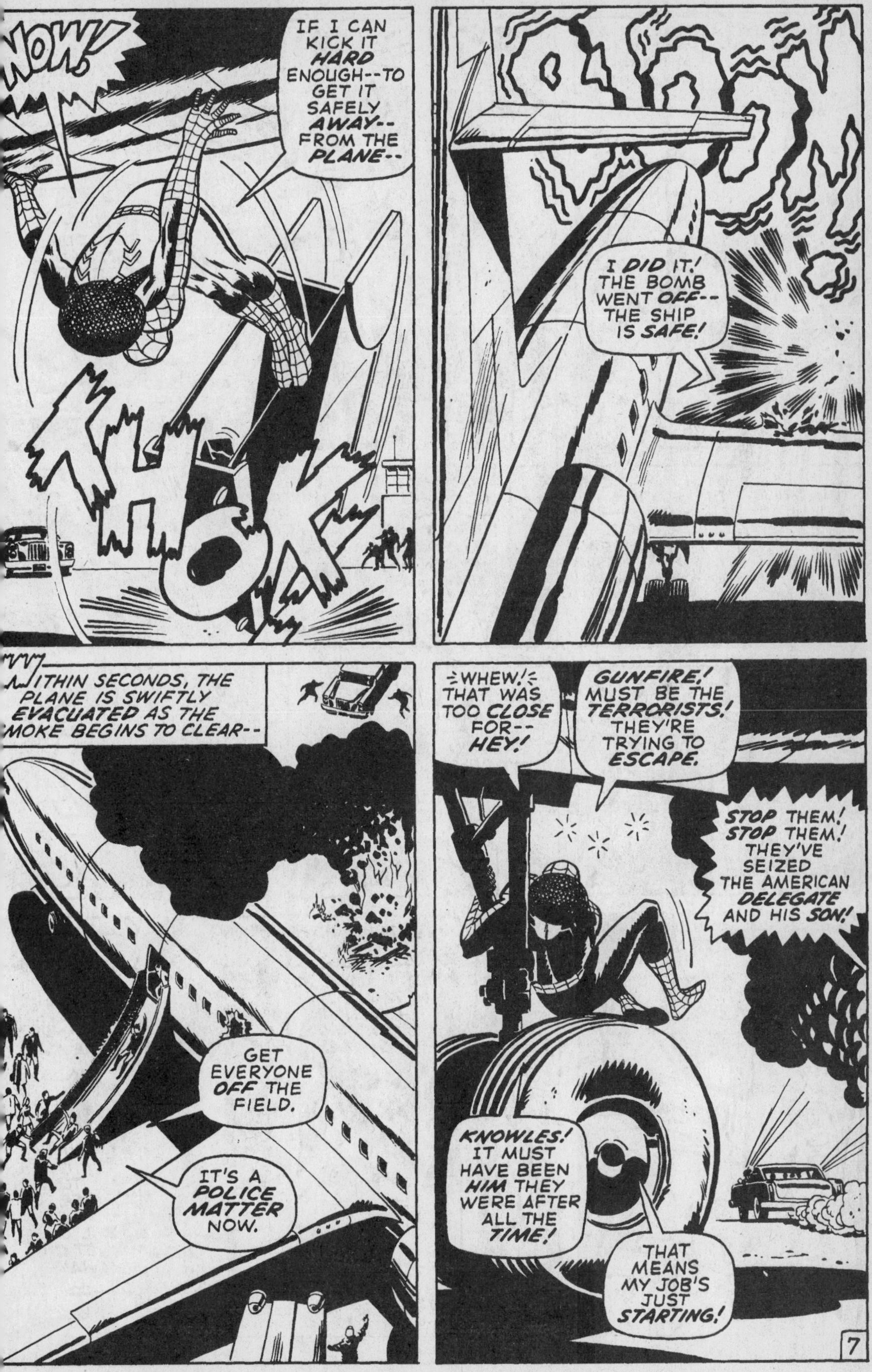
WOW!
IF I CAN KICK IT HARD ENOUGH--TO GET IT SAFELY AWAY--FROM THE PLANE--
KICK
I DID IT! THE BOMB WENT OFF--THE SHIP IS SAFE!
WITHIN SECONDS, THE PLANE IS SWIFTLY EVACUATED AS THE SMOKE BEGINS TO CLEAR--
GET EVERYONE OFF THE FIELD.
IT'S A POLICE MATTER NOW.
WHEW! THAT WAS TOO CLOSE FOR--HEY!
GUNFIRE! MUST BE THE TERRORISTS! THEY'RE TRYING TO ESCAPE.
STOP THEM! STOP THEM! THEY'VE SEIZED THE AMERICAN DELEGATE AND HIS SON!
KNOWLES! IT MUST HAVE BEEN HIM THEY WERE AFTER ALL THE TIME!
THAT MEANS MY JOB'S JUST STARTING!
7

NO *WONDER* THEY CALL 'EM *TERROR-ISTS.* ANYONE WHO'D THREATEN A PLANELOAD OF INNOCENT PEOPLE WITH *BOMBING*--

AND *KIDNAP* A MAN AND HIS *SON*--

I'VE GOT TO *GET* THEM-- AND GET 'EM *GOOD!*

THWIPP

THEY'VE BEEN WATCHING TOO MANY *WESTERNS*-- WHERE THE HERO SHOOTS *PISTOLS* OUT OF OUTLAWS *HANDS*--

--FROM THE BACK OF A RACING *PONY*.

BUT THIS IS NO *MOVIE!*

AND *I'M* NO STAGE-PROP *PISTOL!*

KRAK!

KRAK!

THEY CAN'T *SEE* ME NOW-- --'CAUSE I'M DIRECTLY *OVERHEAD.*

SO HERE GOES--

THEY MUST HAVE HEARD ME *LAND*-- BUT I SHOULD WORRY. --JUST SO LONG AS I GET MY *SPIDEY TRACER* PLANTED.

THERE! NOW I CAN JUST-- *UH OH!*

LUCKY I *TINGLED* JUST IN TIME.

THE WAY YOU FELLAS WASTE AMMO, YOU MUST GET IT *WHOLE-SALE.*

BUKKA BUK! BUK!

DOG! YOU WILL INTERFERE WITH US NO *LONGER.*

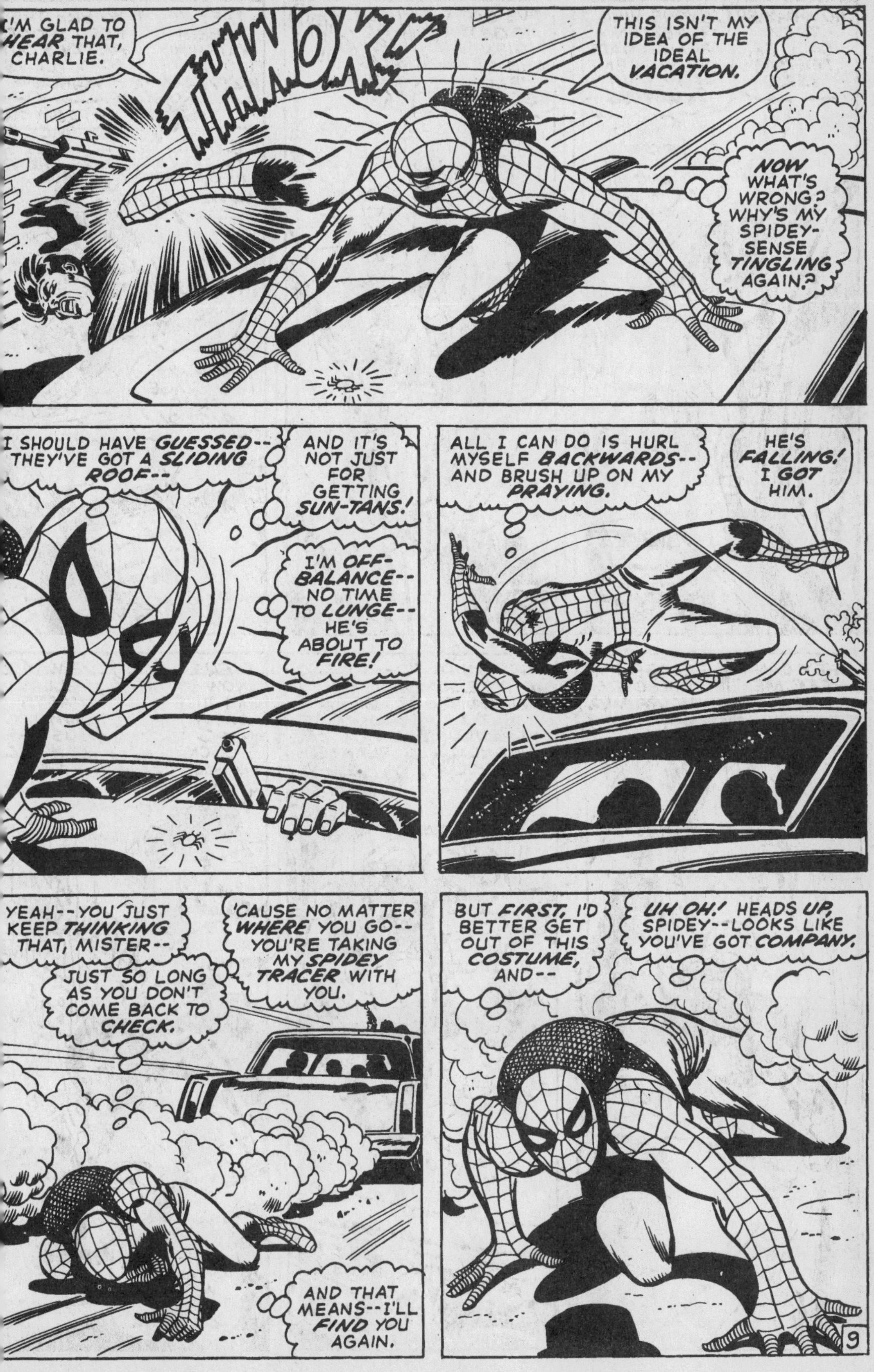

I'M GLAD TO HEAR THAT, CHARLIE.
THWOK!
THIS ISN'T MY IDEA OF THE IDEAL VACATION.
NOW WHAT'S WRONG? WHY'S MY SPIDEY-SENSE TINGLING AGAIN?
I SHOULD HAVE GUESSED-- THEY'VE GOT A SLIDING ROOF--
AND IT'S NOT JUST FOR GETTING SUN-TANS!
I'M OFF-BALANCE-- NO TIME TO LUNGE-- HE'S ABOUT TO FIRE!
ALL I CAN DO IS HURL MYSELF BACKWARDS-- AND BRUSH UP ON MY PRAYING.
HE'S FALLING! I GOT HIM.
YEAH--YOU JUST KEEP THINKING THAT, MISTER--
JUST SO LONG AS YOU DON'T COME BACK TO CHECK.
'CAUSE NO MATTER WHERE YOU GO-- YOU'RE TAKING MY SPIDEY TRACER WITH YOU.
AND THAT MEANS--I'LL FIND YOU AGAIN.
BUT FIRST, I'D BETTER GET OUT OF THIS COSTUME, AND--
UH OH! HEADS UP, SPIDEY--LOOKS LIKE YOU'VE GOT COMPANY.
9

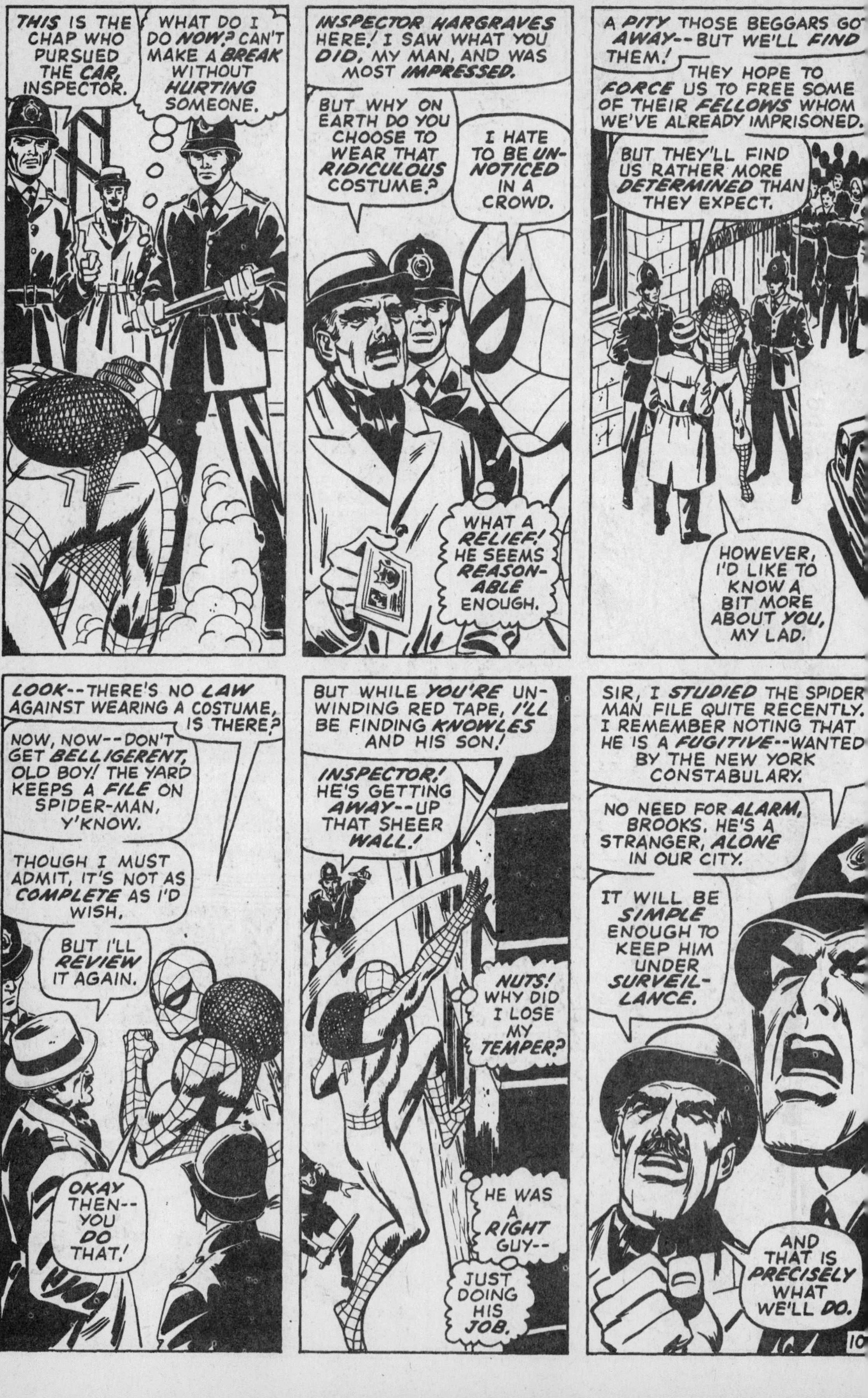

THIS IS THE CHAP WHO PURSUED THE CAR, INSPECTOR.
WHAT DO I DO NOW? CAN'T MAKE A BREAK WITHOUT HURTING SOMEONE.
INSPECTOR HARGRAVES HERE! I SAW WHAT YOU DID, MY MAN, AND WAS MOST IMPRESSED.
BUT WHY ON EARTH DO YOU CHOOSE TO WEAR THAT RIDICULOUS COSTUME?
I HATE TO BE UN-NOTICED IN A CROWD.
WHAT A RELIEF! HE SEEMS REASON-ABLE ENOUGH.
A PITY THOSE BEGGARS GOT AWAY--BUT WE'LL FIND THEM!
THEY HOPE TO FORCE US TO FREE SOME OF THEIR FELLOWS WHOM WE'VE ALREADY IMPRISONED.
BUT THEY'LL FIND US RATHER MORE DETERMINED THAN THEY EXPECT.
HOWEVER, I'D LIKE TO KNOW A BIT MORE ABOUT YOU, MY LAD.
LOOK--THERE'S NO LAW AGAINST WEARING A COSTUME, IS THERE?
NOW, NOW--DON'T GET BELLIGERENT, OLD BOY! THE YARD KEEPS A FILE ON SPIDER-MAN, Y'KNOW.
THOUGH I MUST ADMIT, IT'S NOT AS COMPLETE AS I'D WISH.
BUT I'LL REVIEW IT AGAIN.
OKAY THEN--YOU DO THAT!
BUT WHILE YOU'RE UN-WINDING RED TAPE, I'LL BE FINDING KNOWLES AND HIS SON!
INSPECTOR! HE'S GETTING AWAY--UP THAT SHEER WALL!
NUTS! WHY DID I LOSE MY TEMPER?
HE WAS A RIGHT GUY--
JUST DOING HIS JOB.
SIR, I STUDIED THE SPIDER-MAN FILE QUITE RECENTLY. I REMEMBER NOTING THAT HE IS A FUGITIVE--WANTED BY THE NEW YORK CONSTABULARY.
NO NEED FOR ALARM, BROOKS. HE'S A STRANGER, ALONE IN OUR CITY.
IT WILL BE SIMPLE ENOUGH TO KEEP HIM UNDER SURVEIL-LANCE.
AND THAT IS PRECISELY WHAT WE'LL DO.
10

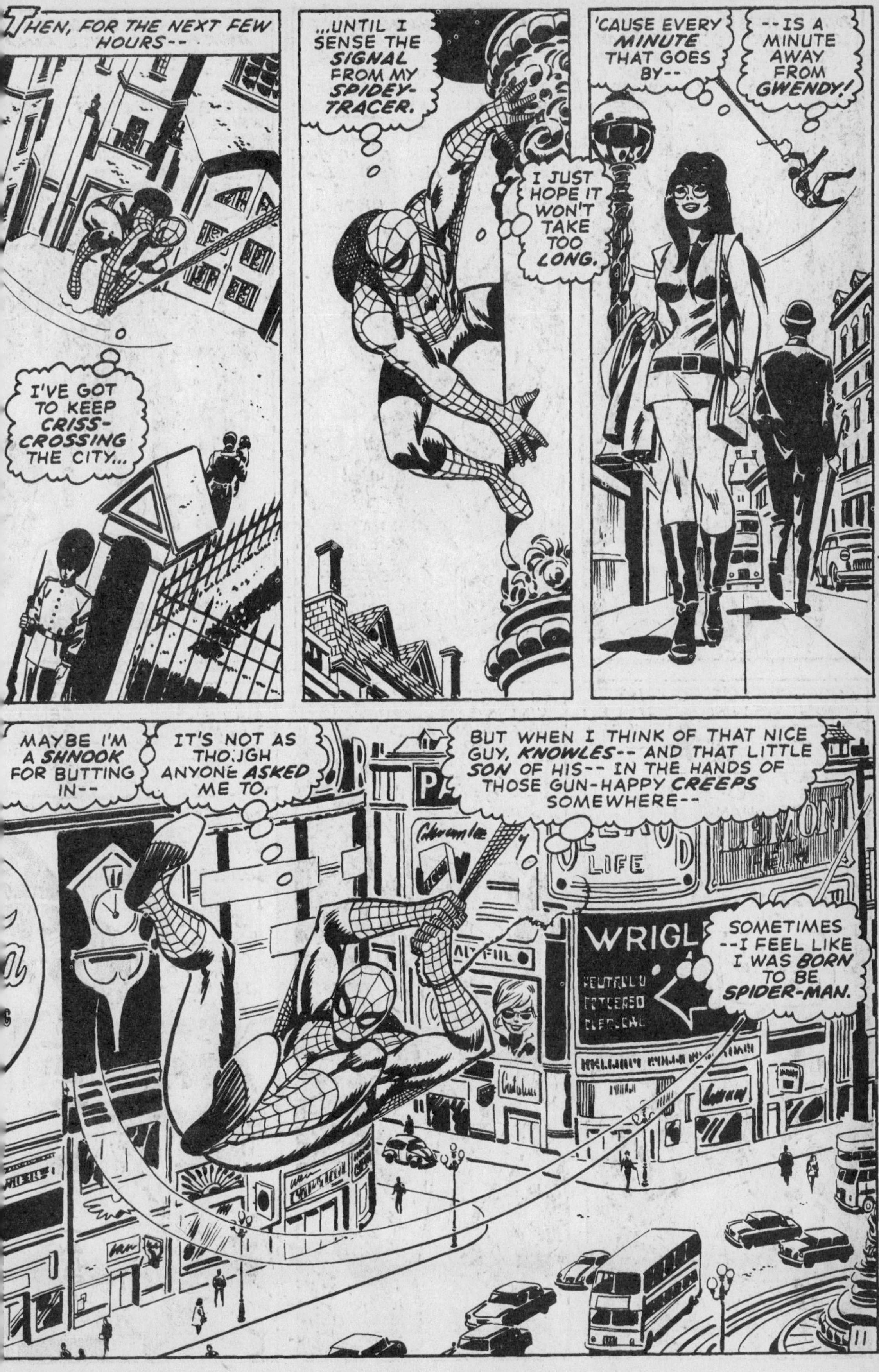

THEN, FOR THE NEXT FEW HOURS--
I'VE GOT TO KEEP CRISS-CROSSING THE CITY...
...UNTIL I SENSE THE SIGNAL FROM MY SPIDEY-TRACER.
I JUST HOPE IT WON'T TAKE TOO LONG.
'CAUSE EVERY MINUTE THAT GOES BY--
--IS A MINUTE AWAY FROM GWENDY!
MAYBE I'M A SHNOOK FOR BUTTING IN--
IT'S NOT AS THOUGH ANYONE ASKED ME TO.
BUT WHEN I THINK OF THAT NICE GUY, KNOWLES-- AND THAT LITTLE SON OF HIS-- IN THE HANDS OF THOSE GUN-HAPPY CREEPS SOMEWHERE--
SOMETIMES --I FEEL LIKE I WAS BORN TO BE SPIDER-MAN.
LIFE
WRIGL

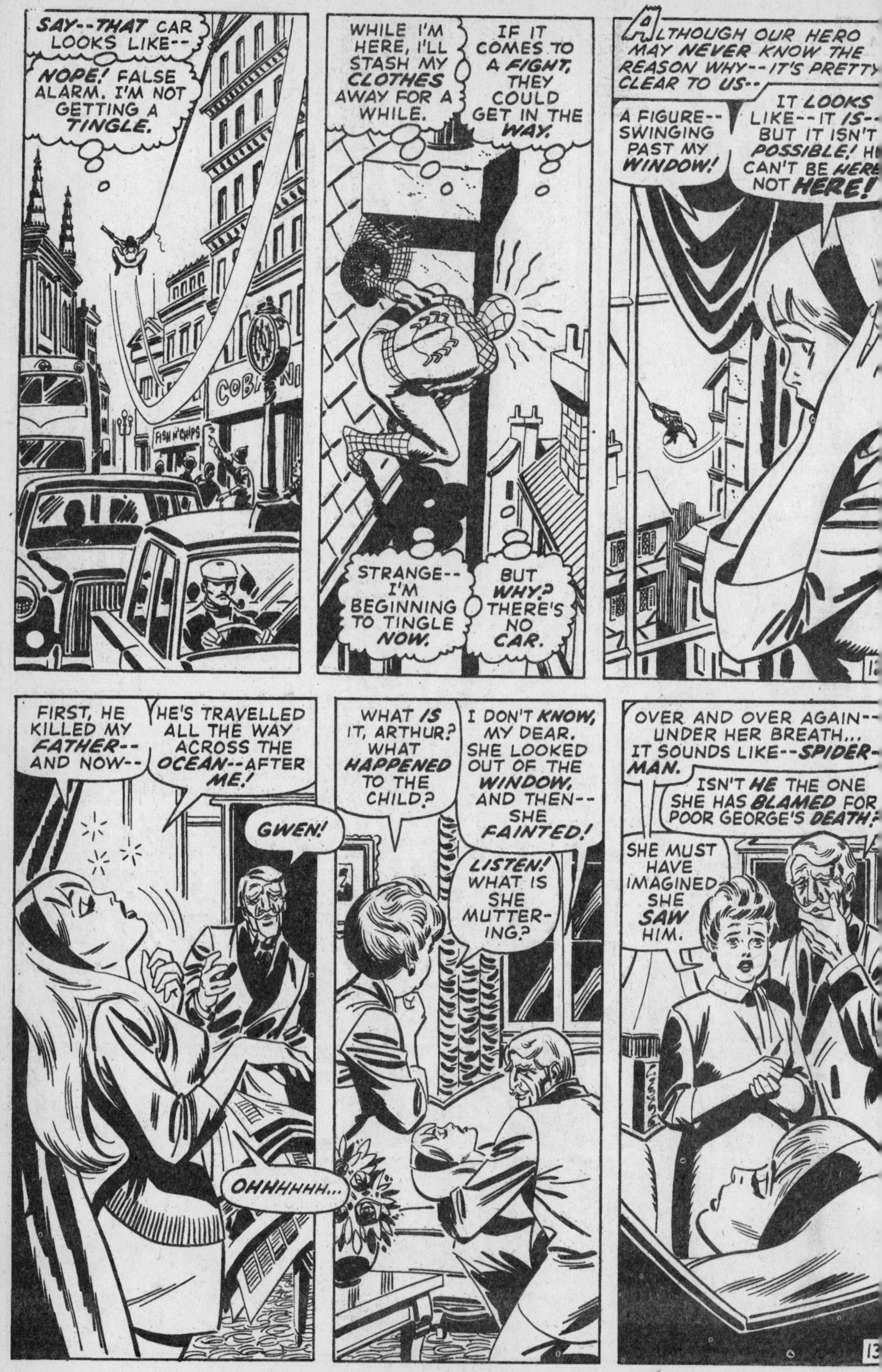
SAY--THAT CAR LOOKS LIKE--
NOPE! FALSE ALARM. I'M NOT GETTING A TINGLE.
FISH N' CHIPS
WHILE I'M HERE, I'LL STASH MY CLOTHES AWAY FOR A WHILE.
IF IT COMES TO A FIGHT, THEY COULD GET IN THE WAY.
STRANGE--I'M BEGINNING TO TINGLE NOW.
BUT WHY? THERE'S NO CAR.
ALTHOUGH OUR HERO MAY NEVER KNOW THE REASON WHY--IT'S PRETTY CLEAR TO US--
A FIGURE--SWINGING PAST MY WINDOW!
IT LOOKS LIKE--IT IS--BUT IT ISN'T POSSIBLE! HE CAN'T BE HERE NOT HERE!
FIRST, HE KILLED MY FATHER--AND NOW--
HE'S TRAVELLED ALL THE WAY ACROSS THE OCEAN--AFTER ME!
GWEN!
OHHHHHH...
WHAT IS IT, ARTHUR? WHAT HAPPENED TO THE CHILD?
I DON'T KNOW, MY DEAR. SHE LOOKED OUT OF THE WINDOW, AND THEN--SHE FAINTED!
LISTEN! WHAT IS SHE MUTTERING?
OVER AND OVER AGAIN--UNDER HER BREATH... IT SOUNDS LIKE--SPIDER-MAN.
ISN'T HE THE ONE SHE HAS BLAMED FOR POOR GEORGE'S DEATH?
SHE MUST HAVE IMAGINED SHE SAW HIM.

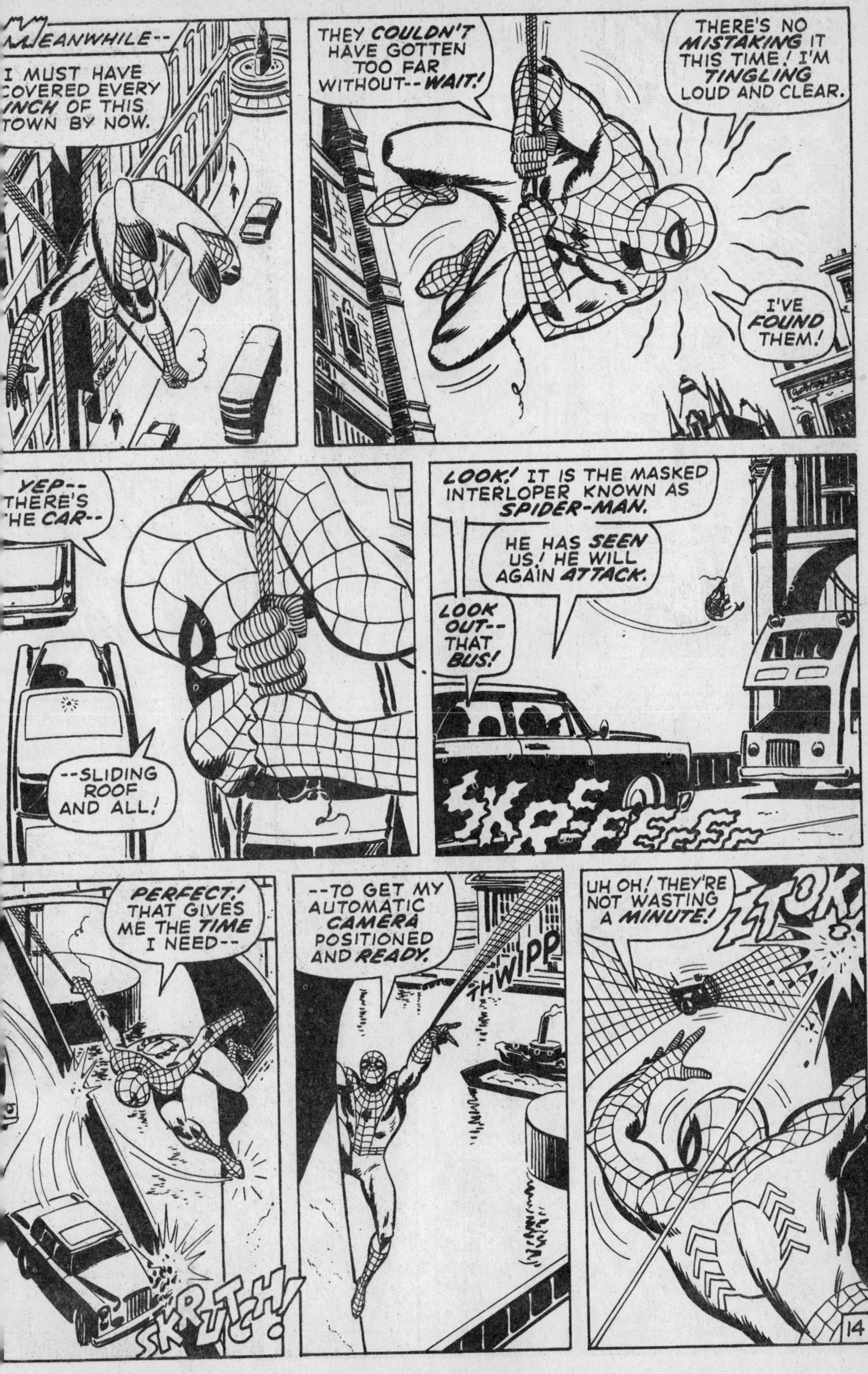

MEANWHILE--
I MUST HAVE COVERED EVERY INCH OF THIS TOWN BY NOW.
THEY COULDN'T HAVE GOTTEN TOO FAR WITHOUT--WAIT!
THERE'S NO MISTAKING IT THIS TIME! I'M TINGLING LOUD AND CLEAR.
I'VE FOUND THEM!
YEP-- THERE'S THE CAR--
--SLIDING ROOF AND ALL!
LOOK! IT IS THE MASKED INTERLOPER KNOWN AS SPIDER-MAN.
HE HAS SEEN US! HE WILL AGAIN ATTACK.
LOOK OUT-- THAT BUS!
PERFECT! THAT GIVES ME THE TIME I NEED--
SKRUTCH!
--TO GET MY AUTOMATIC CAMERA POSITIONED AND READY.
THWIPP
UH OH! THEY'RE NOT WASTING A MINUTE!
TOK!

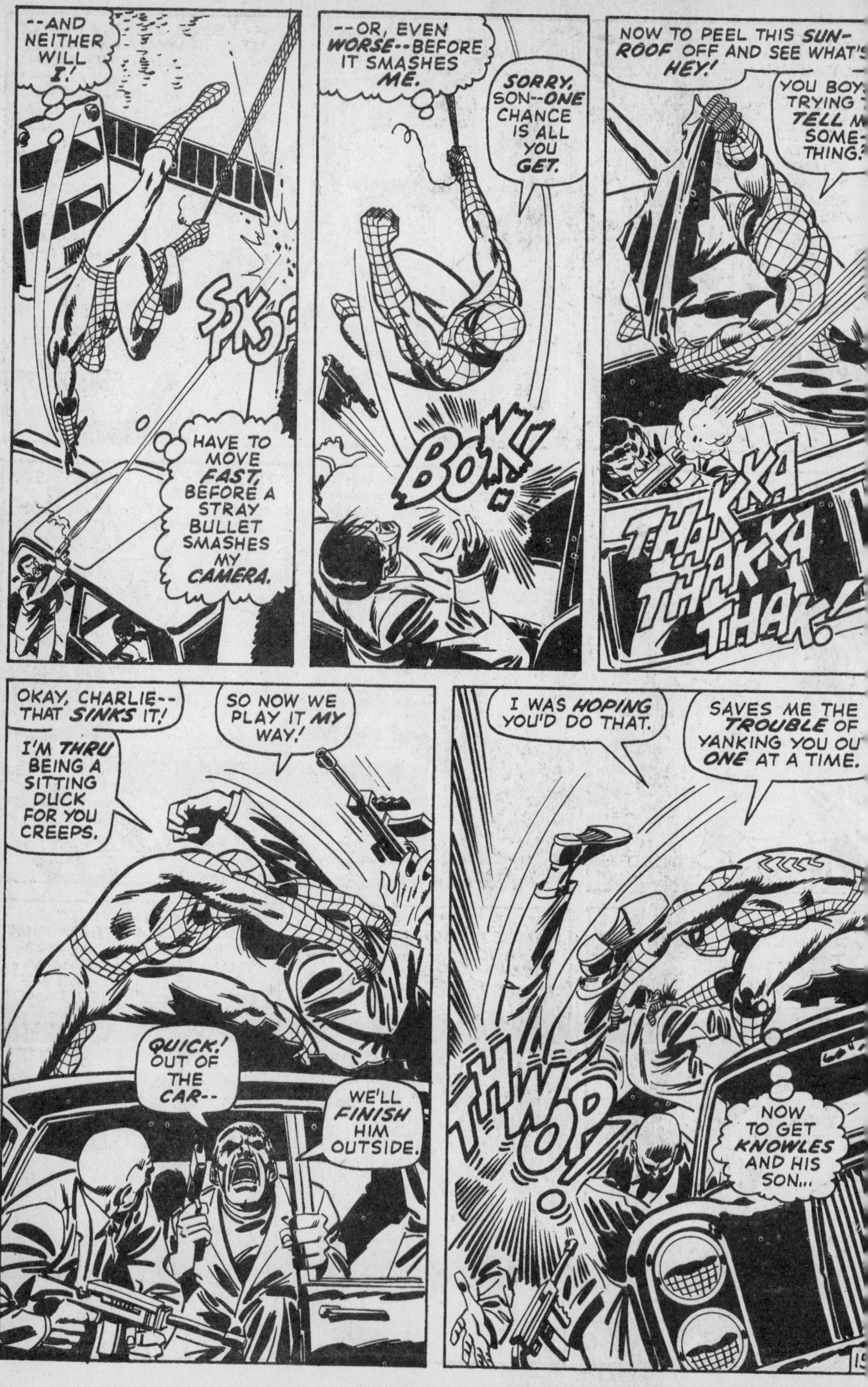

--AND NEITHER WILL I!
SPKSP
HAVE TO MOVE FAST, BEFORE A STRAY BULLET SMASHES MY CAMERA.
--OR, EVEN WORSE--BEFORE IT SMASHES ME.
SORRY, SON--ONE CHANCE IS ALL YOU GET.
BOK!
NOW TO PEEL THIS SUN-ROOF OFF AND SEE WHAT'S HEY!
YOU BOYS TRYING TELL SOME-THING?
THAKKA THAKKA THAKKA THAK!
OKAY, CHARLIE--THAT SINKS IT!
I'M THRU BEING A SITTING DUCK FOR YOU CREEPS.
SO NOW WE PLAY IT MY WAY!
QUICK! OUT OF THE CAR--
WE'LL FINISH HIM OUTSIDE.
I WAS HOPING YOU'D DO THAT.
SAVES ME THE TROUBLE OF YANKING YOU OUT ONE AT A TIME.
THWOOP
NOW TO GET KNOWLES AND HIS SON...

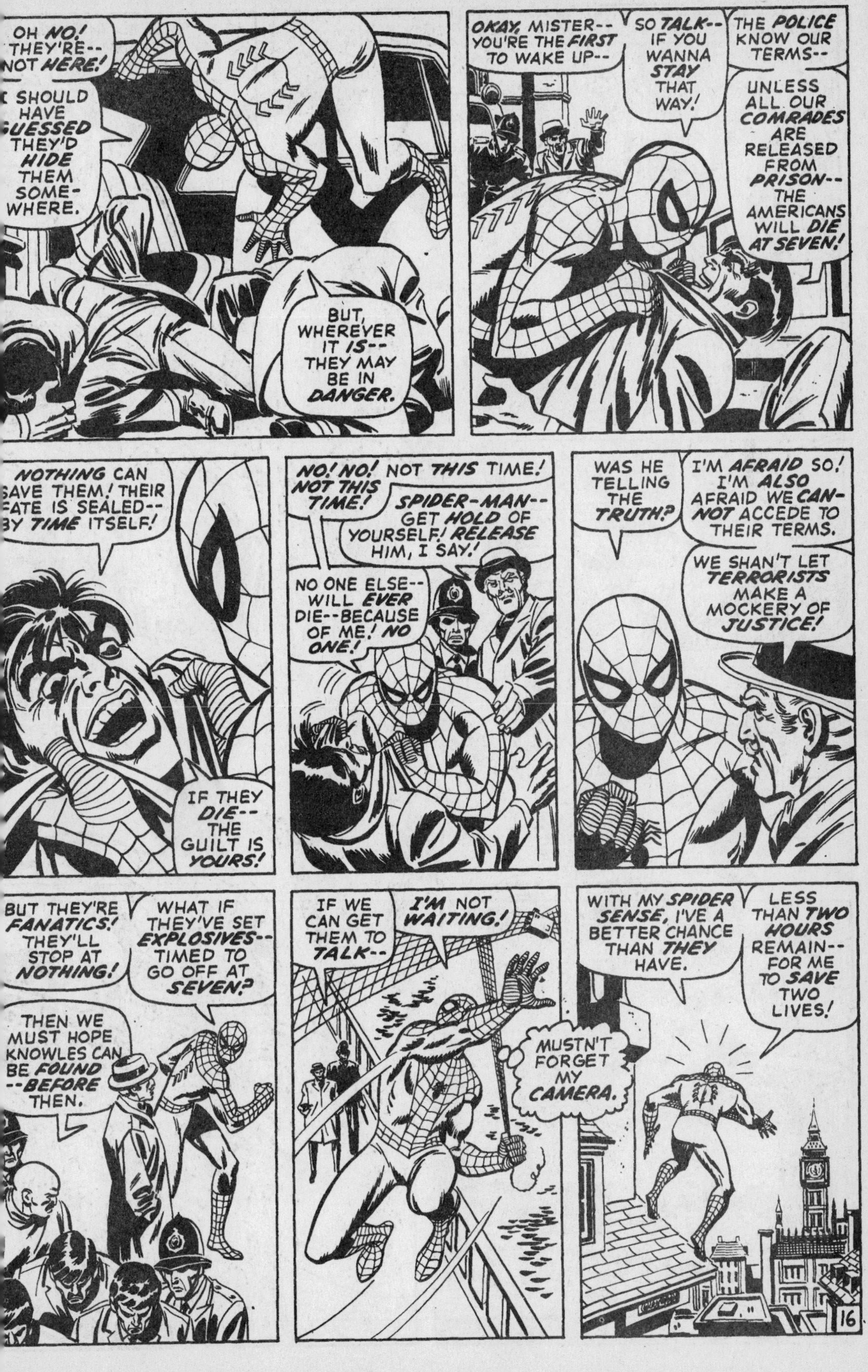
OH NO! THEY'RE-- NOT HERE!
I SHOULD HAVE GUESSED THEY'D HIDE THEM SOME-WHERE.
BUT, WHEREVER IT IS-- THEY MAY BE IN DANGER.
OKAY, MISTER-- YOU'RE THE FIRST TO WAKE UP--
SO TALK-- IF YOU WANNA STAY THAT WAY!
THE POLICE KNOW OUR TERMS--
UNLESS ALL OUR COMRADES ARE RELEASED FROM PRISON-- THE AMERICANS WILL DIE AT SEVEN!
NOTHING CAN SAVE THEM! THEIR FATE IS SEALED-- BY TIME ITSELF!
IF THEY DIE-- THE GUILT IS YOURS!
NO! NO! NOT THIS TIME! NOT THIS TIME!
SPIDER-MAN-- GET HOLD OF YOURSELF! RELEASE HIM, I SAY!
NO ONE ELSE-- WILL EVER DIE--BECAUSE OF ME! NO ONE!
WAS HE TELLING THE TRUTH?
I'M AFRAID SO! I'M ALSO AFRAID WE CAN-NOT ACCEDE TO THEIR TERMS.
WE SHAN'T LET TERRORISTS MAKE A MOCKERY OF JUSTICE!
BUT THEY'RE FANATICS! THEY'LL STOP AT NOTHING!
WHAT IF THEY'VE SET EXPLOSIVES-- TIMED TO GO OFF AT SEVEN?
THEN WE MUST HOPE KNOWLES CAN BE FOUND --BEFORE THEN.
IF WE CAN GET THEM TO TALK--
I'M NOT WAITING!
MUSTN'T FORGET MY CAMERA.
WITH MY SPIDER SENSE, I'VE A BETTER CHANCE THAN THEY HAVE.
LESS THAN TWO HOURS REMAIN-- FOR ME TO SAVE TWO LIVES!
16

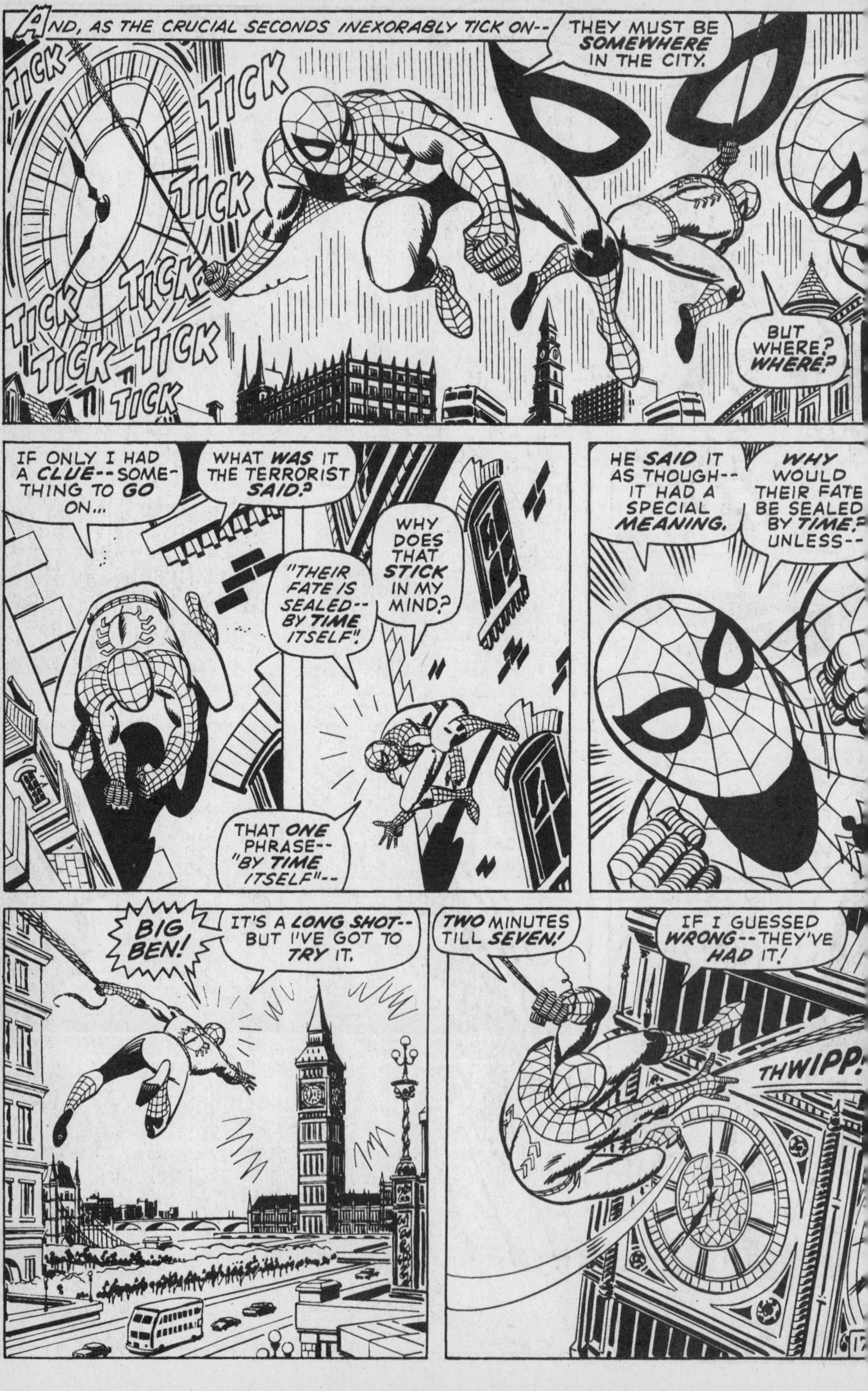
AND, AS THE CRUCIAL SECONDS INEXORABLY TICK ON--
TICK TICK TICK TICK TICK TICK TICK TICK
THEY MUST BE SOMEWHERE IN THE CITY.
BUT WHERE? WHERE?
IF ONLY I HAD A CLUE--SOMETHING TO GO ON...
WHAT WAS IT THE TERRORIST SAID?
"THEIR FATE IS SEALED--BY TIME ITSELF".
WHY DOES THAT STICK IN MY MIND?
THAT ONE PHRASE--"BY TIME ITSELF"--
HE SAID IT AS THOUGH--IT HAD A SPECIAL MEANING.
WHY WOULD THEIR FATE BE SEALED BY TIME? UNLESS--
BIG BEN!
IT'S A LONG SHOT--BUT I'VE GOT TO TRY IT.
TWO MINUTES TILL SEVEN!
IF I GUESSED WRONG--THEY'VE HAD IT!
THWIPP!

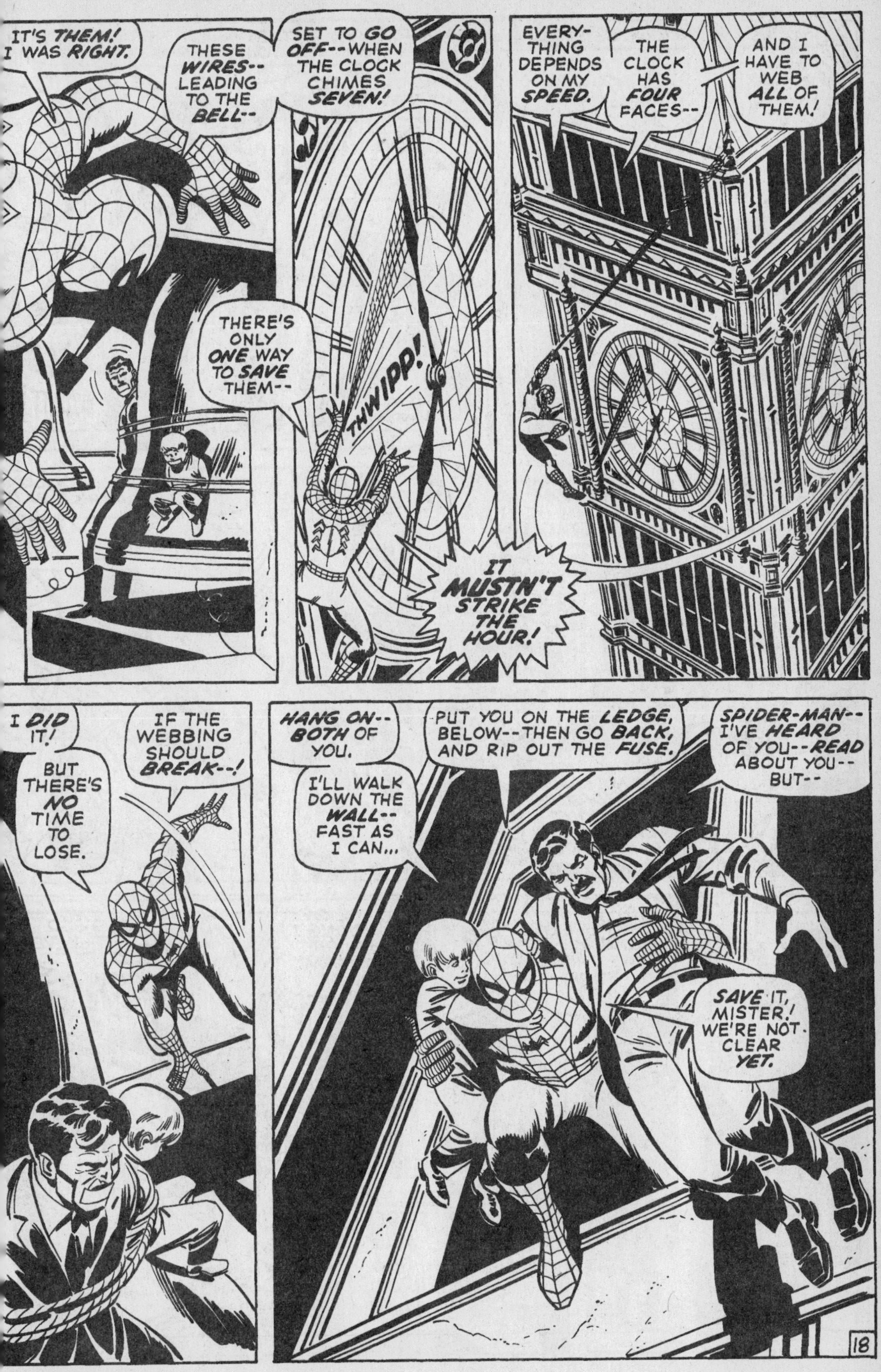
IT'S THEM! I WAS RIGHT.
THESE WIRES-- LEADING TO THE BELL--
SET TO GO OFF--WHEN THE CLOCK CHIMES SEVEN!
THERE'S ONLY ONE WAY TO SAVE THEM--
THWIPP!
EVERY-THING DEPENDS ON MY SPEED.
THE CLOCK HAS FOUR FACES--
AND I HAVE TO WEB ALL OF THEM!
IT MUSTN'T STRIKE THE HOUR!
I DID IT!
BUT THERE'S NO TIME TO LOSE.
IF THE WEBBING SHOULD BREAK--!
HANG ON-- BOTH OF YOU.
I'LL WALK DOWN THE WALL-- FAST AS I CAN...
PUT YOU ON THE LEDGE, BELOW--THEN GO BACK, AND RIP OUT THE FUSE.
SPIDER-MAN-- I'VE HEARD OF YOU--READ ABOUT YOU-- BUT--
SAVE IT, MISTER! WE'RE NOT CLEAR YET.
18

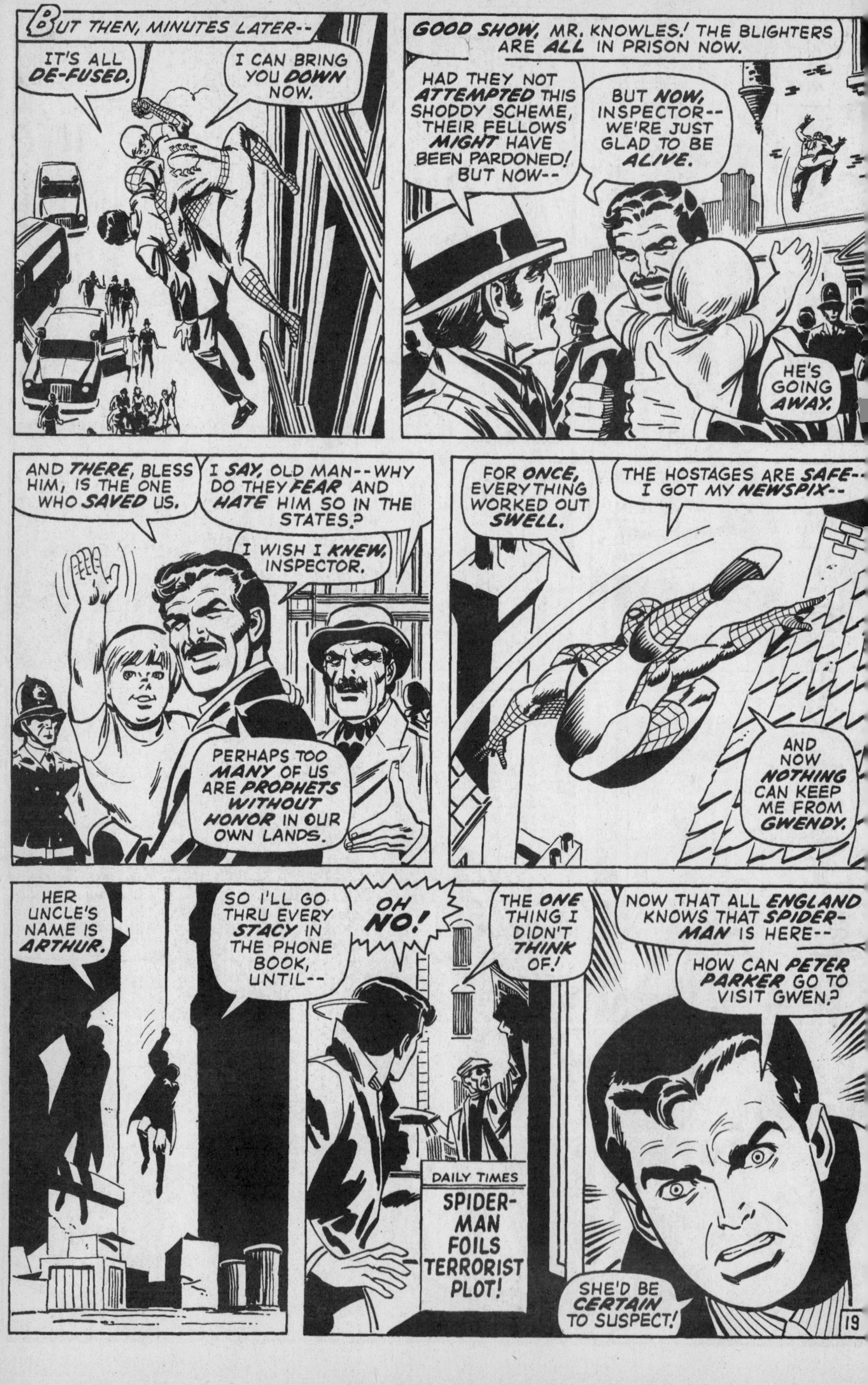
BUT THEN, MINUTES LATER--
IT'S ALL DE-FUSED.
I CAN BRING YOU DOWN NOW.
GOOD SHOW, MR. KNOWLES! THE BLIGHTERS ARE ALL IN PRISON NOW.
HAD THEY NOT ATTEMPTED THIS SHODDY SCHEME, THEIR FELLOWS MIGHT HAVE BEEN PARDONED! BUT NOW--
BUT NOW, INSPECTOR-- WE'RE JUST GLAD TO BE ALIVE.
HE'S GOING AWAY.
AND THERE, BLESS HIM, IS THE ONE WHO SAVED US.
I SAY, OLD MAN--WHY DO THEY FEAR AND HATE HIM SO IN THE STATES?
I WISH I KNEW, INSPECTOR.
PERHAPS TOO MANY OF US ARE PROPHETS WITHOUT HONOR IN OUR OWN LANDS.
FOR ONCE, EVERYTHING WORKED OUT SWELL.
THE HOSTAGES ARE SAFE-- I GOT MY NEWSPIX--
AND NOW NOTHING CAN KEEP ME FROM GWENDY.
HER UNCLE'S NAME IS ARTHUR.
SO I'LL GO THRU EVERY STACY IN THE PHONE BOOK, UNTIL--
OH NO!
THE ONE THING I DIDN'T THINK OF!
DAILY TIMES
SPIDER-MAN FOILS TERRORIST PLOT!
NOW THAT ALL ENGLAND KNOWS THAT SPIDER-MAN IS HERE--
HOW CAN PETER PARKER GO TO VISIT GWEN?
SHE'D BE CERTAIN TO SUSPECT!

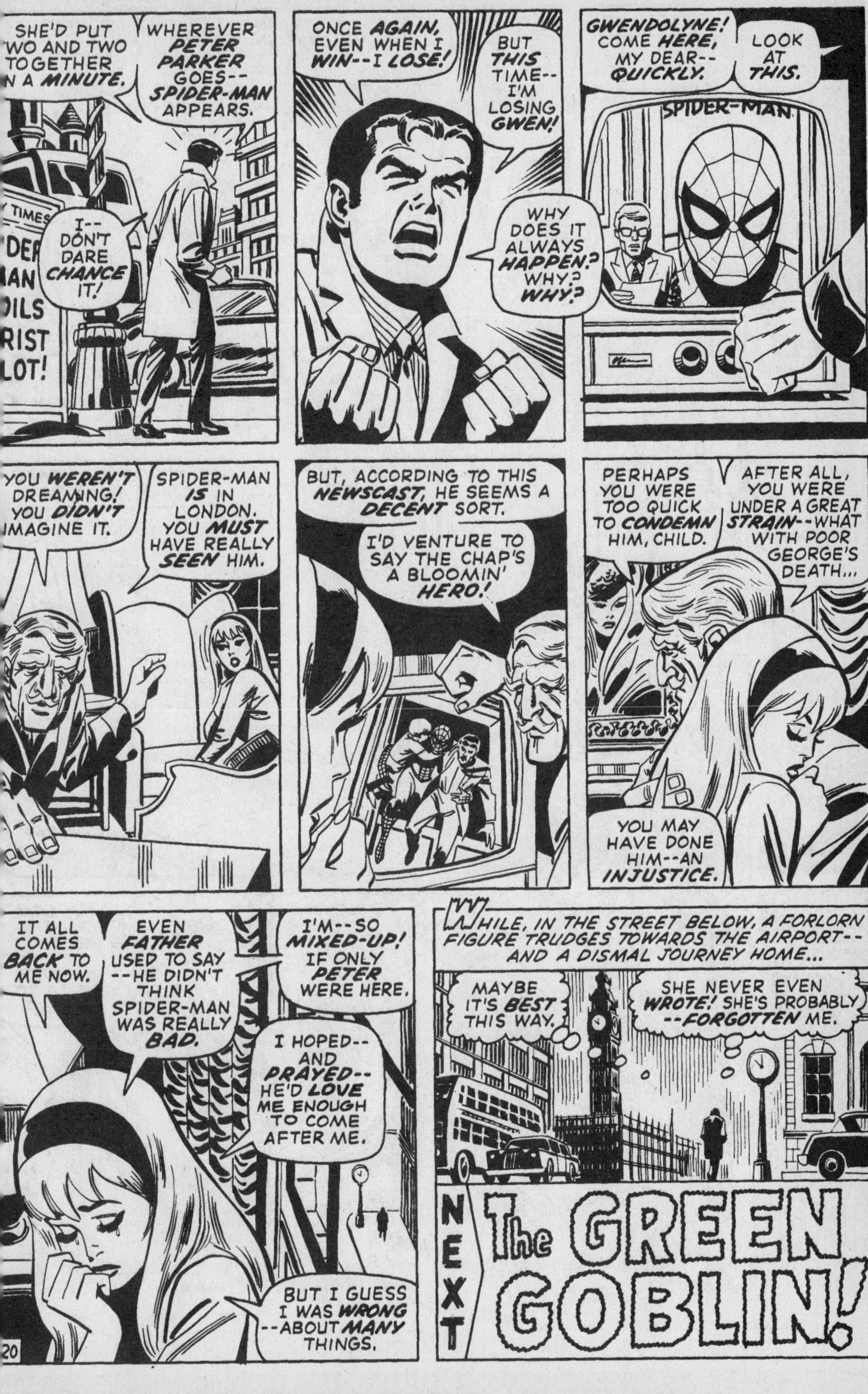
SHE'D PUT TWO AND TWO TOGETHER IN A MINUTE.
WHEREVER PETER PARKER GOES-- SPIDER-MAN APPEARS.
TIMES
DER
AN
ILS
RIST
LOT!
I-- DON'T DARE CHANCE IT!
ONCE AGAIN, EVEN WHEN I WIN--I LOSE!
BUT THIS TIME-- I'M LOSING GWEN!
WHY DOES IT ALWAYS HAPPEN? WHY? WHY?
GWENDOLYNE! COME HERE, MY DEAR-- QUICKLY.
LOOK AT THIS.
SPIDER-MAN
YOU WEREN'T DREAMING! YOU DIDN'T IMAGINE IT.
SPIDER-MAN IS IN LONDON. YOU MUST HAVE REALLY SEEN HIM.
BUT, ACCORDING TO THIS NEWSCAST, HE SEEMS A DECENT SORT.
I'D VENTURE TO SAY THE CHAP'S A BLOOMIN' HERO!
PERHAPS YOU WERE TOO QUICK TO CONDEMN HIM, CHILD.
AFTER ALL, YOU WERE UNDER A GREAT STRAIN--WHAT WITH POOR GEORGE'S DEATH...
YOU MAY HAVE DONE HIM--AN INJUSTICE.
IT ALL COMES BACK TO ME NOW.
EVEN FATHER USED TO SAY --HE DIDN'T THINK SPIDER-MAN WAS REALLY BAD.
I'M--SO MIXED-UP! IF ONLY PETER WERE HERE.
I HOPED-- AND PRAYED-- HE'D LOVE ME ENOUGH TO COME AFTER ME.
BUT I GUESS I WAS WRONG --ABOUT MANY THINGS.
WHILE, IN THE STREET BELOW, A FORLORN FIGURE TRUDGES TOWARDS THE AIRPORT-- AND A DISMAL JOURNEY HOME...
MAYBE IT'S BEST THIS WAY.
SHE NEVER EVEN WROTE! SHE'S PROBABLY --FORGOTTEN ME.
NEXT
The GREEN GOBLIN!
20

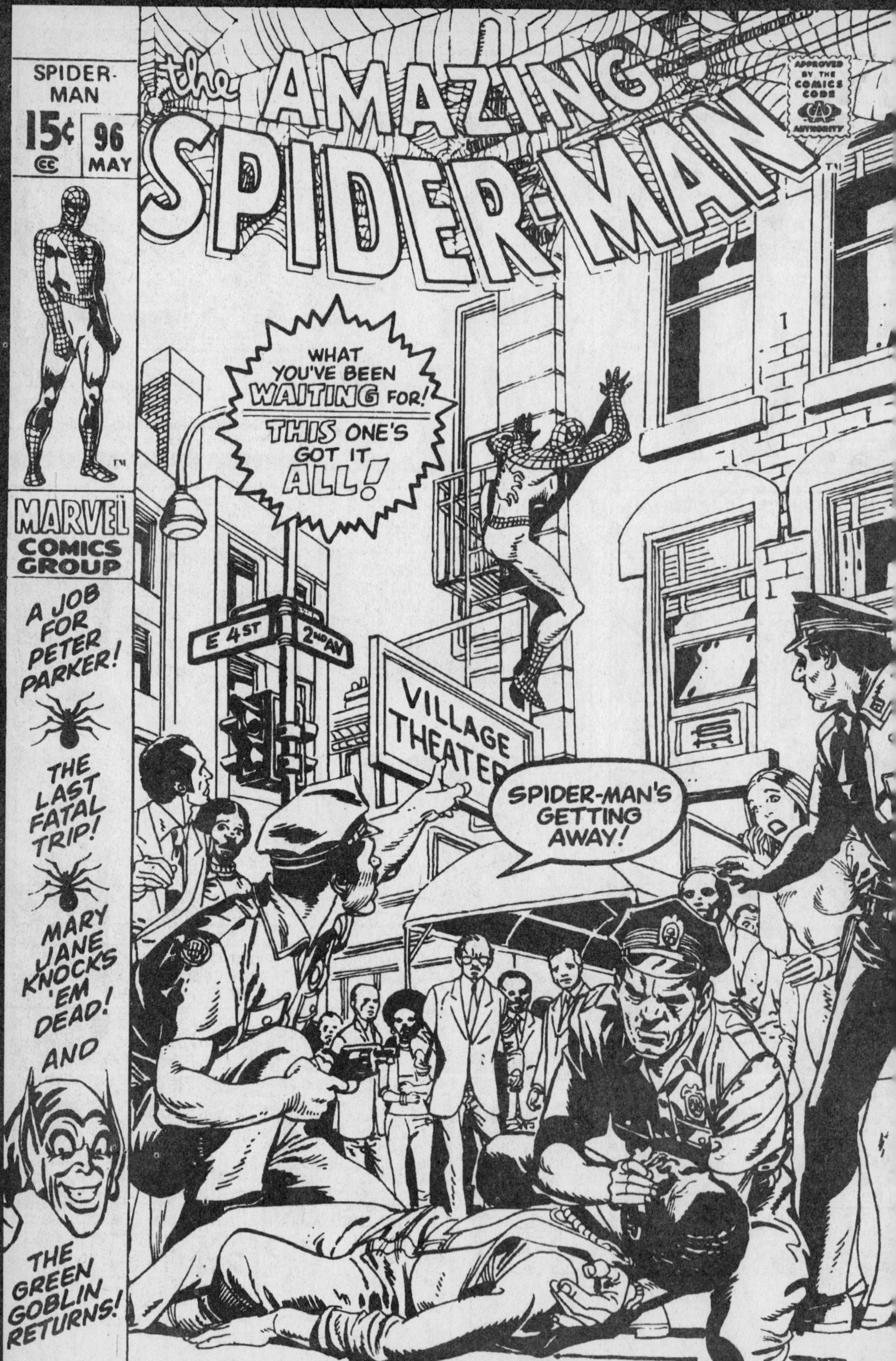

SPIDER-MAN
15¢
96
MAY
the AMAZING SPIDER-MAN
APPROVED BY THE COMICS CODE AUTHORITY
MARVEL COMICS GROUP
A JOB FOR PETER PARKER!
THE LAST FATAL TRIP!
MARY JANE KNOCKS 'EM DEAD!
AND
THE GREEN GOBLIN RETURNS!
WHAT YOU'VE BEEN WAITING FOR!
THIS ONE'S GOT IT ALL!
E 4ST
2ND AV
VILLAGE THEATER
SPIDER-MAN'S GETTING AWAY!

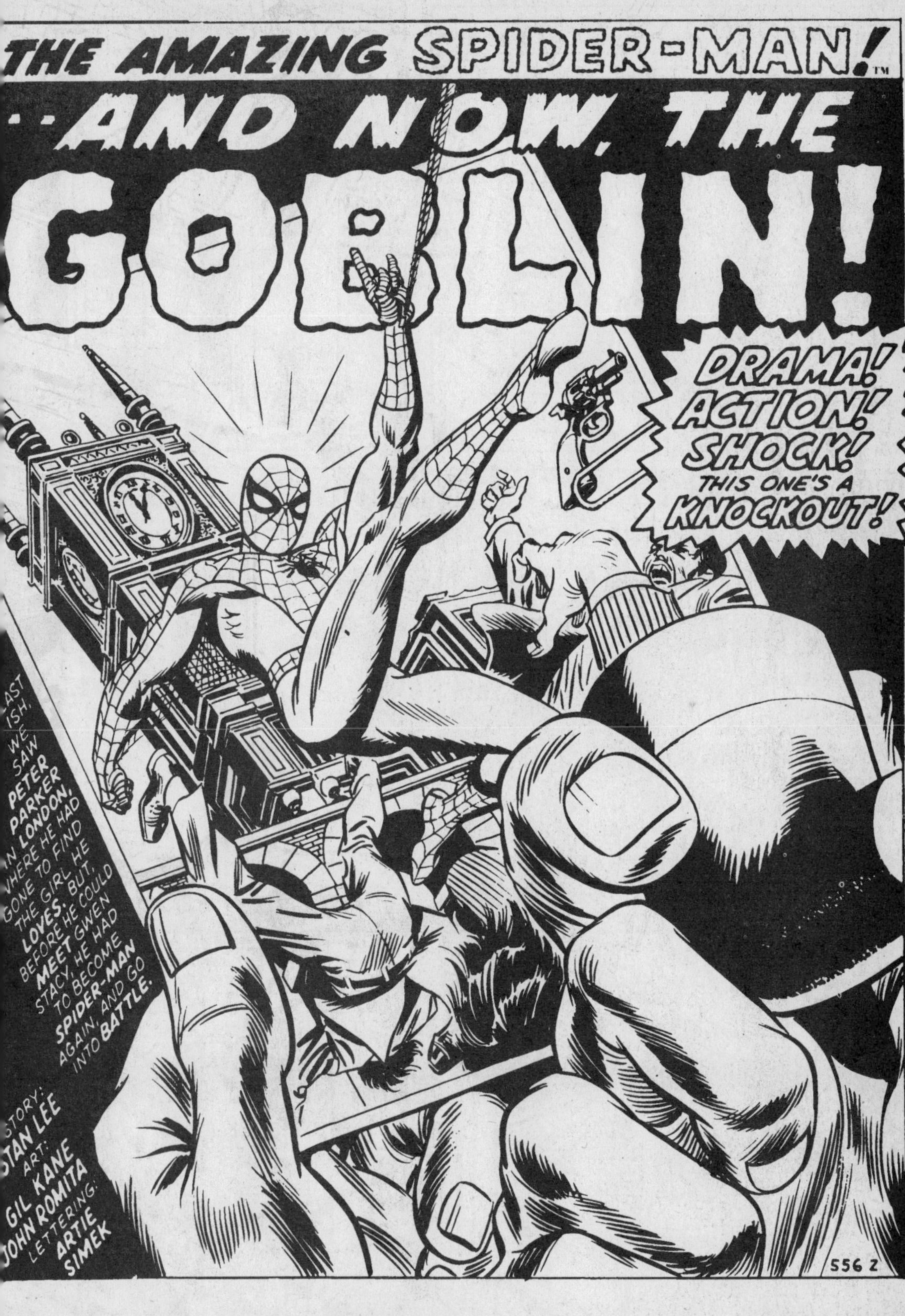
THE AMAZING SPIDER-MAN!™
--AND NOW, THE GOBLIN!
DRAMA! ACTION! SHOCK! THIS ONE'S A KNOCKOUT!
AST ISH, WE SAW PETER PARKER N LONDON, WHERE HE HAD GONE TO FIND THE GIRL HE LOVES. BUT, BEFORE HE COULD MEET GWEN STACY, HE HAD TO BECOME SPIDER-MAN AGAIN, AND GO INTO BATTLE.
STORY: STAN LEE
ART: GIL KANE JOHN ROMITA
LETTERING: ARTIE SIMEK
556 Z

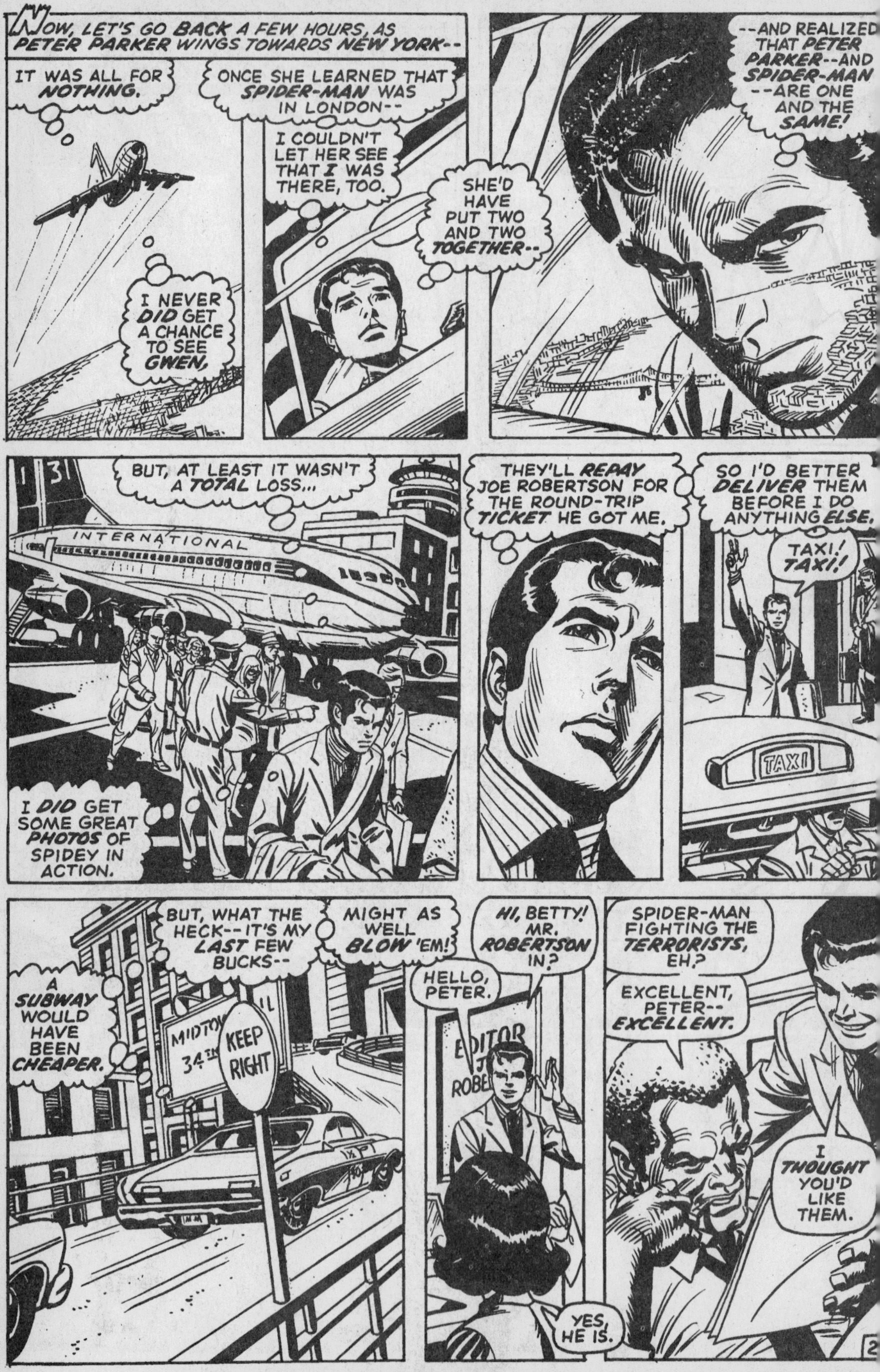
NOW, LET'S GO BACK A FEW HOURS, AS PETER PARKER WINGS TOWARDS NEW YORK--
IT WAS ALL FOR NOTHING.
I NEVER DID GET A CHANCE TO SEE GWEN,
ONCE SHE LEARNED THAT SPIDER-MAN WAS IN LONDON--
I COULDN'T LET HER SEE THAT I WAS THERE, TOO.
SHE'D HAVE PUT TWO AND TWO TOGETHER--
--AND REALIZED THAT PETER PARKER--AND SPIDER-MAN--ARE ONE AND THE SAME!
BUT, AT LEAST IT WASN'T A TOTAL LOSS...
INTERNATIONAL
I DID GET SOME GREAT PHOTOS OF SPIDEY IN ACTION.
THEY'LL REPAY JOE ROBERTSON FOR THE ROUND-TRIP TICKET HE GOT ME.
SO I'D BETTER DELIVER THEM BEFORE I DO ANYTHING ELSE.
TAXI! TAXI!
TAXI
BUT, WHAT THE HECK--IT'S MY LAST FEW BUCKS--
MIGHT AS WELL BLOW 'EM!
A SUBWAY WOULD HAVE BEEN CHEAPER.
KEEP RIGHT
HI, BETTY! MR. ROBERTSON IN?
HELLO, PETER.
YES, HE IS.
SPIDER-MAN FIGHTING THE TERRORISTS, EH?
EXCELLENT, PETER--EXCELLENT.
I THOUGHT YOU'D LIKE THEM.

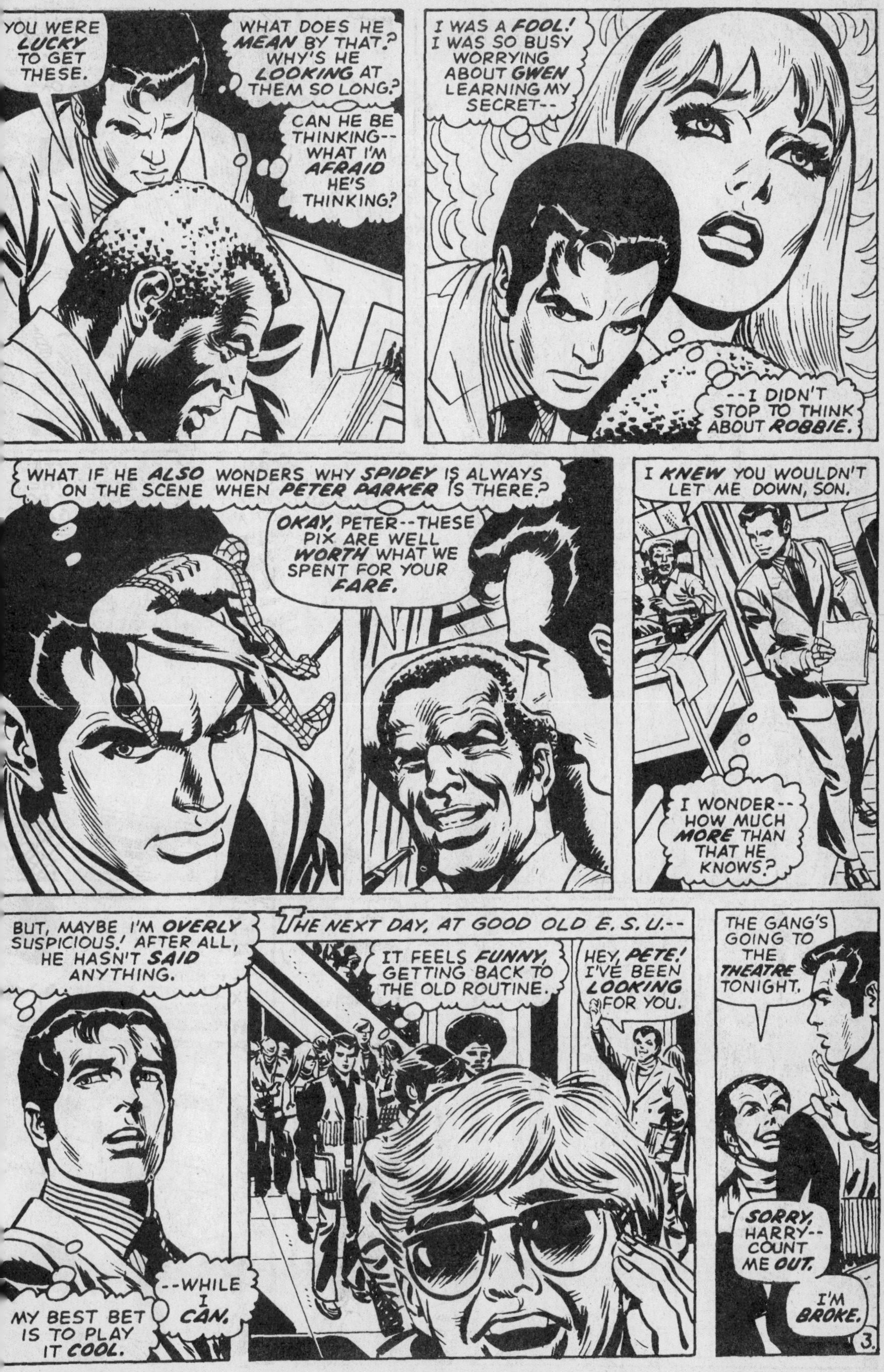

YOU WERE LUCKY TO GET THESE.
WHAT DOES HE MEAN BY THAT? WHY'S HE LOOKING AT THEM SO LONG?
CAN HE BE THINKING-- WHAT I'M AFRAID HE'S THINKING?
I WAS A FOOL! I WAS SO BUSY WORRYING ABOUT GWEN LEARNING MY SECRET--
--I DIDN'T STOP TO THINK ABOUT ROBBIE.
WHAT IF HE ALSO WONDERS WHY SPIDEY IS ALWAYS ON THE SCENE WHEN PETER PARKER IS THERE?
OKAY, PETER--THESE PIX ARE WELL WORTH WHAT WE SPENT FOR YOUR FARE.
I KNEW YOU WOULDN'T LET ME DOWN, SON.
I WONDER-- HOW MUCH MORE THAN THAT HE KNOWS?
BUT, MAYBE I'M OVERLY SUSPICIOUS! AFTER ALL, HE HASN'T SAID ANYTHING.
MY BEST BET IS TO PLAY IT COOL.
--WHILE I CAN.
THE NEXT DAY, AT GOOD OLD E. S. U.--
IT FEELS FUNNY, GETTING BACK TO THE OLD ROUTINE.
HEY, PETE! I'VE BEEN LOOKING FOR YOU.
THE GANG'S GOING TO THE THEATRE TONIGHT.
SORRY, HARRY-- COUNT ME OUT.
I'M BROKE.
3.

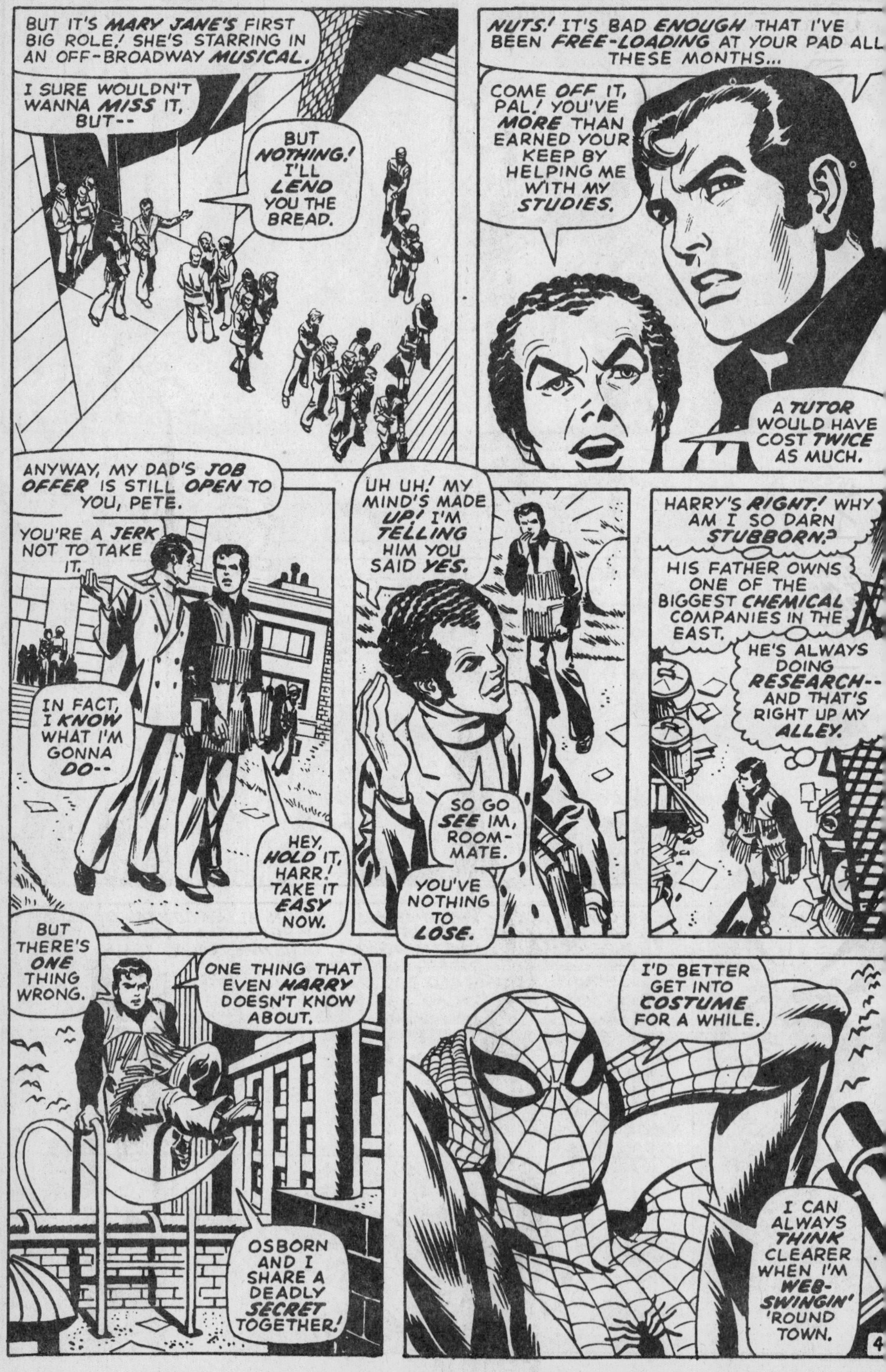

BUT IT'S MARY JANE'S FIRST BIG ROLE! SHE'S STARRING IN AN OFF-BROADWAY MUSICAL.
I SURE WOULDN'T WANNA MISS IT, BUT--
BUT NOTHING! I'LL LEND YOU THE BREAD.
NUTS! IT'S BAD ENOUGH THAT I'VE BEEN FREE-LOADING AT YOUR PAD ALL THESE MONTHS...
COME OFF IT, PAL! YOU'VE MORE THAN EARNED YOUR KEEP BY HELPING ME WITH MY STUDIES.
A TUTOR WOULD HAVE COST TWICE AS MUCH.
ANYWAY, MY DAD'S JOB OFFER IS STILL OPEN TO YOU, PETE.
YOU'RE A JERK NOT TO TAKE IT.
IN FACT, I KNOW WHAT I'M GONNA DO--
HEY, HOLD IT, HARR! TAKE IT EASY NOW.
UH UH! MY MIND'S MADE UP! I'M TELLING HIM YOU SAID YES.
SO GO SEE IM, ROOM-MATE.
YOU'VE NOTHING TO LOSE.
HARRY'S RIGHT! WHY AM I SO DARN STUBBORN?
HIS FATHER OWNS ONE OF THE BIGGEST CHEMICAL COMPANIES IN THE EAST.
HE'S ALWAYS DOING RESEARCH-- AND THAT'S RIGHT UP MY ALLEY.
BUT THERE'S ONE THING WRONG.
ONE THING THAT EVEN HARRY DOESN'T KNOW ABOUT.
OSBORN AND I SHARE A DEADLY SECRET TOGETHER!
I'D BETTER GET INTO COSTUME FOR A WHILE.
I CAN ALWAYS THINK CLEARER WHEN I'M WEB-SWINGIN' 'ROUND TOWN.
4

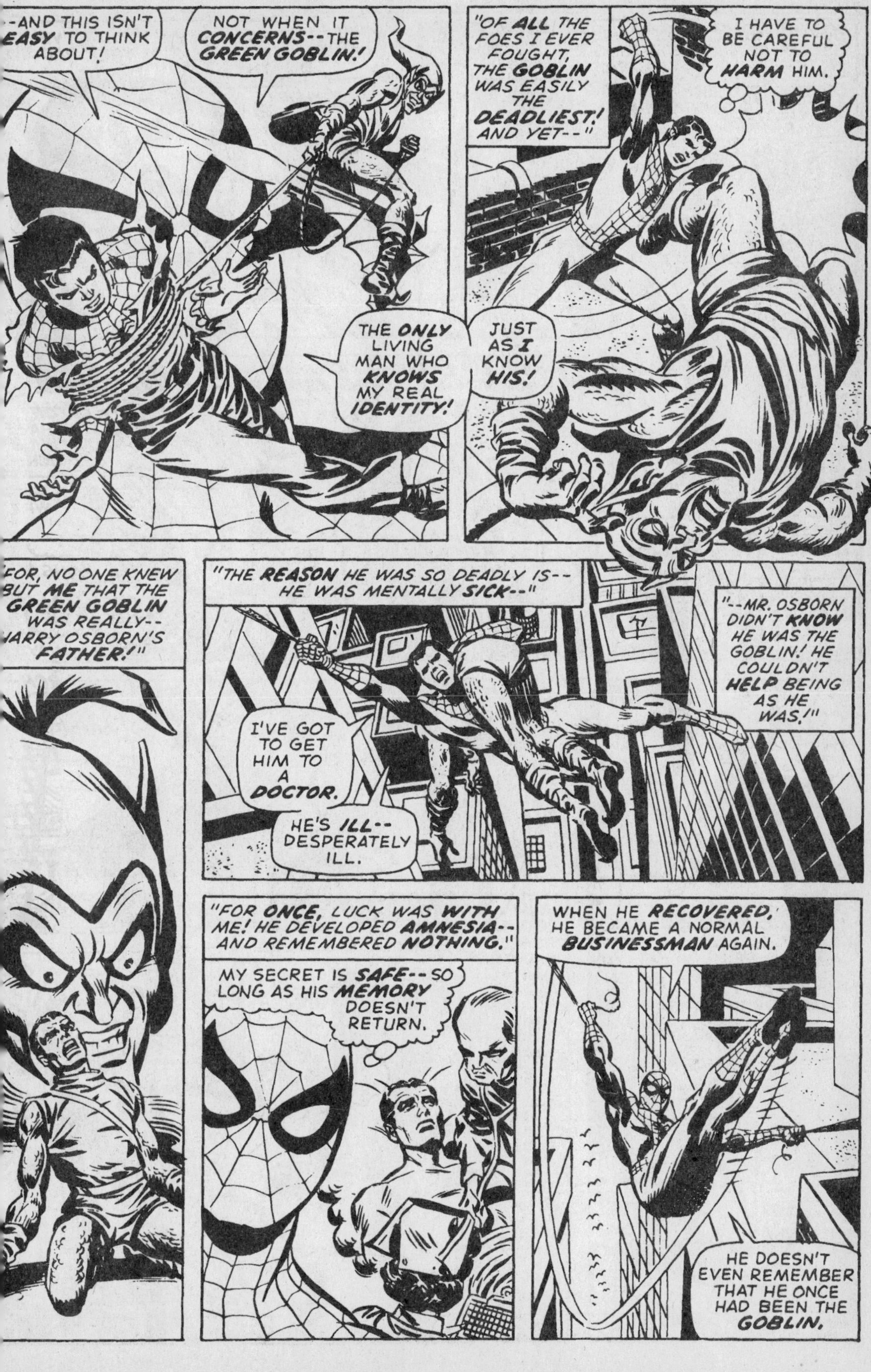

--AND THIS ISN'T EASY TO THINK ABOUT!
NOT WHEN IT CONCERNS--THE GREEN GOBLIN!
THE ONLY LIVING MAN WHO KNOWS MY REAL IDENTITY!
JUST AS I KNOW HIS!
"OF ALL THE FOES I EVER FOUGHT, THE GOBLIN WAS EASILY THE DEADLIEST! AND YET--"
I HAVE TO BE CAREFUL NOT TO HARM HIM.
"FOR, NO ONE KNEW BUT ME THAT THE GREEN GOBLIN WAS REALLY--HARRY OSBORN'S FATHER!"
"THE REASON HE WAS SO DEADLY IS--HE WAS MENTALLY SICK--"
"--MR. OSBORN DIDN'T KNOW HE WAS THE GOBLIN! HE COULDN'T HELP BEING AS HE WAS."
I'VE GOT TO GET HIM TO A DOCTOR.
HE'S ILL--DESPERATELY ILL.
"FOR ONCE, LUCK WAS WITH ME! HE DEVELOPED AMNESIA--AND REMEMBERED NOTHING."
MY SECRET IS SAFE--SO LONG AS HIS MEMORY DOESN'T RETURN.
WHEN HE RECOVERED, HE BECAME A NORMAL BUSINESSMAN AGAIN.
HE DOESN'T EVEN REMEMBER THAT HE ONCE HAD BEEN THE GOBLIN.

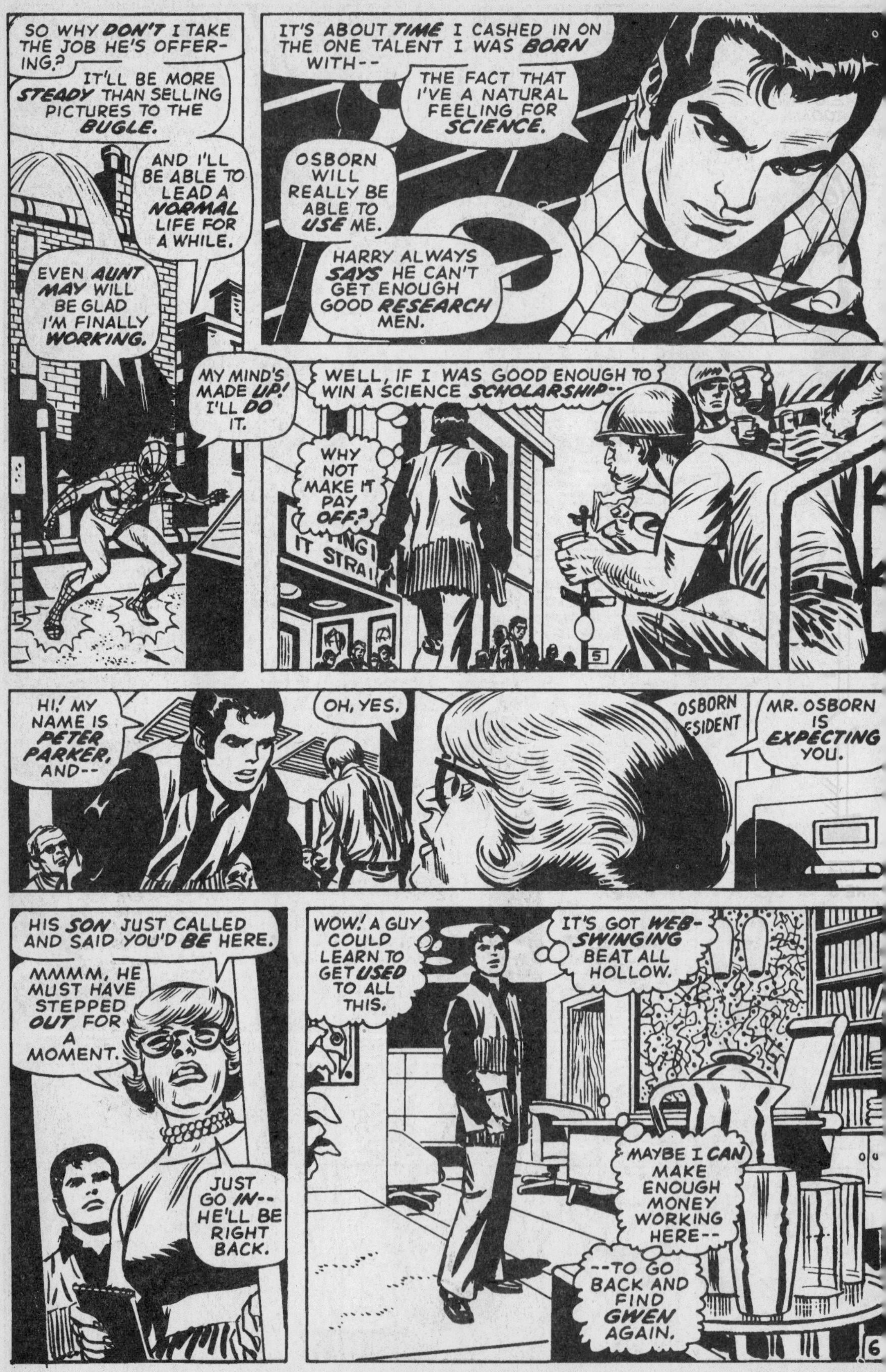
SO WHY DON'T I TAKE THE JOB HE'S OFFERING?
IT'LL BE MORE STEADY THAN SELLING PICTURES TO THE BUGLE.
AND I'LL BE ABLE TO LEAD A NORMAL LIFE FOR A WHILE.
EVEN AUNT MAY WILL BE GLAD I'M FINALLY WORKING.
IT'S ABOUT TIME I CASHED IN ON THE ONE TALENT I WAS BORN WITH--
THE FACT THAT I'VE A NATURAL FEELING FOR SCIENCE.
OSBORN WILL REALLY BE ABLE TO USE ME.
HARRY ALWAYS SAYS HE CAN'T GET ENOUGH GOOD RESEARCH MEN.
MY MIND'S MADE UP! I'LL DO IT.
WELL, IF I WAS GOOD ENOUGH TO WIN A SCIENCE SCHOLARSHIP--
WHY NOT MAKE IT PAY OFF?
IT STRA
5
HI! MY NAME IS PETER PARKER, AND--
OH, YES.
OSBORN
ESIDENT
MR. OSBORN IS EXPECTING YOU.
HIS SON JUST CALLED AND SAID YOU'D BE HERE.
MMMM, HE MUST HAVE STEPPED OUT FOR A MOMENT.
JUST GO IN-- HE'LL BE RIGHT BACK.
WOW! A GUY COULD LEARN TO GET USED TO ALL THIS.
IT'S GOT WEB-SWINGING BEAT ALL HOLLOW.
MAYBE I CAN MAKE ENOUGH MONEY WORKING HERE--
--TO GO BACK AND FIND GWEN AGAIN.
6

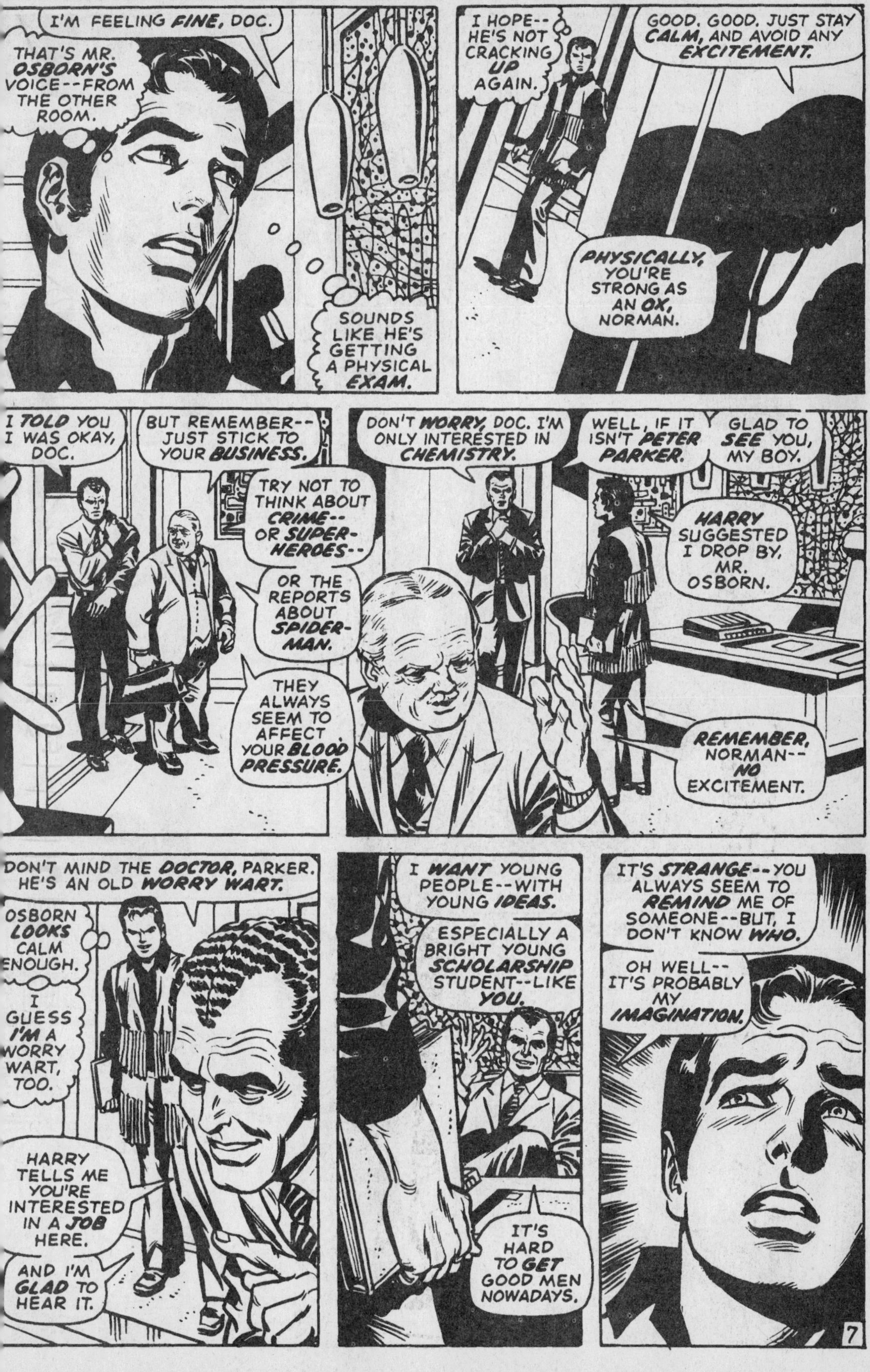
I'M FEELING FINE, DOC.
THAT'S MR. OSBORN'S VOICE--FROM THE OTHER ROOM.
SOUNDS LIKE HE'S GETTING A PHYSICAL EXAM.
I HOPE--HE'S NOT CRACKING UP AGAIN.
GOOD. GOOD. JUST STAY CALM, AND AVOID ANY EXCITEMENT.
PHYSICALLY, YOU'RE STRONG AS AN OX, NORMAN.
I TOLD YOU I WAS OKAY, DOC.
BUT REMEMBER--JUST STICK TO YOUR BUSINESS.
TRY NOT TO THINK ABOUT CRIME--OR SUPER-HEROES--
OR THE REPORTS ABOUT SPIDER-MAN.
THEY ALWAYS SEEM TO AFFECT YOUR BLOOD PRESSURE.
DON'T WORRY, DOC. I'M ONLY INTERESTED IN CHEMISTRY.
WELL, IF IT ISN'T PETER PARKER.
GLAD TO SEE YOU, MY BOY.
HARRY SUGGESTED I DROP BY, MR. OSBORN.
REMEMBER, NORMAN--NO EXCITEMENT.
DON'T MIND THE DOCTOR, PARKER. HE'S AN OLD WORRY WART.
OSBORN LOOKS CALM ENOUGH.
I GUESS I'M A WORRY WART, TOO.
HARRY TELLS ME YOU'RE INTERESTED IN A JOB HERE.
AND I'M GLAD TO HEAR IT.
I WANT YOUNG PEOPLE--WITH YOUNG IDEAS.
ESPECIALLY A BRIGHT YOUNG SCHOLARSHIP STUDENT--LIKE YOU.
IT'S HARD TO GET GOOD MEN NOWADAYS.
IT'S STRANGE--YOU ALWAYS SEEM TO REMIND ME OF SOMEONE--BUT, I DON'T KNOW WHO.
OH WELL--IT'S PROBABLY MY IMAGINATION.
7

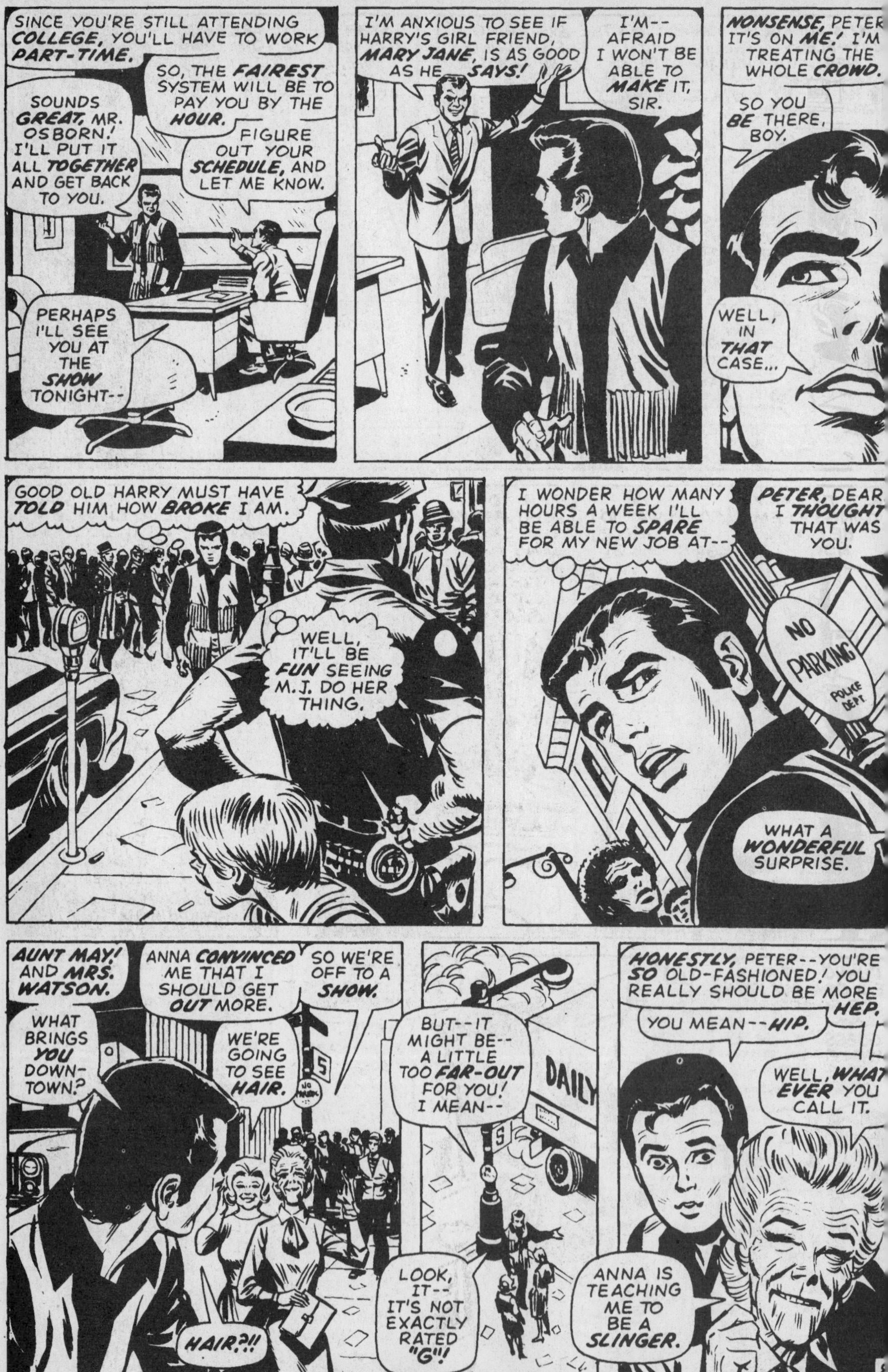
SINCE YOU'RE STILL ATTENDING COLLEGE, YOU'LL HAVE TO WORK PART-TIME.
SO, THE FAIREST SYSTEM WILL BE TO PAY YOU BY THE HOUR.
FIGURE OUT YOUR SCHEDULE, AND LET ME KNOW.
SOUNDS GREAT, MR. OSBORN! I'LL PUT IT ALL TOGETHER AND GET BACK TO YOU.
PERHAPS I'LL SEE YOU AT THE SHOW TONIGHT--
I'M ANXIOUS TO SEE IF HARRY'S GIRL FRIEND, MARY JANE, IS AS GOOD AS HE SAYS!
I'M-- AFRAID I WON'T BE ABLE TO MAKE IT, SIR.
NONSENSE, PETER IT'S ON ME! I'M TREATING THE WHOLE CROWD.
SO YOU BE THERE, BOY.
WELL, IN THAT CASE...
GOOD OLD HARRY MUST HAVE TOLD HIM HOW BROKE I AM.
WELL, IT'LL BE FUN SEEING M.J. DO HER THING.
I WONDER HOW MANY HOURS A WEEK I'LL BE ABLE TO SPARE FOR MY NEW JOB AT--
PETER, DEAR I THOUGHT THAT WAS YOU.
NO PARKING
POLICE DEPT.
WHAT A WONDERFUL SURPRISE.
AUNT MAY! AND MRS. WATSON.
WHAT BRINGS YOU DOWN-TOWN?
ANNA CONVINCED ME THAT I SHOULD GET OUT MORE.
SO WE'RE OFF TO A SHOW.
WE'RE GOING TO SEE HAIR.
HAIR?!!
BUT-- IT MIGHT BE-- A LITTLE TOO FAR-OUT FOR YOU! I MEAN--
DAILY
LOOK, IT-- IT'S NOT EXACTLY RATED "G"!
HONESTLY, PETER--YOU'RE SO OLD-FASHIONED! YOU REALLY SHOULD BE MORE HEP.
YOU MEAN--HIP.
WELL, WHATEVER YOU CALL IT.
ANNA IS TEACHING ME TO BE A SLINGER.

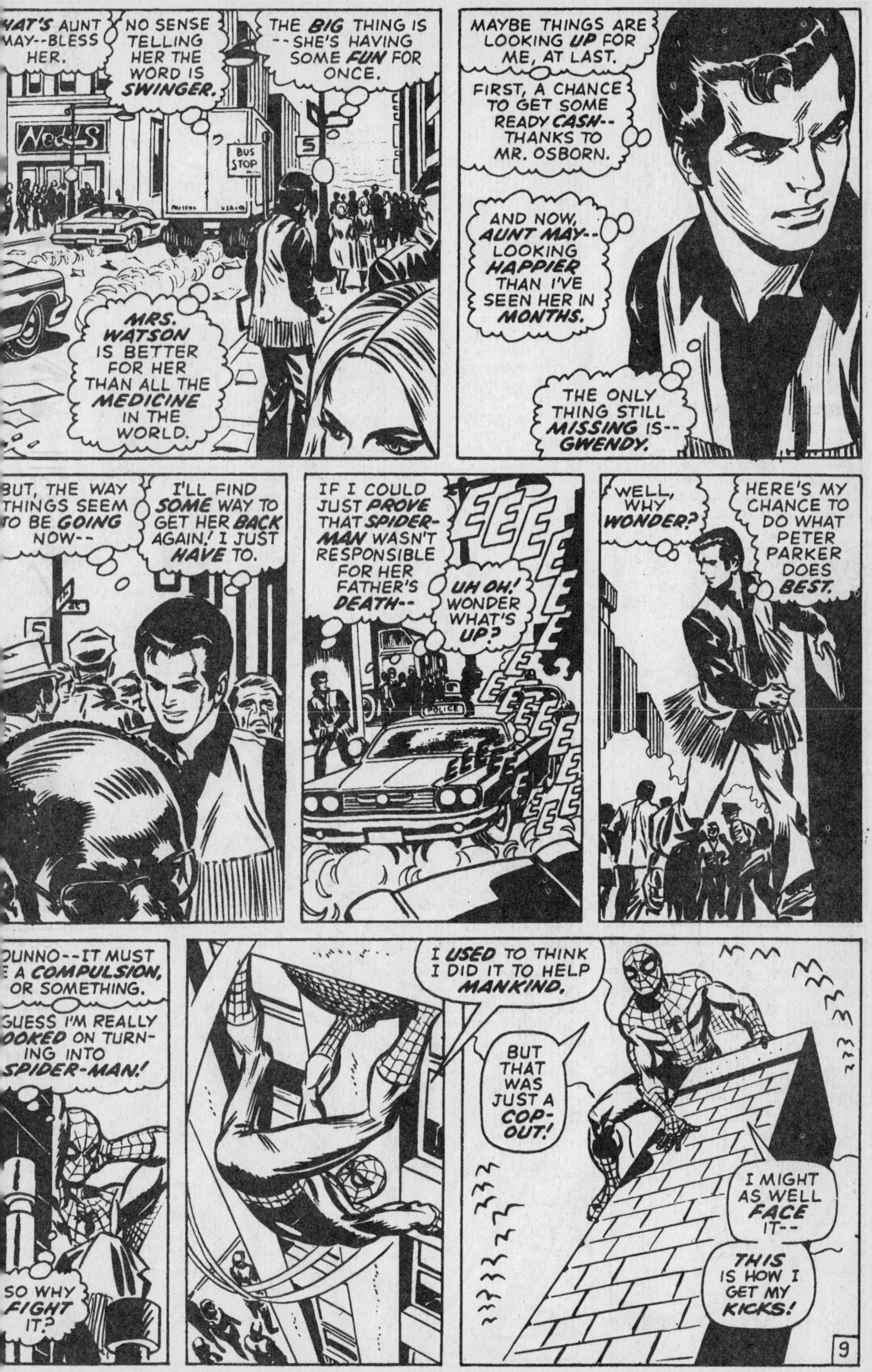

...HAT'S AUNT MAY--BLESS HER.
NO SENSE TELLING HER THE WORD IS SWINGER.
THE BIG THING IS --SHE'S HAVING SOME FUN FOR ONCE.
MRS. WATSON IS BETTER FOR HER THAN ALL THE MEDICINE IN THE WORLD.
BUS STOP
MAYBE THINGS ARE LOOKING UP FOR ME, AT LAST.
FIRST, A CHANCE TO GET SOME READY CASH-- THANKS TO MR. OSBORN.
AND NOW, AUNT MAY-- LOOKING HAPPIER THAN I'VE SEEN HER IN MONTHS.
THE ONLY THING STILL MISSING IS-- GWENDY.
BUT, THE WAY THINGS SEEM TO BE GOING NOW--
I'LL FIND SOME WAY TO GET HER BACK AGAIN! I JUST HAVE TO.
IF I COULD JUST PROVE THAT SPIDER-MAN WASN'T RESPONSIBLE FOR HER FATHER'S DEATH--
EEEEEEEE
UH OH! WONDER WHAT'S UP?
POLICE
WELL, WHY WONDER?
HERE'S MY CHANCE TO DO WHAT PETER PARKER DOES BEST.
...DUNNO--IT MUST ...E A COMPULSION, OR SOMETHING.
...GUESS I'M REALLY ...OOKED ON TURNING INTO SPIDER-MAN!
SO WHY FIGHT IT?
I USED TO THINK I DID IT TO HELP MANKIND.
BUT THAT WAS JUST A COP-OUT!
I MIGHT AS WELL FACE IT--
THIS IS HOW I GET MY KICKS!

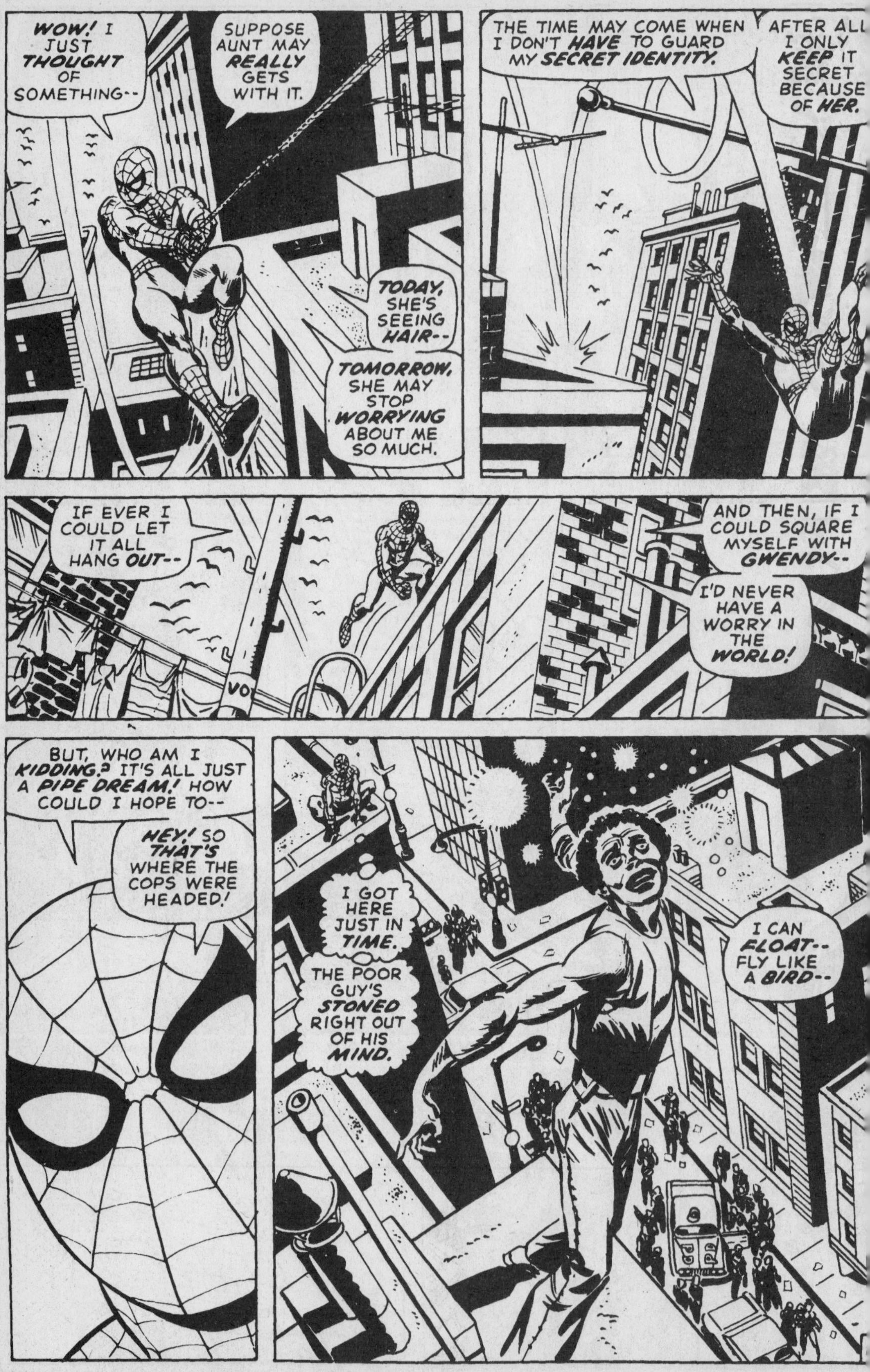
WOW! I JUST THOUGHT OF SOMETHING--
SUPPOSE AUNT MAY REALLY GETS WITH IT.
TODAY, SHE'S SEEING HAIR--
TOMORROW, SHE MAY STOP WORRYING ABOUT ME SO MUCH.
THE TIME MAY COME WHEN I DON'T HAVE TO GUARD MY SECRET IDENTITY.
AFTER ALL I ONLY KEEP IT SECRET BECAUSE OF HER.
IF EVER I COULD LET IT ALL HANG OUT--
AND THEN, IF I COULD SQUARE MYSELF WITH GWENDY--
I'D NEVER HAVE A WORRY IN THE WORLD!
BUT, WHO AM I KIDDING? IT'S ALL JUST A PIPE DREAM! HOW COULD I HOPE TO--
HEY! SO THAT'S WHERE THE COPS WERE HEADED!
I GOT HERE JUST IN TIME.
THE POOR GUY'S STONED RIGHT OUT OF HIS MIND.
I CAN FLOAT-- FLY LIKE A BIRD--

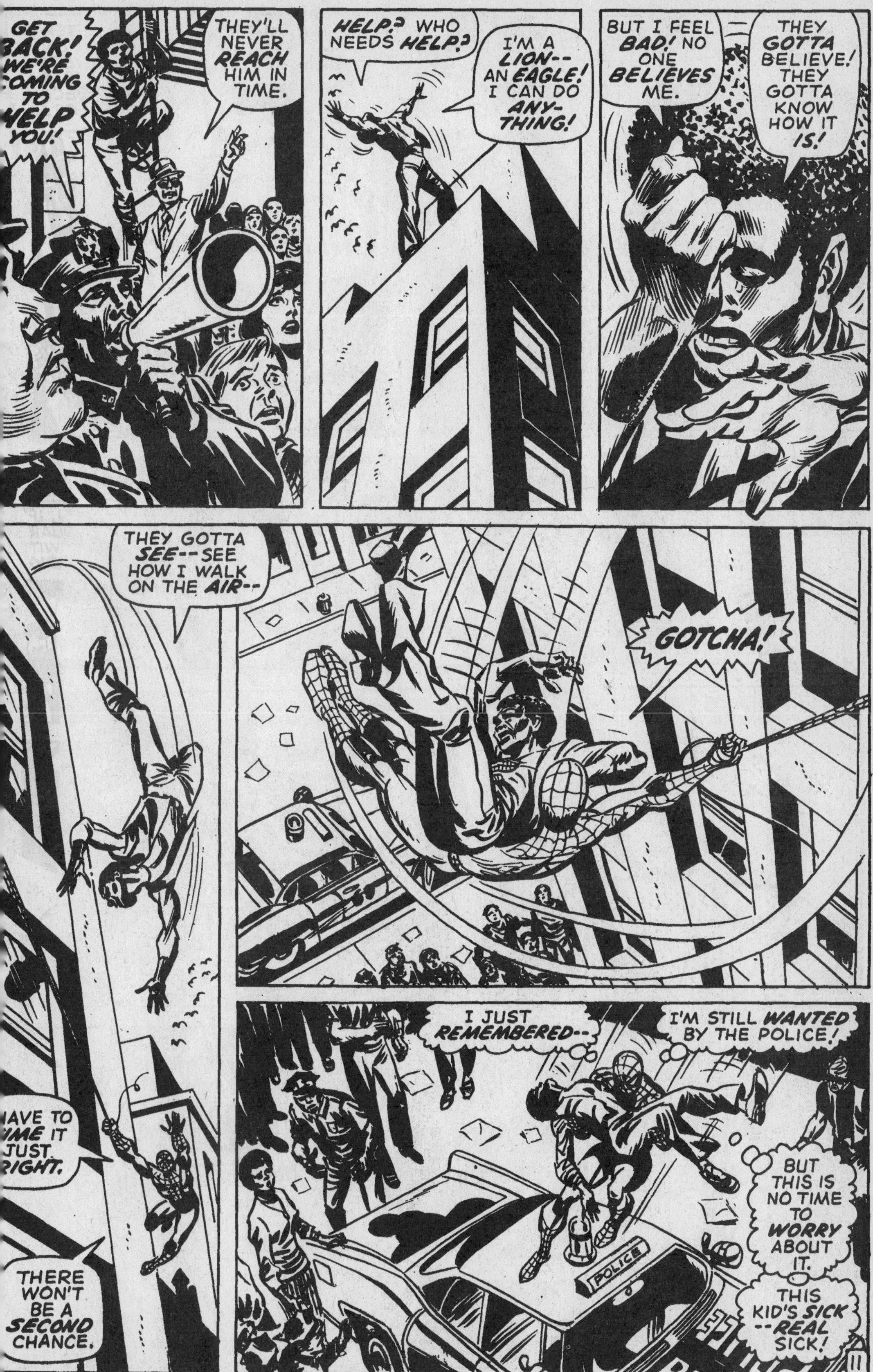
GET BACK! WE'RE COMING TO HELP YOU!
THEY'LL NEVER REACH HIM IN TIME.
HELP? WHO NEEDS HELP?
I'M A LION-- AN EAGLE! I CAN DO ANY-THING!
BUT I FEEL BAD! NO ONE BELIEVES ME.
THEY GOTTA BELIEVE! THEY GOTTA KNOW HOW IT IS!
THEY GOTTA SEE--SEE HOW I WALK ON THE AIR--
HAVE TO TIME IT JUST RIGHT.
THERE WON'T BE A SECOND CHANCE.
GOTCHA!
I JUST REMEMBERED--
I'M STILL WANTED BY THE POLICE!
BUT THIS IS NO TIME TO WORRY ABOUT IT.
THIS KID'S SICK --REAL SICK!
POLICE
11

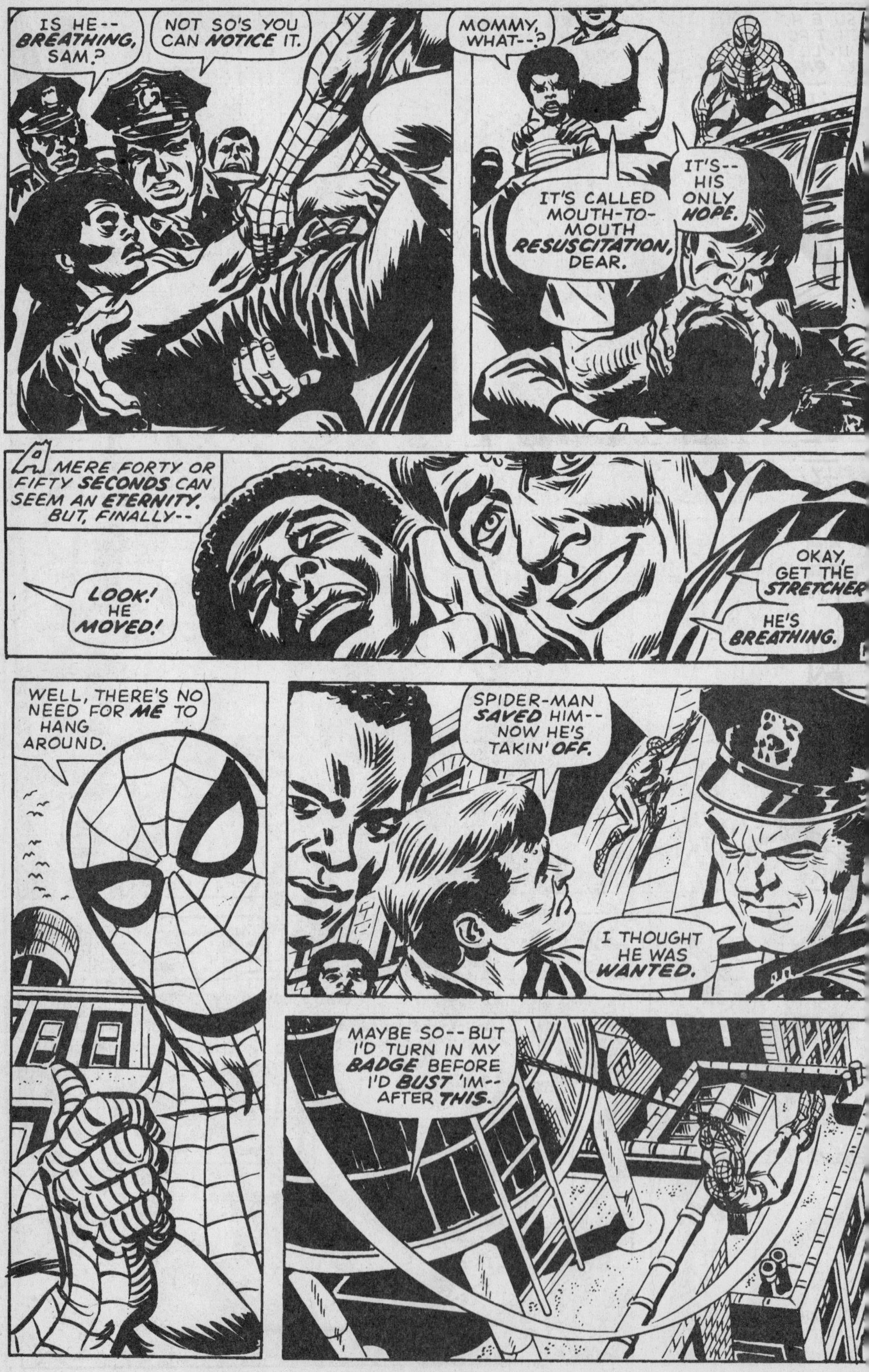
IS HE-- BREATHING, SAM?
NOT SO'S YOU CAN NOTICE IT.
MOMMY, WHAT--?
IT'S CALLED MOUTH-TO-MOUTH RESUSCITATION, DEAR.
IT'S-- HIS ONLY HOPE.
A MERE FORTY OR FIFTY SECONDS CAN SEEM AN ETERNITY. BUT, FINALLY--
LOOK! HE MOVED!
OKAY, GET THE STRETCHER
HE'S BREATHING.
WELL, THERE'S NO NEED FOR ME TO HANG AROUND.
SPIDER-MAN SAVED HIM-- NOW HE'S TAKIN' OFF.
I THOUGHT HE WAS WANTED.
MAYBE SO-- BUT I'D TURN IN MY BADGE BEFORE I'D BUST 'IM-- AFTER THIS.

SURE HOPE THAT POOR GUY'LL BE ALL RIGHT.

--BUT I COULDN'T BET ON IT.

ANY DRUG STRONG ENOUGH TO GIVE YOU THAT KIND OF TRIP--

--CAN DAMAGE YOUR BRAIN--BUT BAD!

BUT HOW DO YOU WARN THE KIDS? HOW DO YOU REACH THEM?

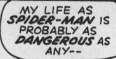

MY LIFE AS SPIDER-MAN IS PROBABLY AS DANGEROUS AS ANY--

BUT I'D RATHER FACE A HUNDRED SUPER-VILLAINS THAN TOSS IT AWAY BY GETTING HOOKED ON HARD DRUGS!

--'CAUSE THAT'S ONE FIGHT YOU CAN'T WIN!

ROBBIE, AND A MILLION OTHER EDITORS, KEEP GRINDING OUT EDITORIALS AGAINST THE DRUG SCENE...

MAYBE IT'S NOT ENOUGH! MAYBE WE'VE GOT TO DO MORE.

IF ONLY SPIDER-MAN COULD...

FINALLY AT SHOW-TIME--

FOR ONCE I'M NOT LATE! THERE'S THE GANG.

BOY! THAT THEATRE ISN'T EXACTLY THE MUSIC HALL!

HOW DO YOU LIKE IT, ROOMMATE?

MY DAD ONCE OWNED THIS BUILDING.

AND NOW, IT'S AN OFF-BROADWAY SHOWPLACE!

IF IT WAS ANY FURTHER OFF BROADWAY --IT WOULD BE IN HOBOKEN!

WELCOME, TIGER.

WHO TOLD ME YOU TOOK THE JOB, PETE.

I'M REAL GLAD FOR YOU.

THANKS, HARRY. I HOPE IT'LL WORK OUT.

HEY! HOW ABOUT PAYING SOME ATTENTION TO THE STAR?

THIS IS MY BIG BREAK, HEAR?

SO WHEN MARVELOUS ME COMES ON THE STAGE, I WANNA HEAR IT, TROOPS!

MMMMM--REMEMBER WHEN THEY USED TO CALL YOU PUNY PARKER?

YOU SURE HAVE CHANGED, PETEY.

I NOTICE YOU DIDN'T BRING A DATE...

IT'S GETTING LATE.

WHAT'RE WE WAITING FOR?

WE'RE JUST WAITING FOR RANDY.

HE'LL BE HERE ANY MINUTE.

WHAT'S MARY JANE TRYING TO DO?

SHE KNOWS HOW HARRY FEELS ABOUT HER! WHY'S SHE PLAYING UP TO ME?

HERE HE IS! HERE COMES RANDY NOW!

HEY, DIDJA HEAR WHAT HAPPENED?

SPIDER-MAN JUST SAVED SOME FREAKED OUT CAT A FEW BLOCKS AWAY.

YEAH, HOW ABOUT THAT!

MAN, THIS DRUG SCENE REALLY BUGS ME!

WHAT DO YOU MEAN, RANDY?

EVERYONE FIGURES IT'S THE BLACK MAN'S BAG --BUT IT AIN'T!

WE'RE THE ONES WHO HATE IT THE MOST!

IT HURTS US MORE THAN ANYONE ELSE--'CAUSE TOO MANY OF US GOT NO HOPE--SO WE'RE EASY PICKIN'S FOR THE PUSHERS.

BUT IT AIN'T JUST OUR PROBLEM, IT'S YOUR TOO!

DON'T LOOK AT ME, SON! I KNOW WHERE IT'S AT.

YOU DO, HUH? YOU SIT ALL DAY IN YOUR IVORY TOWER, COUNTIN' YOUR BREAD--

I WORKED HARD FOR WHAT I GOT, MISTER!

SO WHAT D'YA WANT-- A MEDAL?

ANSWER ME THIS--

EVERYBODY WORKS HARD.

HOW HARD ARE YOU WORKIN' FOR PEOPLE?

WHAT HAVE YOU DONE TO FIGHT DRUGS?

LOOK! I'M JUST ONE MAN! IT'S NOT MY RESPONSIBILITY.

YOU'RE RICH! YOU GOT INFLUENCE! THAT MAKES IT YOUR RESPONSIBILITY.

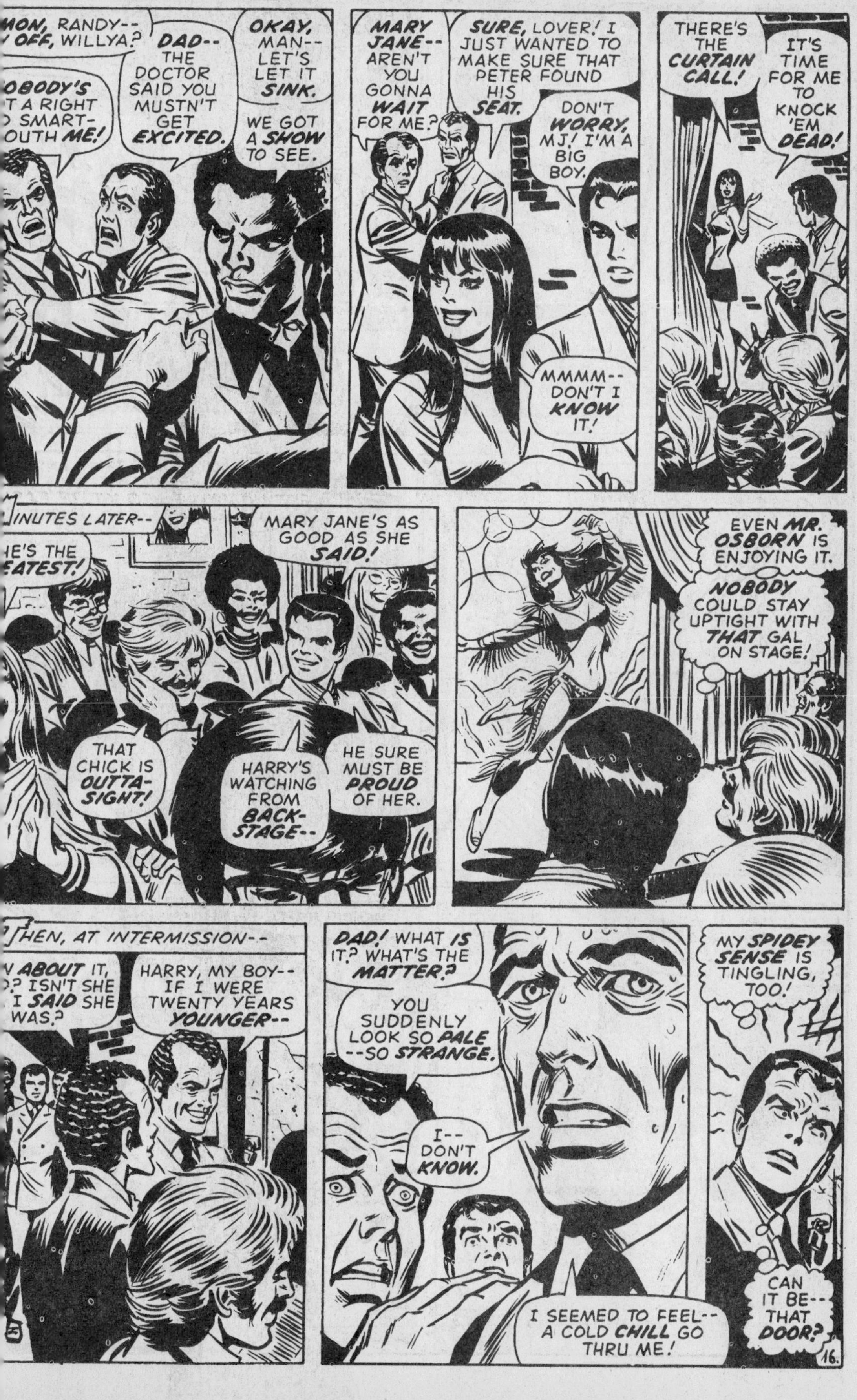

MON, RANDY-- OFF, WILLYA?
OBODY'S T A RIGHT SMART- OUTH ME!
DAD-- THE DOCTOR SAID YOU MUSTN'T GET EXCITED.
OKAY, MAN-- LET'S LET IT SINK.
WE GOT A SHOW TO SEE.
MARY JANE-- AREN'T YOU GONNA WAIT FOR ME?
SURE, LOVER! I JUST WANTED TO MAKE SURE THAT PETER FOUND HIS SEAT.
DON'T WORRY, MJ! I'M A BIG BOY.
MMMM-- DON'T I KNOW IT!
THERE'S THE CURTAIN CALL!
IT'S TIME FOR ME TO KNOCK 'EM DEAD!
INUTES LATER--
E'S THE EATEST!
MARY JANE'S AS GOOD AS SHE SAID!
THAT CHICK IS OUTTA-SIGHT!
HARRY'S WATCHING FROM BACK-STAGE--
HE SURE MUST BE PROUD OF HER.
EVEN MR. OSBORN IS ENJOYING IT.
NOBODY COULD STAY UPTIGHT WITH THAT GAL ON STAGE!
THEN, AT INTERMISSION--
ABOUT IT, ? ISN'T SHE I SAID SHE WAS?
HARRY, MY BOY-- IF I WERE TWENTY YEARS YOUNGER--
DAD! WHAT IS IT? WHAT'S THE MATTER?
YOU SUDDENLY LOOK SO PALE --SO STRANGE.
I-- DON'T KNOW.
I SEEMED TO FEEL-- A COLD CHILL GO THRU ME!
MY SPIDEY SENSE IS TINGLING, TOO!
CAN IT BE-- THAT DOOR?
16.

NO TIME TO CHECK IT OUT *NOW*-- BUT I'D BETTER KEEP MY *EYE* ON HIM-- JUST IN *CASE.*

I'VE GOT TO KNOW WHAT *AFFECTED* HIM THAT WAY.

AND AS THE SHOW ROLLS ON... BUT *THIS* TIME MR. OSBORN ISN' *WITH* IT!

THE *LAST* ACT'S THE BEST OF *ALL.*

MJ IS TOO *MUCH!*

THEN, AFTER THE FINAL CURTAIN CALL--

HE LOOKED LIKE HE WANTED TO *OPEN* THAT DOOR-- BUT HE'S WALKING *PAST* IT-- NERVOUSLY.

IT'S PROBABLY NONE OF MY *BUSINESS!* AND YET--

GREAT SHOW, EH?

YOU CAN *HAVE* THE *SHOW*-- BUT THAT *MARY JANE!*

I'M TINGLING *AGAIN!*

IT *HAS* TO BE THAT *DOOR.*

I'VE *GOT* TO COME *BACK* AND SEE WHA INSIDE.

HOW'D YOU *LIKE* IT? HOW *WAS* I?

DID YOU *HEAR* THE *CHEERS*-- AND THE *APPLAUSE?*

DID WE *HEAR* IT, HONEY? WE WERE *DOING* IT!

I TOOK A *DOZEN* CURTAIN CALLS-- AND *BOWS!*

DO YOU KNOW WHAT THAT *MEANS?*

SURE! YOU'LL HAVE A SORE *BACK* TOMORROW.

WE'V GOT T CELE BRAT LAD

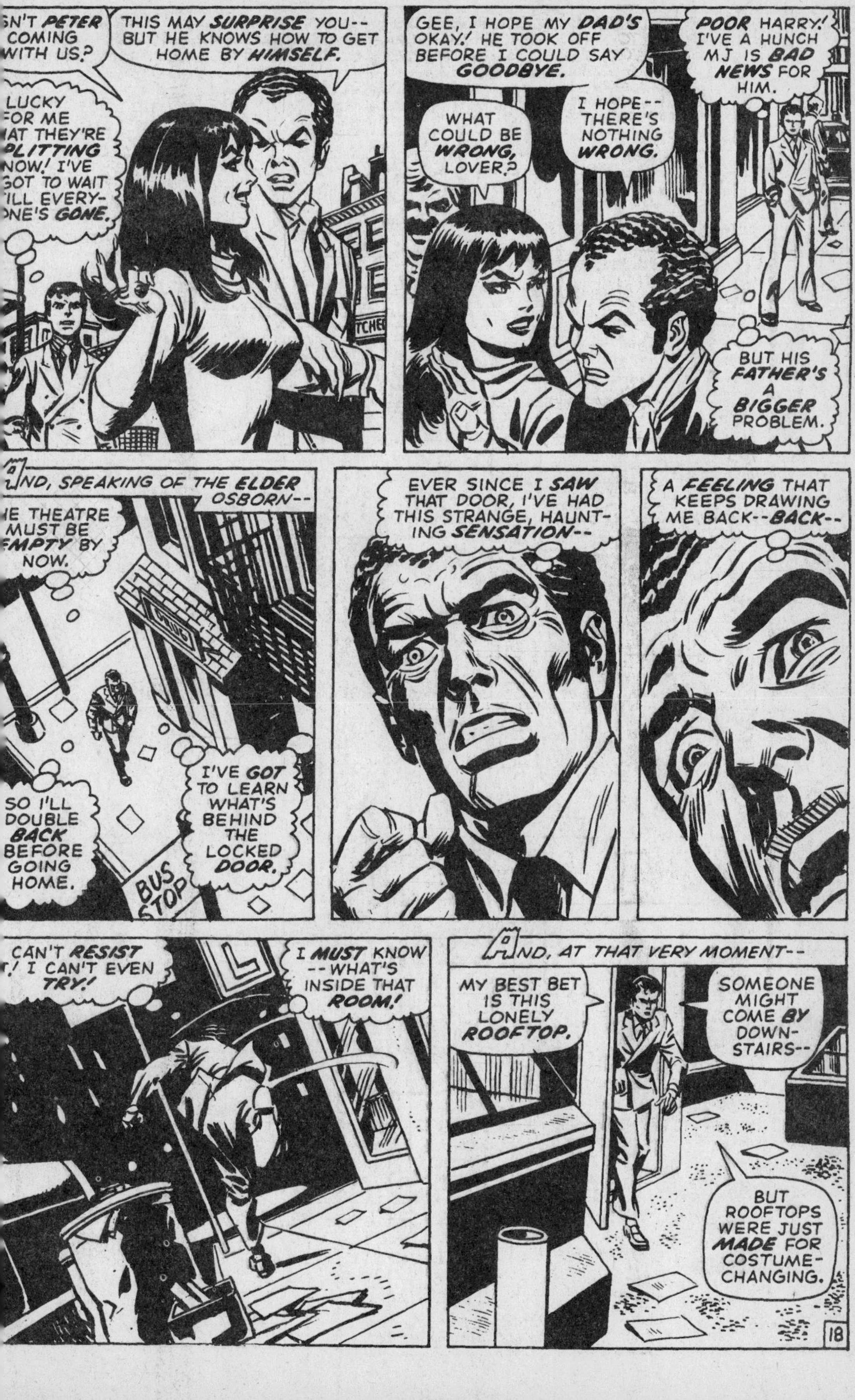

SN'T PETER COMING WITH US?
THIS MAY SURPRISE YOU-- BUT HE KNOWS HOW TO GET HOME BY HIMSELF.
LUCKY FOR ME AT THEY'RE PLITTING NOW! I'VE GOT TO WAIT ILL EVERY-ONE'S GONE.
GEE, I HOPE MY DAD'S OKAY! HE TOOK OFF BEFORE I COULD SAY GOODBYE.
WHAT COULD BE WRONG, LOVER?
I HOPE-- THERE'S NOTHING WRONG.
POOR HARRY! I'VE A HUNCH MJ IS BAD NEWS FOR HIM.
BUT HIS FATHER'S A BIGGER PROBLEM.
AND, SPEAKING OF THE ELDER OSBORN--
HE THEATRE MUST BE EMPTY BY NOW.
SO I'LL DOUBLE BACK BEFORE GOING HOME.
I'VE GOT TO LEARN WHAT'S BEHIND THE LOCKED DOOR.
BUS STOP
EVER SINCE I SAW THAT DOOR, I'VE HAD THIS STRANGE, HAUNTING SENSATION--
A FEELING THAT KEEPS DRAWING ME BACK--BACK--
CAN'T RESIST T! I CAN'T EVEN TRY!
I MUST KNOW --WHAT'S INSIDE THAT ROOM!
AND, AT THAT VERY MOMENT--
MY BEST BET IS THIS LONELY ROOFTOP.
SOMEONE MIGHT COME BY DOWN-STAIRS--
BUT ROOFTOPS WERE JUST MADE FOR COSTUME-CHANGING.

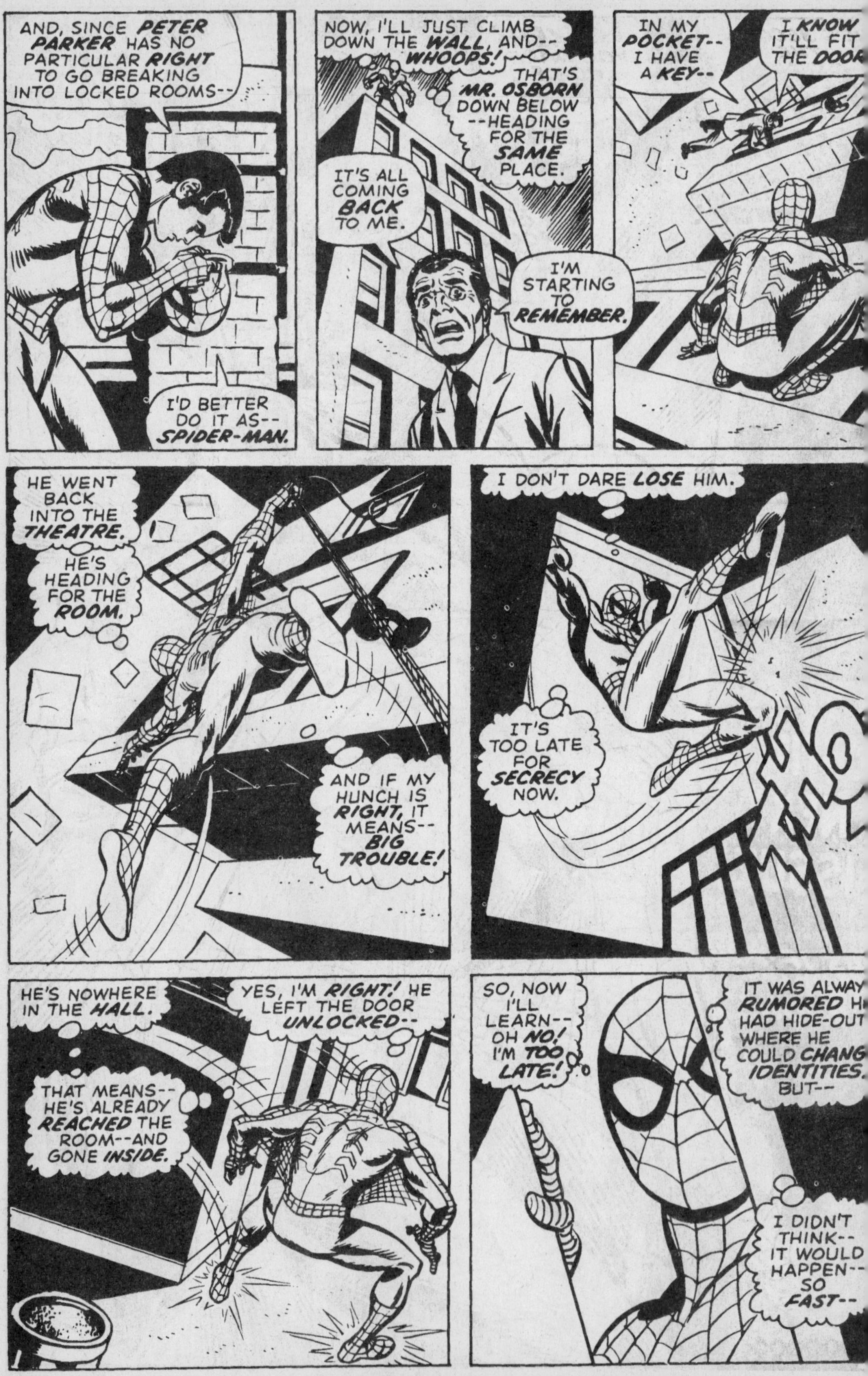
AND, SINCE PETER PARKER HAS NO PARTICULAR RIGHT TO GO BREAKING INTO LOCKED ROOMS--
I'D BETTER DO IT AS-- SPIDER-MAN.
NOW, I'LL JUST CLIMB DOWN THE WALL, AND-- WHOOPS!
THAT'S MR. OSBORN DOWN BELOW --HEADING FOR THE SAME PLACE.
IT'S ALL COMING BACK TO ME.
I'M STARTING TO REMEMBER.
IN MY POCKET-- I HAVE A KEY--
I KNOW IT'LL FIT THE DOOR
HE WENT BACK INTO THE THEATRE.
HE'S HEADING FOR THE ROOM.
AND IF MY HUNCH IS RIGHT, IT MEANS-- BIG TROUBLE!
I DON'T DARE LOSE HIM.
IT'S TOO LATE FOR SECRECY NOW.
HE'S NOWHERE IN THE HALL.
YES, I'M RIGHT! HE LEFT THE DOOR UNLOCKED--
THAT MEANS-- HE'S ALREADY REACHED THE ROOM--AND GONE INSIDE.
SO, NOW I'LL LEARN-- OH NO! I'M TOO LATE!
IT WAS ALWAY RUMORED H HAD HIDE-OUT WHERE HE COULD CHANG IDENTITIES. BUT--
I DIDN'T THINK-- IT WOULD HAPPEN-- SO FAST--

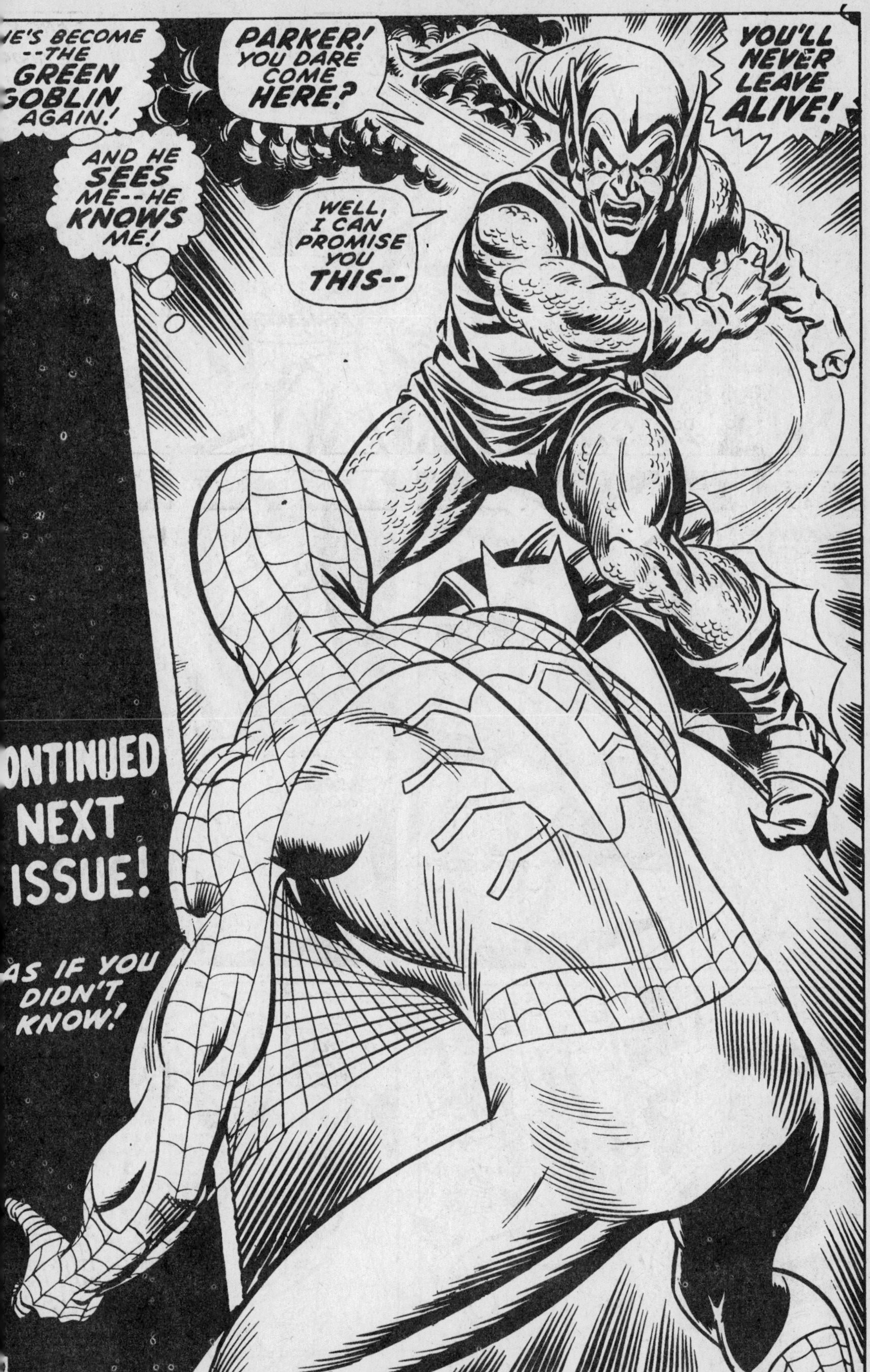

E'S BECOME --THE GREEN GOBLIN AGAIN.!
AND HE SEES ME--HE KNOWS ME!
PARKER! YOU DARE COME HERE?
WELL, I CAN PROMISE YOU THIS--
YOU'LL NEVER LEAVE ALIVE!
ONTINUED NEXT ISSUE!
AS IF YOU DIDN'T KNOW!

SPIDER-MAN
15¢
97
JUNE
the AMAZING SPIDER-MAN
MARVEL COMICS GROUP
ROMITA
SPIDEY FIGHTS THE GOBLIN-- AND LOTS, LOTS MORE! 'NUFF SAID!

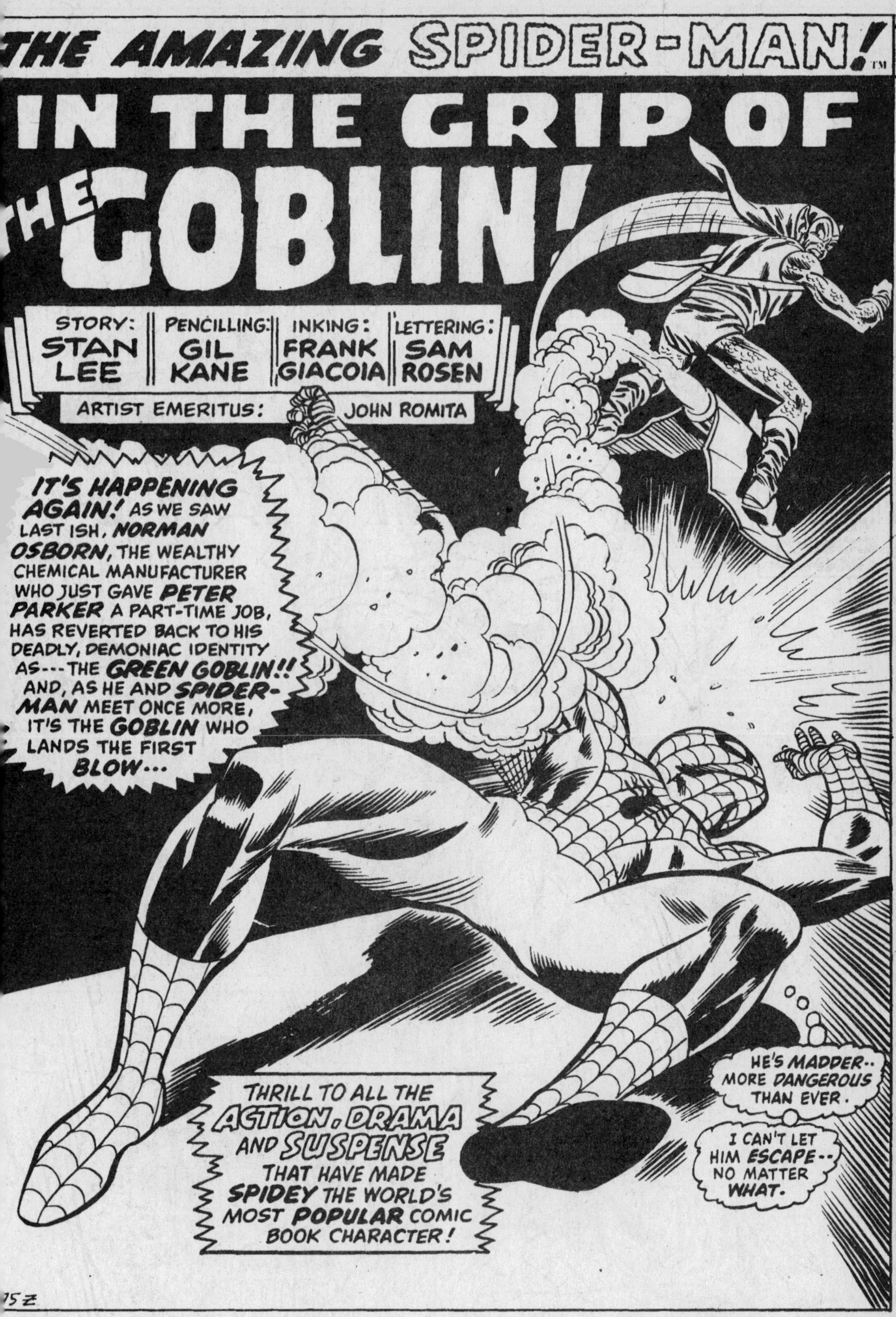
THE AMAZING SPIDER-MAN!
IN THE GRIP OF THE GOBLIN!
STORY: STAN LEE
PENCILLING: GIL KANE
INKING: FRANK GIACOIA
LETTERING: SAM ROSEN
ARTIST EMERITUS: JOHN ROMITA
IT'S HAPPENING AGAIN! AS WE SAW LAST ISH, NORMAN OSBORN, THE WEALTHY CHEMICAL MANUFACTURER WHO JUST GAVE PETER PARKER A PART-TIME JOB, HAS REVERTED BACK TO HIS DEADLY, DEMONIAC IDENTITY AS--- THE GREEN GOBLIN!! AND, AS HE AND SPIDER-MAN MEET ONCE MORE, IT'S THE GOBLIN WHO LANDS THE FIRST BLOW...
HE'S MADDER.. MORE DANGEROUS THAN EVER.
I CAN'T LET HIM ESCAPE-- NO MATTER WHAT.
THRILL TO ALL THE ACTION, DRAMA AND SUSPENSE THAT HAVE MADE SPIDEY THE WORLD'S MOST POPULAR COMIC BOOK CHARACTER!

THIS'LL STOP HIM!

:WHOOPFF!:

SO! YOU'RE TEMPTING ME TO DESTROY YOU AT ONCE, EH?

THWIPP!

OH NO! I FORGOT HIS WEAPONS -- IN HIS GOBLIN BAG.

THIS LITTLE PUMPKIN SHOULD AFFORD US SOME AMUSE-MENT--

--ONCE I REMOVE ITS LITTLE HEAD PLUG.

IF IT'S AN EXPLOSIVE, IT'LL GET YOU, TOO!

WHAT'S HAPPENING? I SEE LOTS OF GOBLINS NOW---

EVERYTHING SPINNING AROUND! TH VAPOR-- IT A GAS!

I--SHOULD HAVE HELD MY BREATH

YOU SHOULD HAVE KNOWN--- THE GOBLIN WOULD NEVER USE ANYTHING AS CRUDE AS EXPLOSIVES--

--WHEN I CAN USE HALLUCI-GEN GAS!

BUT, THIS BARREN ROOM IS CRAMP-ING MY STYLE.

SO I'LL WAIT FOR YOU OUT-SIDE!

I'M SURE YOU WON'T DISAPPOIN ME---

GAS-- MUST HAVE WEAKENED ME! I-- REALLY FELT-- THAT BLOW---

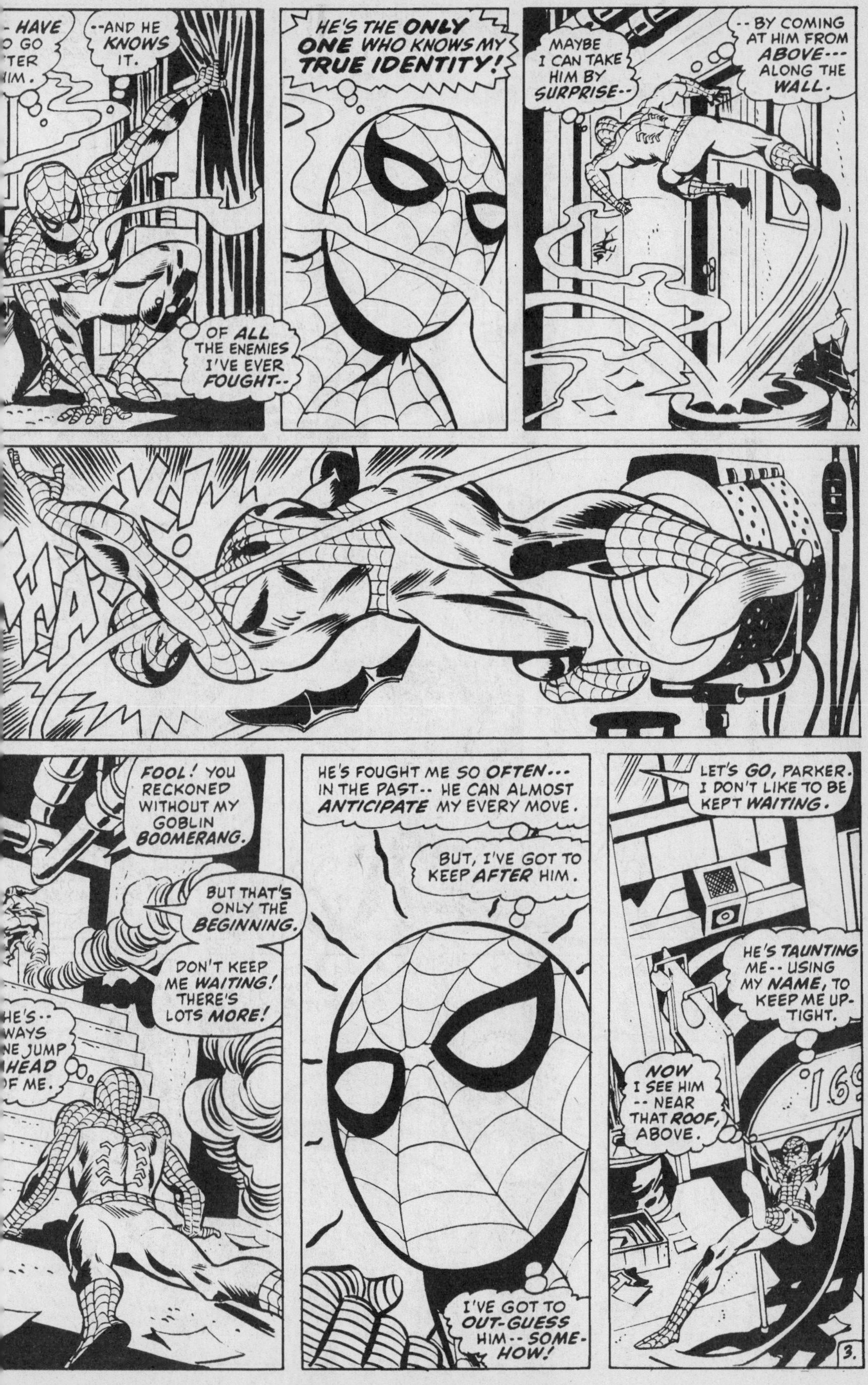

-- HAVE
TO GO
AFTER
HIM.
--AND HE KNOWS IT.
OF ALL THE ENEMIES I'VE EVER FOUGHT--
HE'S THE ONLY ONE WHO KNOWS MY TRUE IDENTITY!
MAYBE I CAN TAKE HIM BY SURPRISE--
-- BY COMING AT HIM FROM ABOVE--- ALONG THE WALL.
FOOL! YOU RECKONED WITHOUT MY GOBLIN BOOMERANG.
BUT THAT'S ONLY THE BEGINNING.
DON'T KEEP ME WAITING! THERE'S LOTS MORE!
HE'S-- ALWAYS ONE JUMP AHEAD OF ME.
HE'S FOUGHT ME SO OFTEN--- IN THE PAST-- HE CAN ALMOST ANTICIPATE MY EVERY MOVE.
BUT, I'VE GOT TO KEEP AFTER HIM.
I'VE GOT TO OUT-GUESS HIM-- SOME-HOW!
LET'S GO, PARKER. I DON'T LIKE TO BE KEPT WAITING.
HE'S TAUNTING ME-- USING MY NAME, TO KEEP ME UP-TIGHT.
NOW I SEE HIM -- NEAR THAT ROOF, ABOVE.

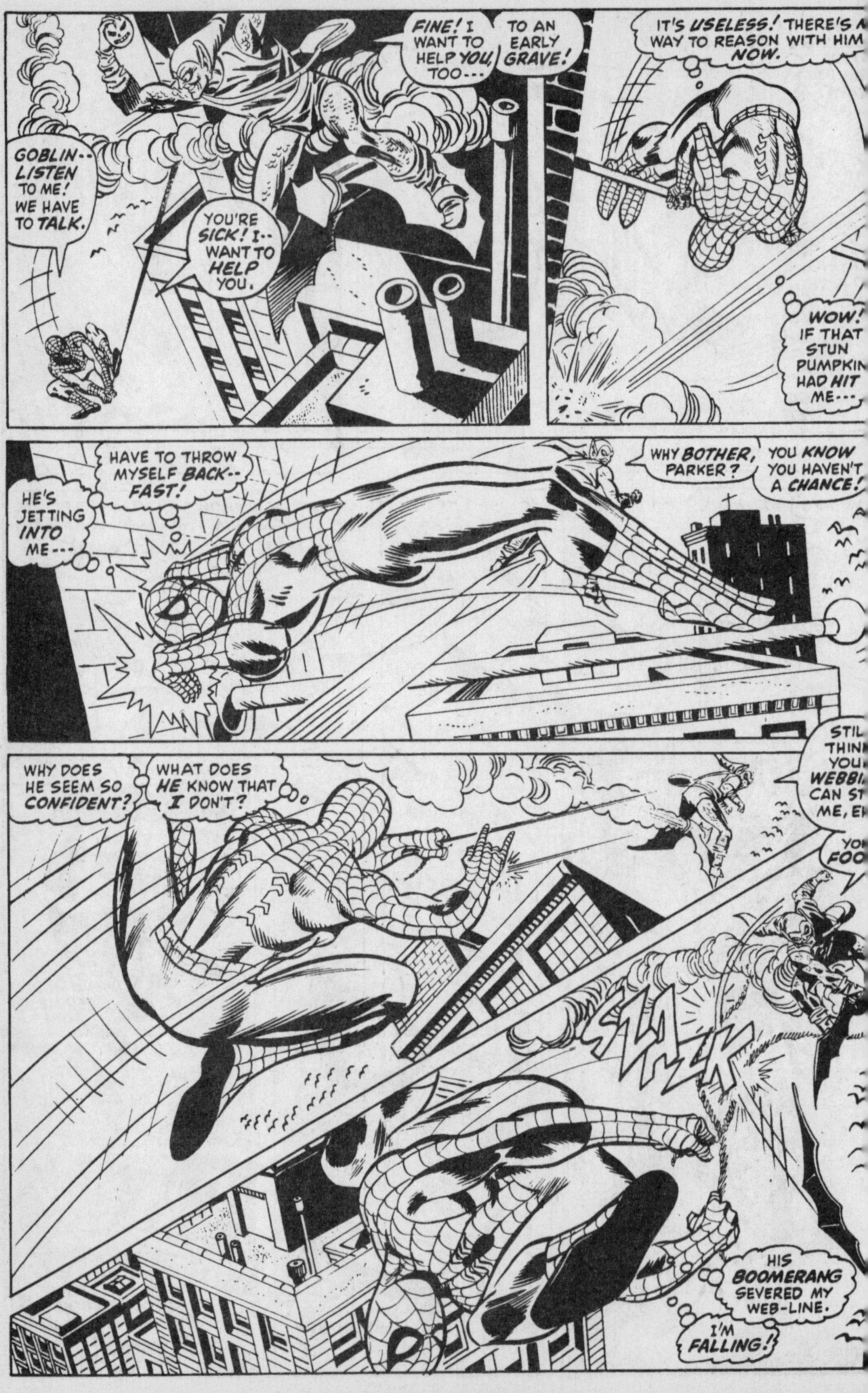
GOBLIN-- LISTEN TO ME! WE HAVE TO TALK.
YOU'RE SICK! I-- WANT TO HELP YOU.
FINE! I WANT TO HELP YOU, TOO---
TO AN EARLY GRAVE!
IT'S USELESS! THERE'S
WAY TO REASON WITH HIM NOW.
WOW! IF THAT STUN PUMPKIN HAD HIT ME---
HE'S JETTING INTO ME---
HAVE TO THROW MYSELF BACK-- FAST!
WHY BOTHER, PARKER?
YOU KNOW YOU HAVEN'T A CHANCE!
WHY DOES HE SEEM SO CONFIDENT?
WHAT DOES HE KNOW THAT I DON'T?
SLAK
HIS BOOMERANG SEVERED MY WEB-LINE.
I'M FALLING!

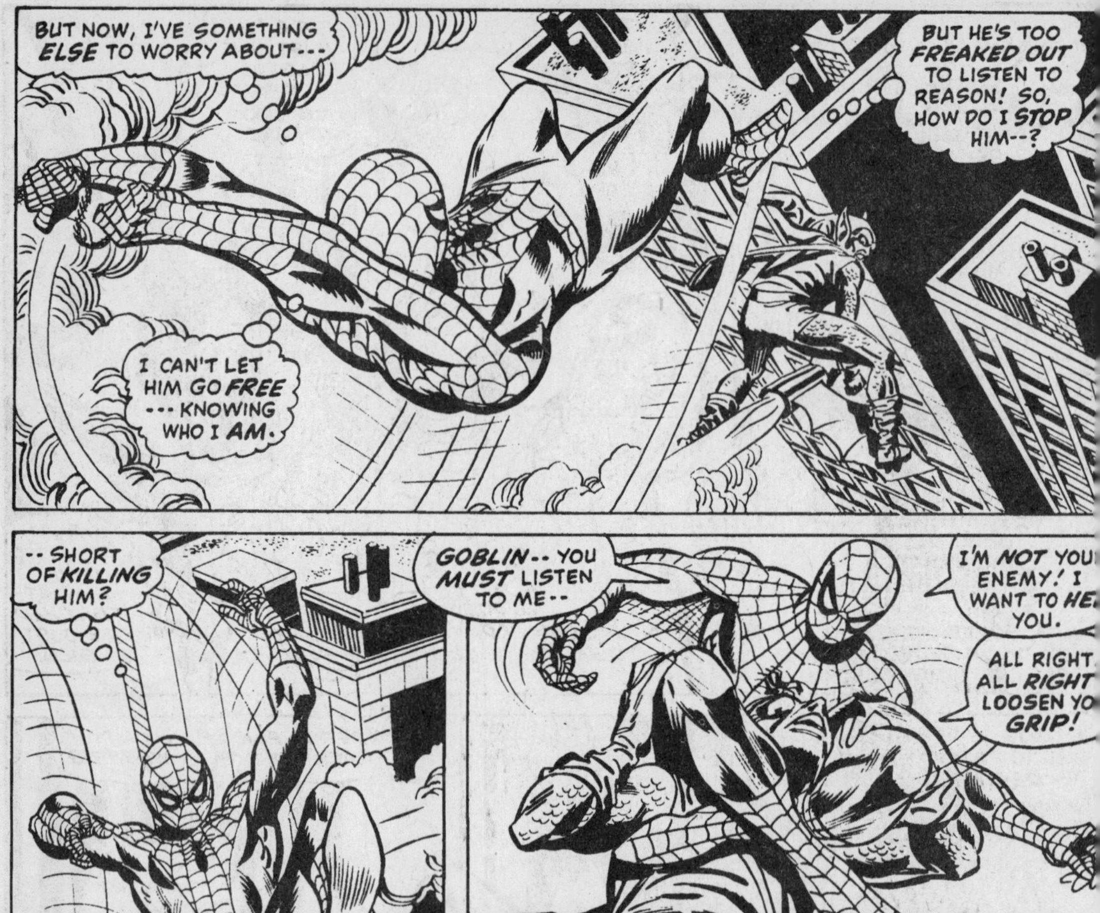

BUT NOW, I'VE SOMETHING ELSE TO WORRY ABOUT---
BUT HE'S TOO FREAKED OUT TO LISTEN TO REASON! SO, HOW DO I STOP HIM--?
I CAN'T LET HIM GO FREE --- KNOWING WHO I AM.
-- SHORT OF KILLING HIM?
BACK FOR MORE OF THE SAME, PARKER?
GOBLIN-- YOU MUST LISTEN TO ME--
I'M NOT YOU ENEMY! I WANT TO HE YOU.
ALL RIGHT ALL RIGHT LOOSEN YO GRIP!
HAH! THANK YOU, YOU CLOD.
NOW I CAN BLIND YOU WITH MY SPARKLER SPRAY.
HE-- HAS A WEAPON--- FOR EVERY-THING.
CAN'T SEE! IT'S LIKE-- A MILLION PIN-WHEELS--- DANCING IN MY BRAIN.
THIS TIME YOU'VE HAD IT.

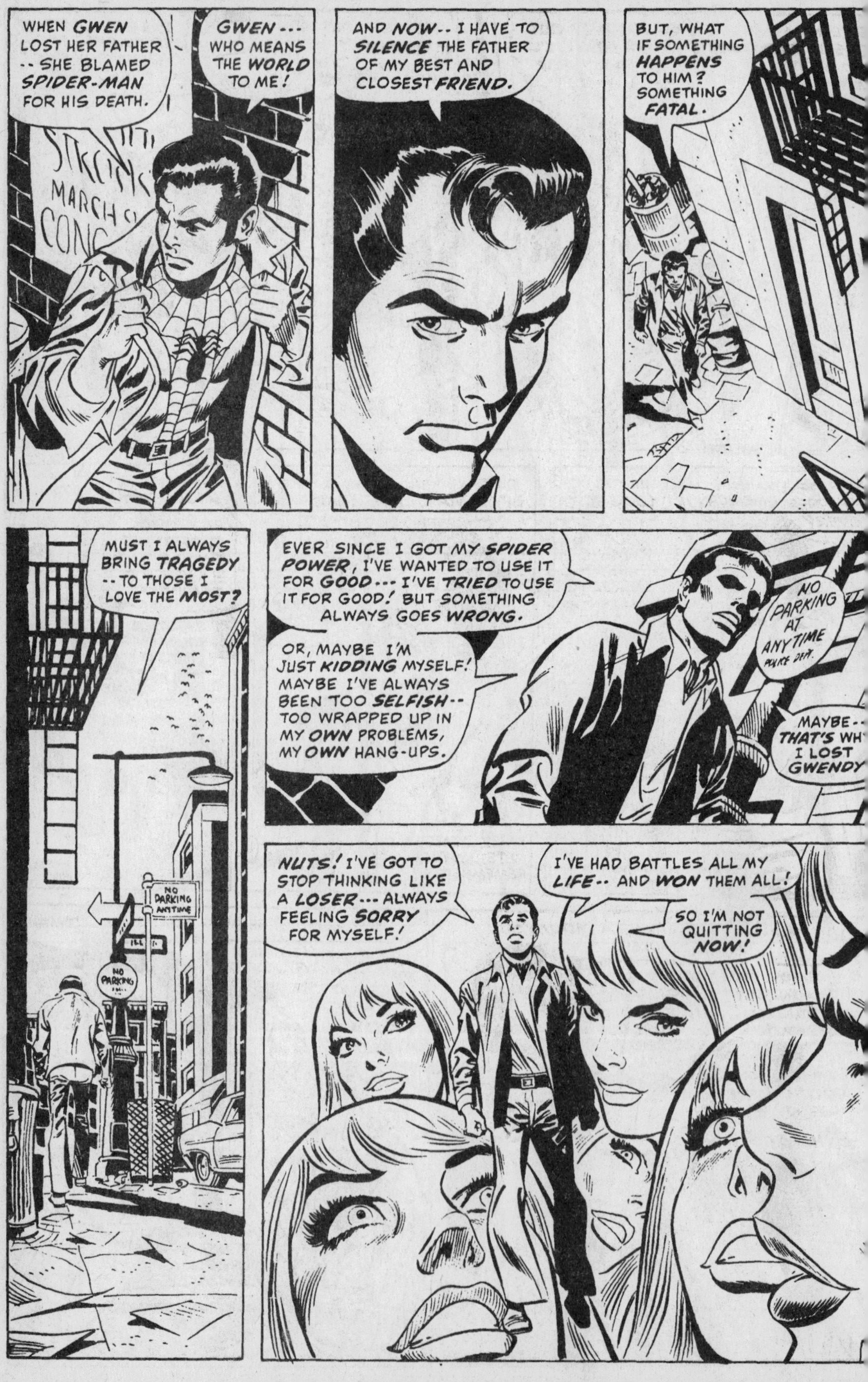
WHEN GWEN LOST HER FATHER -- SHE BLAMED SPIDER-MAN FOR HIS DEATH.
GWEN --- WHO MEANS THE WORLD TO ME!
AND NOW -- I HAVE TO SILENCE THE FATHER OF MY BEST AND CLOSEST FRIEND.
BUT, WHAT IF SOMETHING HAPPENS TO HIM? SOMETHING FATAL.
MUST I ALWAYS BRING TRAGEDY -- TO THOSE I LOVE THE MOST?
NO PARKING ANYTIME
NO PARKING
EVER SINCE I GOT MY SPIDER POWER, I'VE WANTED TO USE IT FOR GOOD --- I'VE TRIED TO USE IT FOR GOOD! BUT SOMETHING ALWAYS GOES WRONG.
OR, MAYBE I'M JUST KIDDING MYSELF! MAYBE I'VE ALWAYS BEEN TOO SELFISH -- TOO WRAPPED UP IN MY OWN PROBLEMS, MY OWN HANG-UPS.
NO PARKING AT ANYTIME POLICE DEPT.
MAYBE -- THAT'S WH I LOST GWENDY
NUTS! I'VE GOT TO STOP THINKING LIKE A LOSER --- ALWAYS FEELING SORRY FOR MYSELF!
I'VE HAD BATTLES ALL MY LIFE -- AND WON THEM ALL!
SO I'M NOT QUITTING NOW!

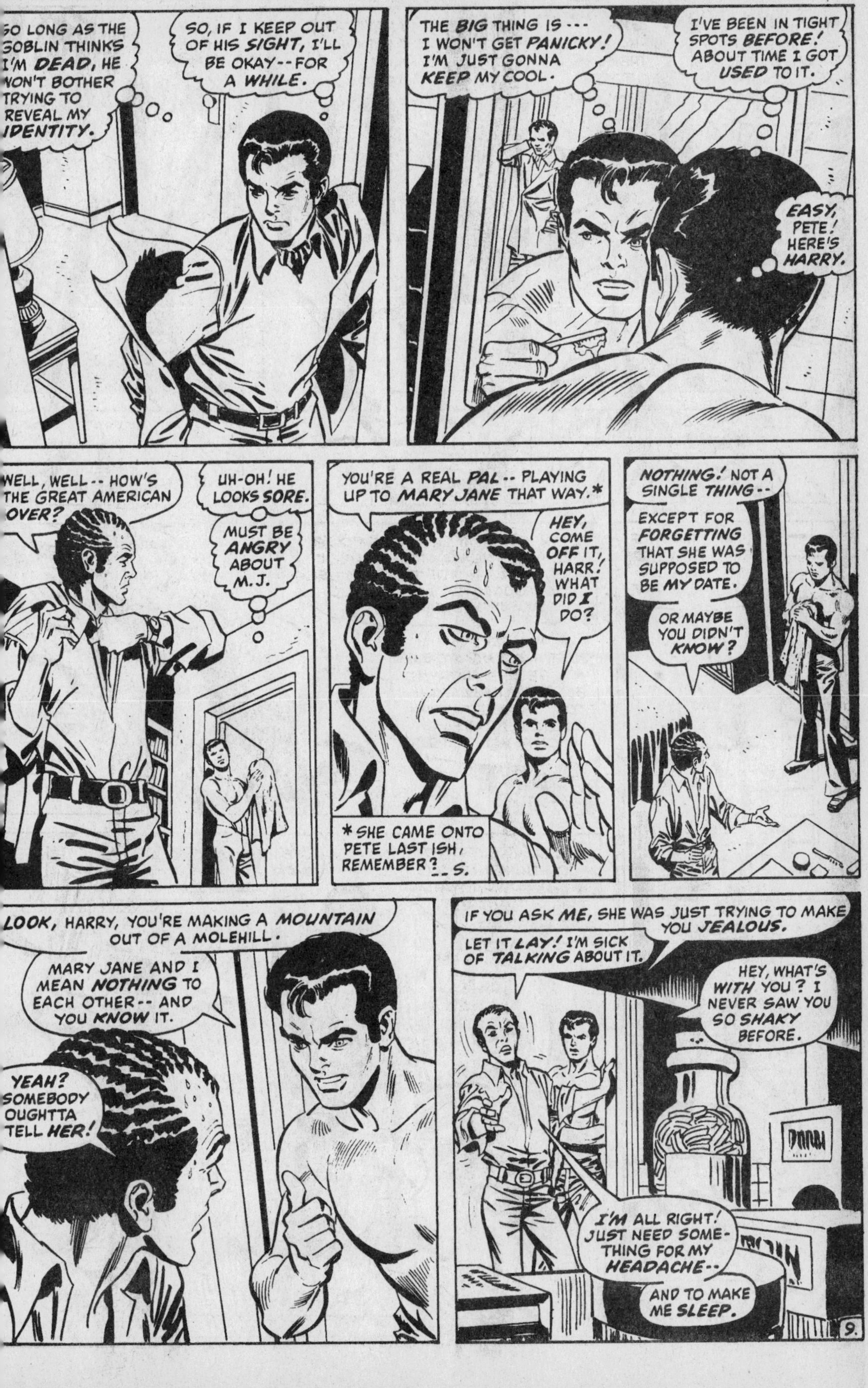
SO LONG AS THE GOBLIN THINKS I'M DEAD, HE WON'T BOTHER TRYING TO REVEAL MY IDENTITY.
SO, IF I KEEP OUT OF HIS SIGHT, I'LL BE OKAY--FOR A WHILE.
THE BIG THING IS--- I WON'T GET PANICKY! I'M JUST GONNA KEEP MY COOL.
I'VE BEEN IN TIGHT SPOTS BEFORE! ABOUT TIME I GOT USED TO IT.
EASY, PETE! HERE'S HARRY.
WELL, WELL--HOW'S THE GREAT AMERICAN LOVER?
UH-OH! HE LOOKS SORE.
MUST BE ANGRY ABOUT M.J.
YOU'RE A REAL PAL--PLAYING UP TO MARY JANE THAT WAY.*
HEY, COME OFF IT, HARR! WHAT DID I DO?
*SHE CAME ONTO PETE LAST ISH, REMEMBER?--S.
NOTHING! NOT A SINGLE THING--
EXCEPT FOR FORGETTING THAT SHE WAS SUPPOSED TO BE MY DATE.
OR MAYBE YOU DIDN'T KNOW?
LOOK, HARRY, YOU'RE MAKING A MOUNTAIN OUT OF A MOLEHILL.
MARY JANE AND I MEAN NOTHING TO EACH OTHER--AND YOU KNOW IT.
YEAH? SOMEBODY OUGHTTA TELL HER!
IF YOU ASK ME, SHE WAS JUST TRYING TO MAKE YOU JEALOUS.
LET IT LAY! I'M SICK OF TALKING ABOUT IT.
HEY, WHAT'S WITH YOU? I NEVER SAW YOU SO SHAKY BEFORE.
I'M ALL RIGHT! JUST NEED SOMETHING FOR MY HEADACHE--
AND TO MAKE ME SLEEP.
9.

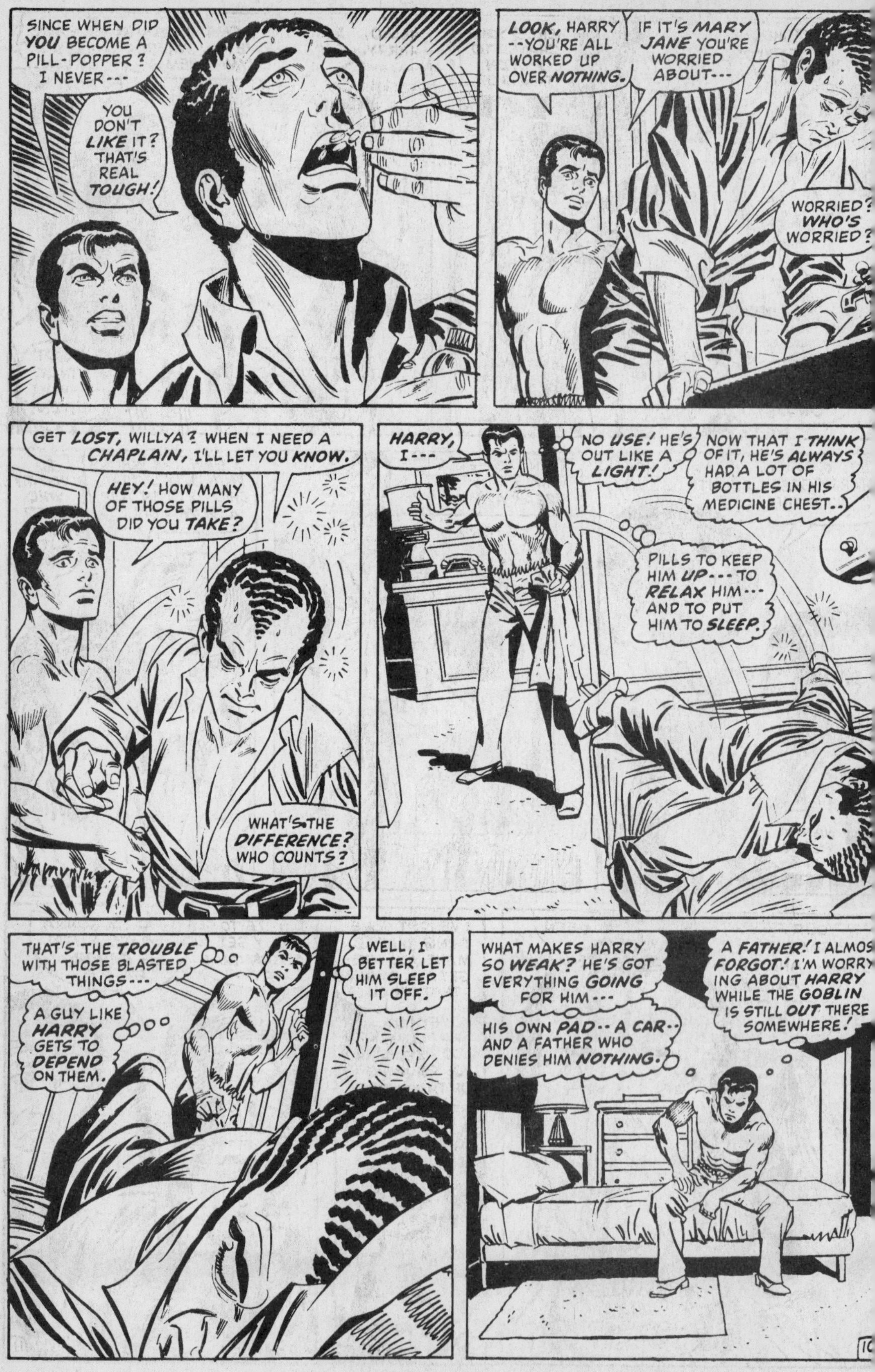
SINCE WHEN DID YOU BECOME A PILL-POPPER? I NEVER---
YOU DON'T LIKE IT? THAT'S REAL TOUGH!
LOOK, HARRY --YOU'RE ALL WORKED UP OVER NOTHING.
IF IT'S MARY JANE YOU'RE WORRIED ABOUT---
WORRIED? WHO'S WORRIED?
GET LOST, WILLYA? WHEN I NEED A CHAPLAIN, I'LL LET YOU KNOW.
HEY! HOW MANY OF THOSE PILLS DID YOU TAKE?
WHAT'S THE DIFFERENCE? WHO COUNTS?
HARRY, I---
NO USE! HE'S OUT LIKE A LIGHT!
NOW THAT I THINK OF IT, HE'S ALWAYS HAD A LOT OF BOTTLES IN HIS MEDICINE CHEST..
PILLS TO KEEP HIM UP---TO RELAX HIM---AND TO PUT HIM TO SLEEP.
THAT'S THE TROUBLE WITH THOSE BLASTED THINGS---
A GUY LIKE HARRY GETS TO DEPEND ON THEM.
WELL, I BETTER LET HIM SLEEP IT OFF.
WHAT MAKES HARRY SO WEAK? HE'S GOT EVERYTHING GOING FOR HIM---
HIS OWN PAD--A CAR--AND A FATHER WHO DENIES HIM NOTHING.
A FATHER! I ALMOS FORGOT! I'M WORRY ING ABOUT HARRY WHILE THE GOBLIN IS STILL OUT THERE SOMEWHERE!
10

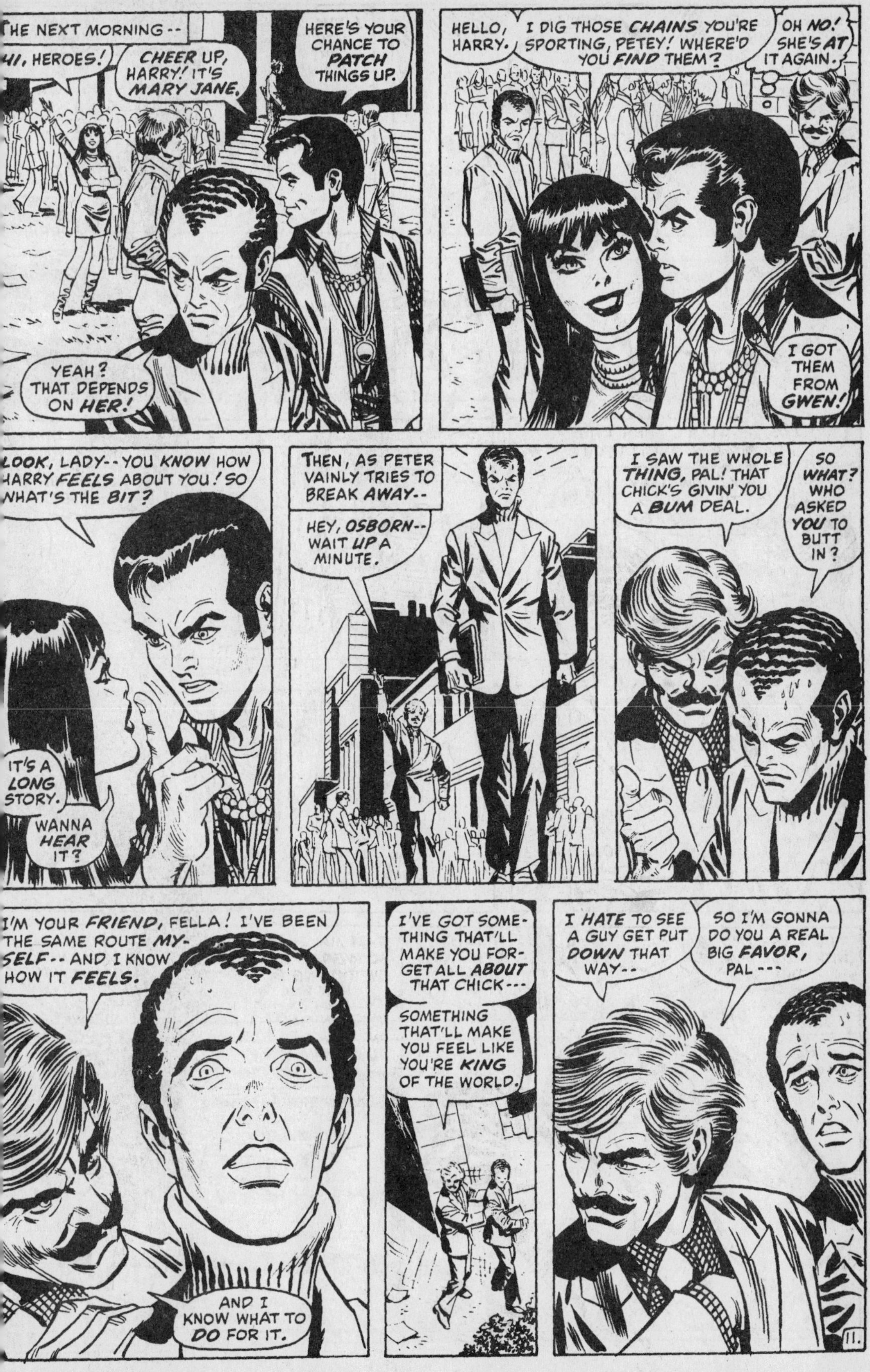
THE NEXT MORNING --
HI, HEROES!
CHEER UP, HARRY! IT'S MARY JANE.
HERE'S YOUR CHANCE TO PATCH THINGS UP.
YEAH? THAT DEPENDS ON HER!
HELLO, HARRY.
I DIG THOSE CHAINS YOU'RE SPORTING, PETEY! WHERE'D YOU FIND THEM?
OH NO! SHE'S AT IT AGAIN.
I GOT THEM FROM GWEN!
LOOK, LADY-- YOU KNOW HOW HARRY FEELS ABOUT YOU! SO WHAT'S THE BIT?
IT'S A LONG STORY.
WANNA HEAR IT?
THEN, AS PETER VAINLY TRIES TO BREAK AWAY--
HEY, OSBORN-- WAIT UP A MINUTE.
I SAW THE WHOLE THING, PAL! THAT CHICK'S GIVIN' YOU A BUM DEAL.
SO WHAT? WHO ASKED YOU TO BUTT IN?
I'M YOUR FRIEND, FELLA! I'VE BEEN THE SAME ROUTE MY-SELF-- AND I KNOW HOW IT FEELS.
AND I KNOW WHAT TO DO FOR IT.
I'VE GOT SOME-THING THAT'LL MAKE YOU FOR-GET ALL ABOUT THAT CHICK---
SOMETHING THAT'LL MAKE YOU FEEL LIKE YOU'RE KING OF THE WORLD.
I HATE TO SEE A GUY GET PUT DOWN THAT WAY--
SO I'M GONNA DO YOU A REAL BIG FAVOR, PAL---
11.

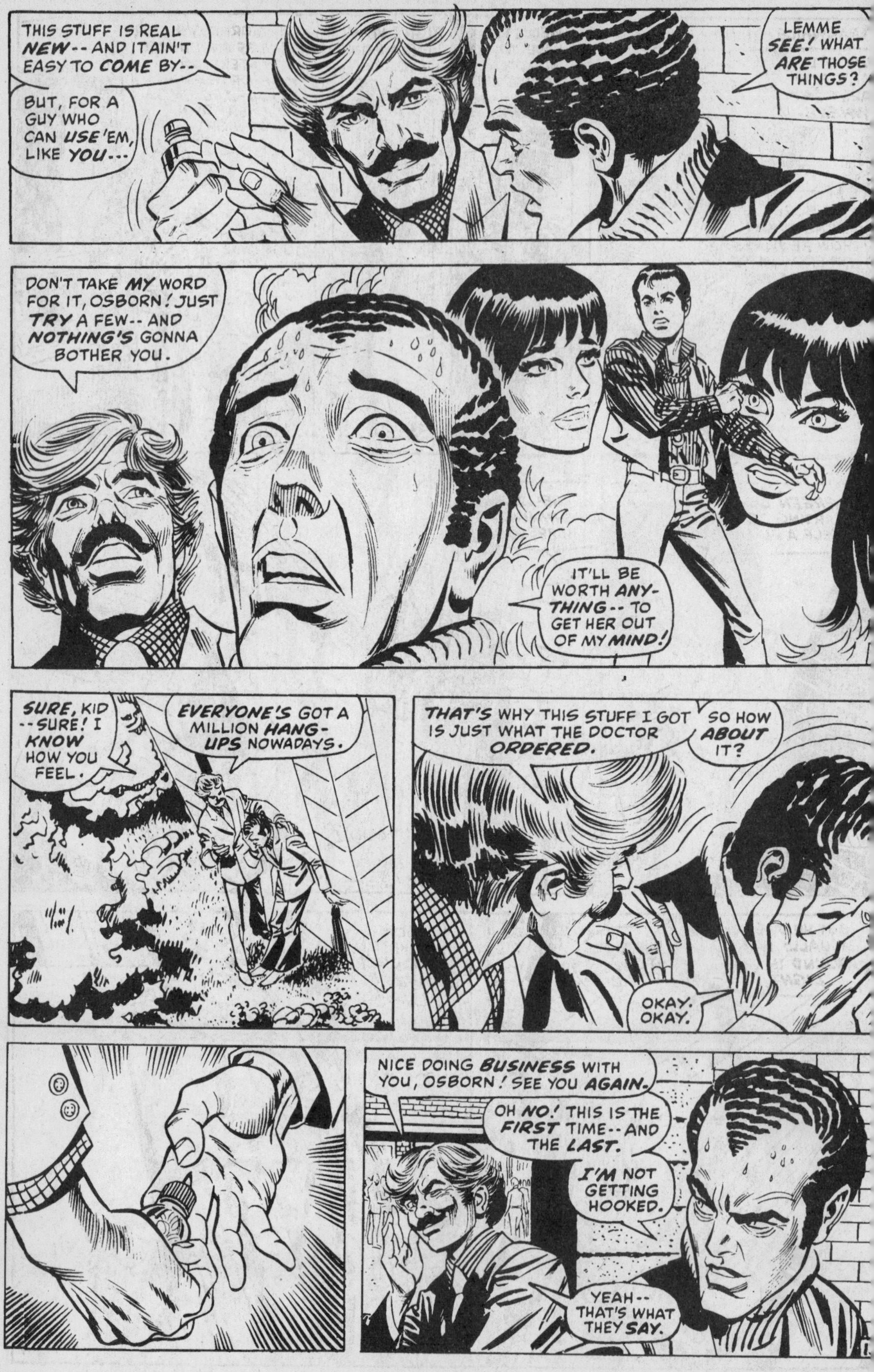
THIS STUFF IS REAL NEW-- AND IT AIN'T EASY TO COME BY--
BUT, FOR A GUY WHO CAN USE 'EM, LIKE YOU...
LEMME SEE! WHAT ARE THOSE THINGS?
DON'T TAKE MY WORD FOR IT, OSBORN! JUST TRY A FEW-- AND NOTHING'S GONNA BOTHER YOU.
IT'LL BE WORTH ANYTHING-- TO GET HER OUT OF MY MIND!
SURE, KID --SURE! I KNOW HOW YOU FEEL.
EVERYONE'S GOT A MILLION HANG-UPS NOWADAYS.
THAT'S WHY THIS STUFF I GOT IS JUST WHAT THE DOCTOR ORDERED.
SO HOW ABOUT IT?
OKAY. OKAY.
NICE DOING BUSINESS WITH YOU, OSBORN! SEE YOU AGAIN.
OH NO! THIS IS THE FIRST TIME-- AND THE LAST.
I'M NOT GETTING HOOKED.
YEAH-- THAT'S WHAT THEY SAY.

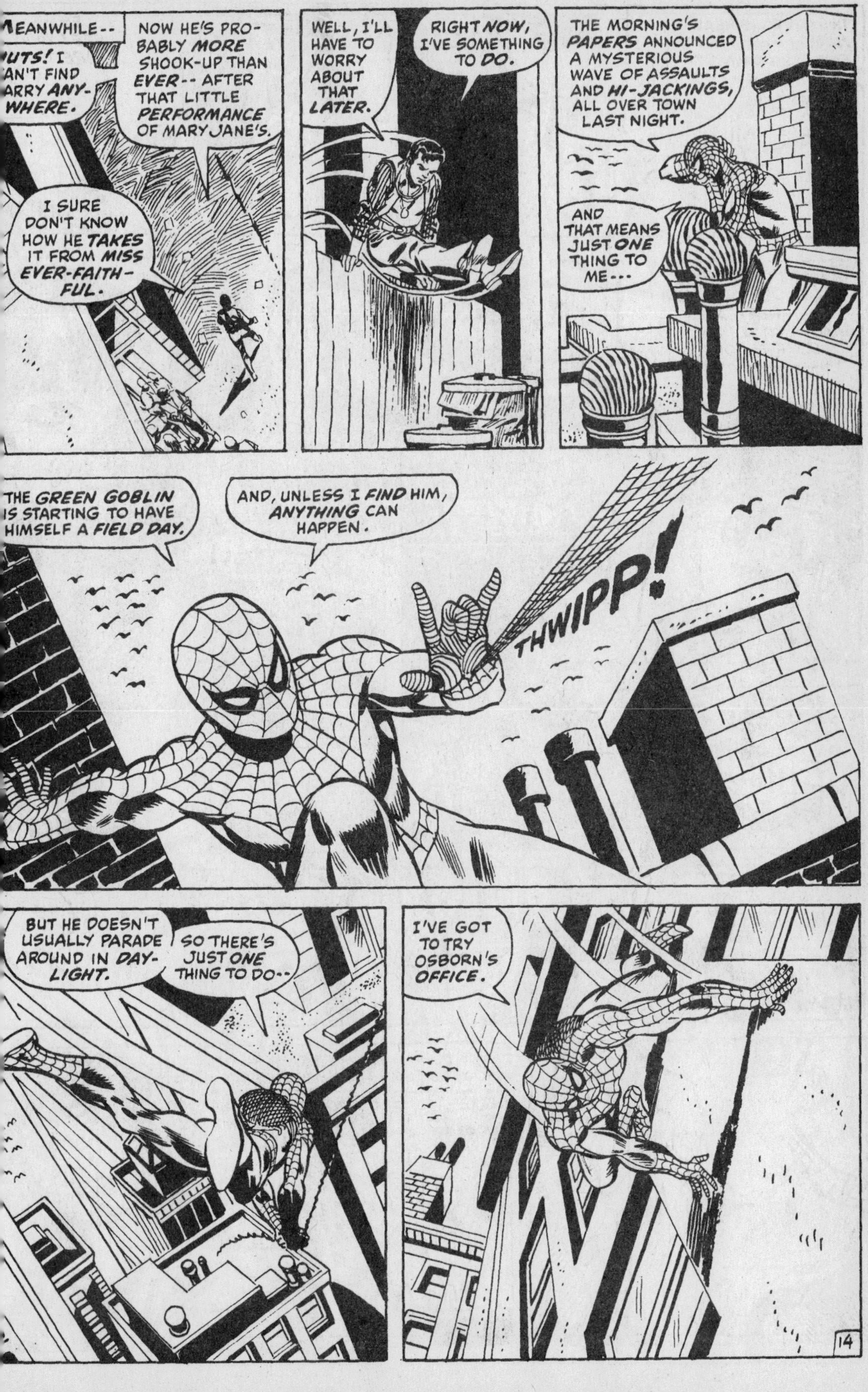
MEANWHILE--
NUTS! I CAN'T FIND HARRY ANYWHERE.
NOW HE'S PROBABLY MORE SHOOK-UP THAN EVER-- AFTER THAT LITTLE PERFORMANCE OF MARY JANE'S.
I SURE DON'T KNOW HOW HE TAKES IT FROM MISS EVER-FAITHFUL.
WELL, I'LL HAVE TO WORRY ABOUT THAT LATER.
RIGHT NOW, I'VE SOMETHING TO DO.
THE MORNING'S PAPERS ANNOUNCED A MYSTERIOUS WAVE OF ASSAULTS AND HI-JACKINGS, ALL OVER TOWN LAST NIGHT.
AND THAT MEANS JUST ONE THING TO ME---
THE GREEN GOBLIN IS STARTING TO HAVE HIMSELF A FIELD DAY.
AND, UNLESS I FIND HIM, ANYTHING CAN HAPPEN.
THWIPP!
BUT HE DOESN'T USUALLY PARADE AROUND IN DAYLIGHT.
SO THERE'S JUST ONE THING TO DO--
I'VE GOT TO TRY OSBORN'S OFFICE.
14

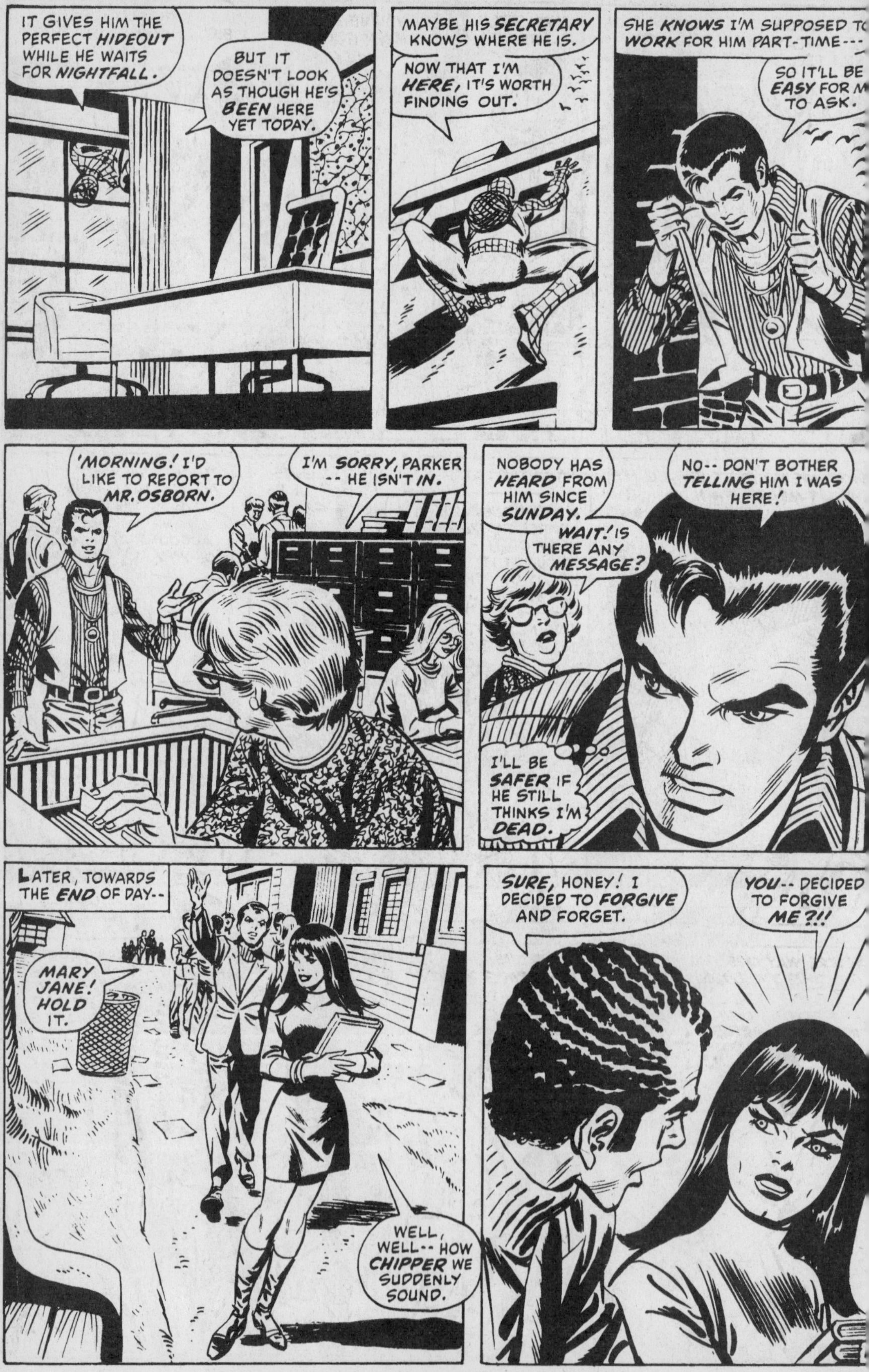

IT GIVES HIM THE PERFECT HIDEOUT WHILE HE WAITS FOR NIGHTFALL.
BUT IT DOESN'T LOOK AS THOUGH HE'S BEEN HERE YET TODAY.
MAYBE HIS SECRETARY KNOWS WHERE HE IS.
NOW THAT I'M HERE, IT'S WORTH FINDING OUT.
SHE KNOWS I'M SUPPOSED TO WORK FOR HIM PART-TIME---
SO IT'LL BE EASY FOR ME TO ASK.
'MORNING! I'D LIKE TO REPORT TO MR. OSBORN.
I'M SORRY, PARKER -- HE ISN'T IN.
NOBODY HAS HEARD FROM HIM SINCE SUNDAY.
WAIT! IS THERE ANY MESSAGE?
NO-- DON'T BOTHER TELLING HIM I WAS HERE!
I'LL BE SAFER IF HE STILL THINKS I'M DEAD.
LATER, TOWARDS THE END OF DAY--
MARY JANE! HOLD IT.
WELL, WELL-- HOW CHIPPER WE SUDDENLY SOUND.
SURE, HONEY! I DECIDED TO FORGIVE AND FORGET.
YOU-- DECIDED TO FORGIVE ME?!!

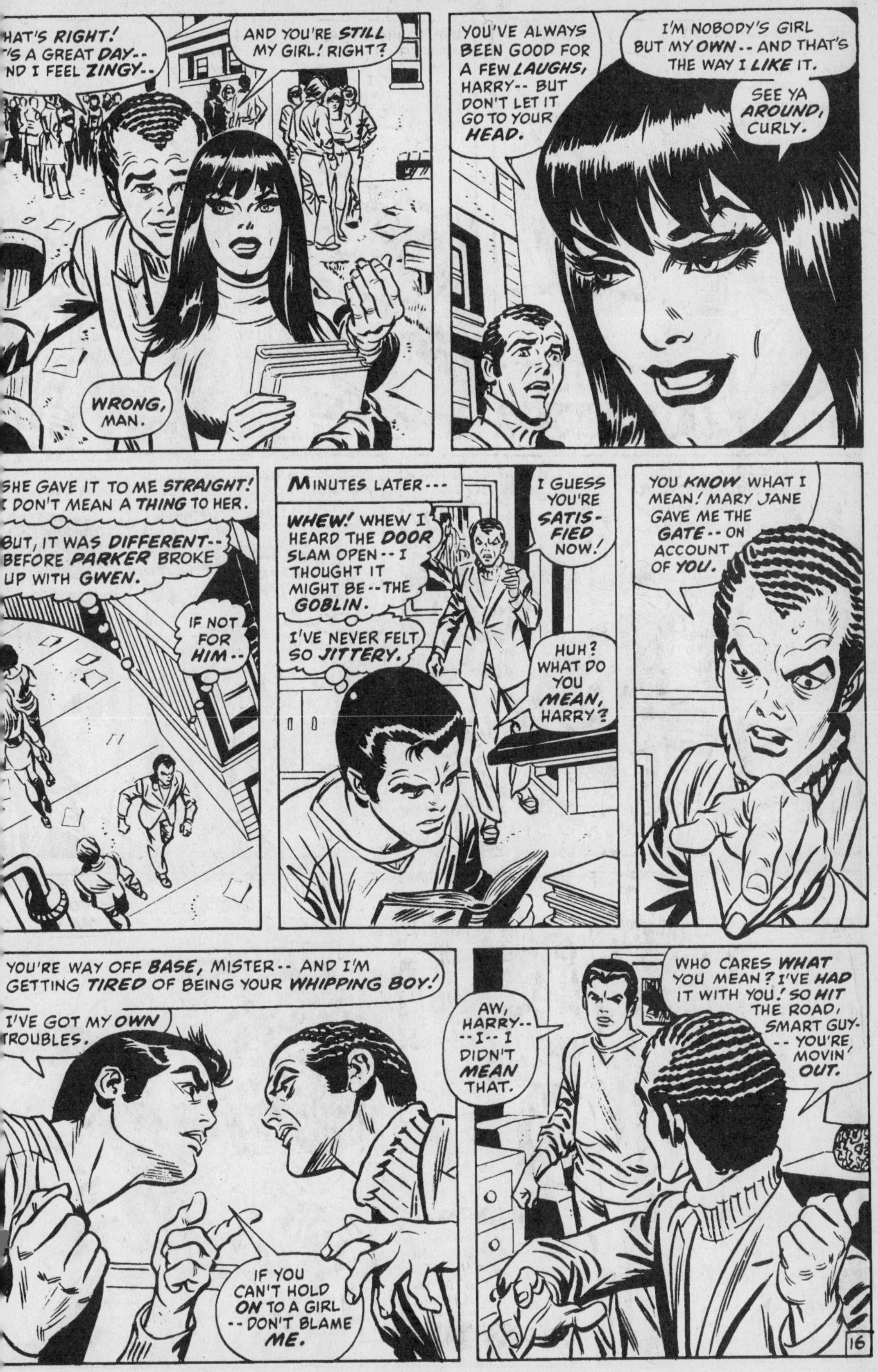

HAT'S RIGHT! T'S A GREAT DAY-- ND I FEEL ZINGY--
AND YOU'RE STILL MY GIRL! RIGHT?
WRONG, MAN.
YOU'VE ALWAYS BEEN GOOD FOR A FEW LAUGHS, HARRY-- BUT DON'T LET IT GO TO YOUR HEAD.
I'M NOBODY'S GIRL BUT MY OWN-- AND THAT'S THE WAY I LIKE IT.
SEE YA AROUND, CURLY.
SHE GAVE IT TO ME STRAIGHT! DON'T MEAN A THING TO HER.
BUT, IT WAS DIFFERENT-- BEFORE PARKER BROKE UP WITH GWEN.
IF NOT FOR HIM--
MINUTES LATER---
WHEW! WHEW I HEARD THE DOOR SLAM OPEN-- I THOUGHT IT MIGHT BE--THE GOBLIN.
I'VE NEVER FELT SO JITTERY.
I GUESS YOU'RE SATIS-FIED NOW!
HUH? WHAT DO YOU MEAN, HARRY?
YOU KNOW WHAT I MEAN! MARY JANE GAVE ME THE GATE-- ON ACCOUNT OF YOU.
YOU'RE WAY OFF BASE, MISTER-- AND I'M GETTING TIRED OF BEING YOUR WHIPPING BOY!
I'VE GOT MY OWN TROUBLES.
IF YOU CAN'T HOLD ON TO A GIRL --DON'T BLAME ME.
AW, HARRY-- --I-- I DIDN'T MEAN THAT.
WHO CARES WHAT YOU MEAN? I'VE HAD IT WITH YOU! SO HIT THE ROAD, SMART GUY- --YOU'RE MOVIN' OUT.
16

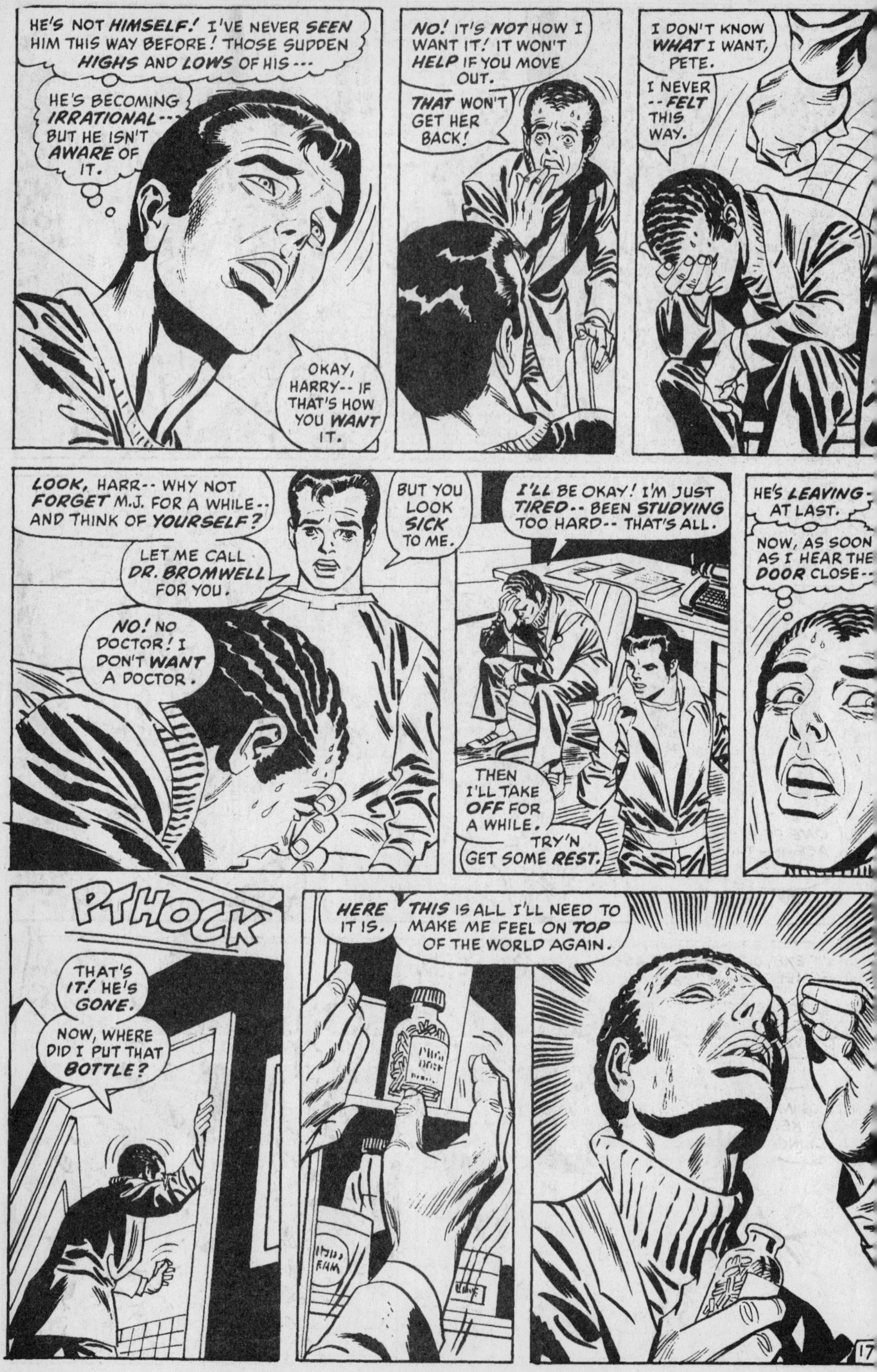
HE'S NOT HIMSELF! I'VE NEVER SEEN HIM THIS WAY BEFORE! THOSE SUDDEN HIGHS AND LOWS OF HIS---
HE'S BECOMING IRRATIONAL-- BUT HE ISN'T AWARE OF IT.
OKAY, HARRY-- IF THAT'S HOW YOU WANT IT.
NO! IT'S NOT HOW I WANT IT! IT WON'T HELP IF YOU MOVE OUT.
THAT WON'T GET HER BACK!
I DON'T KNOW WHAT I WANT, PETE.
I NEVER --FELT THIS WAY.
LOOK, HARR-- WHY NOT FORGET M.J. FOR A WHILE-- AND THINK OF YOURSELF?
LET ME CALL DR. BROMWELL FOR YOU.
NO! NO DOCTOR! I DON'T WANT A DOCTOR.
BUT YOU LOOK SICK TO ME.
I'LL BE OKAY! I'M JUST TIRED-- BEEN STUDYING TOO HARD-- THAT'S ALL.
THEN I'LL TAKE OFF FOR A WHILE.
TRY'N GET SOME REST.
HE'S LEAVING-- AT LAST.
NOW, AS SOON AS I HEAR THE DOOR CLOSE--
PTHOCK
THAT'S IT! HE'S GONE.
NOW, WHERE DID I PUT THAT BOTTLE?
HERE IT IS.
THIS IS ALL I'LL NEED TO MAKE ME FEEL ON TOP OF THE WORLD AGAIN.

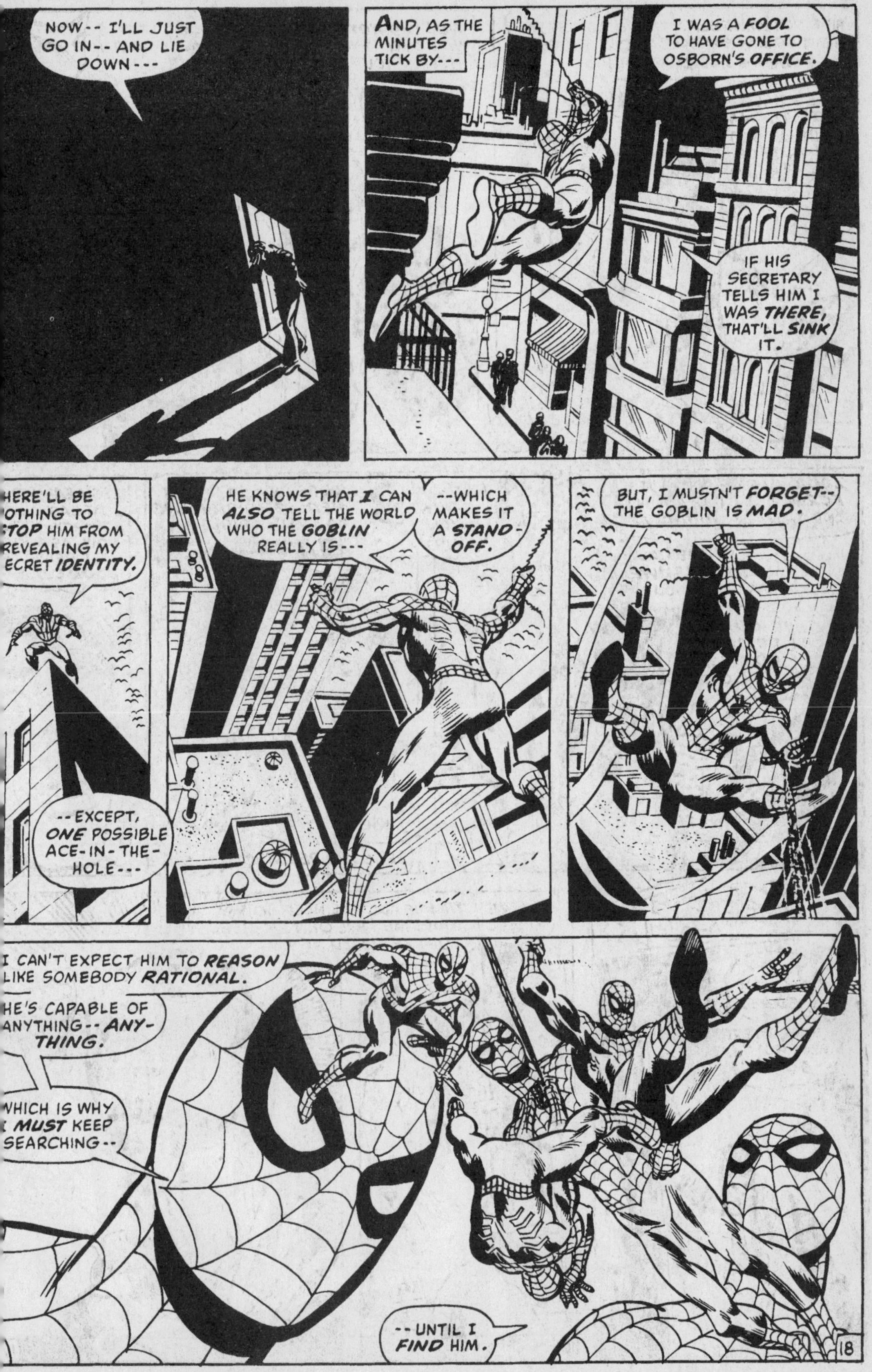

NOW-- I'LL JUST GO IN-- AND LIE DOWN---
AND, AS THE MINUTES TICK BY---
I WAS A FOOL TO HAVE GONE TO OSBORN'S OFFICE.
IF HIS SECRETARY TELLS HIM I WAS THERE, THAT'LL SINK IT.
HERE'LL BE OTHING TO STOP HIM FROM REVEALING MY ECRET IDENTITY.
--EXCEPT, ONE POSSIBLE ACE-IN-THE-HOLE---
HE KNOWS THAT I CAN ALSO TELL THE WORLD WHO THE GOBLIN REALLY IS---
--WHICH MAKES IT A STAND-OFF.
BUT, I MUSTN'T FORGET-- THE GOBLIN IS MAD.
I CAN'T EXPECT HIM TO REASON LIKE SOMEBODY RATIONAL.
HE'S CAPABLE OF ANYTHING-- ANY-THING.
WHICH IS WHY I MUST KEEP SEARCHING--
-- UNTIL I FIND HIM.
18

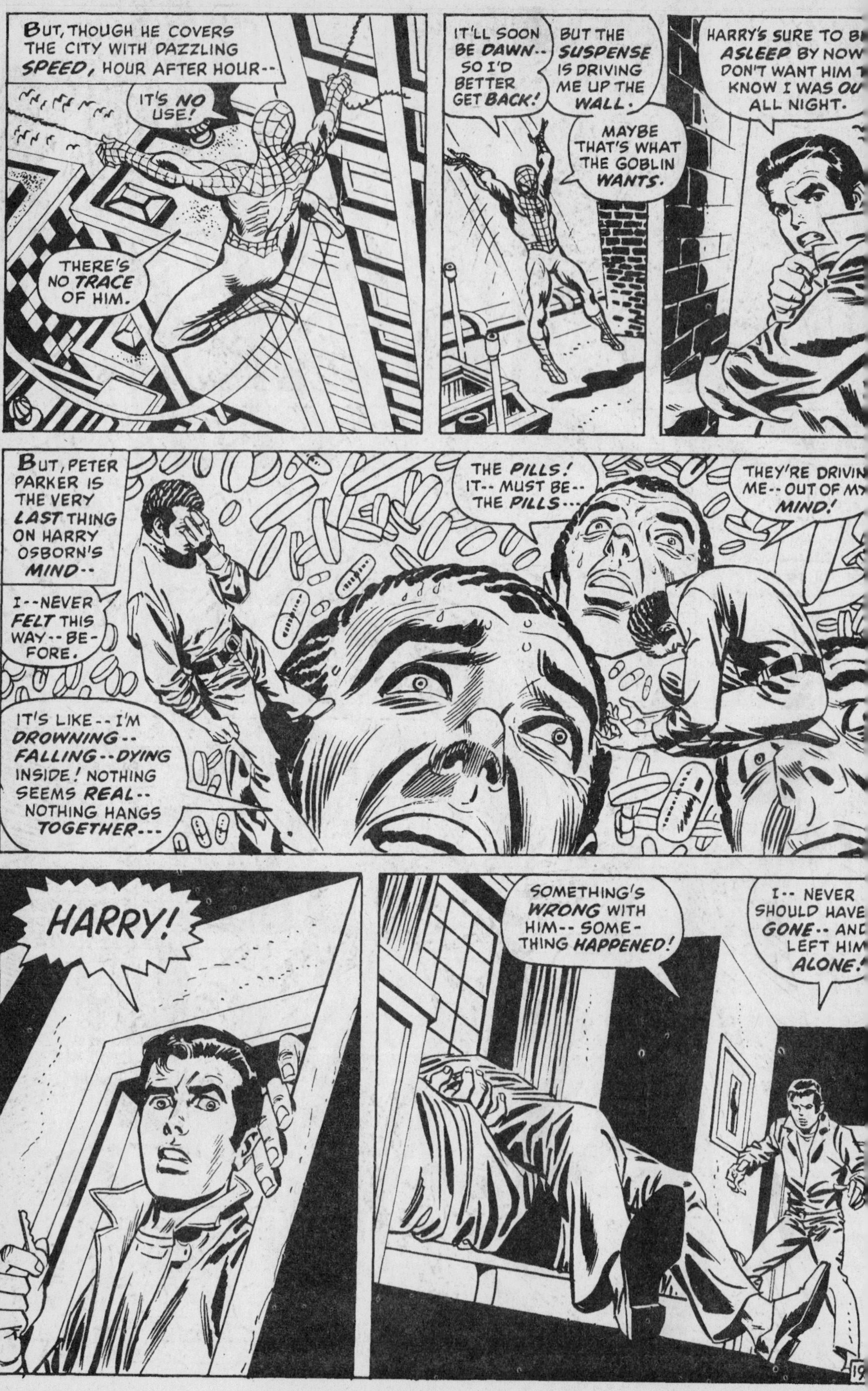
BUT, THOUGH HE COVERS THE CITY WITH DAZZLING SPEED, HOUR AFTER HOUR--
IT'S NO USE!
THERE'S NO TRACE OF HIM.
IT'LL SOON BE DAWN-- SO I'D BETTER GET BACK!
BUT THE SUSPENSE IS DRIVING ME UP THE WALL.
MAYBE THAT'S WHAT THE GOBLIN WANTS.
HARRY'S SURE TO B
ASLEEP BY NOW
DON'T WANT HIM T
KNOW I WAS OU
ALL NIGHT.
BUT, PETER PARKER IS THE VERY LAST THING ON HARRY OSBORN'S MIND--
I--NEVER FELT THIS WAY--BE-FORE.
IT'S LIKE--I'M DROWNING--FALLING--DYING INSIDE! NOTHING SEEMS REAL-- NOTHING HANGS TOGETHER---
THE PILLS! IT-- MUST BE-- THE PILLS---
THEY'RE DRIVIN
ME--OUT OF M
MIND!
HARRY!
SOMETHING'S WRONG WITH HIM-- SOME-THING HAPPENED!
I-- NEVER
SHOULD HAVE
GONE-- AN
LEFT HIM
ALONE!
19

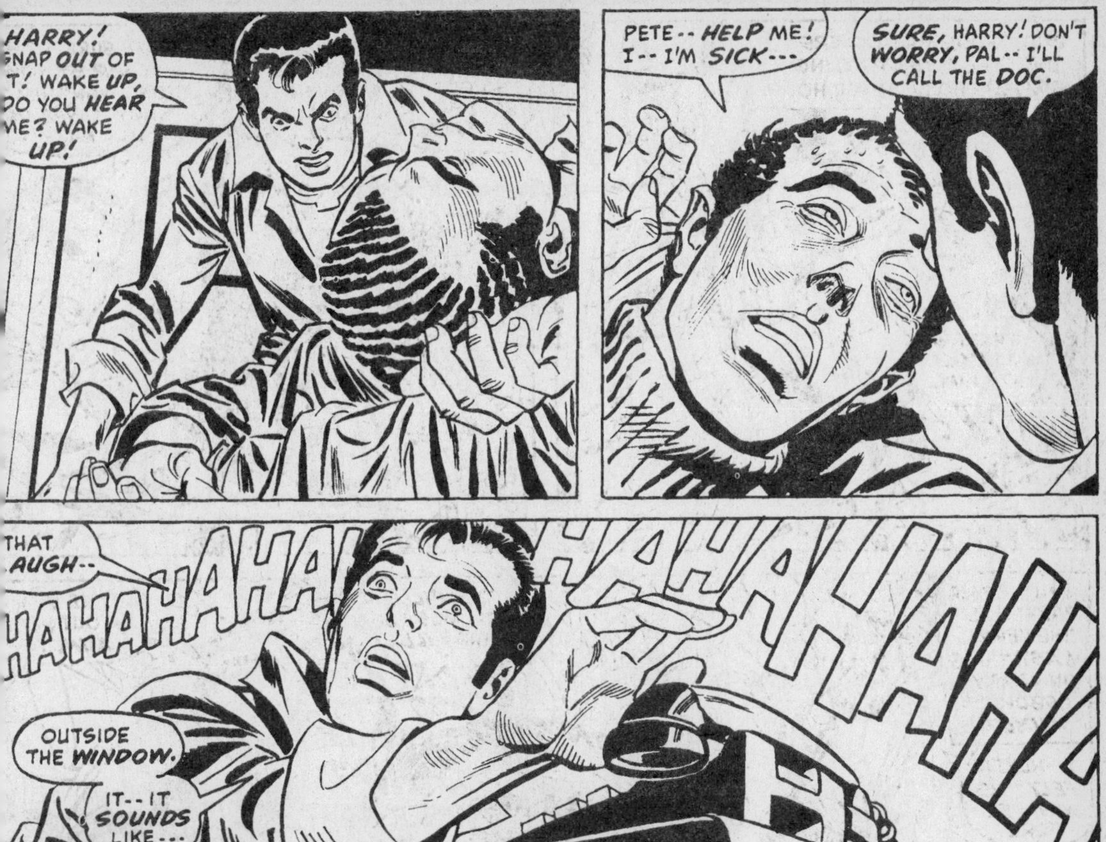

HARRY! SNAP OUT OF IT! WAKE UP, DO YOU HEAR ME? WAKE UP!
PETE-- HELP ME! I-- I'M SICK---
SURE, HARRY! DON'T WORRY, PAL-- I'LL CALL THE DOC.
THAT LAUGH--
HAHAHAHAHAHAHAHAHA
OUTSIDE THE WINDOW.
IT-- IT SOUNDS LIKE---
THE GOBLIN!
DID YOU THINK I WOULDN'T FIND YOU, PARKER?
DID YOU EXPECT THE GREEN GOBLIN TO LET SPIDER-MAN LIVE?
NEXT ISSUE: THE GOBLIN'S POWER!
20

SPIDER MAN
15¢ 98 JULY
the AMAZING SPIDER-MAN
APPROVED BY THE COMICS CODE AUTHORITY
THE GOBLIN'S POWER!
MARVEL COMICS GROUP
LOSING YOUR GRIP, SPIDER-MAN?
IT HAD TO HAPPEN..
I PLANNED IT THIS WAY!

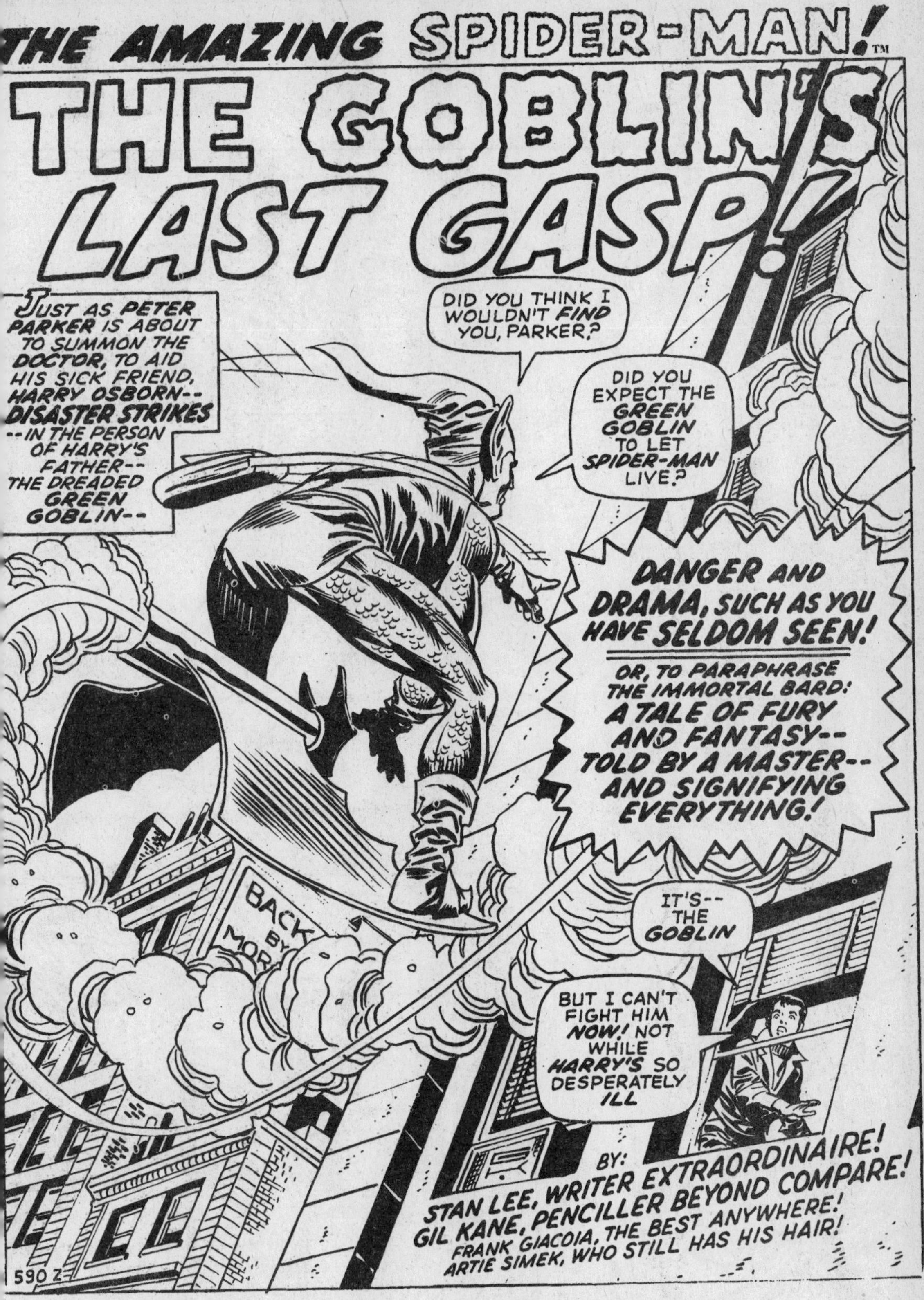
THE AMAZING SPIDER-MAN!™
THE GOBLIN'S LAST GASP!
JUST AS PETER PARKER IS ABOUT TO SUMMON THE DOCTOR, TO AID HIS SICK FRIEND, HARRY OSBORN-- DISASTER STRIKES --IN THE PERSON OF HARRY'S FATHER-- THE DREADED GREEN GOBLIN--
DID YOU THINK I WOULDN'T FIND YOU, PARKER?
DID YOU EXPECT THE GREEN GOBLIN TO LET SPIDER-MAN LIVE?
DANGER AND DRAMA, SUCH AS YOU HAVE SELDOM SEEN!
OR, TO PARAPHRASE THE IMMORTAL BARD: A TALE OF FURY AND FANTASY-- TOLD BY A MASTER-- AND SIGNIFYING EVERYTHING!
BACK BY MOR
IT'S-- THE GOBLIN
BUT I CAN'T FIGHT HIM NOW! NOT WHILE HARRY'S SO DESPERATELY ILL
BY:
STAN LEE, WRITER EXTRAORDINAIRE!
GIL KANE, PENCILLER BEYOND COMPARE!
FRANK GIACOIA, THE BEST ANYWHERE!
ARTIE SIMEK, WHO STILL HAS HIS HAIR!
590 Z

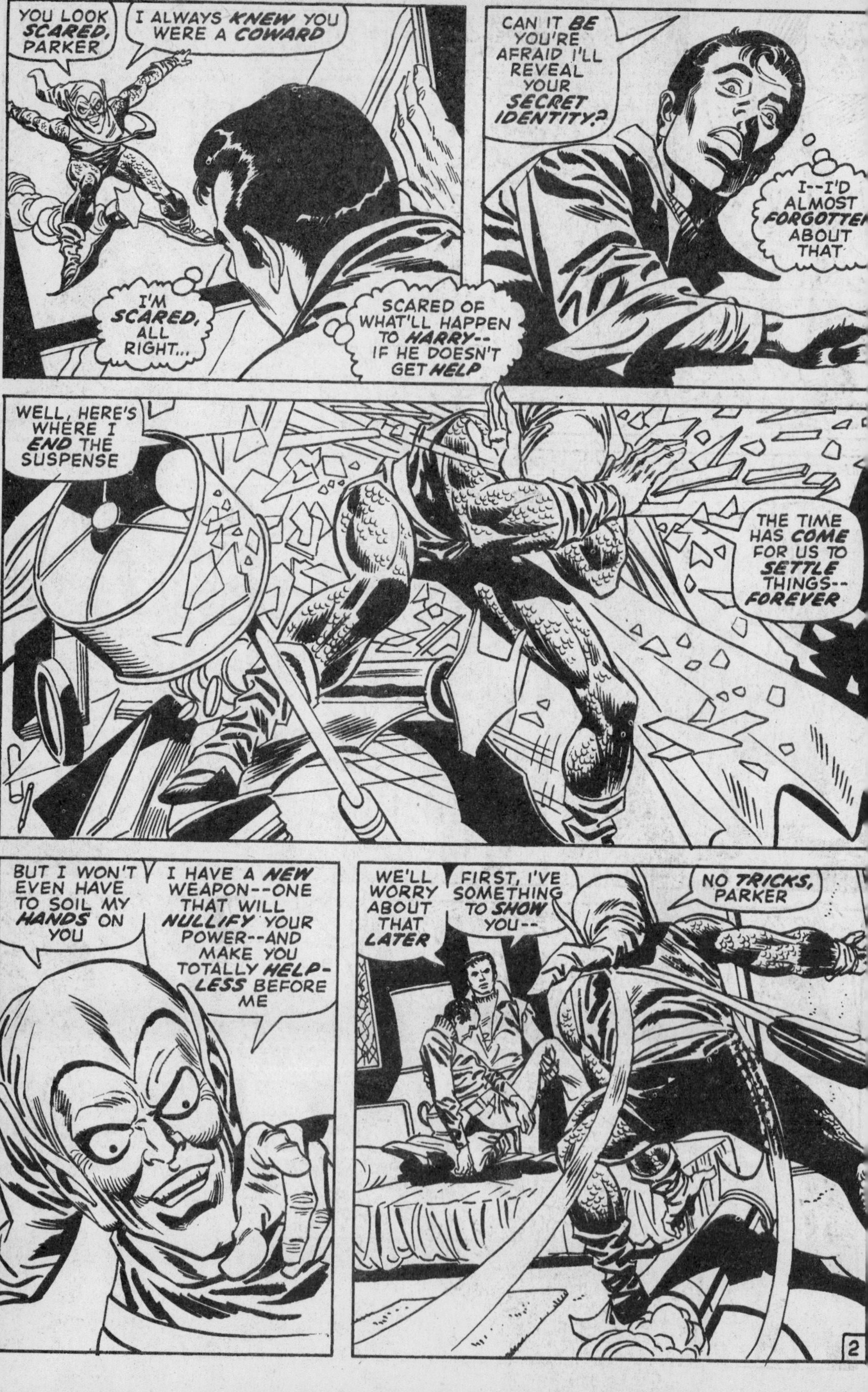
YOU LOOK SCARED, PARKER
I ALWAYS KNEW YOU WERE A COWARD
I'M SCARED, ALL RIGHT...
SCARED OF WHAT'LL HAPPEN TO HARRY-- IF HE DOESN'T GET HELP
CAN IT BE YOU'RE AFRAID I'LL REVEAL YOUR SECRET IDENTITY?
I--I'D ALMOST FORGOTTEN ABOUT THAT
WELL, HERE'S WHERE I END THE SUSPENSE
THE TIME HAS COME FOR US TO SETTLE THINGS-- FOREVER
BUT I WON'T EVEN HAVE TO SOIL MY HANDS ON YOU
I HAVE A NEW WEAPON--ONE THAT WILL NULLIFY YOUR POWER--AND MAKE YOU TOTALLY HELP-LESS BEFORE ME
WE'LL WORRY ABOUT THAT LATER
FIRST, I'VE SOMETHING TO SHOW YOU--
NO TRICKS, PARKER

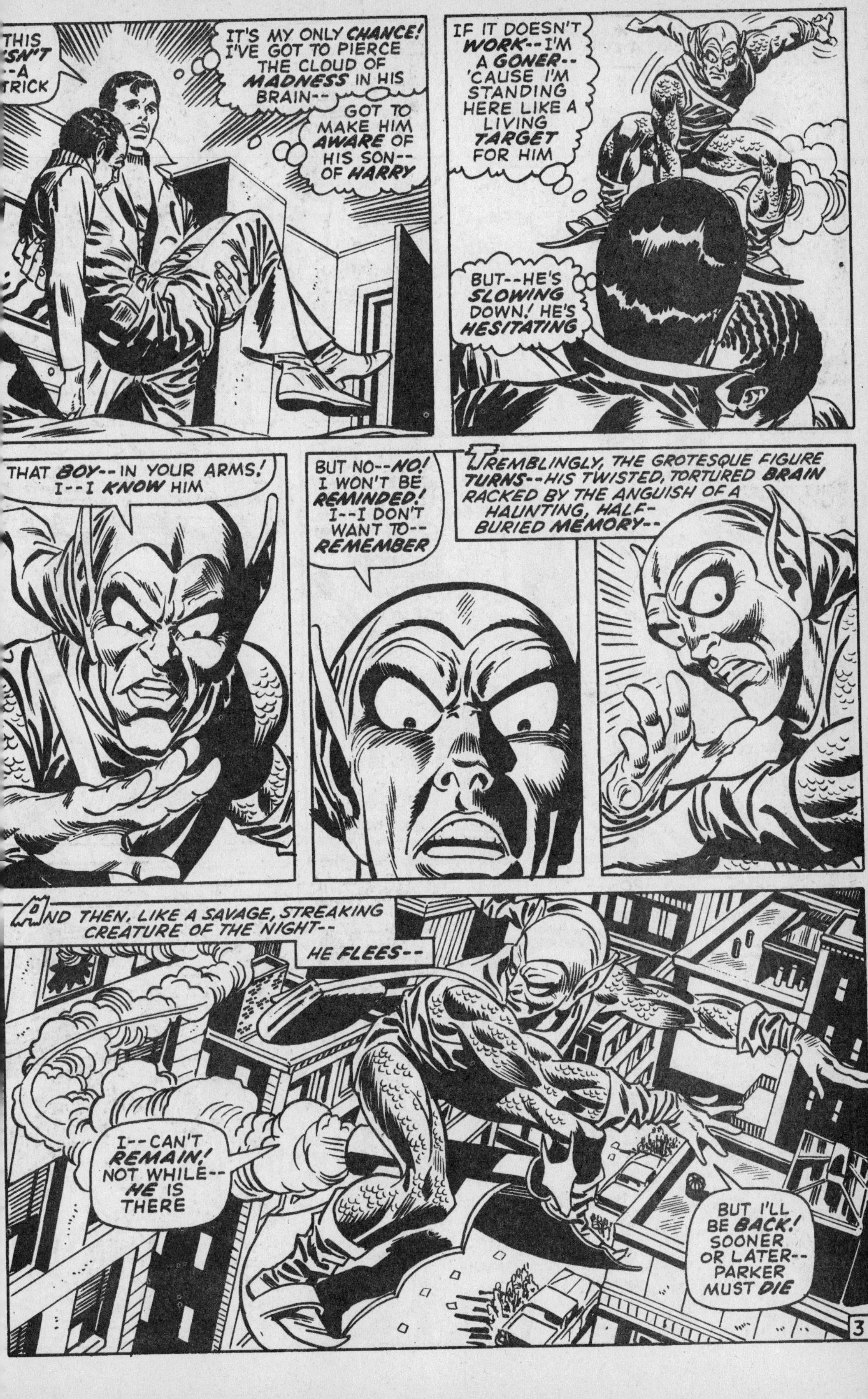
THIS SN'T --A TRICK
IT'S MY ONLY CHANCE! I'VE GOT TO PIERCE THE CLOUD OF MADNESS IN HIS BRAIN--
GOT TO MAKE HIM AWARE OF HIS SON-- OF HARRY
IF IT DOESN'T WORK--I'M A GONER-- 'CAUSE I'M STANDING HERE LIKE A LIVING TARGET FOR HIM
BUT--HE'S SLOWING DOWN! HE'S HESITATING
THAT BOY--IN YOUR ARMS! I--I KNOW HIM
BUT NO--NO! I WON'T BE REMINDED! I--I DON'T WANT TO-- REMEMBER
TREMBLINGLY, THE GROTESQUE FIGURE TURNS--HIS TWISTED, TORTURED BRAIN RACKED BY THE ANGUISH OF A HAUNTING, HALF-BURIED MEMORY--
AND THEN, LIKE A SAVAGE, STREAKING CREATURE OF THE NIGHT--
HE FLEES--
I--CAN'T REMAIN! NOT WHILE-- HE IS THERE
BUT I'LL BE BACK! SOONER OR LATER-- PARKER MUST DIE
3

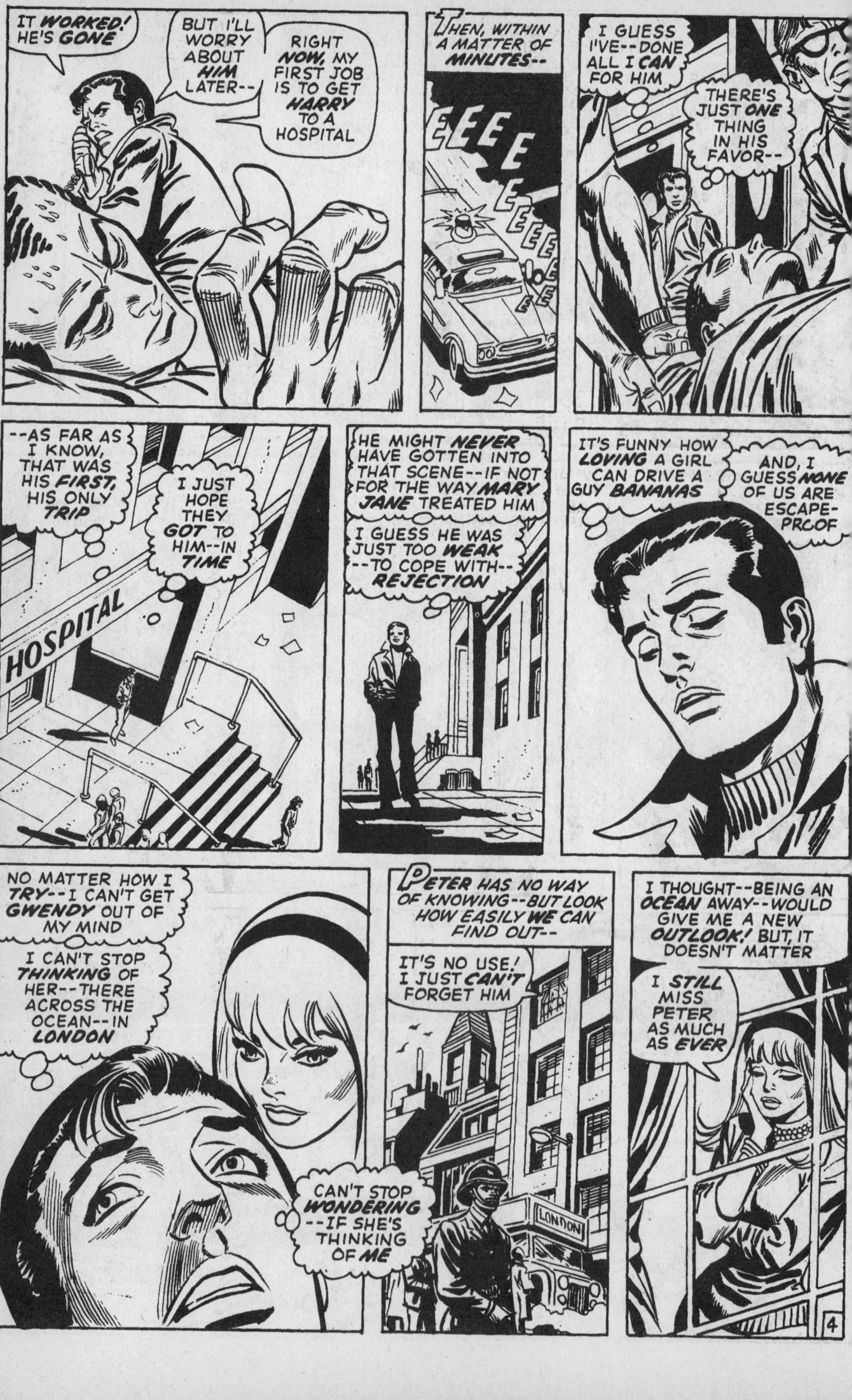

IT WORKED! HE'S GONE
BUT I'LL WORRY ABOUT HIM LATER--
RIGHT NOW, MY FIRST JOB IS TO GET HARRY TO A HOSPITAL
THEN, WITHIN A MATTER OF MINUTES--
EEEEEEEEEEEEE
I GUESS I'VE--DONE ALL I CAN FOR HIM
THERE'S JUST ONE THING IN HIS FAVOR--
--AS FAR AS I KNOW, THAT WAS HIS FIRST, HIS ONLY TRIP
I JUST HOPE THEY GOT TO HIM--IN TIME
HOSPITAL
HE MIGHT NEVER HAVE GOTTEN INTO THAT SCENE--IF NOT FOR THE WAY MARY JANE TREATED HIM
I GUESS HE WAS JUST TOO WEAK --TO COPE WITH-- REJECTION
IT'S FUNNY HOW LOVING A GIRL CAN DRIVE A GUY BANANAS
AND, I GUESS NONE OF US ARE ESCAPE-PROOF
NO MATTER HOW I TRY--I CAN'T GET GWENDY OUT OF MY MIND
I CAN'T STOP THINKING OF HER--THERE ACROSS THE OCEAN--IN LONDON
CAN'T STOP WONDERING --IF SHE'S THINKING OF ME
PETER HAS NO WAY OF KNOWING--BUT LOOK HOW EASILY WE CAN FIND OUT--
IT'S NO USE! I JUST CAN'T FORGET HIM
LONDON
I THOUGHT--BEING AN OCEAN AWAY--WOULD GIVE ME A NEW OUTLOOK! BUT, IT DOESN'T MATTER
I STILL MISS PETER AS MUCH AS EVER

UNCLE ARTHUR-- AND AUNT NANCY-- HAVE BEEN *WONDERFUL* TO ME

THEY'VE TREATED ME LIKE THEIR *OWN* DAUGHTER

THEY'VE TRIED TO MAKE ME FEEL AS THOUGH THIS IS MY *HOME*

BUT, IT'S NOT THE SAME AS IT *WAS* --WHEN *DAD* WAS ALIVE

AND, NOW THAT I'M ALONE, *NO* PLACE CAN FEEL LIKE HOME TO ME--

IF *PETER* ISN'T IN THE PICTURE

I HAVE TO GET *OUT!* I HAVE TO *WALK--THINK* --CLEAR AWAY THE *COBWEBS* SOMEHOW--

WHAT *RIGHT* HAD I TO BE *ANGRY* AT PETER BECAUSE HE DIDN'T PROPOSE *MARRIAGE* TO ME?

I *KNOW* HE LOVES ME-- AS I LOVE *HIM!* I JUST *KNOW* IT

A BOY DOESN'T WANT TO FEEL *PRESSURED*-- DOESN'T WANT TO FEEL *TRAPPED* BY A GIRL

MAYBE I PUSHED TOO *HARD!* MAYBE --I SCARED HIM *AWAY*

I WAS A *FOOL* TO RUN OFF THE WAY I DID

BUT, MAYBE IT'S NOT TOO *LATE*--TO SET THINGS *RIGHT* AGAIN

I LET MY *GRIEF*-- MY HATRED OF *SPIDER-MAN*--AFFECT THE WAY I FELT ABOUT POOR *PETER*

5

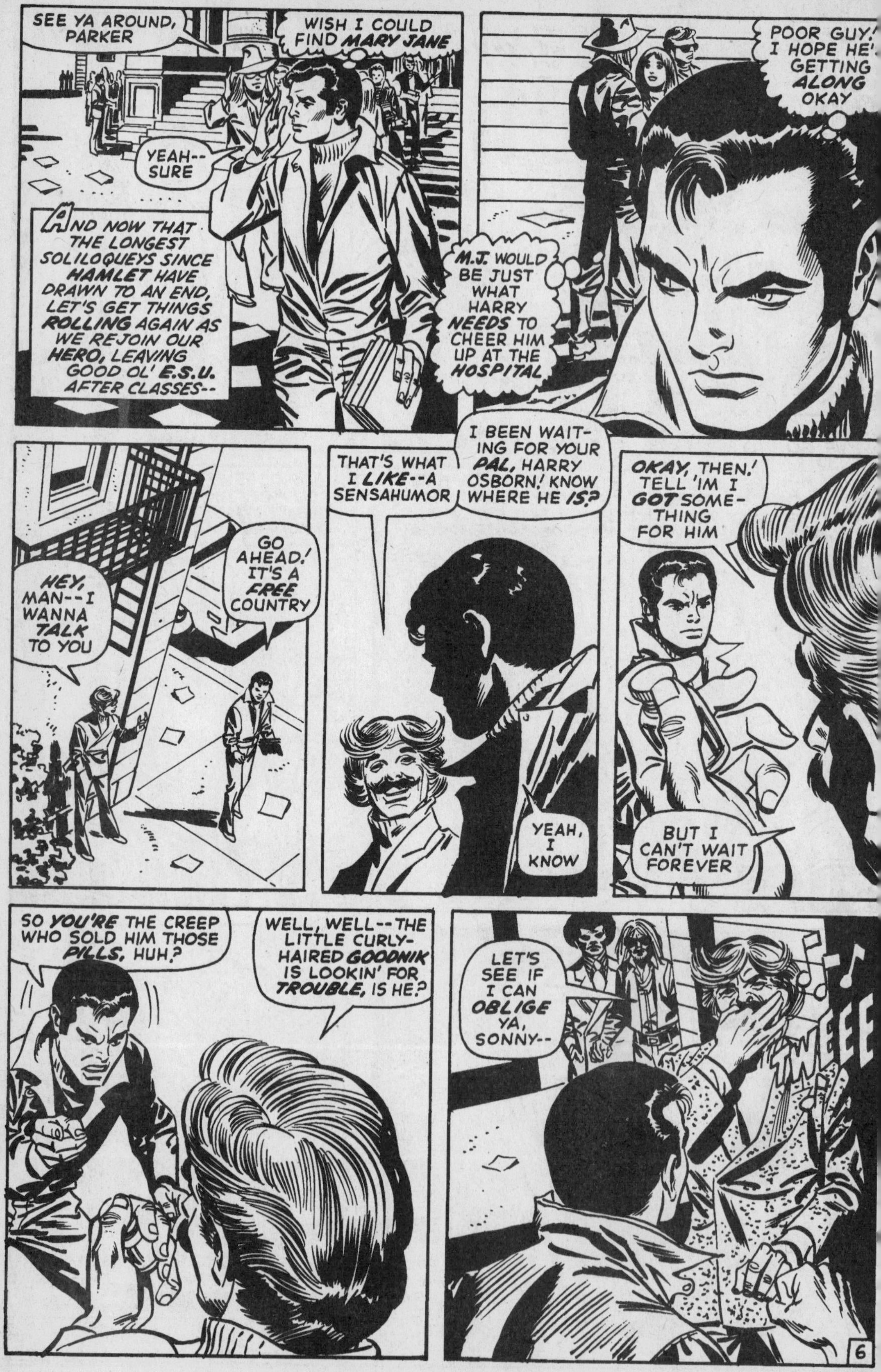

SEE YA AROUND, PARKER
WISH I COULD FIND MARY JANE
YEAH-- SURE
AND NOW THAT THE LONGEST SOLILOQUEYS SINCE HAMLET HAVE DRAWN TO AN END, LET'S GET THINGS ROLLING AGAIN AS WE REJOIN OUR HERO, LEAVING GOOD OL' E.S.U. AFTER CLASSES--
POOR GUY! I HOPE HE'S GETTING ALONG OKAY
M.J. WOULD BE JUST WHAT HARRY NEEDS TO CHEER HIM UP AT THE HOSPITAL
HEY, MAN--I WANNA TALK TO YOU
GO AHEAD! IT'S A FREE COUNTRY
THAT'S WHAT I LIKE--A SENSAHUMOR
I BEEN WAIT-ING FOR YOUR PAL, HARRY OSBORN! KNOW WHERE HE IS?
YEAH, I KNOW
OKAY, THEN! TELL 'IM I GOT SOME-THING FOR HIM
BUT I CAN'T WAIT FOREVER
SO YOU'RE THE CREEP WHO SOLD HIM THOSE PILLS, HUH?
WELL, WELL--THE LITTLE CURLY-HAIRED GOODNIK IS LOOKIN' FOR TROUBLE, IS HE?
LET'S SEE IF I CAN OBLIGE YA, SONNY--
TWEEE

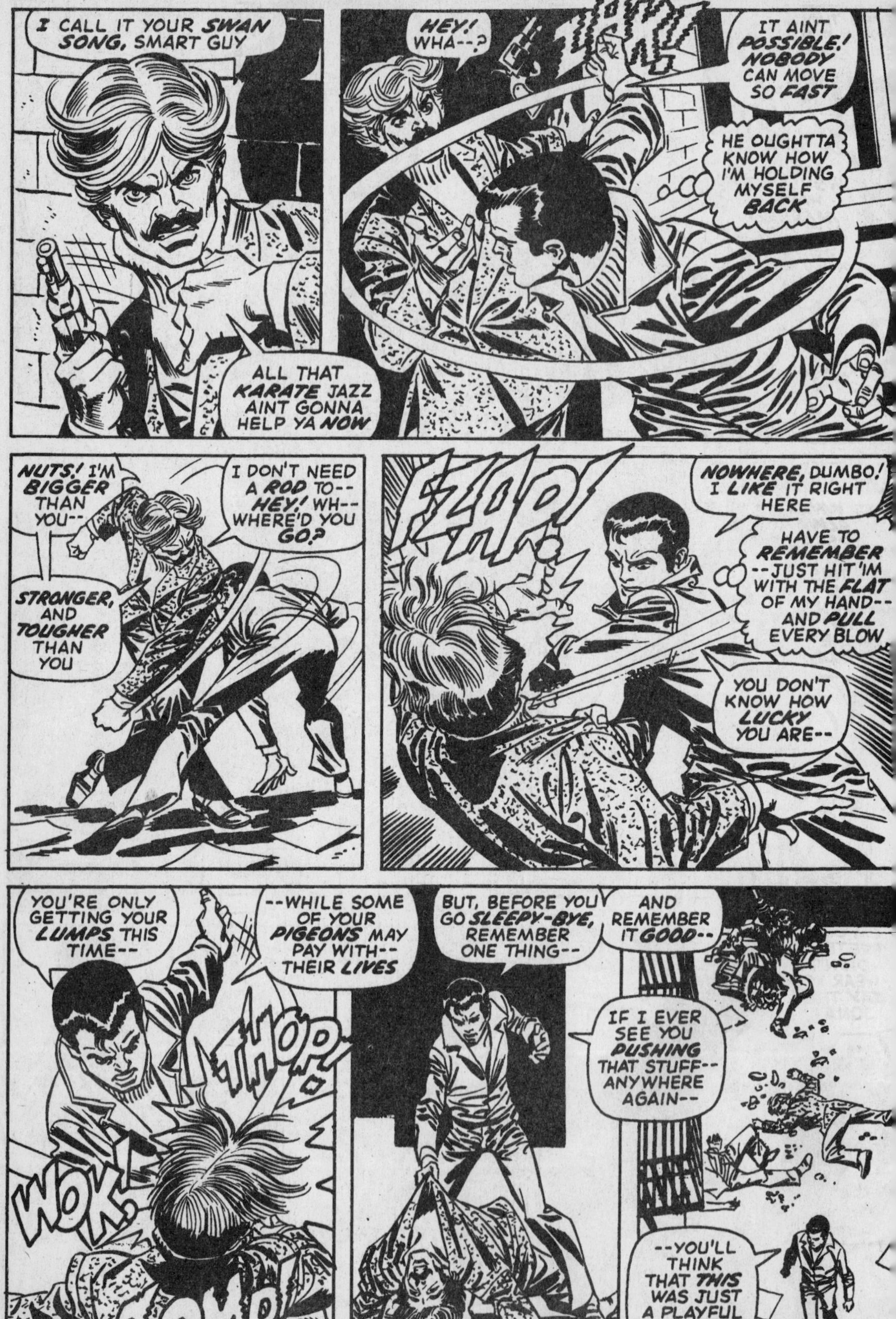

I CALL IT YOUR SWAN SONG, SMART GUY
ALL THAT KARATE JAZZ AINT GONNA HELP YA NOW
HEY! WHA--?
IT AINT POSSIBLE! NOBODY CAN MOVE SO FAST
HE OUGHTTA KNOW HOW I'M HOLDING MYSELF BACK
NUTS! I'M BIGGER THAN YOU--
STRONGER, AND TOUGHER THAN YOU
I DON'T NEED A ROD TO-- HEY! WH-- WHERE'D YOU GO?
FZAP!
NOWHERE, DUMBO! I LIKE IT RIGHT HERE
HAVE TO REMEMBER --JUST HIT 'IM WITH THE FLAT OF MY HAND-- AND PULL EVERY BLOW
YOU DON'T KNOW HOW LUCKY YOU ARE--
YOU'RE ONLY GETTING YOUR LUMPS THIS TIME--
--WHILE SOME OF YOUR PIGEONS MAY PAY WITH-- THEIR LIVES
THOP!
WOK!
ZOMP!
BUT, BEFORE YOU GO SLEEPY-BYE, REMEMBER ONE THING--
AND REMEMBER IT GOOD--
IF I EVER SEE YOU PUSHING THAT STUFF-- ANYWHERE AGAIN--
--YOU'LL THINK THAT THIS WAS JUST A PLAYFUL PICNIC

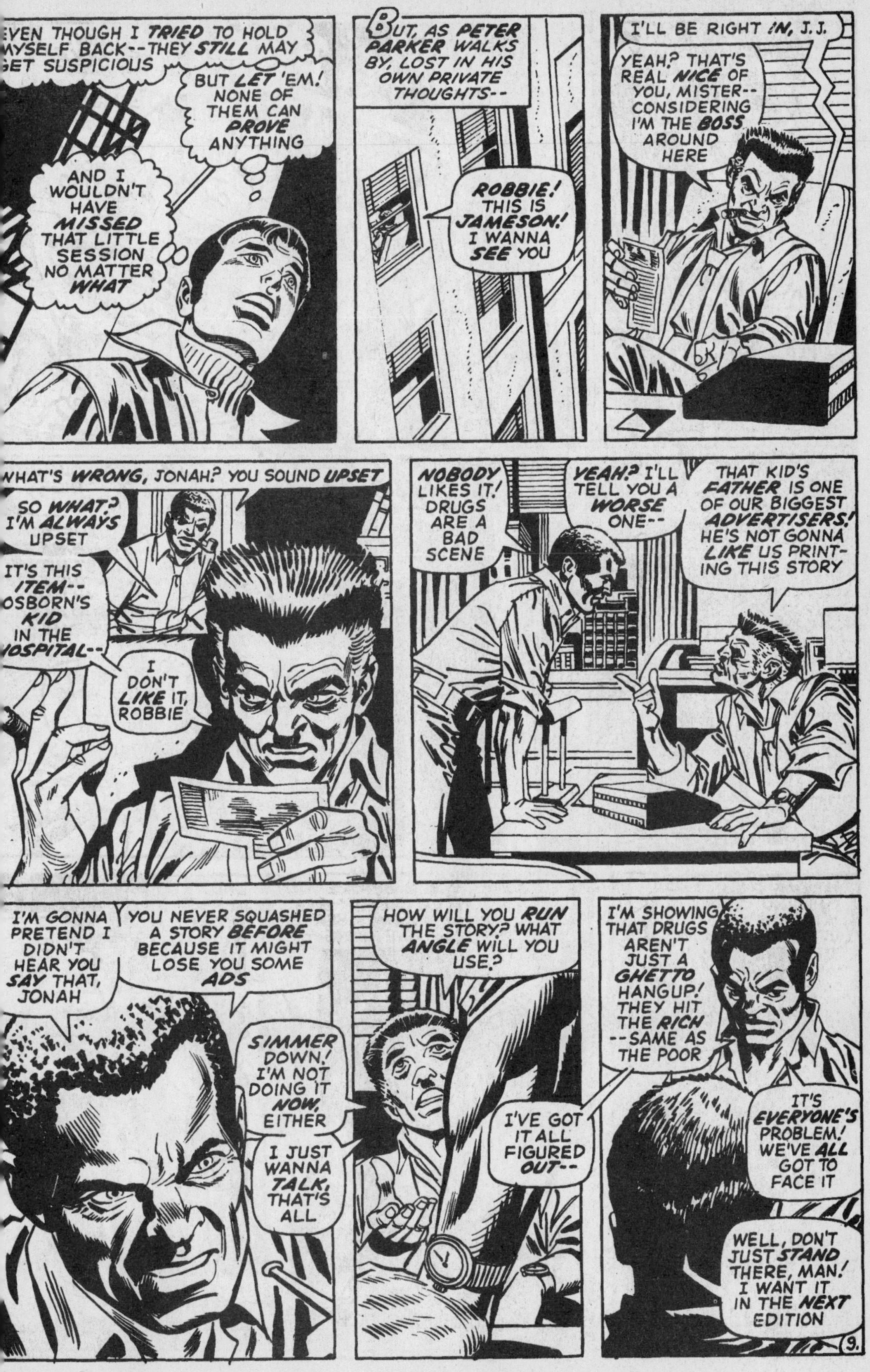

EVEN THOUGH I TRIED TO HOLD MYSELF BACK--THEY STILL MAY GET SUSPICIOUS
BUT LET 'EM! NONE OF THEM CAN PROVE ANYTHING
AND I WOULDN'T HAVE MISSED THAT LITTLE SESSION NO MATTER WHAT
BUT, AS PETER PARKER WALKS BY, LOST IN HIS OWN PRIVATE THOUGHTS--
ROBBIE! THIS IS JAMESON! I WANNA SEE YOU
I'LL BE RIGHT IN, J.J.
YEAH? THAT'S REAL NICE OF YOU, MISTER--CONSIDERING I'M THE BOSS AROUND HERE
WHAT'S WRONG, JONAH? YOU SOUND UPSET
SO WHAT? I'M ALWAYS UPSET
IT'S THIS ITEM--OSBORN'S KID IN THE HOSPITAL--
I DON'T LIKE IT, ROBBIE
NOBODY LIKES IT! DRUGS ARE A BAD SCENE
YEAH? I'LL TELL YOU A WORSE ONE--
THAT KID'S FATHER IS ONE OF OUR BIGGEST ADVERTISERS! HE'S NOT GONNA LIKE US PRINTING THIS STORY
I'M GONNA PRETEND I DIDN'T HEAR YOU SAY THAT, JONAH
YOU NEVER SQUASHED A STORY BEFORE BECAUSE IT MIGHT LOSE YOU SOME ADS
SIMMER DOWN! I'M NOT DOING IT NOW, EITHER
I JUST WANNA TALK, THAT'S ALL
HOW WILL YOU RUN THE STORY? WHAT ANGLE WILL YOU USE?
I'VE GOT IT ALL FIGURED OUT--
I'M SHOWING THAT DRUGS AREN'T JUST A GHETTO HANGUP! THEY HIT THE RICH--SAME AS THE POOR
IT'S EVERYONE'S PROBLEM! WE'VE ALL GOT TO FACE IT
WELL, DON'T JUST STAND THERE, MAN! I WANT IT IN THE NEXT EDITION
9.

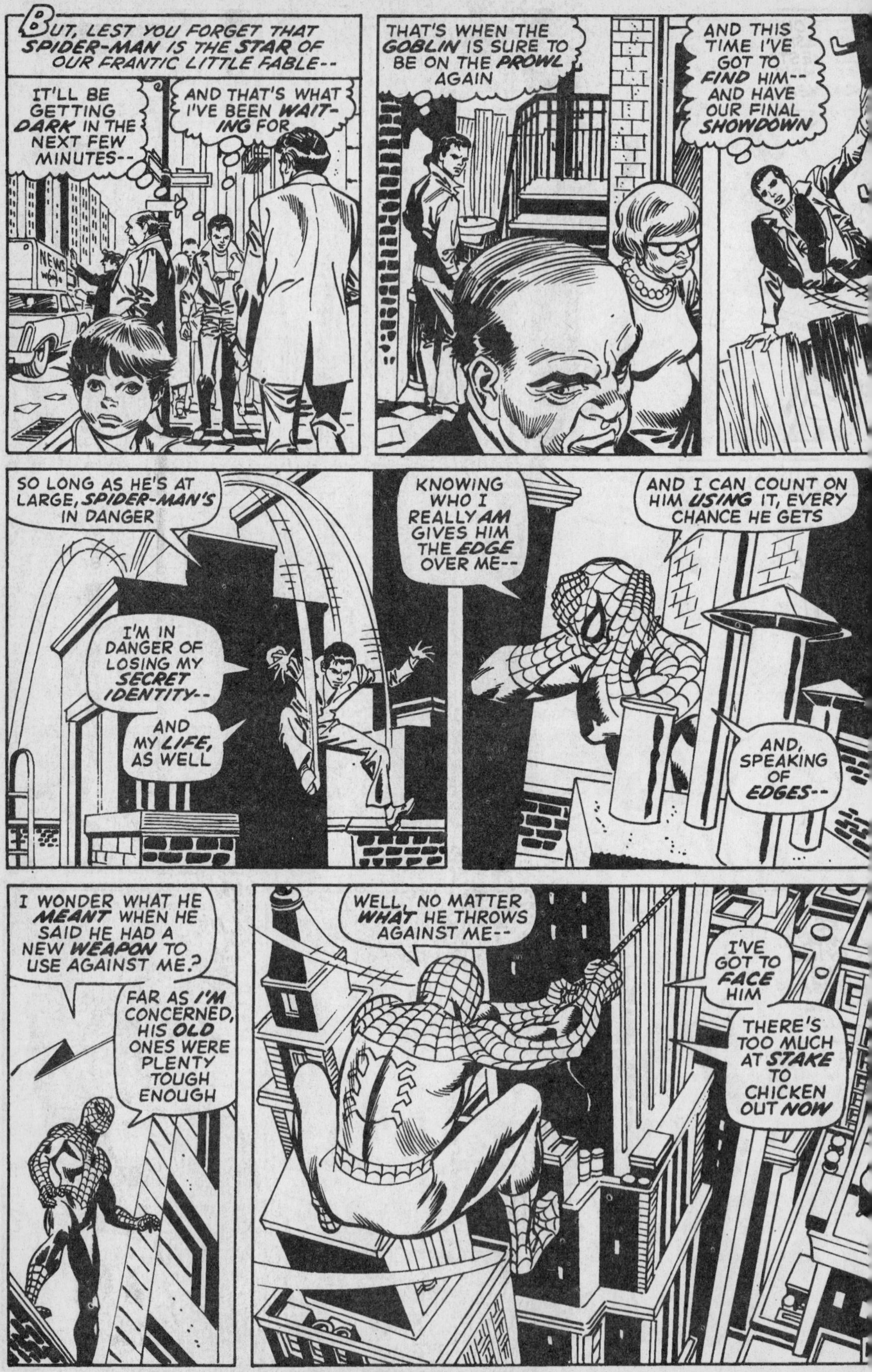
BUT, LEST YOU FORGET THAT SPIDER-MAN IS THE STAR OF OUR FRANTIC LITTLE FABLE--
IT'LL BE GETTING DARK IN THE NEXT FEW MINUTES--
AND THAT'S WHAT I'VE BEEN WAITING FOR
NEWS
THAT'S WHEN THE GOBLIN IS SURE TO BE ON THE PROWL AGAIN
AND THIS TIME I'VE GOT TO FIND HIM-- AND HAVE OUR FINAL SHOWDOWN
SO LONG AS HE'S AT LARGE, SPIDER-MAN'S IN DANGER
I'M IN DANGER OF LOSING MY SECRET IDENTITY--
AND MY LIFE, AS WELL
KNOWING WHO I REALLY AM GIVES HIM THE EDGE OVER ME--
AND I CAN COUNT ON HIM USING IT, EVERY CHANCE HE GETS
AND, SPEAKING OF EDGES--
I WONDER WHAT HE MEANT WHEN HE SAID HE HAD A NEW WEAPON TO USE AGAINST ME?
FAR AS I'M CONCERNED, HIS OLD ONES WERE PLENTY TOUGH ENOUGH
WELL, NO MATTER WHAT HE THROWS AGAINST ME--
I'VE GOT TO FACE HIM
THERE'S TOO MUCH AT STAKE TO CHICKEN OUT NOW

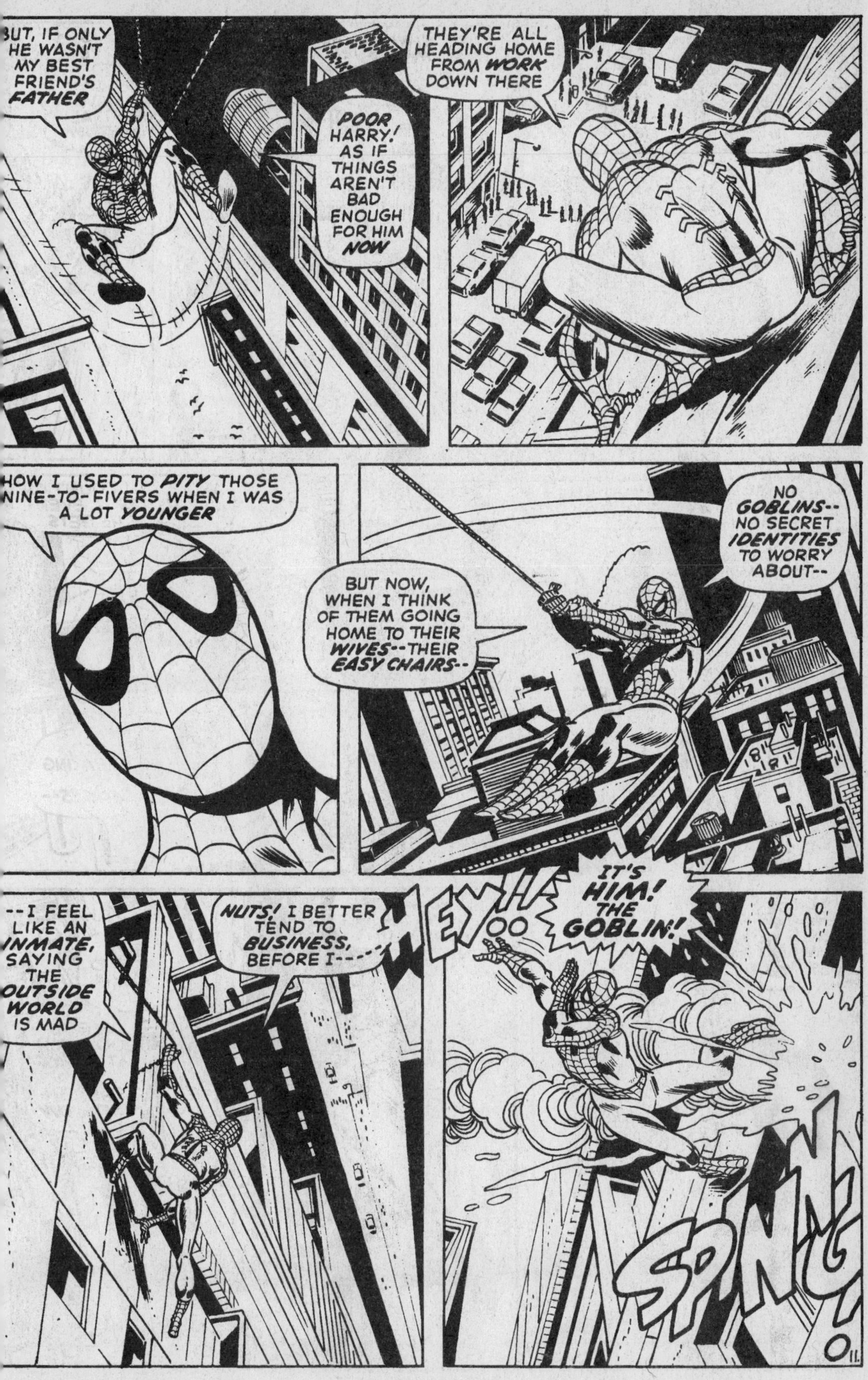
BUT, IF ONLY HE WASN'T MY BEST FRIEND'S FATHER
POOR HARRY! AS IF THINGS AREN'T BAD ENOUGH FOR HIM NOW
THEY'RE ALL HEADING HOME FROM WORK DOWN THERE
HOW I USED TO PITY THOSE NINE-TO-FIVERS WHEN I WAS A LOT YOUNGER
BUT NOW, WHEN I THINK OF THEM GOING HOME TO THEIR WIVES--THEIR EASY CHAIRS--
NO GOBLINS--NO SECRET IDENTITIES TO WORRY ABOUT--
--I FEEL LIKE AN INMATE, SAYING THE OUTSIDE WORLD IS MAD
NUTS! I BETTER TEND TO BUSINESS, BEFORE I---
HEY!!
IT'S HIM! THE GOBLIN!
SPANG

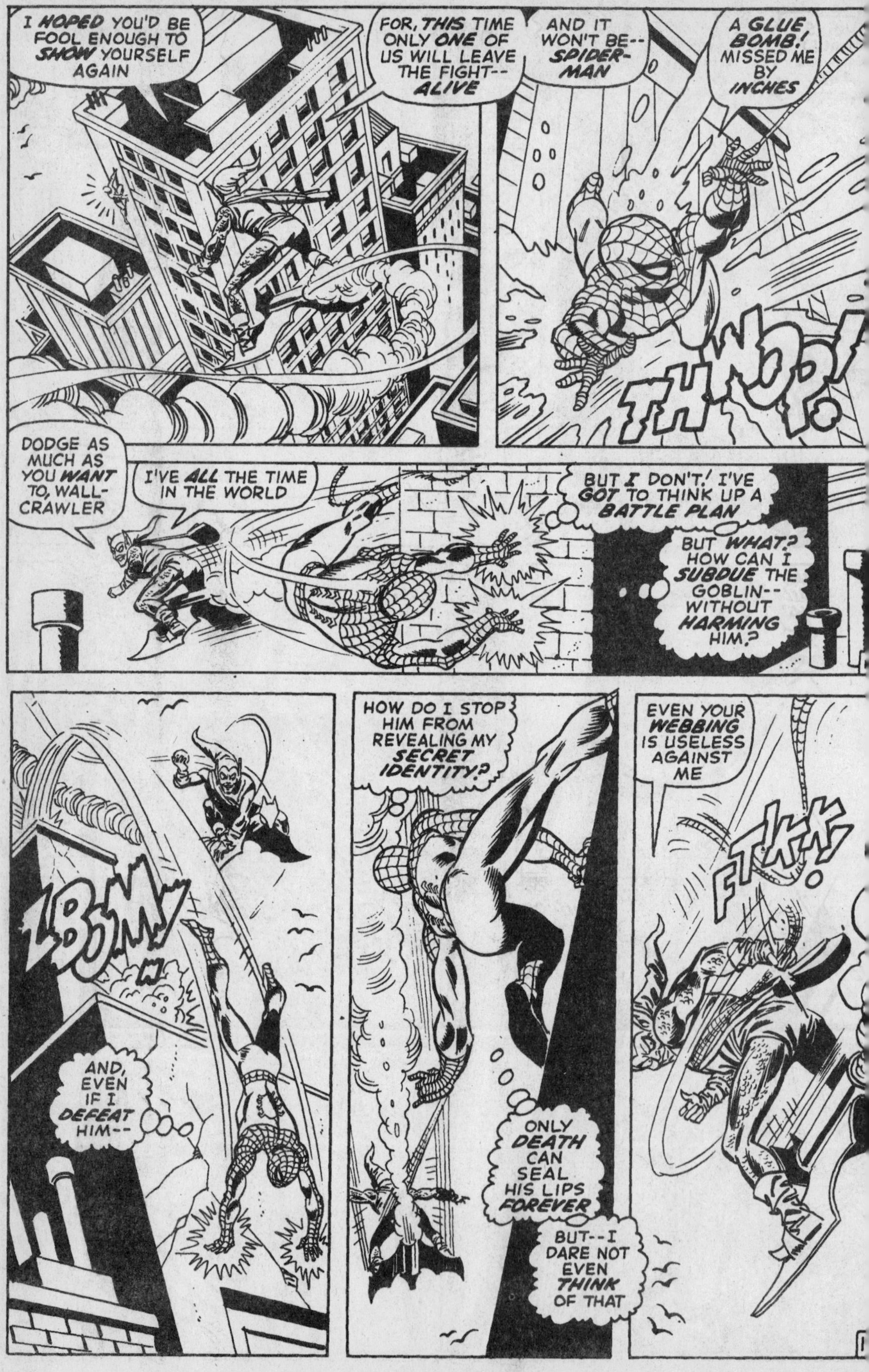

I HOPED YOU'D BE FOOL ENOUGH TO SHOW YOURSELF AGAIN
FOR, THIS TIME ONLY ONE OF US WILL LEAVE THE FIGHT-- ALIVE
AND IT WON'T BE-- SPIDER-MAN
A GLUE BOMB! MISSED ME BY INCHES
THWOP!
DODGE AS MUCH AS YOU WANT TO, WALL-CRAWLER
I'VE ALL THE TIME IN THE WORLD
BUT I DON'T! I'VE GOT TO THINK UP A BATTLE PLAN
BUT WHAT? HOW CAN I SUBDUE THE GOBLIN-- WITHOUT HARMING HIM?
BOOM
AND, EVEN IF I DEFEAT HIM--
HOW DO I STOP HIM FROM REVEALING MY SECRET IDENTITY?
ONLY DEATH CAN SEAL HIS LIPS FOREVER
BUT--I DARE NOT EVEN THINK OF THAT
EVEN YOUR WEBBING IS USELESS AGAINST ME
FTKKK!

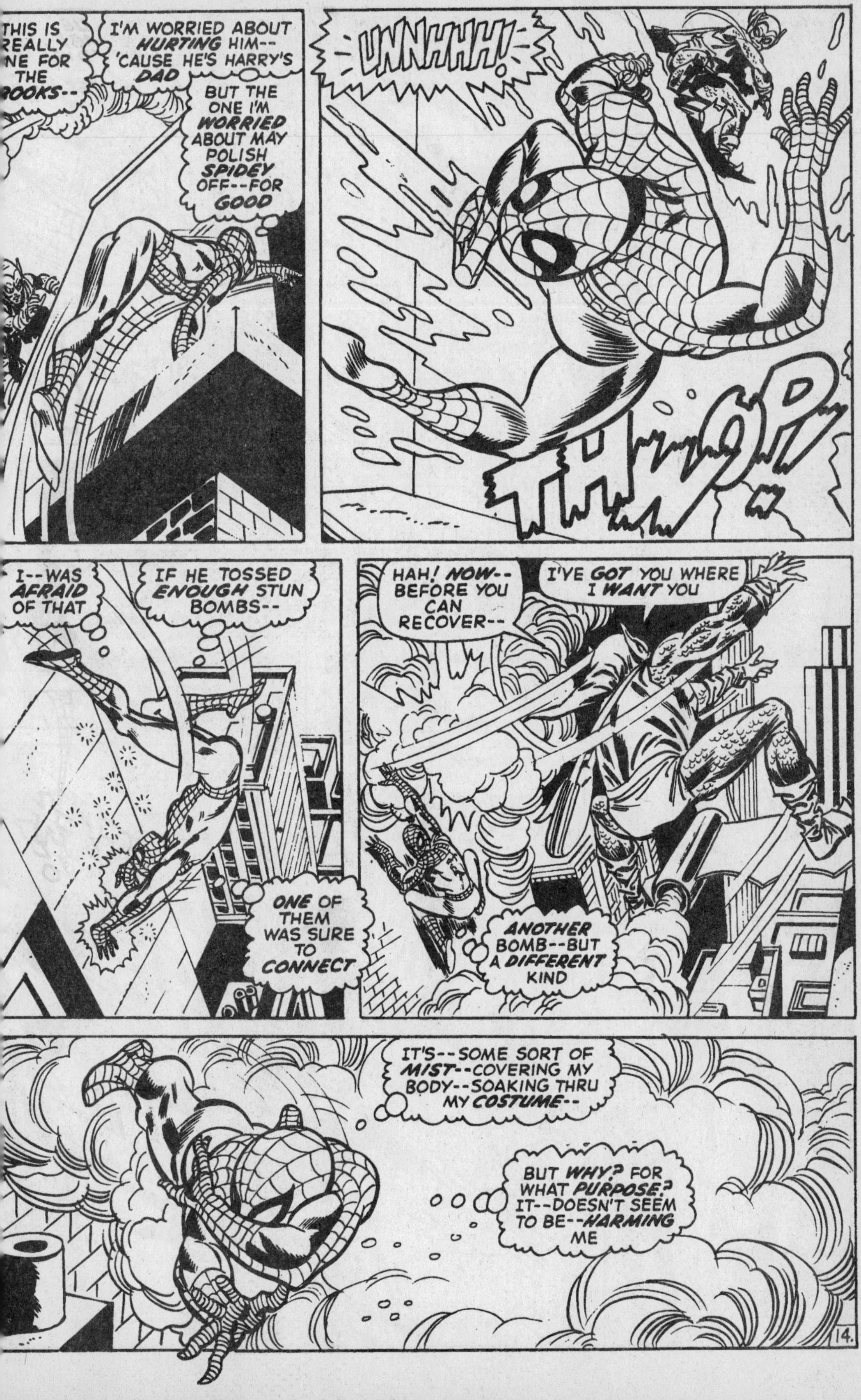
THIS IS REALLY NE FOR THE ROOKS--
I'M WORRIED ABOUT HURTING HIM-- 'CAUSE HE'S HARRY'S DAD
BUT THE ONE I'M WORRIED ABOUT MAY POLISH SPIDEY OFF--FOR GOOD
UNNHHH!
THWOP!
I--WAS AFRAID OF THAT
IF HE TOSSED ENOUGH STUN BOMBS--
ONE OF THEM WAS SURE TO CONNECT
HAH! NOW-- BEFORE YOU CAN RECOVER--
I'VE GOT YOU WHERE I WANT YOU
ANOTHER BOMB--BUT A DIFFERENT KIND
IT'S--SOME SORT OF MIST--COVERING MY BODY--SOAKING THRU MY COSTUME--
BUT WHY? FOR WHAT PURPOSE? IT--DOESN'T SEEM TO BE--HARMING ME
14.

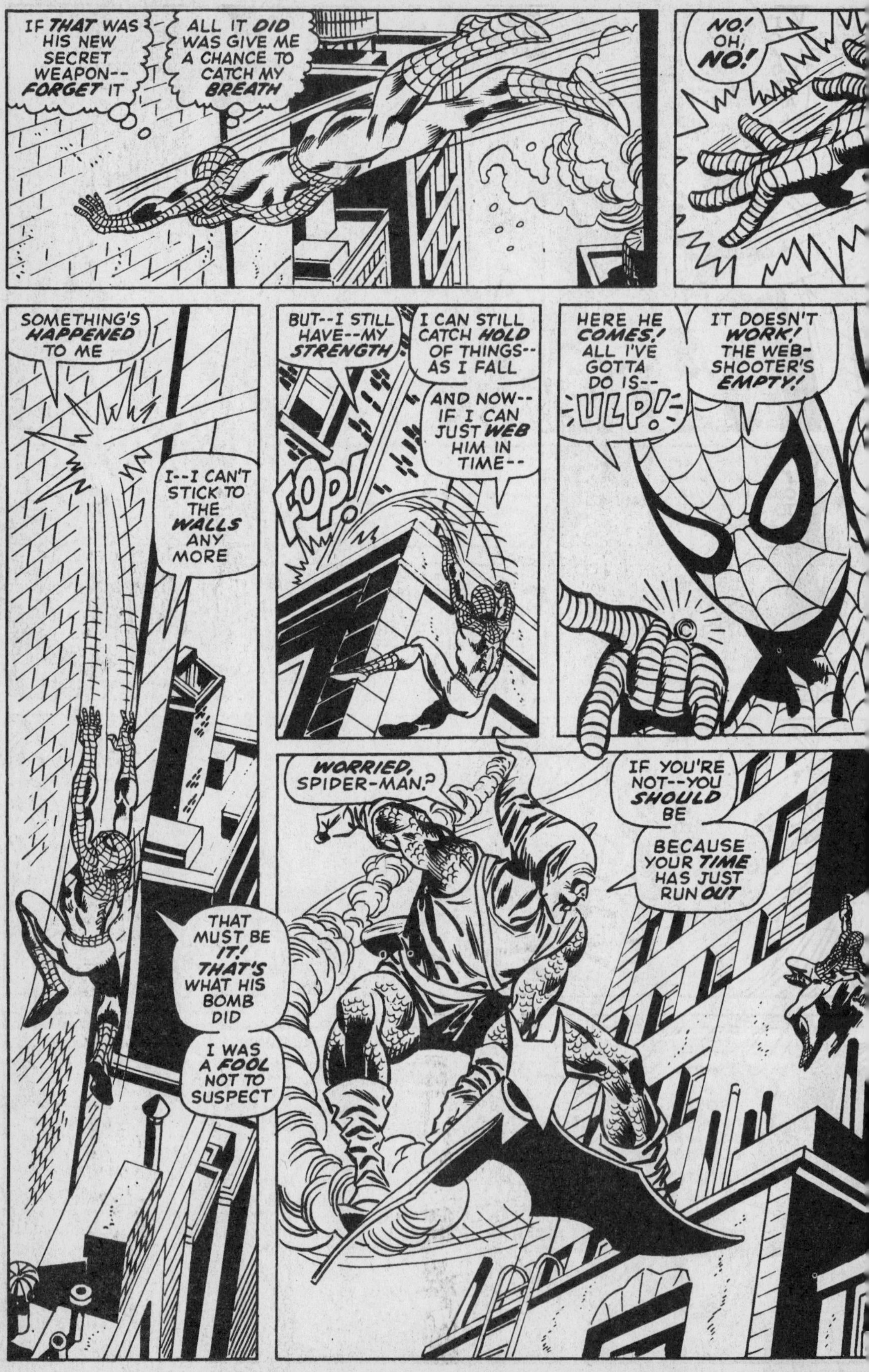
IF THAT WAS HIS NEW SECRET WEAPON--FORGET IT
ALL IT DID WAS GIVE ME A CHANCE TO CATCH MY BREATH
NO! OH, NO!
SOMETHING'S HAPPENED TO ME
I--I CAN'T STICK TO THE WALLS ANY MORE
THAT MUST BE IT! THAT'S WHAT HIS BOMB DID
I WAS A FOOL NOT TO SUSPECT
BUT--I STILL HAVE--MY STRENGTH
I CAN STILL CATCH HOLD OF THINGS--AS I FALL
AND NOW--IF I CAN JUST WEB HIM IN TIME--
FOP!
HERE HE COMES! ALL I'VE GOTTA DO IS--
ULP!
IT DOESN'T WORK! THE WEB-SHOOTER'S EMPTY!
WORRIED, SPIDER-MAN?
IF YOU'RE NOT--YOU SHOULD BE
BECAUSE YOUR TIME HAS JUST RUN OUT

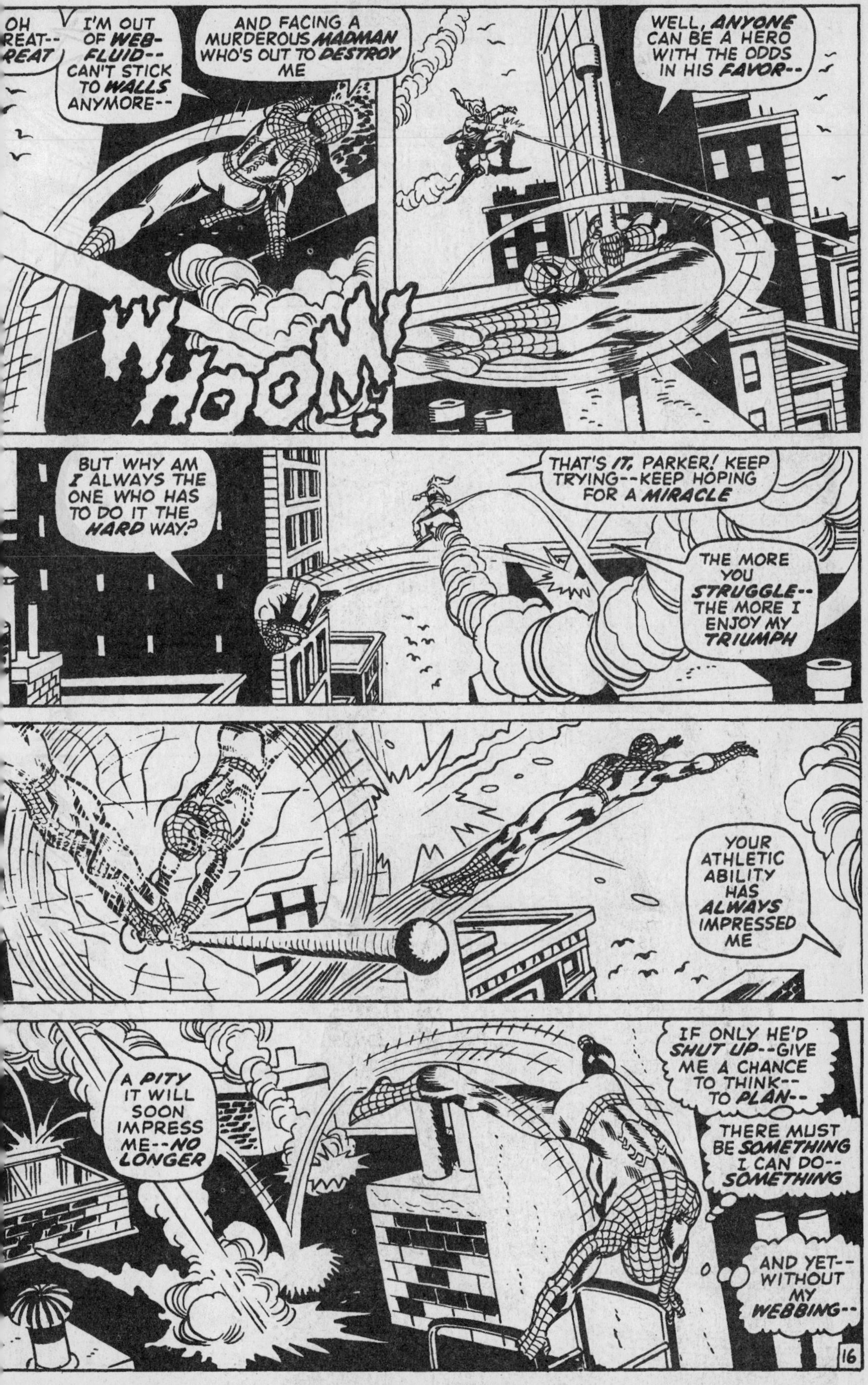

OH
REAT--
REAT
I'M OUT OF WEB-FLUID--CAN'T STICK TO WALLS ANYMORE--
AND FACING A MURDEROUS MADMAN WHO'S OUT TO DESTROY ME
WHOOM!
WELL, ANYONE CAN BE A HERO WITH THE ODDS IN HIS FAVOR--
BUT WHY AM I ALWAYS THE ONE WHO HAS TO DO IT THE HARD WAY?
THAT'S IT, PARKER! KEEP TRYING--KEEP HOPING FOR A MIRACLE
THE MORE YOU STRUGGLE--THE MORE I ENJOY MY TRIUMPH
YOUR ATHLETIC ABILITY HAS ALWAYS IMPRESSED ME
A PITY IT WILL SOON IMPRESS ME--NO LONGER
IF ONLY HE'D SHUT UP--GIVE ME A CHANCE TO THINK--TO PLAN--
THERE MUST BE SOMETHING I CAN DO--SOMETHING
AND YET--WITHOUT MY WEBBING--
16

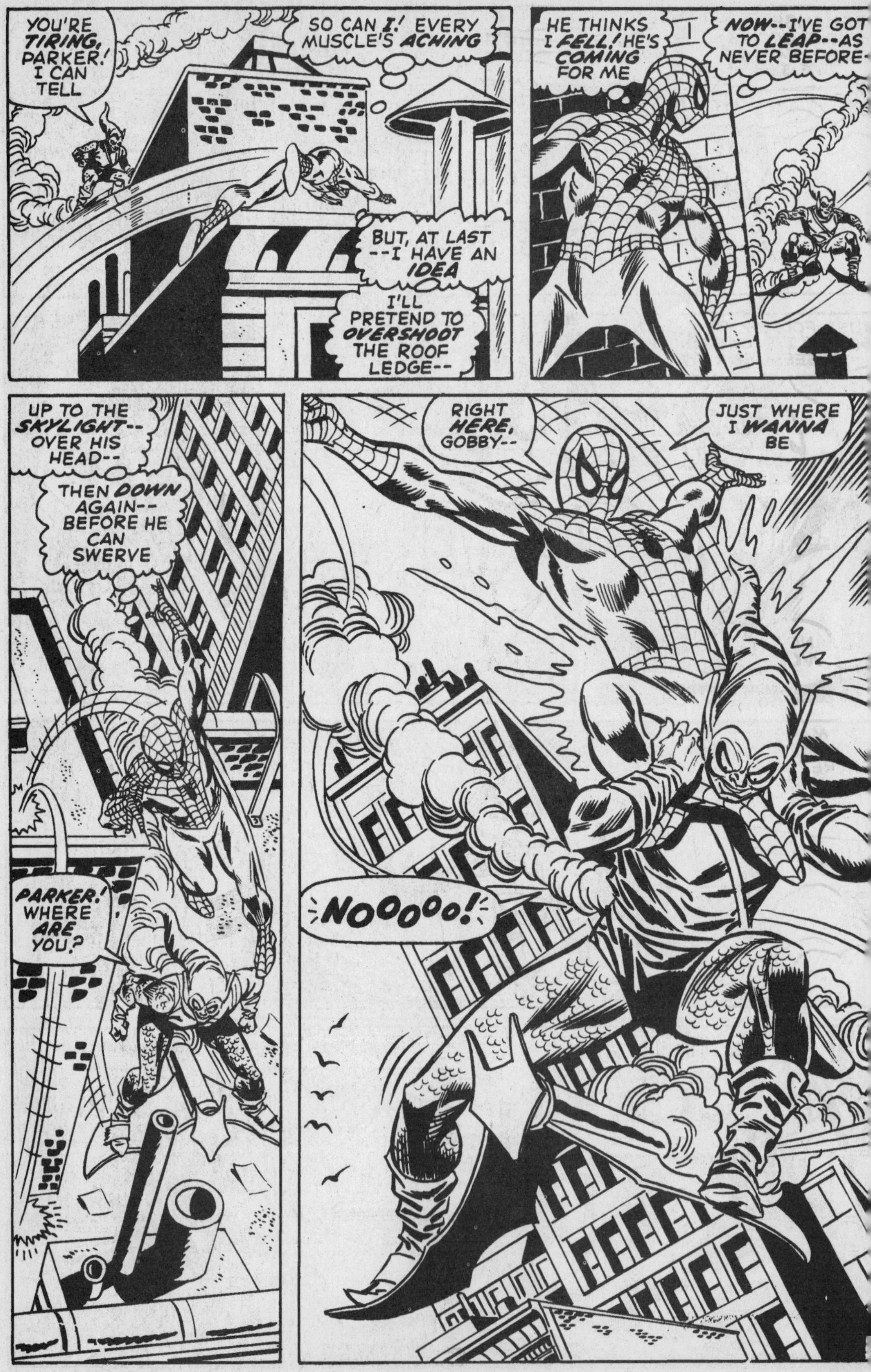

YOU'RE TIRING, PARKER! I CAN TELL
SO CAN I! EVERY MUSCLE'S ACHING
BUT, AT LAST --I HAVE AN IDEA
I'LL PRETEND TO OVERSHOOT THE ROOF LEDGE--
HE THINKS I FELL! HE'S COMING FOR ME
NOW--I'VE GOT TO LEAP--AS NEVER BEFORE--
UP TO THE SKYLIGHT-- OVER HIS HEAD--
THEN DOWN AGAIN-- BEFORE HE CAN SWERVE
PARKER! WHERE ARE YOU?
RIGHT HERE, GOBBY--
JUST WHERE I WANNA BE
NOOOOOO!

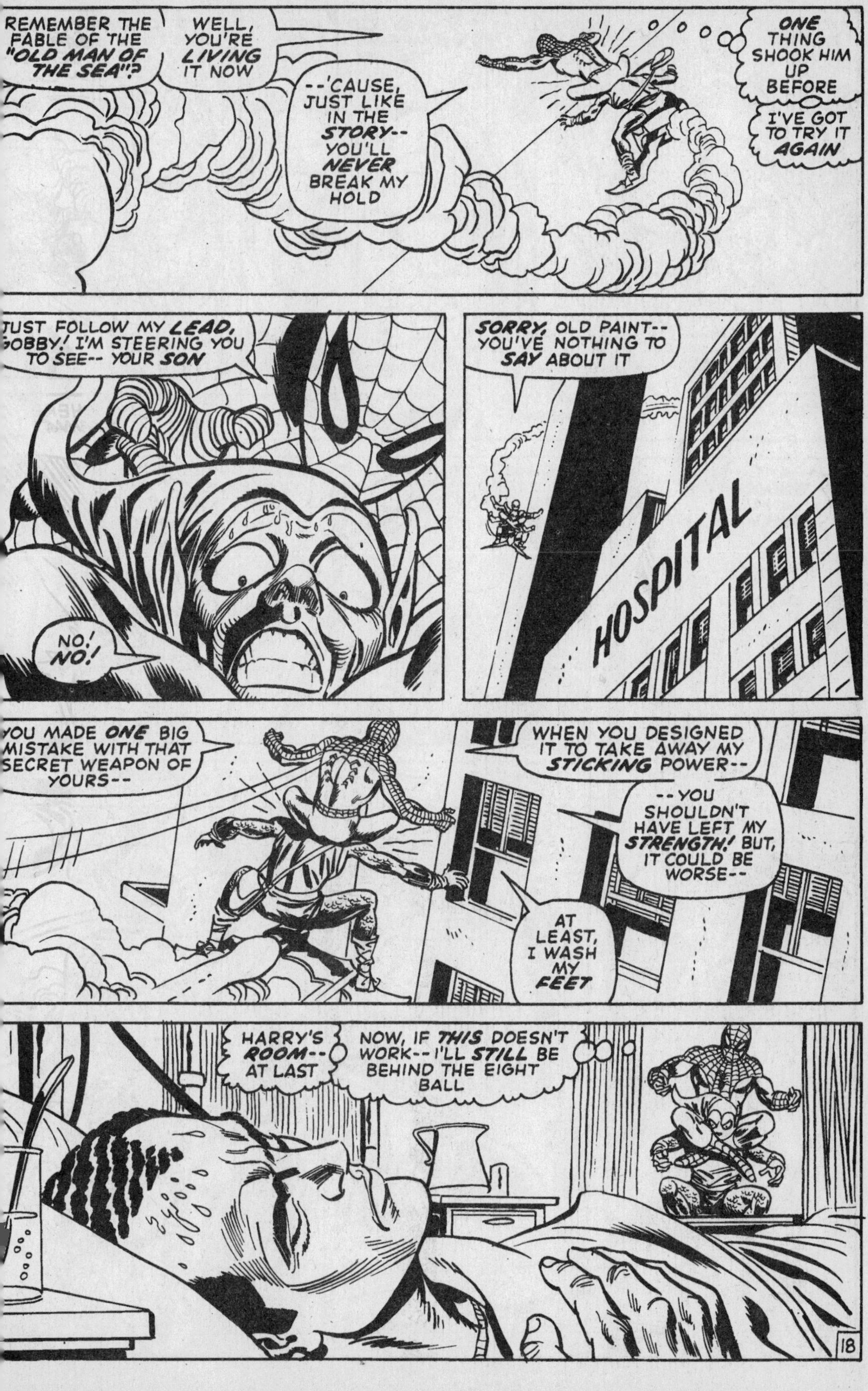
REMEMBER THE FABLE OF THE "OLD MAN OF THE SEA"?
WELL, YOU'RE LIVING IT NOW
--'CAUSE, JUST LIKE IN THE STORY-- YOU'LL NEVER BREAK MY HOLD
ONE THING SHOOK HIM UP BEFORE
I'VE GOT TO TRY IT AGAIN
JUST FOLLOW MY LEAD, GOBBY! I'M STEERING YOU TO SEE-- YOUR SON
NO! NO!
SORRY, OLD PAINT-- YOU'VE NOTHING TO SAY ABOUT IT
HOSPITAL
YOU MADE ONE BIG MISTAKE WITH THAT SECRET WEAPON OF YOURS--
WHEN YOU DESIGNED IT TO TAKE AWAY MY STICKING POWER--
--YOU SHOULDN'T HAVE LEFT MY STRENGTH! BUT, IT COULD BE WORSE--
AT LEAST, I WASH MY FEET
HARRY'S ROOM-- AT LAST
NOW, IF THIS DOESN'T WORK--I'LL STILL BE BEHIND THE EIGHT BALL

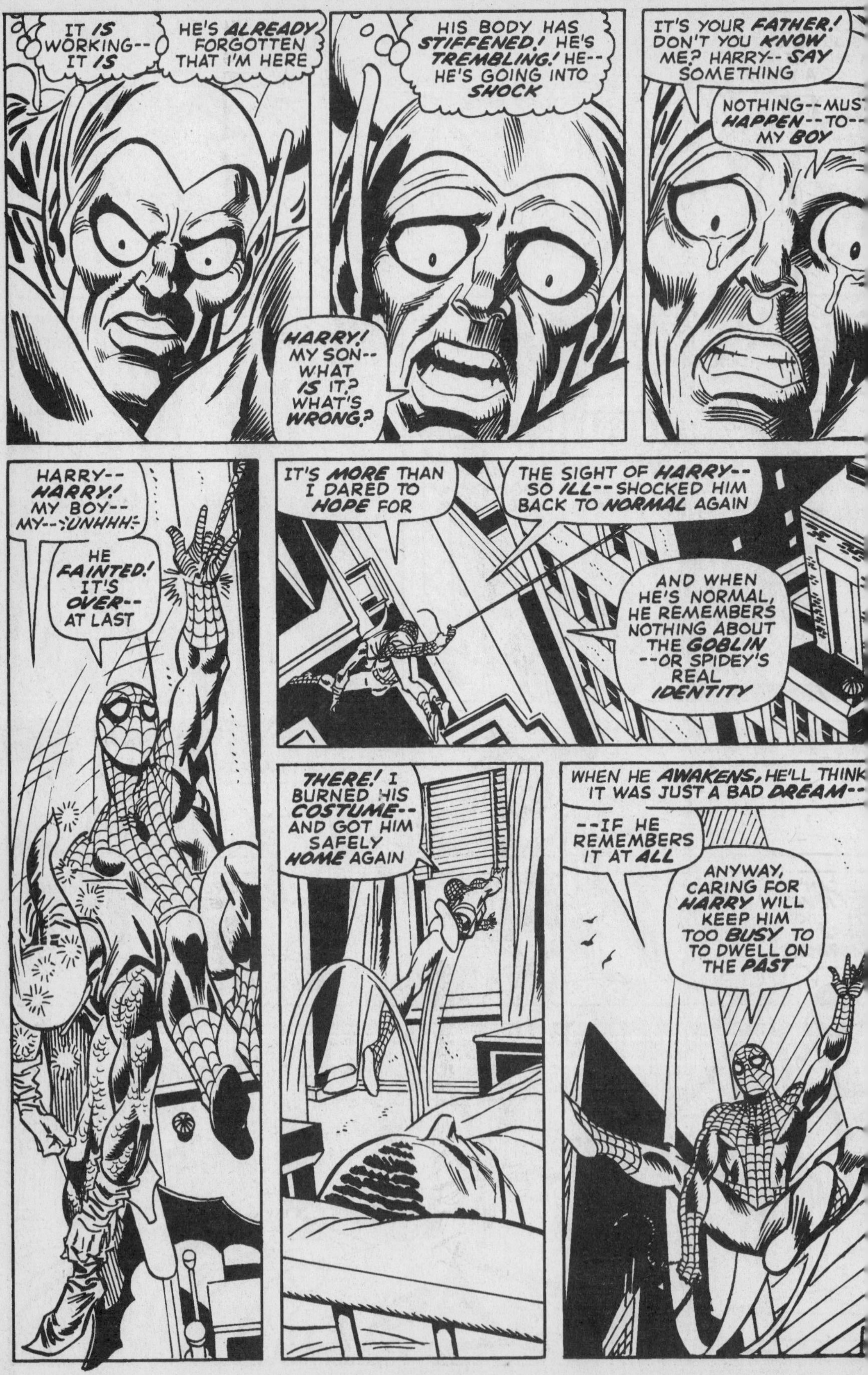

IT IS WORKING-- IT IS
HE'S ALREADY FORGOTTEN THAT I'M HERE
HIS BODY HAS STIFFENED! HE'S TREMBLING! HE-- HE'S GOING INTO SHOCK
HARRY! MY SON-- WHAT IS IT? WHAT'S WRONG?
IT'S YOUR FATHER! DON'T YOU KNOW ME? HARRY-- SAY SOMETHING
NOTHING--MUST HAPPEN--TO-- MY BOY
HARRY-- HARRY! MY BOY-- MY--UNHHH
HE FAINTED! IT'S OVER-- AT LAST
IT'S MORE THAN I DARED TO HOPE FOR
THE SIGHT OF HARRY-- SO ILL--SHOCKED HIM BACK TO NORMAL AGAIN
AND WHEN HE'S NORMAL, HE REMEMBERS NOTHING ABOUT THE GOBLIN --OR SPIDEY'S REAL IDENTITY
THERE! I BURNED HIS COSTUME-- AND GOT HIM SAFELY HOME AGAIN
WHEN HE AWAKENS, HE'LL THINK IT WAS JUST A BAD DREAM--
--IF HE REMEMBERS IT AT ALL
ANYWAY, CARING FOR HARRY WILL KEEP HIM TOO BUSY TO TO DWELL ON THE PAST

NO, MY IDENTITY IS *SAFE* ONCE MORE--AT LEAST, FOR A WHILE

NOW, ALL THAT REMAINS IS TO HOPE THAT POOR *HARRY* WILL SOON BE ALL RIGHT

AND, TO HOPE THAT HE'S LEARNED YOU CAN'T SOLVE YOUR PROBLEMS WITH *PILLS*

AS FOR ME, I'M RIGHT BACK WHERE I STARTED--

NOTHING TO LOOK *FORWARD* TO--EXCEPT DULL AND EMPTY *LONELINESS*--WITHOUT *GWEN*

OH *NO!* AM I--STARTING TO *CRACK UP?*

I--SUDDENLY IMAGINE--THAT I HEAR--

--HER *VOICE*--CALLING ME

PETER! PETER! I'M *BACK!* I--HAD TO RETURN

IT--IT *IS* YOU! IT *IS!* *GWENDY!*

I CAN'T *BELIEVE* IT! IT'S LIKE A *DREAM*--A *MIRACLE*

IT'S *TRUE*, PETER! I *COULDN'T* STAY AWAY

AND NOW, BEFORE WE EAGERLY COUNT THE DAYS TILL NEXT ISSUE, WE JUST WANT TO ASK YOU ONE LITTLE QUESTION--

--WHO SAYS WE NEVER GIVE SPIDEY A *HAPPY ENDING?*

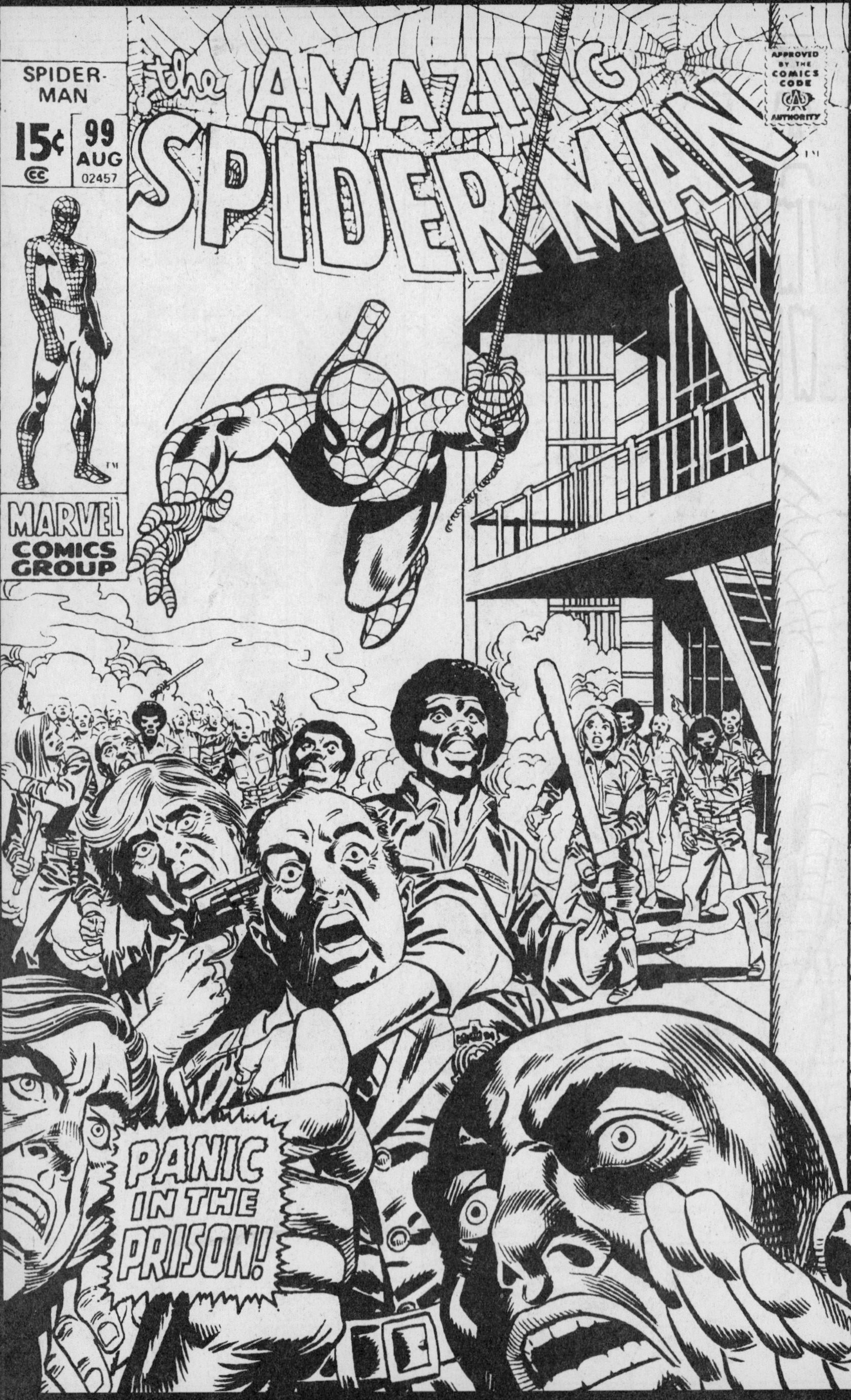

SPIDER-MAN
15¢
99
AUG
02457
the AMAZING SPIDER-MAN
APPROVED BY THE COMICS CODE AUTHORITY
MARVEL COMICS GROUP
PANIC IN THE PRISON!

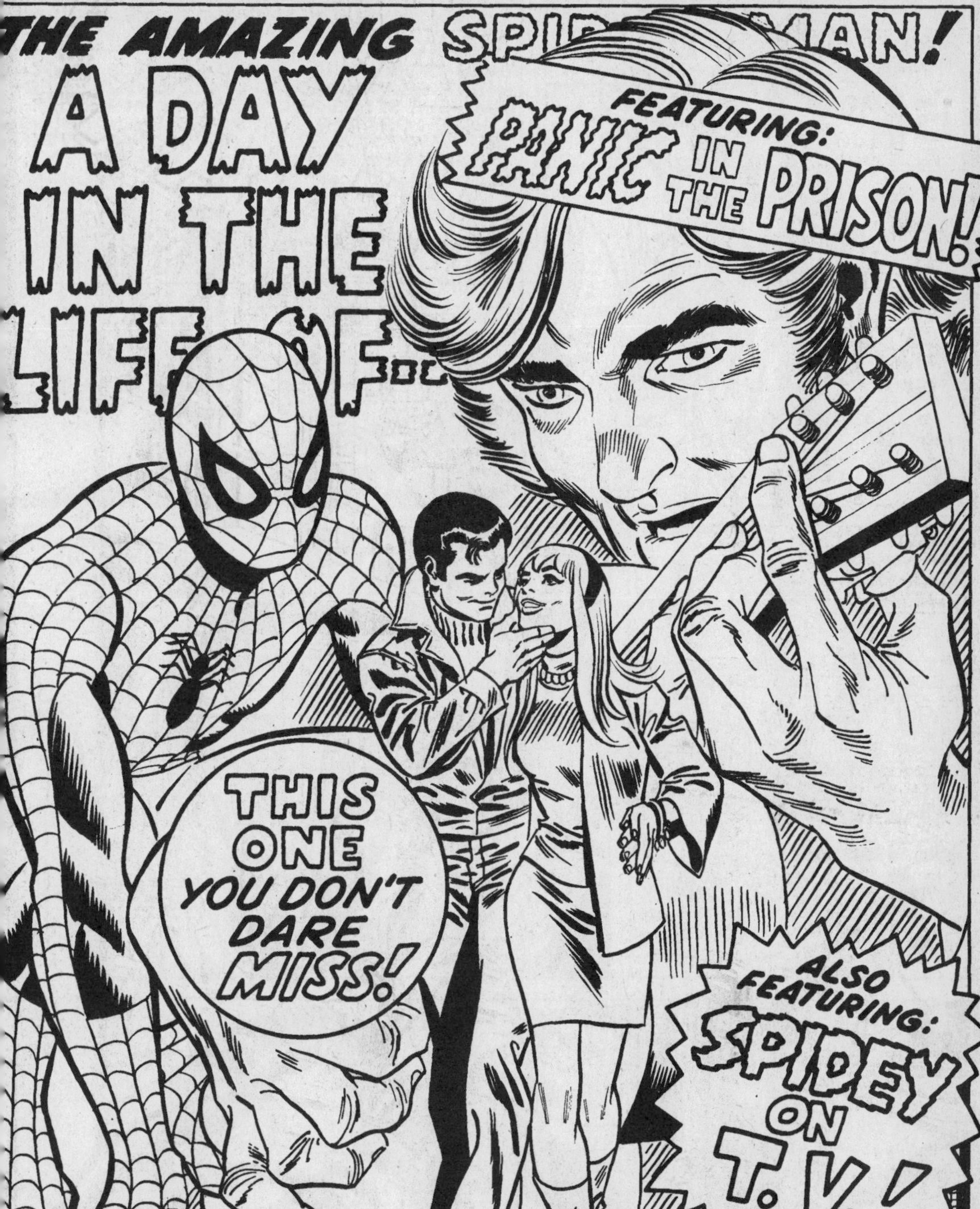
THE AMAZING SPIDER-MAN!
A DAY IN THE LIFE OF...
FEATURING: PANIC IN THE PRISON!
THIS ONE YOU DON'T DARE MISS!
ALSO FEATURING: SPIDEY ON T.V.!
BY:
TAN LEE UTHOR
GIL KANE PENCILLER
FRANK GIACOIA INKER
ARTIE SIMEK LETTERER
609Z.

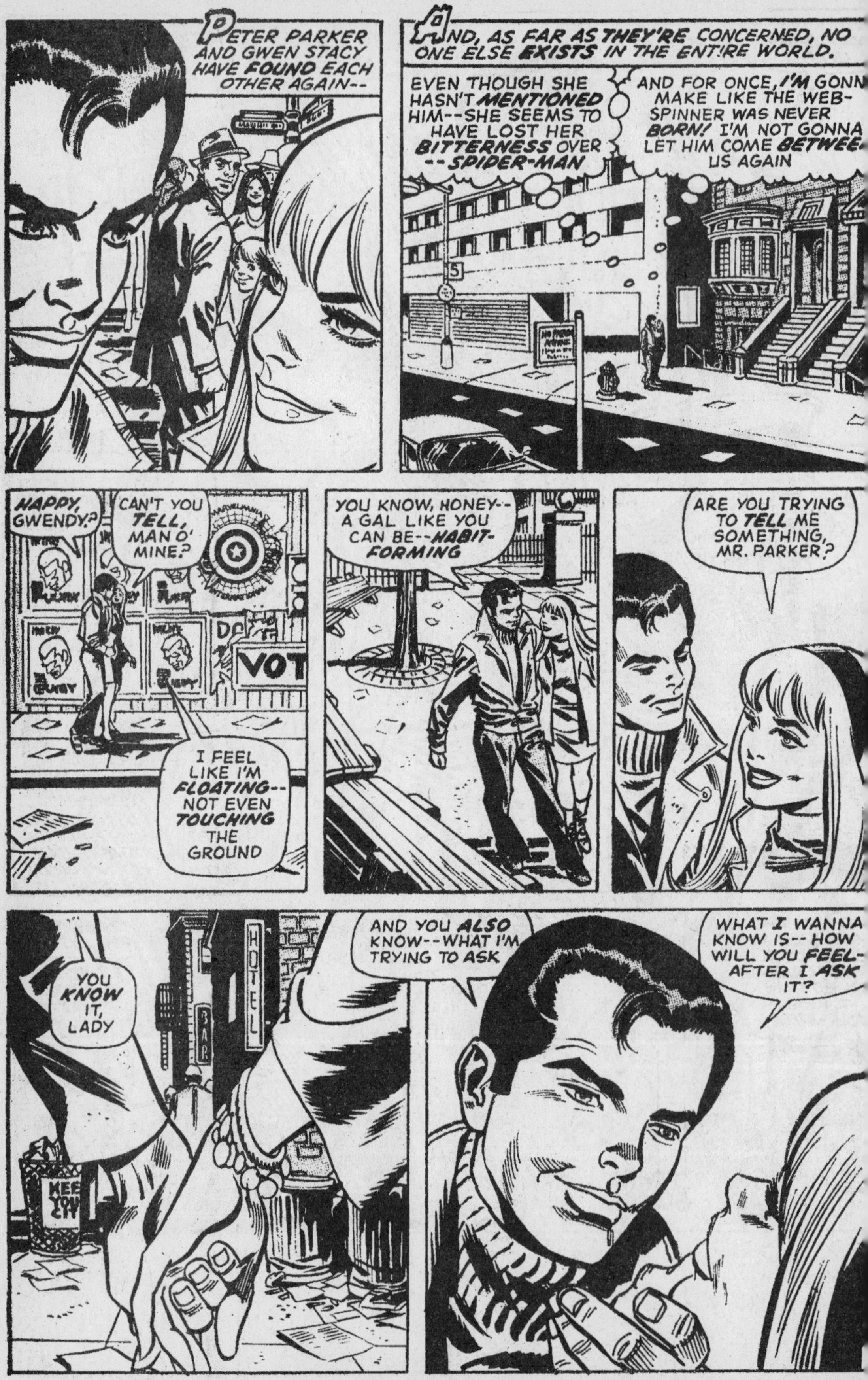
PETER PARKER AND GWEN STACY HAVE FOUND EACH OTHER AGAIN--
AND, AS FAR AS THEY'RE CONCERNED, NO ONE ELSE EXISTS IN THE ENTIRE WORLD.
EVEN THOUGH SHE HASN'T MENTIONED HIM--SHE SEEMS TO HAVE LOST HER BITTERNESS OVER --SPIDER-MAN
AND FOR ONCE, I'M GONN MAKE LIKE THE WEB-SPINNER WAS NEVER BORN! I'M NOT GONNA LET HIM COME BETWEE US AGAIN
HAPPY, GWENDY?
CAN'T YOU TELL, MAN O' MINE?
I FEEL LIKE I'M FLOATING-- NOT EVEN TOUCHING THE GROUND
VOT
YOU KNOW, HONEY-- A GAL LIKE YOU CAN BE--HABIT-FORMING
ARE YOU TRYING TO TELL ME SOMETHING, MR. PARKER?
YOU KNOW IT, LADY
HOTEL
BAR
AND YOU ALSO KNOW--WHAT I'M TRYING TO ASK
WHAT I WANNA KNOW IS--HOW WILL YOU FEEL-AFTER I ASK IT?

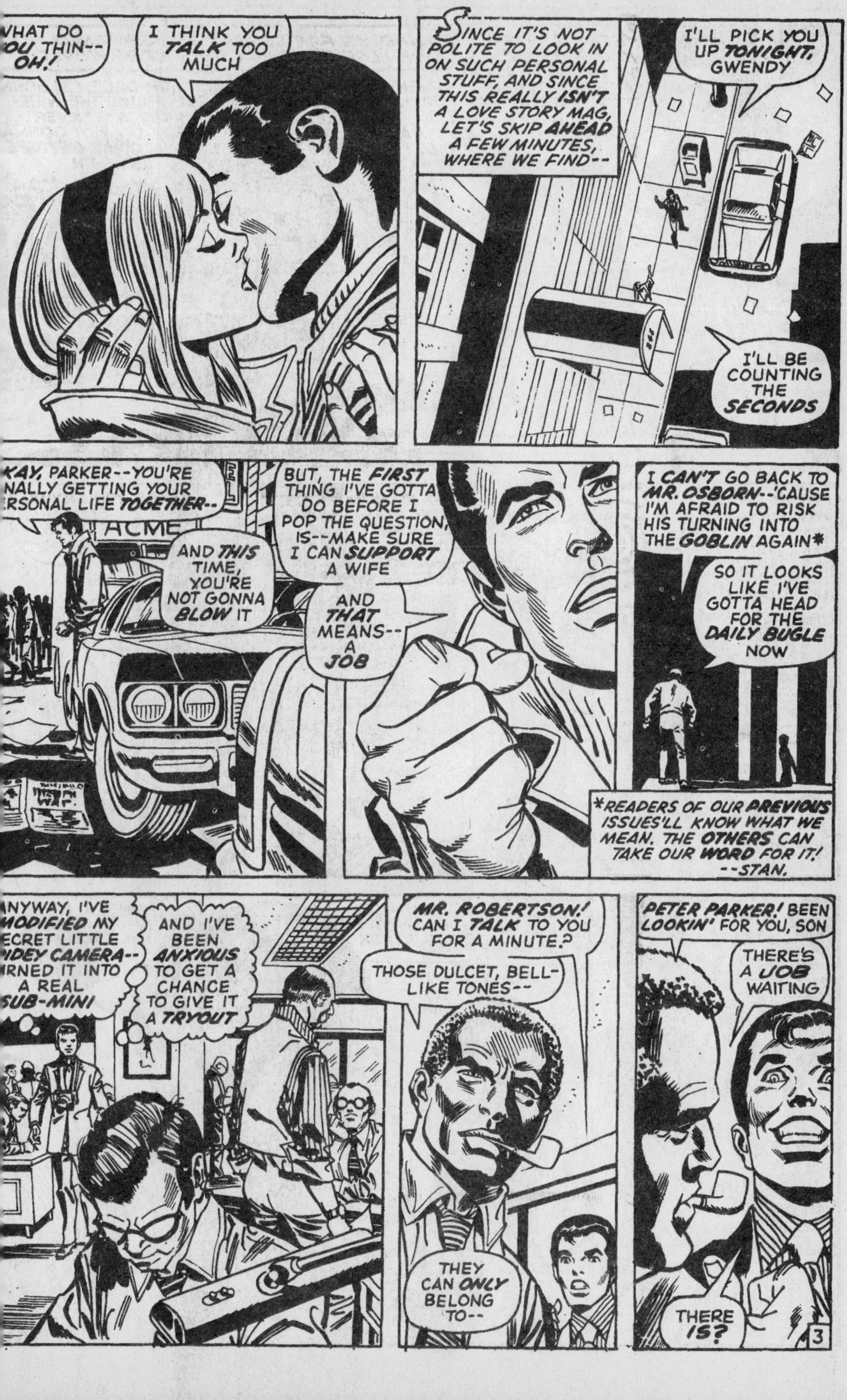

WHAT DO YOU THIN-- OH!
I THINK YOU TALK TOO MUCH
SINCE IT'S NOT POLITE TO LOOK IN ON SUCH PERSONAL STUFF, AND SINCE THIS REALLY ISN'T A LOVE STORY MAG, LET'S SKIP AHEAD A FEW MINUTES, WHERE WE FIND--
I'LL PICK YOU UP TONIGHT, GWENDY
I'LL BE COUNTING THE SECONDS
KAY, PARKER--YOU'RE NALLY GETTING YOUR RSONAL LIFE TOGETHER--
AND THIS TIME, YOU'RE NOT GONNA BLOW IT
BUT, THE FIRST THING I'VE GOTTA DO BEFORE I POP THE QUESTION, IS--MAKE SURE I CAN SUPPORT A WIFE
AND THAT MEANS-- A JOB
I CAN'T GO BACK TO MR. OSBORN--'CAUSE I'M AFRAID TO RISK HIS TURNING INTO THE GOBLIN AGAIN*
SO IT LOOKS LIKE I'VE GOTTA HEAD FOR THE DAILY BUGLE NOW
*READERS OF OUR PREVIOUS ISSUES'LL KNOW WHAT WE MEAN. THE OTHERS CAN TAKE OUR WORD FOR IT! --STAN.
NYWAY, I'VE MODIFIED MY ECRET LITTLE IDEY CAMERA-- RNED IT INTO A REAL SUB-MINI
AND I'VE BEEN ANXIOUS TO GET A CHANCE TO GIVE IT A TRYOUT
MR. ROBERTSON! CAN I TALK TO YOU FOR A MINUTE?
THOSE DULCET, BELL-LIKE TONES--
THEY CAN ONLY BELONG TO--
PETER PARKER! BEEN LOOKIN' FOR YOU, SON
THERE'S A JOB WAITING
THERE IS?

LEMME JUST CHECK IT OUT WITH *JAMESON*

IS THAT *PRISON ASSIGNMENT* STILL UP FOR GRABS, J.J.?

YEAH! ALL OUR TOP CAMERAMEN ARE EITHER *SICK* OR IN THE *FIELD*

I'M TRYING TO GET HOLD OF A GOOD *FREELANCER* NOW, BUT--

SAVE YOUR *DIME*, JONAH! YOUR WORRIES ARE *OVER*

PETER PARKER JUST DROPPED IN

PARKER, HUH? I *WONDERED* WHERE THAT KID HAD BEEN?

WELL, HE'S BETTER THAN *NOBODY*

COME *OFF* IT, MAN! HE'S GOOD AS THEY *COME*-- AND YOU *KNOW* IT

YEAH, BUT I DON'T WANNA TELL *HIM*

AWRIGHT! THERE'S A *RIOT* AT THE *CITY PEN*-- THEY'RE HOLDING THE *WARDEN* HOSTAGE

I NEED *PICTURES!* SO GET *GOING*

FIRST, LET'S TALK *MONEY*

THIS IS NO TIME TO *HASSLE!* YOU WANT EVERY OTHER PAPER TO *SCOOP* ME?

SPARE ME THE *CRYING ACT*, MISTER

I'M *THRU* SELLING MY SHOTS TO YOU FOR *CHICKEN FEED*

SO SETTLE THE PRICE *NOW*, OR NO DEAL

LOOK! CHANCES ARE *SPIDER-MAN* MAY BE ON THE SCENE

AND THAT MEANS I'LL BE RISKING MY *LIFE* FOR THOSE PHOTOS

WITH *ME* YOU GET TOUGH? WITH *ME*?

SO MY *PRICE* JUST WENT U

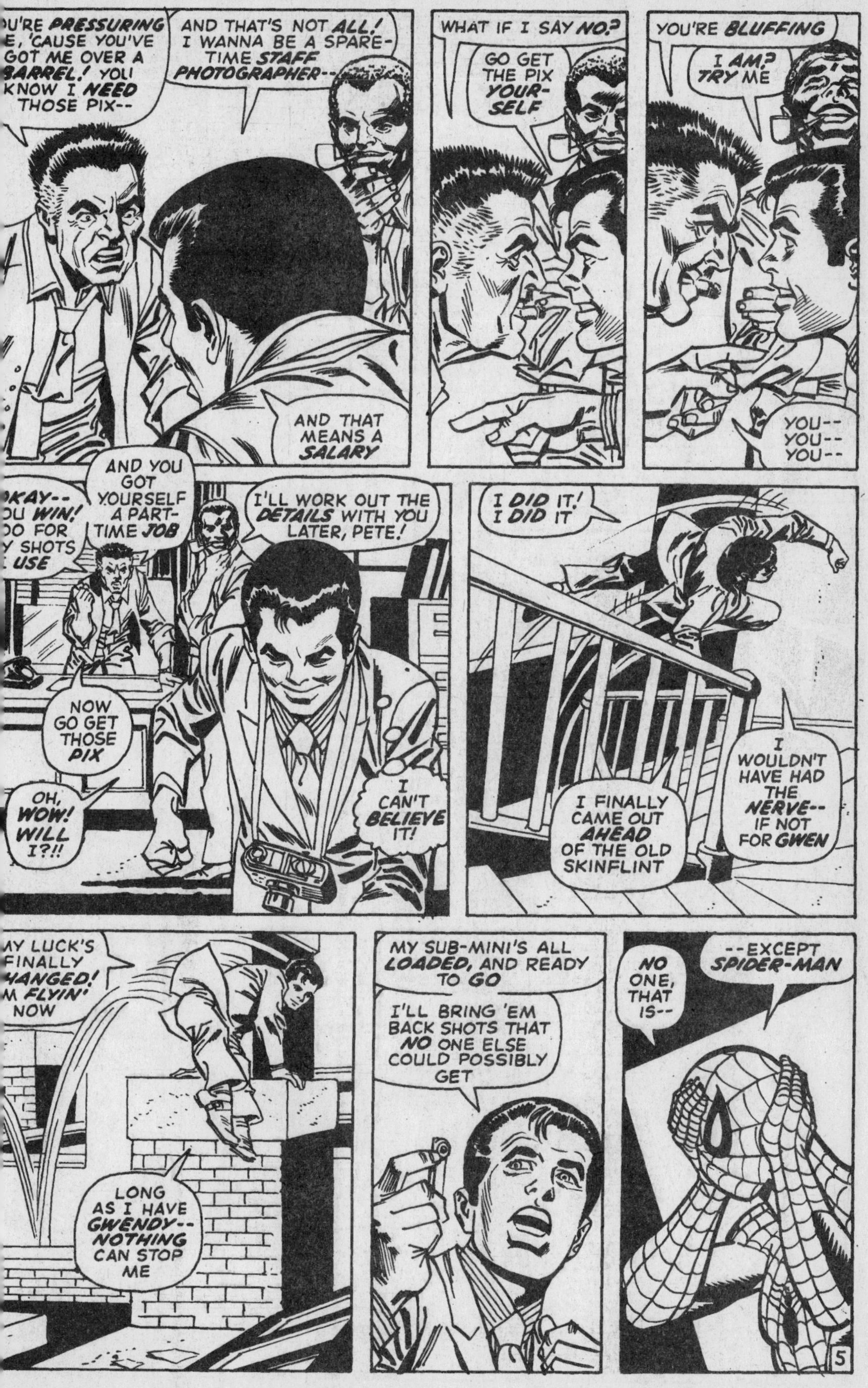

OU'RE PRESSURING E, 'CAUSE YOU'VE GOT ME OVER A BARREL! YOU KNOW I NEED THOSE PIX--
AND THAT'S NOT ALL! I WANNA BE A SPARE-TIME STAFF PHOTOGRAPHER--
AND THAT MEANS A SALARY
WHAT IF I SAY NO?
GO GET THE PIX YOURSELF
YOU'RE BLUFFING
I AM? TRY ME
YOU-- YOU-- YOU--
OKAY-- OU WIN! OO FOR Y SHOTS USE
AND YOU GOT YOURSELF A PART-TIME JOB
I'LL WORK OUT THE DETAILS WITH YOU LATER, PETE!
NOW GO GET THOSE PIX
OH, WOW! WILL I?!!
I CAN'T BELIEVE IT!
I DID IT! I DID IT
I FINALLY CAME OUT AHEAD OF THE OLD SKINFLINT
I WOULDN'T HAVE HAD THE NERVE-- IF NOT FOR GWEN
MY LUCK'S FINALLY HANGED! M FLYIN' NOW
LONG AS I HAVE GWENDY-- NOTHING CAN STOP ME
MY SUB-MINI'S ALL LOADED, AND READY TO GO
I'LL BRING 'EM BACK SHOTS THAT NO ONE ELSE COULD POSSIBLY GET
NO ONE, THAT IS--
--EXCEPT SPIDER-MAN
5

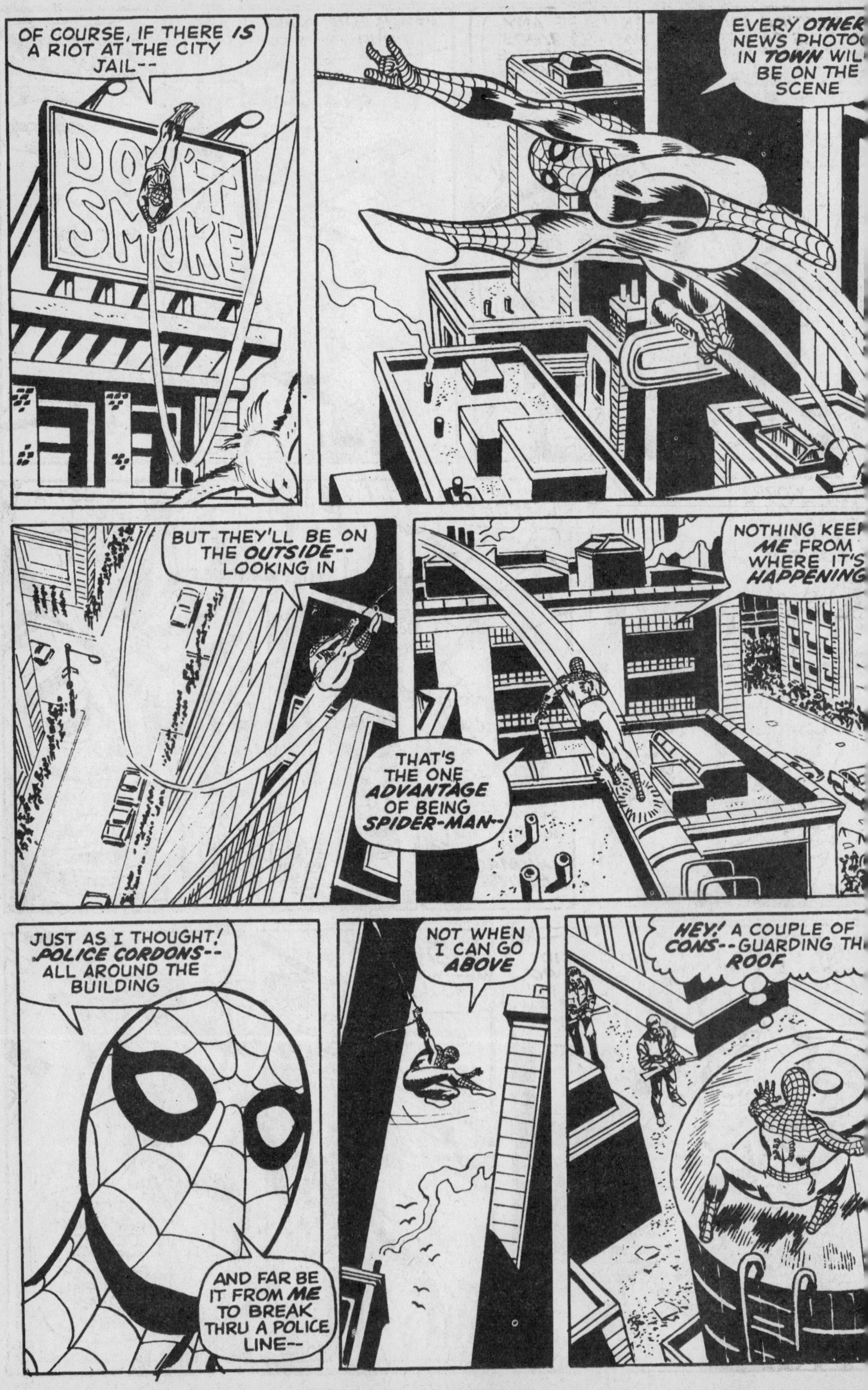
OF COURSE, IF THERE IS A RIOT AT THE CITY JAIL--
DON'T SMOKE
EVERY OTHER NEWS PHOTO IN TOWN WIL BE ON THE SCENE
BUT THEY'LL BE ON THE OUTSIDE-- LOOKING IN
NOTHING KEEP ME FROM WHERE IT'S HAPPENING
THAT'S THE ONE ADVANTAGE OF BEING SPIDER-MAN--
JUST AS I THOUGHT! POLICE CORDONS-- ALL AROUND THE BUILDING
AND FAR BE IT FROM ME TO BREAK THRU A POLICE LINE--
NOT WHEN I CAN GO ABOVE
HEY! A COUPLE OF CONS--GUARDING TH ROOF

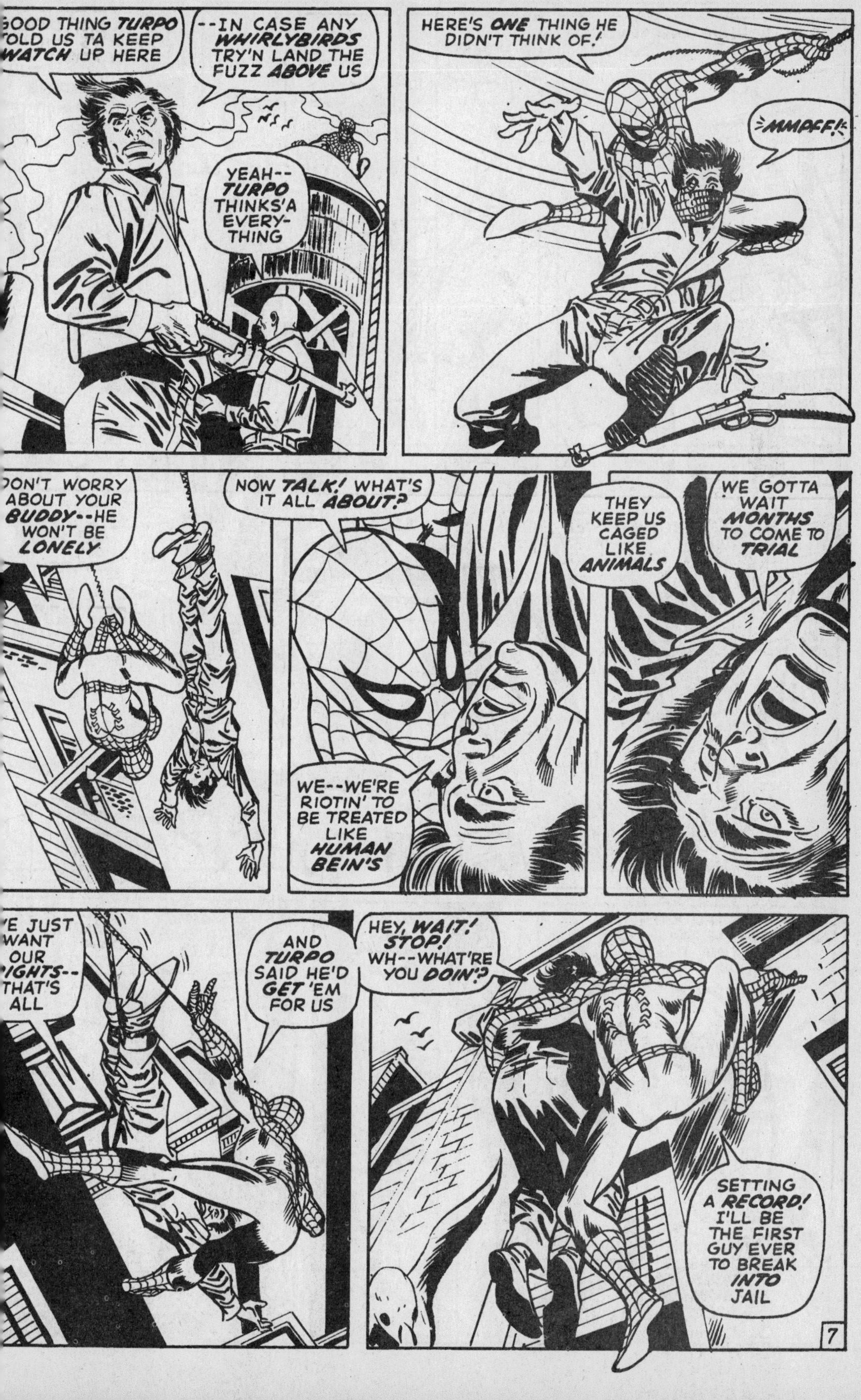

GOOD THING TURPO TOLD US TA KEEP WATCH UP HERE
--IN CASE ANY WHIRLYBIRDS TRY'N LAND THE FUZZ ABOVE US
YEAH--TURPO THINKS'A EVERY-THING
HERE'S ONE THING HE DIDN'T THINK OF!
MMPFF!
DON'T WORRY ABOUT YOUR BUDDY--HE WON'T BE LONELY
NOW TALK! WHAT'S IT ALL ABOUT?
WE--WE'RE RIOTIN' TO BE TREATED LIKE HUMAN BEIN'S
THEY KEEP US CAGED LIKE ANIMALS
WE GOTTA WAIT MONTHS TO COME TO TRIAL
WE JUST WANT OUR RIGHTS--THAT'S ALL
AND TURPO SAID HE'D GET 'EM FOR US
HEY, WAIT! STOP! WH--WHAT'RE YOU DOIN'?
SETTING A RECORD! I'LL BE THE FIRST GUY EVER TO BREAK INTO JAIL

NOW, *YOU* STAY THERE AND THINK NICE THOUGHTS-- WHILE I GO FIND OUR FRIEND *TURPO*

AND, SINCE I'M NOT APT TO WIN ANY *POPULARITY PRIZES* IN A PLACE LIKE THIS--

THE LESS ANY-ONE *SEES* OF ME, THE *BETTER*

ANY WORD FROM *TURPO* YET?

NO! HE'S STILL IN WITH THE *WARDEN*

THE WARDEN BETTER COME *ACROSS*-- OR *ELSE*

SO THAT'S THE *SIZE* OF IT, HUH?

LOOKS LIKE I'D BETTER *GET* TO THE WARDEN-- BUT *FAST*

THOSE *CONS* IN THERE ARE PLAYING FOR *KEEPS*

THE ONE I *SPOKE* TO WAS *LEVELLING* WITH ME

HE REALLY *MEANT* IT ABOUT THOSE GRIPES

BUT-- WHERE DOES THE *BLAME* LIE?

DO AS WE *TELL* YA, MAN

YOU CAN'T GET *AWAY* WITH THIS, TURPO

YOU'RE SELLING THOSE CO— DOWN TH— *RIVER*

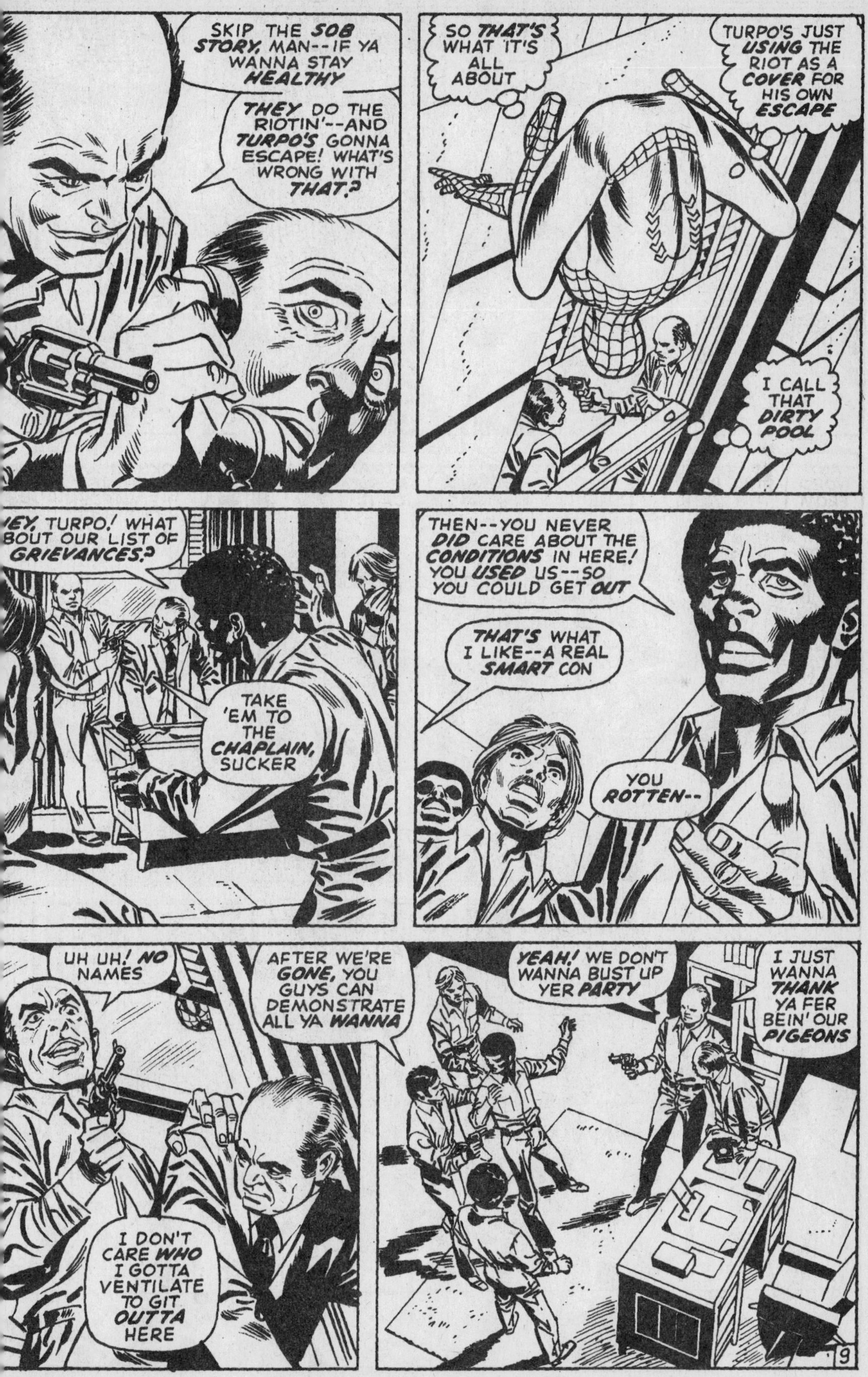
SKIP THE SOB STORY, MAN--IF YA WANNA STAY HEALTHY
THEY DO THE RIOTIN'--AND TURPO'S GONNA ESCAPE! WHAT'S WRONG WITH THAT?
SO THAT'S WHAT IT'S ALL ABOUT
TURPO'S JUST USING THE RIOT AS A COVER FOR HIS OWN ESCAPE
I CALL THAT DIRTY POOL
EY, TURPO! WHAT BOUT OUR LIST OF GRIEVANCES?
TAKE 'EM TO THE CHAPLAIN, SUCKER
THEN--YOU NEVER DID CARE ABOUT THE CONDITIONS IN HERE! YOU USED US--SO YOU COULD GET OUT
THAT'S WHAT I LIKE--A REAL SMART CON
YOU ROTTEN--
UH UH! NO NAMES
I DON'T CARE WHO I GOTTA VENTILATE TO GIT OUTTA HERE
AFTER WE'RE GONE, YOU GUYS CAN DEMONSTRATE ALL YA WANNA
YEAH! WE DON'T WANNA BUST UP YER PARTY
I JUST WANNA THANK YA FER BEIN' OUR PIGEONS
9

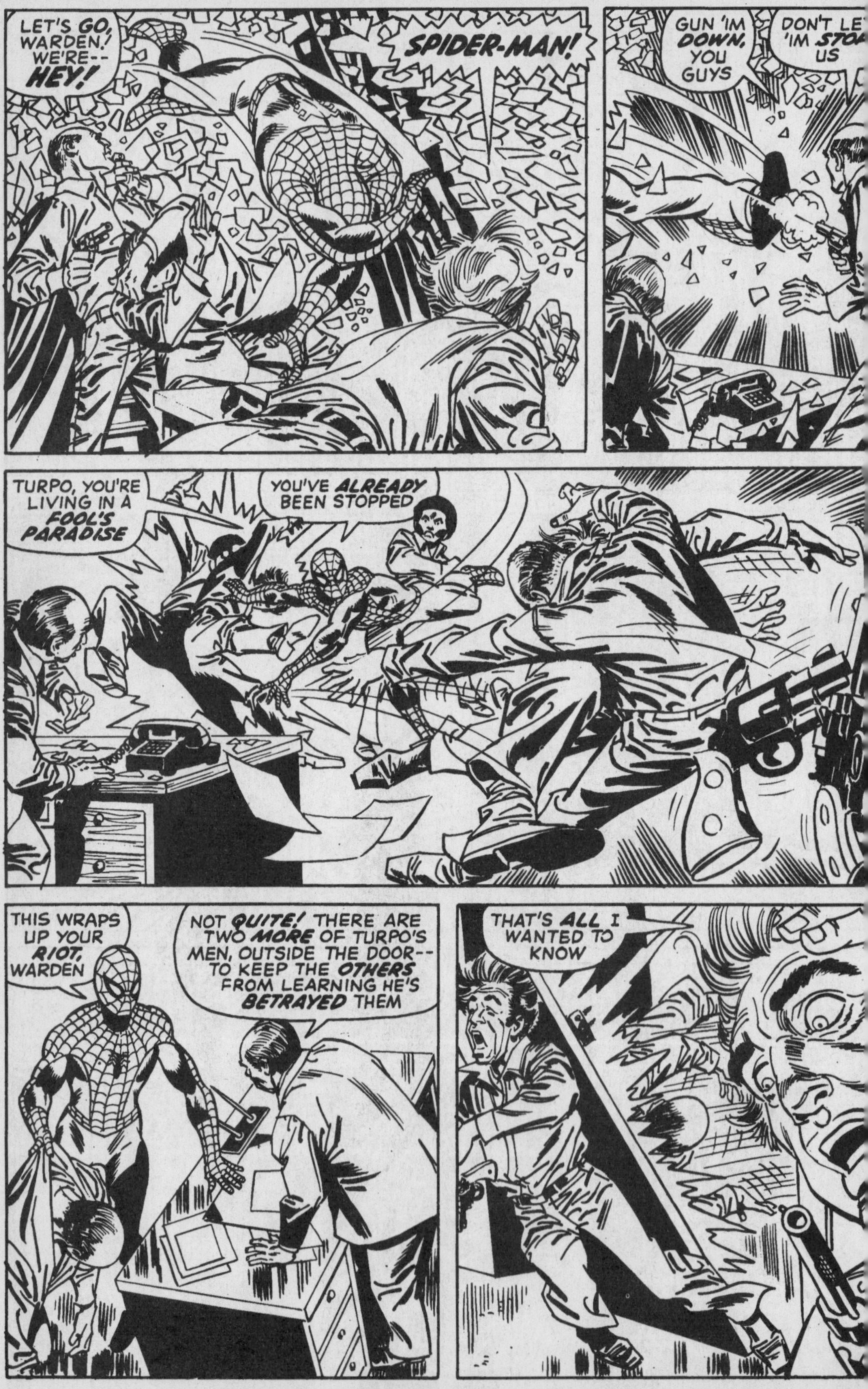

LET'S GO, WARDEN! WE'RE-- HEY!
SPIDER-MAN!
GUN 'IM DOWN, YOU GUYS
DON'T LE 'IM STO US
TURPO, YOU'RE LIVING IN A FOOL'S PARADISE
YOU'VE ALREADY BEEN STOPPED
THIS WRAPS UP YOUR RIOT, WARDEN
NOT QUITE! THERE ARE TWO MORE OF TURPO'S MEN, OUTSIDE THE DOOR-- TO KEEP THE OTHERS FROM LEARNING HE'S BETRAYED THEM
THAT'S ALL I WANTED TO KNOW

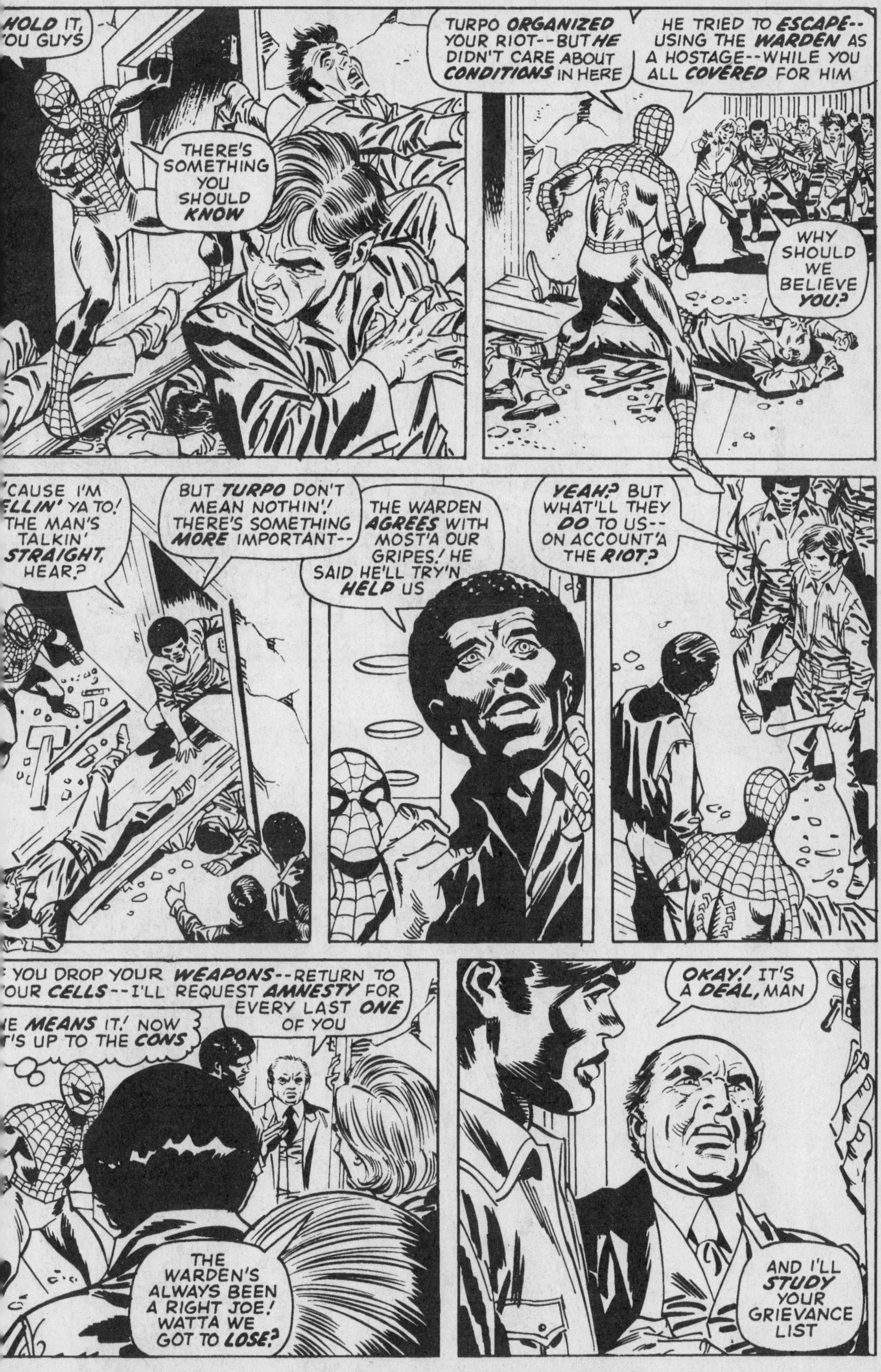
HOLD IT, YOU GUYS
THERE'S SOMETHING YOU SHOULD KNOW
TURPO ORGANIZED YOUR RIOT--BUT HE DIDN'T CARE ABOUT CONDITIONS IN HERE
HE TRIED TO ESCAPE--USING THE WARDEN AS A HOSTAGE--WHILE YOU ALL COVERED FOR HIM
WHY SHOULD WE BELIEVE YOU?
'CAUSE I'M ELLIN' YA TO! THE MAN'S TALKIN' STRAIGHT, HEAR?
BUT TURPO DON'T MEAN NOTHIN'! THERE'S SOMETHING MORE IMPORTANT--
THE WARDEN AGREES WITH MOST'A OUR GRIPES! HE SAID HE'LL TRY'N HELP US
YEAH? BUT WHAT'LL THEY DO TO US--ON ACCOUNT'A THE RIOT?
YOU DROP YOUR WEAPONS--RETURN TO YOUR CELLS--I'LL REQUEST AMNESTY FOR EVERY LAST ONE OF YOU
E MEANS IT! NOW T'S UP TO THE CONS
THE WARDEN'S ALWAYS BEEN A RIGHT JOE! WATTA WE GOT TO LOSE?
OKAY! IT'S A DEAL, MAN
AND I'LL STUDY YOUR GRIEVANCE LIST

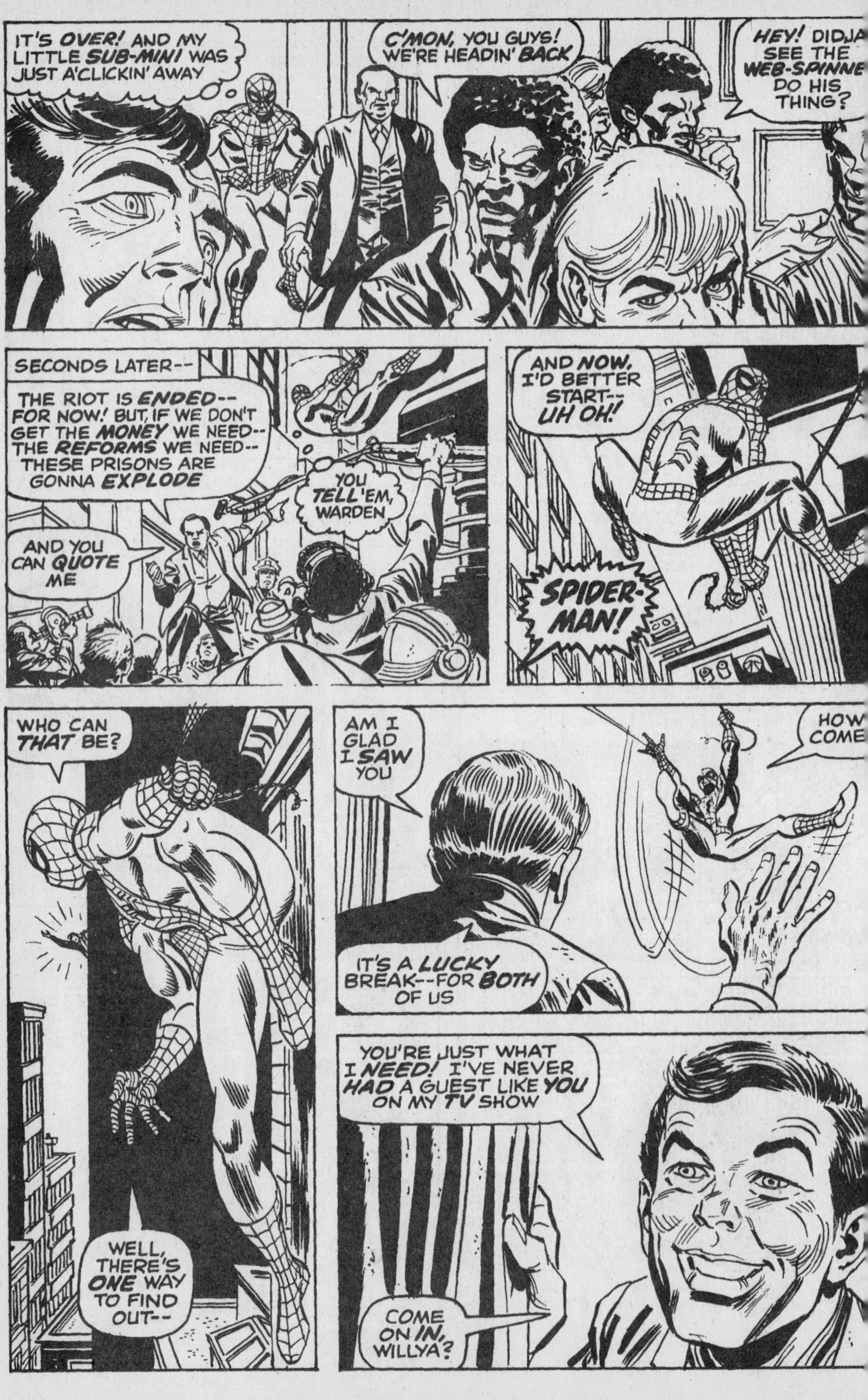
IT'S OVER! AND MY LITTLE SUB-MINI WAS JUST A'CLICKIN' AWAY
C'MON, YOU GUYS! WE'RE HEADIN' BACK
HEY! DIDJA SEE THE WEB-SPINNE DO HIS THING?
SECONDS LATER--
THE RIOT IS ENDED--FOR NOW! BUT, IF WE DON'T GET THE MONEY WE NEED--THE REFORMS WE NEED--THESE PRISONS ARE GONNA EXPLODE
YOU TELL 'EM, WARDEN
AND YOU CAN QUOTE ME
AND NOW, I'D BETTER START--UH OH!
SPIDER-MAN!
WHO CAN THAT BE?
WELL, THERE'S ONE WAY TO FIND OUT--
AM I GLAD I SAW YOU
HOW COME
IT'S A LUCKY BREAK--FOR BOTH OF US
YOU'RE JUST WHAT I NEED! I'VE NEVER HAD A GUEST LIKE YOU ON MY TV SHOW
COME ON IN, WILLYA?

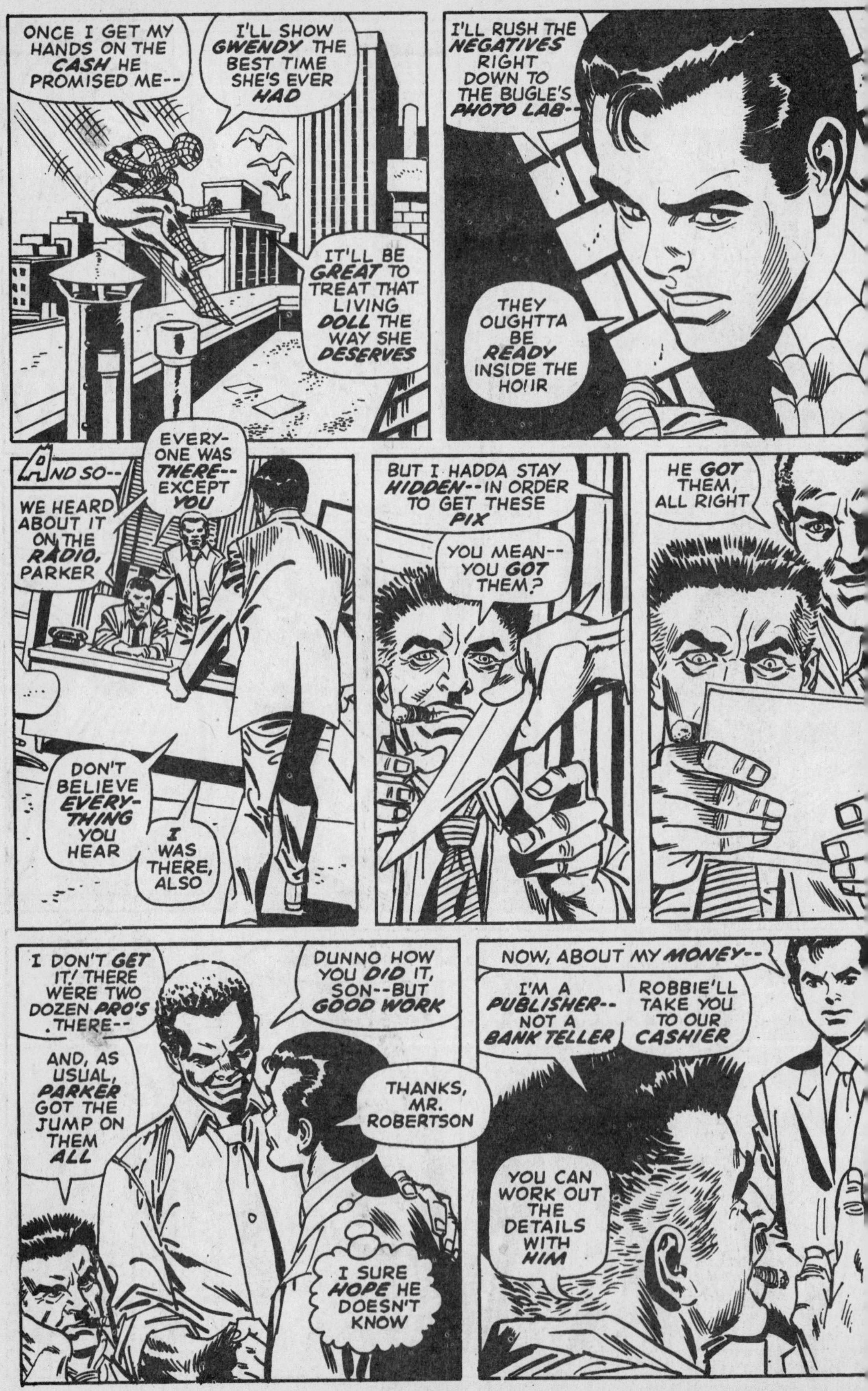
ONCE I GET MY HANDS ON THE CASH HE PROMISED ME--
I'LL SHOW GWENDY THE BEST TIME SHE'S EVER HAD
IT'LL BE GREAT TO TREAT THAT LIVING DOLL THE WAY SHE DESERVES
I'LL RUSH THE NEGATIVES RIGHT DOWN TO THE BUGLE'S PHOTO LAB--
THEY OUGHTTA BE READY INSIDE THE HOUR
AND SO--
WE HEARD ABOUT IT ON THE RADIO, PARKER
EVERY-ONE WAS THERE--EXCEPT YOU
DON'T BELIEVE EVERY-THING YOU HEAR
I WAS THERE, ALSO
BUT I HADDA STAY HIDDEN--IN ORDER TO GET THESE PIX
YOU MEAN--YOU GOT THEM?
HE GOT THEM, ALL RIGHT
I DON'T GET IT! THERE WERE TWO DOZEN PRO'S THERE--
AND, AS USUAL, PARKER GOT THE JUMP ON THEM ALL
DUNNO HOW YOU DID IT, SON--BUT GOOD WORK
THANKS, MR. ROBERTSON
I SURE HOPE HE DOESN'T KNOW
NOW, ABOUT MY MONEY--
I'M A PUBLISHER--NOT A BANK TELLER
ROBBIE'LL TAKE YOU TO OUR CASHIER
YOU CAN WORK OUT THE DETAILS WITH HIM

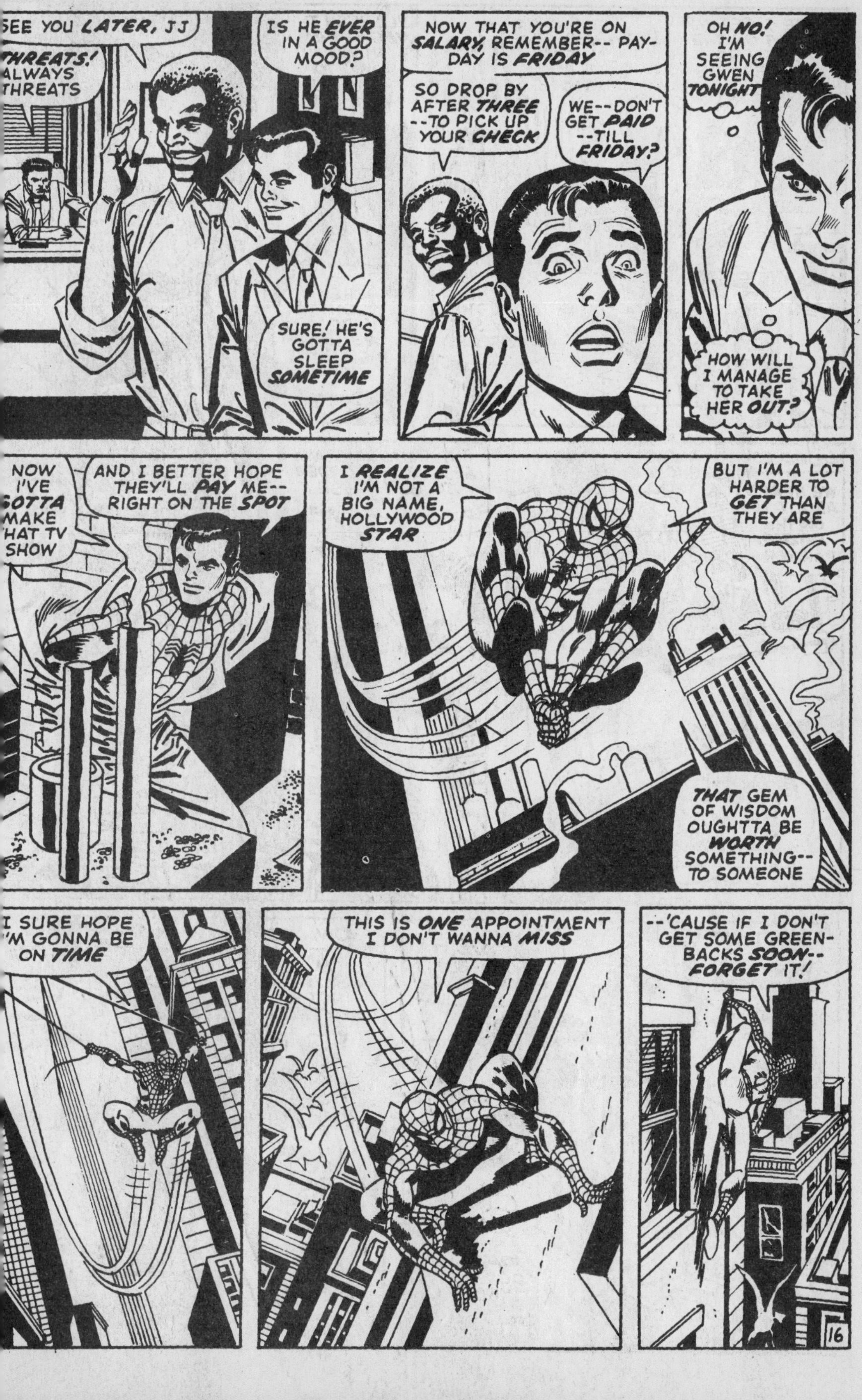
SEE YOU LATER, JJ
THREATS! ALWAYS THREATS
IS HE EVER IN A GOOD MOOD?
SURE! HE'S GOTTA SLEEP SOMETIME
NOW THAT YOU'RE ON SALARY, REMEMBER-- PAY-DAY IS FRIDAY
SO DROP BY AFTER THREE --TO PICK UP YOUR CHECK
WE--DON'T GET PAID --TILL FRIDAY?
OH NO! I'M SEEING GWEN TONIGHT
HOW WILL I MANAGE TO TAKE HER OUT?
NOW I'VE GOTTA MAKE THAT TV SHOW
AND I BETTER HOPE THEY'LL PAY ME-- RIGHT ON THE SPOT
I REALIZE I'M NOT A BIG NAME, HOLLYWOOD STAR
BUT I'M A LOT HARDER TO GET THAN THEY ARE
THAT GEM OF WISDOM OUGHTTA BE WORTH SOMETHING-- TO SOMEONE
I SURE HOPE I'M GONNA BE ON TIME
THIS IS ONE APPOINTMENT I DON'T WANNA MISS
--'CAUSE IF I DON'T GET SOME GREEN-BACKS SOON-- FORGET IT!

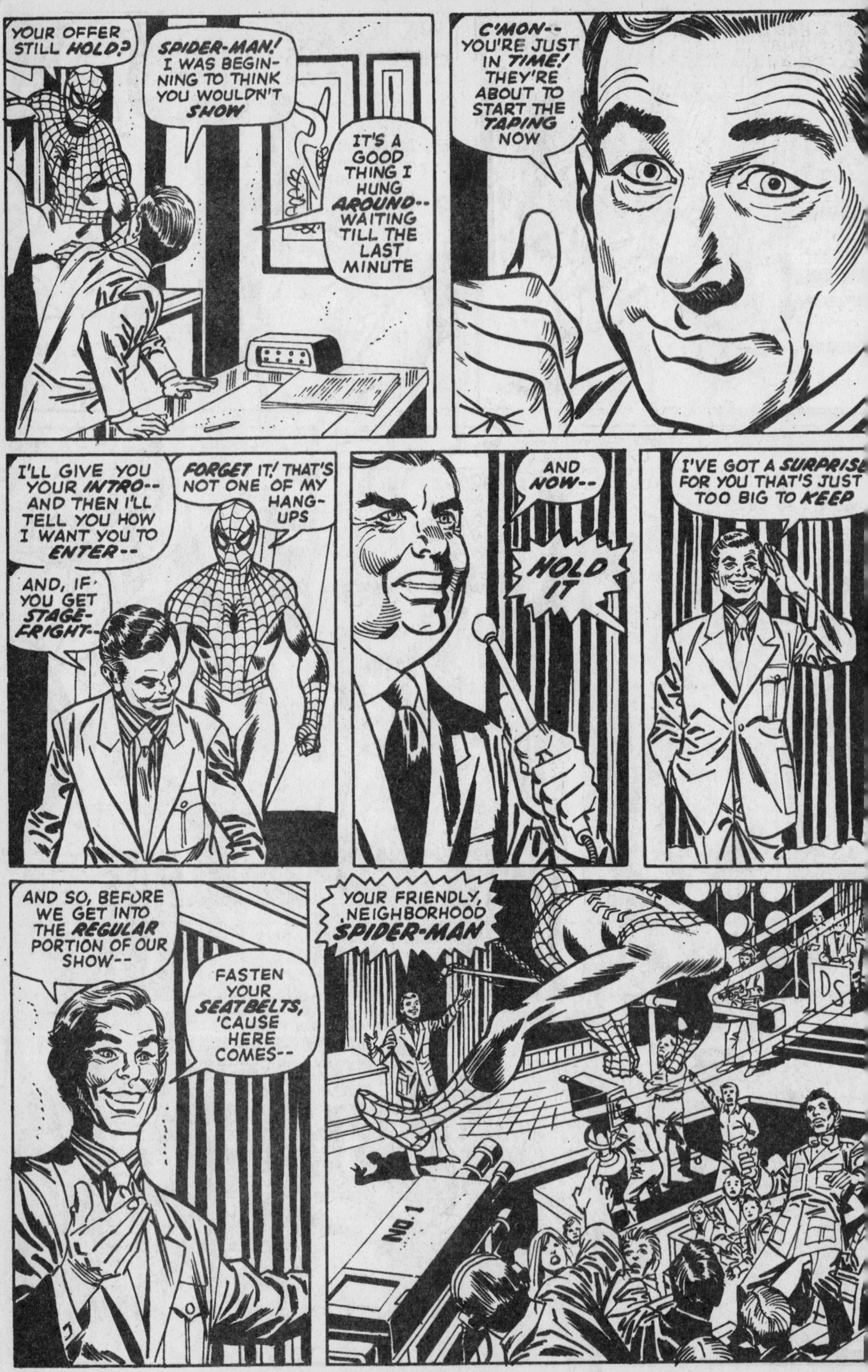
YOUR OFFER STILL HOLD?
SPIDER-MAN! I WAS BEGINNING TO THINK YOU WOULDN'T SHOW
IT'S A GOOD THING I HUNG AROUND-- WAITING TILL THE LAST MINUTE
C'MON-- YOU'RE JUST IN TIME! THEY'RE ABOUT TO START THE TAPING NOW
I'LL GIVE YOU YOUR INTRO-- AND THEN I'LL TELL YOU HOW I WANT YOU TO ENTER--
FORGET IT! THAT'S NOT ONE OF MY HANG-UPS
AND, IF YOU GET STAGE-FRIGHT--
AND NOW--
HOLD IT
I'VE GOT A SURPRISE FOR YOU THAT'S JUST TOO BIG TO KEEP
AND SO, BEFORE WE GET INTO THE REGULAR PORTION OF OUR SHOW--
FASTEN YOUR SEATBELTS, 'CAUSE HERE COMES--
YOUR FRIENDLY, NEIGHBORHOOD SPIDER-MAN
DS
NO. 1

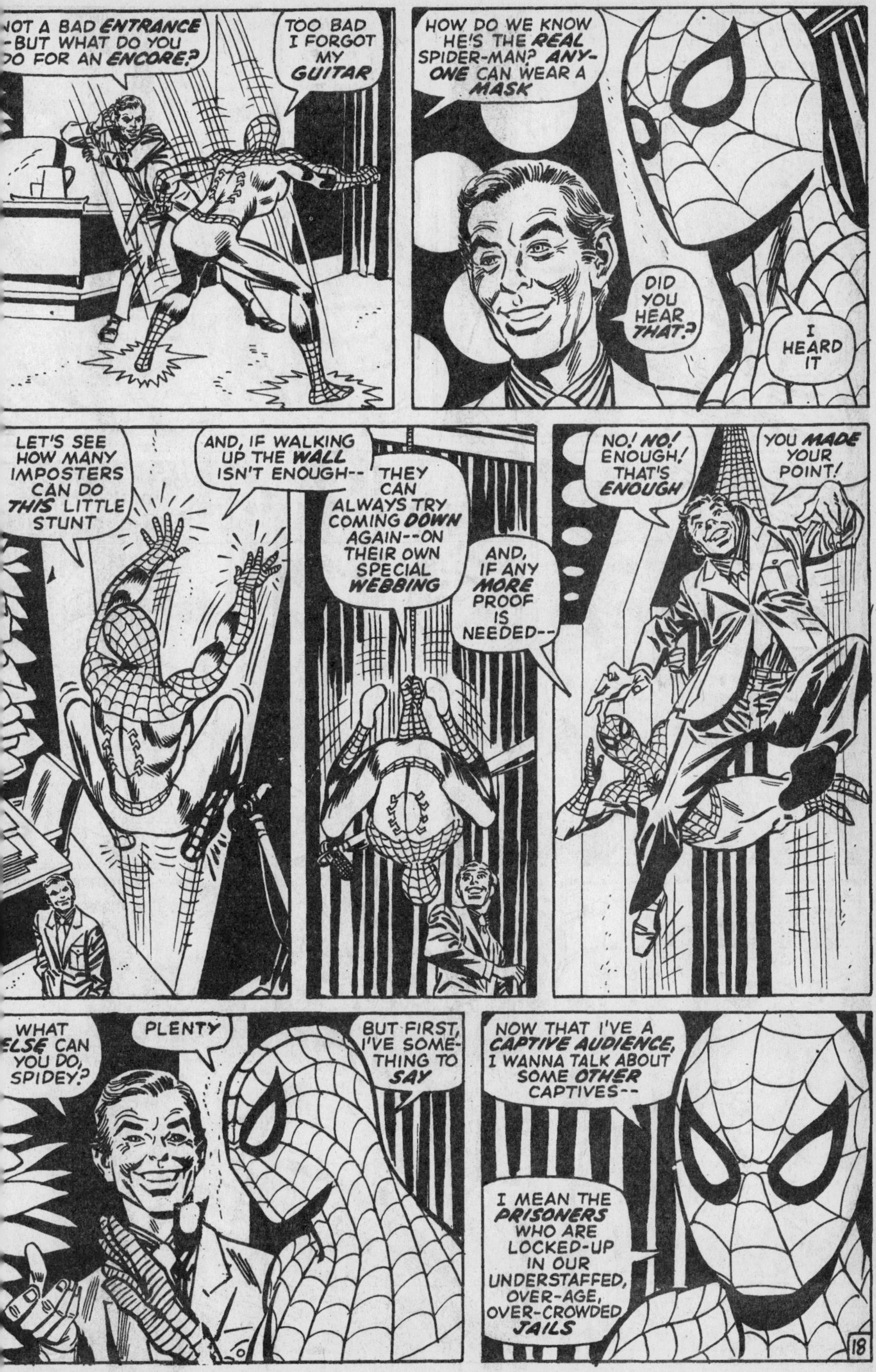
NOT A BAD ENTRANCE --BUT WHAT DO YOU DO FOR AN ENCORE?
TOO BAD I FORGOT MY GUITAR
HOW DO WE KNOW HE'S THE REAL SPIDER-MAN? ANY-ONE CAN WEAR A MASK
DID YOU HEAR THAT?
I HEARD IT
LET'S SEE HOW MANY IMPOSTERS CAN DO THIS LITTLE STUNT
AND, IF WALKING UP THE WALL ISN'T ENOUGH--
THEY CAN ALWAYS TRY COMING DOWN AGAIN--ON THEIR OWN SPECIAL WEBBING
AND, IF ANY MORE PROOF IS NEEDED--
NO! NO! ENOUGH! THAT'S ENOUGH
YOU MADE YOUR POINT!
WHAT ELSE CAN YOU DO, SPIDEY?
PLENTY
BUT FIRST, I'VE SOME-THING TO SAY
NOW THAT I'VE A CAPTIVE AUDIENCE, I WANNA TALK ABOUT SOME OTHER CAPTIVES--
I MEAN THE PRISONERS WHO ARE LOCKED-UP IN OUR UNDERSTAFFED, OVER-AGE, OVER-CROWDED JAILS
18

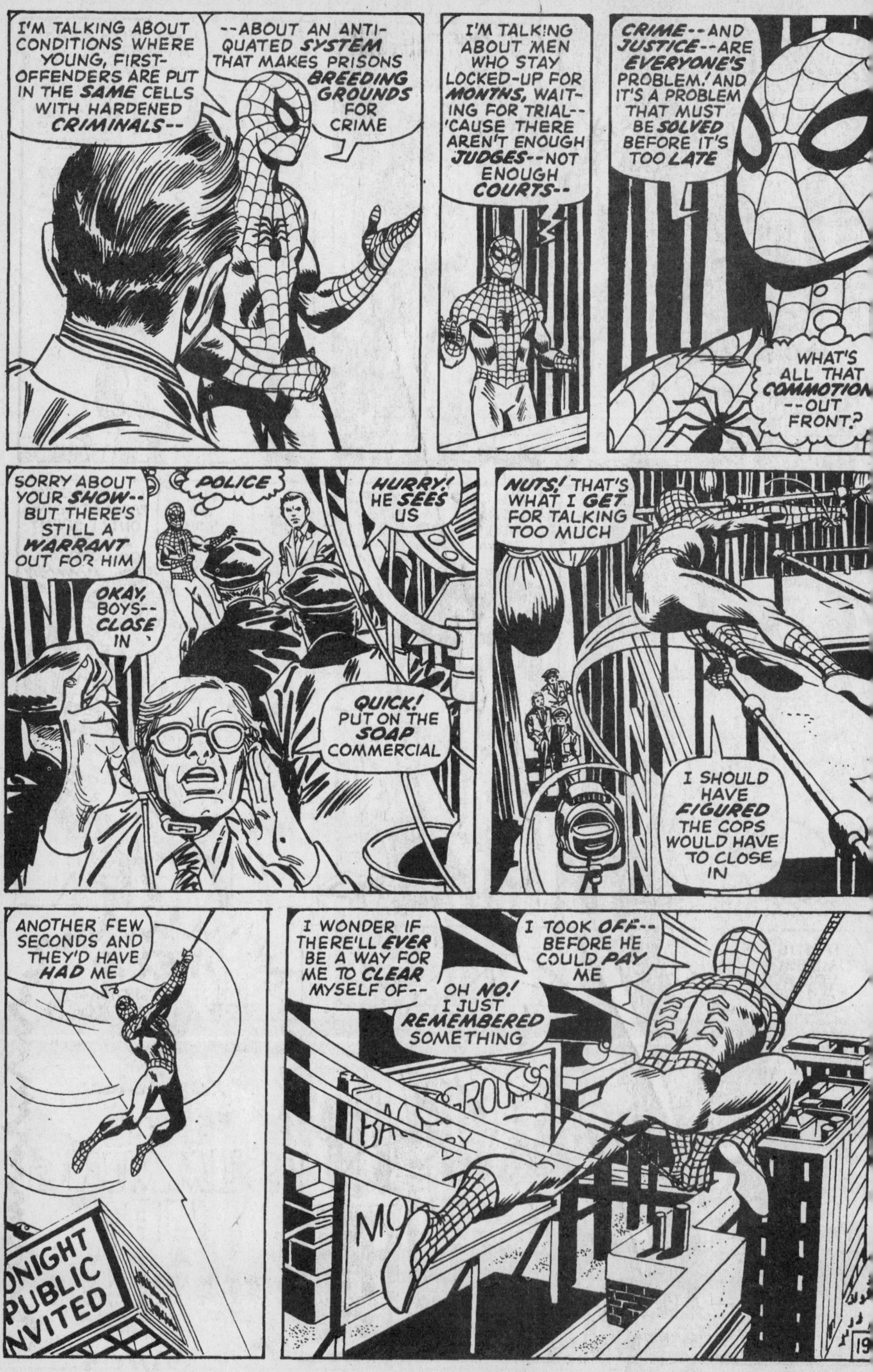
I'M TALKING ABOUT CONDITIONS WHERE YOUNG, FIRST-OFFENDERS ARE PUT IN THE SAME CELLS WITH HARDENED CRIMINALS--
--ABOUT AN ANTI-QUATED SYSTEM THAT MAKES PRISONS BREEDING GROUNDS FOR CRIME
I'M TALKING ABOUT MEN WHO STAY LOCKED-UP FOR MONTHS, WAITING FOR TRIAL--'CAUSE THERE AREN'T ENOUGH JUDGES--NOT ENOUGH COURTS--
CRIME--AND JUSTICE--ARE EVERYONE'S PROBLEM! AND IT'S A PROBLEM THAT MUST BE SOLVED BEFORE IT'S TOO LATE
WHAT'S ALL THAT COMMOTION--OUT FRONT?
SORRY ABOUT YOUR SHOW--BUT THERE'S STILL A WARRANT OUT FOR HIM
POLICE
HURRY! HE SEES US
OKAY, BOYS--CLOSE IN
QUICK! PUT ON THE SOAP COMMERCIAL
NUTS! THAT'S WHAT I GET FOR TALKING TOO MUCH
I SHOULD HAVE FIGURED THE COPS WOULD HAVE TO CLOSE IN
ANOTHER FEW SECONDS AND THEY'D HAVE HAD ME
ONIGHT PUBLIC NVITED
I WONDER IF THERE'LL EVER BE A WAY FOR ME TO CLEAR MYSELF OF--
OH NO! I JUST REMEMBERED SOMETHING
I TOOK OFF--BEFORE HE COULD PAY ME
19

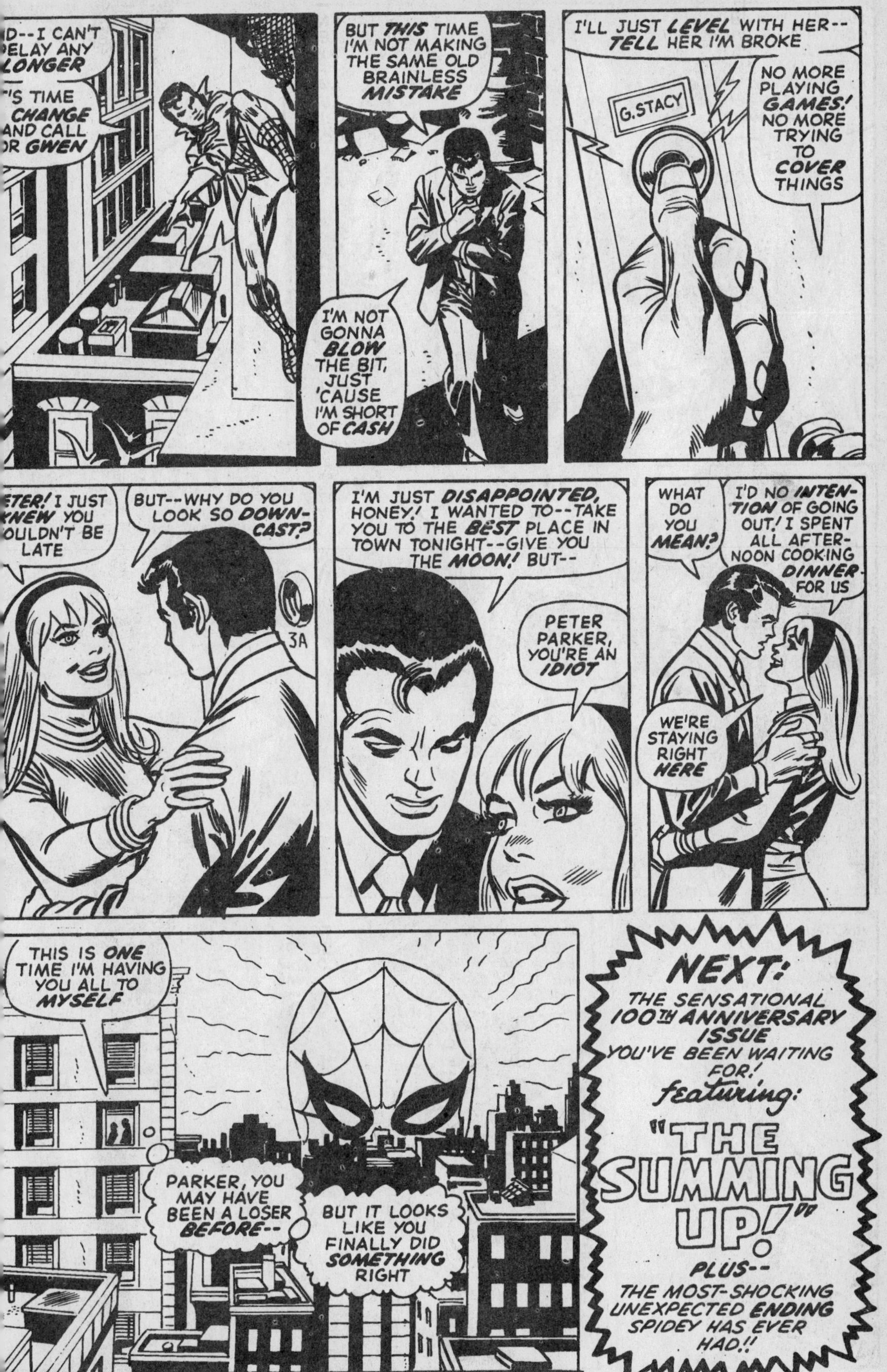

D--I CAN'T DELAY ANY LONGER
'S TIME CHANGE AND CALL OR GWEN
BUT THIS TIME I'M NOT MAKING THE SAME OLD BRAINLESS MISTAKE
I'M NOT GONNA BLOW THE BIT, JUST 'CAUSE I'M SHORT OF CASH
I'LL JUST LEVEL WITH HER--TELL HER I'M BROKE
G. STACY
NO MORE PLAYING GAMES! NO MORE TRYING TO COVER THINGS
ETER! I JUST KNEW YOU OULDN'T BE LATE
BUT--WHY DO YOU LOOK SO DOWN-CAST?
3A
I'M JUST DISAPPOINTED, HONEY! I WANTED TO--TAKE YOU TO THE BEST PLACE IN TOWN TONIGHT--GIVE YOU THE MOON! BUT--
PETER PARKER, YOU'RE AN IDIOT
WHAT DO YOU MEAN?
I'D NO INTENTION OF GOING OUT! I SPENT ALL AFTERNOON COOKING DINNER FOR US
WE'RE STAYING RIGHT HERE
THIS IS ONE TIME I'M HAVING YOU ALL TO MYSELF
PARKER, YOU MAY HAVE BEEN A LOSER BEFORE--
BUT IT LOOKS LIKE YOU FINALLY DID SOMETHING RIGHT
NEXT:
THE SENSATIONAL 100TH ANNIVERSARY ISSUE YOU'VE BEEN WAITING FOR!
featuring:
"THE SUMMING UP!"
PLUS--
THE MOST-SHOCKING UNEXPECTED ENDING SPIDEY HAS EVER HAD!!

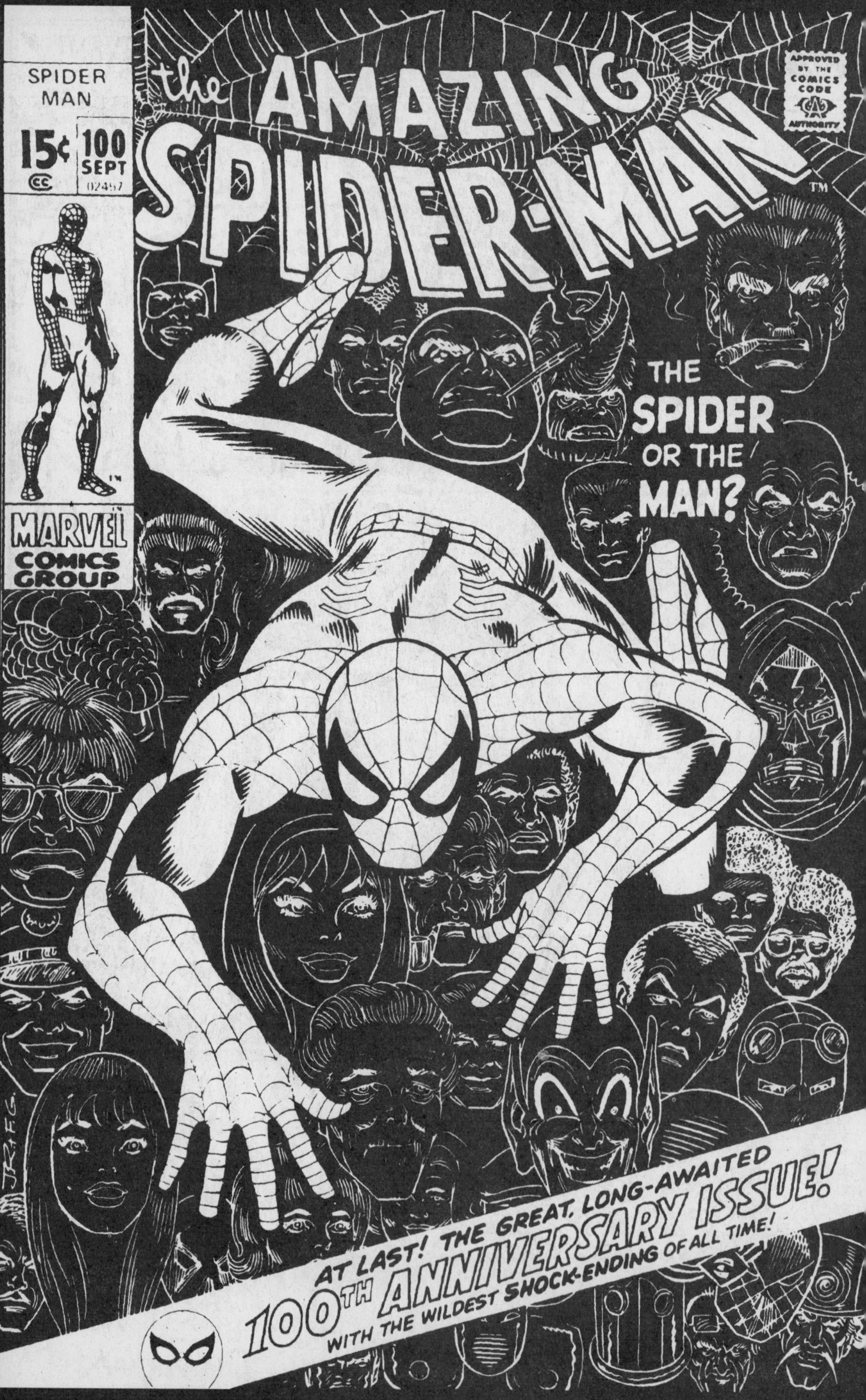
SPIDER MAN
15¢ 100 SEPT
02457
MARVEL COMICS GROUP
the AMAZING SPIDER-MAN
APPROVED BY THE COMICS CODE AUTHORITY
THE SPIDER OR THE MAN?
AT LAST! THE GREAT, LONG-AWAITED
100TH ANNIVERSARY ISSUE!
WITH THE WILDEST SHOCK-ENDING OF ALL TIME!

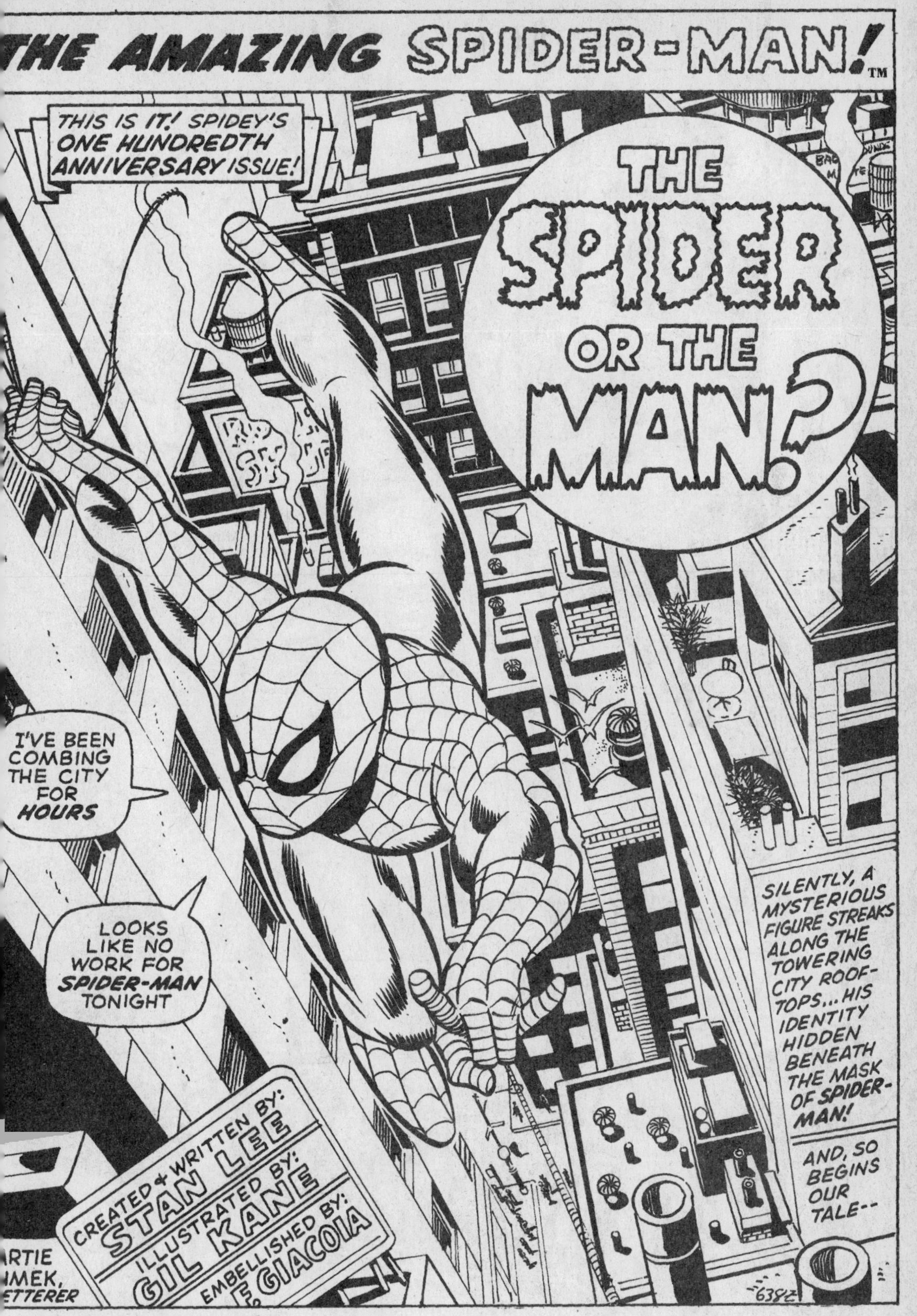
THE AMAZING SPIDER-MAN! TM
THIS IS IT! SPIDEY'S ONE HUNDREDTH ANNIVERSARY ISSUE!
THE SPIDER OR THE MAN?
I'VE BEEN COMBING THE CITY FOR HOURS
LOOKS LIKE NO WORK FOR SPIDER-MAN TONIGHT
SILENTLY, A MYSTERIOUS FIGURE STREAKS ALONG THE TOWERING CITY ROOF-TOPS... HIS IDENTITY HIDDEN BENEATH THE MASK OF SPIDER-MAN!
AND, SO BEGINS OUR TALE--
CREATED & WRITTEN BY: STAN LEE
ILLUSTRATED BY: GIL KANE
EMBELLISHED BY: F. GIACOIA
ARTIE SIMEK, LETTERER

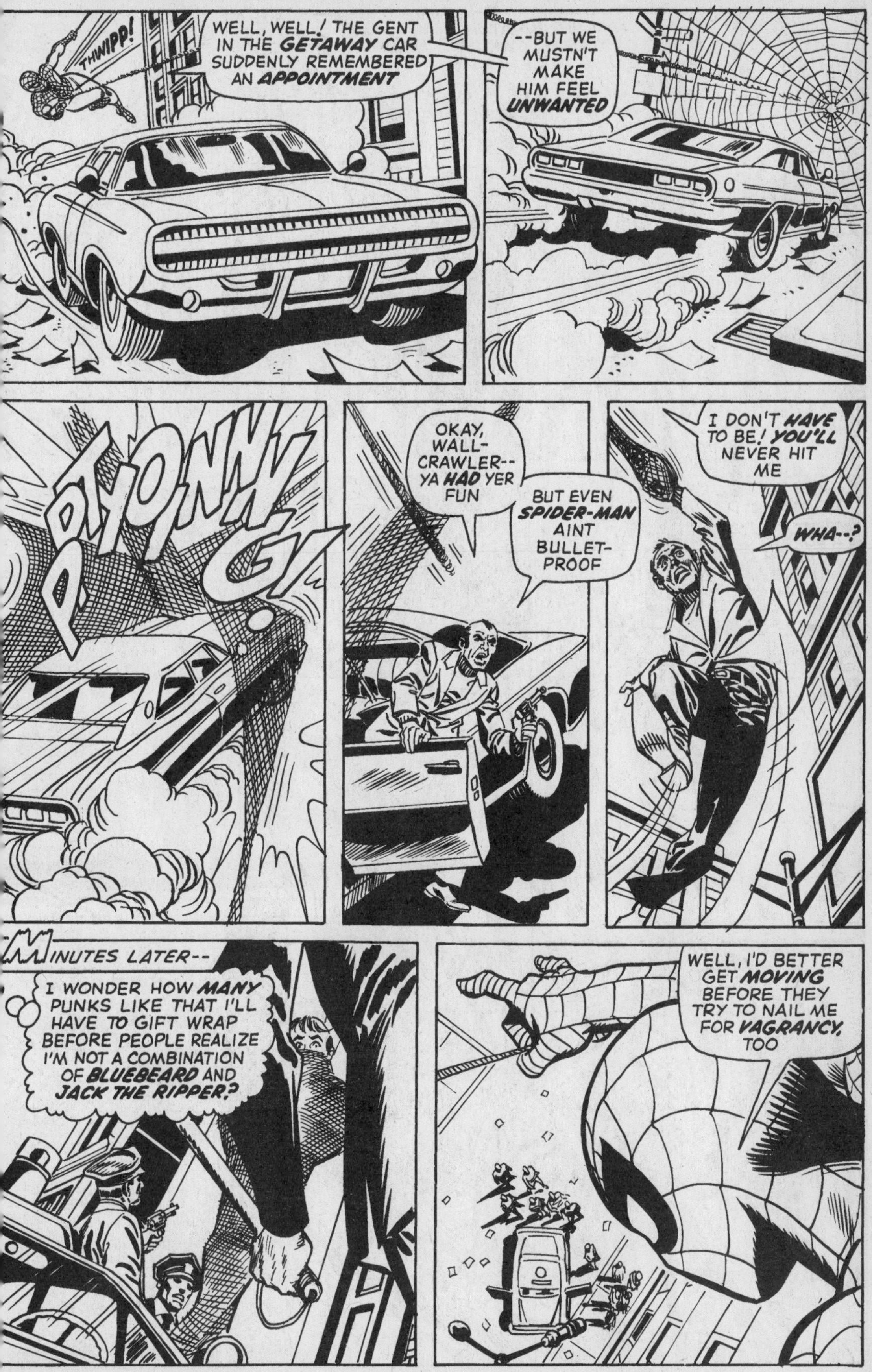
THWIPP!
WELL, WELL! THE GENT IN THE GETAWAY CAR SUDDENLY REMEMBERED AN APPOINTMENT
--BUT WE MUSTN'T MAKE HIM FEEL UNWANTED
PTYONNNG!
OKAY, WALL-CRAWLER--YA HAD YER FUN
BUT EVEN SPIDER-MAN AINT BULLET-PROOF
I DON'T HAVE TO BE! YOU'LL NEVER HIT ME
WHA--?
MINUTES LATER--
I WONDER HOW MANY PUNKS LIKE THAT I'LL HAVE TO GIFT WRAP BEFORE PEOPLE REALIZE I'M NOT A COMBINATION OF BLUEBEARD AND JACK THE RIPPER?
WELL, I'D BETTER GET MOVING BEFORE THEY TRY TO NAIL ME FOR VAGRANCY, TOO

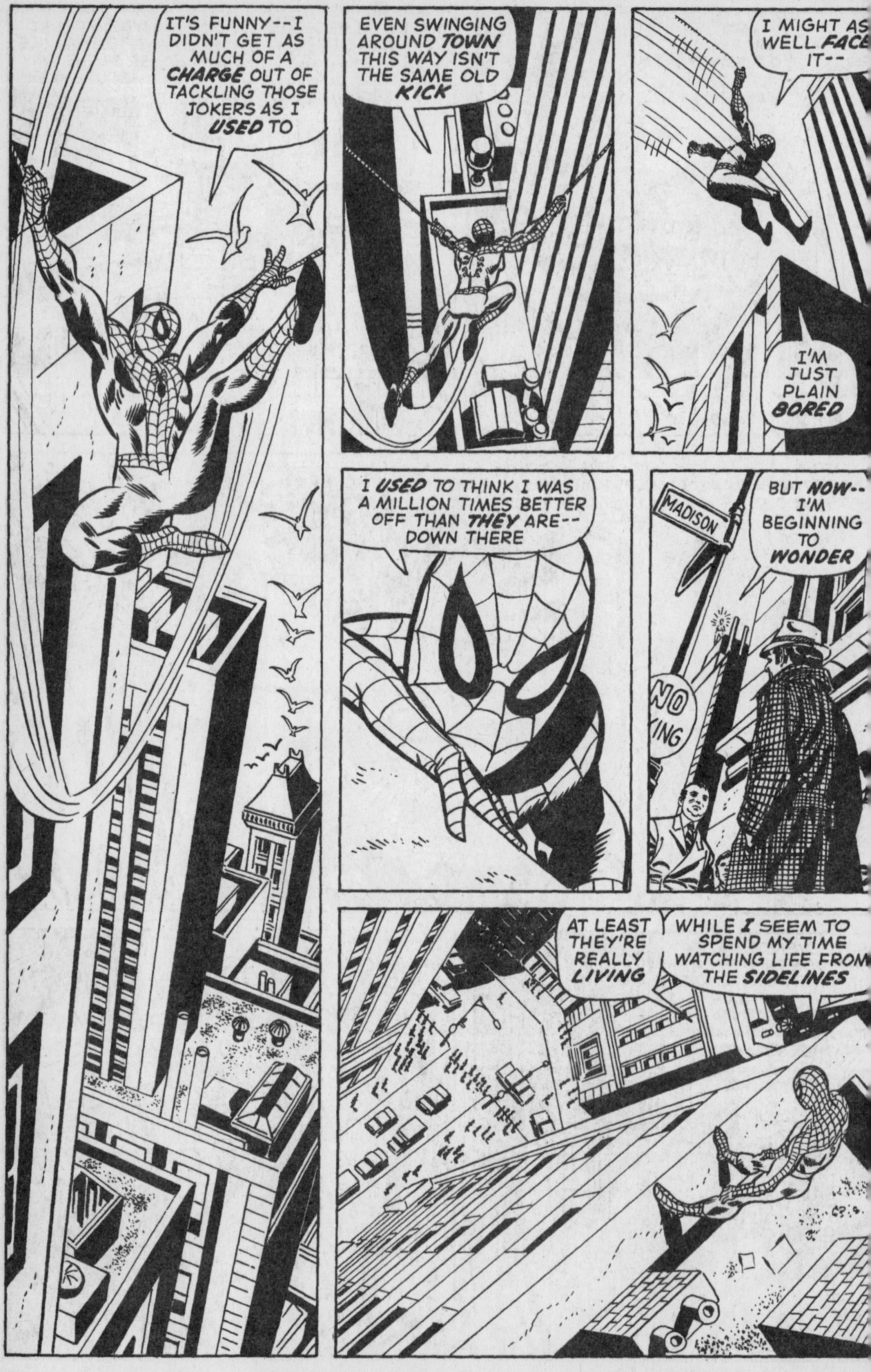

IT'S FUNNY--I DIDN'T GET AS MUCH OF A CHARGE OUT OF TACKLING THOSE JOKERS AS I USED TO
EVEN SWINGING AROUND TOWN THIS WAY ISN'T THE SAME OLD KICK
I MIGHT AS WELL FACE IT--
I'M JUST PLAIN BORED
I USED TO THINK I WAS A MILLION TIMES BETTER OFF THAN THEY ARE--DOWN THERE
MADISON
BUT NOW--I'M BEGINNING TO WONDER
AT LEAST THEY'RE REALLY LIVING
WHILE I SEEM TO SPEND MY TIME WATCHING LIFE FROM THE SIDELINES

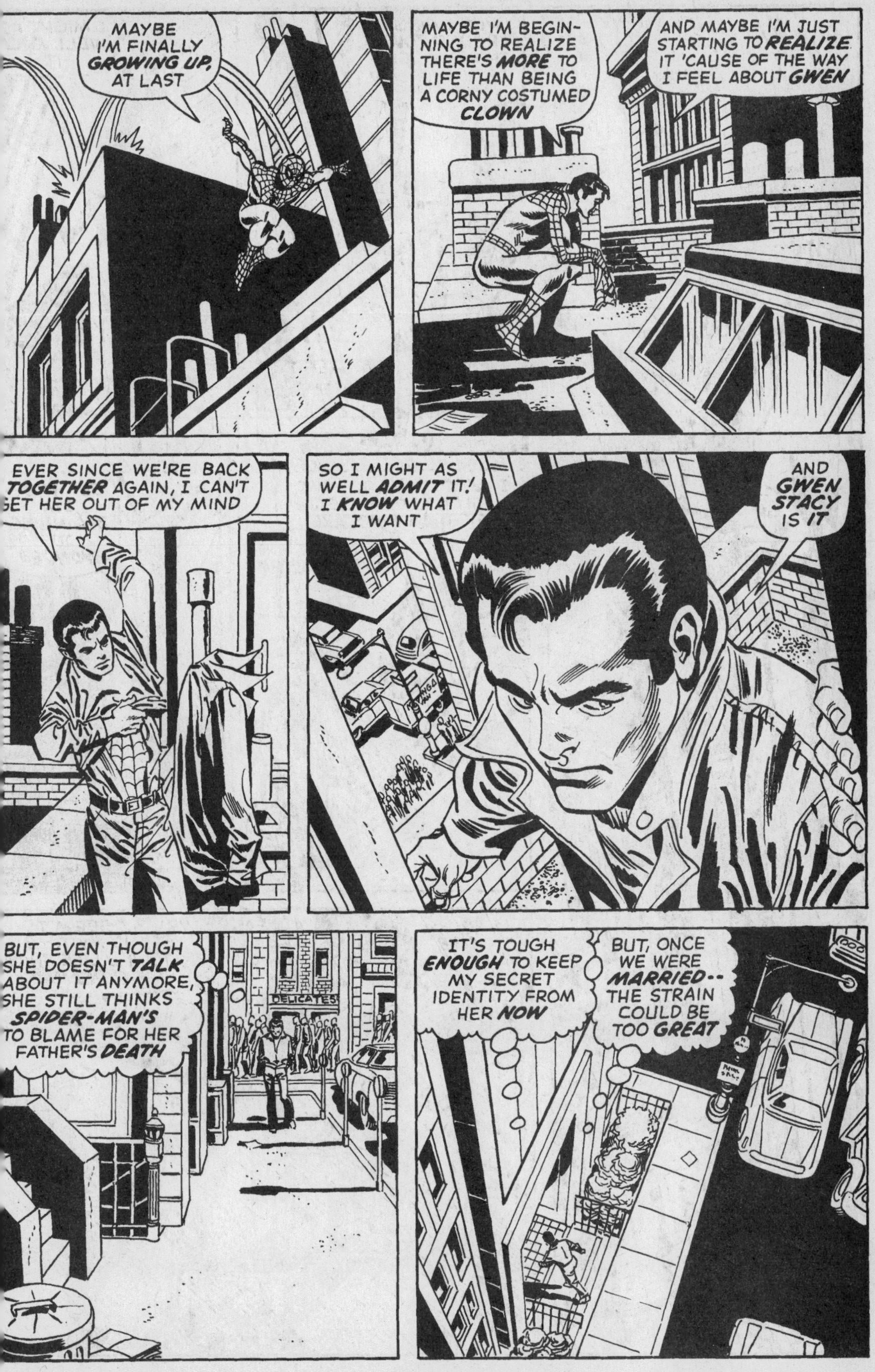
MAYBE I'M FINALLY GROWING UP, AT LAST
MAYBE I'M BEGINNING TO REALIZE THERE'S MORE TO LIFE THAN BEING A CORNY COSTUMED CLOWN
AND MAYBE I'M JUST STARTING TO REALIZE IT 'CAUSE OF THE WAY I FEEL ABOUT GWEN
EVER SINCE WE'RE BACK TOGETHER AGAIN, I CAN'T GET HER OUT OF MY MIND
SO I MIGHT AS WELL ADMIT IT! I KNOW WHAT I WANT
AND GWEN STACY IS IT
BUT, EVEN THOUGH SHE DOESN'T TALK ABOUT IT ANYMORE, SHE STILL THINKS SPIDER-MAN'S TO BLAME FOR HER FATHER'S DEATH
DELICATES
IT'S TOUGH ENOUGH TO KEEP MY SECRET IDENTITY FROM HER NOW
BUT, ONCE WE WERE MARRIED-- THE STRAIN COULD BE TOO GREAT

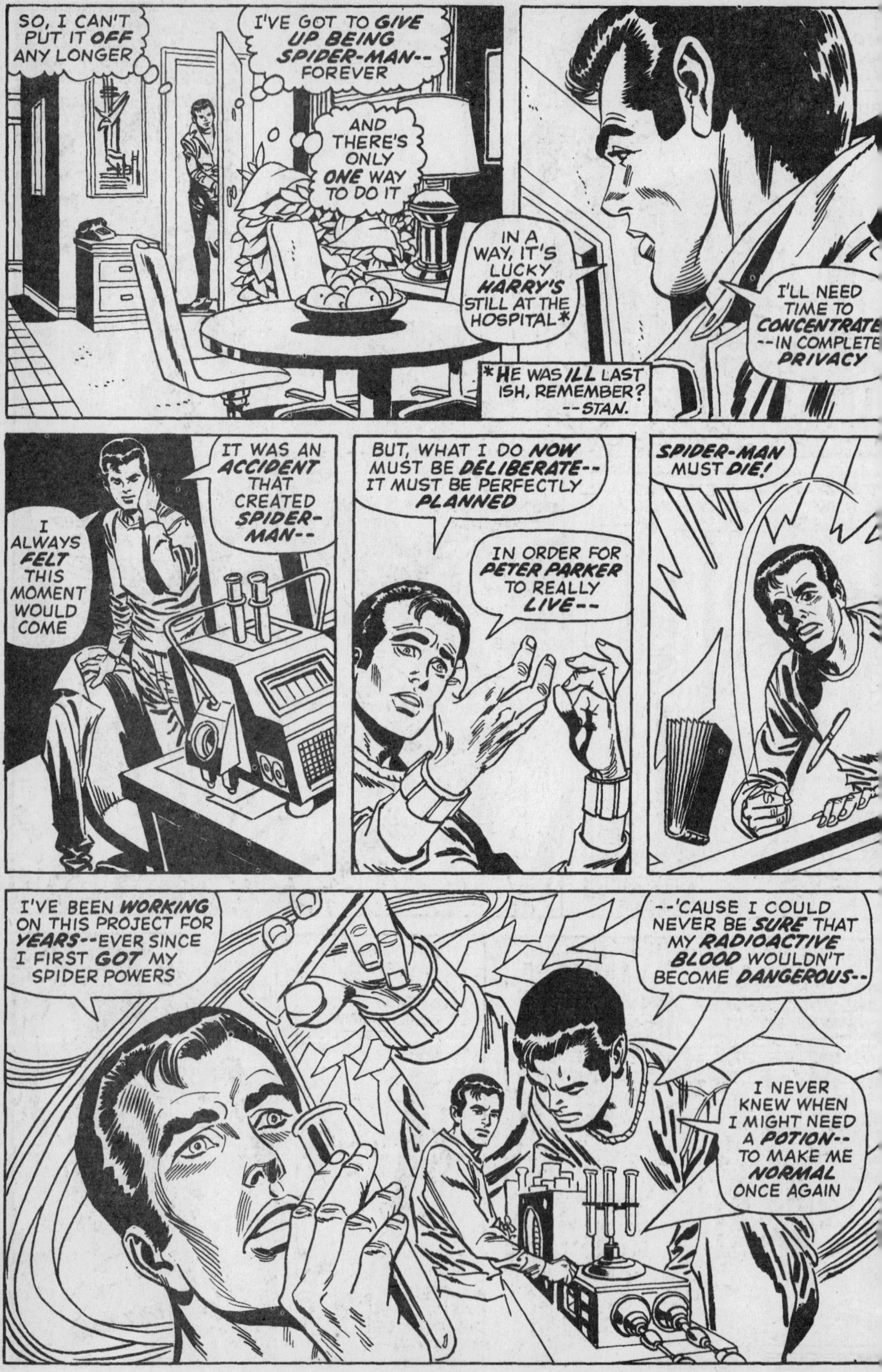
SO, I CAN'T PUT IT OFF ANY LONGER
I'VE GOT TO GIVE UP BEING SPIDER-MAN-- FOREVER
AND THERE'S ONLY ONE WAY TO DO IT
IN A WAY, IT'S LUCKY HARRY'S STILL AT THE HOSPITAL*
*HE WAS ILL LAST ISH, REMEMBER? --STAN.
I'LL NEED TIME TO CONCENTRATE --IN COMPLETE PRIVACY
IT WAS AN ACCIDENT THAT CREATED SPIDER-MAN--
I ALWAYS FELT THIS MOMENT WOULD COME
BUT, WHAT I DO NOW MUST BE DELIBERATE-- IT MUST BE PERFECTLY PLANNED
IN ORDER FOR PETER PARKER TO REALLY LIVE--
SPIDER-MAN MUST DIE!
I'VE BEEN WORKING ON THIS PROJECT FOR YEARS--EVER SINCE I FIRST GOT MY SPIDER POWERS
--'CAUSE I COULD NEVER BE SURE THAT MY RADIOACTIVE BLOOD WOULDN'T BECOME DANGEROUS--
I NEVER KNEW WHEN I MIGHT NEED A POTION-- TO MAKE ME NORMAL ONCE AGAIN

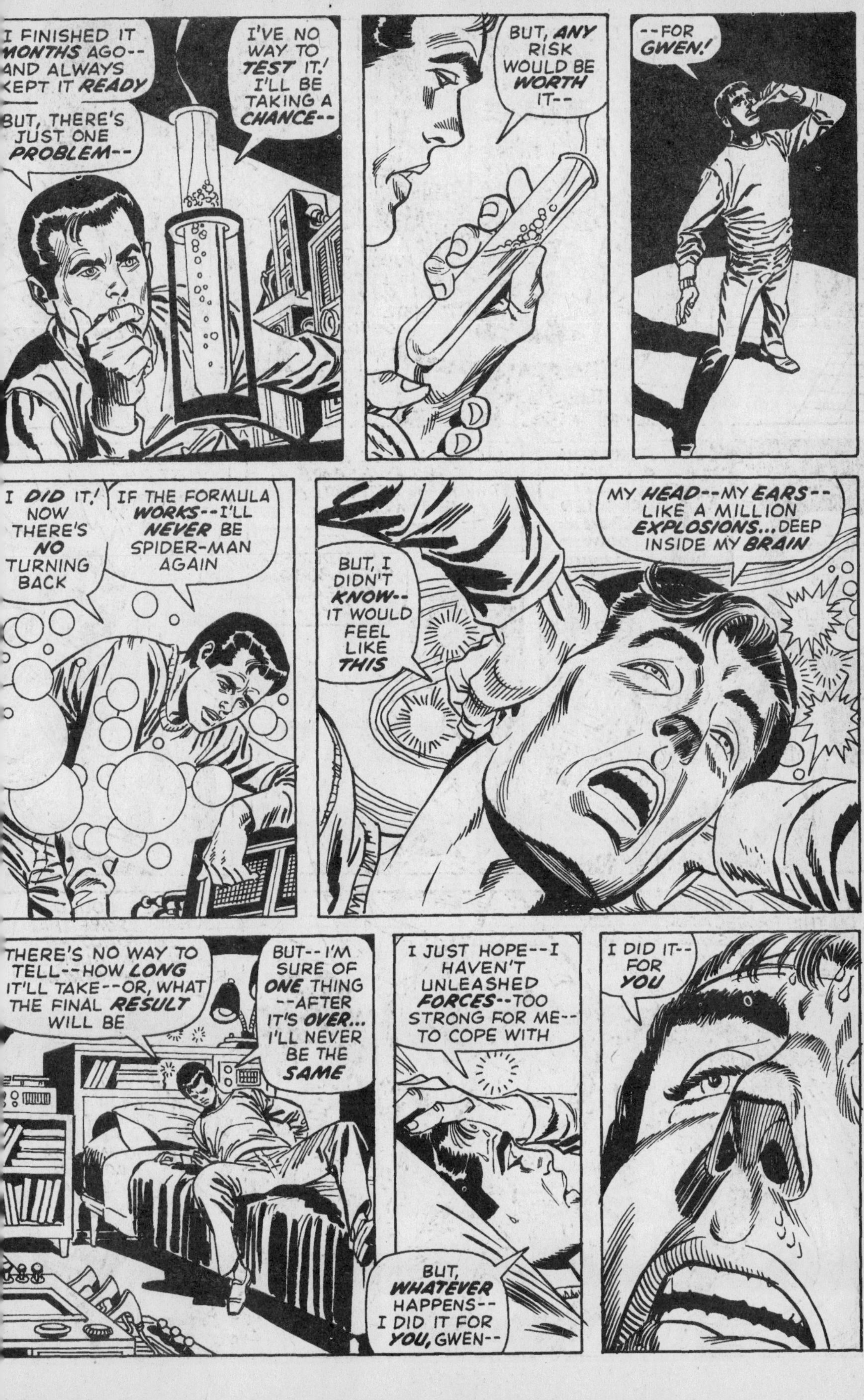

I FINISHED IT MONTHS AGO--AND ALWAYS KEPT IT READY
BUT, THERE'S JUST ONE PROBLEM--
I'VE NO WAY TO TEST IT! I'LL BE TAKING A CHANCE--
BUT, ANY RISK WOULD BE WORTH IT--
--FOR GWEN!
I DID IT! NOW THERE'S NO TURNING BACK
IF THE FORMULA WORKS--I'LL NEVER BE SPIDER-MAN AGAIN
MY HEAD--MY EARS--LIKE A MILLION EXPLOSIONS...DEEP INSIDE MY BRAIN
BUT, I DIDN'T KNOW--IT WOULD FEEL LIKE THIS
THERE'S NO WAY TO TELL--HOW LONG IT'LL TAKE--OR, WHAT THE FINAL RESULT WILL BE
BUT--I'M SURE OF ONE THING--AFTER IT'S OVER... I'LL NEVER BE THE SAME
I JUST HOPE--I HAVEN'T UNLEASHED FORCES--TOO STRONG FOR ME--TO COPE WITH
BUT, WHATEVER HAPPENS--I DID IT FOR YOU, GWEN--
I DID IT--FOR YOU

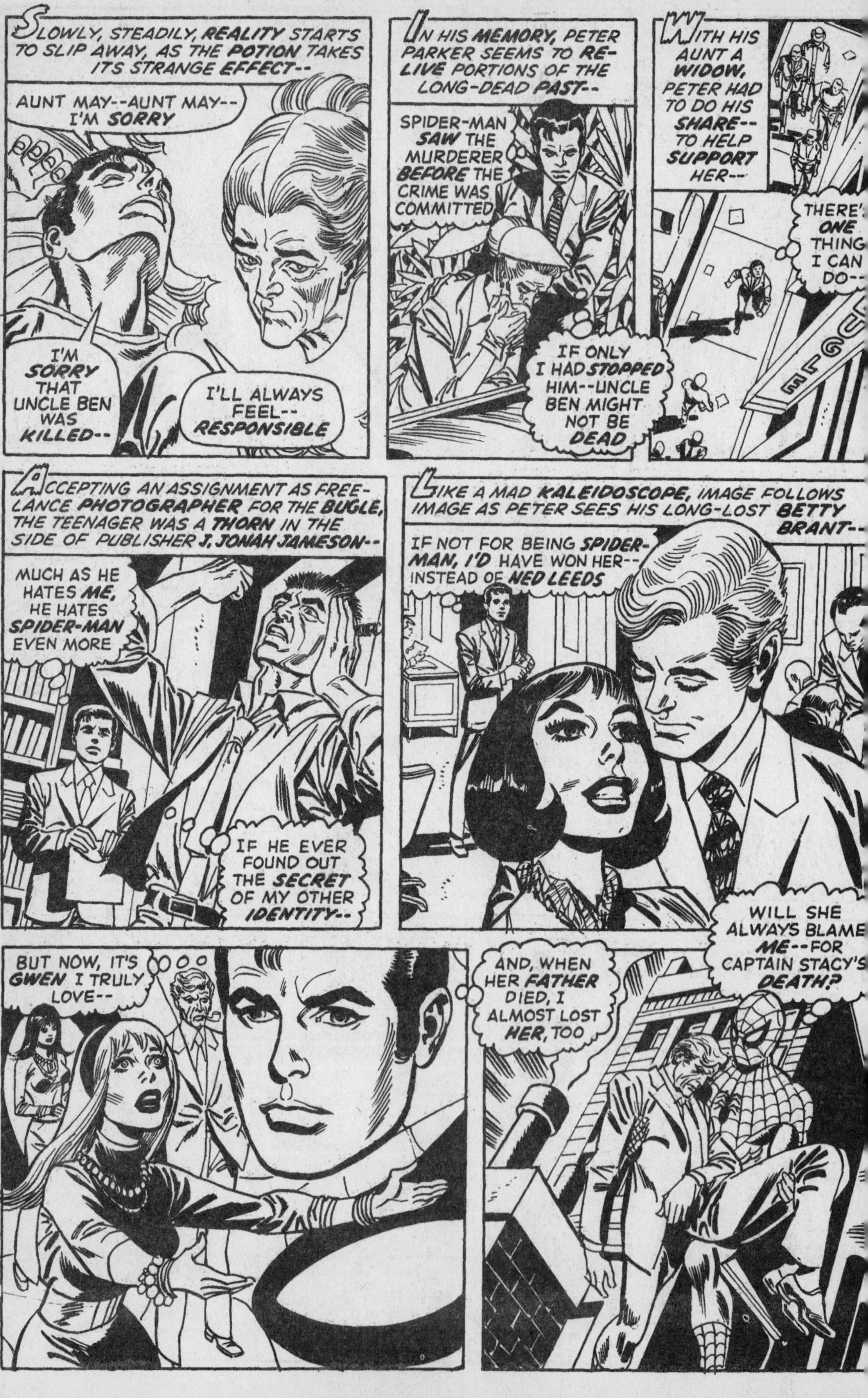
SLOWLY, STEADILY, REALITY STARTS TO SLIP AWAY, AS THE POTION TAKES ITS STRANGE EFFECT--
AUNT MAY--AUNT MAY-- I'M SORRY
I'M SORRY THAT UNCLE BEN WAS KILLED--
I'LL ALWAYS FEEL-- RESPONSIBLE
IN HIS MEMORY, PETER PARKER SEEMS TO RE-LIVE PORTIONS OF THE LONG-DEAD PAST--
SPIDER-MAN SAW THE MURDERER BEFORE THE CRIME WAS COMMITTED
IF ONLY I HAD STOPPED HIM--UNCLE BEN MIGHT NOT BE DEAD
WITH HIS AUNT A WIDOW, PETER HAD TO DO HIS SHARE-- TO HELP SUPPORT HER--
THERE'S ONE THING I CAN DO--
ACCEPTING AN ASSIGNMENT AS FREE-LANCE PHOTOGRAPHER FOR THE BUGLE, THE TEENAGER WAS A THORN IN THE SIDE OF PUBLISHER J. JONAH JAMESON--
MUCH AS HE HATES ME, HE HATES SPIDER-MAN EVEN MORE
IF HE EVER FOUND OUT THE SECRET OF MY OTHER IDENTITY--
LIKE A MAD KALEIDOSCOPE, IMAGE FOLLOWS IMAGE AS PETER SEES HIS LONG-LOST BETTY BRANT--
IF NOT FOR BEING SPIDER-MAN, I'D HAVE WON HER-- INSTEAD OF NED LEEDS
BUT NOW, IT'S GWEN I TRULY LOVE--
AND, WHEN HER FATHER DIED, I ALMOST LOST HER, TOO
WILL SHE ALWAYS BLAME ME--FOR CAPTAIN STACY'S DEATH?

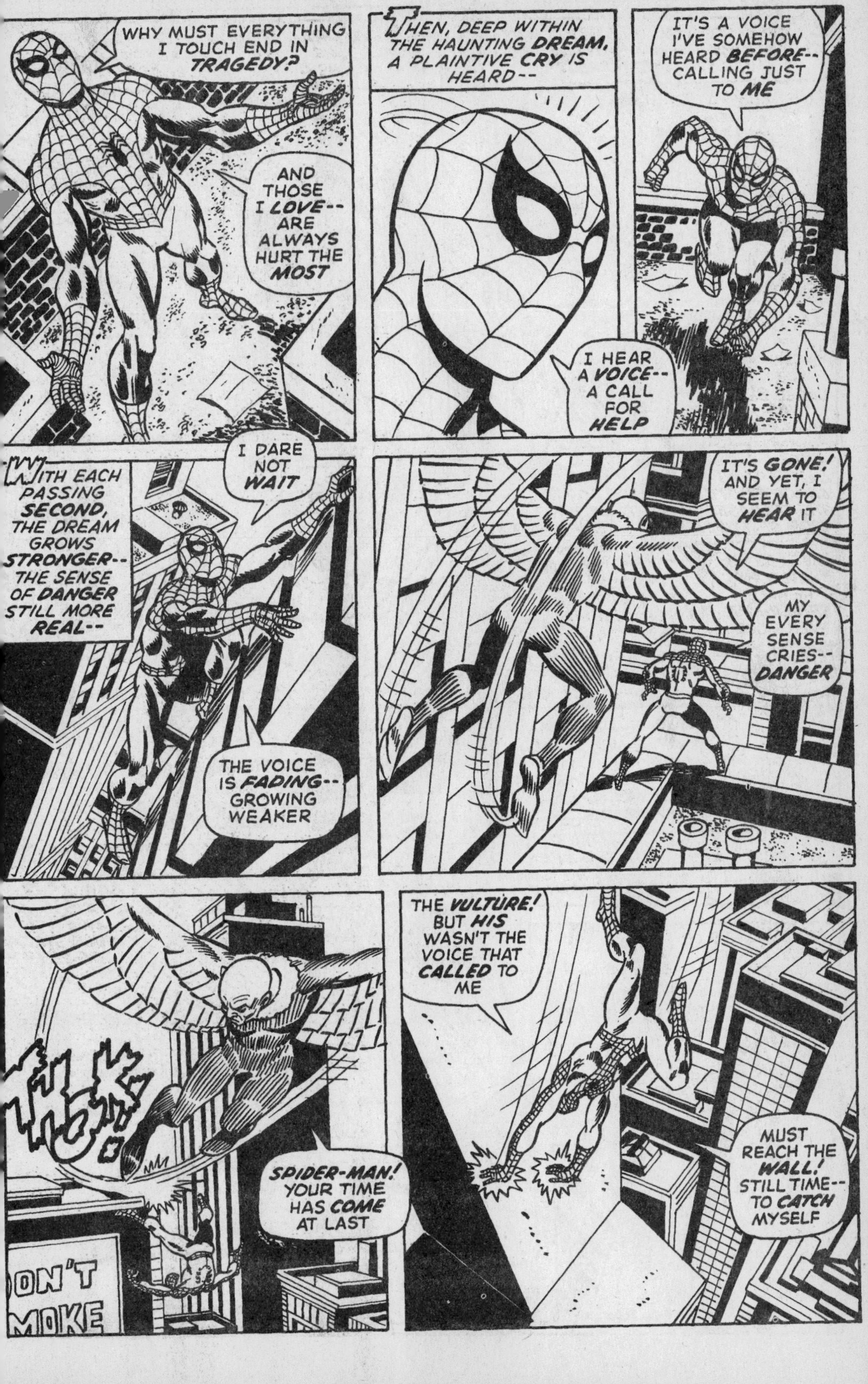
WHY MUST EVERYTHING I TOUCH END IN TRAGEDY?
AND THOSE I LOVE-- ARE ALWAYS HURT THE MOST
THEN, DEEP WITHIN THE HAUNTING DREAM, A PLAINTIVE CRY IS HEARD--
I HEAR A VOICE-- A CALL FOR HELP
IT'S A VOICE I'VE SOMEHOW HEARD BEFORE-- CALLING JUST TO ME
WITH EACH PASSING SECOND, THE DREAM GROWS STRONGER-- THE SENSE OF DANGER STILL MORE REAL--
I DARE NOT WAIT
THE VOICE IS FADING-- GROWING WEAKER
IT'S GONE! AND YET, I SEEM TO HEAR IT
MY EVERY SENSE CRIES-- DANGER
SPIDER-MAN! YOUR TIME HAS COME AT LAST
ON'T
MOKE
THE VULTURE! BUT HIS WASN'T THE VOICE THAT CALLED TO ME
MUST REACH THE WALL! STILL TIME-- TO CATCH MYSELF

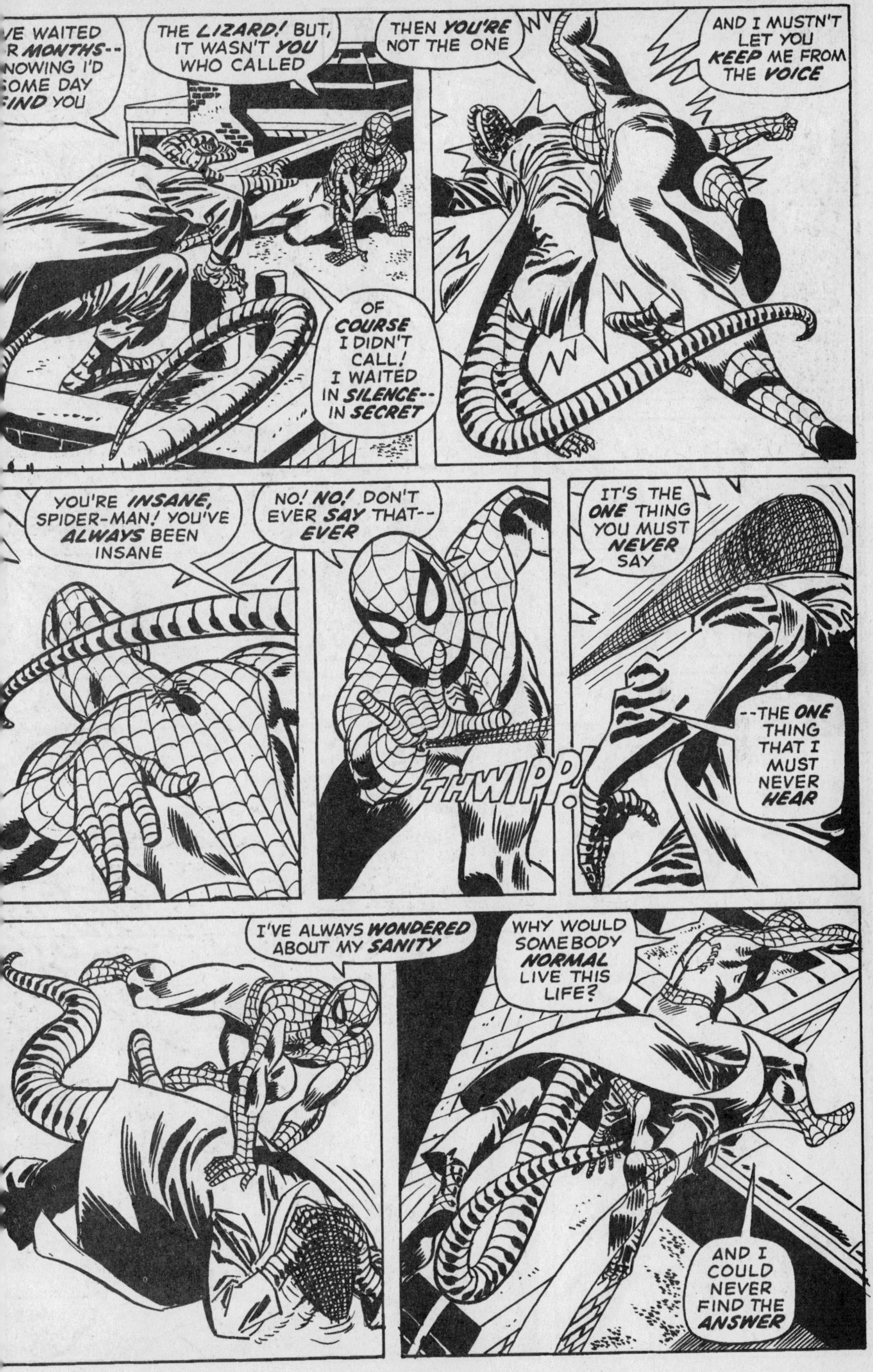

VE WAITED R MONTHS-- NOWING I'D SOME DAY FIND YOU
THE LIZARD! BUT, IT WASN'T YOU WHO CALLED
OF COURSE I DIDN'T CALL! I WAITED IN SILENCE-- IN SECRET
THEN YOU'RE NOT THE ONE
AND I MUSTN'T LET YOU KEEP ME FROM THE VOICE
YOU'RE INSANE, SPIDER-MAN! YOU'VE ALWAYS BEEN INSANE
NO! NO! DON'T EVER SAY THAT-- EVER
THWIPP!
IT'S THE ONE THING YOU MUST NEVER SAY
--THE ONE THING THAT I MUST NEVER HEAR
I'VE ALWAYS WONDERED ABOUT MY SANITY
WHY WOULD SOME BODY NORMAL LIVE THIS LIFE?
AND I COULD NEVER FIND THE ANSWER

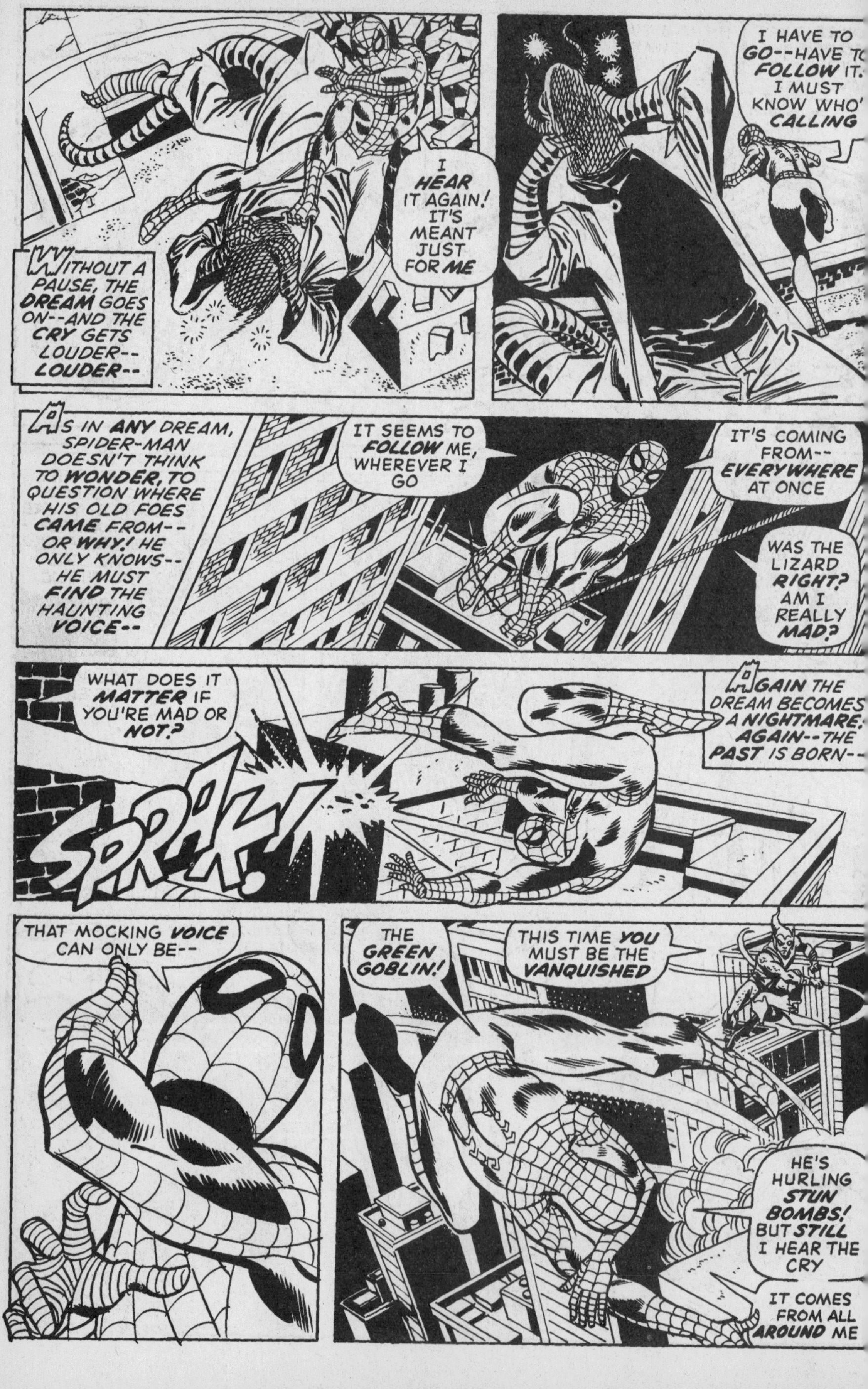
I HEAR IT AGAIN! IT'S MEANT JUST FOR ME
WITHOUT A PAUSE, THE DREAM GOES ON--AND THE CRY GETS LOUDER--LOUDER--
I HAVE TO GO--HAVE TO FOLLOW IT. I MUST KNOW WHO' CALLING
AS IN ANY DREAM, SPIDER-MAN DOESN'T THINK TO WONDER, TO QUESTION WHERE HIS OLD FOES CAME FROM--OR WHY! HE ONLY KNOWS--HE MUST FIND THE HAUNTING VOICE--
IT SEEMS TO FOLLOW ME, WHEREVER I GO
IT'S COMING FROM--EVERYWHERE AT ONCE
WAS THE LIZARD RIGHT? AM I REALLY MAD?
WHAT DOES IT MATTER IF YOU'RE MAD OR NOT?
AGAIN THE DREAM BECOMES A NIGHTMARE. AGAIN--THE PAST IS BORN--
SPRAK!
THAT MOCKING VOICE CAN ONLY BE--
THE GREEN GOBLIN!
THIS TIME YOU MUST BE THE VANQUISHED
HE'S HURLING STUN BOMBS! BUT STILL I HEAR THE CRY
IT COMES FROM ALL AROUND ME

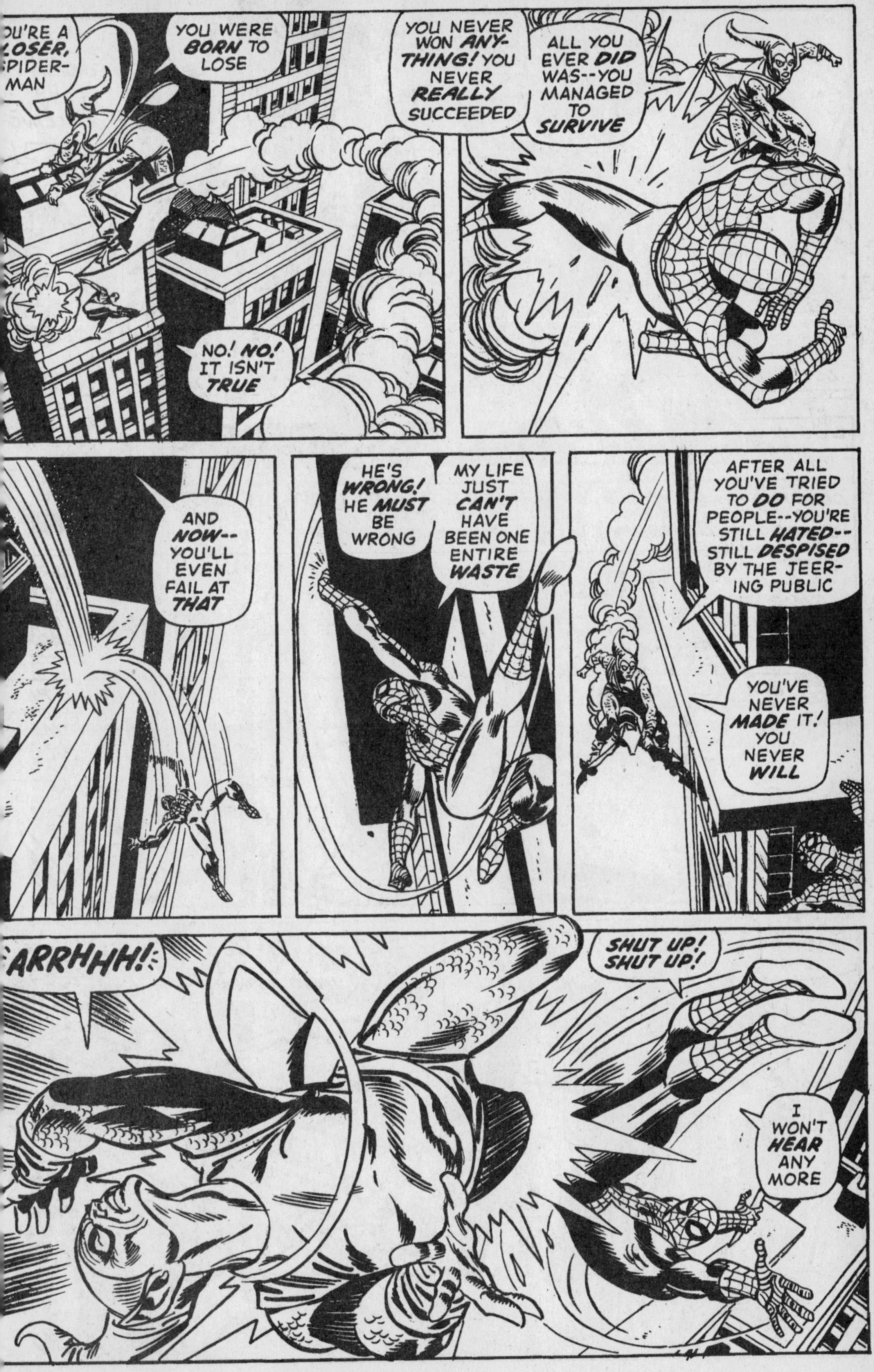

OU'RE A LOSER, SPIDER-MAN
YOU WERE BORN TO LOSE
YOU NEVER WON ANY-THING! YOU NEVER REALLY SUCCEEDED
ALL YOU EVER DID WAS--YOU MANAGED TO SURVIVE
NO! NO! IT ISN'T TRUE
AND NOW-- YOU'LL EVEN FAIL AT THAT
HE'S WRONG! HE MUST BE WRONG
MY LIFE JUST CAN'T HAVE BEEN ONE ENTIRE WASTE
AFTER ALL YOU'VE TRIED TO DO FOR PEOPLE--YOU'RE STILL HATED-- STILL DESPISED BY THE JEERING PUBLIC
YOU'VE NEVER MADE IT! YOU NEVER WILL
ARRHHH!
SHUT UP! SHUT UP!
I WON'T HEAR ANY MORE

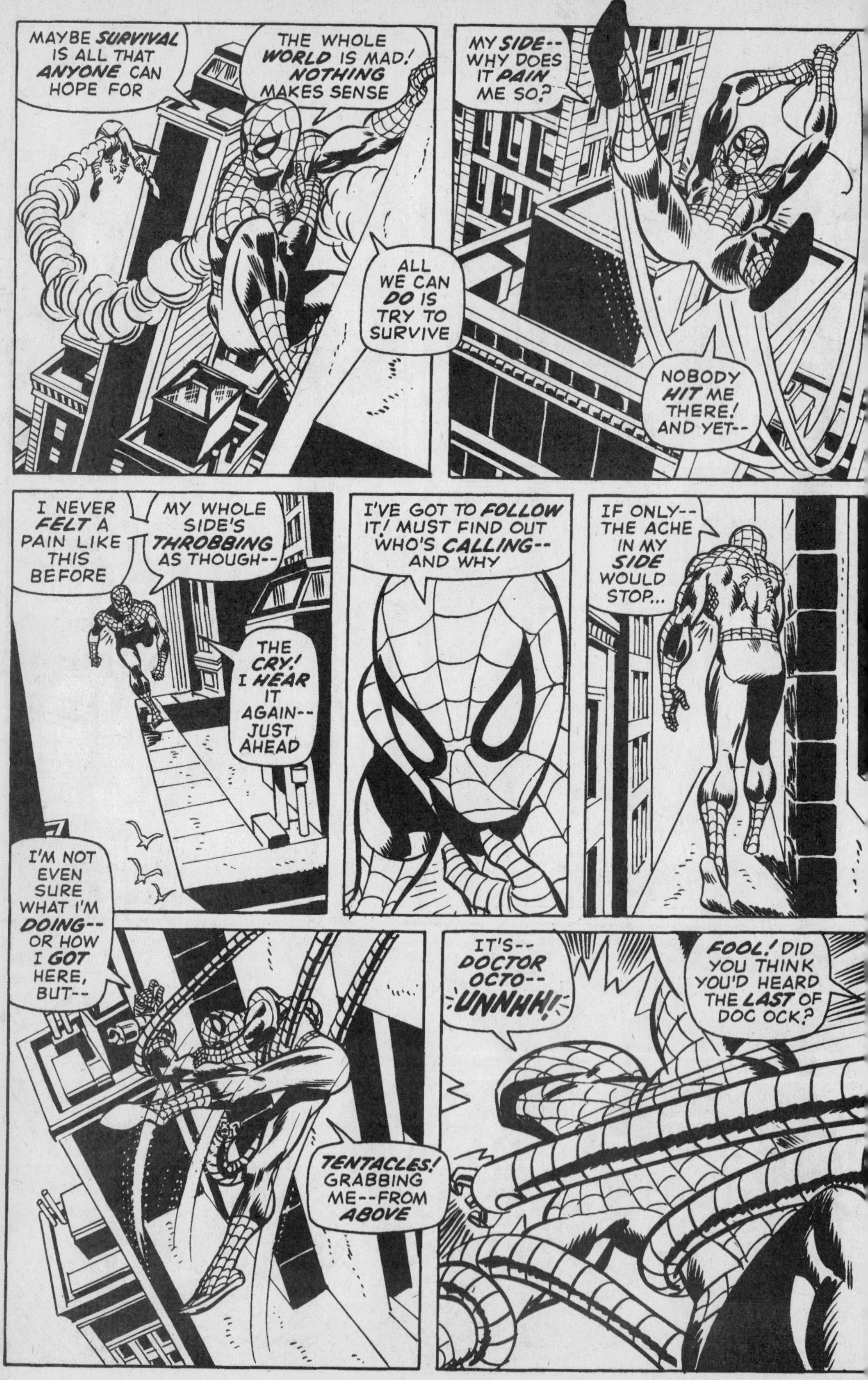
MAYBE SURVIVAL IS ALL THAT ANYONE CAN HOPE FOR
THE WHOLE WORLD IS MAD! NOTHING MAKES SENSE
ALL WE CAN DO IS TRY TO SURVIVE
MY SIDE--WHY DOES IT PAIN ME SO?
NOBODY HIT ME THERE! AND YET--
I NEVER FELT A PAIN LIKE THIS BEFORE
MY WHOLE SIDE'S THROBBING AS THOUGH--
THE CRY! I HEAR IT AGAIN--JUST AHEAD
I'VE GOT TO FOLLOW IT! MUST FIND OUT WHO'S CALLING--AND WHY
IF ONLY--THE ACHE IN MY SIDE WOULD STOP...
I'M NOT EVEN SURE WHAT I'M DOING--OR HOW I GOT HERE, BUT--
TENTACLES! GRABBING ME--FROM ABOVE
IT'S--DOCTOR OCTO--UNNHH!
FOOL! DID YOU THINK YOU'D HEARD THE LAST OF DOC OCK?

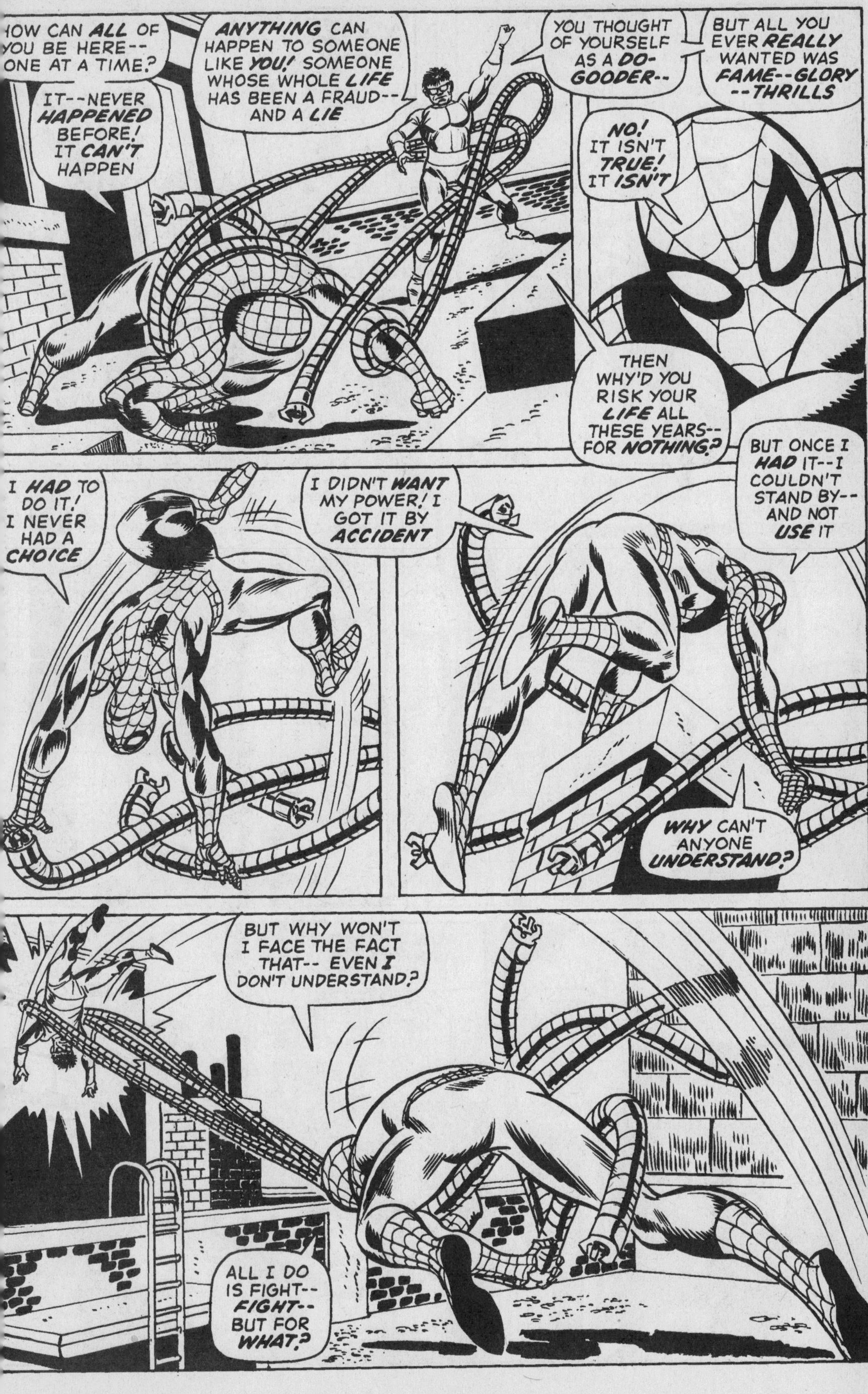
HOW CAN ALL OF YOU BE HERE-- ONE AT A TIME?
IT--NEVER HAPPENED BEFORE! IT CAN'T HAPPEN
ANYTHING CAN HAPPEN TO SOMEONE LIKE YOU! SOMEONE WHOSE WHOLE LIFE HAS BEEN A FRAUD-- AND A LIE
YOU THOUGHT OF YOURSELF AS A DO-GOODER--
BUT ALL YOU EVER REALLY WANTED WAS FAME--GLORY --THRILLS
NO! IT ISN'T TRUE! IT ISN'T
THEN WHY'D YOU RISK YOUR LIFE ALL THESE YEARS-- FOR NOTHING?
I HAD TO DO IT! I NEVER HAD A CHOICE
I DIDN'T WANT MY POWER! I GOT IT BY ACCIDENT
BUT ONCE I HAD IT--I COULDN'T STAND BY-- AND NOT USE IT
WHY CAN'T ANYONE UNDERSTAND?
BUT WHY WON'T I FACE THE FACT THAT-- EVEN I DON'T UNDERSTAND?
ALL I DO IS FIGHT-- FIGHT-- BUT FOR WHAT?

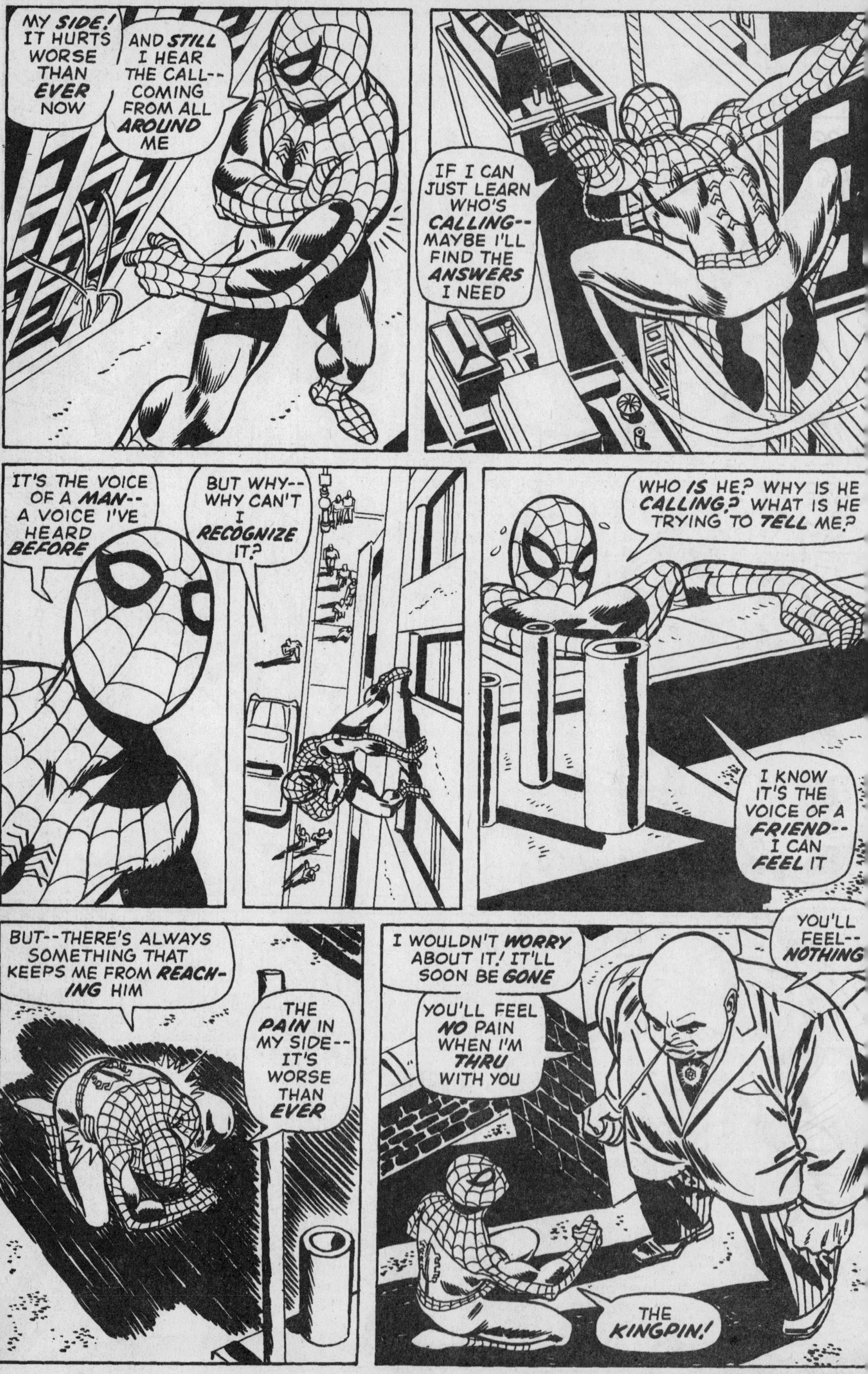

MY SIDE! IT HURTS WORSE THAN EVER NOW
AND STILL I HEAR THE CALL-- COMING FROM ALL AROUND ME
IF I CAN JUST LEARN WHO'S CALLING-- MAYBE I'LL FIND THE ANSWERS I NEED
IT'S THE VOICE OF A MAN-- A VOICE I'VE HEARD BEFORE
BUT WHY-- WHY CAN'T I RECOGNIZE IT?
WHO IS HE? WHY IS HE CALLING? WHAT IS HE TRYING TO TELL ME?
I KNOW IT'S THE VOICE OF A FRIEND-- I CAN FEEL IT
BUT--THERE'S ALWAYS SOMETHING THAT KEEPS ME FROM REACHING HIM
THE PAIN IN MY SIDE-- IT'S WORSE THAN EVER
I WOULDN'T WORRY ABOUT IT! IT'LL SOON BE GONE
YOU'LL FEEL NO PAIN WHEN I'M THRU WITH YOU
YOU'LL FEEL-- NOTHING
THE KINGPIN!

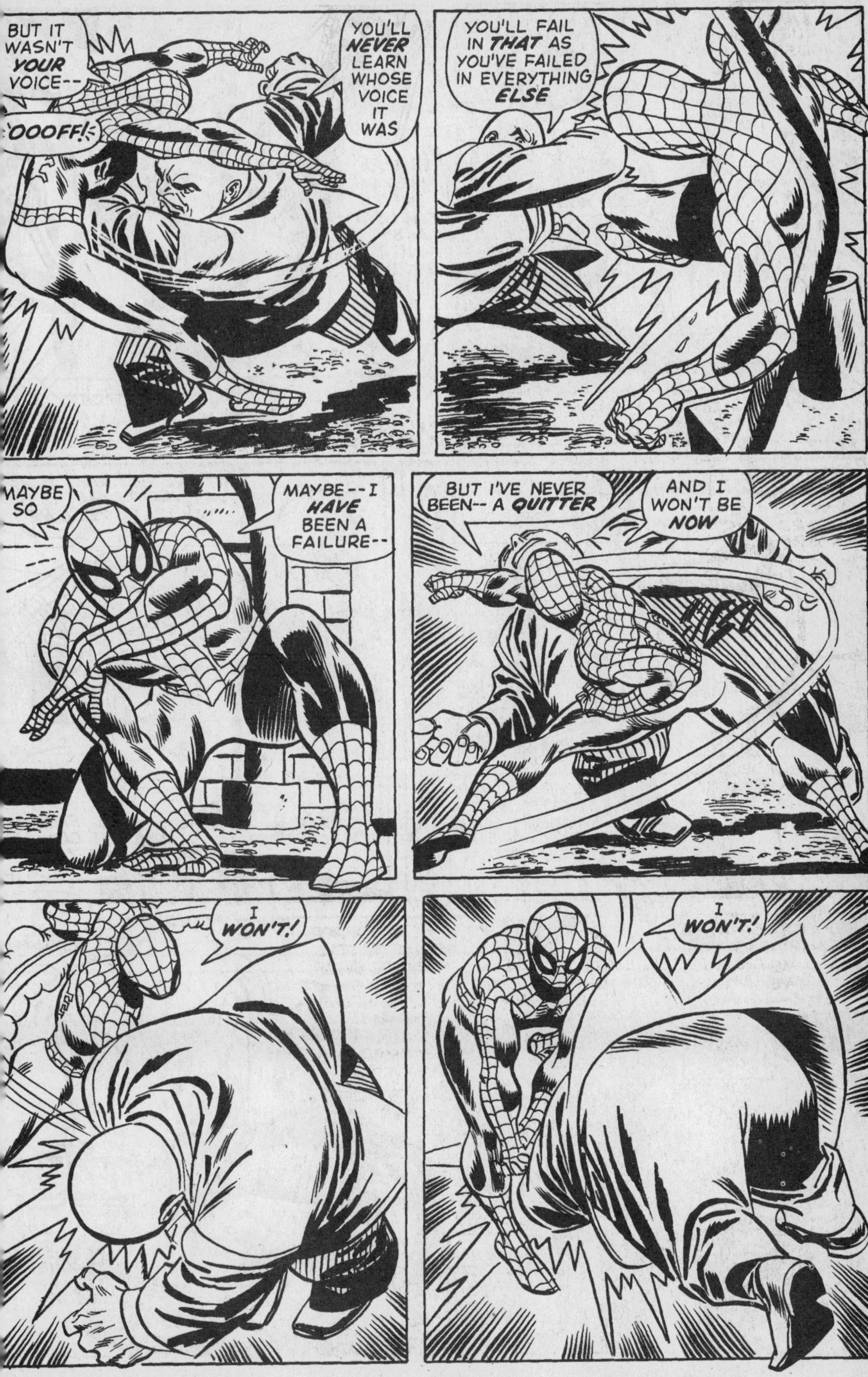

BUT IT WASN'T YOUR VOICE--
YOU'LL NEVER LEARN WHOSE VOICE IT WAS
'OOOFF!'
YOU'LL FAIL IN THAT AS YOU'VE FAILED IN EVERYTHING ELSE
MAYBE SO
MAYBE--I HAVE BEEN A FAILURE--
BUT I'VE NEVER BEEN-- A QUITTER
AND I WON'T BE NOW
I WON'T!
I WON'T!

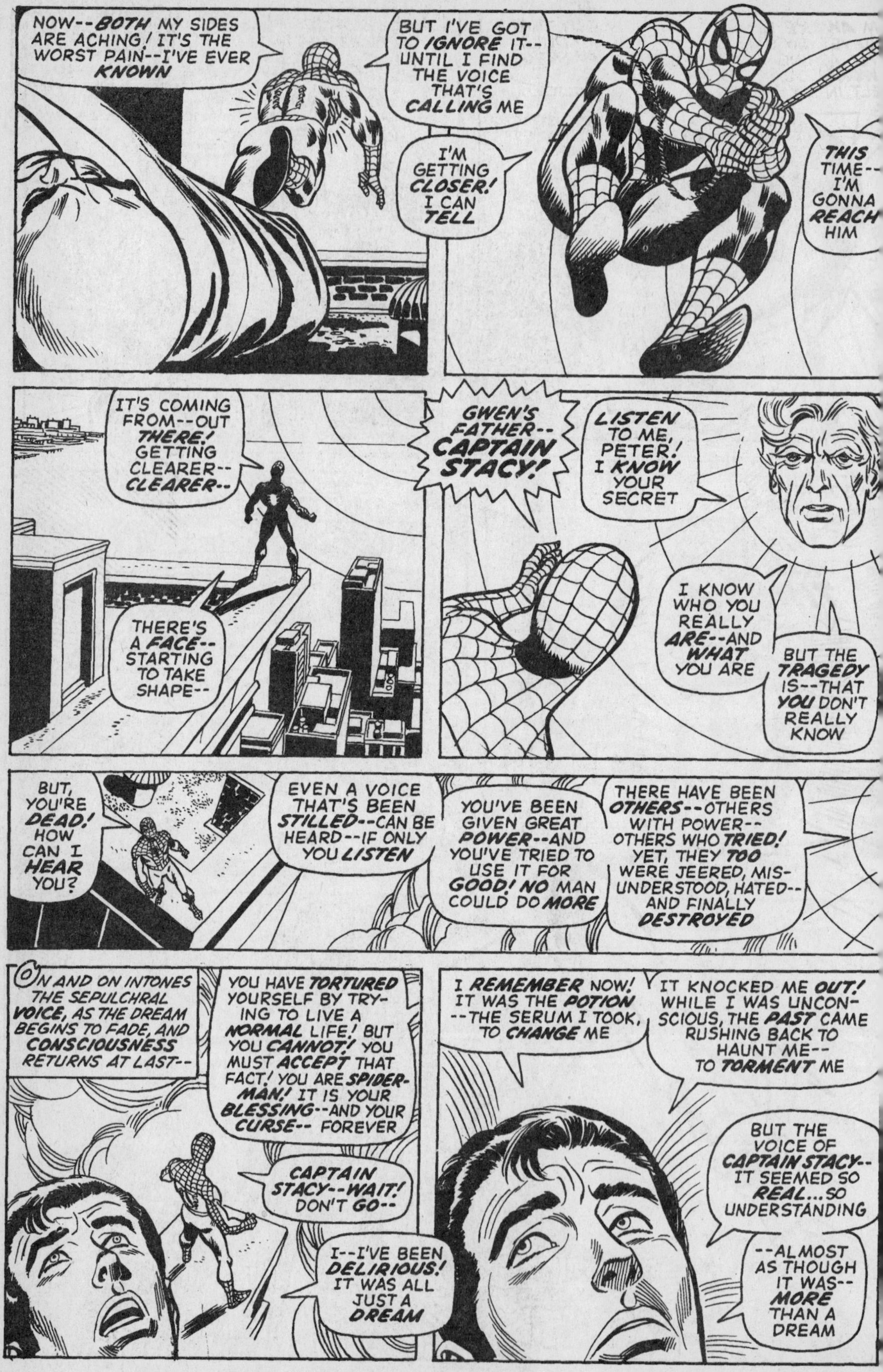
NOW--BOTH MY SIDES ARE ACHING! IT'S THE WORST PAIN--I'VE EVER KNOWN
BUT I'VE GOT TO IGNORE IT--UNTIL I FIND THE VOICE THAT'S CALLING ME
I'M GETTING CLOSER! I CAN TELL
THIS TIME--I'M GONNA REACH HIM
IT'S COMING FROM--OUT THERE! GETTING CLEARER--CLEARER--
THERE'S A FACE--STARTING TO TAKE SHAPE--
GWEN'S FATHER--CAPTAIN STACY!
LISTEN TO ME, PETER! I KNOW YOUR SECRET
I KNOW WHO YOU REALLY ARE--AND WHAT YOU ARE
BUT THE TRAGEDY IS--THAT YOU DON'T REALLY KNOW
BUT, YOU'RE DEAD! HOW CAN I HEAR YOU?
EVEN A VOICE THAT'S BEEN STILLED--CAN BE HEARD--IF ONLY YOU LISTEN
YOU'VE BEEN GIVEN GREAT POWER--AND YOU'VE TRIED TO USE IT FOR GOOD! NO MAN COULD DO MORE
THERE HAVE BEEN OTHERS--OTHERS WITH POWER--OTHERS WHO TRIED! YET, THEY TOO WERE JEERED, MISUNDERSTOOD, HATED--AND FINALLY DESTROYED
ON AND ON INTONES THE SEPULCHRAL VOICE, AS THE DREAM BEGINS TO FADE, AND CONSCIOUSNESS RETURNS AT LAST--
YOU HAVE TORTURED YOURSELF BY TRYING TO LIVE A NORMAL LIFE! BUT YOU CANNOT! YOU MUST ACCEPT THAT FACT! YOU ARE SPIDER-MAN! IT IS YOUR BLESSING--AND YOUR CURSE-- FOREVER
CAPTAIN STACY--WAIT! DON'T GO--
I--I'VE BEEN DELIRIOUS! IT WAS ALL JUST A DREAM
I REMEMBER NOW! IT WAS THE POTION--THE SERUM I TOOK, TO CHANGE ME
IT KNOCKED ME OUT! WHILE I WAS UNCONSCIOUS, THE PAST CAME RUSHING BACK TO HAUNT ME--TO TORMENT ME
BUT THE VOICE OF CAPTAIN STACY--IT SEEMED SO REAL...SO UNDERSTANDING
--ALMOST AS THOUGH IT WAS--MORE THAN A DREAM

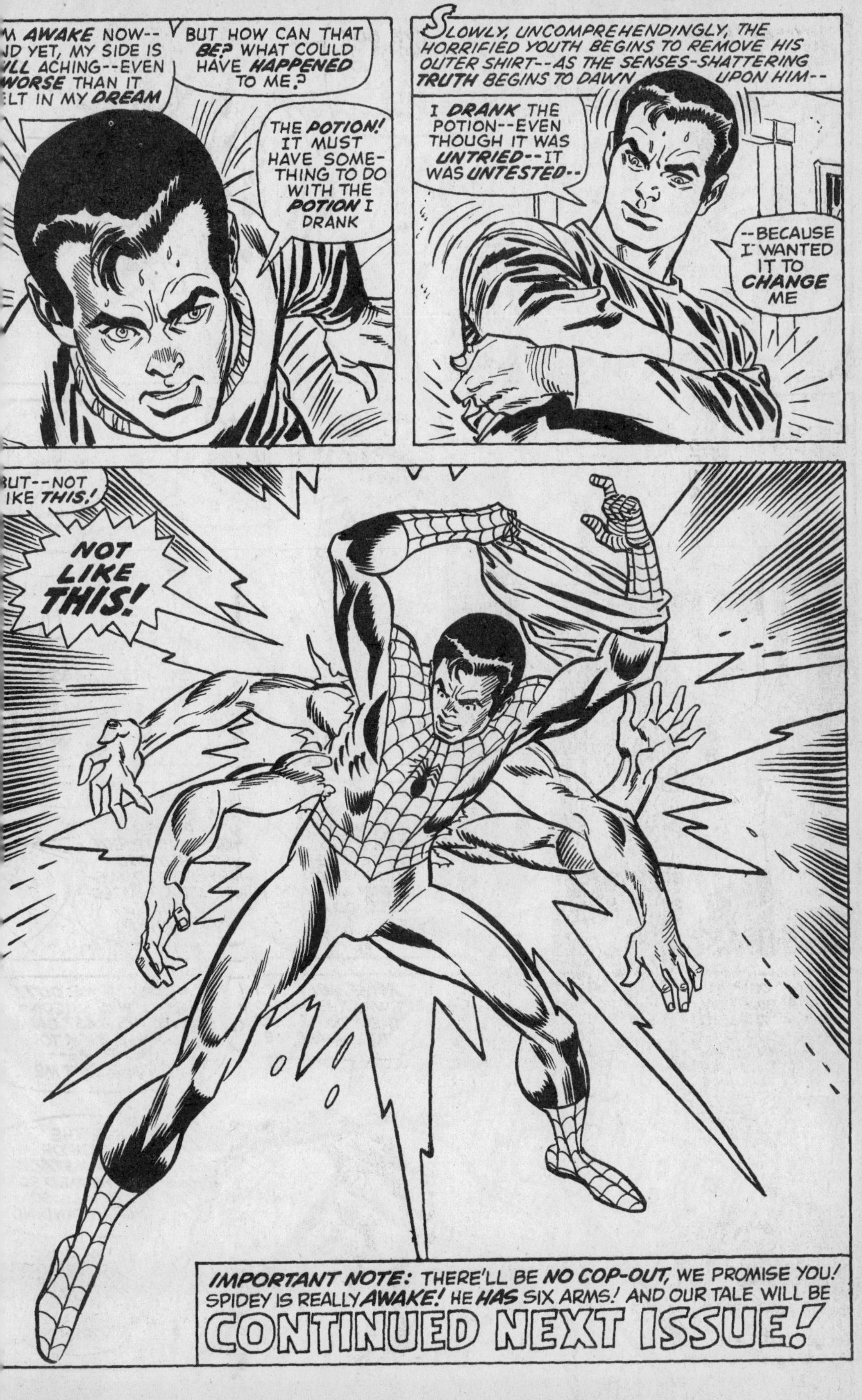

M AWAKE NOW-- ND YET, MY SIDE IS LL ACHING--EVEN WORSE THAN IT ELT IN MY DREAM
BUT HOW CAN THAT BE? WHAT COULD HAVE HAPPENED TO ME?
THE POTION! IT MUST HAVE SOMETHING TO DO WITH THE POTION I DRANK
SLOWLY, UNCOMPREHENDINGLY, THE HORRIFIED YOUTH BEGINS TO REMOVE HIS OUTER SHIRT--AS THE SENSES-SHATTERING TRUTH BEGINS TO DAWN UPON HIM--
I DRANK THE POTION--EVEN THOUGH IT WAS UNTRIED--IT WAS UNTESTED--
--BECAUSE I WANTED IT TO CHANGE ME
BUT--NOT IKE THIS!
NOT LIKE THIS!
IMPORTANT NOTE: THERE'LL BE NO COP-OUT, WE PROMISE YOU! SPIDEY IS REALLY AWAKE! HE HAS SIX ARMS! AND OUR TALE WILL BE
CONTINUED NEXT ISSUE!

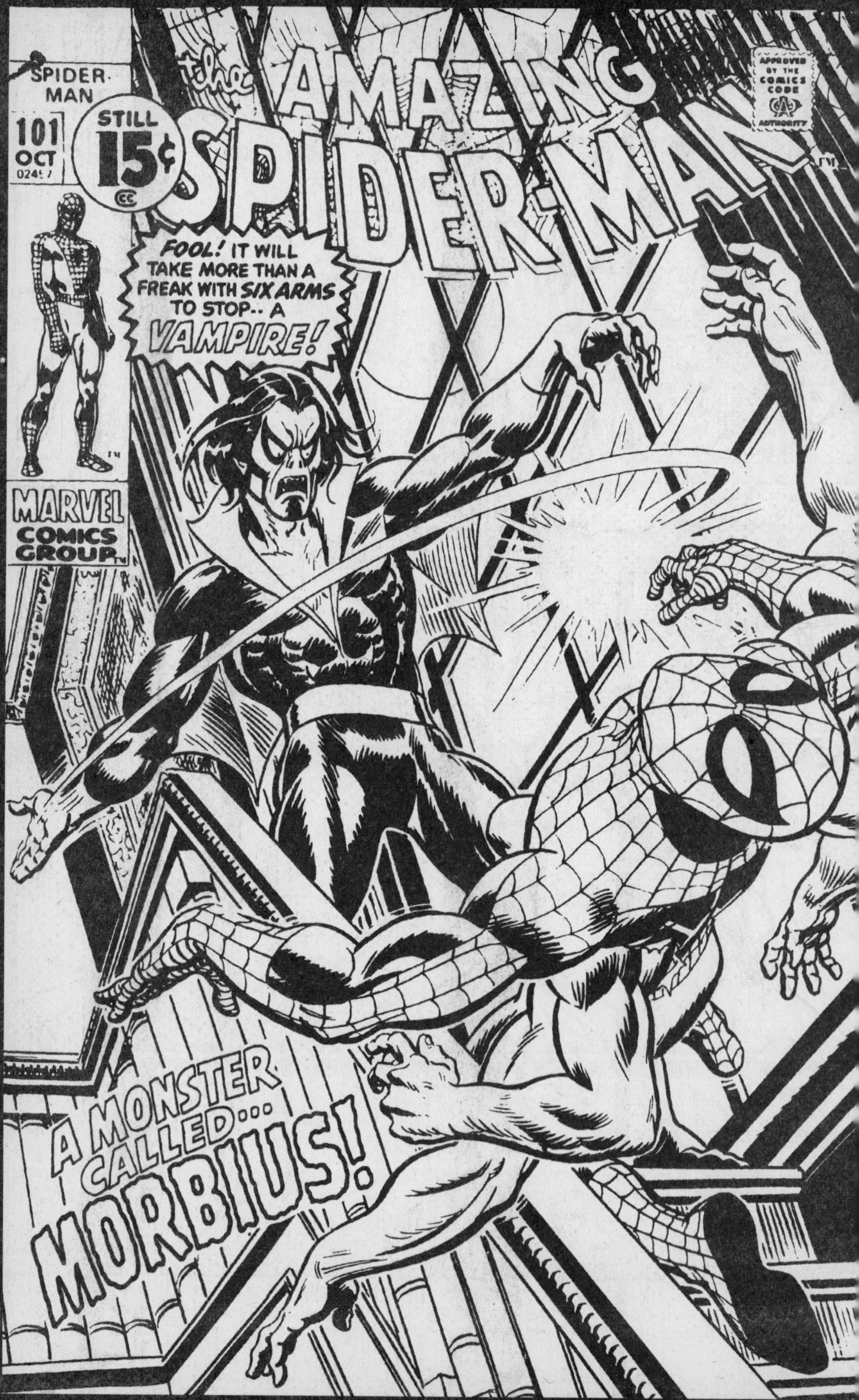

SPIDER-MAN
101
OCT
STILL 15¢
the AMAZING SPIDER-MAN
APPROVED BY THE COMICS CODE AUTHORITY
FOOL! IT WILL TAKE MORE THAN A FREAK WITH SIX ARMS TO STOP.. A VAMPIRE!
MARVEL COMICS GROUP
A MONSTER CALLED... MORBIUS!

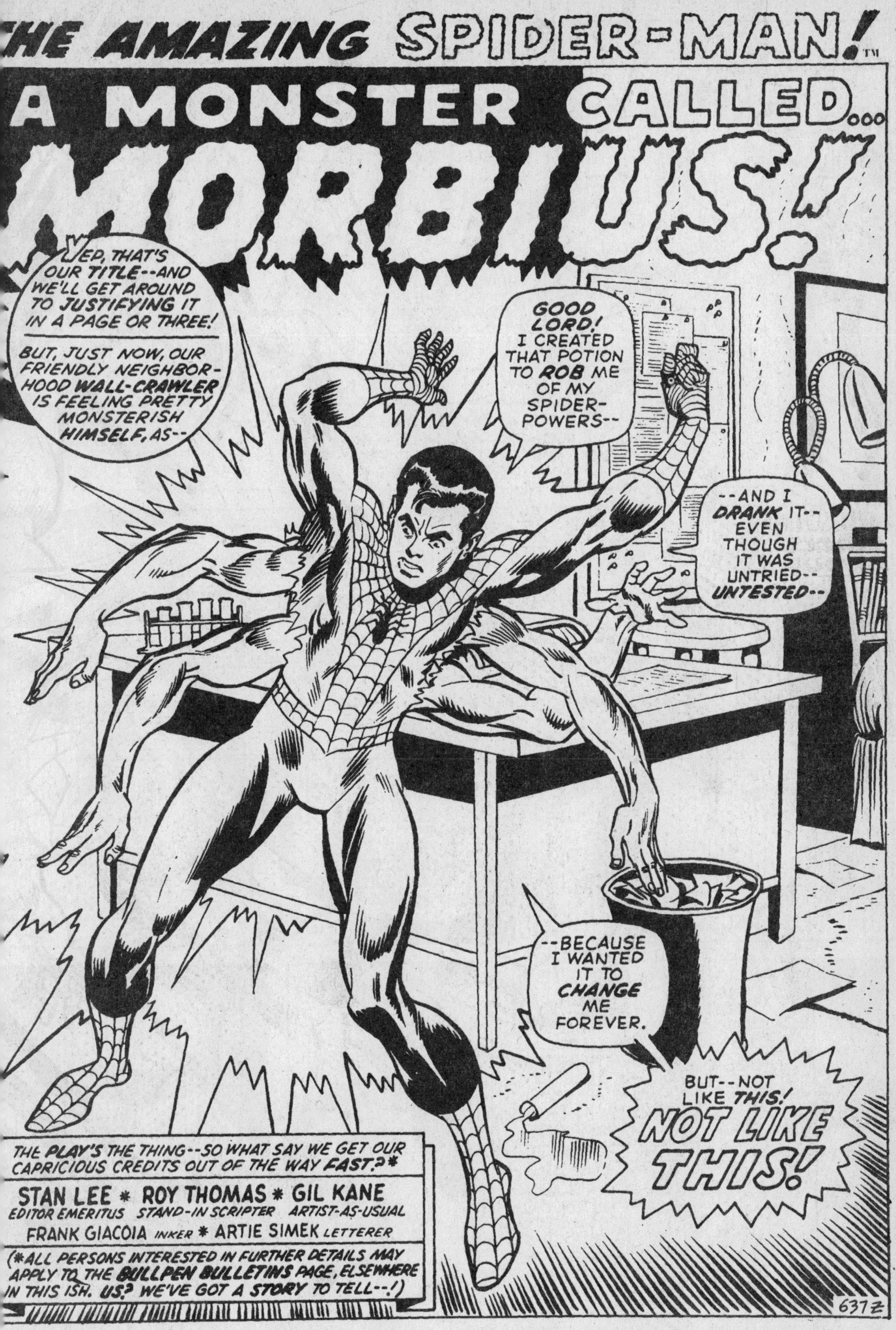
THE AMAZING SPIDER-MAN!™
A MONSTER CALLED...
MORBIUS!
YEP, THAT'S OUR TITLE--AND WE'LL GET AROUND TO JUSTIFYING IT IN A PAGE OR THREE!
BUT, JUST NOW, OUR FRIENDLY NEIGHBOR-HOOD WALL-CRAWLER IS FEELING PRETTY MONSTERISH HIMSELF, AS--
GOOD LORD! I CREATED THAT POTION TO ROB ME OF MY SPIDER-POWERS--
--AND I DRANK IT--EVEN THOUGH IT WAS UNTRIED--UNTESTED--
--BECAUSE I WANTED IT TO CHANGE ME FOREVER.
BUT--NOT LIKE THIS! NOT LIKE THIS!
THE PLAY'S THE THING--SO WHAT SAY WE GET OUR CAPRICIOUS CREDITS OUT OF THE WAY FAST?*
STAN LEE * ROY THOMAS * GIL KANE
EDITOR EMERITUS STAND-IN SCRIPTER ARTIST-AS-USUAL
FRANK GIACOIA INKER * ARTIE SIMEK LETTERER
(*ALL PERSONS INTERESTED IN FURTHER DETAILS MAY APPLY TO THE BULLPEN BULLETINS PAGE, ELSEWHERE IN THIS ISH. US? WE'VE GOT A STORY TO TELL--!)
637Z

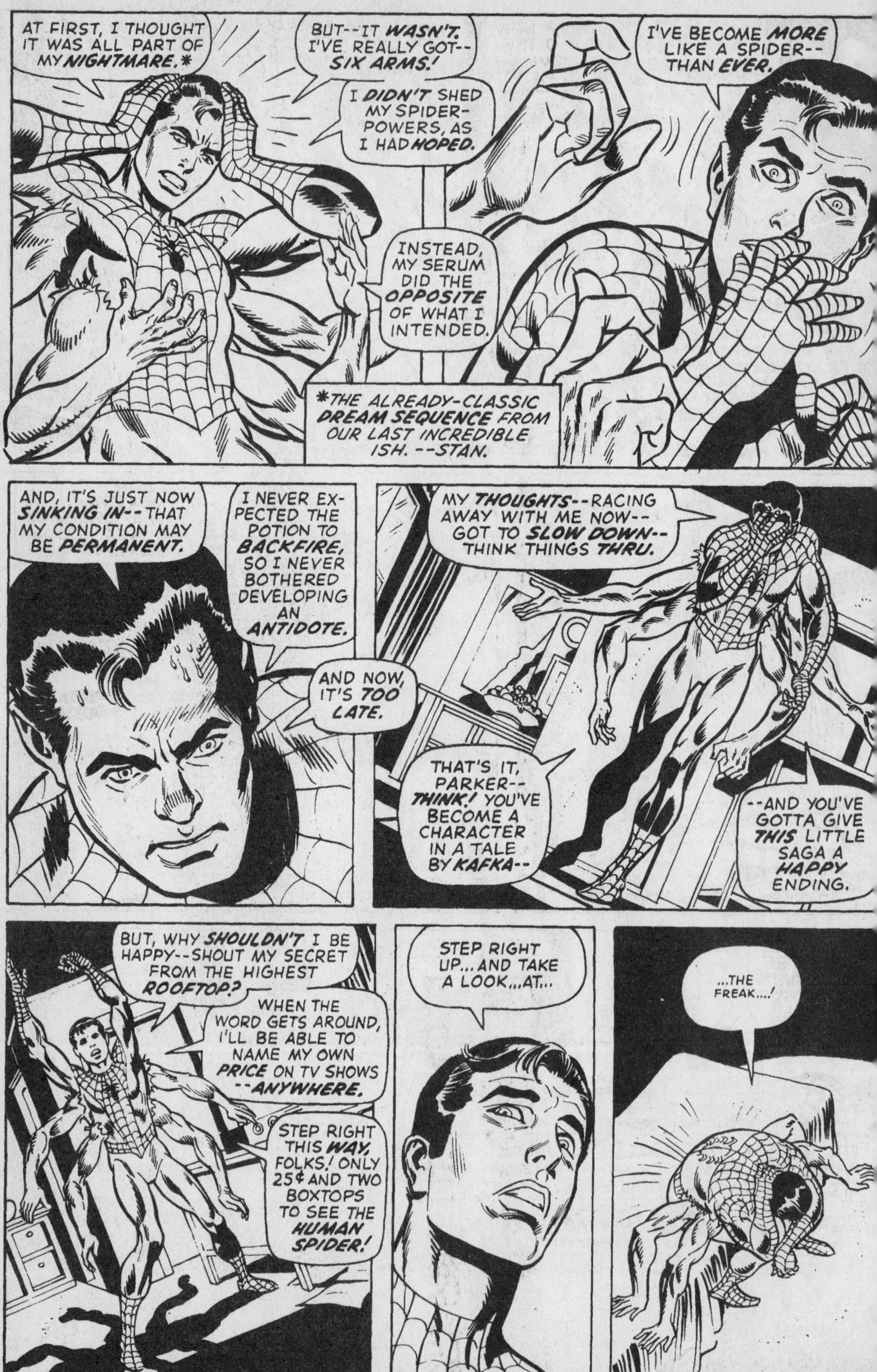

AT FIRST, I THOUGHT IT WAS ALL PART OF MY NIGHTMARE.*
BUT--IT WASN'T. I'VE REALLY GOT--SIX ARMS!
I DIDN'T SHED MY SPIDER-POWERS, AS I HAD HOPED.
INSTEAD, MY SERUM DID THE OPPOSITE OF WHAT I INTENDED.
I'VE BECOME MORE LIKE A SPIDER--THAN EVER.
*THE ALREADY-CLASSIC DREAM SEQUENCE FROM OUR LAST INCREDIBLE ISH. --STAN.
AND, IT'S JUST NOW SINKING IN--THAT MY CONDITION MAY BE PERMANENT.
I NEVER EXPECTED THE POTION TO BACKFIRE, SO I NEVER BOTHERED DEVELOPING AN ANTIDOTE.
AND NOW, IT'S TOO LATE.
MY THOUGHTS--RACING AWAY WITH ME NOW--GOT TO SLOW DOWN--THINK THINGS THRU.
THAT'S IT, PARKER--THINK! YOU'VE BECOME A CHARACTER IN A TALE BY KAFKA--
--AND YOU'VE GOTTA GIVE THIS LITTLE SAGA A HAPPY ENDING.
BUT, WHY SHOULDN'T I BE HAPPY--SHOUT MY SECRET FROM THE HIGHEST ROOFTOP?
WHEN THE WORD GETS AROUND, I'LL BE ABLE TO NAME MY OWN PRICE ON TV SHOWS --ANYWHERE.
STEP RIGHT THIS WAY, FOLKS! ONLY 25¢ AND TWO BOXTOPS TO SEE THE HUMAN SPIDER!
STEP RIGHT UP... AND TAKE A LOOK... AT...
...THE FREAK...!

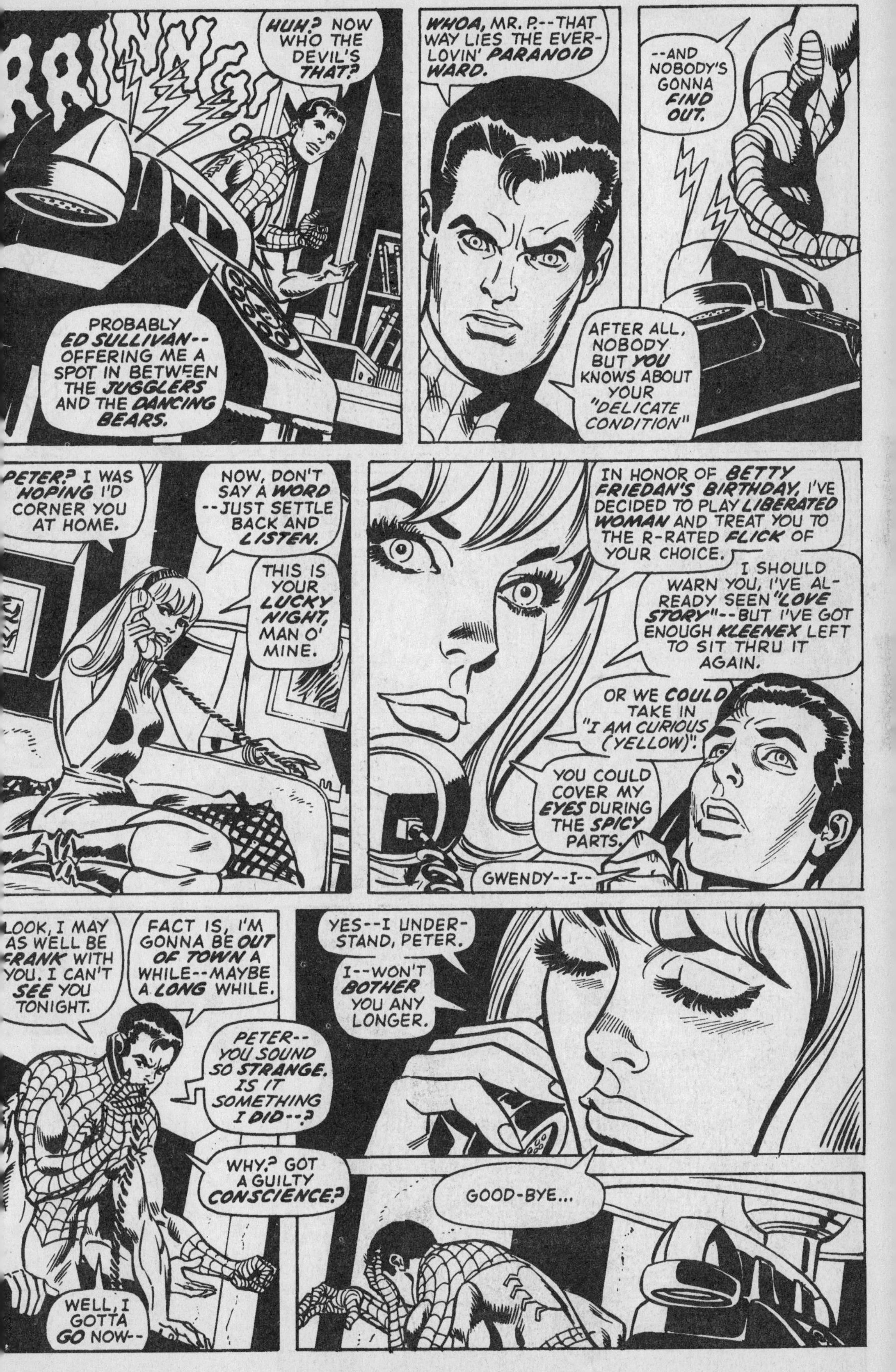

BRRINNNG!
HUH? NOW WHO THE DEVIL'S THAT?
PROBABLY ED SULLIVAN-- OFFERING ME A SPOT IN BETWEEN THE JUGGLERS AND THE DANCING BEARS.
WHOA, MR. P.--THAT WAY LIES THE EVER-LOVIN' PARANOID WARD.
AFTER ALL, NOBODY BUT YOU KNOWS ABOUT YOUR "DELICATE CONDITION"
--AND NOBODY'S GONNA FIND OUT.
PETER? I WAS HOPING I'D CORNER YOU AT HOME.
NOW, DON'T SAY A WORD --JUST SETTLE BACK AND LISTEN.
THIS IS YOUR LUCKY NIGHT, MAN O' MINE.
IN HONOR OF BETTY FRIEDAN'S BIRTHDAY, I'VE DECIDED TO PLAY LIBERATED WOMAN AND TREAT YOU TO THE R-RATED FLICK OF YOUR CHOICE.
I SHOULD WARN YOU, I'VE AL-READY SEEN "LOVE STORY"--BUT I'VE GOT ENOUGH KLEENEX LEFT TO SIT THRU IT AGAIN.
OR WE COULD TAKE IN "I AM CURIOUS (YELLOW)".
YOU COULD COVER MY EYES DURING THE SPICY PARTS.
GWENDY--I--
LOOK, I MAY AS WELL BE FRANK WITH YOU. I CAN'T SEE YOU TONIGHT.
FACT IS, I'M GONNA BE OUT OF TOWN A WHILE--MAYBE A LONG WHILE.
PETER-- YOU SOUND SO STRANGE. IS IT SOMETHING I DID--?
WHY? GOT A GUILTY CONSCIENCE?
WELL, I GOTTA GO NOW--
YES--I UNDER-STAND, PETER.
I--WON'T BOTHER YOU ANY LONGER.
GOOD-BYE...

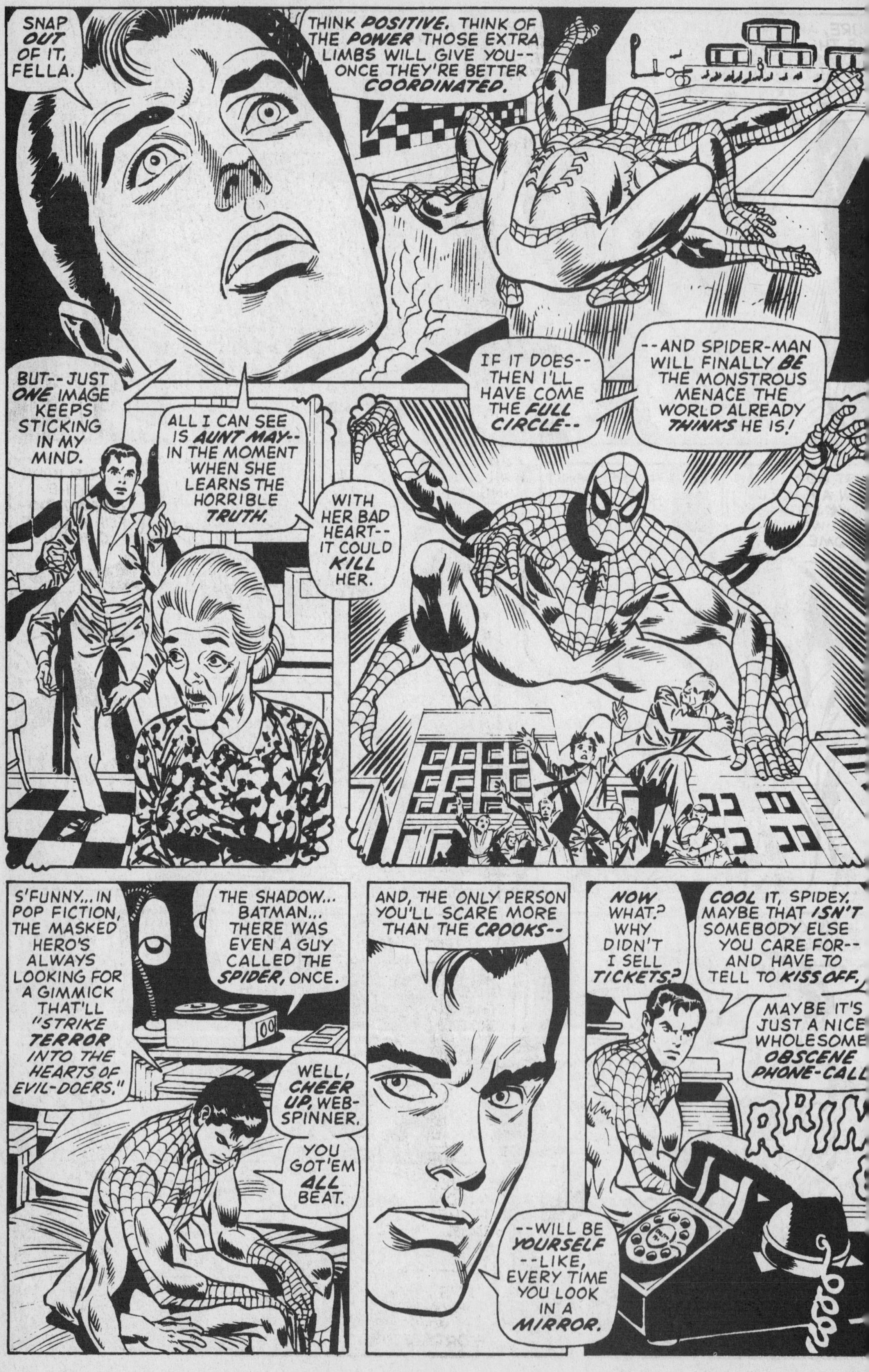

SNAP OUT OF IT, FELLA.
THINK POSITIVE. THINK OF THE POWER THOSE EXTRA LIMBS WILL GIVE YOU-- ONCE THEY'RE BETTER COORDINATED.
BUT--JUST ONE IMAGE KEEPS STICKING IN MY MIND.
ALL I CAN SEE IS AUNT MAY-- IN THE MOMENT WHEN SHE LEARNS THE HORRIBLE TRUTH.
WITH HER BAD HEART-- IT COULD KILL HER.
IF IT DOES-- THEN I'LL HAVE COME THE FULL CIRCLE--
--AND SPIDER-MAN WILL FINALLY BE THE MONSTROUS MENACE THE WORLD ALREADY THINKS HE IS!
S'FUNNY...IN POP FICTION, THE MASKED HERO'S ALWAYS LOOKING FOR A GIMMICK THAT'LL "STRIKE TERROR INTO THE HEARTS OF EVIL-DOERS."
THE SHADOW... BATMAN... THERE WAS EVEN A GUY CALLED THE SPIDER, ONCE.
WELL, CHEER UP, WEB-SPINNER.
YOU GOT'EM ALL BEAT.
AND, THE ONLY PERSON YOU'LL SCARE MORE THAN THE CROOKS--
--WILL BE YOURSELF --LIKE, EVERY TIME YOU LOOK IN A MIRROR.
NOW WHAT? WHY DIDN'T I SELL TICKETS?
COOL IT, SPIDEY. MAYBE THAT ISN'T SOMEBODY ELSE YOU CARE FOR-- AND HAVE TO TELL TO KISS OFF.
MAYBE IT'S JUST A NICE WHOLESOME OBSCENE PHONE-CALL

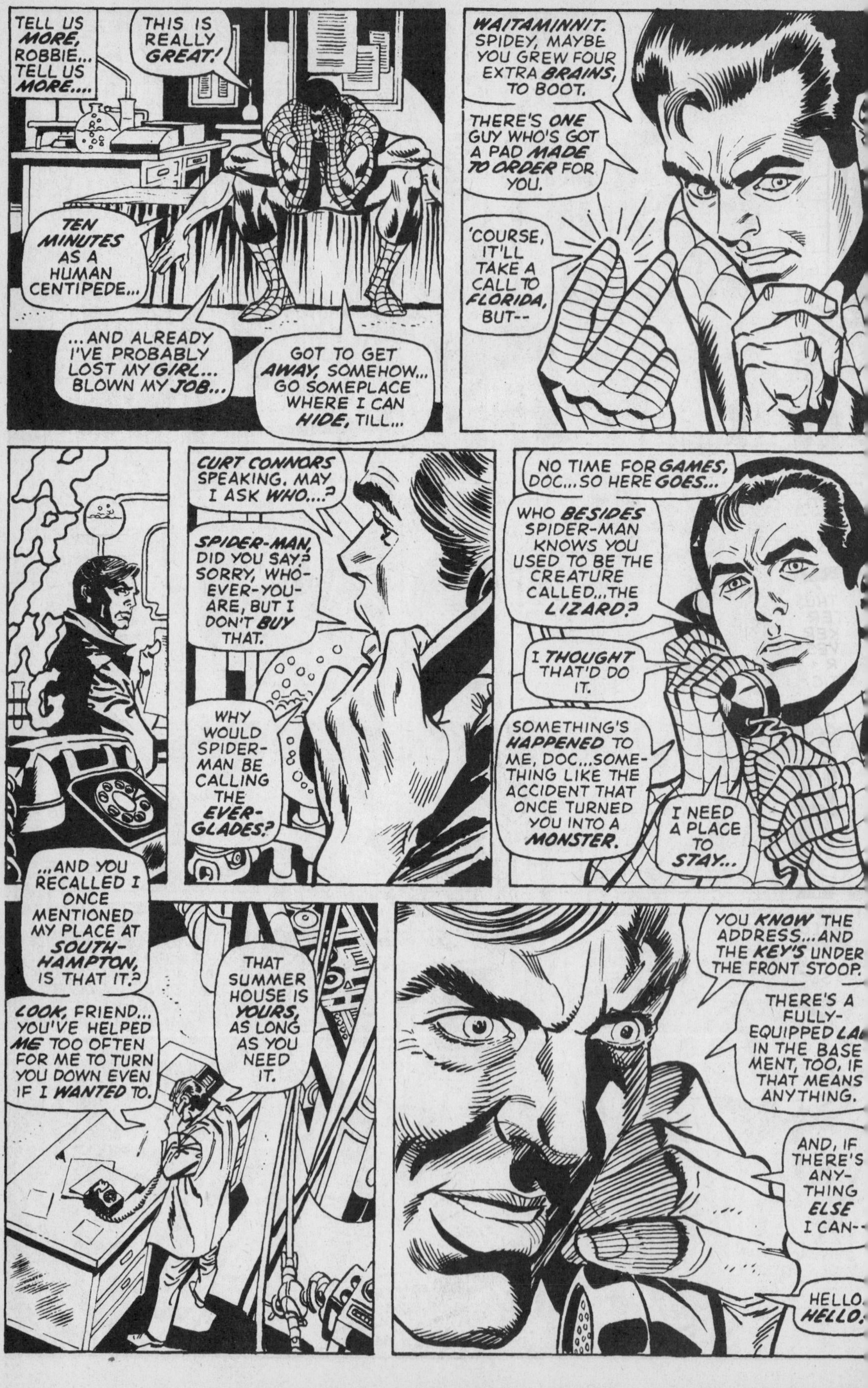

TELL US MORE, ROBBIE... TELL US MORE....
THIS IS REALLY GREAT!
TEN MINUTES AS A HUMAN CENTIPEDE...
...AND ALREADY I'VE PROBABLY LOST MY GIRL... BLOWN MY JOB...
GOT TO GET AWAY, SOMEHOW... GO SOMEPLACE WHERE I CAN HIDE, TILL...
WAITAMINNIT. SPIDEY, MAYBE YOU GREW FOUR EXTRA BRAINS, TO BOOT.
THERE'S ONE GUY WHO'S GOT A PAD MADE TO ORDER FOR YOU.
'COURSE, IT'LL TAKE A CALL TO FLORIDA, BUT--
CURT CONNORS SPEAKING. MAY I ASK WHO...?
SPIDER-MAN, DID YOU SAY? SORRY, WHO-EVER-YOU-ARE, BUT I DON'T BUY THAT.
WHY WOULD SPIDER-MAN BE CALLING THE EVER-GLADES?
NO TIME FOR GAMES, DOC...SO HERE GOES...
WHO BESIDES SPIDER-MAN KNOWS YOU USED TO BE THE CREATURE CALLED...THE LIZARD?
I THOUGHT THAT'D DO IT.
SOMETHING'S HAPPENED TO ME, DOC...SOME-THING LIKE THE ACCIDENT THAT ONCE TURNED YOU INTO A MONSTER.
I NEED A PLACE TO STAY...
...AND YOU RECALLED I ONCE MENTIONED MY PLACE AT SOUTH-HAMPTON, IS THAT IT?
LOOK, FRIEND... YOU'VE HELPED ME TOO OFTEN FOR ME TO TURN YOU DOWN EVEN IF I WANTED TO.
THAT SUMMER HOUSE IS YOURS, AS LONG AS YOU NEED IT.
YOU KNOW THE ADDRESS...AND THE KEY'S UNDER THE FRONT STOOP.
THERE'S A FULLY-EQUIPPED LA IN THE BASE-MENT, TOO, IF THAT MEANS ANYTHING.
AND, IF THERE'S ANY-THING ELSE I CAN--
HELLO. HELLO.

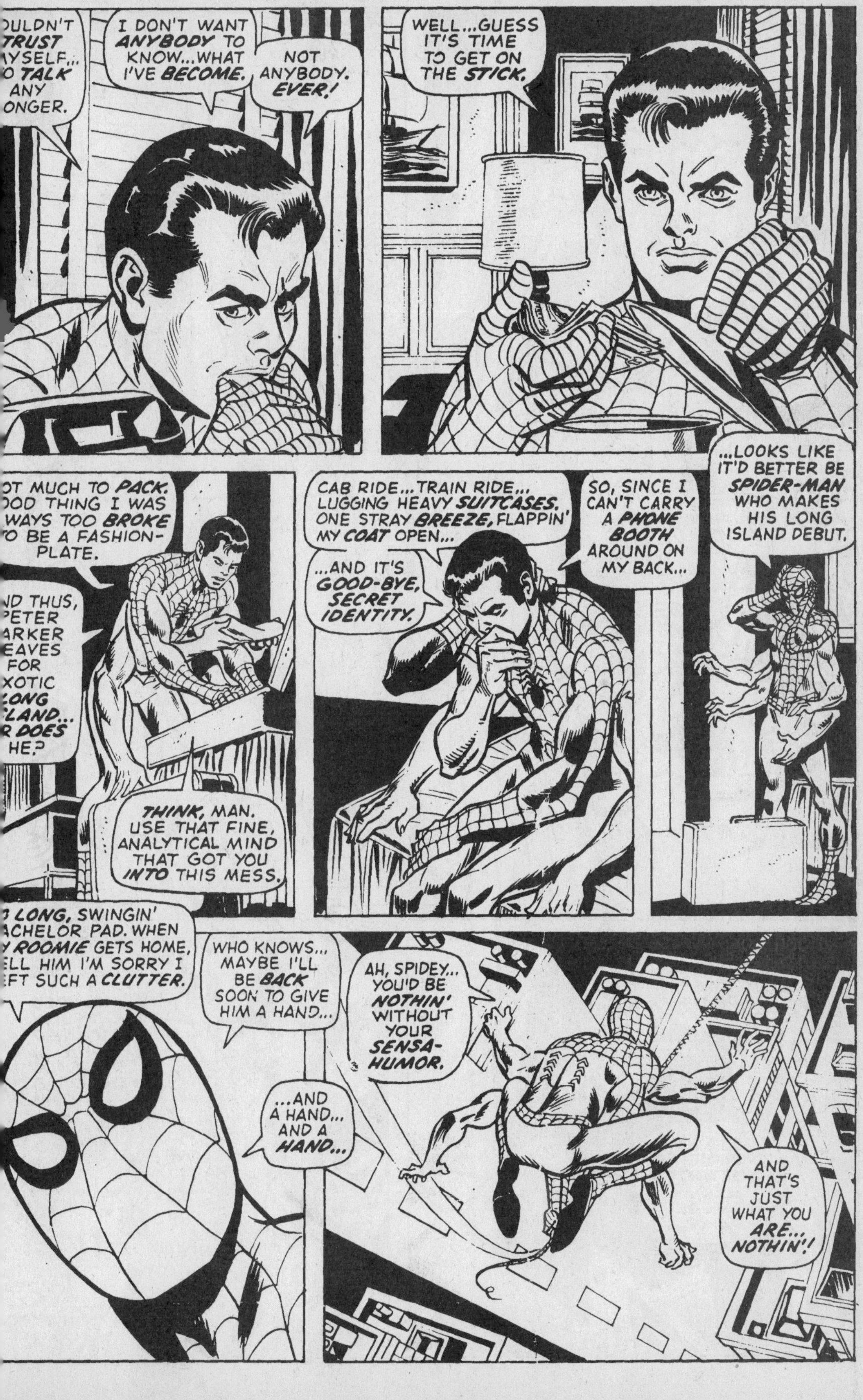

OULDN'T TRUST MYSELF... O TALK ANY ONGER.
I DON'T WANT ANYBODY TO KNOW...WHAT I'VE BECOME.
NOT ANYBODY. EVER!
WELL...GUESS IT'S TIME TO GET ON THE STICK.
OT MUCH TO PACK. OOD THING I WAS WAYS TOO BROKE TO BE A FASHION-PLATE.
ND THUS, PETER ARKER EAVES FOR XOTIC LONG SLAND... R DOES HE?
THINK, MAN. USE THAT FINE, ANALYTICAL MIND THAT GOT YOU INTO THIS MESS.
CAB RIDE...TRAIN RIDE... LUGGING HEAVY SUITCASES. ONE STRAY BREEZE, FLAPPIN' MY COAT OPEN...
...AND IT'S GOOD-BYE, SECRET IDENTITY.
SO, SINCE I CAN'T CARRY A PHONE BOOTH AROUND ON MY BACK...
...LOOKS LIKE IT'D BETTER BE SPIDER-MAN WHO MAKES HIS LONG ISLAND DEBUT.
O LONG, SWINGIN' ACHELOR PAD. WHEN Y ROOMIE GETS HOME, ELL HIM I'M SORRY I EFT SUCH A CLUTTER.
WHO KNOWS... MAYBE I'LL BE BACK SOON TO GIVE HIM A HAND...
...AND A HAND... AND A HAND...
AH, SPIDEY... YOU'D BE NOTHIN' WITHOUT YOUR SENSA-HUMOR.
AND THAT'S JUST WHAT YOU ARE... NOTHIN'!

HUH?

NOW WHAT IN--?

≥WHEW!≤ LUCKY I'M NOT A WALL-CRAWLER IN *NAME* ONLY.

SMEK!

STILL, WONDE WHAT MAD ME LOSE MY-

WISE UP, WEBHEAD. HOW MANY *TIMES* DOES A WALL HAVE TO FALL ON YOU?

IT'S THESE EXTRA *ARMS* OF YOURS, FLAILING AROUND LIKE CRAZY.

THEY'RE FOULING UP YOUR *TIMING*, SOMETHING FIERCE.

WELL, GET *USED* TO 'EM, KID.

THEY MIGHT JUST BE AROUND FOR A LONG LONG *WHILE*.

I GUESS--I SHOULD HAVE *PRACTICED* WITH ALL SIX ARMS-- BEFORE I MADE LIKE *KA-ZAR*.

BUT, MY SPIRO AGNEW *WRIST WATCH* TELLS ME IT'S NEARLY *DAWN*...

AND, SOMETHING TELLS ME IF I'M NOT OUT OF TOWN BY *SUN-UP*...

THIS IS *ONE* DAWN THAT'S *REALLY* GONNA COME UP LIKE THUNDER!

THWIPP

NOW PLAYI BLACKM

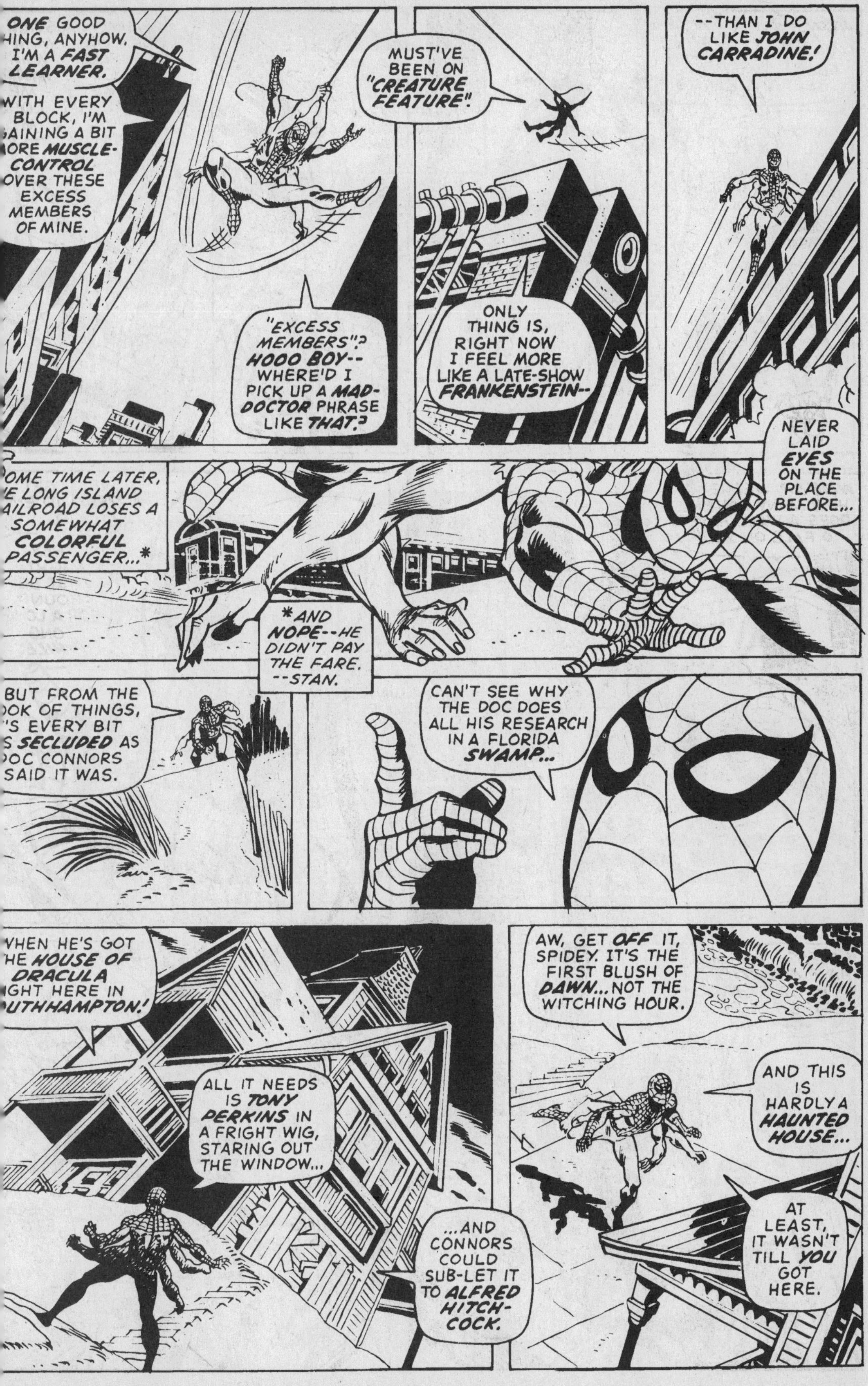
ONE GOOD HING, ANYHOW, I'M A FAST LEARNER.
WITH EVERY BLOCK, I'M AINING A BIT ORE MUSCLE-CONTROL OVER THESE EXCESS MEMBERS OF MINE.
"EXCESS MEMBERS"? HOOO BOY-- WHERE'D I PICK UP A MAD-DOCTOR PHRASE LIKE THAT?
MUST'VE BEEN ON "CREATURE FEATURE".
ONLY THING IS, RIGHT NOW I FEEL MORE LIKE A LATE-SHOW FRANKENSTEIN--
--THAN I DO LIKE JOHN CARRADINE!
OME TIME LATER, E LONG ISLAND AILROAD LOSES A SOMEWHAT COLORFUL PASSENGER...*
NEVER LAID EYES ON THE PLACE BEFORE...
*AND NOPE--HE DIDN'T PAY THE FARE. --STAN.
BUT FROM THE OOK OF THINGS, 'S EVERY BIT S SECLUDED AS OC CONNORS SAID IT WAS.
CAN'T SEE WHY THE DOC DOES ALL HIS RESEARCH IN A FLORIDA SWAMP...
VHEN HE'S GOT HE HOUSE OF DRACULA IGHT HERE IN UTHHAMPTON!
ALL IT NEEDS IS TONY PERKINS IN A FRIGHT WIG, STARING OUT THE WINDOW...
...AND CONNORS COULD SUB-LET IT TO ALFRED HITCH-COCK.
AW, GET OFF IT, SPIDEY. IT'S THE FIRST BLUSH OF DAWN... NOT THE WITCHING HOUR.
AND THIS IS HARDLY A HAUNTED HOUSE...
AT LEAST, IT WASN'T TILL YOU GOT HERE.

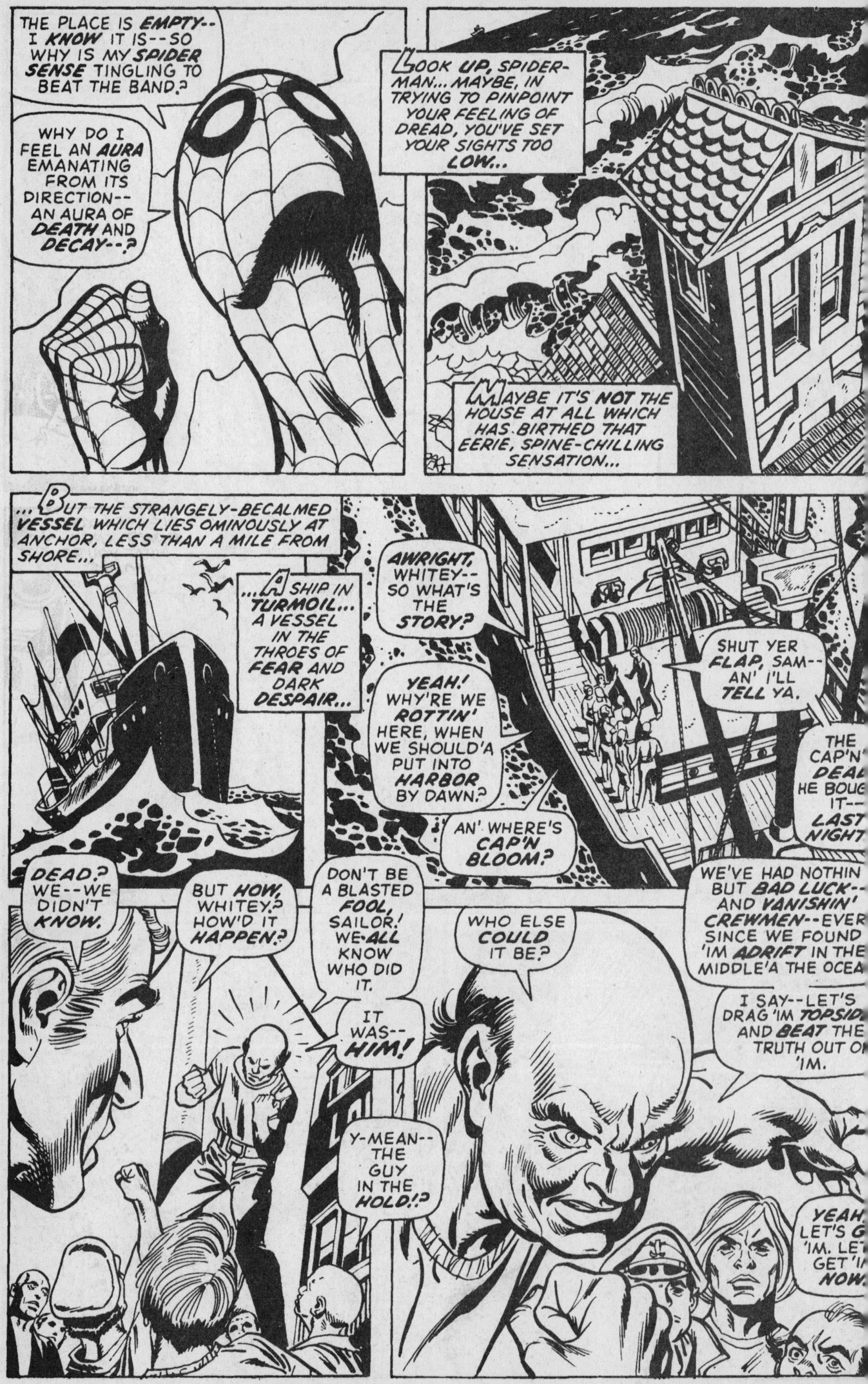
THE PLACE IS EMPTY-- I KNOW IT IS--SO WHY IS MY SPIDER SENSE TINGLING TO BEAT THE BAND?
WHY DO I FEEL AN AURA EMANATING FROM ITS DIRECTION-- AN AURA OF DEATH AND DECAY--?
LOOK UP, SPIDER-MAN... MAYBE, IN TRYING TO PINPOINT YOUR FEELING OF DREAD, YOU'VE SET YOUR SIGHTS TOO LOW...
MAYBE IT'S NOT THE HOUSE AT ALL WHICH HAS BIRTHED THAT EERIE, SPINE-CHILLING SENSATION...
...BUT THE STRANGELY-BECALMED VESSEL WHICH LIES OMINOUSLY AT ANCHOR, LESS THAN A MILE FROM SHORE...
...A SHIP IN TURMOIL... A VESSEL IN THE THROES OF FEAR AND DARK DESPAIR...
AWRIGHT, WHITEY-- SO WHAT'S THE STORY?
YEAH! WHY'RE WE ROTTIN' HERE, WHEN WE SHOULD'A PUT INTO HARBOR BY DAWN?
AN' WHERE'S CAP'N BLOOM?
SHUT YER FLAP, SAM-- AN' I'LL TELL YA.
THE CAP'N' DEAD HE BOUG IT-- LAST NIGHT
DEAD? WE--WE DIDN'T KNOW.
BUT HOW, WHITEY? HOW'D IT HAPPEN?
DON'T BE A BLASTED FOOL, SAILOR! WE ALL KNOW WHO DID IT.
WHO ELSE COULD IT BE?
IT WAS-- HIM!
WE'VE HAD NOTHIN BUT BAD LUCK-- AND VANISHIN' CREWMEN--EVER SINCE WE FOUND 'IM ADRIFT IN THE MIDDLE'A THE OCEA
I SAY--LET'S DRAG 'IM TOPSID AND BEAT THE TRUTH OUT O 'IM.
Y-MEAN-- THE GUY IN THE HOLD!?
YEAH LET'S G 'IM. LE GET 'I NOW

HURRY! DON'T LET 'IM GET AWAY.

WHERE'S HE GONNA RUN TO-- A MILE OUT AT SEA?

C'MON-- HE MUST BE HIDIN' OUT IN THE ENGINE ROOM.

THERE HE IS!

NO--PLEASE-- GO BACK.

I--JUST WANT-- TO GET TO SHORE.

I DON'T-- WANT TO HURT YOU--!

DIDJA HEAR THAT, MATES?

HE DON'T WANNA HURT US.

PLEASE--YOU DON'T KNOW-- WHAT YOU'RE DOING.

WE'RE MAKIN' SURE WE AINT ALL MURDERED IN OUR BUNKS, BUDDY-- AN' THAT'S ENOUGH.

PIPES! THIS GUY MOVES LIKE HE'S HALF ASLEEP--AN' WE STILL CAN'T PUT A DENT IN HIM.

KEEP POUNDIN' AWAY AT 'IM! REMEMBER WHAT HAPPENED TO THE CAP'N.

HOLD 'IM DOWN! HE'S-- TRYIN' TO BREAK FREE.

CORRECTION-- SWINE--

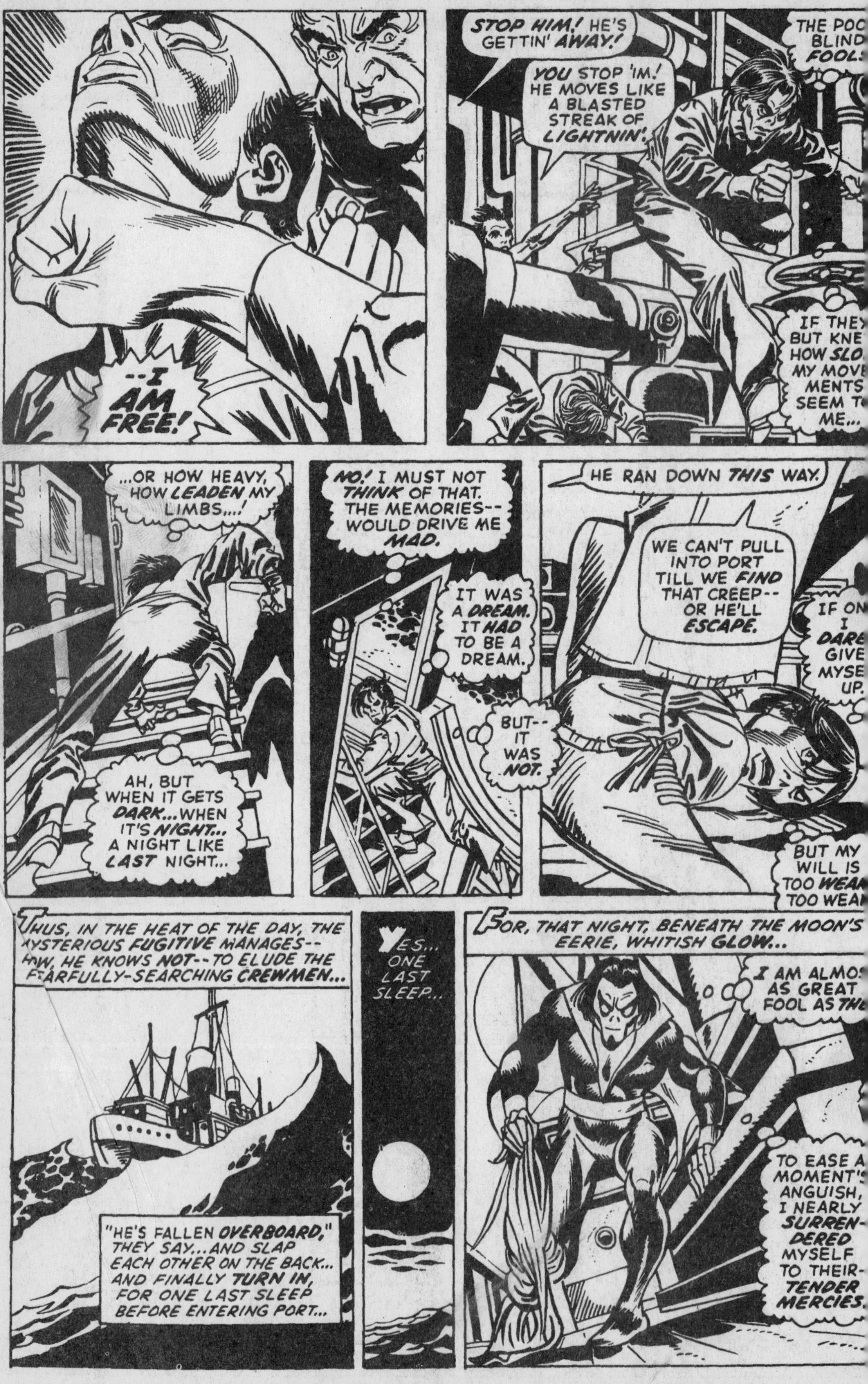
--I AM FREE!
STOP HIM! HE'S GETTIN' AWAY!
YOU STOP 'IM! HE MOVES LIKE A BLASTED STREAK OF LIGHTNIN'!
THE POO BLIND FOOLS
IF THEY BUT KNE HOW SLO MY MOVE MENTS SEEM T ME...
...OR HOW HEAVY, HOW LEADEN MY LIMBS...!
AH, BUT WHEN IT GETS DARK...WHEN IT'S NIGHT... A NIGHT LIKE LAST NIGHT...
NO! I MUST NOT THINK OF THAT. THE MEMORIES--WOULD DRIVE ME MAD.
IT WAS A DREAM. IT HAD TO BE A DREAM.
BUT--IT WAS NOT.
HE RAN DOWN THIS WAY.
WE CAN'T PULL INTO PORT TILL WE FIND THAT CREEP--OR HE'LL ESCAPE.
IF ON I DARE GIVE MYSE UP.
BUT MY WILL IS TOO WEA TOO WEA
THUS, IN THE HEAT OF THE DAY, THE MYSTERIOUS FUGITIVE MANAGES--HOW, HE KNOWS NOT--TO ELUDE THE FEARFULLY-SEARCHING CREWMEN...
"HE'S FALLEN OVERBOARD," THEY SAY...AND SLAP EACH OTHER ON THE BACK... AND FINALLY TURN IN, FOR ONE LAST SLEEP BEFORE ENTERING PORT...
YES... ONE LAST SLEEP...
FOR, THAT NIGHT, BENEATH THE MOON'S EERIE, WHITISH GLOW...
I AM ALMOS AS GREAT FOOL AS THE
TO EASE A MOMENT'S ANGUISH, I NEARLY SURRENDERED MYSELF TO THEIR TENDER MERCIES.

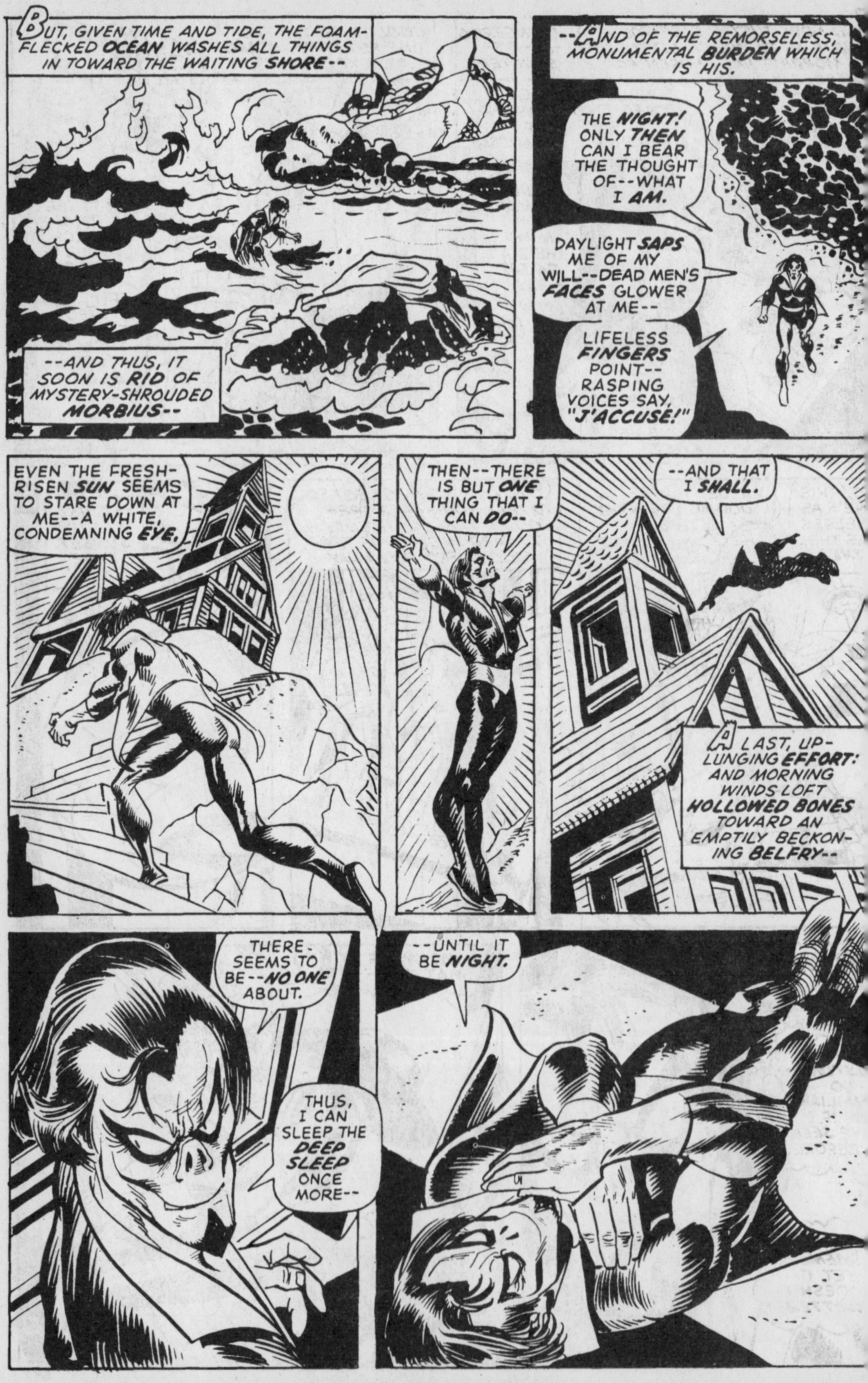
BUT, GIVEN TIME AND TIDE, THE FOAM-FLECKED OCEAN WASHES ALL THINGS IN TOWARD THE WAITING SHORE--
--AND THUS, IT SOON IS RID OF MYSTERY-SHROUDED MORBIUS--
--AND OF THE REMORSELESS, MONUMENTAL BURDEN WHICH IS HIS.
THE NIGHT! ONLY THEN CAN I BEAR THE THOUGHT OF--WHAT I AM.
DAYLIGHT SAPS ME OF MY WILL--DEAD MEN'S FACES GLOWER AT ME--
LIFELESS FINGERS POINT--RASPING VOICES SAY, "J'ACCUSE!"
EVEN THE FRESH-RISEN SUN SEEMS TO STARE DOWN AT ME--A WHITE, CONDEMNING EYE.
THEN--THERE IS BUT ONE THING THAT I CAN DO--
--AND THAT I SHALL.
A LAST, UP-LUNGING EFFORT: AND MORNING WINDS LOFT HOLLOWED BONES TOWARD AN EMPTILY BECKONING BELFRY--
THERE SEEMS TO BE--NO ONE ABOUT.
THUS, I CAN SLEEP THE DEEP SLEEP ONCE MORE--
--UNTIL IT BE NIGHT.

AND NOW, JUST IN CASE YOU'VE ANY LINGERING DOUBTS AS TO *WHICH* LITTLE VILLA-BY-THE-SEA MORBIUS HAS CHOSEN FOR HIS SINISTER SOMNOLENCE--

WE'VE BEEN HERE *TWO DAYS*--AND WE'VE ACCOMPLISHED *EXACTLY NOTHING.*

UNLESS YOU GET *CREDIT* FOR WASTING A VATFUL OF EXPENSIVE *CHEMICALS.*

DOC CONNORS WON'T *MIND.* HE'S A *GREAT* GUY.

WISH I COULD GIVE HIM ONE OF *THESE* ARMS --TO REPLACE THE ONE HE *LOST.*

COOL IT, SPIDEY--NO TIME FOR *PIPE-DREAMS.* GOTTA KEEP *TRUCKIN'!*

MAYBE *THIS* BATCH WILL BE THE ONE.

IF IT *IS,* MY THEORY SAYS IT SHOULD TURN *BLUE*--

NO! THIS ONE'S AS *USELESS AS* THE *OTHERS.*

MAYBE--MAYBE I'M *DOOMED* TO *STAY* THIS WAY--

--FOR THE REST OF MY *LIFE!*

OH, AND WE *NEGLECTED* TO TELL YOU--THE FORE-GOING TABLEAU OCCURS TOWARD THE *END* OF THAT SECOND *FRUITLESS* DAY--

--*JUST BEFORE SUNSET,* TO BE *EXACT.*

WHAT MANNER OF *PLACE* IS THIS? THAT MAN HAS-- *SIX ARMS.*

YET--HIS *COSTUME*--SO *FAMILIAR,* AS IF I HAVE *SEEN* IT BEFORE.

I--*CANNOT REMEMBER.* YET, IT *DOESN'T MATTER*--

NOTHING MATTERS--

--EXCEPT THE *RAVENING THIRST* OF MORBIUS!

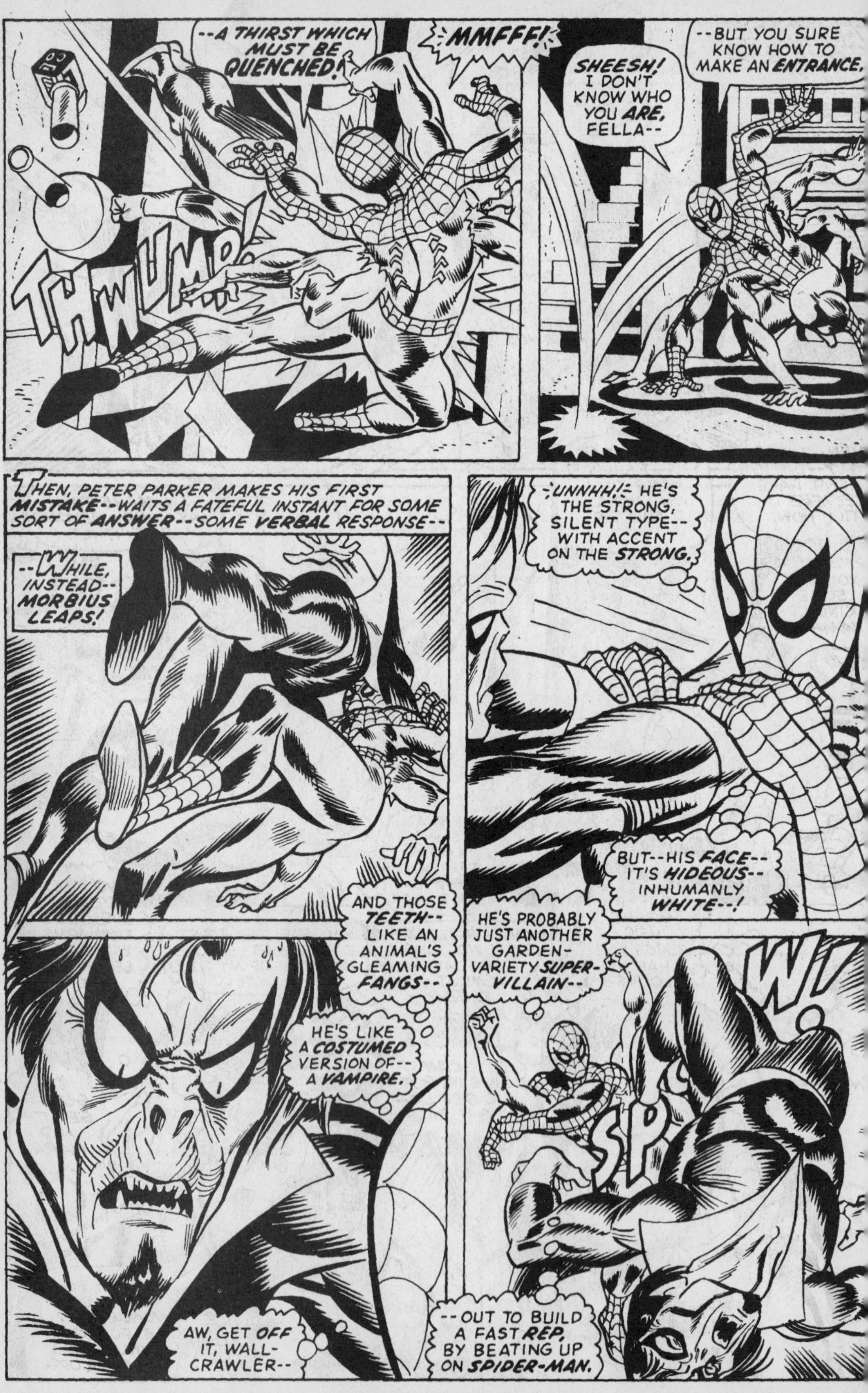
--A THIRST WHICH MUST BE QUENCHED!
MMFFF!
THWUMP
SHEESH! I DON'T KNOW WHO YOU ARE, FELLA--
--BUT YOU SURE KNOW HOW TO MAKE AN ENTRANCE.
THEN, PETER PARKER MAKES HIS FIRST MISTAKE--WAITS A FATEFUL INSTANT FOR SOME SORT OF ANSWER--SOME VERBAL RESPONSE--
--WHILE, INSTEAD--MORBIUS LEAPS!
UNNHH! HE'S THE STRONG, SILENT TYPE--WITH ACCENT ON THE STRONG.
BUT--HIS FACE--IT'S HIDEOUS--INHUMANLY WHITE--!
AND THOSE TEETH--LIKE AN ANIMAL'S GLEAMING FANGS--
HE'S LIKE A COSTUMED VERSION OF--A VAMPIRE.
AW, GET OFF IT, WALL-CRAWLER--
HE'S PROBABLY JUST ANOTHER GARDEN-VARIETY SUPER-VILLAIN--
--OUT TO BUILD A FAST REP, BY BEATING UP ON SPIDER-MAN.

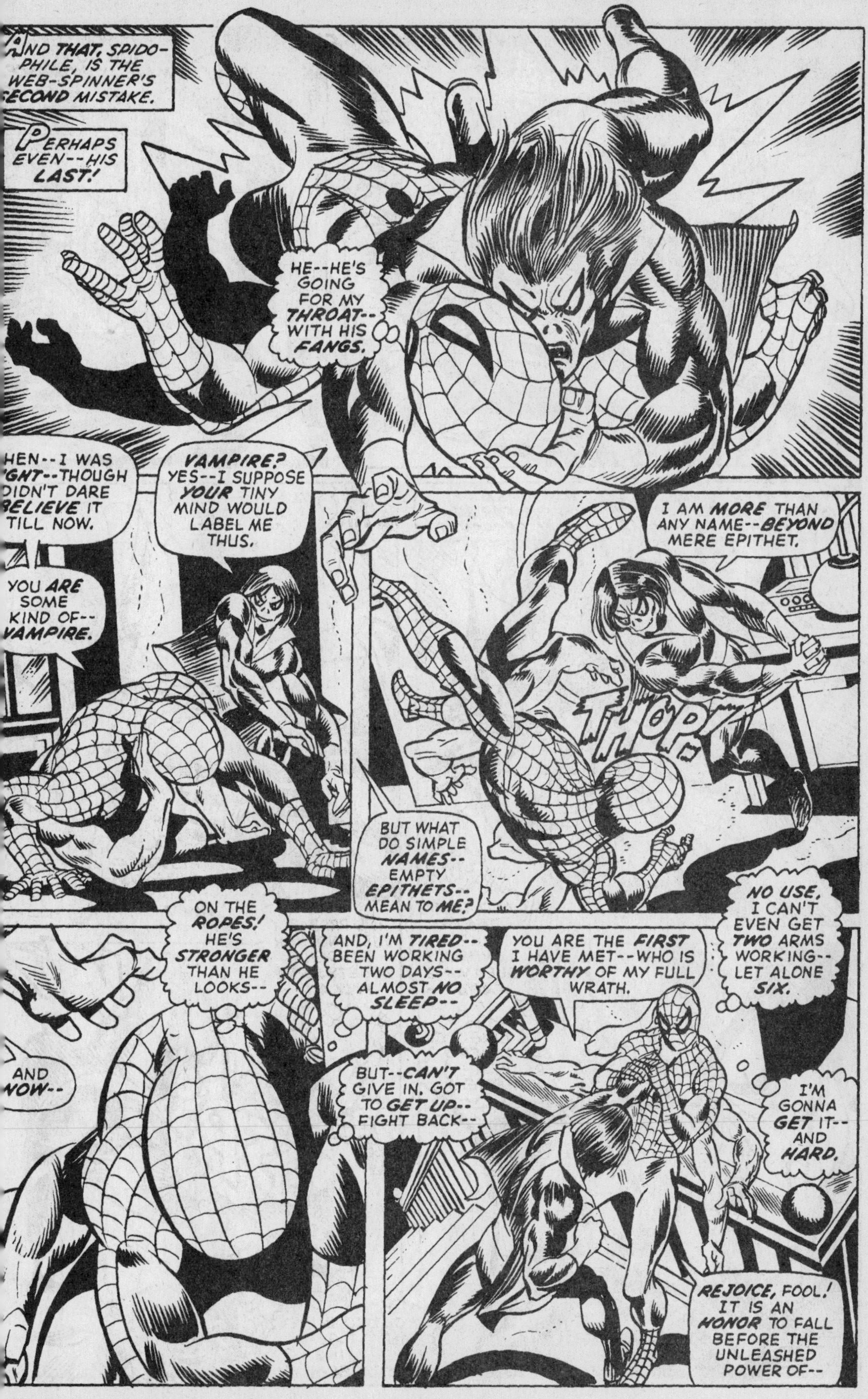

AND THAT, SPIDO-PHILE, IS THE WEB-SPINNER'S SECOND MISTAKE.
PERHAPS EVEN--HIS LAST!
HE--HE'S GOING FOR MY THROAT--WITH HIS FANGS.
HEN--I WAS IGHT--THOUGH DIDN'T DARE BELIEVE IT TILL NOW.
YOU ARE SOME KIND OF--VAMPIRE.
VAMPIRE? YES--I SUPPOSE YOUR TINY MIND WOULD LABEL ME THUS.
I AM MORE THAN ANY NAME--BEYOND MERE EPITHET.
THOP!
BUT WHAT DO SIMPLE NAMES--EMPTY EPITHETS--MEAN TO ME?
AND NOW--
ON THE ROPES! HE'S STRONGER THAN HE LOOKS--
AND, I'M TIRED--BEEN WORKING TWO DAYS--ALMOST NO SLEEP--
BUT--CAN'T GIVE IN. GOT TO GET UP--FIGHT BACK--
YOU ARE THE FIRST I HAVE MET--WHO IS WORTHY OF MY FULL WRATH.
NO USE. I CAN'T EVEN GET TWO ARMS WORKING--LET ALONE SIX.
I'M GONNA GET IT--AND HARD.
REJOICE, FOOL! IT IS AN HONOR TO FALL BEFORE THE UNLEASHED POWER OF--

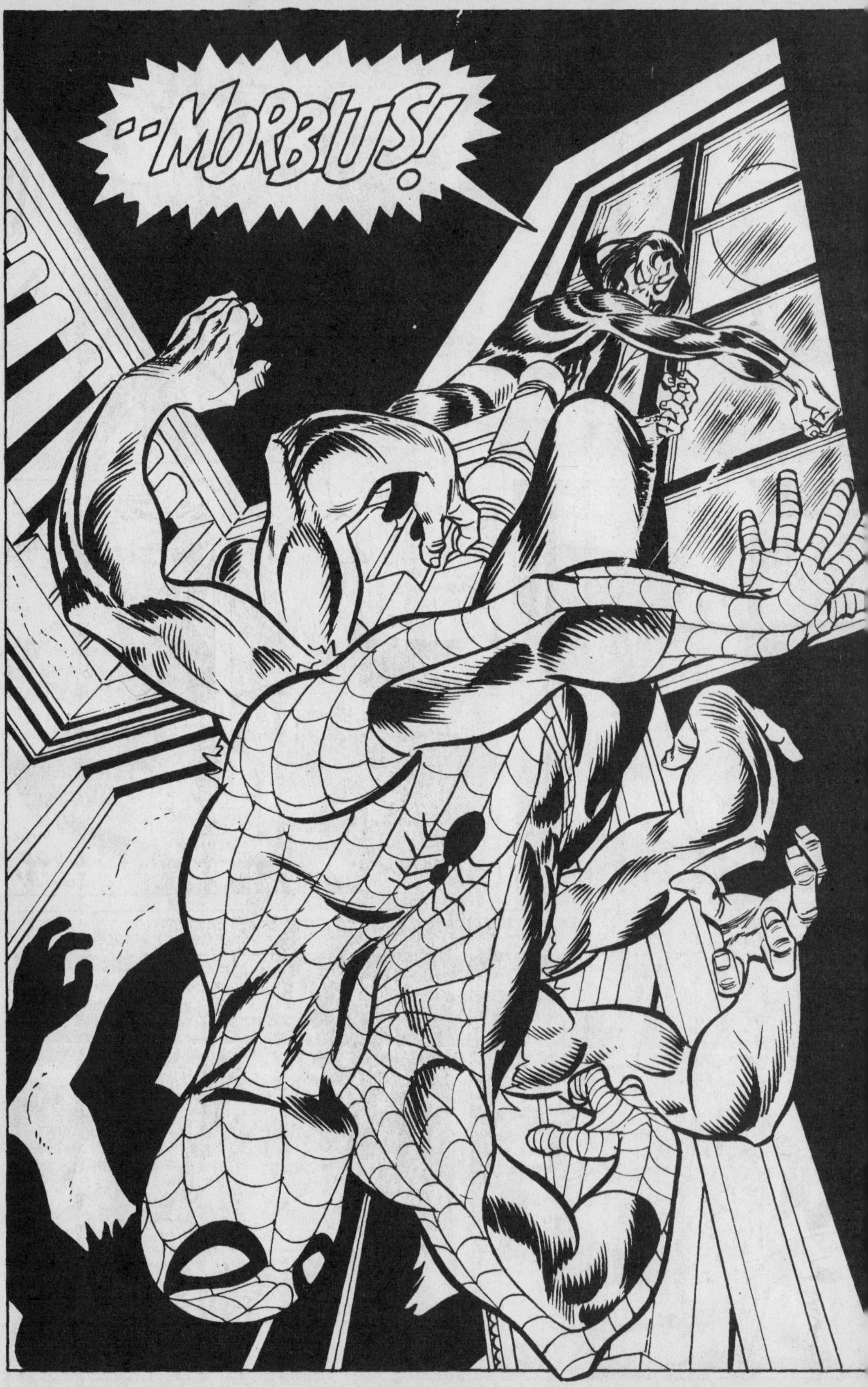
--MORBIUS!

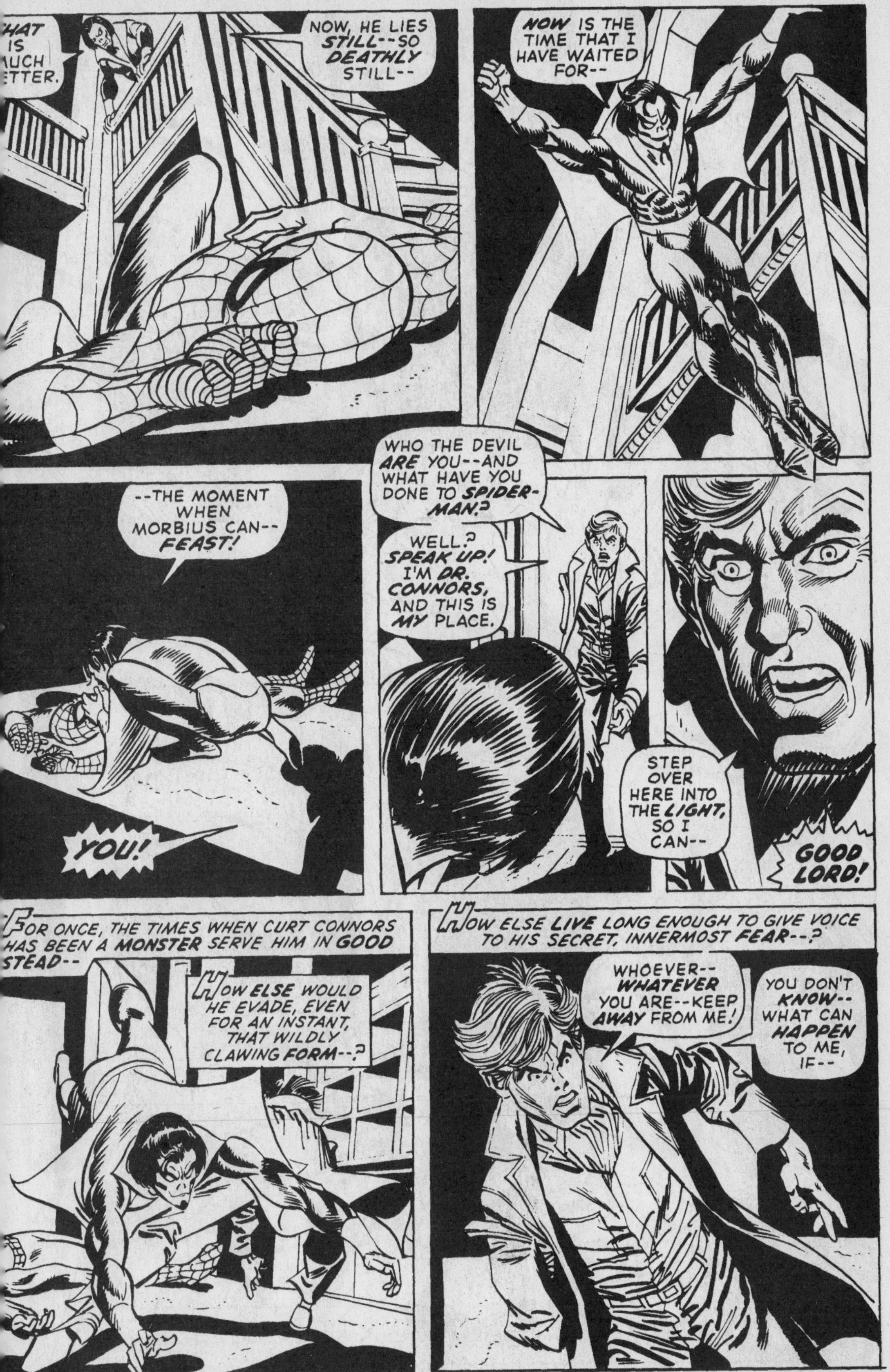

HAT IS UCH ETTER.
NOW, HE LIES STILL--SO DEATHLY STILL--
NOW IS THE TIME THAT I HAVE WAITED FOR--
--THE MOMENT WHEN MORBIUS CAN-- FEAST!
YOU!
WHO THE DEVIL ARE YOU--AND WHAT HAVE YOU DONE TO SPIDER-MAN?
WELL? SPEAK UP! I'M DR. CONNORS, AND THIS IS MY PLACE.
STEP OVER HERE INTO THE LIGHT, SO I CAN--
GOOD LORD!
FOR ONCE, THE TIMES WHEN CURT CONNORS HAS BEEN A MONSTER SERVE HIM IN GOOD STEAD--
HOW ELSE WOULD HE EVADE, EVEN FOR AN INSTANT, THAT WILDLY CLAWING FORM--?
HOW ELSE LIVE LONG ENOUGH TO GIVE VOICE TO HIS SECRET, INNERMOST FEAR--?
WHOEVER-- WHATEVER YOU ARE--KEEP AWAY FROM ME!
YOU DON'T KNOW-- WHAT CAN HAPPEN TO ME, IF--

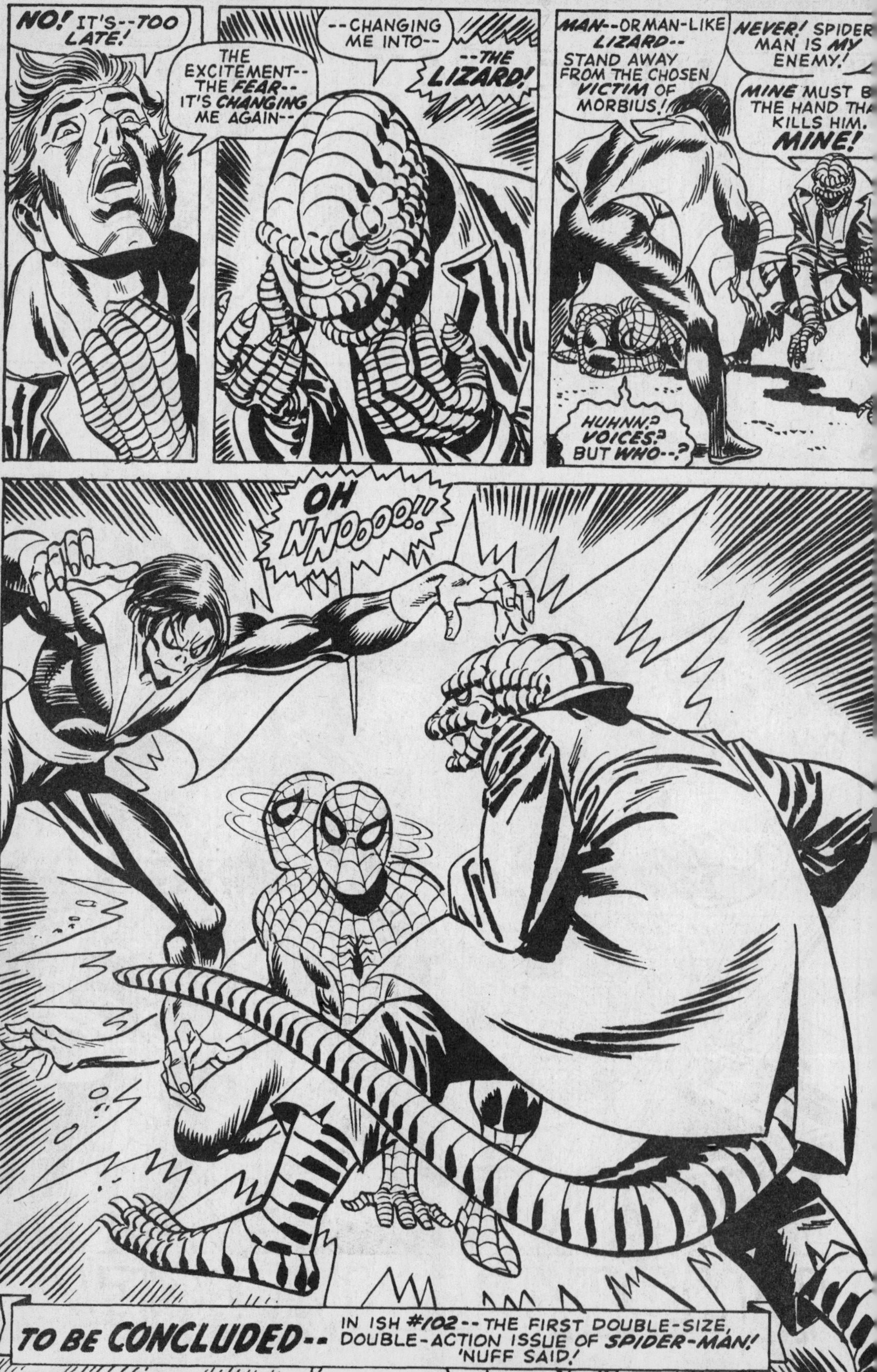
NO! IT'S--TOO LATE!
THE EXCITEMENT--THE FEAR--IT'S CHANGING ME AGAIN--
--CHANGING ME INTO--
--THE LIZARD!
MAN--OR MAN-LIKE LIZARD--STAND AWAY FROM THE CHOSEN VICTIM OF MORBIUS!
NEVER! SPIDER MAN IS MY ENEMY!
MINE MUST B THE HAND THA KILLS HIM. MINE!
HUHNN? VOICES? BUT WHO--?
OH NNOOOO!!
TO BE CONCLUDED-- IN ISH #102--THE FIRST DOUBLE-SIZE, DOUBLE-ACTION ISSUE OF SPIDER-MAN! 'NUFF SAID!

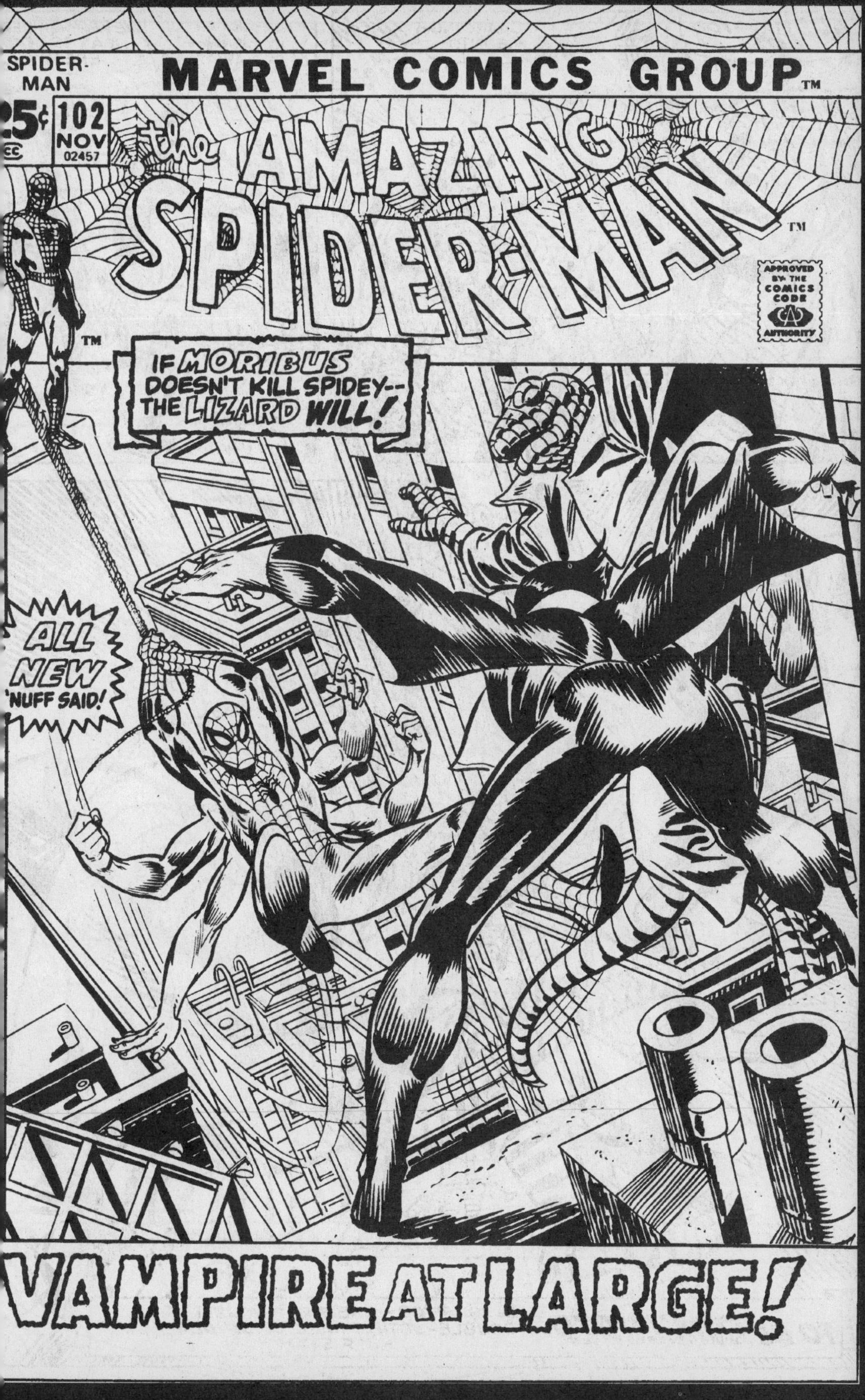
SPIDER-MAN
MARVEL COMICS GROUP
25¢ 102 NOV 02457
the AMAZING SPIDER-MAN
APPROVED BY THE COMICS CODE AUTHORITY
IF MORIBUS DOESN'T KILL SPIDEY-- THE LIZARD WILL!
ALL NEW 'NUFF SAID!
VAMPIRE AT LARGE!

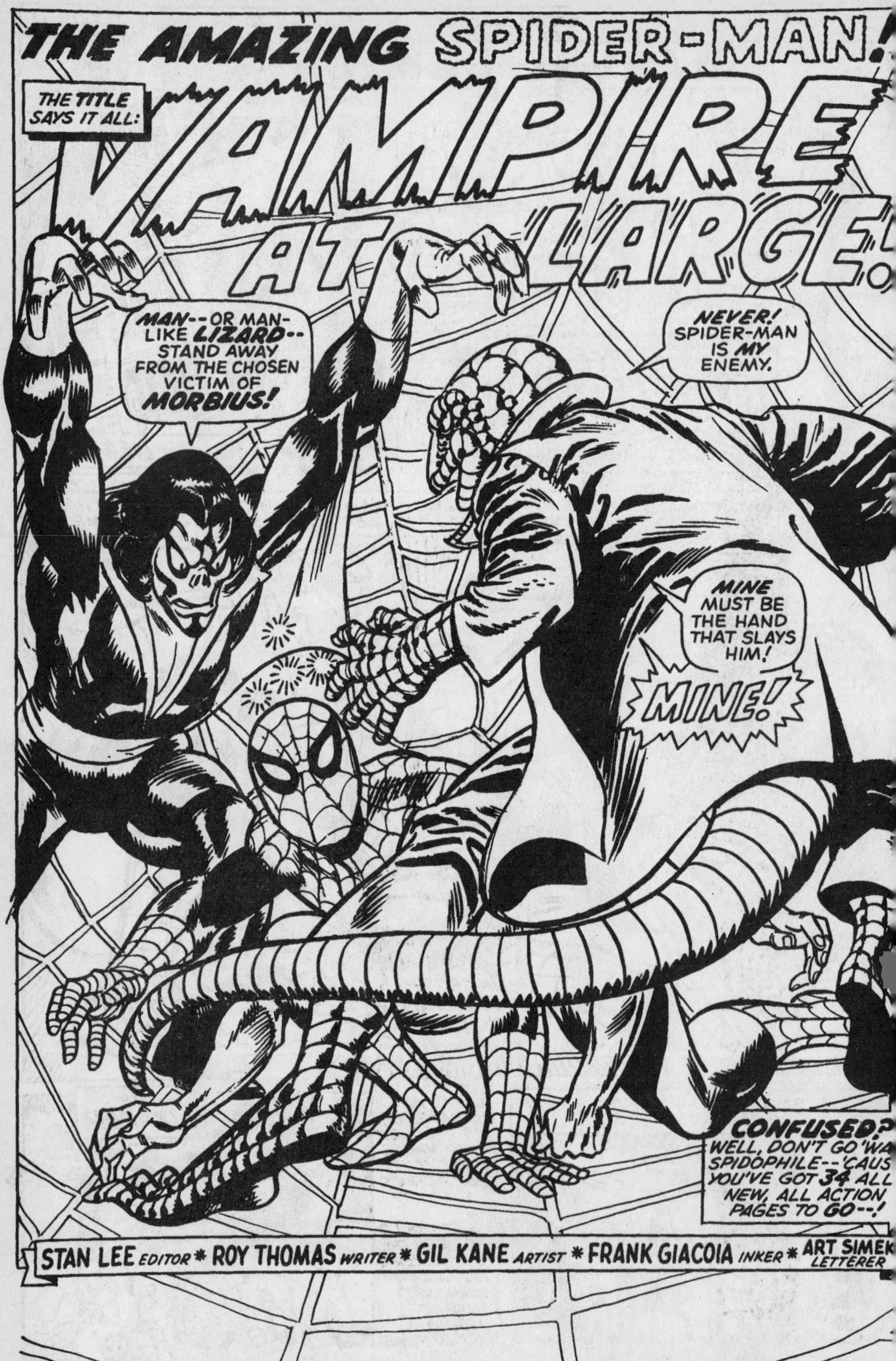

THE AMAZING SPIDER-MAN!
THE TITLE SAYS IT ALL:
VAMPIRE AT LARGE!
MAN--OR MAN-LIKE LIZARD--STAND AWAY FROM THE CHOSEN VICTIM OF MORBIUS!
NEVER! SPIDER-MAN IS MY ENEMY.
MINE MUST BE THE HAND THAT SLAYS HIM!
MINE!
CONFUSED? WELL, DON'T GO 'WA SPIDOPHILE--'CAUS YOU'VE GOT 34 ALL NEW, ALL ACTION PAGES TO GO--!
STAN LEE EDITOR * ROY THOMAS WRITER * GIL KANE ARTIST * FRANK GIACOIA INKER * ART SIMEK LETTERER

FALLEN, GROGGY **SPIDER-MAN**--MYSTERY-SHROUDED **MORBIUS**--AND THE REPTILIAN THING THEY CALL THE **LIZARD**--

HOW CAME THEY **HERE**, TO FORM SUCH A SINISTER **TABLEAU**--?

--**H**ERE, TO DR. CURT CONNORS' DESERTED **SUMMER-HOUSE**, ON THE SEAWARD TIP OF LONG ISLAND--?

CALL IT DESTINY-- THE WILL OF HEAVEN-- KISMET--

HOW DID IT ALL **BEGIN**??

FOR PETER PARKER, HORROR CAME IN A BUBBLING **VIAL**--A SERUM CREATED TO **RID** HIM FOREVER OF HIS UNWANTED SPIDER-POWERS--BUT WHICH LEFT HIM, INSTEAD, AN AWESOME EIGHT-LIMBED MONSTROSITY--

--IN TRUTH-- A **HUMAN SPIDER!**

A**ND MORBIUS**--HE WHO WAFTED IN FROM A SHIP OF **DEAD MEN**, OUT AT SEA--

WHAT ARE HIS **ORIGINS**, THIS TALONED **FIEND** WHOSE **FANGS** ACHED FOR PETER'S THROAT?

WHAT WOULD HAVE BEEN THE WEB-SPINNER'S **FATE**, IF **CURT CONNORS** HAD NOT ARRIVED, JUST IN TIME TO BE STARTLED INTO BECOMING--

--**THE LIZARD!?**

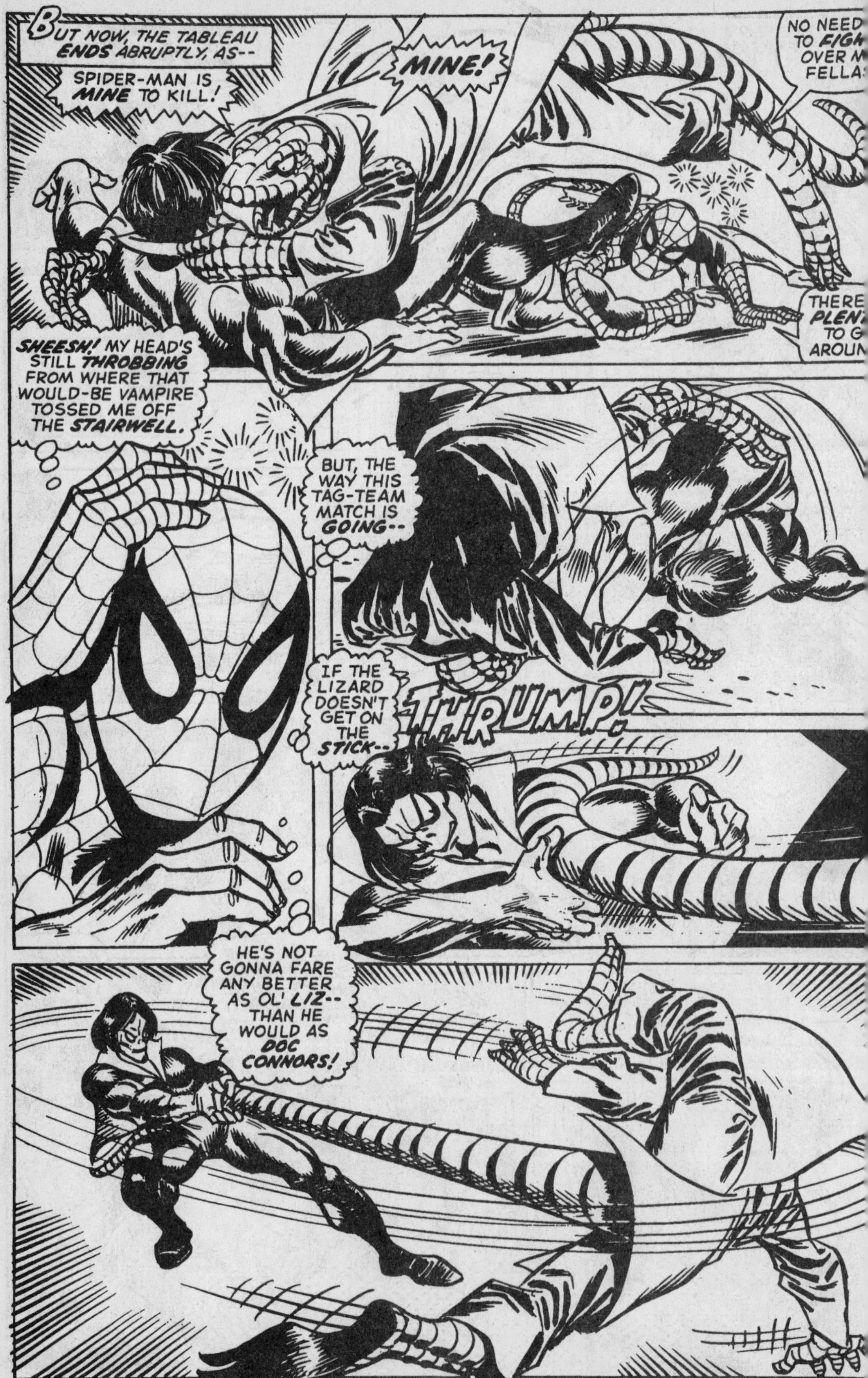
BUT NOW, THE TABLEAU ENDS ABRUPTLY, AS--
SPIDER-MAN IS MINE TO KILL!
MINE!
NO NEED TO FIGH OVER M FELLA
THERE PLEN TO G AROUN
SHEESH! MY HEAD'S STILL THROBBING FROM WHERE THAT WOULD-BE VAMPIRE TOSSED ME OFF THE STAIRWELL.
BUT, THE WAY THIS TAG-TEAM MATCH IS GOING--
IF THE LIZARD DOESN'T GET ON THE STICK--
THRUMP!
HE'S NOT GONNA FARE ANY BETTER AS OL' LIZ-- THAN HE WOULD AS DOC CONNORS!

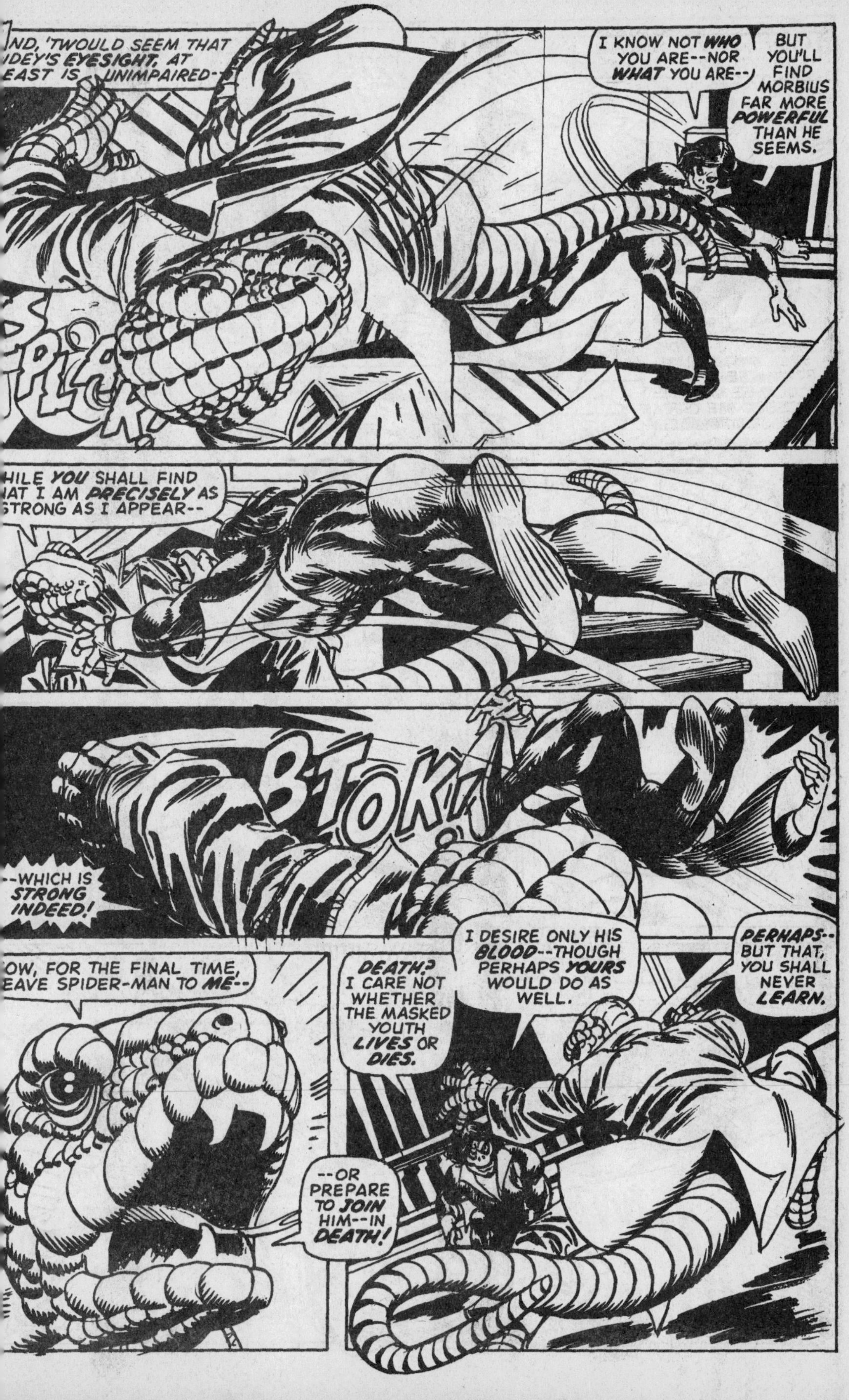
ND, 'TWOULD SEEM THAT
IDEY'S EYESIGHT, AT
EAST IS UNIMPAIRED--
I KNOW NOT WHO YOU ARE--NOR WHAT YOU ARE--
BUT YOU'LL FIND MORBIUS FAR MORE POWERFUL THAN HE SEEMS.
SPLAK!
HILE YOU SHALL FIND
HAT I AM PRECISELY AS
STRONG AS I APPEAR--
BTOK!
--WHICH IS STRONG INDEED!
OW, FOR THE FINAL TIME,
EAVE SPIDER-MAN TO ME--
DEATH? I CARE NOT WHETHER THE MASKED YOUTH LIVES OR DIES.
I DESIRE ONLY HIS BLOOD--THOUGH PERHAPS YOURS WOULD DO AS WELL.
PERHAPS--BUT THAT, YOU SHALL NEVER LEARN.
--OR PREPARE TO JOIN HIM--IN DEATH!

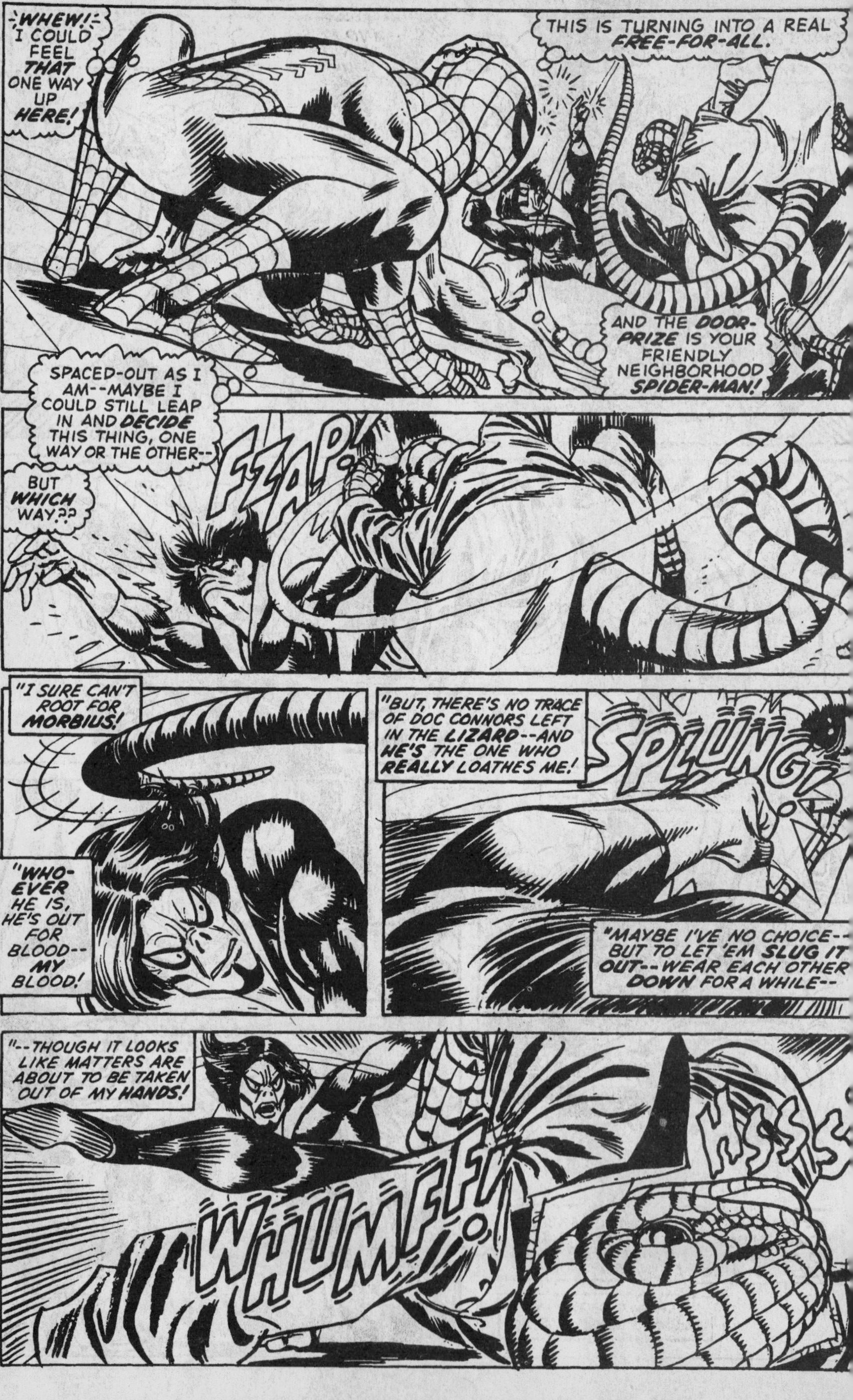

-WHEW!- I COULD FEEL THAT ONE WAY UP HERE!
THIS IS TURNING INTO A REAL FREE-FOR-ALL.
AND THE DOOR-PRIZE IS YOUR FRIENDLY NEIGHBORHOOD SPIDER-MAN!
SPACED-OUT AS I AM--MAYBE I COULD STILL LEAP IN AND DECIDE THIS THING, ONE WAY OR THE OTHER--
BUT WHICH WAY??
FZAP!
"I SURE CAN'T ROOT FOR MORBIUS!
"WHO-EVER HE IS, HE'S OUT FOR BLOOD--MY BLOOD!
"BUT, THERE'S NO TRACE OF DOC CONNORS LEFT IN THE LIZARD--AND HE'S THE ONE WHO REALLY LOATHES ME!
SPLUNG!
"MAYBE I'VE NO CHOICE--BUT TO LET 'EM SLUG IT OUT--WEAR EACH OTHER DOWN FOR A WHILE--
"--THOUGH IT LOOKS LIKE MATTERS ARE ABOUT TO BE TAKEN OUT OF MY HANDS!
WHUMFF!
HSSS

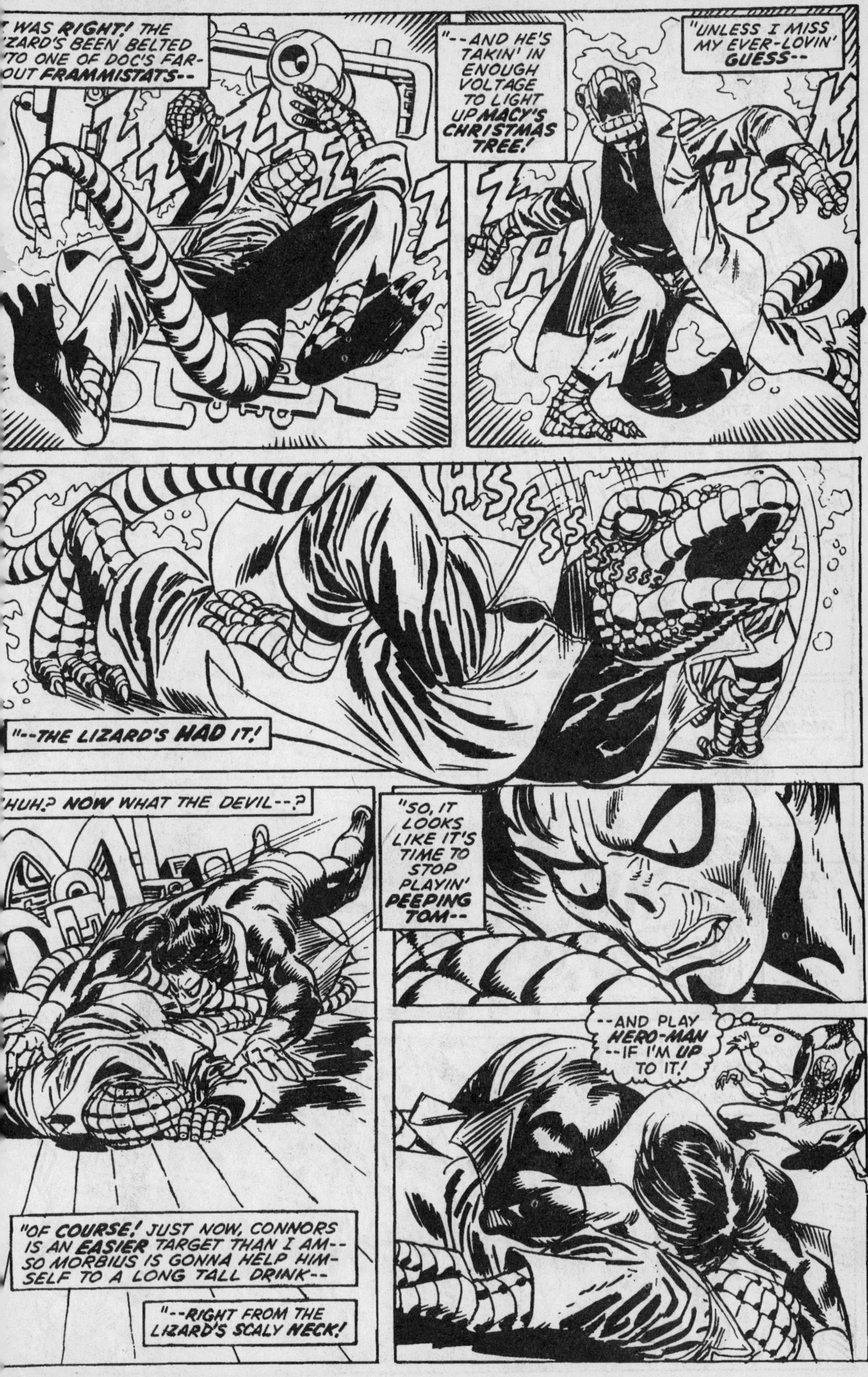

WAS RIGHT! THE IZARD'S BEEN BELTED TO ONE OF DOC'S FAR-OUT FRAMMISTATS--
"--AND HE'S TAKIN' IN ENOUGH VOLTAGE TO LIGHT UP MACY'S CHRISTMAS TREE!
"UNLESS I MISS MY EVER-LOVIN' GUESS--
HSSSS
"--THE LIZARD'S HAD IT!
HUH? NOW WHAT THE DEVIL--?
"SO, IT LOOKS LIKE IT'S TIME TO STOP PLAYIN' PEEPING TOM--
"OF COURSE! JUST NOW, CONNORS IS AN EASIER TARGET THAN I AM--SO MORBIUS IS GONNA HELP HIMSELF TO A LONG TALL DRINK--
"--RIGHT FROM THE LIZARD'S SCALY NECK!
--AND PLAY HERO-MAN --IF I'M UP TO IT!

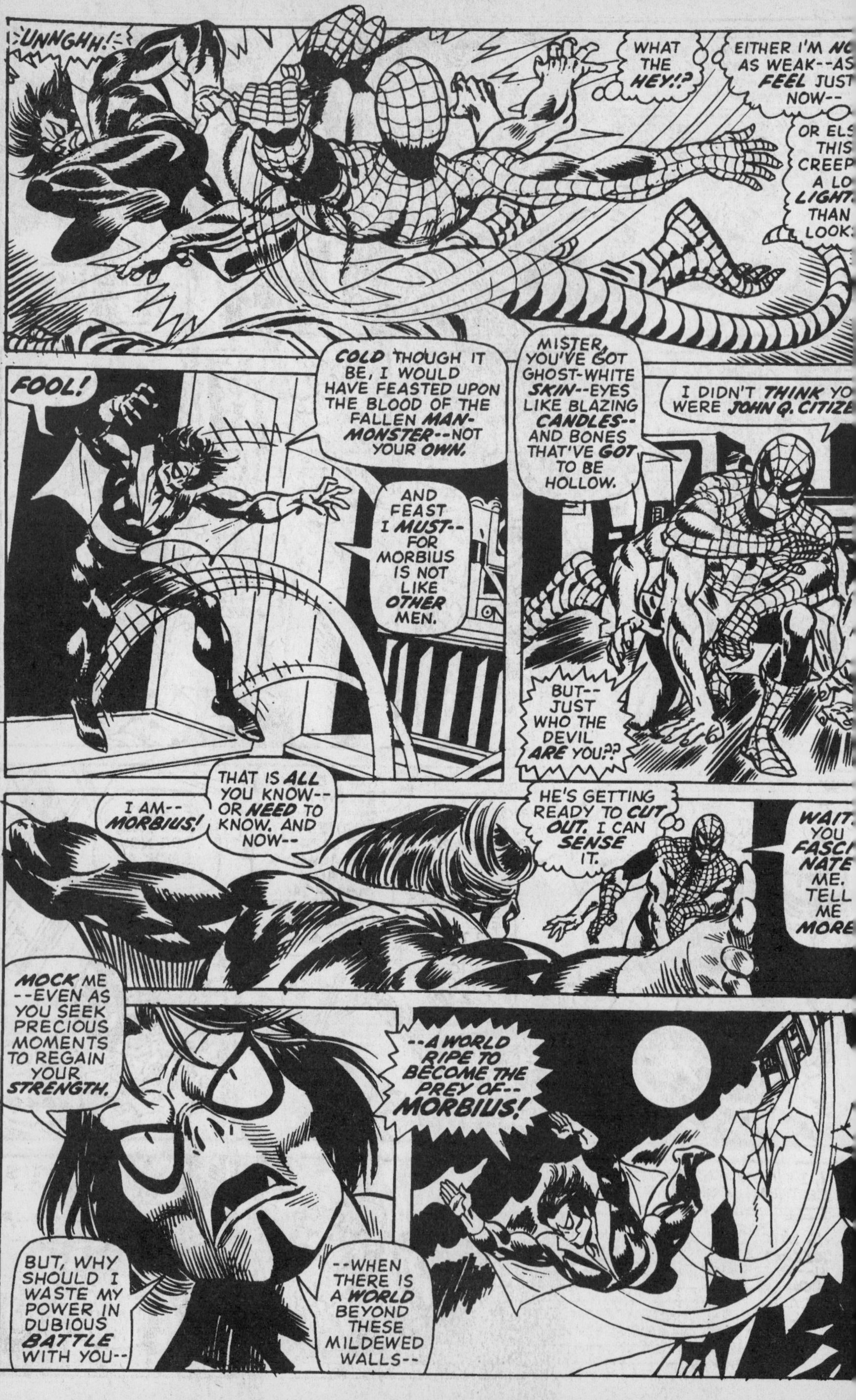
UNNGHH!
WHAT THE HEY!!?
EITHER I'M NO AS WEAK--AS FEEL JUST NOW--
OR ELS THIS CREEP A LO LIGHT THAN LOOK
FOOL!
COLD THOUGH IT BE, I WOULD HAVE FEASTED UPON THE BLOOD OF THE FALLEN MAN-MONSTER--NOT YOUR OWN.
AND FEAST I MUST--FOR MORBIUS IS NOT LIKE OTHER MEN.
MISTER, YOU'VE GOT GHOST-WHITE SKIN--EYES LIKE BLAZING CANDLES--AND BONES THAT'VE GOT TO BE HOLLOW.
I DIDN'T THINK YO WERE JOHN Q. CITIZE
BUT--JUST WHO THE DEVIL ARE YOU??
I AM--MORBIUS!
THAT IS ALL YOU KNOW--OR NEED TO KNOW. AND NOW--
HE'S GETTING READY TO CUT OUT. I CAN SENSE IT.
WAIT. YOU FASCI NATE ME. TELL ME MORE
MOCK ME--EVEN AS YOU SEEK PRECIOUS MOMENTS TO REGAIN YOUR STRENGTH.
BUT, WHY SHOULD I WASTE MY POWER IN DUBIOUS BATTLE WITH YOU--
--WHEN THERE IS A WORLD BEYOND THESE MILDEWED WALLS--
--A WORLD RIPE TO BECOME THE PREY OF--MORBIUS!

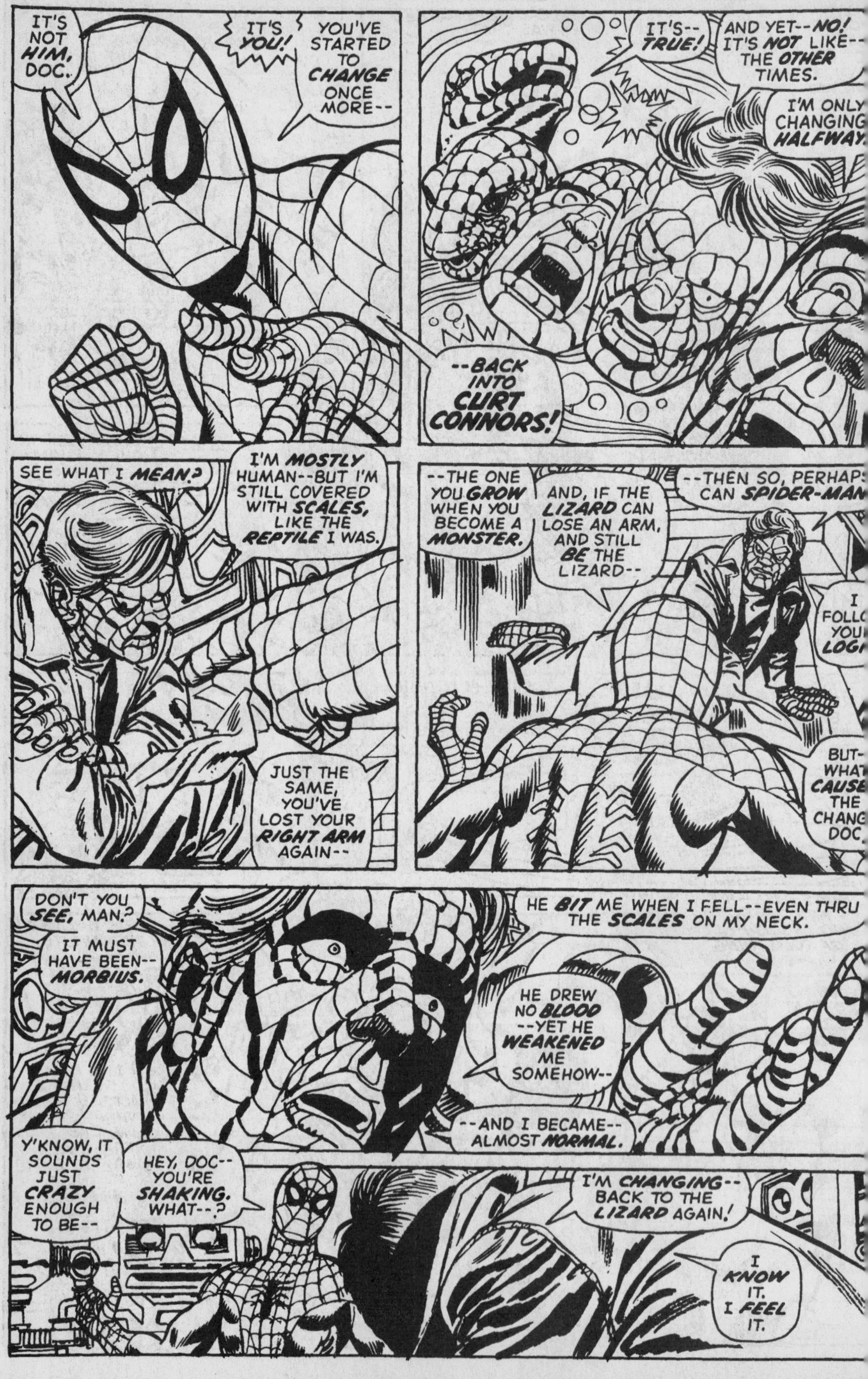

IT'S NOT HIM, DOC..
IT'S YOU!
YOU'VE STARTED TO CHANGE ONCE MORE--
IT'S--TRUE!
AND YET--NO! IT'S NOT LIKE--THE OTHER TIMES.
I'M ONLY CHANGING HALFWAY
--BACK INTO CURT CONNORS!
SEE WHAT I MEAN?
I'M MOSTLY HUMAN--BUT I'M STILL COVERED WITH SCALES, LIKE THE REPTILE I WAS.
JUST THE SAME, YOU'VE LOST YOUR RIGHT ARM AGAIN--
--THE ONE YOU GROW WHEN YOU BECOME A MONSTER.
AND, IF THE LIZARD CAN LOSE AN ARM, AND STILL BE THE LIZARD--
--THEN SO, PERHAPS CAN SPIDER-MAN
I FOLLO YOU LOGI
BUT-WHAT CAUSE THE CHANG DOC
DON'T YOU SEE, MAN?
IT MUST HAVE BEEN--MORBIUS.
HE BIT ME WHEN I FELL--EVEN THRU THE SCALES ON MY NECK.
HE DREW NO BLOOD--YET HE WEAKENED ME SOMEHOW--
--AND I BECAME--ALMOST NORMAL.
Y'KNOW, IT SOUNDS JUST CRAZY ENOUGH TO BE--
HEY, DOC--YOU'RE SHAKING. WHAT--?
I'M CHANGING--BACK TO THE LIZARD AGAIN!
I KNOW IT. I FEEL IT.

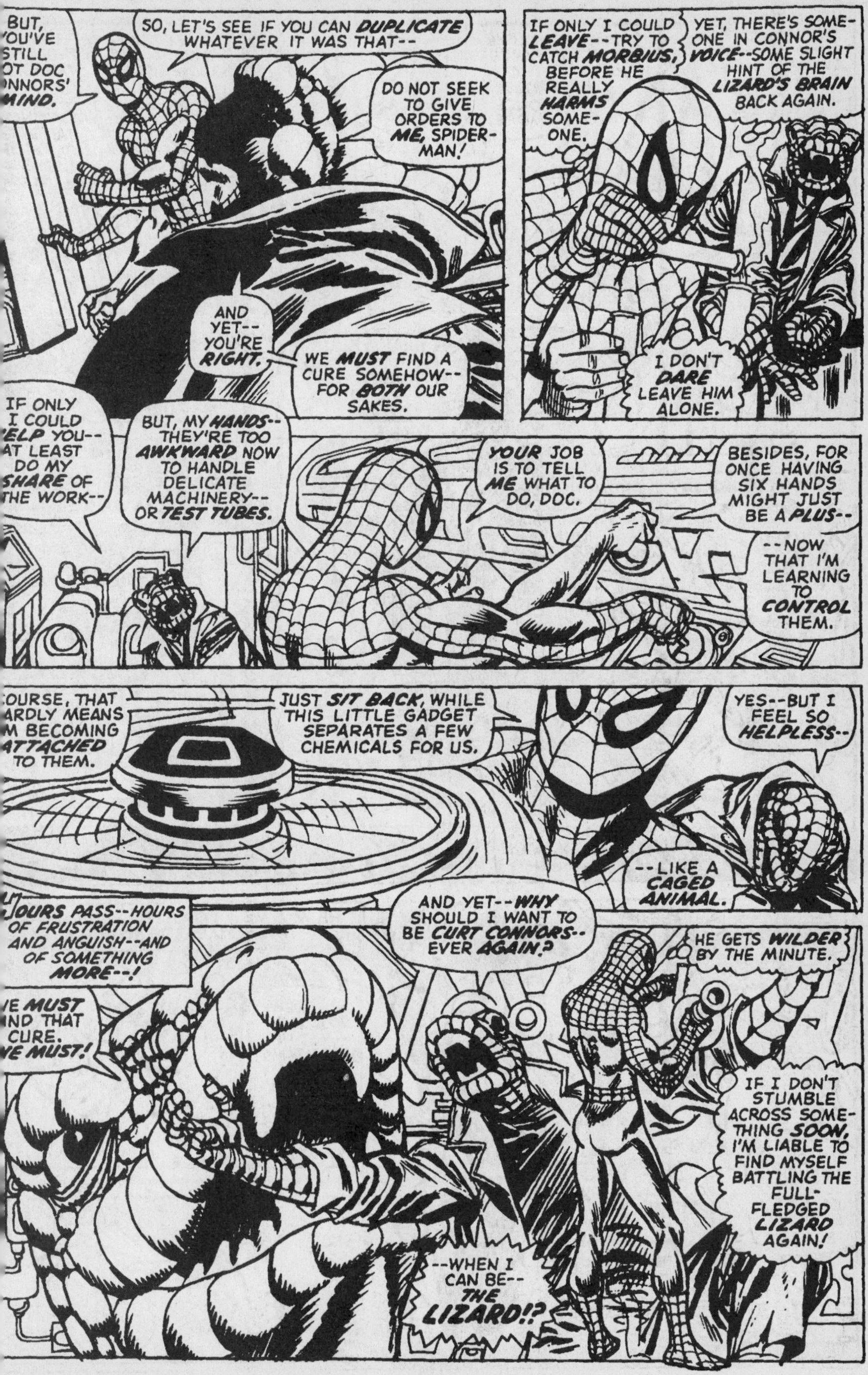
BUT, OU'VE STILL OT DOC ONNORS' MIND.
SO, LET'S SEE IF YOU CAN DUPLICATE WHATEVER IT WAS THAT--
DO NOT SEEK TO GIVE ORDERS TO ME, SPIDER-MAN!
AND YET--YOU'RE RIGHT.
WE MUST FIND A CURE SOMEHOW--FOR BOTH OUR SAKES.
IF ONLY I COULD LEAVE--TRY TO CATCH MORBIUS, BEFORE HE REALLY HARMS SOME-ONE.
YET, THERE'S SOME-ONE IN CONNOR'S VOICE--SOME SLIGHT HINT OF THE LIZARD'S BRAIN BACK AGAIN.
I DON'T DARE LEAVE HIM ALONE.
IF ONLY I COULD ELP YOU--AT LEAST DO MY SHARE OF THE WORK--
BUT, MY HANDS--THEY'RE TOO AWKWARD NOW TO HANDLE DELICATE MACHINERY--OR TEST TUBES.
YOUR JOB IS TO TELL ME WHAT TO DO, DOC.
BESIDES, FOR ONCE HAVING SIX HANDS MIGHT JUST BE A PLUS--
--NOW THAT I'M LEARNING TO CONTROL THEM.
COURSE, THAT ARDLY MEANS M BECOMING ATTACHED TO THEM.
JUST SIT BACK, WHILE THIS LITTLE GADGET SEPARATES A FEW CHEMICALS FOR US.
YES--BUT I FEEL SO HELPLESS--
--LIKE A CAGED ANIMAL.
OURS PASS--HOURS OF FRUSTRATION AND ANGUISH--AND OF SOMETHING MORE--!
E MUST IND THAT CURE. E MUST!
AND YET--WHY SHOULD I WANT TO BE CURT CONNORS--EVER AGAIN?
--WHEN I CAN BE--THE LIZARD!?
HE GETS WILDER BY THE MINUTE.
IF I DON'T STUMBLE ACROSS SOME-THING SOON, I'M LIABLE TO FIND MYSELF BATTLING THE FULL-FLEDGED LIZARD AGAIN!

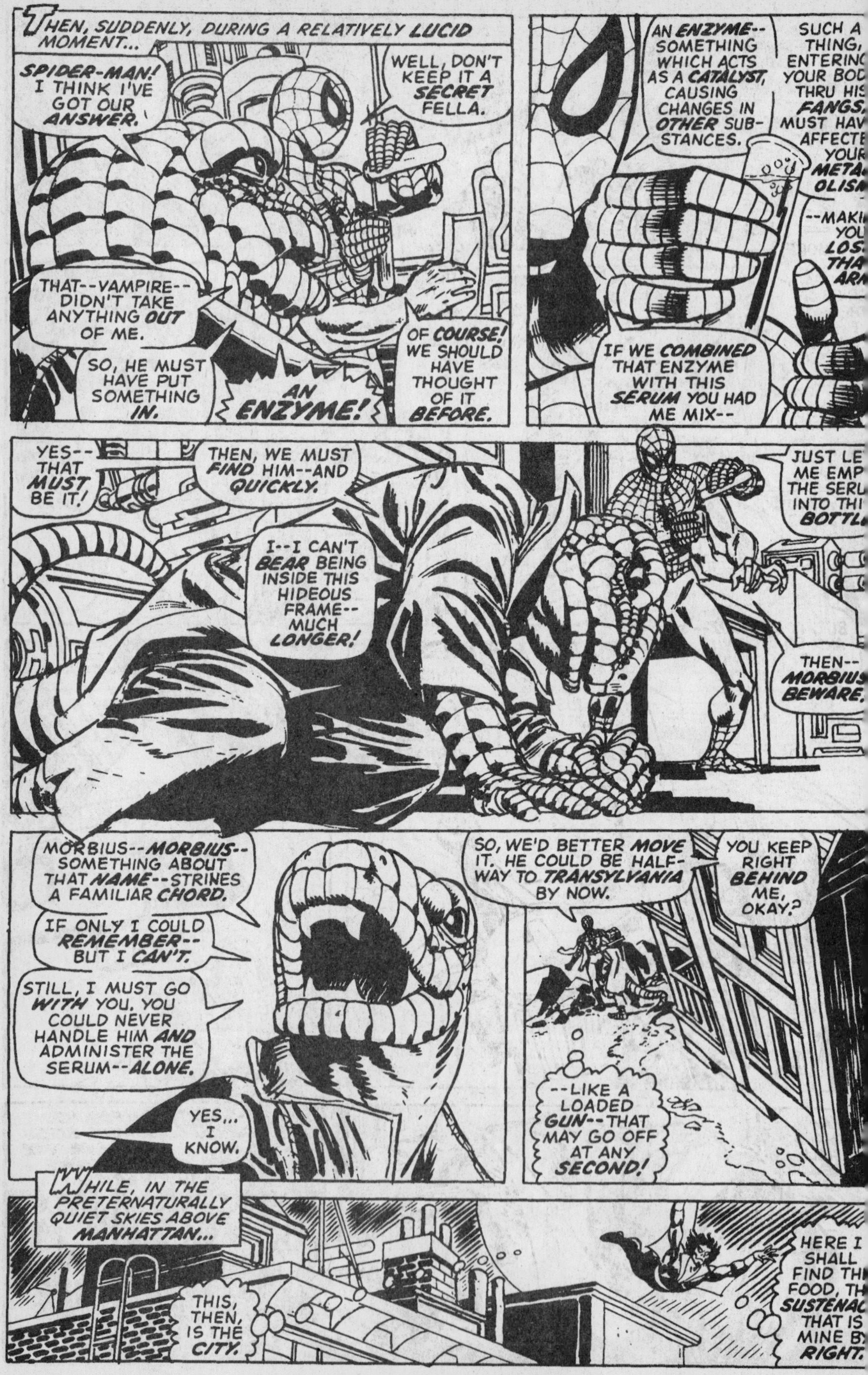
THEN, SUDDENLY, DURING A RELATIVELY LUCID MOMENT...
SPIDER-MAN! I THINK I'VE GOT OUR ANSWER.
WELL, DON'T KEEP IT A SECRET FELLA.
THAT--VAMPIRE--DIDN'T TAKE ANYTHING OUT OF ME.
SO, HE MUST HAVE PUT SOMETHING IN.
AN ENZYME!
OF COURSE! WE SHOULD HAVE THOUGHT OF IT BEFORE.
AN ENZYME--SOMETHING WHICH ACTS AS A CATALYST, CAUSING CHANGES IN OTHER SUBSTANCES.
IF WE COMBINED THAT ENZYME WITH THIS SERUM YOU HAD ME MIX--
YES--THAT MUST BE IT!
THEN, WE MUST FIND HIM--AND QUICKLY.
I--I CAN'T BEAR BEING INSIDE THIS HIDEOUS FRAME--MUCH LONGER!
MORBIUS--MORBIUS--SOMETHING ABOUT THAT NAME--STRINES A FAMILIAR CHORD.
IF ONLY I COULD REMEMBER--BUT I CAN'T.
STILL, I MUST GO WITH YOU. YOU COULD NEVER HANDLE HIM AND ADMINISTER THE SERUM--ALONE.
YES... I KNOW.
SO, WE'D BETTER MOVE IT. HE COULD BE HALF-WAY TO TRANSYLVANIA BY NOW.
YOU KEEP RIGHT BEHIND ME, OKAY?
--LIKE A LOADED GUN--THAT MAY GO OFF AT ANY SECOND!
WHILE, IN THE PRETERNATURALLY QUIET SKIES ABOVE MANHATTAN...
THIS, THEN, IS THE CITY.

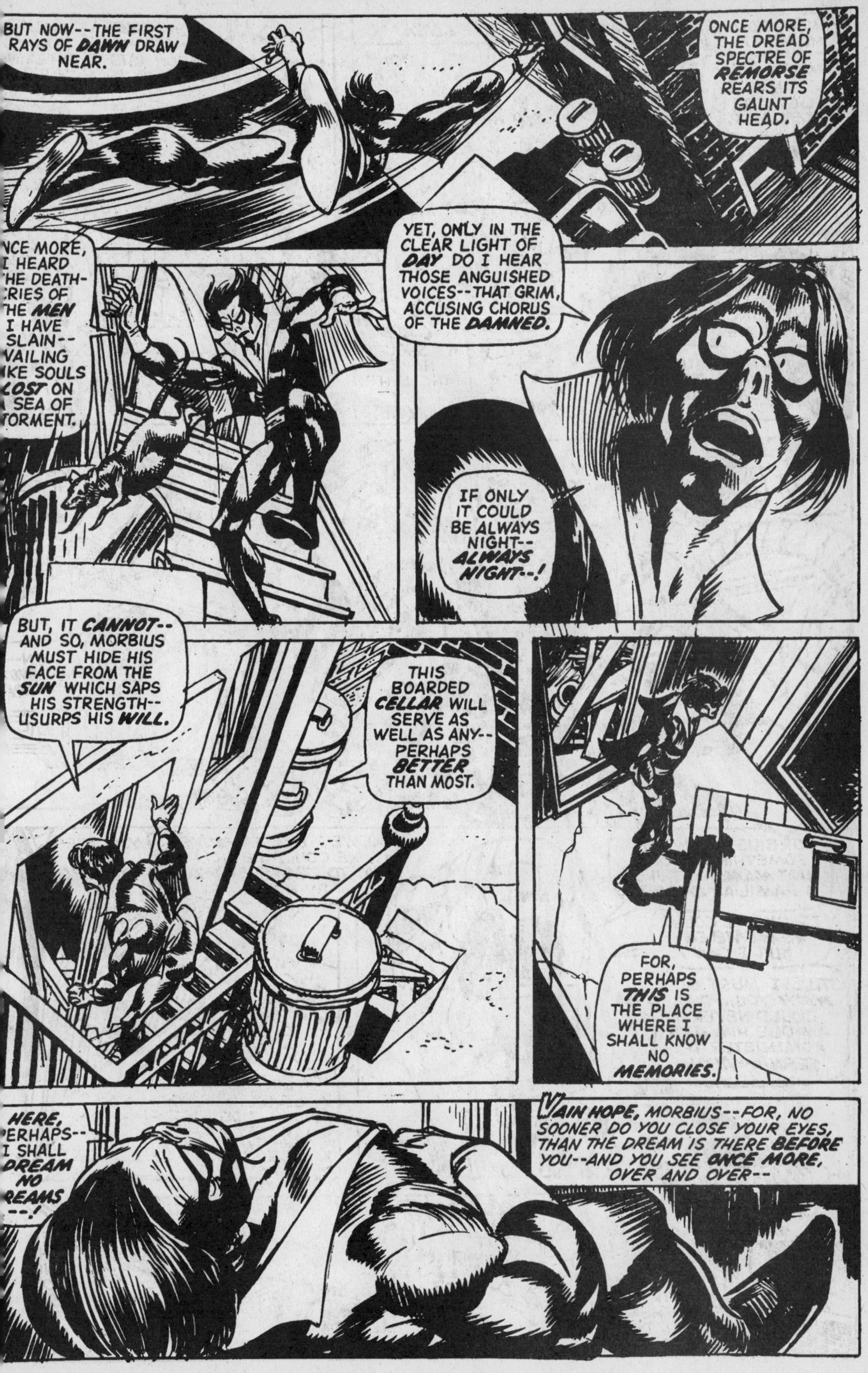
BUT NOW--THE FIRST RAYS OF DAWN DRAW NEAR.
ONCE MORE, THE DREAD SPECTRE OF REMORSE REARS ITS GAUNT HEAD.
NCE MORE, I HEARD THE DEATH-CRIES OF THE MEN I HAVE SLAIN--WAILING IKE SOULS LOST ON A SEA OF TORMENT.
YET, ONLY IN THE CLEAR LIGHT OF DAY DO I HEAR THOSE ANGUISHED VOICES--THAT GRIM, ACCUSING CHORUS OF THE DAMNED.
IF ONLY IT COULD BE ALWAYS NIGHT--ALWAYS NIGHT--!
BUT, IT CANNOT--AND SO, MORBIUS MUST HIDE HIS FACE FROM THE SUN WHICH SAPS HIS STRENGTH--USURPS HIS WILL.
THIS BOARDED CELLAR WILL SERVE AS WELL AS ANY--PERHAPS BETTER THAN MOST.
FOR, PERHAPS THIS IS THE PLACE WHERE I SHALL KNOW NO MEMORIES.
HERE, PERHAPS--I SHALL DREAM NO REAMS--!
VAIN HOPE, MORBIUS--FOR, NO SOONER DO YOU CLOSE YOUR EYES, THAN THE DREAM IS THERE BEFORE YOU--AND YOU SEE ONCE MORE, OVER AND OVER--

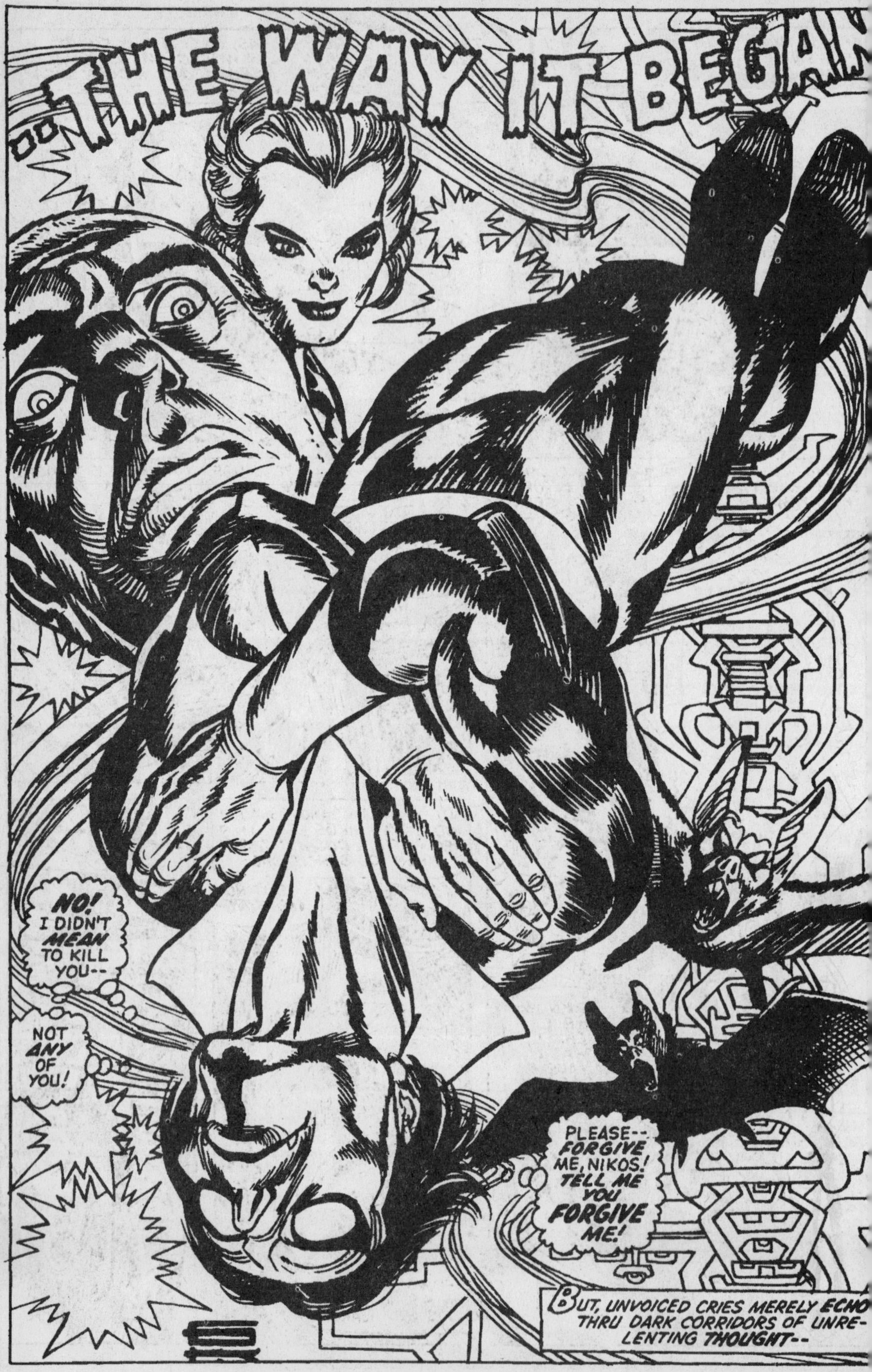

..THE WAY IT BEGAN
NO! I DIDN'T MEAN TO KILL YOU--
NOT ANY OF YOU!
PLEASE-- FORGIVE ME, NIKOS! TELL ME YOU FORGIVE ME!
BUT, UNVOICED CRIES MERELY ECHO THRU DARK CORRIDORS OF UNRE-LENTING THOUGHT--

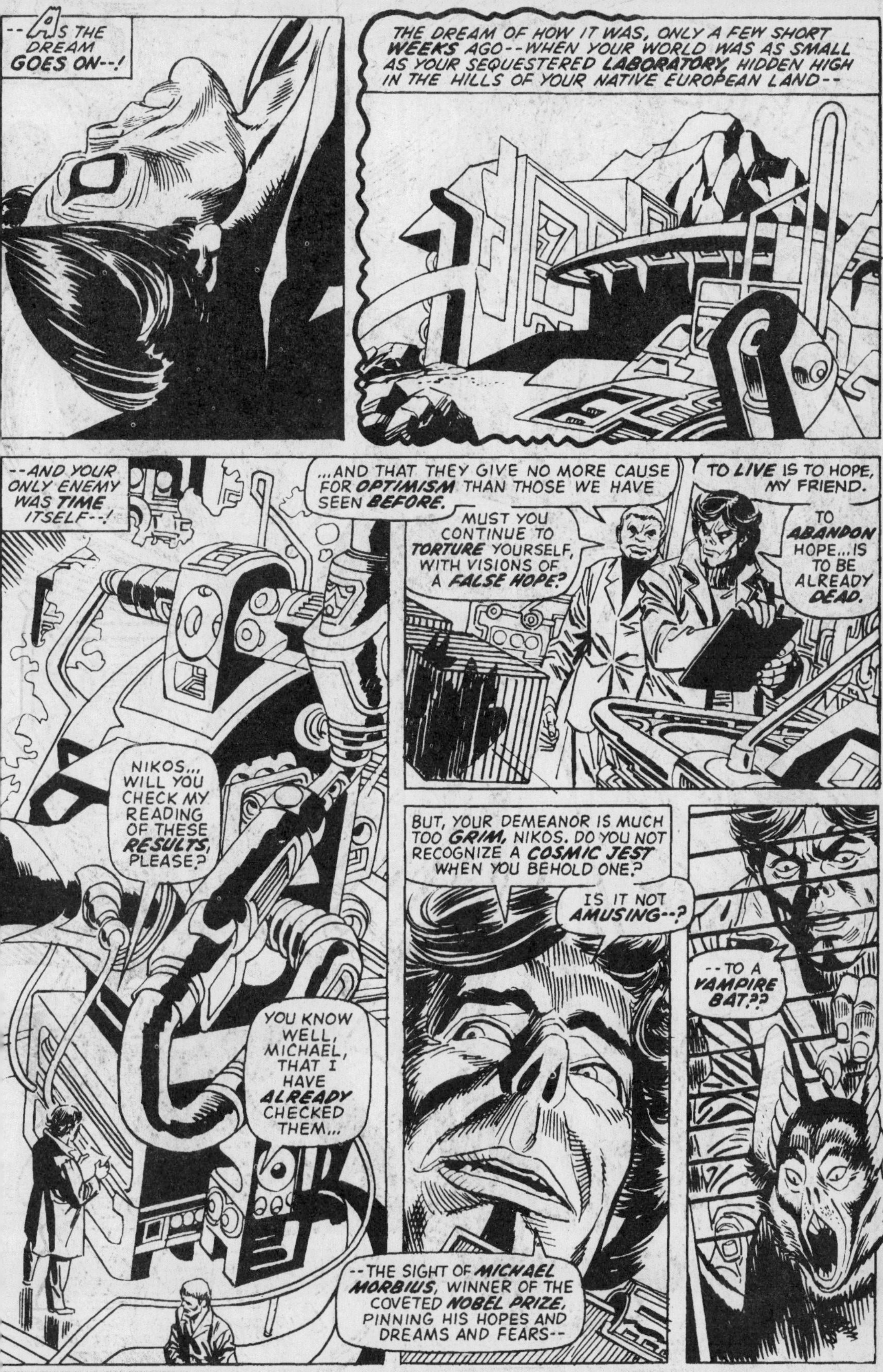
--AS THE DREAM GOES ON--!
THE DREAM OF HOW IT WAS, ONLY A FEW SHORT WEEKS AGO--WHEN YOUR WORLD WAS AS SMALL AS YOUR SEQUESTERED LABORATORY, HIDDEN HIGH IN THE HILLS OF YOUR NATIVE EUROPEAN LAND--
--AND YOUR ONLY ENEMY WAS TIME ITSELF--!
NIKOS... WILL YOU CHECK MY READING OF THESE RESULTS, PLEASE?
YOU KNOW WELL, MICHAEL, THAT I HAVE ALREADY CHECKED THEM...
...AND THAT THEY GIVE NO MORE CAUSE FOR OPTIMISM THAN THOSE WE HAVE SEEN BEFORE.
MUST YOU CONTINUE TO TORTURE YOURSELF, WITH VISIONS OF A FALSE HOPE?
TO LIVE IS TO HOPE, MY FRIEND.
TO ABANDON HOPE...IS TO BE ALREADY DEAD.
BUT, YOUR DEMEANOR IS MUCH TOO GRIM, NIKOS. DO YOU NOT RECOGNIZE A COSMIC JEST WHEN YOU BEHOLD ONE?
IS IT NOT AMUSING--?
--THE SIGHT OF MICHAEL MORBIUS, WINNER OF THE COVETED NOBEL PRIZE, PINNING HIS HOPES AND DREAMS AND FEARS--
--TO A VAMPIRE BAT??

HELLO DOWN THERE. AM I INTERRUPTING ANYTHING?

NOTHING... IMPORTANT, MY DEAR.

I KNOW YOU TWO PREFER TO WORK IN SECRET OUT HERE. BUT SOMETIMES, A WOMAN GETS LONELY...

AND SHALL, I FEAR, GET LONELIER STILL.

I HAVE DECIDED THE NEXT PHASE OF MY RESEARCH MUST BE DONE...AT SEA.

A PLACE WHERE SECURITY WILL BE TOTAL... AND CERTAIN.

REMEMBER, NIKOS, NOT A WORD TO MARTINE ABOUT...

WHATEVER YOU WISH, MICHAEL.

THEN, I'M COMING WITH YOU.

NO! IS IT NOT ENOUGH THAT FOOLS SNICKER BEHIND YOUR BACK, BECAUSE YOU LOVE ONE AS HIDEOUS AS MYSELF?

WOULD YOU NOW RISK YOUR LIFE AS WELL, KNOWING THE DEADLY RADIOACTIVE MATERIALS WITH WHICH I WORK?

I CARE FOR YOU...IF YOU DO NOT CARE FOR YOURSELF.

YOU WILL STAY HERE, DO YOU HEAR ME?

YES...I HEAR YOU, MICHAEL.

AND NOW, IF YOU'RE QUITE FINISHED, I MUST GO UPSTAIRS AND PACK.

SAY WHAT YOU WILL MARTINE.

FOR WHEN YOUR SHIP LEAVES PORT... I'LL BE ON THAT DECK WITH YOU.

NIKOS AND I MUST SAIL... ALONE.

BUT YOU COULDN'T LEAVE HER BEHIND, COULD YOU, MORBIUS?

NOT THE GIRL WHOSE LOVE FLOWED LIKE BLOOD THRU YOUR VEINS...!

YOU'LL NEVER KEEP ME FROM YOUR SIDE, MICHAEL... NOT AS LONG AS YOU LIVE.

YOU KNOW THAT, DON'T YOU?

YES...I SUPPOSE I DO.

AS LONG ...AS I LIVE...

THE IRONY OF MARTINE'S WORDS HAUNTED YOU, MORBIUS...HAUNTED YOU THE LENGTH AND BREADTH OF THE SUN-DRENCHED MEDITERRANEAN...

--I CAN'T STAND IT ANY LONGER.

I'M TURNING THIS ACCURSED THING OFF-- NOW!

ARE YOU ALL RIGHT? YOU SCREAMED--!

YES, I--I AM FINE. BUT WEAK... SO WEAK...

HELP ME... REMOVE THIS SUIT...!

.IT IS DONE, MY FRIEND. BUT, WHAT OF THIS SUIT WHICH YOU WORE AS SECONDARY INSULATION AGAINST THE SHOCK....?

NO...LET IT BE.

FOR NOW, I FEEL...SO COLD.

AND... THE LIGHTS IN THIS PLACE...

THEY SEEM... MUCH TOO BRIGHT...!

IN HERE, MICHAEL. YOU CAN REST IN HERE.

YES... REST. THAT IS ALL I NEED... A FEW MOMENTS' REST...

YOU MEANT THAT WHEN YOU SAID IT, MORBIUS...

YOU REALLY DID...

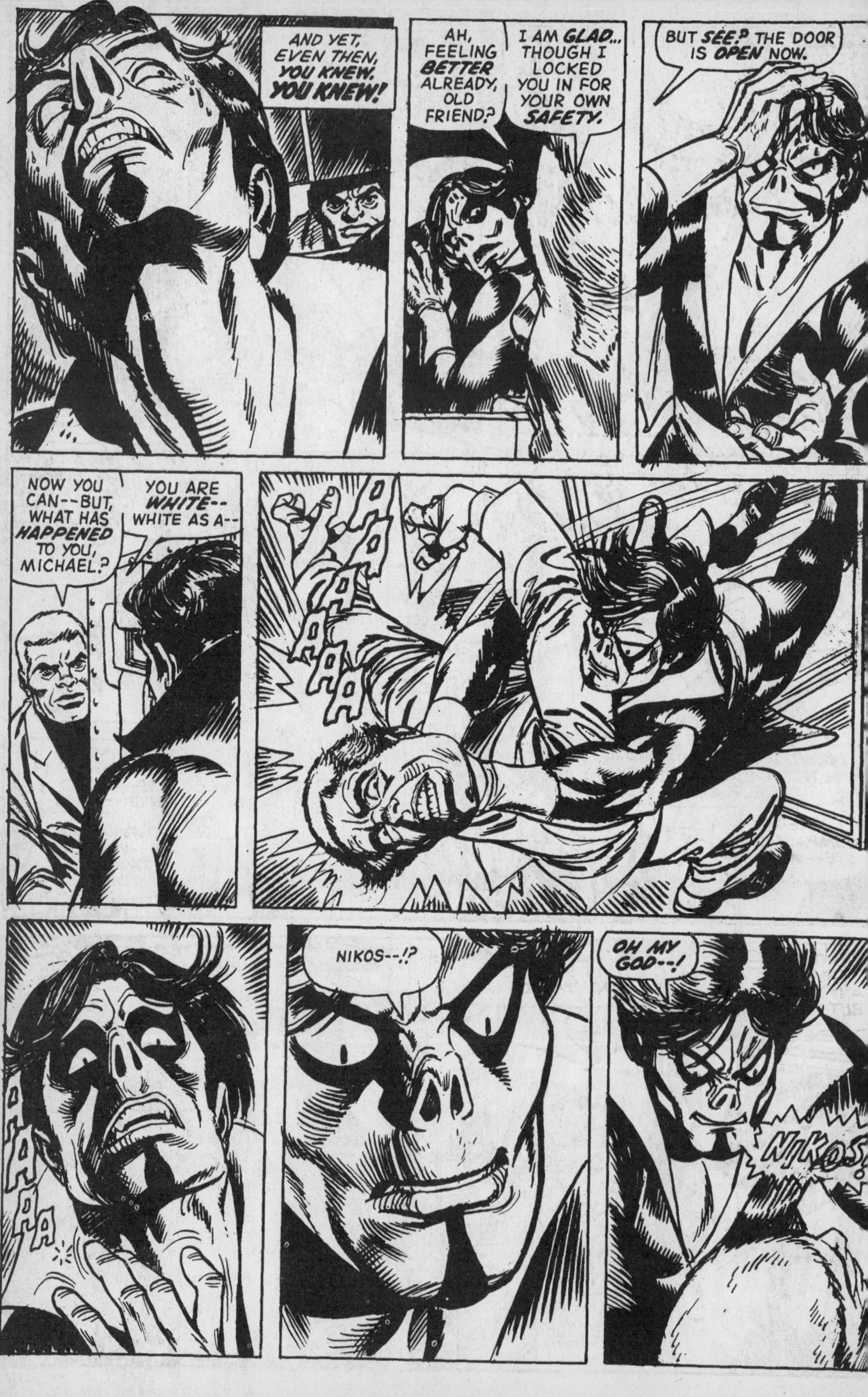
AND YET, EVEN THEN, YOU KNEW. YOU KNEW!
AH, FEELING BETTER ALREADY, OLD FRIEND?
I AM GLAD... THOUGH I LOCKED YOU IN FOR YOUR OWN SAFETY.
BUT SEE? THE DOOR IS OPEN NOW.
NOW YOU CAN--BUT, WHAT HAS HAPPENED TO YOU, MICHAEL?
YOU ARE WHITE-- WHITE AS A--
NIKOS--!?
OH MY GOD--!
NIKOS

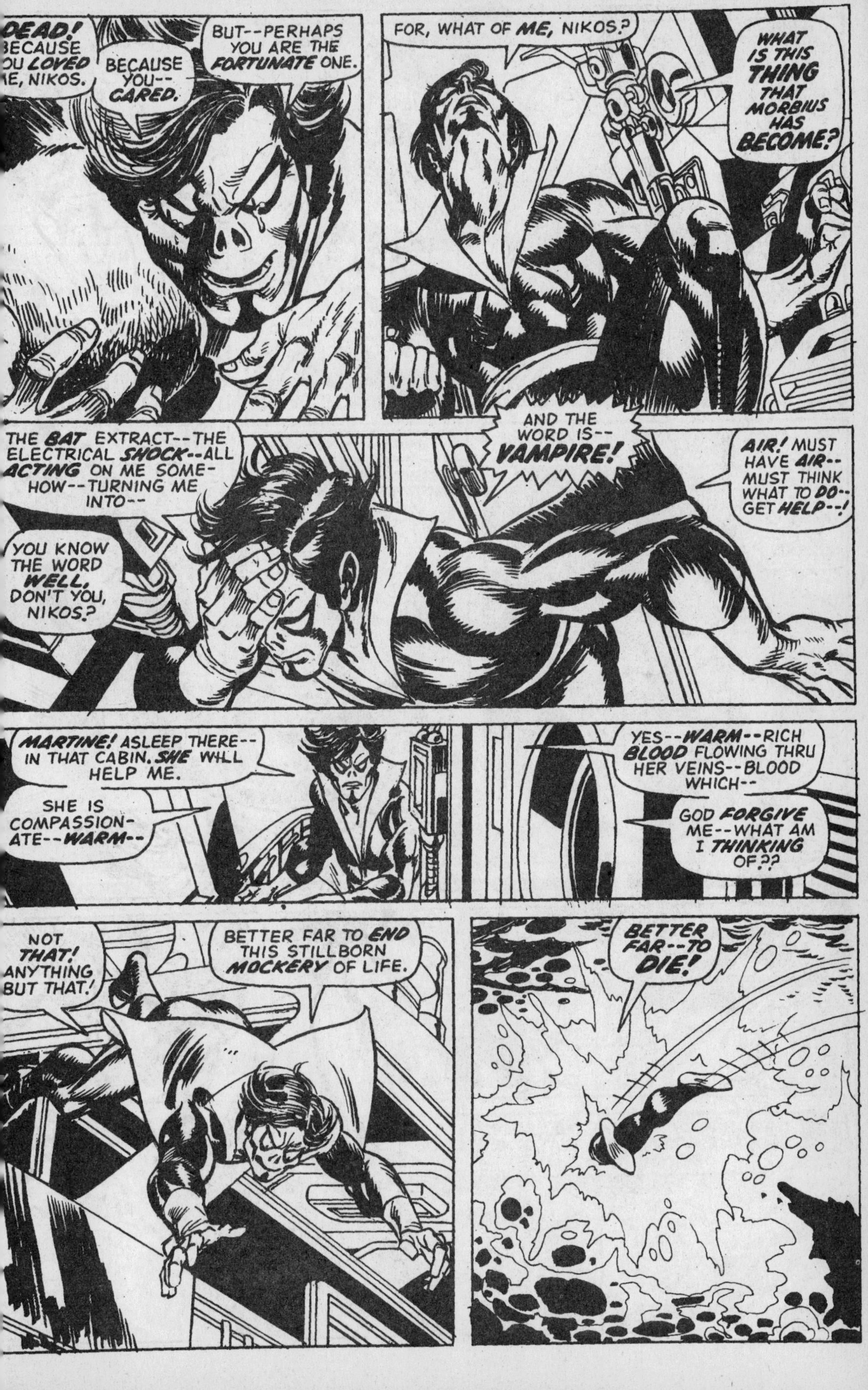
DEAD! BECAUSE YOU LOVED ME, NIKOS.
BECAUSE YOU-- CARED.
BUT--PERHAPS YOU ARE THE FORTUNATE ONE.
FOR, WHAT OF ME, NIKOS?
WHAT IS THIS THING THAT MORBIUS HAS BECOME?
THE BAT EXTRACT--THE ELECTRICAL SHOCK--ALL ACTING ON ME SOME-HOW--TURNING ME INTO--
YOU KNOW THE WORD WELL, DON'T YOU, NIKOS?
AND THE WORD IS-- VAMPIRE!
AIR! MUST HAVE AIR--MUST THINK WHAT TO DO--GET HELP--!
MARTINE! ASLEEP THERE-- IN THAT CABIN. SHE WILL HELP ME.
SHE IS COMPASSION-ATE--WARM--
YES--WARM--RICH BLOOD FLOWING THRU HER VEINS--BLOOD WHICH--
GOD FORGIVE ME--WHAT AM I THINKING OF??
NOT THAT! ANYTHING BUT THAT!
BETTER FAR TO END THIS STILLBORN MOCKERY OF LIFE.
BETTER FAR--TO DIE!

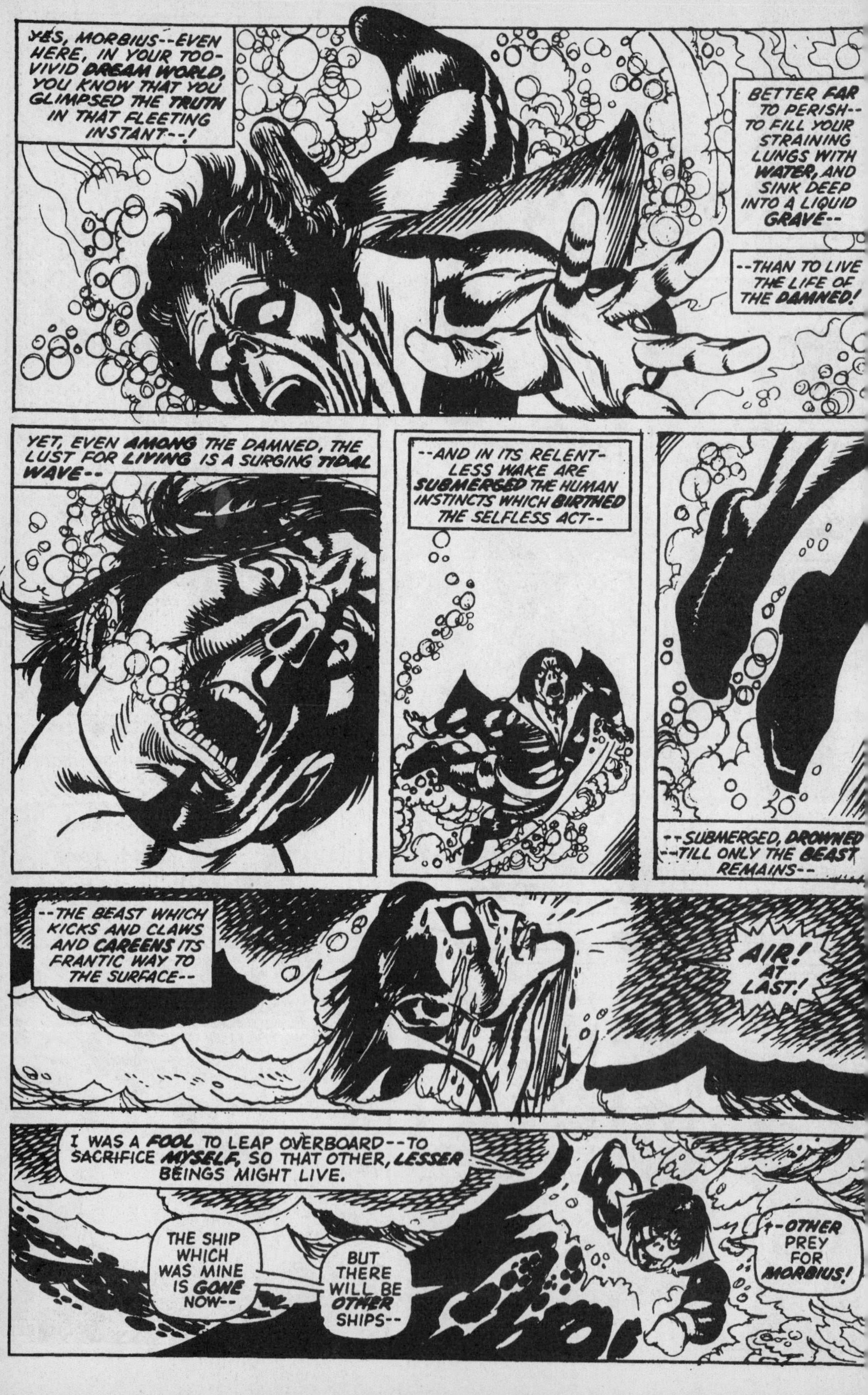

YES, MORBIUS--EVEN HERE, IN YOUR TOO-VIVID DREAM WORLD, YOU KNOW THAT YOU GLIMPSED THE TRUTH IN THAT FLEETING INSTANT--!
BETTER FAR TO PERISH--TO FILL YOUR STRAINING LUNGS WITH WATER, AND SINK DEEP INTO A LIQUID GRAVE--
--THAN TO LIVE THE LIFE OF THE DAMNED!
YET, EVEN AMONG THE DAMNED, THE LUST FOR LIVING IS A SURGING TIDAL WAVE--
--AND IN ITS RELENTLESS WAKE ARE SUBMERGED THE HUMAN INSTINCTS WHICH BIRTHED THE SELFLESS ACT--
--SUBMERGED, DROWNED --TILL ONLY THE BEAST REMAINS--
--THE BEAST WHICH KICKS AND CLAWS AND CAREENS ITS FRANTIC WAY TO THE SURFACE--
AIR! AT LAST!
I WAS A FOOL TO LEAP OVERBOARD--TO SACRIFICE MYSELF, SO THAT OTHER, LESSER BEINGS MIGHT LIVE.
THE SHIP WHICH WAS MINE IS GONE NOW--
BUT THERE WILL BE OTHER SHIPS--
--OTHER PREY FOR MORBIUS!

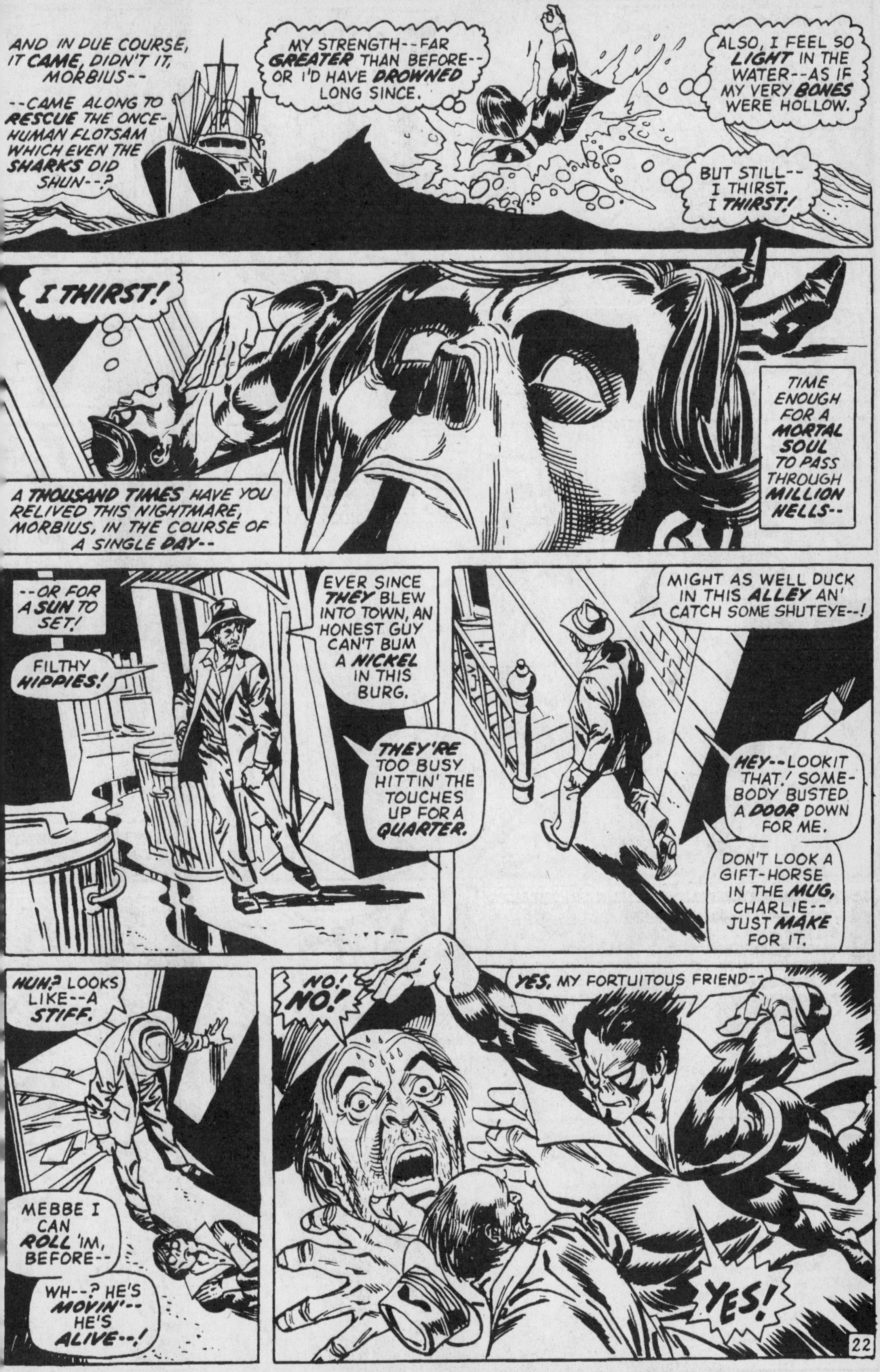
AND IN DUE COURSE, IT CAME, DIDN'T IT, MORBIUS--
--CAME ALONG TO RESCUE THE ONCE-HUMAN FLOTSAM WHICH EVEN THE SHARKS DID SHUN--?
MY STRENGTH--FAR GREATER THAN BEFORE--OR I'D HAVE DROWNED LONG SINCE.
ALSO, I FEEL SO LIGHT IN THE WATER--AS IF MY VERY BONES WERE HOLLOW.
BUT STILL--I THIRST. I THIRST!
I THIRST!
A THOUSAND TIMES HAVE YOU RELIVED THIS NIGHTMARE, MORBIUS, IN THE COURSE OF A SINGLE DAY--
TIME ENOUGH FOR A MORTAL SOUL TO PASS THROUGH MILLION HELLS--
--OR FOR A SUN TO SET!
FILTHY HIPPIES!
EVER SINCE THEY BLEW INTO TOWN, AN HONEST GUY CAN'T BUM A NICKEL IN THIS BURG.
THEY'RE TOO BUSY HITTIN' THE TOUCHES UP FOR A QUARTER.
MIGHT AS WELL DUCK IN THIS ALLEY AN' CATCH SOME SHUTEYE--!
HEY--LOOKIT THAT! SOMEBODY BUSTED A DOOR DOWN FOR ME.
DON'T LOOK A GIFT-HORSE IN THE MUG, CHARLIE--JUST MAKE FOR IT.
HUH? LOOKS LIKE--A STIFF.
MEBBE I CAN ROLL 'IM, BEFORE--
WH--? HE'S MOVIN'--HE'S ALIVE--!
NO! NO!
YES, MY FORTUITOUS FRIEND--
YES!
22

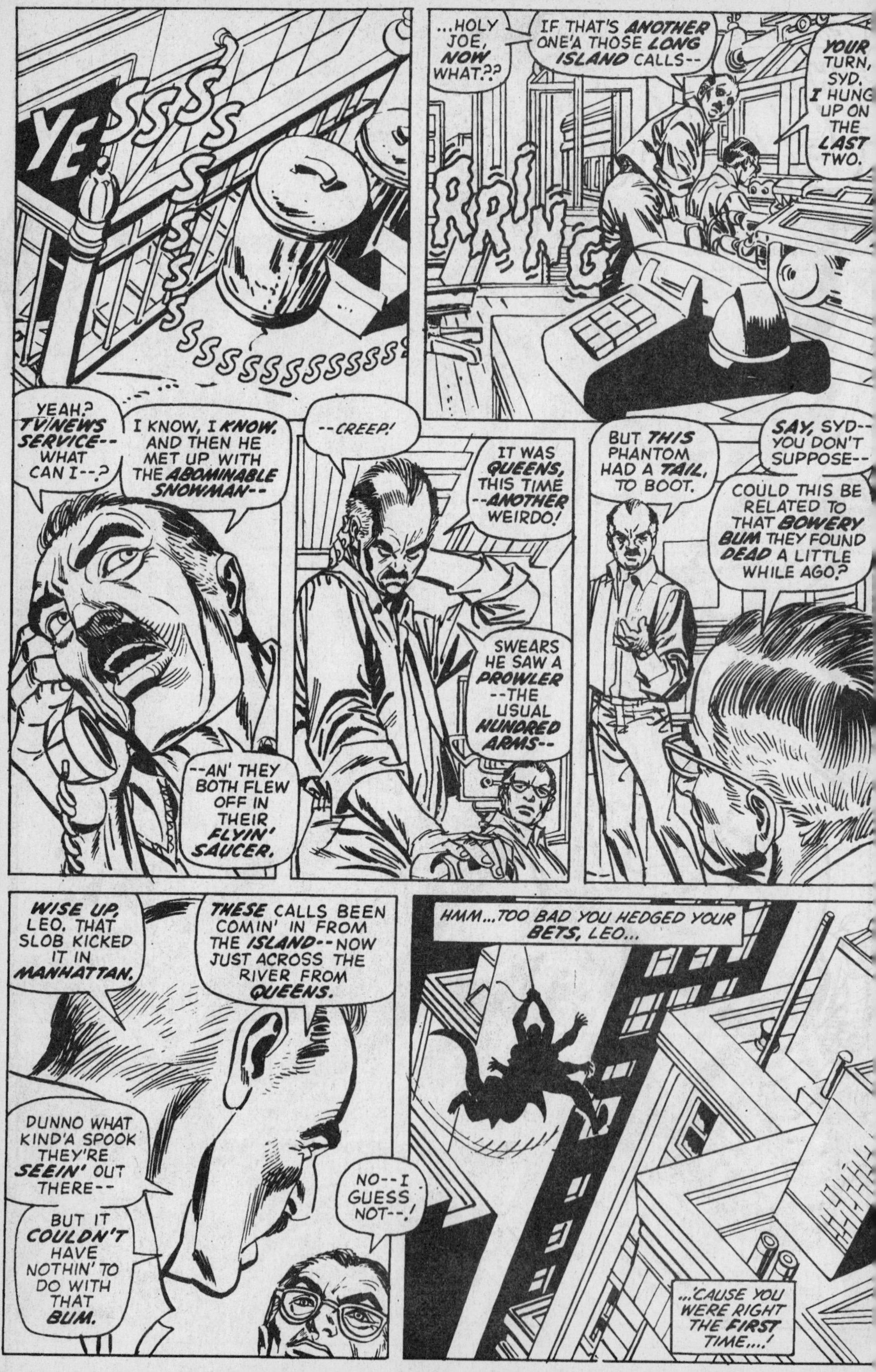
YE
SSSSSSSSSSSSSSSSSSSSS
...HOLY JOE, NOW WHAT??
IF THAT'S ANOTHER ONE'A THOSE LONG ISLAND CALLS--
YOUR TURN, SYD. I HUNG UP ON THE LAST TWO.
RRING
YEAH? TV/NEWS SERVICE-- WHAT CAN I--?
I KNOW, I KNOW. AND THEN HE MET UP WITH THE ABOMINABLE SNOWMAN--
--AN' THEY BOTH FLEW OFF IN THEIR FLYIN' SAUCER.
--CREEP!
IT WAS QUEENS, THIS TIME --ANOTHER WEIRDO!
SWEARS HE SAW A PROWLER --THE USUAL HUNDRED ARMS--
BUT THIS PHANTOM HAD A TAIL, TO BOOT.
SAY, SYD-- YOU DON'T SUPPOSE--
COULD THIS BE RELATED TO THAT BOWERY BUM THEY FOUND DEAD A LITTLE WHILE AGO?
WISE UP, LEO. THAT SLOB KICKED IT IN MANHATTAN.
THESE CALLS BEEN COMIN' IN FROM THE ISLAND-- NOW JUST ACROSS THE RIVER FROM QUEENS.
DUNNO WHAT KIND'A SPOOK THEY'RE SEEIN' OUT THERE--
BUT IT COULDN'T HAVE NOTHIN' TO DO WITH THAT BUM.
NO--I GUESS NOT--!
HMM...TOO BAD YOU HEDGED YOUR BETS, LEO...
...'CAUSE YOU WERE RIGHT THE FIRST TIME....!

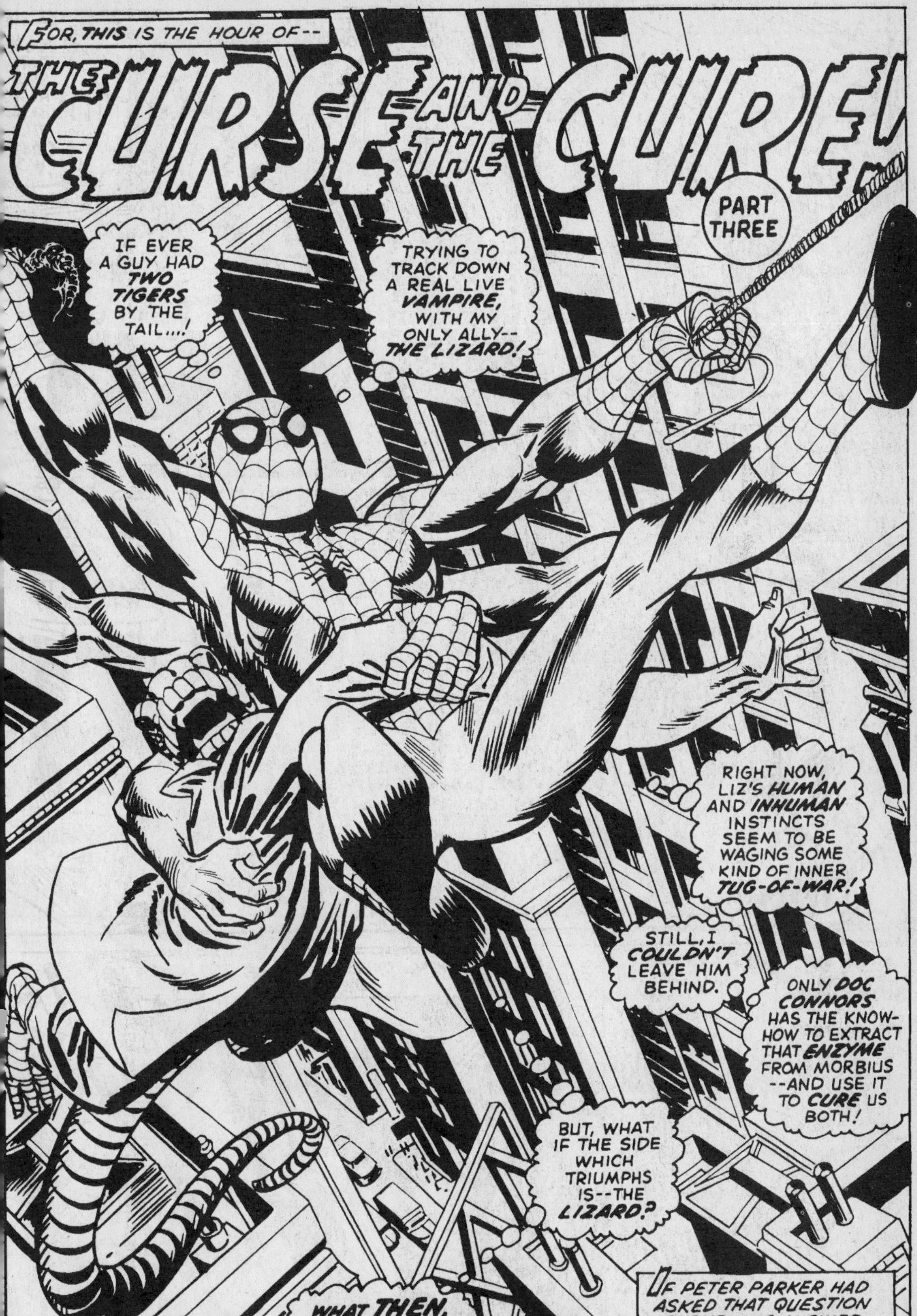
FOR, THIS IS THE HOUR OF--
THE CURSE AND THE CURE!
PART THREE
IF EVER A GUY HAD TWO TIGERS BY THE TAIL....!
TRYING TO TRACK DOWN A REAL LIVE VAMPIRE, WITH MY ONLY ALLY-- THE LIZARD!
RIGHT NOW, LIZ'S HUMAN AND INHUMAN INSTINCTS SEEM TO BE WAGING SOME KIND OF INNER TUG-OF-WAR!
STILL, I COULDN'T LEAVE HIM BEHIND.
ONLY DOC CONNORS HAS THE KNOW-HOW TO EXTRACT THAT ENZYME FROM MORBIUS --AND USE IT TO CURE US BOTH!
BUT, WHAT IF THE SIDE WHICH TRIUMPHS IS--THE LIZARD?
WHAT THEN, WEB-SLINGER?
IF PETER PARKER HAD ASKED THAT QUESTION ALOUD, HIS ANSWER WOULD HAVE BEEN MOCKING ECHOES, ROLLING THRU CANYONS OF STEEL--
24

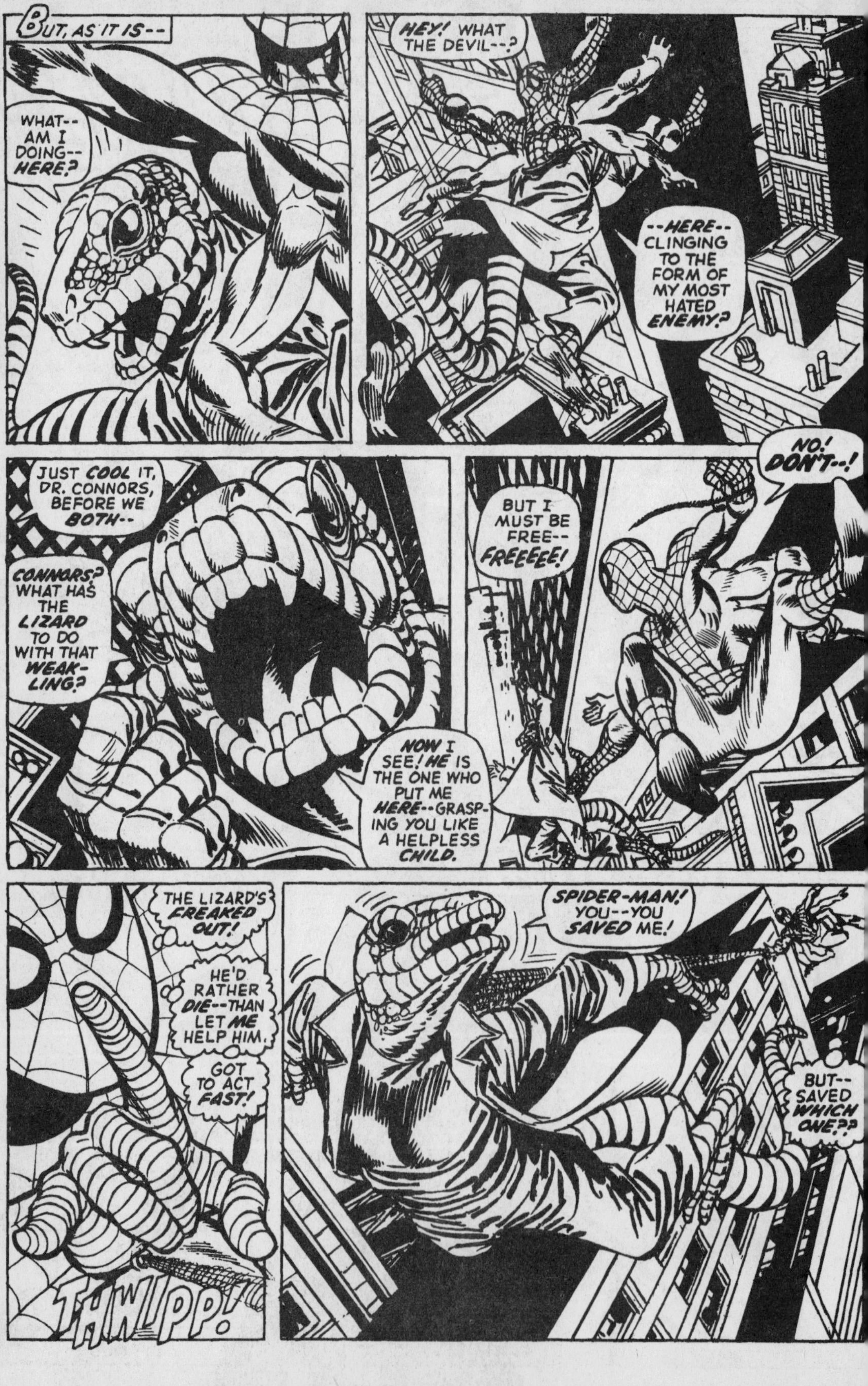
BUT, AS IT IS--
WHAT-- AM I DOING-- HERE?
HEY! WHAT THE DEVIL--?
--HERE-- CLINGING TO THE FORM OF MY MOST HATED ENEMY?
JUST COOL IT, DR. CONNORS, BEFORE WE BOTH--
CONNORS? WHAT HAS THE LIZARD TO DO WITH THAT WEAK-LING?
BUT I MUST BE FREE-- FREEEEEE!
NO! DON'T--!
NOW I SEE! HE IS THE ONE WHO PUT ME HERE--GRASP-ING YOU LIKE A HELPLESS CHILD.
THE LIZARD'S FREAKED OUT!
HE'D RATHER DIE--THAN LET ME HELP HIM.
GOT TO ACT FAST!
THWIPP!
SPIDER-MAN! YOU--YOU SAVED ME!
BUT-- SAVED WHICH ONE??

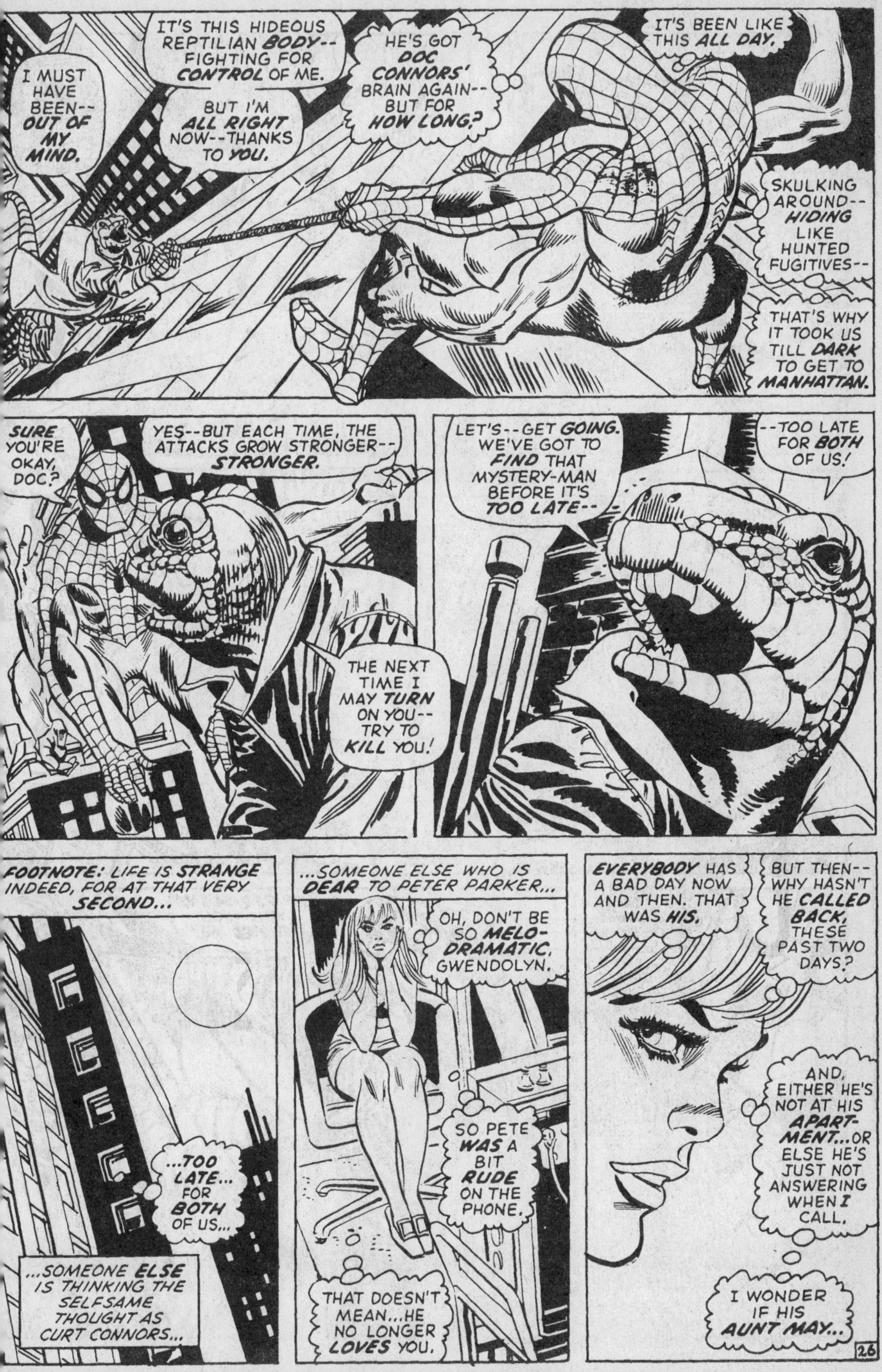
I MUST HAVE BEEN-- OUT OF MY MIND.
IT'S THIS HIDEOUS REPTILIAN BODY-- FIGHTING FOR CONTROL OF ME.
BUT I'M ALL RIGHT NOW--THANKS TO YOU.
HE'S GOT DOC CONNORS' BRAIN AGAIN-- BUT FOR HOW LONG?
IT'S BEEN LIKE THIS ALL DAY.
SKULKING AROUND-- HIDING LIKE HUNTED FUGITIVES--
THAT'S WHY IT TOOK US TILL DARK TO GET TO MANHATTAN.
SURE YOU'RE OKAY, DOC?
YES--BUT EACH TIME, THE ATTACKS GROW STRONGER-- STRONGER.
THE NEXT TIME I MAY TURN ON YOU-- TRY TO KILL YOU!
LET'S--GET GOING. WE'VE GOT TO FIND THAT MYSTERY-MAN BEFORE IT'S TOO LATE--
--TOO LATE FOR BOTH OF US!
FOOTNOTE: LIFE IS STRANGE INDEED, FOR AT THAT VERY SECOND...
...TOO LATE... FOR BOTH OF US...
...SOMEONE ELSE IS THINKING THE SELFSAME THOUGHT AS CURT CONNORS...
...SOMEONE ELSE WHO IS DEAR TO PETER PARKER...
OH, DON'T BE SO MELO-DRAMATIC, GWENDOLYN.
SO PETE WAS A BIT RUDE ON THE PHONE.
THAT DOESN'T MEAN...HE NO LONGER LOVES YOU.
EVERYBODY HAS A BAD DAY NOW AND THEN. THAT WAS HIS.
BUT THEN-- WHY HASN'T HE CALLED BACK, THESE PAST TWO DAYS?
AND, EITHER HE'S NOT AT HIS APART-MENT...OR ELSE HE'S JUST NOT ANSWERING WHEN I CALL.
I WONDER IF HIS AUNT MAY...
26

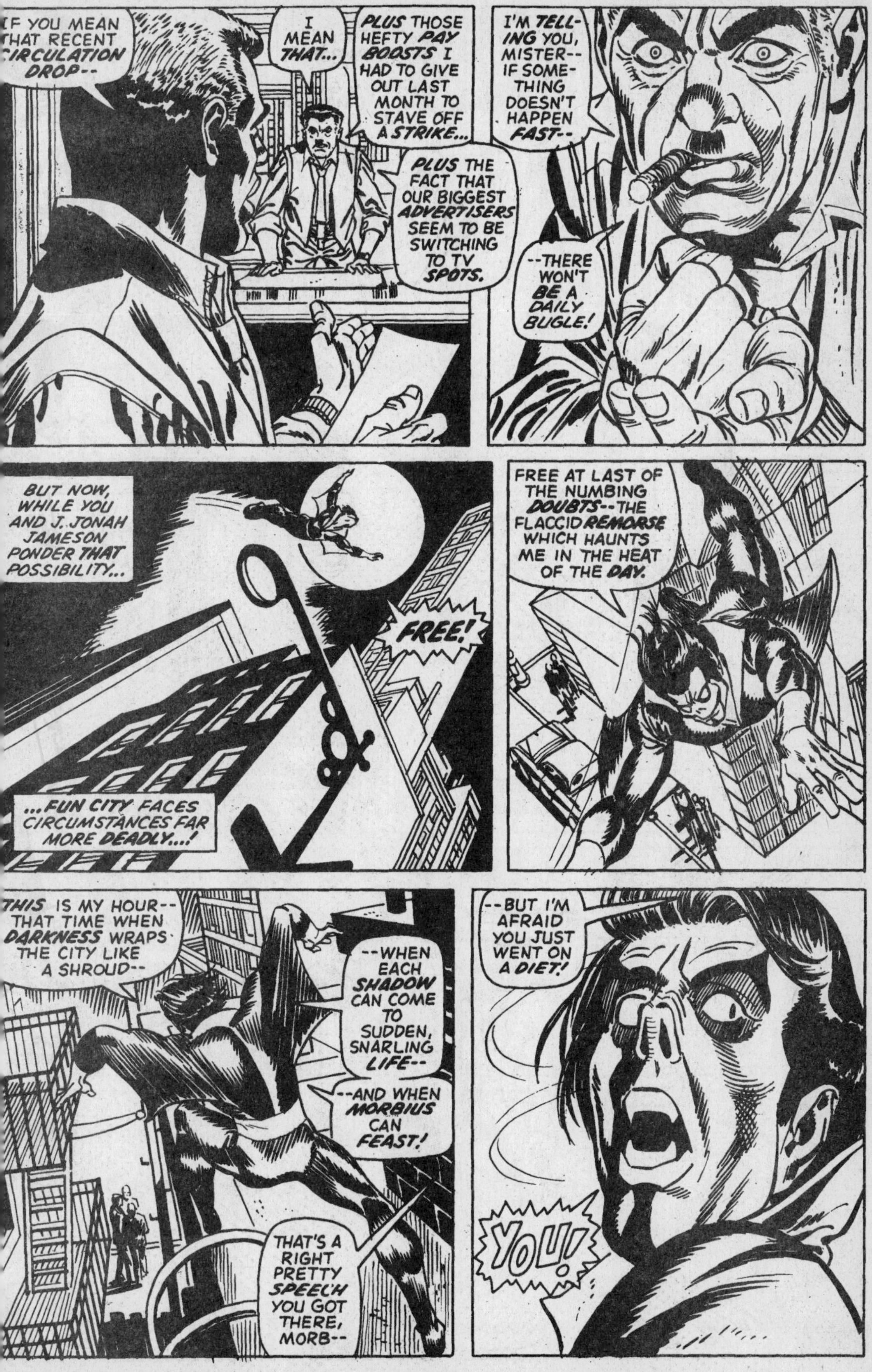
IF YOU MEAN THAT RECENT CIRCULATION DROP--
I MEAN THAT...
PLUS THOSE HEFTY PAY BOOSTS I HAD TO GIVE OUT LAST MONTH TO STAVE OFF A STRIKE...
PLUS THE FACT THAT OUR BIGGEST ADVERTISERS SEEM TO BE SWITCHING TO TV SPOTS.
I'M TELLING YOU, MISTER-- IF SOMETHING DOESN'T HAPPEN FAST--
--THERE WON'T BE A DAILY BUGLE!
BUT NOW, WHILE YOU AND J. JONAH JAMESON PONDER THAT POSSIBILITY...
FREE!
...FUN CITY FACES CIRCUMSTANCES FAR MORE DEADLY...!
FREE AT LAST OF THE NUMBING DOUBTS--THE FLACCID REMORSE WHICH HAUNTS ME IN THE HEAT OF THE DAY.
THIS IS MY HOUR-- THAT TIME WHEN DARKNESS WRAPS THE CITY LIKE A SHROUD--
--WHEN EACH SHADOW CAN COME TO SUDDEN, SNARLING LIFE--
--AND WHEN MORBIUS CAN FEAST!
THAT'S A RIGHT PRETTY SPEECH YOU GOT THERE, MORB--
--BUT I'M AFRAID YOU JUST WENT ON A DIET!
YOU!

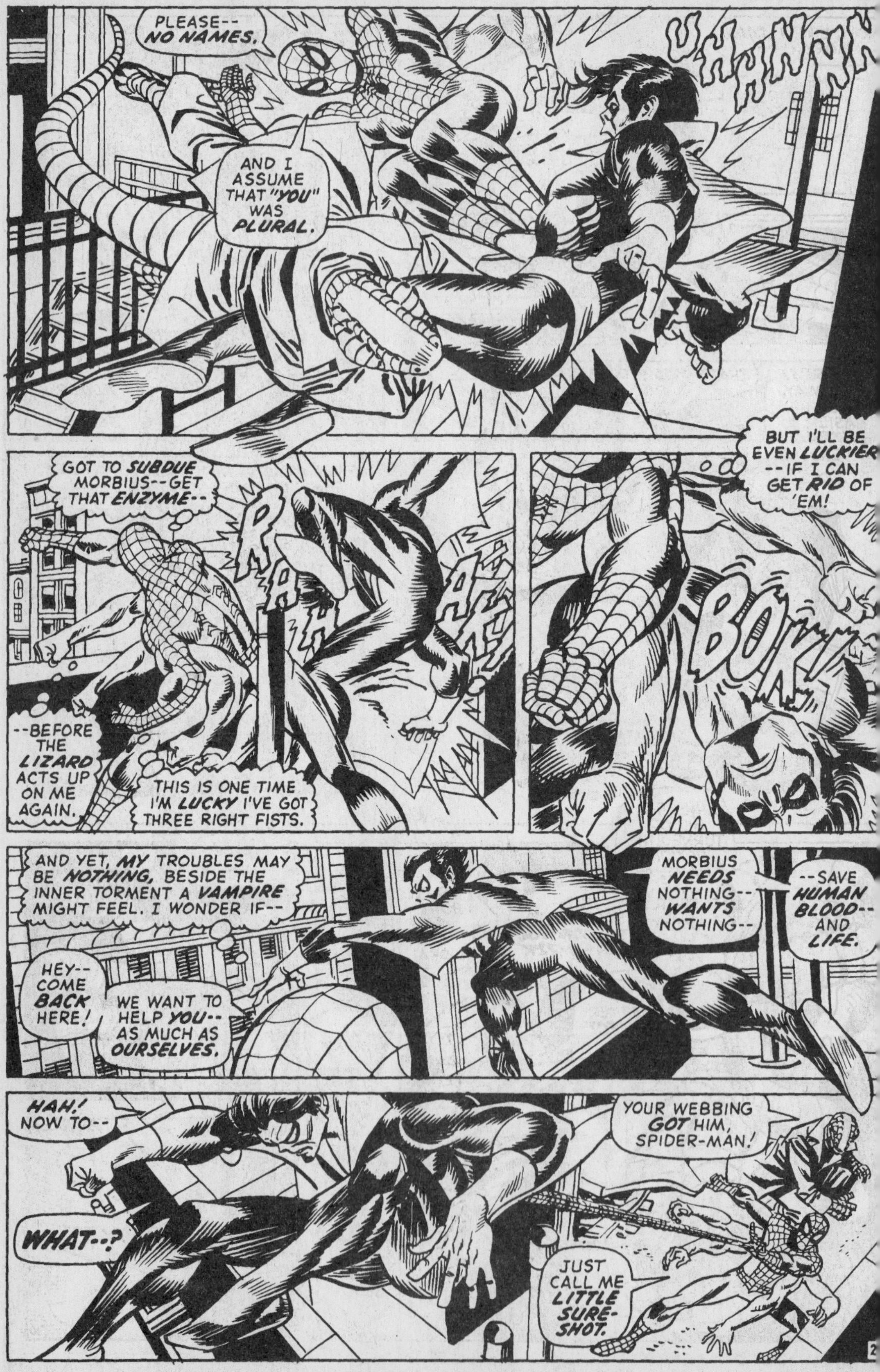
PLEASE--
NO NAMES.
UHHNNK
AND I ASSUME THAT "YOU" WAS PLURAL.
GOT TO SUBDUE MORBIUS--GET THAT ENZYME--
--BEFORE THE LIZARD ACTS UP ON ME AGAIN.
RAK
THIS IS ONE TIME I'M LUCKY I'VE GOT THREE RIGHT FISTS.
BUT I'LL BE EVEN LUCKIER --IF I CAN GET RID OF 'EM!
BOK!
AND YET, MY TROUBLES MAY BE NOTHING, BESIDE THE INNER TORMENT A VAMPIRE MIGHT FEEL. I WONDER IF--
MORBIUS NEEDS NOTHING-- WANTS NOTHING--
--SAVE HUMAN BLOOD-- AND LIFE.
HEY-- COME BACK HERE!
WE WANT TO HELP YOU-- AS MUCH AS OURSELVES.
HAH! NOW TO--
WHAT--?
YOUR WEBBING GOT HIM, SPIDER-MAN!
JUST CALL ME LITTLE SURE-SHOT.

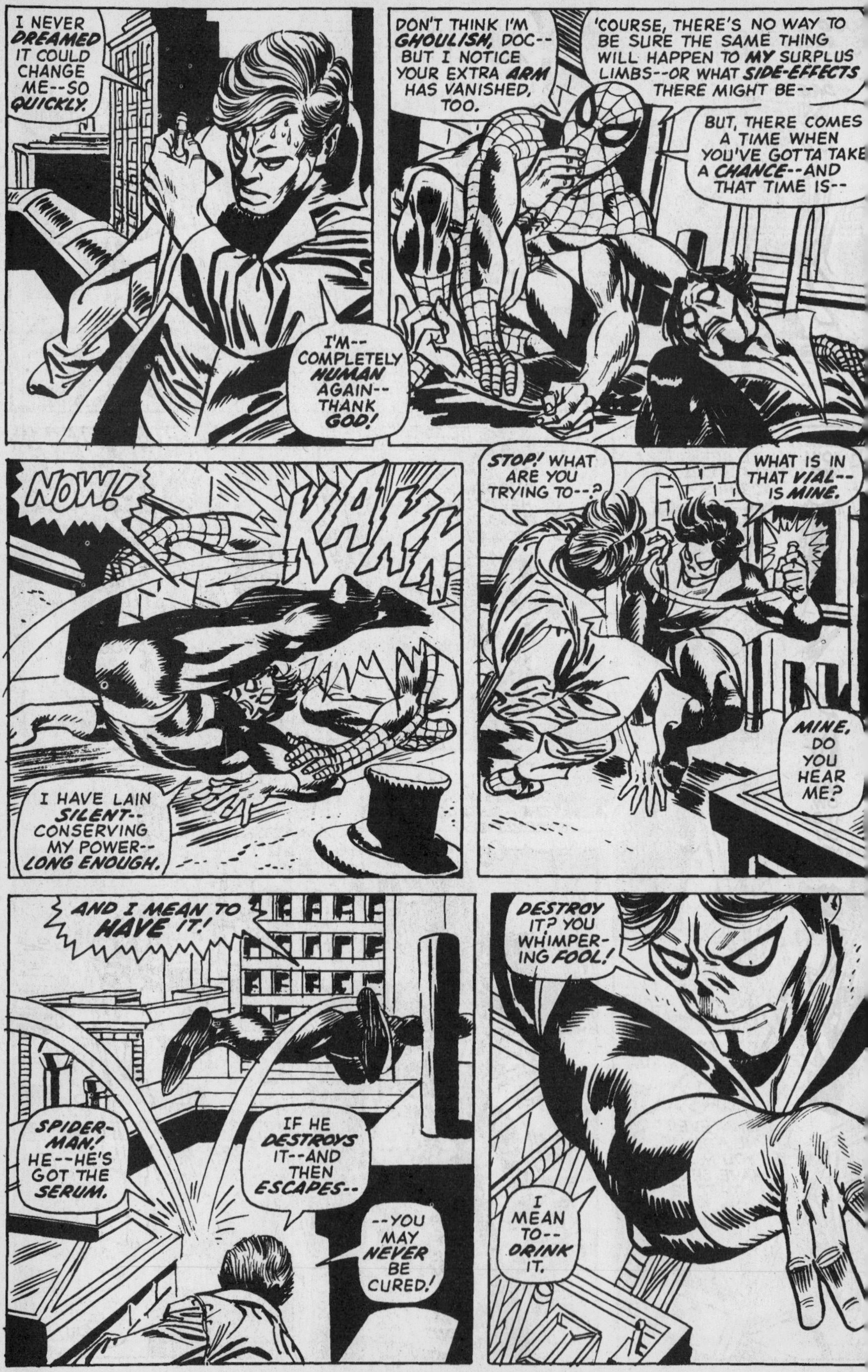
I NEVER DREAMED IT COULD CHANGE ME--SO QUICKLY.
I'M--COMPLETELY HUMAN AGAIN--THANK GOD!
DON'T THINK I'M GHOULISH, DOC--BUT I NOTICE YOUR EXTRA ARM HAS VANISHED, TOO.
'COURSE, THERE'S NO WAY TO BE SURE THE SAME THING WILL HAPPEN TO MY SURPLUS LIMBS--OR WHAT SIDE-EFFECTS THERE MIGHT BE--
BUT, THERE COMES A TIME WHEN YOU'VE GOTTA TAKE A CHANCE--AND THAT TIME IS--
NOW!
KAKK
I HAVE LAIN SILENT--CONSERVING MY POWER--LONG ENOUGH.
STOP! WHAT ARE YOU TRYING TO--?
WHAT IS IN THAT VIAL--IS MINE.
MINE. DO YOU HEAR ME?
AND I MEAN TO HAVE IT!
SPIDER-MAN! HE--HE'S GOT THE SERUM.
IF HE DESTROYS IT--AND THEN ESCAPES--
--YOU MAY NEVER BE CURED!
DESTROY IT? YOU WHIMPERING FOOL!
I MEAN TO--DRINK IT.

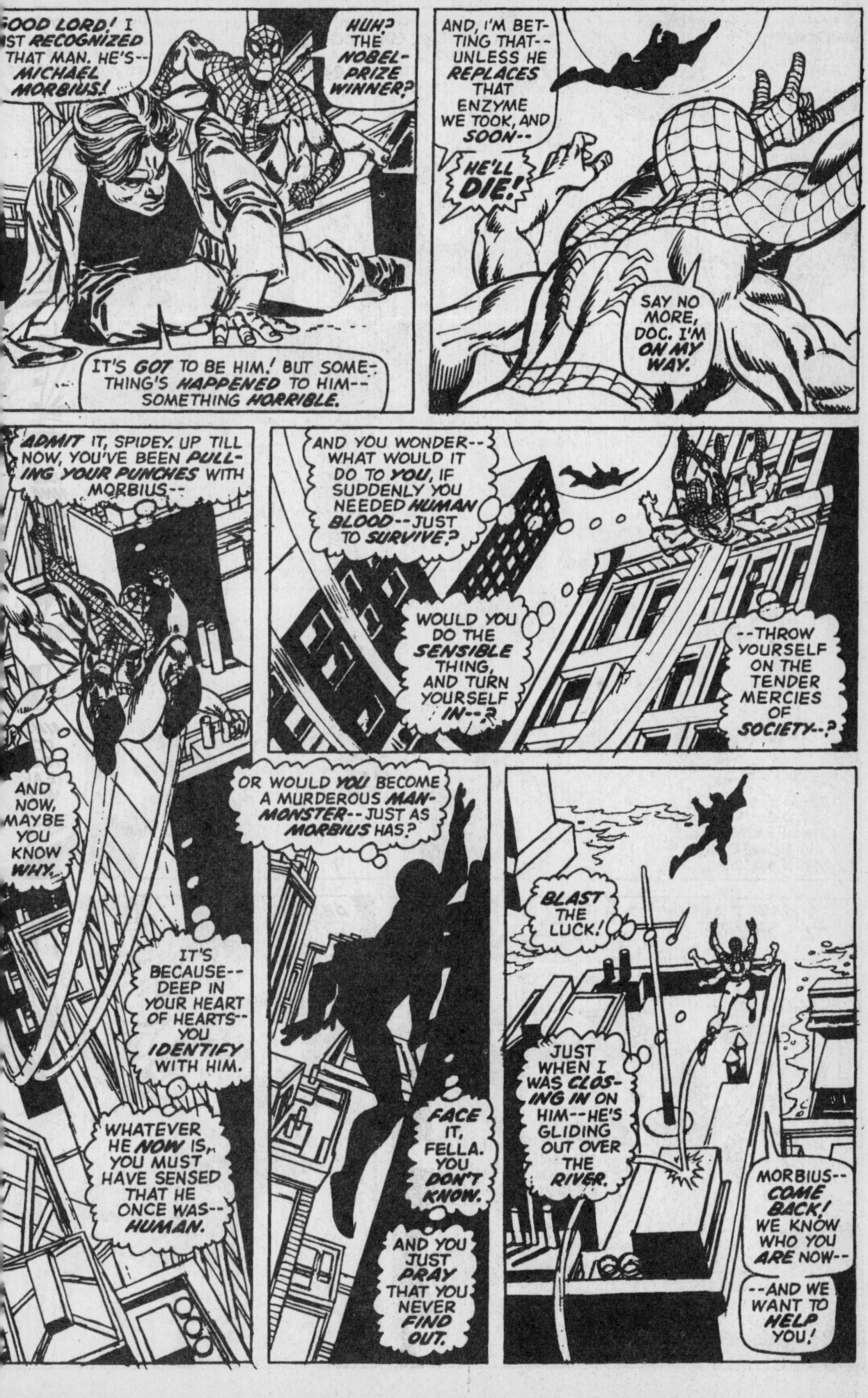
GOOD LORD! I JUST RECOGNIZED THAT MAN. HE'S-- MICHAEL MORBIUS!
HUH? THE NOBEL-PRIZE WINNER?
IT'S GOT TO BE HIM! BUT SOMETHING'S HAPPENED TO HIM-- SOMETHING HORRIBLE.
AND, I'M BETTING THAT-- UNLESS HE REPLACES THAT ENZYME WE TOOK, AND SOON--
HE'LL DIE!
SAY NO MORE, DOC. I'M ON MY WAY.
ADMIT IT, SPIDEY. UP TILL NOW, YOU'VE BEEN PULLING YOUR PUNCHES WITH MORBIUS--
AND NOW, MAYBE YOU KNOW WHY.
IT'S BECAUSE-- DEEP IN YOUR HEART OF HEARTS-- YOU IDENTIFY WITH HIM.
WHATEVER HE NOW IS, YOU MUST HAVE SENSED THAT HE ONCE WAS-- HUMAN.
AND YOU WONDER-- WHAT WOULD IT DO TO YOU, IF SUDDENLY YOU NEEDED HUMAN BLOOD--JUST TO SURVIVE?
WOULD YOU DO THE SENSIBLE THING, AND TURN YOURSELF IN--?
--THROW YOURSELF ON THE TENDER MERCIES OF SOCIETY--?
OR WOULD YOU BECOME A MURDEROUS MAN-MONSTER--JUST AS MORBIUS HAS?
FACE IT, FELLA. YOU DON'T KNOW.
AND YOU JUST PRAY THAT YOU NEVER FIND OUT.
BLAST THE LUCK!
JUST WHEN I WAS CLOSING IN ON HIM--HE'S GLIDING OUT OVER THE RIVER.
MORBIUS-- COME BACK! WE KNOW WHO YOU ARE NOW--
--AND WE WANT TO HELP YOU!

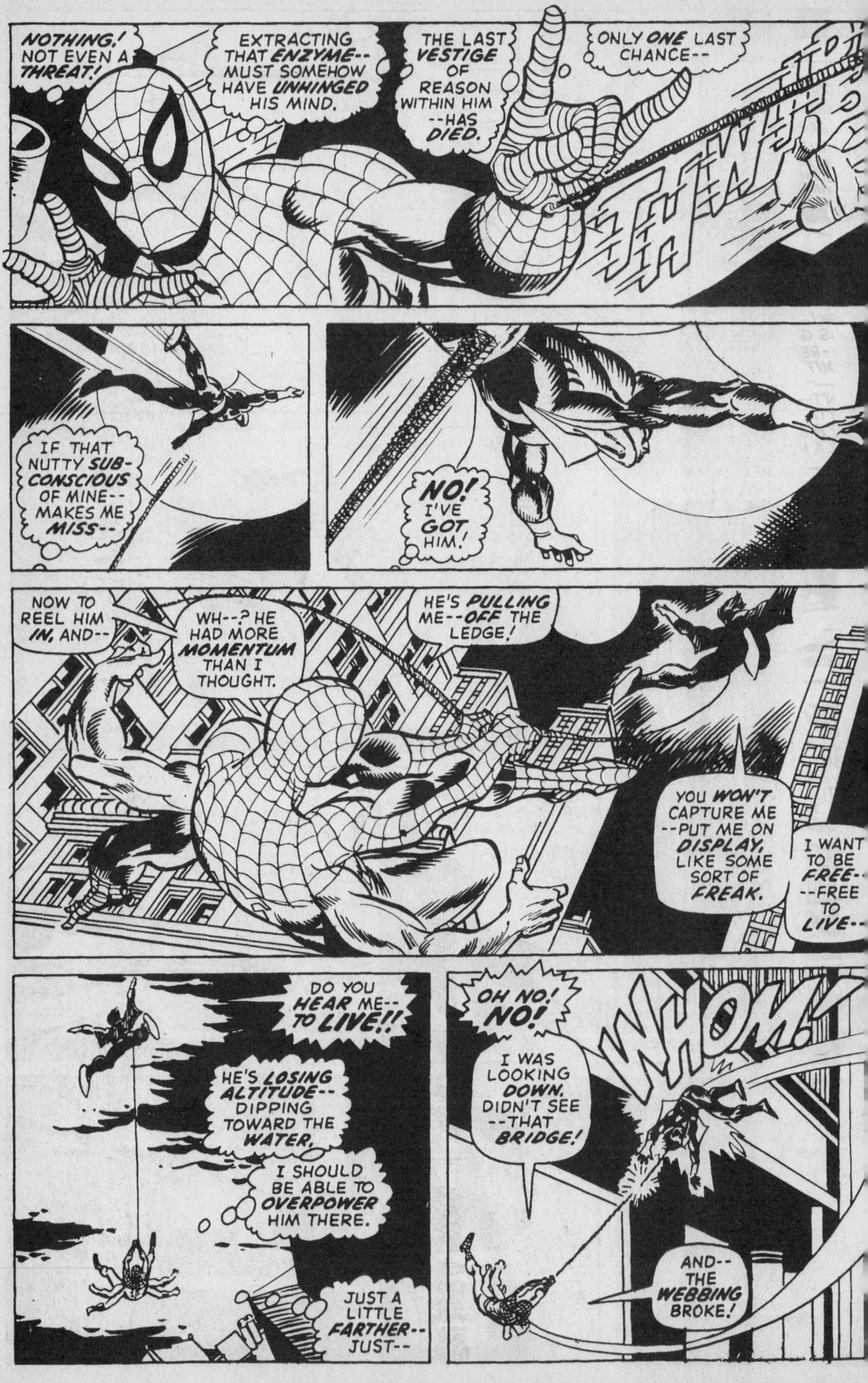
NOTHING! NOT EVEN A THREAT!
EXTRACTING THAT ENZYME--MUST SOMEHOW HAVE UNHINGED HIS MIND.
THE LAST VESTIGE OF REASON WITHIN HIM--HAS DIED.
ONLY ONE LAST CHANCE--
THWIP
THTHTHTHT
IF THAT NUTTY SUB-CONSCIOUS OF MINE--MAKES ME MISS--
NO! I'VE GOT HIM!
NOW TO REEL HIM IN, AND--
WH--? HE HAD MORE MOMENTUM THAN I THOUGHT.
HE'S PULLING ME--OFF THE LEDGE!
YOU WON'T CAPTURE ME--PUT ME ON DISPLAY, LIKE SOME SORT OF FREAK.
I WANT TO BE FREE--FREE TO LIVE--
DO YOU HEAR ME--TO LIVE!!
HE'S LOSING ALTITUDE--DIPPING TOWARD THE WATER.
I SHOULD BE ABLE TO OVERPOWER HIM THERE.
JUST A LITTLE FARTHER--JUST--
OH NO! NO!
WHOM!
I WAS LOOKING DOWN. DIDN'T SEE--THAT BRIDGE!
AND--THE WEBBING BROKE!

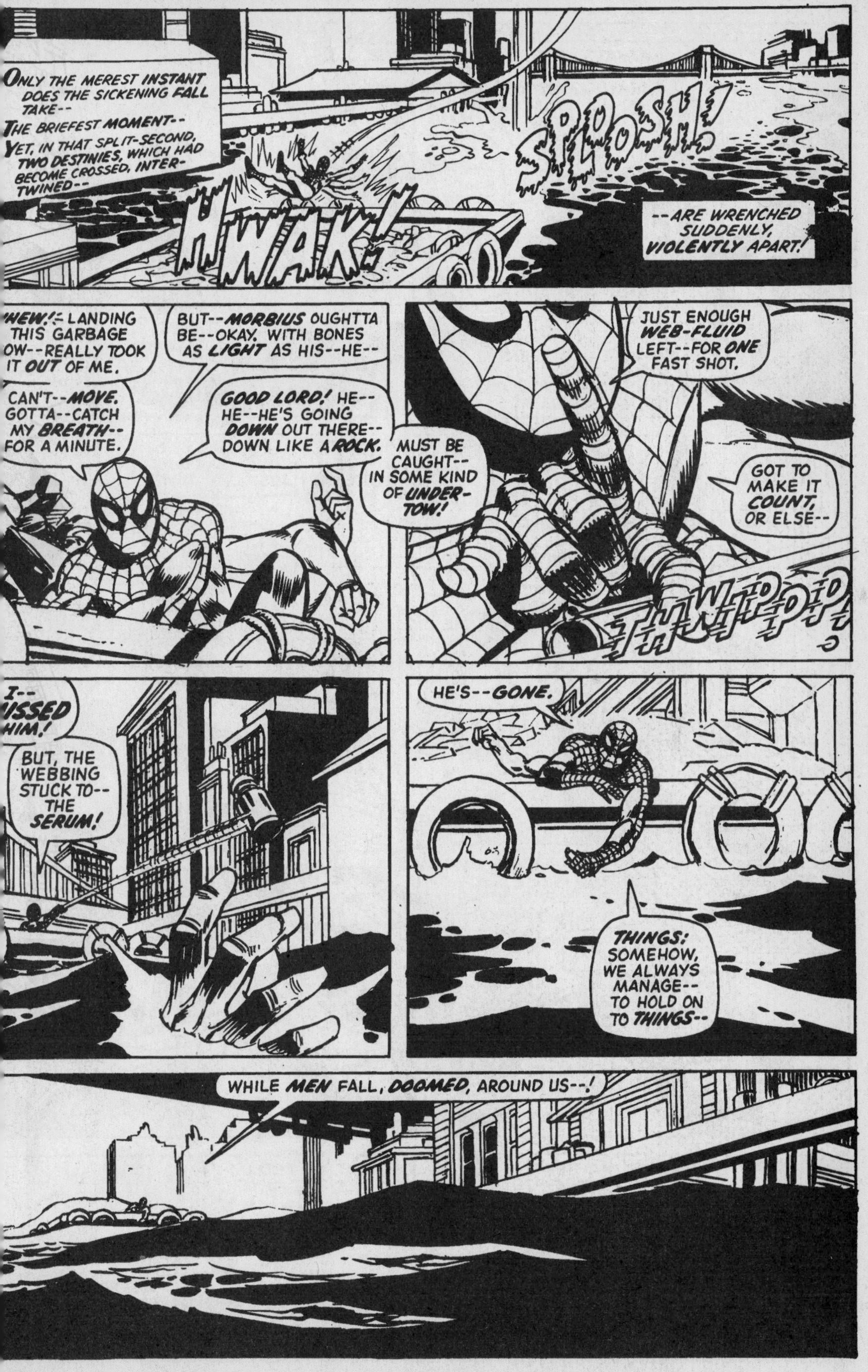
ONLY THE MEREST INSTANT DOES THE SICKENING FALL TAKE--
THE BRIEFEST MOMENT--
YET, IN THAT SPLIT-SECOND, TWO DESTINIES, WHICH HAD BECOME CROSSED, INTER-TWINED--
HWAK!
SPLOOSH!
--ARE WRENCHED SUDDENLY, VIOLENTLY APART!
WHEW!--LANDING THIS GARBAGE SCOW--REALLY TOOK IT OUT OF ME.
CAN'T--MOVE. GOTTA--CATCH MY BREATH--FOR A MINUTE.
BUT--MORBIUS OUGHTTA BE--OKAY. WITH BONES AS LIGHT AS HIS--HE--
GOOD LORD! HE--HE--HE'S GOING DOWN OUT THERE--DOWN LIKE A ROCK.
MUST BE CAUGHT--IN SOME KIND OF UNDER-TOW!
JUST ENOUGH WEB-FLUID LEFT--FOR ONE FAST SHOT.
GOT TO MAKE IT COUNT, OR ELSE--
THWIPPP
I--MISSED HIM!
BUT, THE WEBBING STUCK TO--THE SERUM!
HE'S--GONE.
THINGS: SOMEHOW, WE ALWAYS MANAGE--TO HOLD ON TO THINGS--
WHILE MEN FALL, DOOMED, AROUND US--!

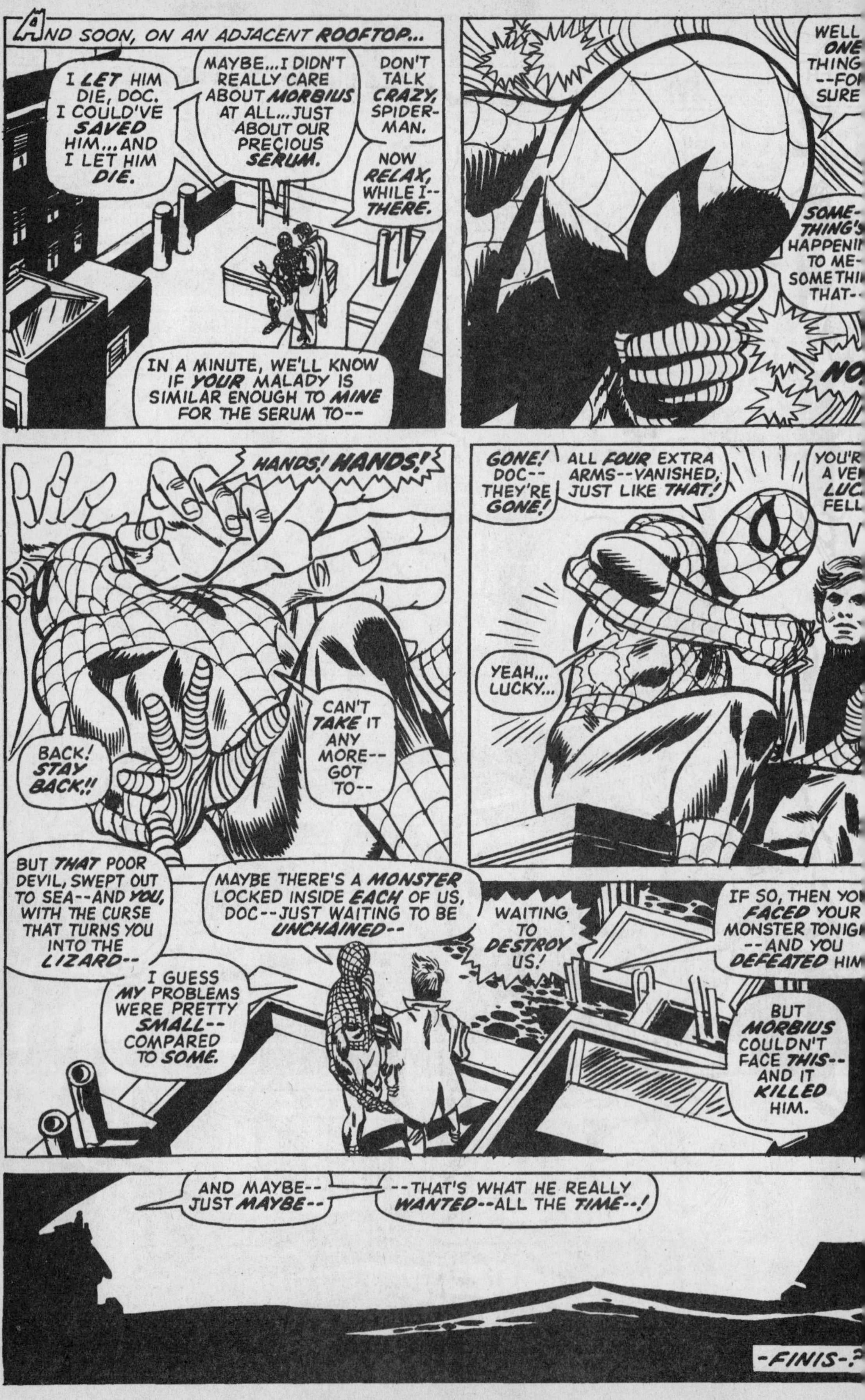
AND SOON, ON AN ADJACENT ROOFTOP...
I LET HIM DIE, DOC. I COULD'VE SAVED HIM... AND I LET HIM DIE.
MAYBE... I DIDN'T REALLY CARE ABOUT MORBIUS AT ALL... JUST ABOUT OUR PRECIOUS SERUM.
DON'T TALK CRAZY, SPIDER-MAN.
NOW RELAX, WHILE I-- THERE.
IN A MINUTE, WE'LL KNOW IF YOUR MALADY IS SIMILAR ENOUGH TO MINE FOR THE SERUM TO--
WELL
HANDS! HANDS!
BACK! STAY BACK!!
CAN'T TAKE IT ANY MORE-- GOT TO--
GONE! DOC-- THEY'RE GONE!
ALL FOUR EXTRA ARMS--VANISHED, JUST LIKE THAT!
YEAH... LUCKY...
BUT THAT POOR DEVIL, SWEPT OUT TO SEA--AND YOU, WITH THE CURSE THAT TURNS YOU INTO THE LIZARD--
I GUESS MY PROBLEMS WERE PRETTY SMALL-- COMPARED TO SOME.
MAYBE THERE'S A MONSTER LOCKED INSIDE EACH OF US, DOC--JUST WAITING TO BE UNCHAINED--
WAITING TO DESTROY US!
BUT MORBIUS COULDN'T FACE THIS-- AND IT KILLED HIM.
AND MAYBE-- JUST MAYBE--
--THAT'S WHAT HE REALLY WANTED--ALL THE TIME--!

MARVEL COMICS GROUP
20¢
the AMAZING SPIDER-MAN
APPROVED BY THE COMICS CODE AUTHORITY
ALL NEW ..AND ALL GREAT!!
GUEST-STARRING: KA-ZAR and ZABU THE SABRE-TOOTH!
GOG! HE WHO WALKS THE SAVAGE LAND!

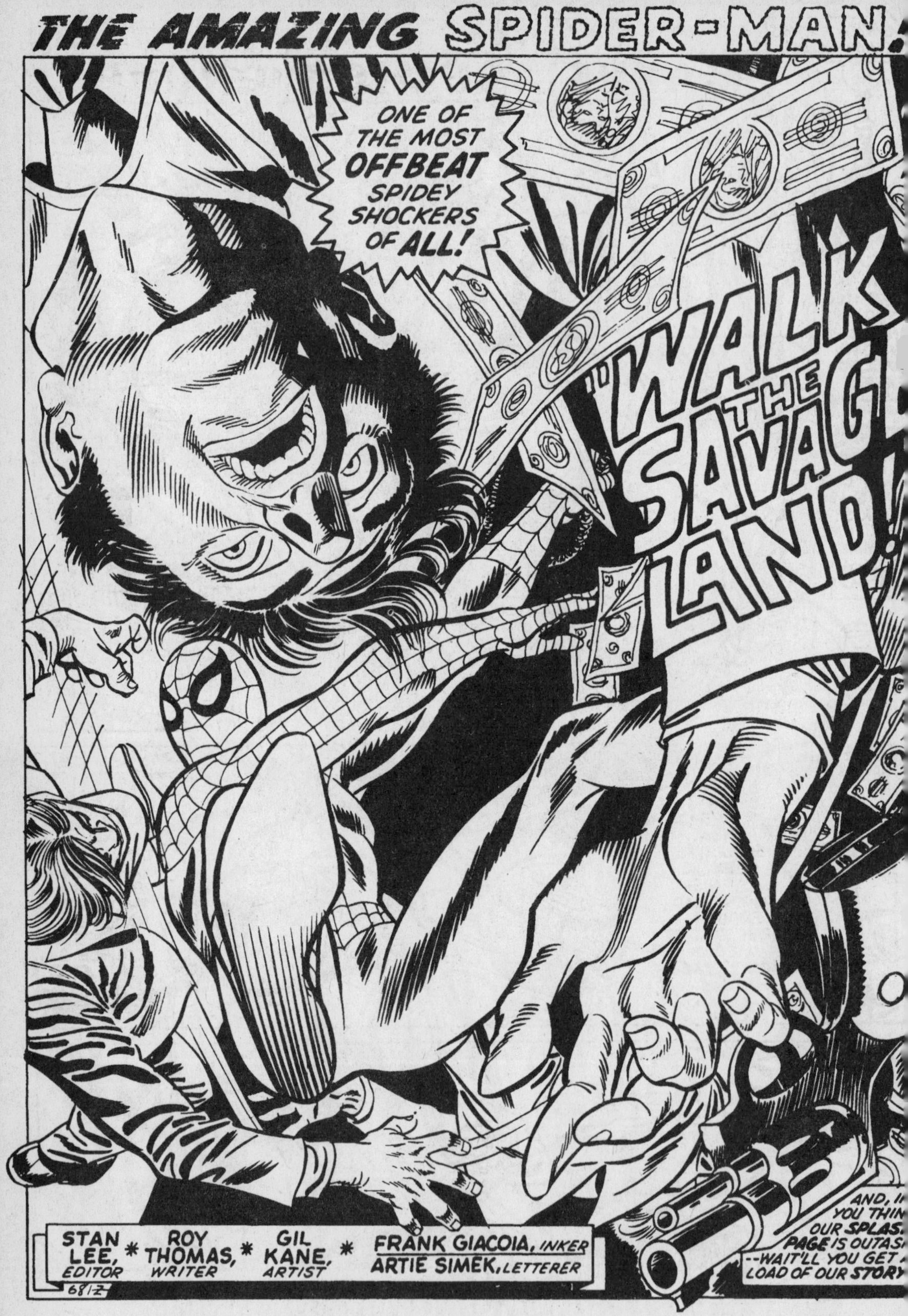

THE AMAZING SPIDER-MAN
ONE OF THE MOST OFFBEAT SPIDEY SHOCKERS OF ALL!
"WALK THE SAVAG LAND!
STAN LEE, EDITOR * ROY THOMAS, WRITER * GIL KANE, ARTIST * FRANK GIACOIA, INKER ARTIE SIMEK, LETTERER
AND, I YOU THIN OUR SPLAS PAGE IS OUTAS --WAIT'LL YOU GET LOAD OF OUR STORY

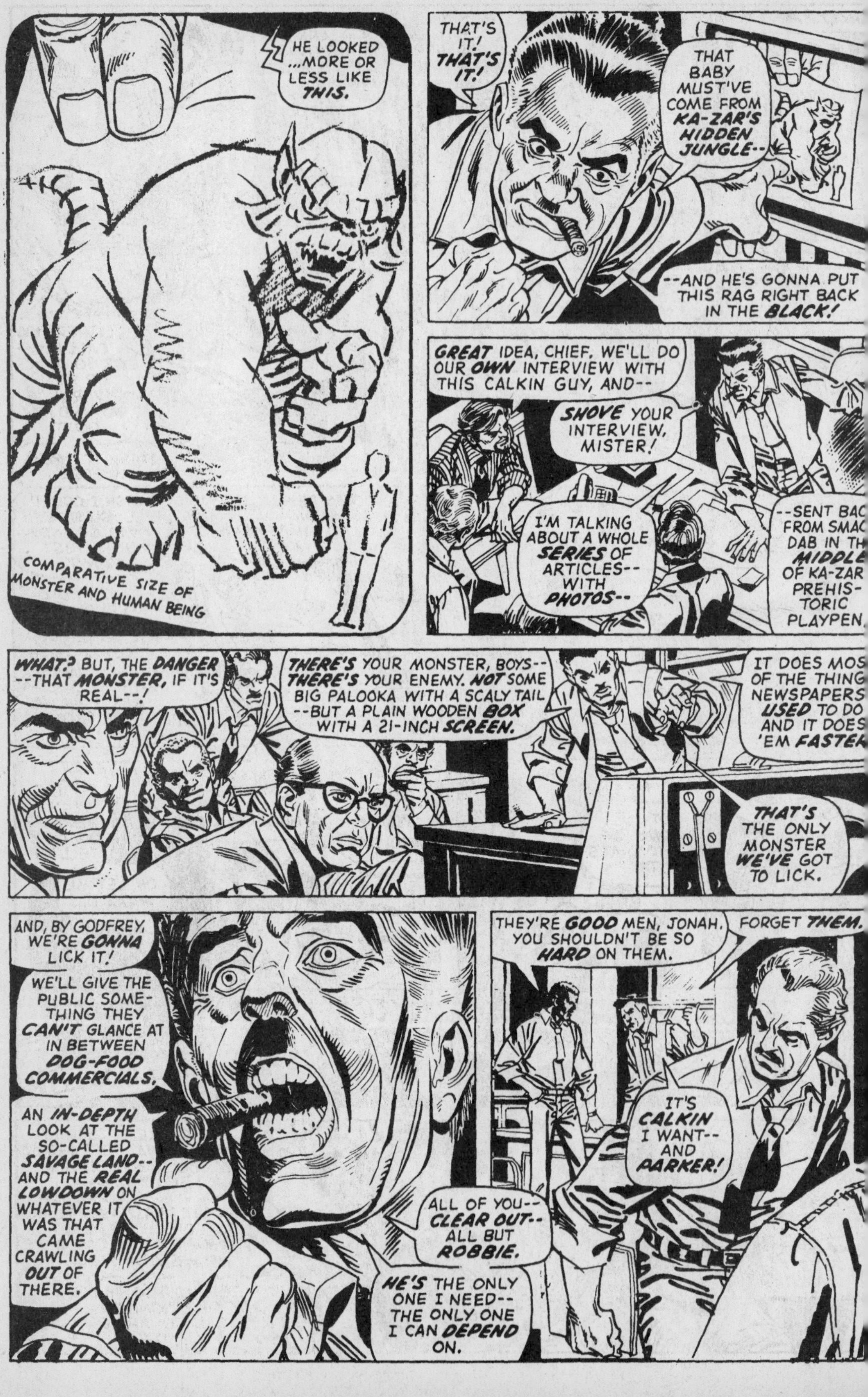
HE LOOKED ...MORE OR LESS LIKE THIS.
COMPARATIVE SIZE OF MONSTER AND HUMAN BEING
THAT'S IT! THAT'S IT!
THAT BABY MUST'VE COME FROM KA-ZAR'S HIDDEN JUNGLE--
--AND HE'S GONNA PUT THIS RAG RIGHT BACK IN THE BLACK!
GREAT IDEA, CHIEF. WE'LL DO OUR OWN INTERVIEW WITH THIS CALKIN GUY, AND--
SHOVE YOUR INTERVIEW, MISTER!
I'M TALKING ABOUT A WHOLE SERIES OF ARTICLES-- WITH PHOTOS--
--SENT BAC FROM SMAC DAB IN TH MIDDLE OF KA-ZAR PREHIS-TORIC PLAYPEN.
WHAT? BUT, THE DANGER --THAT MONSTER, IF IT'S REAL--!
THERE'S YOUR MONSTER, BOYS-- THERE'S YOUR ENEMY. NOT SOME BIG PALOOKA WITH A SCALY TAIL --BUT A PLAIN WOODEN BOX WITH A 21-INCH SCREEN.
IT DOES MOS OF THE THING NEWSPAPERS USED TO DO AND IT DOES 'EM FASTER
THAT'S THE ONLY MONSTER WE'VE GOT TO LICK.
AND, BY GODFREY, WE'RE GONNA LICK IT!
WE'LL GIVE THE PUBLIC SOME-THING THEY CAN'T GLANCE AT IN BETWEEN DOG-FOOD COMMERCIALS.
AN IN-DEPTH LOOK AT THE SO-CALLED SAVAGE LAND-- AND THE REAL LOWDOWN ON WHATEVER IT WAS THAT CAME CRAWLING OUT OF THERE.
ALL OF YOU-- CLEAR OUT-- ALL BUT ROBBIE.
HE'S THE ONLY ONE I NEED-- THE ONLY ONE I CAN DEPEND ON.
THEY'RE GOOD MEN, JONAH. YOU SHOULDN'T BE SO HARD ON THEM.
FORGET THEM.
IT'S CALKIN I WANT-- AND PARKER!

WHAT? NO, I WASN'T WATCHING TV LAST NIGHT. BUT--

ANTARCTICA? A LOST JUNGLE? ALL THIS--AND A CASH BONUS BESIDES?

NEVER MIND THE DANGERS, MR. ROBERTSON.

TELL YOUR PENNY-PINCHING BOSS HE'S FOUND HIS SHUTTERBUG!

HEAR THAT, HONEY? I LEAVE IN A COUPLE OF DAYS. THIS COULD BE MY BIG BREAK--

YES, MISTER PARKER-- I DID HEAR--AND I DON'T LIKE IT ONE BIT!

H-HOW COULD YOU SAY YES--NOW, OF ALL TIMES? I--I--

DON'T CRY, GWENDY. IT MEANS MONEY-- MONEY WE COULD USE TO GET MAR--

S'NO USE, GUY.

BUILD ANY WALL OF LOGIC YOU WANT--THAT LITTLE GIRL'S TEARS WILL MELT IT.

PETE-- WH-WHERE ARE YOU DRAGGING ME?

YOU'LL SEE, LADY.

BELIEVE ME-- YOU'LL SEE.

...YOUNG PARKER'S OUTSIDE... CLAIMS HE'S GOT TO SEE YOU RIGHT AWAY.

JONAH-- YOU'VE HARDLY SAID A WORD ALL DAY.

IF IT'S THAT FLARE-UP WE HAD--IF YOU'D RATHER I RESIGN--

BITE YOUR TONGUE, MAN. I'VE ALREADY PUT YOU DOWN FOR A RAISE.

NO, IT'S--THIS MONSTER-HUNT THE BUGLE'S SPONSORING

SOMETHING'S MISSING-- SOMETHING I CAN'T QUITE PUT MY FINGER ON

OH WELL--MAYBE IT'LL COME TO ME

THERE'S--SOMETHING I'VE GOT TO SAY, MR. JAMESON--

--AND I WANTED GWEN TO HEAR IT.

SO SAY, ALREADY. I'VE GOT TOO MANY THINGS ON MY MIND TO--

I'VE GOT IT, BY GEORGE, I'VE GOT IT!

YOU'RE THE MISSING INGREDIENT I'VE BEEN WRACKING MY BRAIN FOR!

YES, I MEAN *YOU*-- --*GWEN STACY!*

I--I DON'T KNOW WHAT YOU'RE *TALKING* ABOUT, MR. JAMESON.

WELL, I *DO*--AND I'M *WARNING* YOU, JONAH--

SAVE IT, ROBBIE. I'M GONNA *LEVEL* WITH THESE KIDS.

THEN, IT'S UP TO *THEM.*

THUS, MINUTES LATER...

SOUNDS GREAT TO *ME*, SIR-- BUT FOR *GWEN*--I DON'T *KNOW*--

WHY, *PETER PARKER*-- *WHAT* A *MALE CHAUVIN-IST PIG* THING TO SAY!

YOU *TELL* 'IM, YOUNG LADY.

A GIRL LIKE YOU IS JUST WHAT MY EXPEDITION *NEEDS.*

GOTTA THINK OF THE *WOMEN'S* ANGLE. THEY BUY PAPERS *TOO*, Y'KNOW.

BESIDES, A PRETTY FACE NEVER SCARED GENTS *AWAY* FROM THE NEWSSTAND.

IT'S--ALL VERY *TEMPTING.* I *COULD* USE THE *MONEY* TOO, AND--

THEN *SAY* YES.

CALKIN'S ON HIS WAY HERE *RIGHT* NOW.

I'VE GOT TO *KNOW.*

MR. JAMESON--*PLEASE*--CAN'T RUSH *INTO* THIS.

GIVE THEM TIME TO *THINK*, JONAH.

THINK? THERE'S NO *TIME* FOR THAT.

DID *ALEXANDER THE GREAT* HAVE TIME TO *THINK?* DID *LUCKY LINDY?*

WELL, GWEN--WADDA YOU *SAY?*

I SAY-- A-OK, MR. J.!

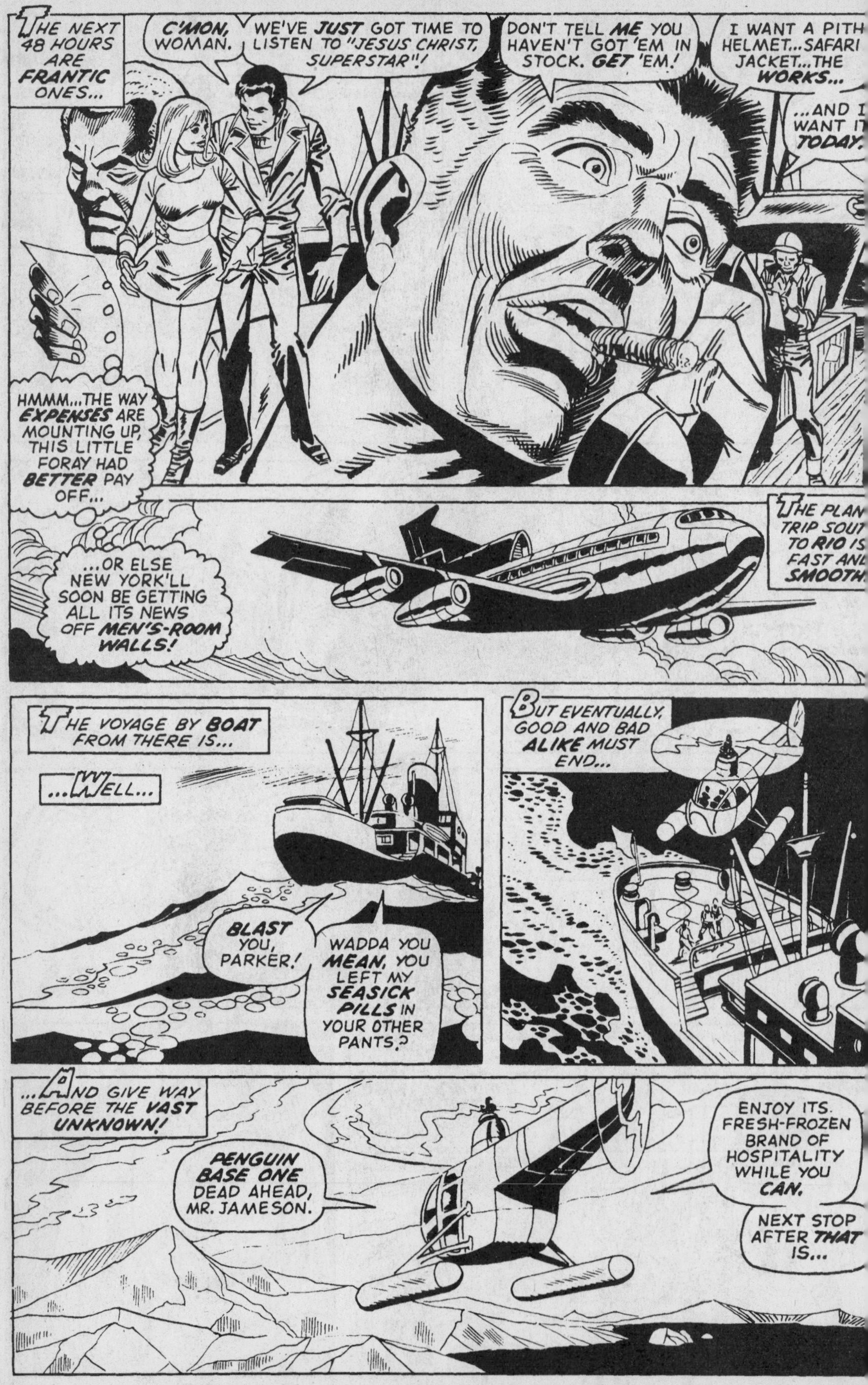
THE NEXT 48 HOURS ARE FRANTIC ONES...
C'MON, WOMAN.
WE'VE JUST GOT TIME TO LISTEN TO "JESUS CHRIST, SUPERSTAR"!
HMMM...THE WAY EXPENSES ARE MOUNTING UP, THIS LITTLE FORAY HAD BETTER PAY OFF...
DON'T TELL ME YOU HAVEN'T GOT 'EM IN STOCK. GET 'EM!
I WANT A PITH HELMET...SAFARI JACKET...THE WORKS...
...AND I WANT IT TODAY.
...OR ELSE NEW YORK'LL SOON BE GETTING ALL ITS NEWS OFF MEN'S-ROOM WALLS!
THE PLAN TRIP SOUT TO RIO IS FAST AN SMOOTH.
THE VOYAGE BY BOAT FROM THERE IS...
...WELL...
BLAST YOU, PARKER!
WADDA YOU MEAN, YOU LEFT MY SEASICK PILLS IN YOUR OTHER PANTS?
BUT EVENTUALLY, GOOD AND BAD ALIKE MUST END...
...AND GIVE WAY BEFORE THE VAST UNKNOWN!
PENGUIN BASE ONE DEAD AHEAD, MR. JAMESON.
ENJOY ITS FRESH-FROZEN BRAND OF HOSPITALITY WHILE YOU CAN.
NEXT STOP AFTER THAT IS...

...THE SAVAGE LAND!

WELCOME! WELCOME. THE BRASS RADIOED US YOU'D BE COMING THRU HERE ON YOUR WILD-GOOSE CHASE.

AND ORDERED YOU TO HUMOR US, HUH? WELL, THAT'S OKAY BY ME.

NOW, IF YOU'VE GOT A MAP OF THIS OPEN-AIR ICEBOX--!

...AFTER DECIMATING OUR CAMP, THE CREATURE STALKED OFF IN THIS DIRECTION, SO...

TELL ME, MR. JAMESON...HASN'T IT OCCURRED TO YOU THAT I MIGHT BE A FRAUD...OR JUST PLAIN LOONEY?

CALKIN, I'VE GOT A MULTI-MILLION-DOLLAR BUSINESS AT STAKE IN THIS LITTLE VENTURE.

AT THIS STAGE I CAN'T AFFORD EVEN TO CONSIDER THAT POSSIBILITY.

THANKS FOR THAT, MY FRIEND.

'CAUSE THAT DEVIL WAS REAL, ALL RIGHT--

AND I ONLY HOPE THE MOMENT NEVER COMES-- WHEN WE WISH IT HADN'T BEEN.

A FINAL RE-FUELING-- A TIGHTENING OF BREATHS--

THEN, THE LAST LIFTOFF FROM THE LAST OUTPOST OF CIVILIZATION--

--IN A LAND WHOSE STARK BEAUTY BEGGARS DESCRIPTION--

--A LAND WHERE WHITE, NOT BLACK, IS THE COLOR OF DEATH!

10.

HOURS PASS...
THE HELICOPTER REACHES THE *LIMITS* OF ITS FUEL, ITS *POINT-OF-NO-RETURN...*

AND THEN, WHITE *UPON* WHITE:

A GLEAMING IVORY WALL OF *MIST,* SUDDENLY LOOMING BEFORE THE HUMMING 'COPTER LIKE A MILKY SHROUD...

IS IT ONLY A WHIPLASH *WIND,* A FREAKISH *UPDRAFT,* WHICH MAKES THE CRAFT *SHUDDER* MOMENTARILY BEFORE PLUNGING INTO THAT MIST...

OR IS IT...SOMETHING *MORE....?*

I CAN'T SEE A *THING* UP AHEAD.

MR. CALKIN-- WHAT'S *WRONG??*

SPEAK UP, MAN--YOU'RE PALE AS A *SHEET!*

--I THINK WE'RE *THERE!*

THAT-- *HIDDEN JUNGLE* WE'RE LOOKING FOR, MR. *JAMESON--*

*W*HAT DEEP-THRUST *MEMORIES* ARE AWAKENED BY THAT SWOOPING *PTEROSAUR,* CAREENING AWAY FROM THE *BUZZING STEEL GNAT* WHICH HAS STARTLED IT?

*F*OR CALKIN: THE MEMORY OF A *RAZED CAMP,* TWO COMRADES ALL BUT *DISMEMBERED...*

*F*OR JAMESON: THE DAY HE FIRST FACED KA-ZAR'S SNARLING *SABRE-TOOTH...*

*B*UT THE YOUNG, BEING YOUNG...HAVE FEWER *MEMORIES...* SO PETE AND GWEN CAN MERELY *REACT,* AND THEN *ACCEPT...*

...*A*S IF THERE WERE, PERHAPS, SOME SUBTLE COSMIC *AFFINITY* BETWEEN THE VERY *YOUNG...* AND THE *AWESOMELY, INESTIMABLY ANCIENT...!*

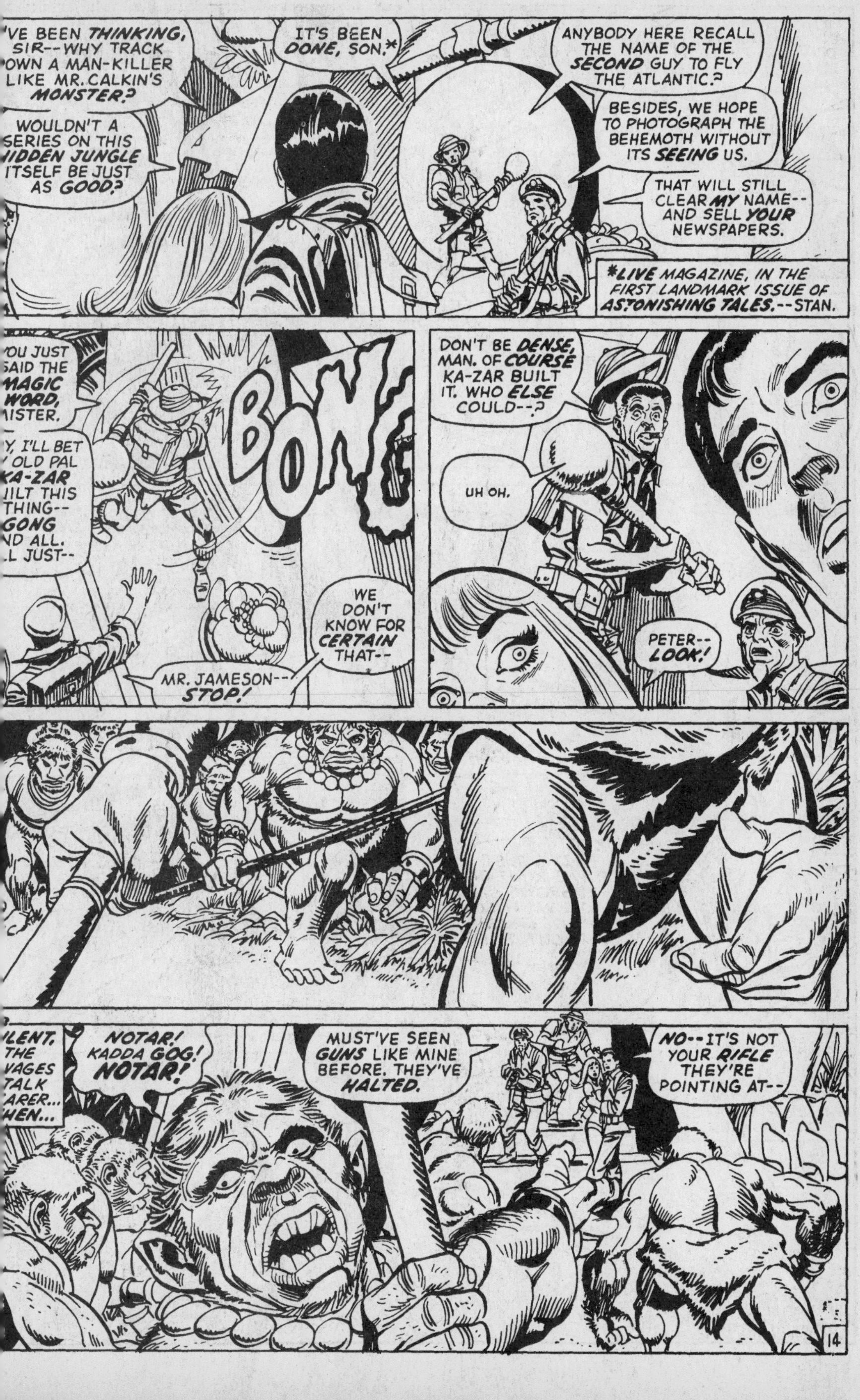
'VE BEEN THINKING, SIR--WHY TRACK OWN A MAN-KILLER LIKE MR. CALKIN'S MONSTER?
WOULDN'T A SERIES ON THIS IDDEN JUNGLE ITSELF BE JUST AS GOOD?
IT'S BEEN DONE, SON.*
ANYBODY HERE RECALL THE NAME OF THE SECOND GUY TO FLY THE ATLANTIC?
BESIDES, WE HOPE TO PHOTOGRAPH THE BEHEMOTH WITHOUT ITS SEEING US.
THAT WILL STILL CLEAR MY NAME--AND SELL YOUR NEWSPAPERS.
*LIVE MAGAZINE, IN THE FIRST LANDMARK ISSUE OF ASTONISHING TALES.--STAN.
OU JUST SAID THE MAGIC WORD, MISTER.
Y, I'LL BET OLD PAL KA-ZAR UILT THIS THING--GONG ND ALL. L JUST--
BONG
WE DON'T KNOW FOR CERTAIN THAT--
MR. JAMESON--STOP!
DON'T BE DENSE, MAN. OF COURSE KA-ZAR BUILT IT. WHO ELSE COULD--?
UH OH.
PETER--LOOK!
LENT, THE VAGES TALK ARER... HEN...
NOTAR! KADDA GOG! NOTAR!
MUST'VE SEEN GUNS LIKE MINE BEFORE. THEY'VE HALTED.
NO--IT'S NOT YOUR RIFLE THEY'RE POINTING AT--
14

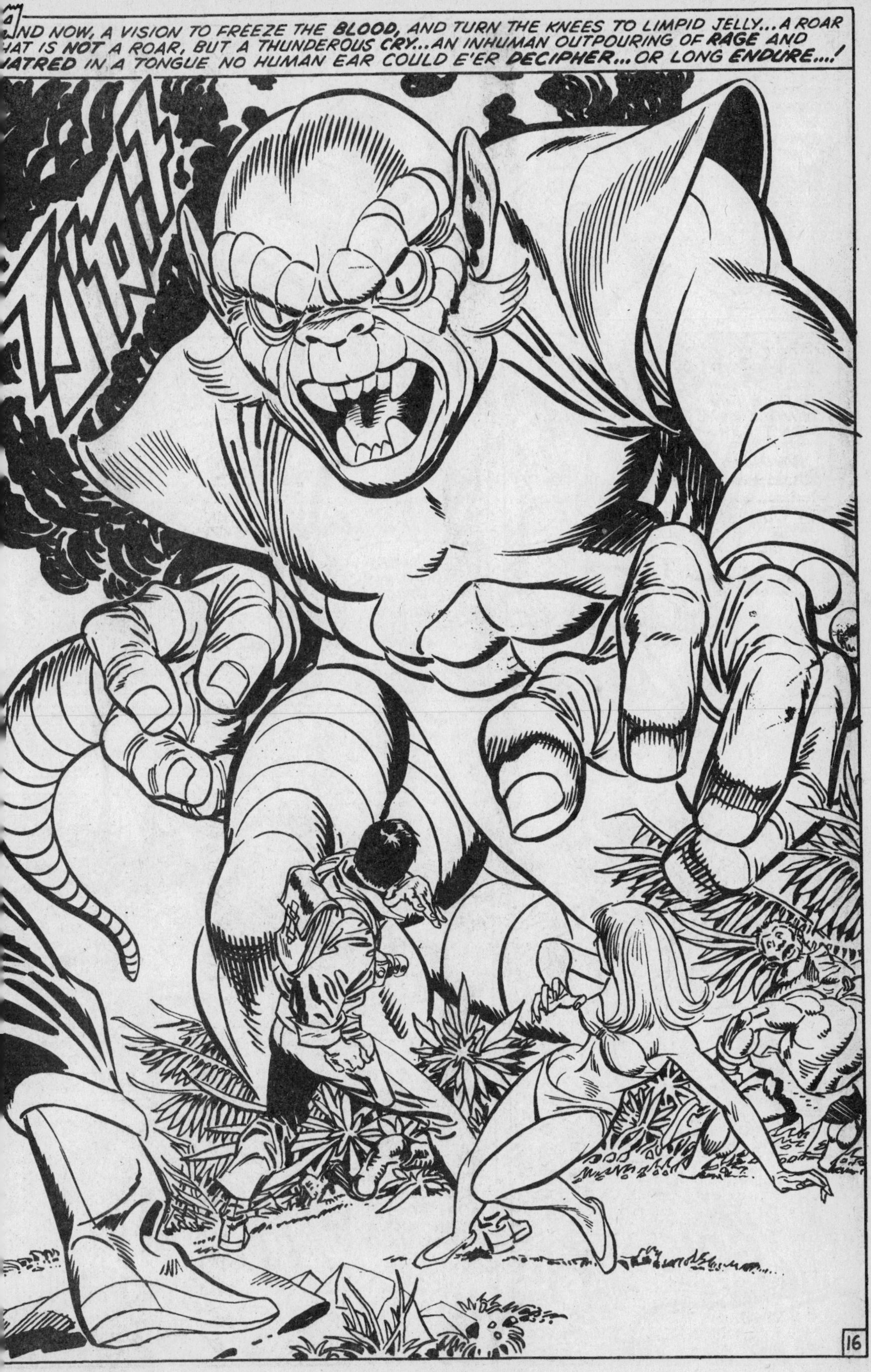
AND NOW, A VISION TO FREEZE THE BLOOD, AND TURN THE KNEES TO LIMPID JELLY... A ROAR THAT IS NOT A ROAR, BUT A THUNDEROUS CRY... AN INHUMAN OUTPOURING OF RAGE AND HATRED IN A TONGUE NO HUMAN EAR COULD E'ER DECIPHER... OR LONG ENDURE...!

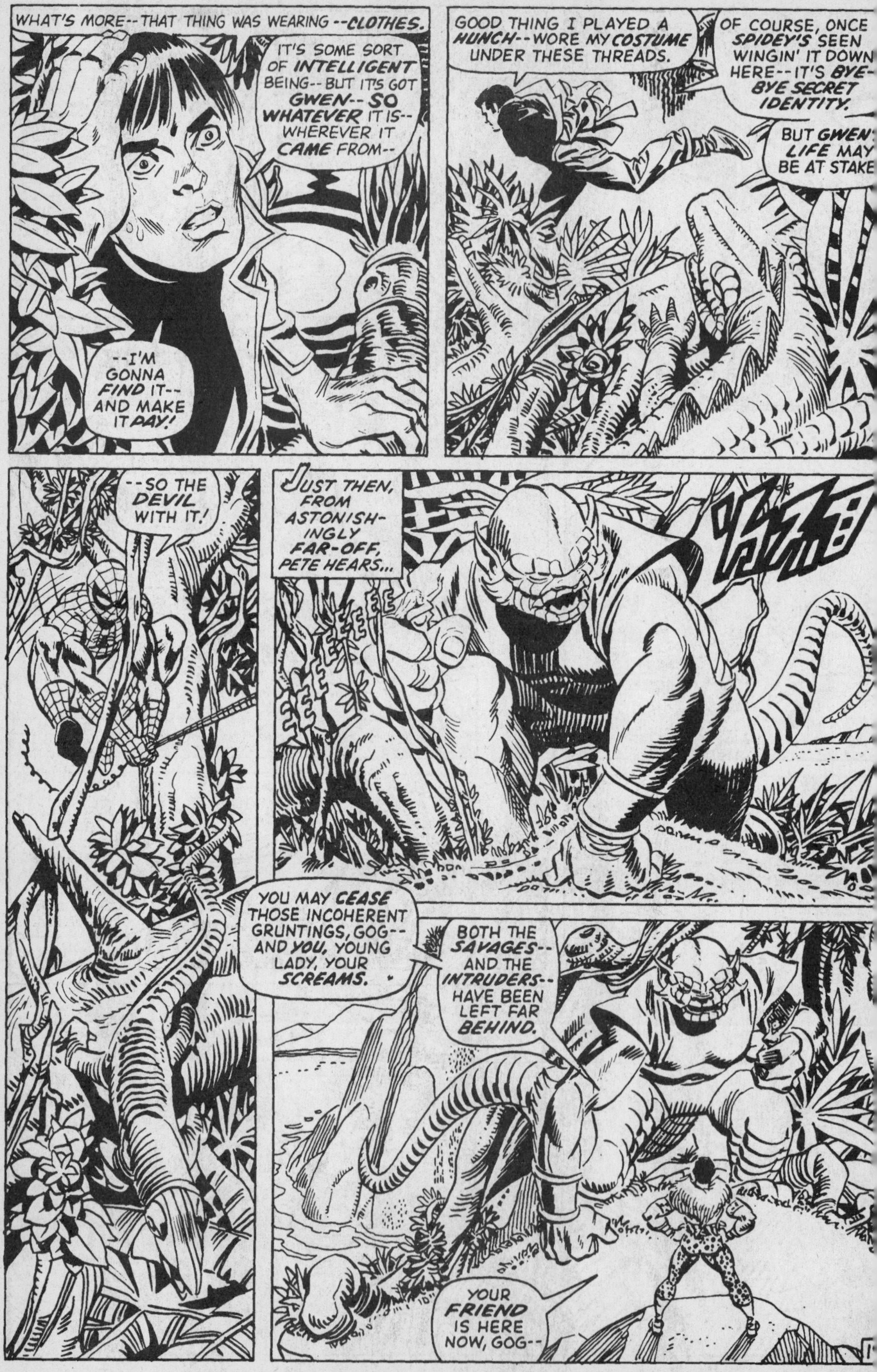

WHAT'S MORE--THAT THING WAS WEARING--CLOTHES.
IT'S SOME SORT OF INTELLIGENT BEING--BUT IT'S GOT GWEN--SO WHATEVER IT IS--WHEREVER IT CAME FROM--
--I'M GONNA FIND IT--AND MAKE IT PAY!
GOOD THING I PLAYED A HUNCH--WORE MY COSTUME UNDER THESE THREADS.
OF COURSE, ONCE SPIDEY'S SEEN WINGIN' IT DOWN HERE--IT'S BYE-BYE SECRET IDENTITY.
BUT GWEN'S LIFE MAY BE AT STAKE
--SO THE DEVIL WITH IT!
JUST THEN, FROM ASTONISHINGLY FAR-OFF, PETE HEARS...
EEEEE
YOU MAY CEASE THOSE INCOHERENT GRUNTINGS, GOG--AND YOU, YOUNG LADY, YOUR SCREAMS.
BOTH THE SAVAGES--AND THE INTRUDERS--HAVE BEEN LEFT FAR BEHIND.
YOUR FRIEND IS HERE NOW, GOG--

YOU'RE [NO]T THE [ONLY] [O]NE, [KA]-ZAR...!

HE'S [L]EAVING [T]RACKS [R]OUGHLY [TH]E SIZE [O]F A [W]ATER-[BE]D.

FROM THE LOOK OF THEM, I MUST BE GAINING ON THAT MONSTER --AND ON GWEN.

'COURSE, THERE'S ALWAYS THE LITTLE MATTER OF WHAT I'LL DO WHEN I--

UH OH! THIS GNARLED LIMB I JUST LANDED ON-- IT'S MOVING UNDER MY FEET.

--WHICH MIGHT JUST MEAN--

--THAT IT ISN'T A TREE-LIMB AT ALL!

IT'S--SOME KIND OF GIGANTIC SERPENT!

HSSSSSS

THAT WAS CLOSE-- [R]EAL CLOSE-- BUT NO [K]EWPIE DOLL.

LOOK, OLIVER J. DRAGON--

MOST DAYS, I'D BE GLAD TO HASSLE WITH YOU FOR A WHILE--

RAKK!

BUT, THE GIRL I LOVE IS UP AHEAD SOMEWHERE, IN DANGER OF HER LIFE--

22

SO I'LL JUST HAVE TO PLAY *DIRTY POOL*--

--AND HOPE THERE ISN'T A LOCAL CHAPTER OF THE *SPCA* IN THE VICINITY!

SK-RUK!

THERE'S A LOT IN WHAT YOU *SAY*, PAL.

PUT IT ALL IN WRITING TO YOUR *CONGRESSMAN*, HUH?

BUT-- I WAS *RIGHT*.

I'M GETTING *CLOSER* TO THAT MONSTER --AND IT'S STILL GOT *GWEN*.

IF ONLY I KNEW *WHAT* IT IS--*WHY* IT GRABBED *GWEN*.

IF IT'S AN *AFFAIR OF THE HEART*, I'M AFRAID IT'S GONNA BE DEFINITELY *ONE-SIDED*.

BUT, A MORE *IMMEDIATE* PROBLEM--

HOW DO I CROSS THIS *STREAM* THAT THING JUST WADED THRU?

I COULD TRY *SWIMMING*--BUT CONSIDERING WHAT MIGHT LIE *BENEATH* THE WATER--

FORGET IT.

AS LONG AS THERE ARE--*UHNNN!*--TOUGH *SAPLINGS* LIKE THIS ONE AROUND--

I CAN ALWAYS-- *AIR-MAIL* MYSELF ACROSS--

SPLANNG!

--SPECIAL DELIVERY, YET!

WILD! I'LL CLEAR THE STREAM WITH ROOM TO *SPARE.*

NOW TO PICK OUT A NICE, SOFT SPOT TO *LAND.*

THAT *PUDDLE* UP AHEAD LOOKS JUST ABOUT RIGHT.

A *FLIP-FLOP* OR TWO-- TO HELP ME *CONTROL* MY DIRECTION--

--AND I SHOULD MAKE A *PERFECT* TWO-POINT LANDING.

SPIDEY, YOU'RE A *WONDER!*

BUT--MY *FEET!?* WHY DO THEY FEEL--LIKE THEY'RE *MIRED* IN THE MUD?

PLOASH!

OH NO! IT WASN'T *MUD* THAT LAY BENEATH THAT PUDDLE--IT WAS--

QUICK-SAND!

IT'S PULLING ME *DOWN--* LIKE SOME STARVING *ANIMAL.*

CAN'T EVEN LATCH ONTO A *LIMB--* TO GAIN *TIME!*

WALL-CRAWLER --YOU'VE *HAD* IT!

CONTINUED! WHAT ELSE?

SPIDER-MAN
MARVEL COMICS GROUP™
20¢
104
JAN
02457
the AMAZING SPIDER-MAN™
APPROVED BY THE COMICS CODE AUTHORITY
IS THIS TO BE THE FINAL HUNT?
KRAVEN THE HUNTER!

THE AMAZING SPIDER-MAN!
STAN LEE EDITOR * ROY THOMAS WRITER * GIL KANE ARTIST * FRANK GIACOIA INKER * ARTIE SIMEK LETTERER
TALK ABOUT CLIFF HANGERS!
LAST ISH, OUR WONDROUS WEB-SPINNER WENT SOARING THRU THE AIR WITH THE GREATEST OF EASE, ONLY TO FIND A FEW MOMENTS LATER THAT HE HAD LANDED IN--
QUICK-SAND!
PULLING ME DOWN-- LIKE SOME STARVING ANIMAL!
WALL-CRAWLER-- IT LOOKS LIKE YOU'VE HAD IT!
THE BEAUTY AND THE BRUTE

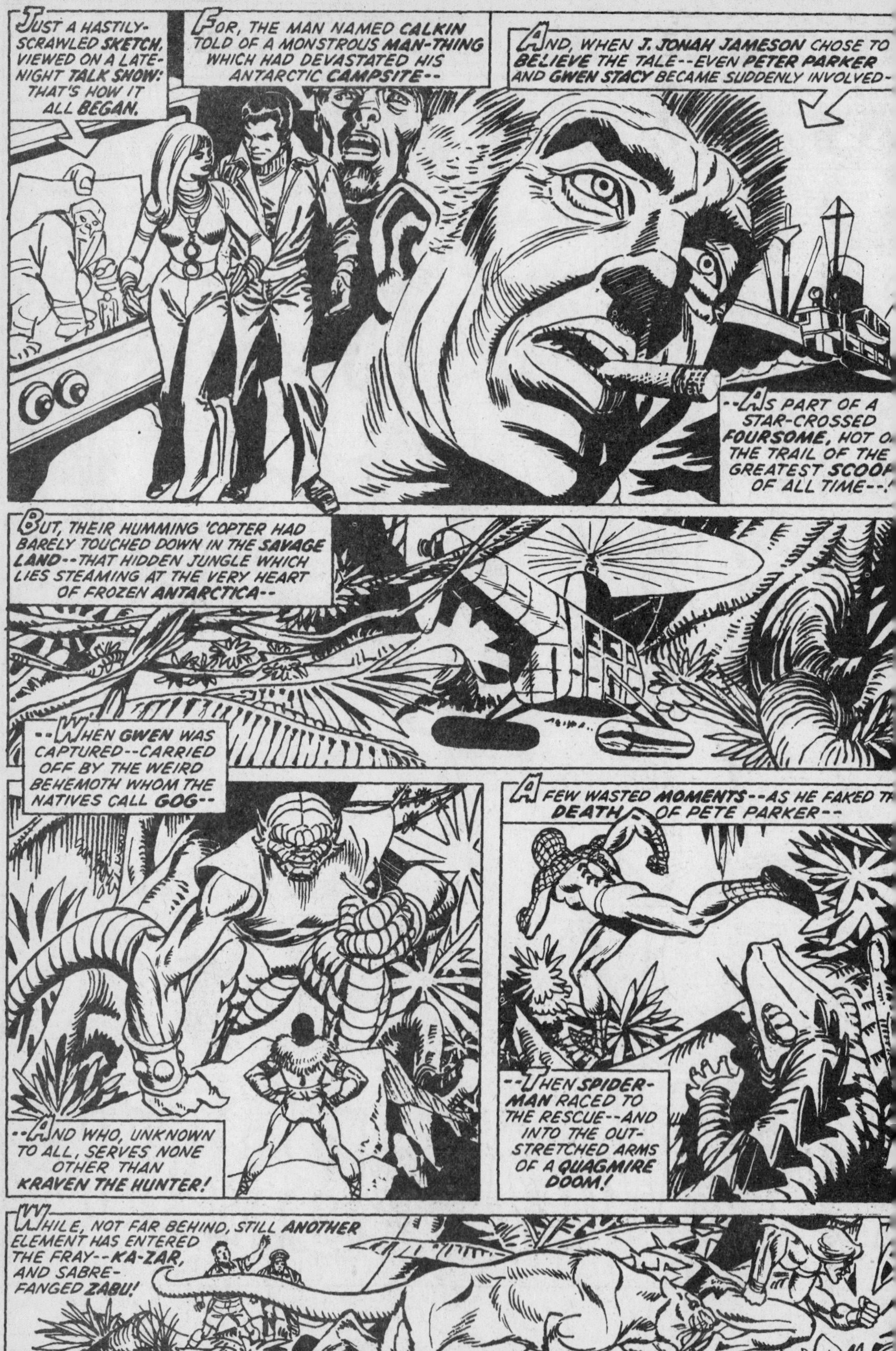
JUST A HASTILY-SCRAWLED SKETCH, VIEWED ON A LATE-NIGHT TALK SHOW: THAT'S HOW IT ALL BEGAN.
FOR, THE MAN NAMED CALKIN TOLD OF A MONSTROUS MAN-THING WHICH HAD DEVASTATED HIS ANTARCTIC CAMPSITE--
AND, WHEN J. JONAH JAMESON CHOSE TO BELIEVE THE TALE--EVEN PETER PARKER AND GWEN STACY BECAME SUDDENLY INVOLVED--
--AS PART OF A STAR-CROSSED FOURSOME, HOT O THE TRAIL OF THE GREATEST SCOOP OF ALL TIME--!
BUT, THEIR HUMMING 'COPTER HAD BARELY TOUCHED DOWN IN THE SAVAGE LAND--THAT HIDDEN JUNGLE WHICH LIES STEAMING AT THE VERY HEART OF FROZEN ANTARCTICA--
--WHEN GWEN WAS CAPTURED--CARRIED OFF BY THE WEIRD BEHEMOTH WHOM THE NATIVES CALL GOG--
--AND WHO, UNKNOWN TO ALL, SERVES NONE OTHER THAN KRAVEN THE HUNTER!
A FEW WASTED MOMENTS--AS HE FAKED TH DEATH OF PETE PARKER--
--THEN SPIDER-MAN RACED TO THE RESCUE--AND INTO THE OUT-STRETCHED ARMS OF A QUAGMIRE DOOM!
WHILE, NOT FAR BEHIND, STILL ANOTHER ELEMENT HAS ENTERED THE FRAY--KA-ZAR, AND SABRE-FANGED ZABU!

TWO SPRAWLING **FORMS**--TUMBLING HEADLONG OVER **ROCKS** AND JAGGED **BOULDERS**--

MOST ANY MEN WOULD SUFFER **GRIEVOUS WOUNDS** --SPLINTERED **BONES**--AMID SUCH VIOLENT **ACTION**--

BUT **ONE** OF THESE TWAIN IS **KRAVEN**, CALLED THE **HUNTER**--

--**A**ND THE OTHER ONE IS--**KA-ZAR!**

B K K K!

MMMFF!--

YOU ARE--MY PHYSICAL **EQUAL**, JUNGLE MAN--

--PERHAPS EVEN-- IN SOME CRUDE WAY--MY **SUPERIOR**.

BUT STILL-- I AM **KRAVEN**--

AND, WHOM **KRAVEN** CANNOT **DEFEAT** ONE WAY--

--HE SHALL BEST **ANOTHER!**

SSFFFSSSS

AMAZING! YOU-- STILL **STAND!**

BUT, THAT VAPOR-BLAST WOULD HAVE FELLED A **BULL** ELEPHANT.

--YES--BECAUSE A MERE **BEAST** WOULD NOT HAVE HELD ITS **BREATH**.

BUT KA-ZAR IS **MORE** THAN BEAST-- PERHAPS EVEN MORE THAN **MAN**.

11

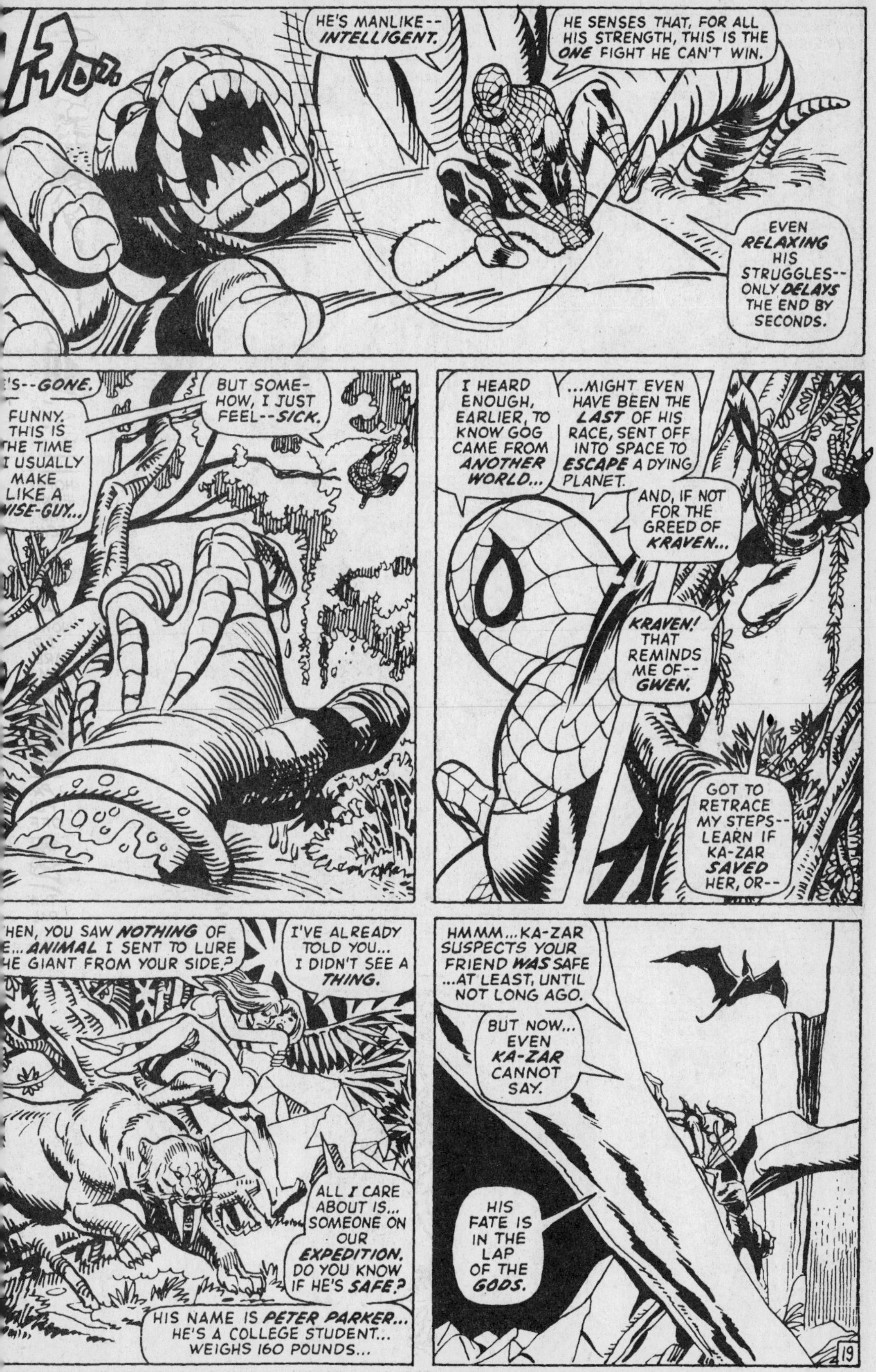

HE'S MANLIKE-- INTELLIGENT.
HE SENSES THAT, FOR ALL HIS STRENGTH, THIS IS THE ONE FIGHT HE CAN'T WIN.
EVEN RELAXING HIS STRUGGLES-- ONLY DELAYS THE END BY SECONDS.
E'S--GONE.
FUNNY. THIS IS THE TIME I USUALLY MAKE LIKE A ISE-GUY...
BUT SOME-HOW, I JUST FEEL--SICK.
I HEARD ENOUGH, EARLIER, TO KNOW GOG CAME FROM ANOTHER WORLD...
...MIGHT EVEN HAVE BEEN THE LAST OF HIS RACE, SENT OFF INTO SPACE TO ESCAPE A DYING PLANET.
AND, IF NOT FOR THE GREED OF KRAVEN...
KRAVEN! THAT REMINDS ME OF--GWEN.
GOT TO RETRACE MY STEPS--LEARN IF KA-ZAR SAVED HER, OR--
HEN, YOU SAW NOTHING OF E...ANIMAL I SENT TO LURE HE GIANT FROM YOUR SIDE?
I'VE ALREADY TOLD YOU... I DIDN'T SEE A THING.
ALL I CARE ABOUT IS... SOMEONE ON OUR EXPEDITION. DO YOU KNOW IF HE'S SAFE?
HIS NAME IS PETER PARKER... HE'S A COLLEGE STUDENT... WEIGHS 160 POUNDS...
HMMM...KA-ZAR SUSPECTS YOUR FRIEND WAS SAFE ...AT LEAST, UNTIL NOT LONG AGO.
BUT NOW... EVEN KA-ZAR CANNOT SAY.
HIS FATE IS IN THE LAP OF THE GODS.
19

PETE...GWEN... BOTH *GONE.* SOMEHOW, I... I STILL CAN'T *BELIEVE* IT.

I'M AFRAID WE'VE BOTH GOT TO FACE THE FACT, JAMESON, THAT WE *DOOMED* THOSE TWO KIDS.

THEY DON'T COME ANY *BETTER...* OR *BRAVER.*

YOU DON'T HAVE TO *REMIND* ME, CALKIN.

WHAT HAVE WE *DONE--* YOU, TO SAVE A REPUTA- TION--ME, TO SAVE A *NEWSPAPER?*

I'D GIVE IT ALL *UP*, JUST TO HEAR GWEN'S VOICE...OR PARKER, HUSTLING ME FOR MORE *MONEY...*

HO, THE CAMP!

THE WAY YOUNG PARKER CHARGED THAT *MONSTER*, WHEN IT GRABBED THE GIRL...

YAHOOO!

IT'S KA-ZAR-- AND HE'S GOT GWEN!

WE SHOULD'V *KNOWN* TH JUNGLE MA WOULDN' LET US DOWN!

A BRIEF, TEARFUL REUNION--THEN--

IT'S SO *WONDERFUL* TO HAVE YOU BACK, GWEN...

KA-ZAR DID IT. I'LL TELL YOU ALL ABOUT IT *LATER.*

BUT... WHERE'S *PETER?*

MR. JAMESON... DIDN'T YOU *HEAR* ME?

I SAID... *WHERE'S PETER??*

I....I GUESS YOU DIDN'T *SEE*, GWEN.

THAT MONSTER *STRUCK* HIM ...KNOCKED HIM OVER A CLIFF, INTO THE *RIVER*, AND.

...AND... WE LOST HIM.

THE MEMORY OF *CARL DENHAM*, ENTREPRENEUR, THIS TWO-PART STORY IS AFFECTIONATELY DEDICATED. --ROY T.

SPIDER-MAN
MARVEL COMICS GROUP
20¢
105
FEB
02457
the AMAZING SPIDER-MAN
APPROVED BY THE COMICS CODE AUTHORITY
THE SPIDER SLAYER!

THE AMAZING SPIDER-MAN! TM
THE SPIDER SLAYER!
WOW! IT FEELS GREAT TO BE BACK IN THE CITY AT LAST.
NOT THAT I DIDN'T DIG THE JUNGLE-- BUT ENOUGH'S ENOUGH.*
NOW THE OL' WEB-SPINNER CAN START DOIN' HIS THING AROUND TOWN.
*IF YOU MISSED LAST ISH, FEATURING SPIDEY AND KA-ZAR, THAT'LL TEACH YA! --UNFORGIVING STAN
STORY BY STAN (WE TOLD YOU HE'D BE BACK!) LEE
PENCILS BY GIL (HE NEVER EVEN LEFT!) KANE
INKS BY FRANK (WE CAN'T GET RID OF 'IM!) GIACOIA
LETTERING BY ARTIE (HE'S REALLY GONE!) SIMEK
EAT

SAY IT FAST! SAY IT SLOW! THE BUGLE'S GOTTA GO!

THE BUGLE DOESN'T CARE ABOUT THE COMMON MAN!

THE BUGLE'S UNFAIR TO MINORITY GROUPS!

OPLE ARE HUNGRY--JOBLESS-- 'GRY--AND WHAT DOES THE BUGLE DO A SERIES ABOUT--?

HE ADVENTURES F KA-ZAR AND OME COSTUMED WEIRDO!

HEY, MAN--LOOK WHO'S HERE.

MY FATHER! I FIGURED HE'D SHOW.

THE BUGLE'S GOTTA GET WITH IT!

JAMESON'S GOT POWER-- HE HAS TO USE IT-- FOR THE PEOPLE!

I'M CITY EDITOR, RANDY! WHY NOT TALK TO ME?

FACE IT, PA--YOU WORK FOR THE MAN.

N'T GIVE ME THAT 'E, SON! YOU KNOW HERE MY HEAD'S AT.

NYWAY, O SAYS 'M NOT 'TH YOU?

NKS, --I 'LL.

DO WHAT YOU WANNA DO, RANDY-- LONG AS YOU BELIEVE IN IT.

BOY! AFTER THEY MADE JOE ROBERTSON, THEY THREW AWAY THE MOLD.

I'VE GOTTA GET TO WORK NOW, SON.

THE ESTABLISH- MENT NEEDS ALL THE HELP IT CAN GET.

DO WHAT YOU MUST, BUT DON'T LOSE YOUR COOL, HEAR?

3

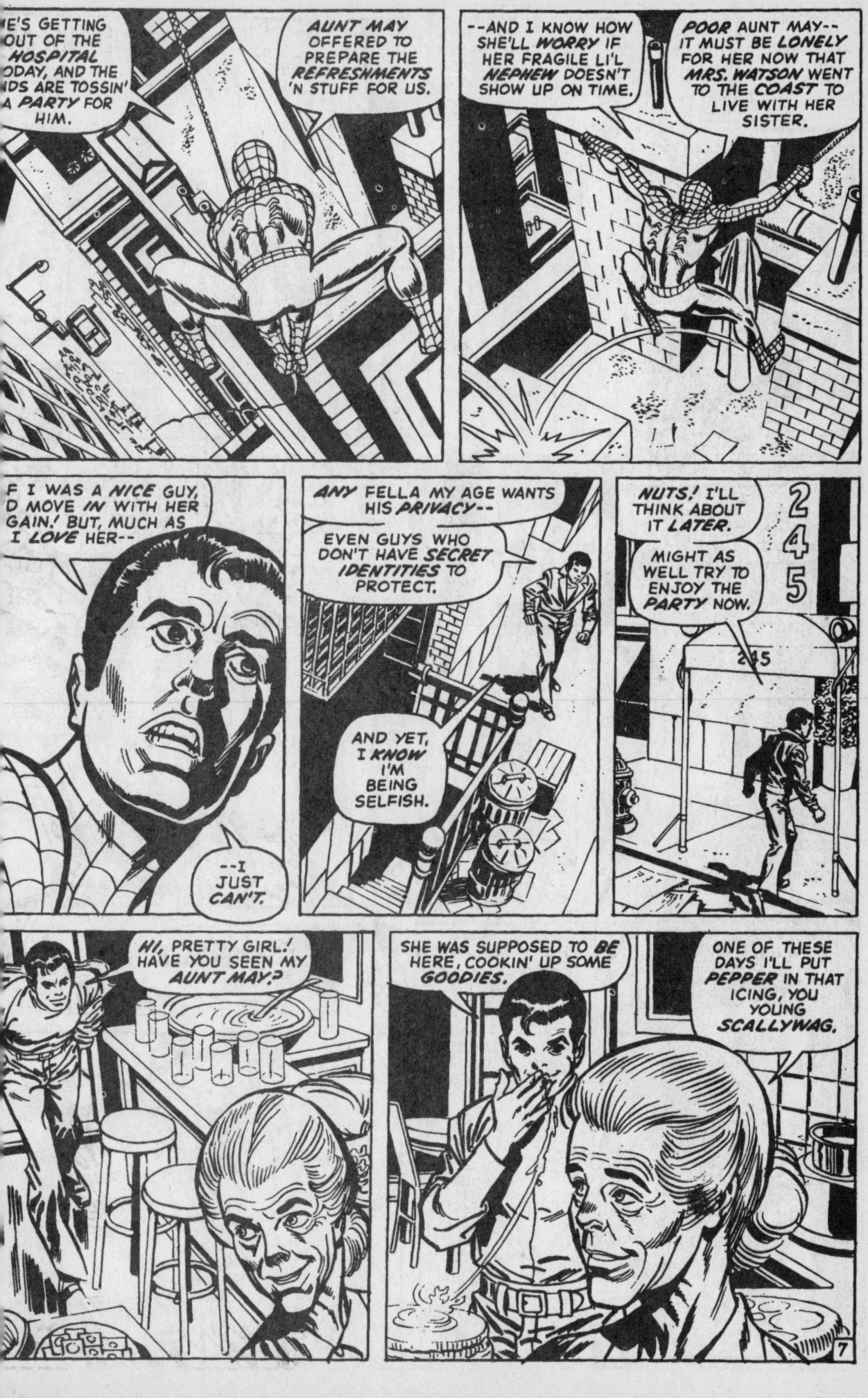
E'S GETTING OUT OF THE HOSPITAL ODAY, AND THE IDS ARE TOSSIN' A PARTY FOR HIM.
AUNT MAY OFFERED TO PREPARE THE REFRESHMENTS 'N STUFF FOR US.
--AND I KNOW HOW SHE'LL WORRY IF HER FRAGILE LI'L NEPHEW DOESN'T SHOW UP ON TIME.
POOR AUNT MAY-- IT MUST BE LONELY FOR HER NOW THAT MRS. WATSON WENT TO THE COAST TO LIVE WITH HER SISTER.
F I WAS A NICE GUY, D MOVE IN WITH HER GAIN! BUT, MUCH AS I LOVE HER--
--I JUST CAN'T.
ANY FELLA MY AGE WANTS HIS PRIVACY--
EVEN GUYS WHO DON'T HAVE SECRET IDENTITIES TO PROTECT.
AND YET, I KNOW I'M BEING SELFISH.
NUTS! I'LL THINK ABOUT IT LATER.
MIGHT AS WELL TRY TO ENJOY THE PARTY NOW.
245
245
HI, PRETTY GIRL! HAVE YOU SEEN MY AUNT MAY?
SHE WAS SUPPOSED TO BE HERE, COOKIN' UP SOME GOODIES.
ONE OF THESE DAYS I'LL PUT PEPPER IN THAT ICING, YOU YOUNG SCALLYWAG.
7

PETER--RE YOU--?

IT'S FOR *YOU*, SON. IT'S A *SURPRISE PARTY.*

OH! THERE-- HERE'S A WHOLE *CROWD* HERE.

WELCOME HOME, ROOMMATE! IT'S *YOUR* TURN TO TAKE OUT THE GARBAGE.

WE *MISSED* YOU, PUSSYCAT--IN CASE YOU HAVEN'T GUESSED.

GOSH, I--I DON'T KNOW WHAT TO *SAY...*

YOU *DON'T?* THEN HOW ABOUT BREATHING ON *JONAH JAMESON?*

MAYBE IT'LL BE *CONTAGIOUS.*

ND LOOK WHO'S *ALSO* BACK-- *ASH THOMPSON!*

IT'S ALL TOO *GOOD* TO BE TRUE.

SOMETHING'S WRONG! I CAN *SENSE* IT.

HARRY'S ON THE ROAD TO RECOVERY. BUT *FLASH*--THERE'S SOMETHING *ABOUT* HIM--SOMETHING *OMINOUS!*

UT, PETE HAS AN EVEN EADLIER PROBLEM--'THOUGH T DOESN'T YET *SUSPECT* IT! T'S FIND OUT BEFORE *HE* DOES--

S *LATE* AND IT'S *ARK.*

NO ONE'S APT TO *SEE* ME HERE.

COME *IN*, JAMESON! EVERY- THING'S *READY.*

IT *SHOULD* BE! I *PAID* YOU ENOUGH.

I'M INTERESTED IN *MORE* THAN MONEY.

IMPOSSIBLE! NOBODY *CAN.*

WHAT ABOUT THE *ROBOT?*

I HATE *SPIDER-MAN* AS MUCH AS *YOU* DO.

IT'S RIGHT *BEHIND* YOU! *LOOK--*

9

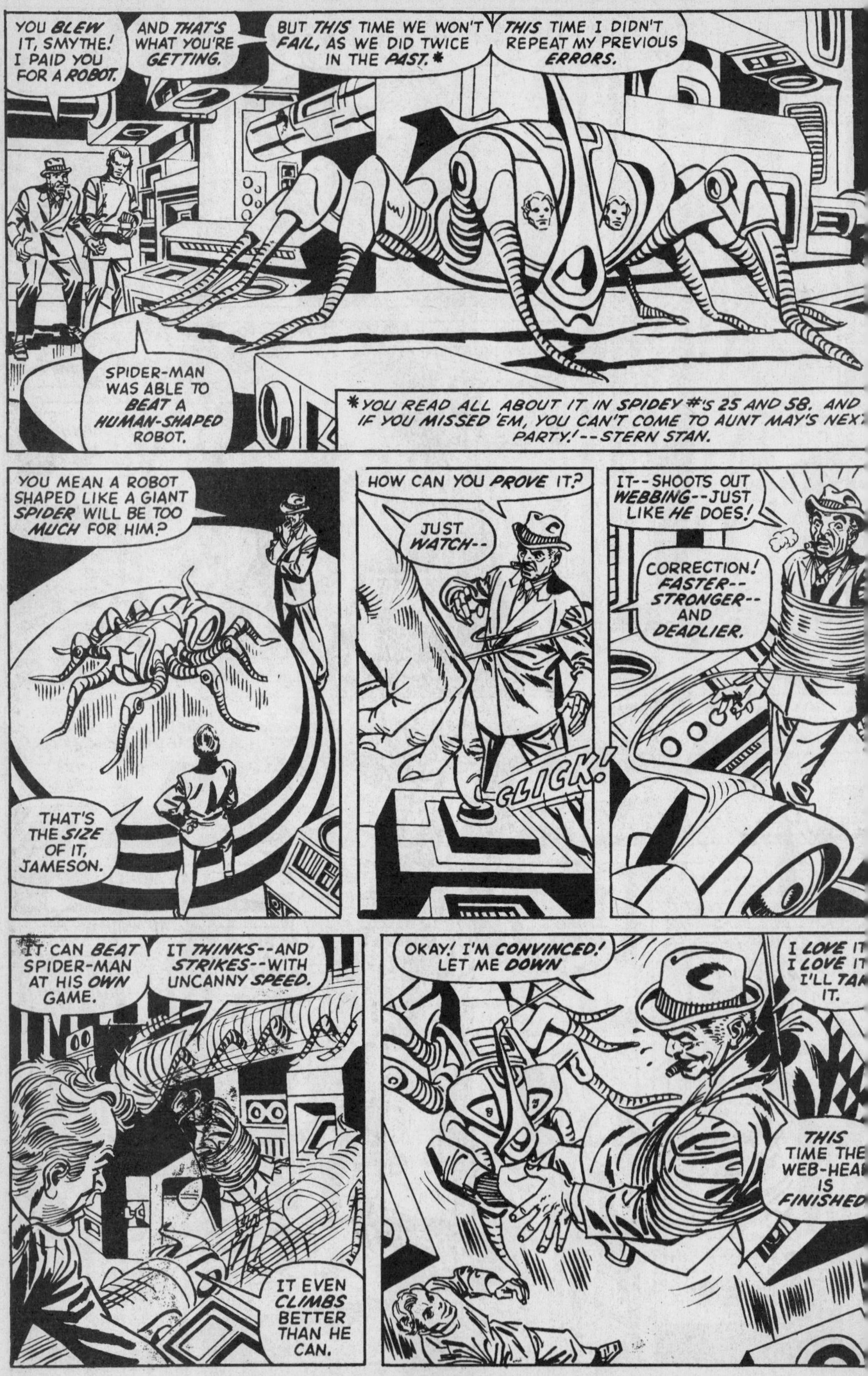

YOU BLEW IT, SMYTHE! I PAID YOU FOR A ROBOT.
AND THAT'S WHAT YOU'RE GETTING.
BUT THIS TIME WE WON'T FAIL, AS WE DID TWICE IN THE PAST.*
THIS TIME I DIDN'T REPEAT MY PREVIOUS ERRORS.
SPIDER-MAN WAS ABLE TO BEAT A HUMAN-SHAPED ROBOT.
*YOU READ ALL ABOUT IT IN SPIDEY #'S 25 AND 58. AND IF YOU MISSED 'EM, YOU CAN'T COME TO AUNT MAY'S NEXT PARTY! --STERN STAN.
YOU MEAN A ROBOT SHAPED LIKE A GIANT SPIDER WILL BE TOO MUCH FOR HIM?
THAT'S THE SIZE OF IT, JAMESON.
HOW CAN YOU PROVE IT?
JUST WATCH--
CLICK!
IT--SHOOTS OUT WEBBING--JUST LIKE HE DOES!
CORRECTION! FASTER--STRONGER--AND DEADLIER.
IT CAN BEAT SPIDER-MAN AT HIS OWN GAME.
IT THINKS--AND STRIKES--WITH UNCANNY SPEED.
IT EVEN CLIMBS BETTER THAN HE CAN.
OKAY! I'M CONVINCED! LET ME DOWN
I LOVE IT I LOVE IT I'LL TA IT.
THIS TIME THE WEB-HEA IS FINISHED

KAY! WE'VE SET THE SCENE AND FINISHED THE TROS. NOW, WHAT SAY WE GET TO THE ACTION? 'S THE NEXT DAY, AND JOLLY JONAH JUST CAN'T AIT TO PLAY WITH HIS STRANGE NEW TOY--

MYTHE WAS A *FOOL* RENT ME THIS OBOT SO *CHEAP.*

HAVE PAID ICE WHAT HE KED ME FOR --BUT I'M NOT ELLING *HIM.*

ANYWAY, IT'S START-ING TO GET *DARK* NOW, SO Y'D BETTER KEEP MY *EYES* OPEN...

IF THAT WALL-CRAWLING WEASEL'S ON THE *PROWL* TONIGHT, THE SPIDER-SLAYER WILL *FIND* HIM.

S GOT ENOUGH BUILT-IN ELECTRONIC IRCUITRY TO ANDLE A *DOZEN* RUMMY MASKED MISFITS.

AT LEAST, THAT'S WHAT *SMYTHE* TOLD ME.

AND, SINCE HE'S THE ONE WHO *BUILT* IT, I GUESS HE OUGHTTA *KNOW.*

WOW! I'M IN LUCK-- HE'S SPOTTED HIM *ALREADY.*

TH-WIPP!

E'S EVEN GOT SOME KIND OF BUILT-IN LLIFIER--SO THAT HE WEB-HEAD WON'T KNOW HE'S BEING *FOLLOWED.*

GOTTA HAND IT TO SMYTHE. HE THINKS OF *EVERYTHING.*

I'LL FIX IT SO I CAPTURE HIM *ALIVE.*

SO I CAN ENJOY LAUGHING IN HIS *FACE* WHEN THE POLICE *UNMASK* HIM.

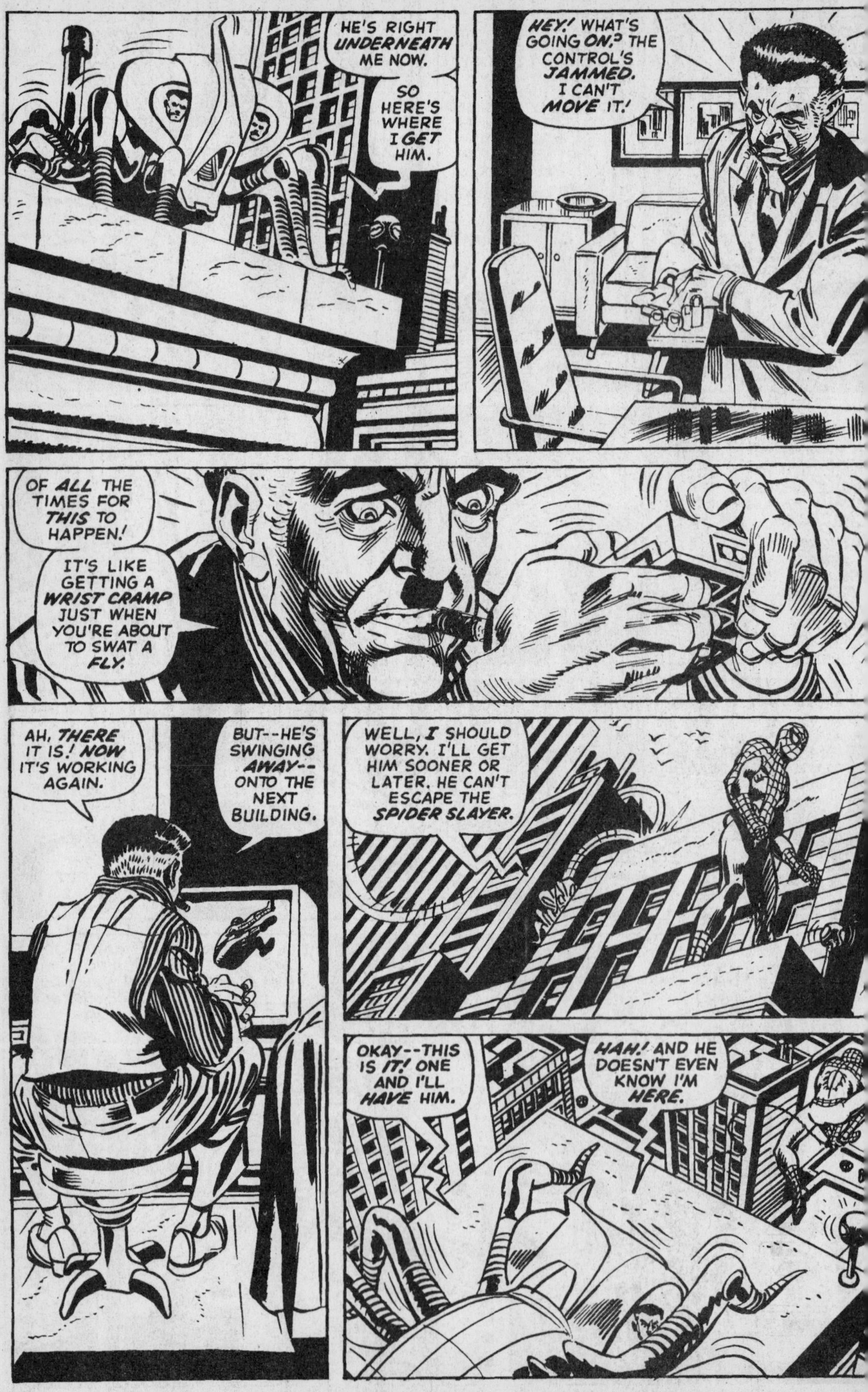
HE'S RIGHT UNDERNEATH ME NOW.
SO HERE'S WHERE I GET HIM.
HEY! WHAT'S GOING ON? THE CONTROL'S JAMMED. I CAN'T MOVE IT!
OF ALL THE TIMES FOR THIS TO HAPPEN!
IT'S LIKE GETTING A WRIST CRAMP JUST WHEN YOU'RE ABOUT TO SWAT A FLY.
AH, THERE IT IS! NOW IT'S WORKING AGAIN.
BUT--HE'S SWINGING AWAY--ONTO THE NEXT BUILDING.
WELL, I SHOULD WORRY. I'LL GET HIM SOONER OR LATER. HE CAN'T ESCAPE THE SPIDER SLAYER.
OKAY--THIS IS IT! ONE AND I'LL HAVE HIM.
HAH! AND HE DOESN'T EVEN KNOW I'M HERE.

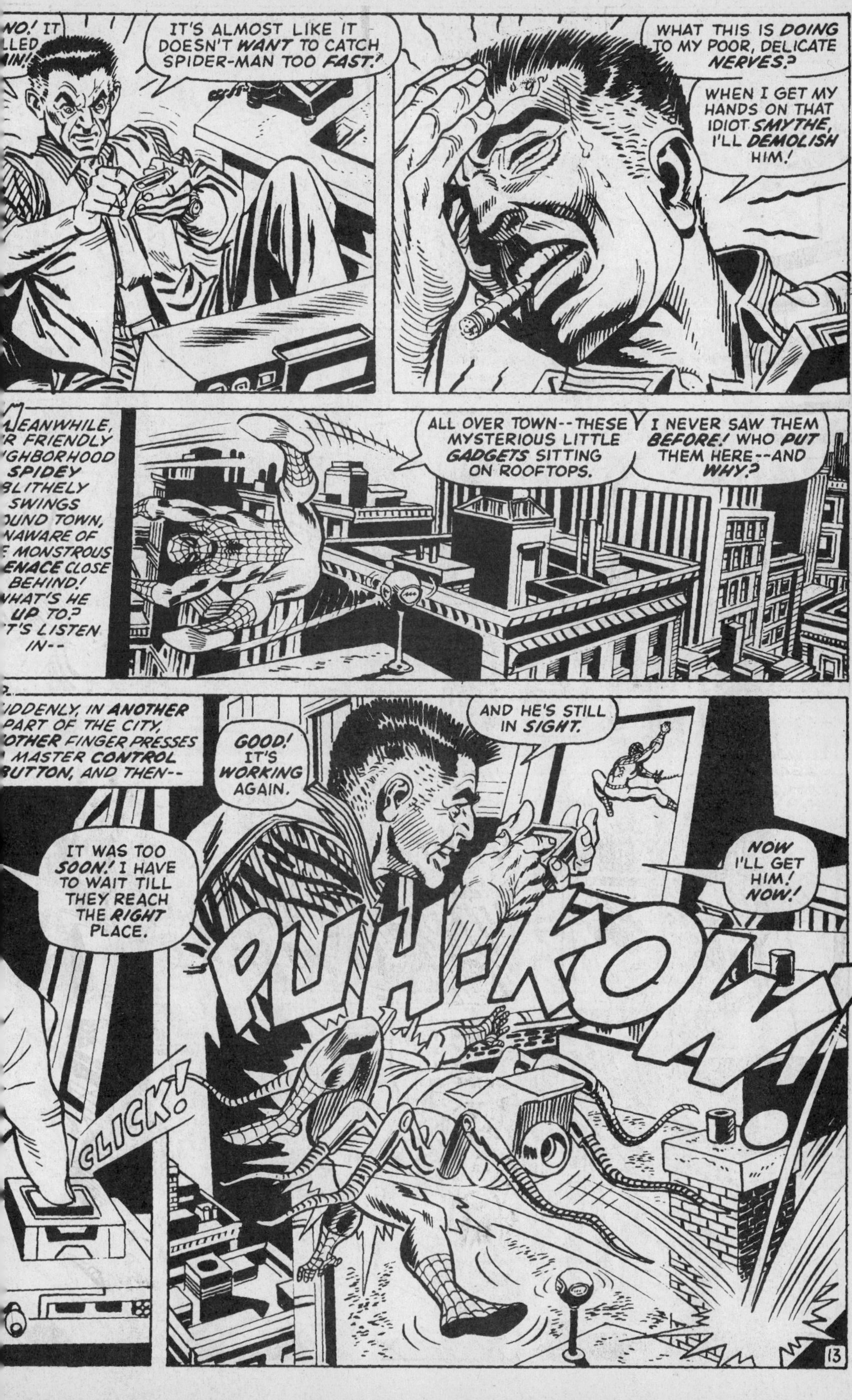

NO! IT
LLED
IN!
IT'S ALMOST LIKE IT DOESN'T WANT TO CATCH SPIDER-MAN TOO FAST!
WHAT THIS IS DOING TO MY POOR, DELICATE NERVES?
WHEN I GET MY HANDS ON THAT IDIOT SMYTHE, I'LL DEMOLISH HIM!
EANWHILE, R FRIENDLY IGHBORHOOD SPIDEY BLITHELY SWINGS OUND TOWN, NAWARE OF E MONSTROUS ENACE CLOSE BEHIND! HAT'S HE UP TO? T'S LISTEN IN--
ALL OVER TOWN--THESE MYSTERIOUS LITTLE GADGETS SITTING ON ROOFTOPS.
I NEVER SAW THEM BEFORE! WHO PUT THEM HERE--AND WHY?
UDDENLY, IN ANOTHER PART OF THE CITY, OTHER FINGER PRESSES MASTER CONTROL BUTTON, AND THEN--
GOOD! IT'S WORKING AGAIN.
AND HE'S STILL IN SIGHT.
IT WAS TOO SOON! I HAVE TO WAIT TILL THEY REACH THE RIGHT PLACE.
NOW I'LL GET HIM! NOW!
PUH-KOW
CLICK!

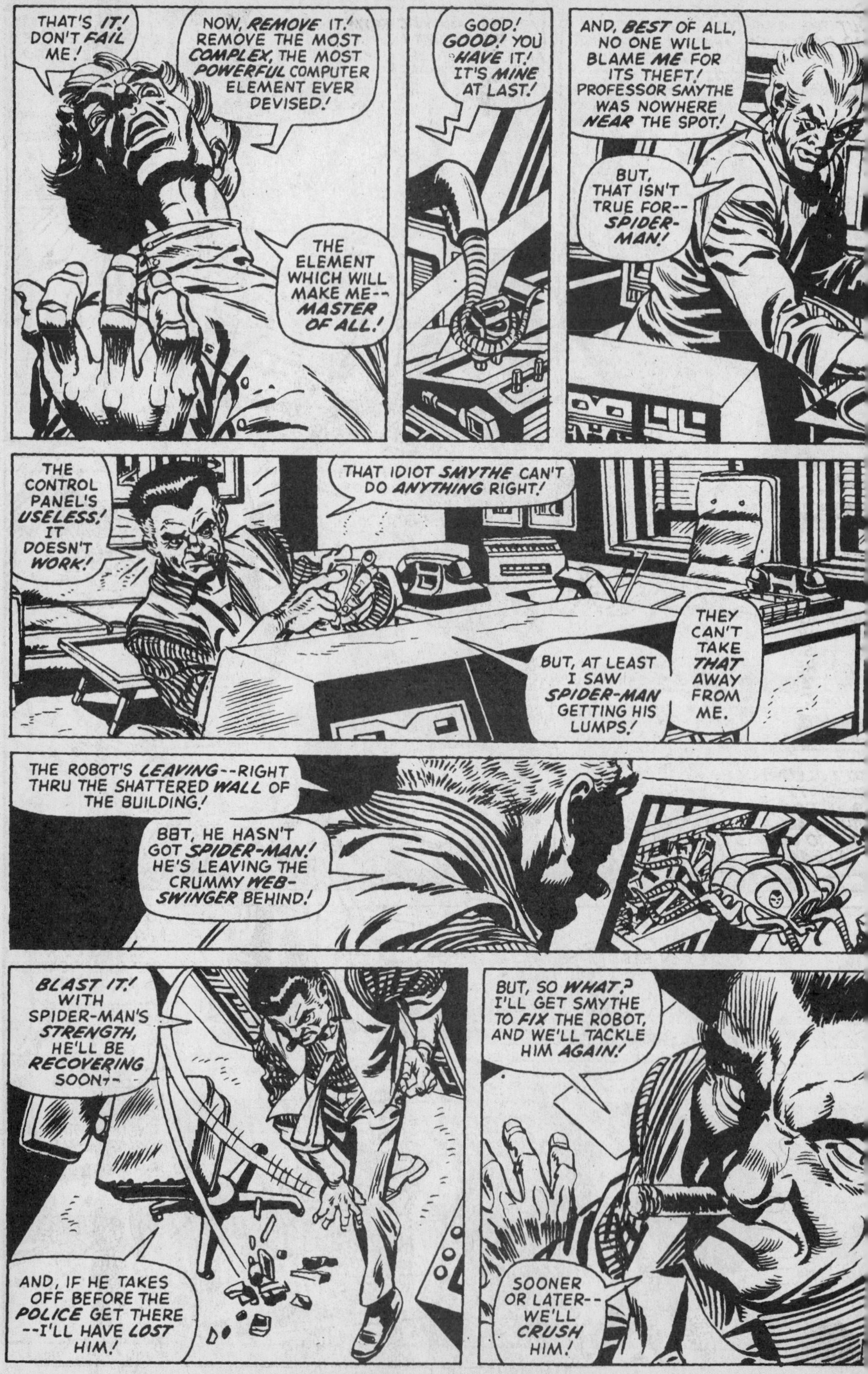
THAT'S IT! DON'T FAIL ME!
NOW, REMOVE IT! REMOVE THE MOST COMPLEX, THE MOST POWERFUL COMPUTER ELEMENT EVER DEVISED!
THE ELEMENT WHICH WILL MAKE ME-- MASTER OF ALL!
GOOD! GOOD! YOU HAVE IT! IT'S MINE AT LAST!
AND, BEST OF ALL, NO ONE WILL BLAME ME FOR ITS THEFT! PROFESSOR SMYTHE WAS NOWHERE NEAR THE SPOT!
BUT, THAT ISN'T TRUE FOR-- SPIDER-MAN!
THE CONTROL PANEL'S USELESS! IT DOESN'T WORK!
THAT IDIOT SMYTHE CAN'T DO ANYTHING RIGHT!
BUT, AT LEAST I SAW SPIDER-MAN GETTING HIS LUMPS!
THEY CAN'T TAKE THAT AWAY FROM ME.
THE ROBOT'S LEAVING--RIGHT THRU THE SHATTERED WALL OF THE BUILDING!
BBT, HE HASN'T GOT SPIDER-MAN! HE'S LEAVING THE CRUMMY WEB-SWINGER BEHIND!
BLAST IT! WITH SPIDER-MAN'S STRENGTH, HE'LL BE RECOVERING SOON--
AND, IF HE TAKES OFF BEFORE THE POLICE GET THERE --I'LL HAVE LOST HIM!
BUT, SO WHAT? I'LL GET SMYTHE TO FIX THE ROBOT, AND WE'LL TACKLE HIM AGAIN!
SOONER OR LATER-- WE'LL CRUSH HIM!

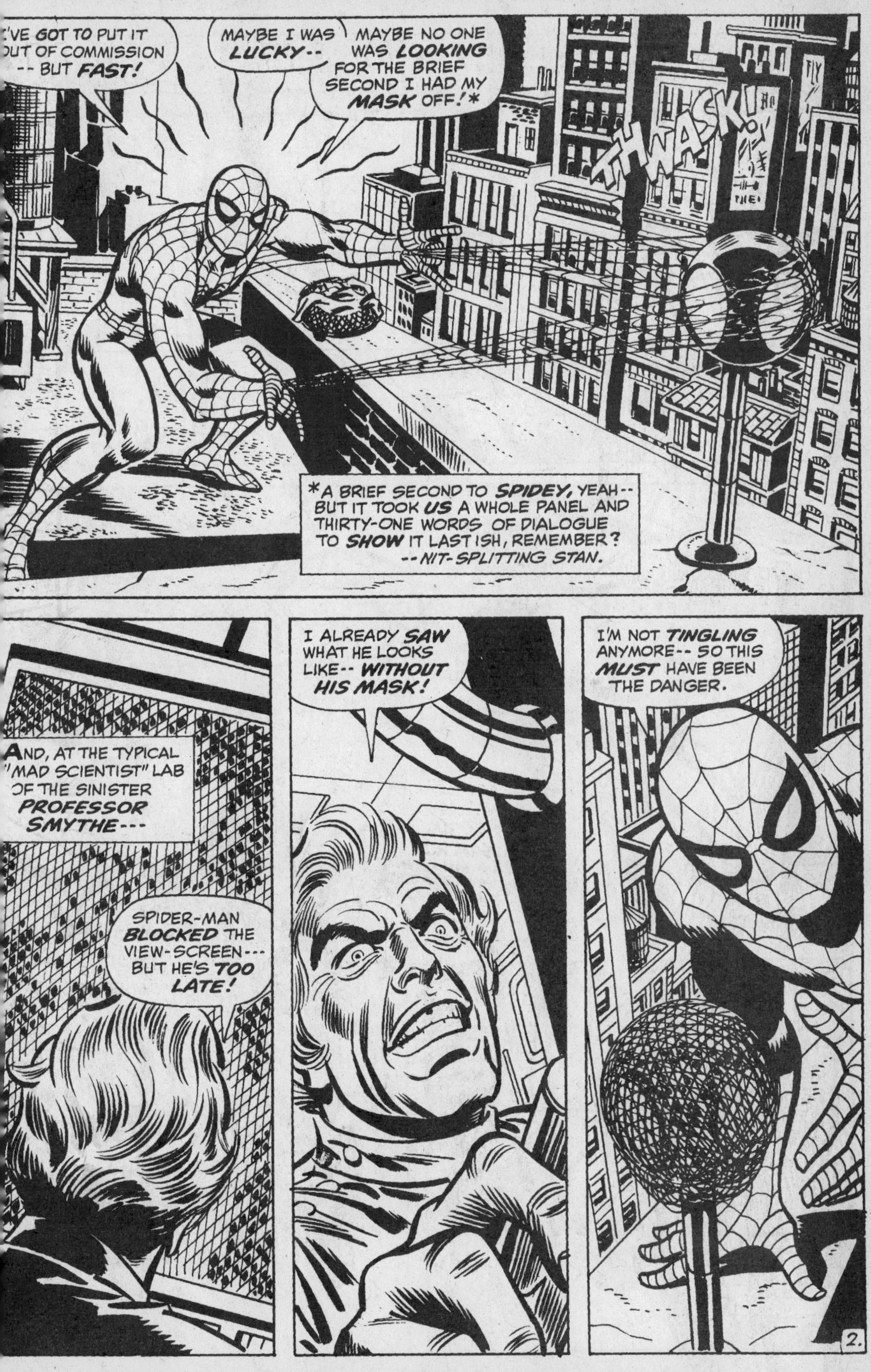
I'VE GOT TO PUT IT OUT OF COMMISSION -- BUT FAST!
MAYBE I WAS LUCKY--
MAYBE NO ONE WAS LOOKING FOR THE BRIEF SECOND I HAD MY MASK OFF!*
THWASK!
*A BRIEF SECOND TO SPIDEY, YEAH-- BUT IT TOOK US A WHOLE PANEL AND THIRTY-ONE WORDS OF DIALOGUE TO SHOW IT LAST ISH, REMEMBER? --NIT-SPLITTING STAN.
AND, AT THE TYPICAL "MAD SCIENTIST" LAB OF THE SINISTER PROFESSOR SMYTHE---
SPIDER-MAN BLOCKED THE VIEW-SCREEN--- BUT HE'S TOO LATE!
I ALREADY SAW WHAT HE LOOKS LIKE-- WITHOUT HIS MASK!
I'M NOT TINGLING ANYMORE-- SO THIS MUST HAVE BEEN THE DANGER.
2.

BUT HOW WILL I **KNOW** WHETHER IT SAW MY **REAL FACE** OR NOT?

NUTS! I OUGHTTA **SMASH** IT INTO THE MIDDLE OF---

HEY! WAIT A MINUTE!

IT SAYS "PROPERTY OF THE N.Y. POLICE DEPT."!

DOES THAT MEAN THE **LAW** BEEN **TRACKING** ME?

I THOUGHT IT WAS **PROFESSOR SMYTHE**---

I FIGURED IT HAD SOMETHING TO DO WITH HIS **ROBOT** ATTACKING ME *

THWIPP

* IT HAPPENED LAST ISH, ALSO, BUT WE DON'T HAVE TO TELL **YOU!** --SMUG STAN

WOW! THERE ARE **OTHER** SCANNERS-- ON ALMOST EVERY ROOFTOP!

CAN'T PUT 'EM **ALL** ON THE BLINK

BUT I CAN'T TAKE **CHANCES!** WHAT IF THEY **DID** SEE MY FACE?

I'VE GOT TO **DO SOME** THING-- **FAST**

MINUTES LATER---

EASY-- EASY-- HAVE TO MAKE A *SOLID* MOLD.

NOW-- JUST A FEW MINUTES AND IT'LL BE *READY.*

IT'LL BE *PERFECT* ONCE I ADD SOME BLACK PAINT FOR THE EYE-BROWS AND HAIR.

THANKS, DOC! YOU WERE A LIFE-SAVER.

I LEFT EVERY-THING JUST LIKE I FOUND IT.

TOO BAD! I WAS HOPING YOU'D *TIDY* THE PLACE UP.

ANYWAY, GLAD I WAS ABLE TO HELP.

IT'S HARD TO BELIEVE THAT HE'S REALLY THE DEADLY *LIZARD.*

OH WELL, THAT'S *ANOTHER* STORY.*

*AND WE HAVEN'T TIME FOR IT NOW -- STAN

NOW, THE *FIRST* THING I'VE GOTTA DO IS UNLOAD MY *THREADS* AGAIN, AND THEN KEEP MY *FINGERS* CROSSED.

BOY! THERE'S NEVER A DULL MOMENT.

AND, SPEAKING OF *DULL MOMENTS,* LET'S VISIT JOLLY OL' *J. JONAH JAMESON*---

BLAST IT! I LOST *CONTROL* OF SMYTHE'S CRUMMY *ROBOT* AGAIN!

WHAT'S GOING O[N] HERE?

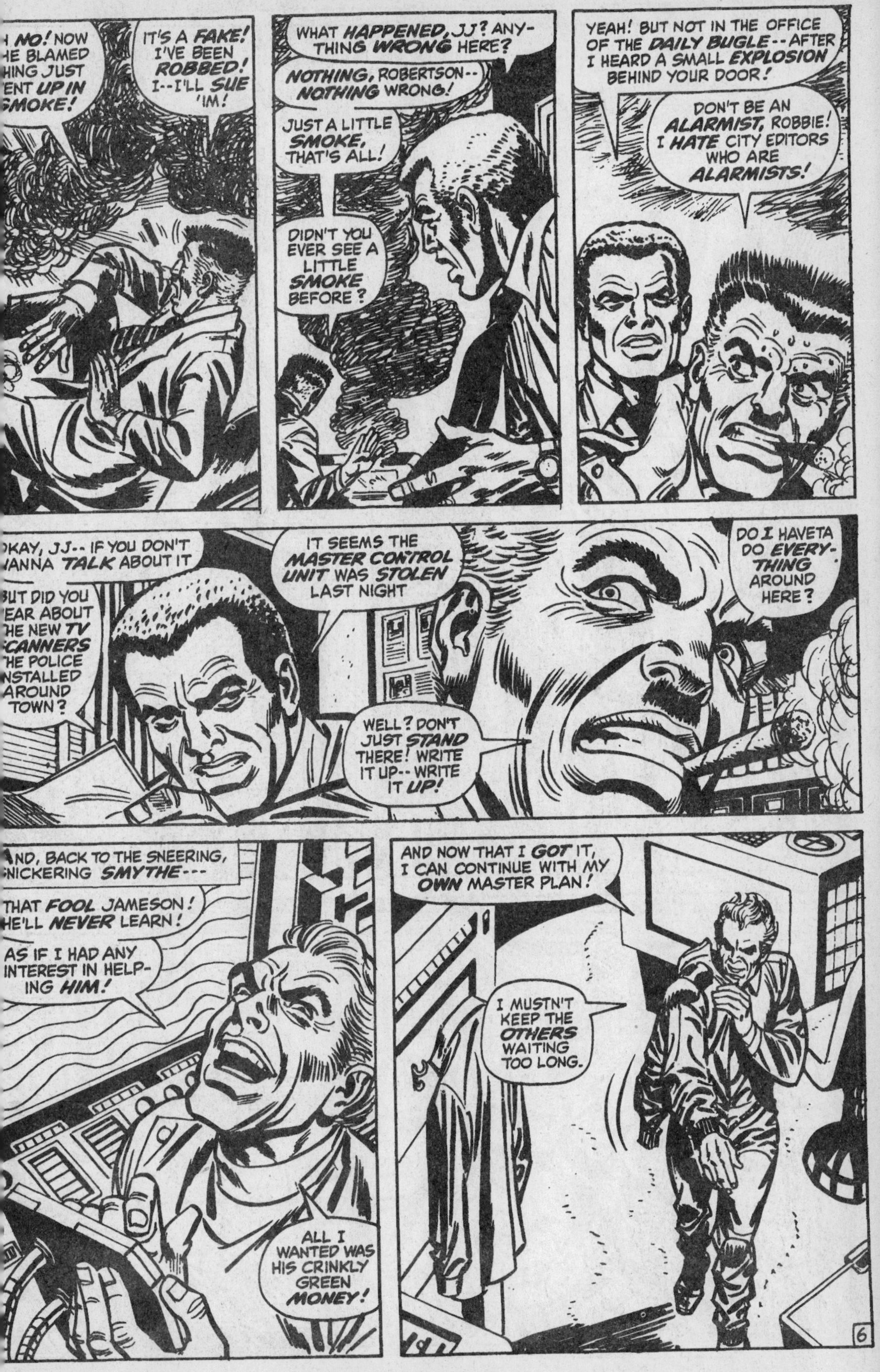

H NO! NOW HE BLAMED HING JUST ENT UP IN SMOKE!
IT'S A FAKE! I'VE BEEN ROBBED! I--I'LL SUE 'IM!
WHAT HAPPENED, JJ? ANY-THING WRONG HERE?
NOTHING, ROBERTSON-- NOTHING WRONG!
JUST A LITTLE SMOKE, THAT'S ALL!
DIDN'T YOU EVER SEE A LITTLE SMOKE BEFORE?
YEAH! BUT NOT IN THE OFFICE OF THE DAILY BUGLE--AFTER I HEARD A SMALL EXPLOSION BEHIND YOUR DOOR!
DON'T BE AN ALARMIST, ROBBIE! I HATE CITY EDITORS WHO ARE ALARMISTS!
OKAY, JJ-- IF YOU DON'T WANNA TALK ABOUT IT
BUT DID YOU EAR ABOUT HE NEW TV SCANNERS THE POLICE NSTALLED AROUND TOWN?
IT SEEMS THE MASTER CONTROL UNIT WAS STOLEN LAST NIGHT
DO I HAVETA DO EVERY-THING AROUND HERE?
WELL? DON'T JUST STAND THERE! WRITE IT UP-- WRITE IT UP!
AND, BACK TO THE SNEERING, SNICKERING SMYTHE---
THAT FOOL JAMESON! HE'LL NEVER LEARN!
AS IF I HAD ANY INTEREST IN HELP-ING HIM!
ALL I WANTED WAS HIS CRINKLY GREEN MONEY!
AND NOW THAT I GOT IT, I CAN CONTINUE WITH MY OWN MASTER PLAN!
I MUSTN'T KEEP THE OTHERS WAITING TOO LONG.
6

DON'T YOU *GET* IT? THIS IS THE *SCANNER SYSTEM* I DESIGNED FOR THE *POLICE DEPARTMENT*--- SO THEY COULD *OBSERVE* EVERYTHING THAT HAPPENS IN THE CITY!

LOOK! AT THE TWIST OF A DIAL WE CAN PICK UP THE ROUTE OF AN *ARMORED CAR* --- WE CAN SEE WHERE THE *COPS* ARE ON GUARD-- AND WHERE THEY'RE *NOT*.

SUPPOSE WE PLAN A *BANK ROBBERY?* BY WATCHING THE *SCANNER*, I CAN RADIO YOUR MEN WHICH *STREETS* TO TAKE IN MAKING THEIR *GETAWAY!*

IN *OTHER* WORDS-- YOU'LL ALWAYS BE A JUMP *AHEAD* OF THE *POLICE!* THEY'LL *NEVER* CATCH YOU!

HEY! IT'S BEGINNIN' TO SOUND *GOOD!*

[B]UT IF YOU DESIGNED THIS FOR [T]HE *FUZZ*-- HOW COME *YOU* GOT CONTROL?

EASY! USING MY *ROBOT*, I MANAGED TO STEAL THE VITAL *MASTER CONTROL UNIT!* THAT MAKES *ME* THE ONLY ONE WHO CAN *OPERATE* IT!

HUH? *WHAT* ROBOT?

WE'LL COME TO *THAT* LATER!

FIRST, LET ME SHOW YOU HOW *NOTHING* CAN ESCAPE ME WHILE I CONTROL MY *SCANNERS*--

A SIMPLE TWIST OF THE *DIAL*, AND I LOCATE *SPIDER-MAN* ONCE AGAIN!

HEY! THAT THING'S *DYNAMITE!*

THERE! WE SEE HIM *UN-MASKED!* HOW'S *THAT* FOR--? *WAIT!* WHAT'S HE *DOING?*

WHY IS HE TUGGING AT HIS *FACE?*

8

UNMASKED, MY *FOOT!* IT *WAS* A MASK HE WUZ WEARIN'! HE'S *WAVIN'* IT LIKE HE *KNOWS* WE'RE WATCHIN'!

THAT AIN'T HIS *REAL* FACE! 'N EVEN IF IT *WAS* -- SO WHAT?

HE LOOKS LIKE ANY OF A *MILLION* GUYS! WE *STILL* WOULDN'T KNOW WHO HE IS.

HE MUSTA *KNOWN* YOU WUZ WATCHIN'! HE'S PUTTIN' YA *ON!*

THE WEB-SLING CLEVER! I UN ESTIMATE HIM.

BUT IT DOESN'T *MATTER!* I CAN TRACK HIM DOWN *ANYTIME!*

THE *IMPORTANT* THING IS-- YOU'VE SEEN HOW THE SCANNER *WORKS*

YEAH, BUT I DO LIKE *SPIDER-MAN* KNOWIN ABOUT IT, *TOO.*

HE'S TOO *DANGEROUS!* WE DON'T TALK *BUSINESS* TILL YA PUT 'IM UNDER *WRAPS!*

I *HOPED* YOU'D SAY THAT!

THAT'S WHERE MY NEW *ROBOT* COMES IN!

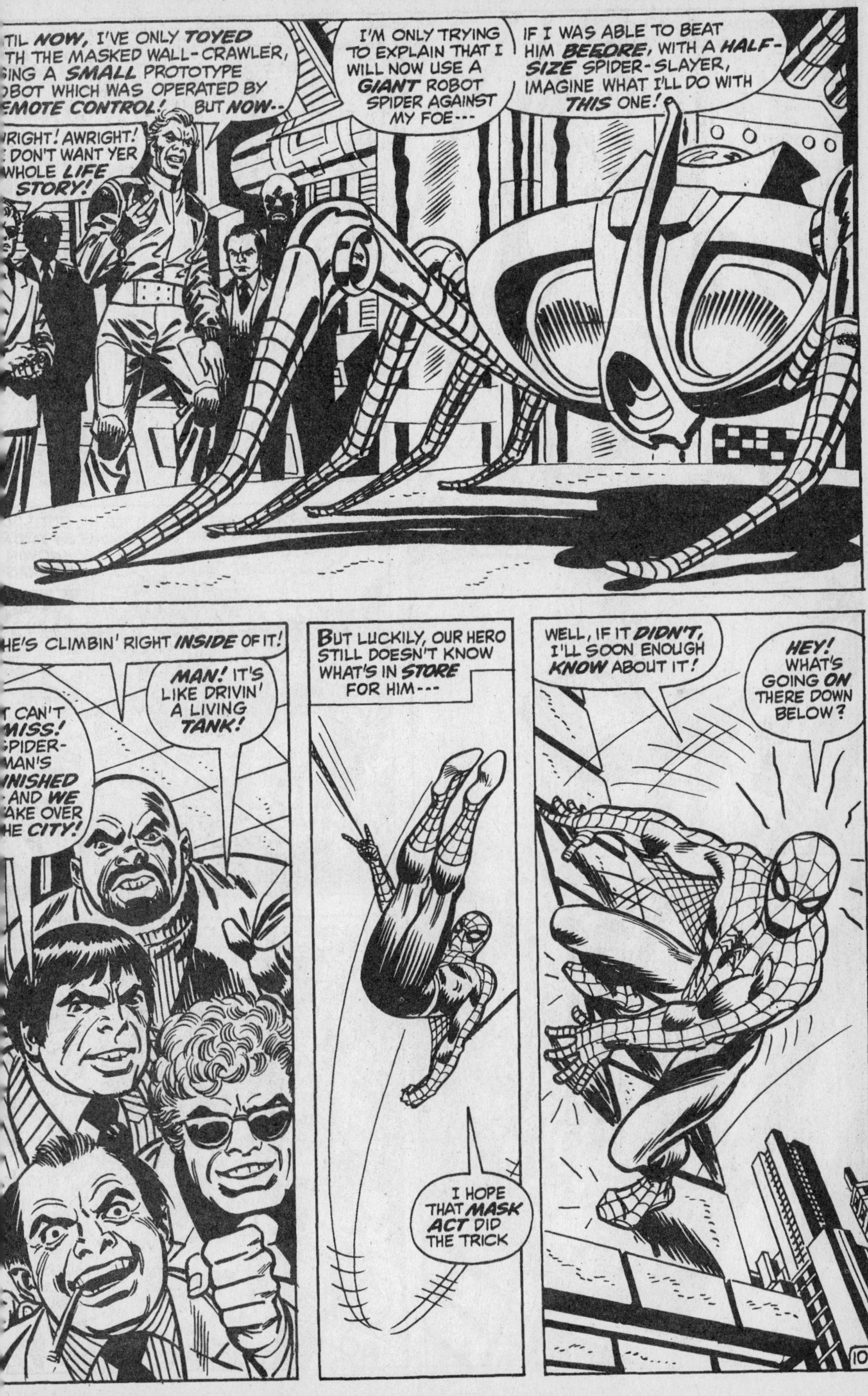

TIL NOW, I'VE ONLY TOYED
TH THE MASKED WALL-CRAWLER,
ING A SMALL PROTOTYPE
OBOT WHICH WAS OPERATED BY
EMOTE CONTROL! BUT NOW..
WRIGHT! AWRIGHT!
DON'T WANT YER
WHOLE LIFE
STORY!
I'M ONLY TRYING TO EXPLAIN THAT I WILL NOW USE A GIANT ROBOT SPIDER AGAINST MY FOE---
IF I WAS ABLE TO BEAT HIM BEEORE, WITH A HALF-SIZE SPIDER-SLAYER, IMAGINE WHAT I'LL DO WITH THIS ONE!
HE'S CLIMBIN' RIGHT INSIDE OF IT!
MAN! IT'S LIKE DRIVIN' A LIVING TANK!
T CAN'T
MISS!
SPIDER-
MAN'S
INISHED
-AND WE
AKE OVER
HE CITY!
BUT LUCKILY, OUR HERO STILL DOESN'T KNOW WHAT'S IN STORE FOR HIM---
I HOPE THAT MASK ACT DID THE TRICK
WELL, IF IT DIDN'T, I'LL SOON ENOUGH KNOW ABOUT IT!
HEY! WHAT'S GOING ON THERE DOWN BELOW?
10

THERE'S ANOTHER *PROTEST RALLY* IN FRONT OF THE *BUGLE!*

I WONDER WHAT *THIS* ONE'S ALL ABOUT?

WELL *WIGGLE MY WEBS* AND CALL ME *SHAKY*-- I CAN'T *BELIEVE* IT!

IT LOOKS LIKE JOLLY JONAH *HIMSELF* IS THE *LEADER* OF THE DEMONSTRATION!

NOW I GET IT! THEY'RE PROTESTING THE *TV SCANNERS* THAT THE POLICE HAVE INSTALLED

SPY 'EYES' COVER CITY

DAILY BUGLE

I GUESS EVEN *JJ* STILL BELIEVES IN *PRIVACY!*

NO SPIES IN THE SKY!

PRIVACY OR ELSE

EYES ON ALL

NO BIG BROTHER

SOUL BROTHER NOT BIG BROTHER

OKAY! WHAT'RE YOU *WAITING* FOR? START *CHANTING*

EY, DAD-- IS THAT FOR *REAL?* OL' AMESON LEADIN' THE PROTESTORS?

OU BETTER *BELIEVE* RANDY! HE'S A UG ON CIVIL IBERTIES

DAIL BUGI

--'LONG AS THEY'RE NOT *SPIDER-MAN'S!*

I GUESS *NO ONE* LIKES BEING SPIED UPON--EVEN IF THE *MOTIVES* ARE GOOD

WOW! I WISH I HAD LOADED MY *CAMERA!*

WHAT A *PICTURE*--- JOE ROBERTSON'S SON, *RANDY*, SIDE-BY-SIDE WITH *J. JONAH* HIMSELF!

MAYBE I OUGHTTA SWING DOWN AND SAY HELLO

PRIVACY OR ELSE!

NO BIG BROTHER

WHAT THE HECK-- I'LL LEND THEM MY *MORAL* SUPPORT

RIGHT ON, GANG! I'M *WITH* YOU ALL THE WAY!

SPIDER-MAN!

STOP HIM! DON'T LET HIM *GET* ME!

STAY WAKE EY ILL!

PRIVAC OR ELSE!

NO BIG BROTHER

JUST SOUL BROTHER

12

13

FIRST, I'VE GOTTA FIND *SMYTHE* AND MAKE SURE HE DOESN'T *TACKLE* ME AGAIN WITH THAT CRUMMY *ROBOT* OF HIS---

MMM--- MY *SPIDEY SENSE* IS QUIET---SO I GUESS NO ONE'S *WATCHING*

AND THAT'S THE WAY I *LIKE* IT

THEY'VE GOT THOSE SCANNERS ON ALMOST *EVERY* ROOFTOP!

I'LL BET IT WAS *SMYTHE* WHO TALKED THEM *INTO* IT

HE'LL FIND *SOME* WAY TO TURN THEM TO HIS *OWN* ADVANTAGE

BUT I BETTER TAKE *OFF* NOW--- WHILE IT'S STILL *SAFE* FOR ME TO GO.

I DON'T WANNA BE LATE FOR MY DATE WITH *GWENDY*

STAIRWAY

OH, *HI* HARRY! DIDN'T THINK YOU'D STILL BE *UP*.

THE *DOC* WANTED YOU TO HAVE LOTS OF *SLEEP*, REMEMBER?

IS-- IS ANYTHING *WRONG?*

NOT *REALLY,* PETE

I *TRIED*, BUT I JUST COULDN'T FALL ASLEEP

I GUESS IT'S THE EXCITEMENT OF BEING BACK FROM THE *HOSPITAL* AND EVERYTHING

ARE YOU *SURE* THAT'S *ALL?*

WELL---

14.

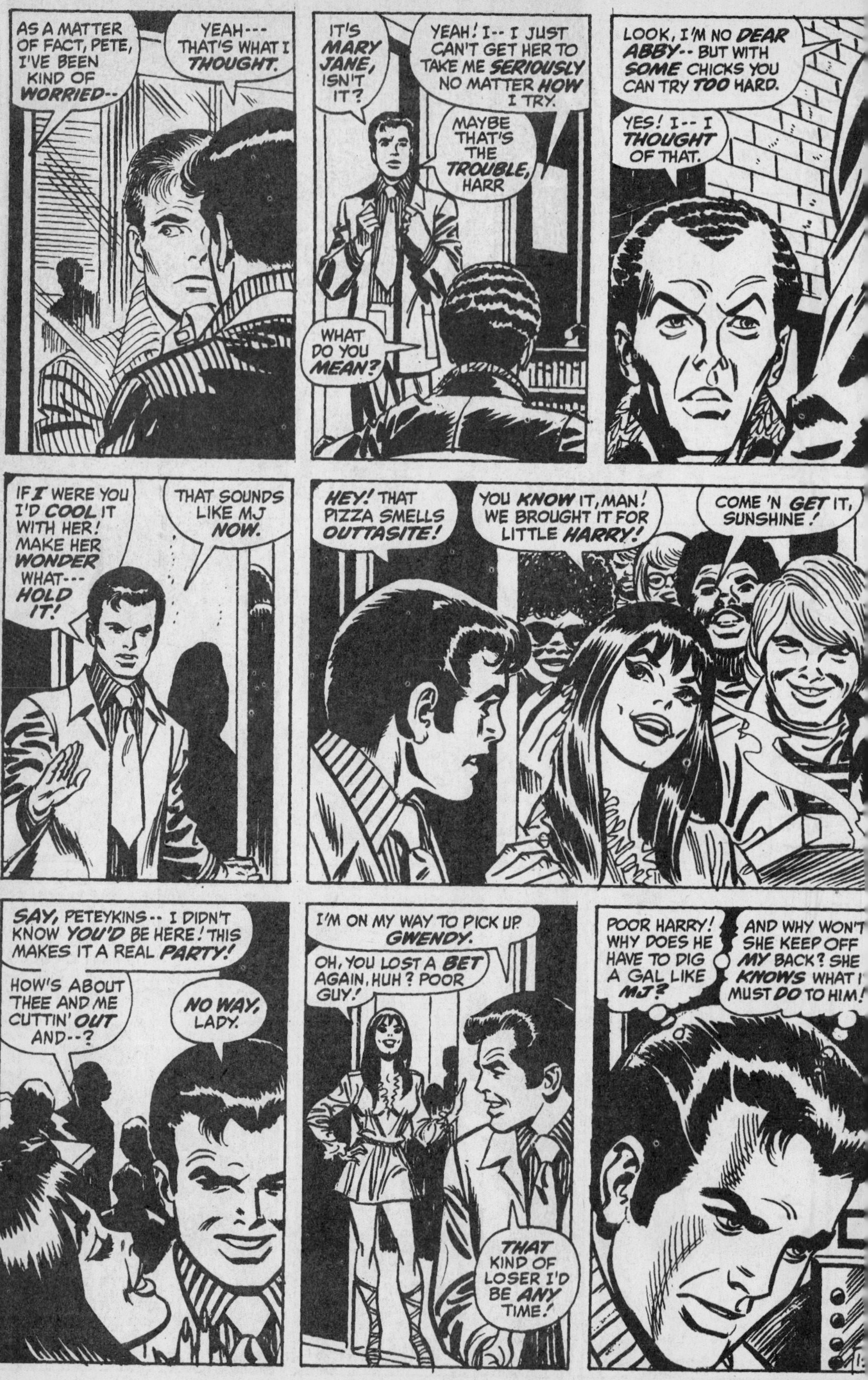

AS A MATTER OF FACT, PETE, I'VE BEEN KIND OF WORRIED--
YEAH--- THAT'S WHAT I THOUGHT.
IT'S MARY JANE, ISN'T IT?
YEAH! I-- I JUST CAN'T GET HER TO TAKE ME SERIOUSLY NO MATTER HOW I TRY.
MAYBE THAT'S THE TROUBLE, HARR
WHAT DO YOU MEAN?
LOOK, I'M NO DEAR ABBY-- BUT WITH SOME CHICKS YOU CAN TRY TOO HARD.
YES! I-- I THOUGHT OF THAT.
IF I WERE YOU I'D COOL IT WITH HER! MAKE HER WONDER WHAT--- HOLD IT!
THAT SOUNDS LIKE MJ NOW.
HEY! THAT PIZZA SMELLS OUTTASITE!
YOU KNOW IT, MAN! WE BROUGHT IT FOR LITTLE HARRY!
COME 'N GET IT, SUNSHINE!
SAY, PETEYKINS-- I DIDN'T KNOW YOU'D BE HERE! THIS MAKES IT A REAL PARTY!
HOW'S ABOUT THEE AND ME CUTTIN' OUT AND--?
NO WAY, LADY.
I'M ON MY WAY TO PICK UP GWENDY.
OH, YOU LOST A BET AGAIN, HUH? POOR GUY!
THAT KIND OF LOSER I'D BE ANY TIME!
POOR HARRY! WHY DOES HE HAVE TO DIG A GAL LIKE MJ?
AND WHY WON'T SHE KEEP OFF MY BACK? SHE KNOWS WHAT I MUST DO TO HIM!

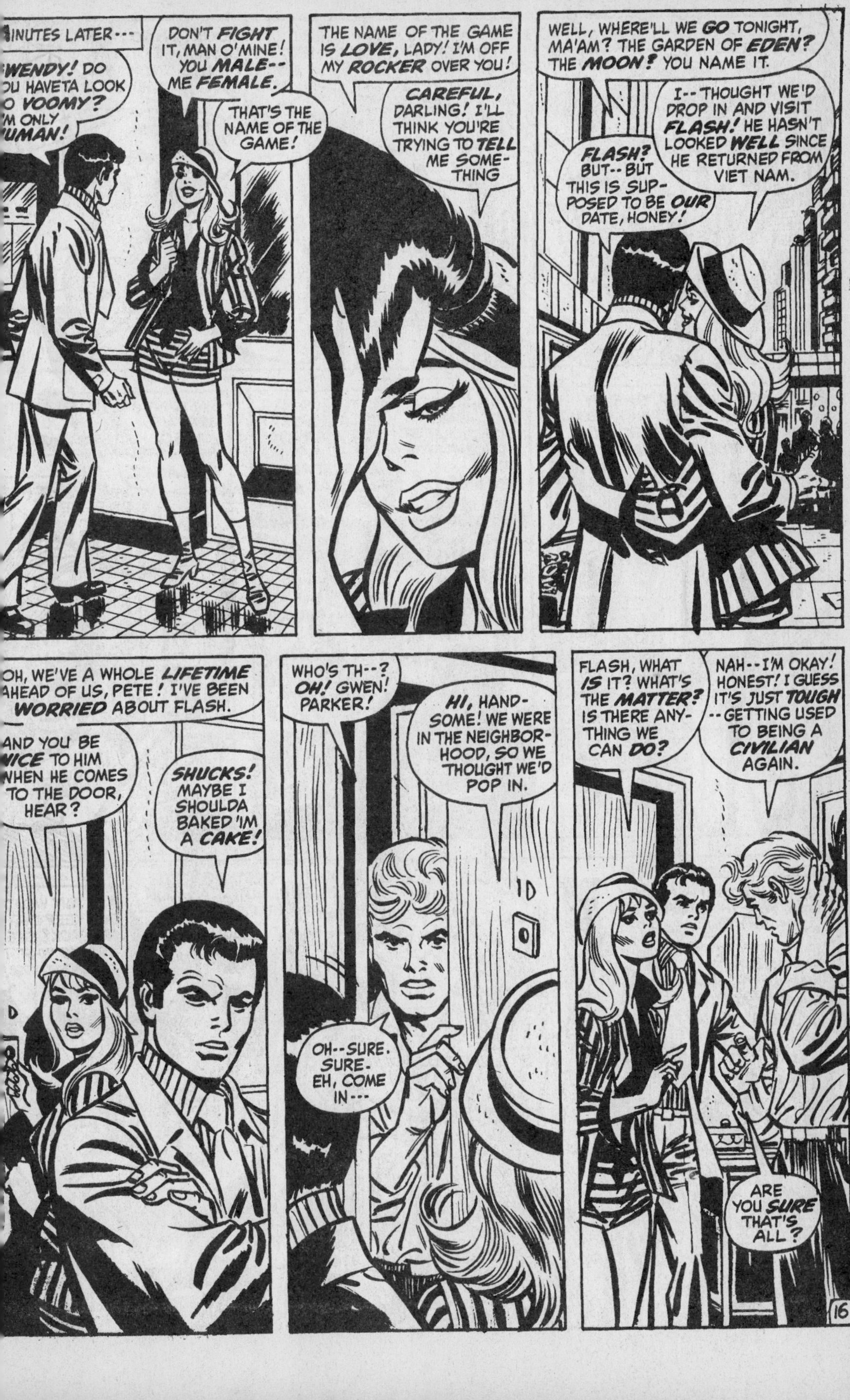

MINUTES LATER---
WENDY! DO YOU HAVETA LOOK SO VOOMY? I'M ONLY HUMAN!
DON'T FIGHT IT, MAN O'MINE! YOU MALE-- ME FEMALE.
THAT'S THE NAME OF THE GAME!
THE NAME OF THE GAME IS LOVE, LADY! I'M OFF MY ROCKER OVER YOU!
CAREFUL, DARLING! I'LL THINK YOU'RE TRYING TO TELL ME SOMETHING
WELL, WHERE'LL WE GO TONIGHT, MA'AM? THE GARDEN OF EDEN? THE MOON? YOU NAME IT.
I--THOUGHT WE'D DROP IN AND VISIT FLASH! HE HASN'T LOOKED WELL SINCE HE RETURNED FROM VIET NAM.
FLASH? BUT--BUT THIS IS SUPPOSED TO BE OUR DATE, HONEY!
OH, WE'VE A WHOLE LIFETIME AHEAD OF US, PETE! I'VE BEEN WORRIED ABOUT FLASH.
AND YOU BE NICE TO HIM WHEN HE COMES TO THE DOOR, HEAR?
SHUCKS! MAYBE I SHOULDA BAKED 'IM A CAKE!
WHO'S TH--? OH! GWEN! PARKER!
HI, HANDSOME! WE WERE IN THE NEIGHBORHOOD, SO WE THOUGHT WE'D POP IN.
1D
OH--SURE. SURE. EH, COME IN---
FLASH, WHAT IS IT? WHAT'S THE MATTER? IS THERE ANYTHING WE CAN DO?
NAH--I'M OKAY! HONEST! I GUESS IT'S JUST TOUGH --GETTING USED TO BEING A CIVILIAN AGAIN.
ARE YOU SURE THAT'S ALL?
16

...EN, AFTER RELUCTANTLY ...LLING IT A NIGHT WITH ...WENDOLYN---

...YBE FLASH ...S STILL ...WAKE

...CAN GET TO ...M FASTER ...--SPIDER-MAN!

THEN I'LL CHANGE *BACK* WHEN I *REACH* HIM!

IF THERE'S ANYTHING *SERIOUSLY* WRONG, HE'S MORE APT TO LEVEL WITH *PETER PARKER* IF GWENDY'S NOT AROUND

GWENDY! BOY, SHE'S THE *GREATEST* THING THAT EVER *HAPPENED* TO ME!

..H OH! ..'S START- ..G TO ..NGLE ..GAIN!

IT'S THE *SCANNER!* SOMEONE'S *WATCHING* ME!

WELL, LET 'IM *WATCH!* IT WON'T TAKE ME LONG TO GET OUT OF *RANGE!*

THWIPP!

OH *NO!* WHAT'S *THAT?*

I'LL JUST SWING AROUND THE *CORNER* AND---

18

THEN, AS THE FUMES FINALLY *CLEAR*--

IT'S--IT'S THE *SPIDER-SLAYER!* BUT *NO!* IT'S FAR *BIGGER*-- FAR MORE *POWER-FUL-LOOKING!*

AND IT'S *TRAPPING* ME-- THE WAY THAT A *REAL* SPIDER CAPTURES-- AND *FREEZES* --ITS VICTIM!

SMYTHE'S FACE IN THE *VIEW-SCREEN!* THEN IT'S *HE* WHO'S CONTROLLING IT!

YOU SEEM *SURPRISED*, WEB-SLINGER

BUT YOU *SHOULDN'T* BE! AFTER ALL, I *SWORE* I WOULD ONE DAY *DESTROY* YOU

YOU HAVEN'T GOT ME *YET*, YOU CACKLING *CRETIN!* I CAN *STILL* OUT-FIGHT A *ROBOT!*

A *ROBOT*, PERHAPS! BUT YOU'RE FIGHTING PROFESSOR *SMYTHE*, AS WELL!

SO *WHAT?* YOU'RE STILL GUIDING IT BY *REMOTE CONTROL*, FROM A SAFE DISTANCE *AWAY!*

THE ADVANTAGE IS *MINE!* I'M RIGHT ON THE *SCENE*-- COMING TO YOU *LIVE!*

THAT'S WHERE YOU MAKE YOUR BIG *MISTAKE!* --YOUR *LAST* MISTAKE!

20

SPIDER-MAN--CAUGHT IN A WEB!

HOW BEAUTIFUL! HOW POETICALLY IRONIC!

YOU THOUGHT YOU'D BE FIGHTING A MERE ROBOT AGAIN!

BUT I FOOLED YOU! I MADE MY SPIDER SLAYER BIG ENOUGH FOR ME TO DRIVE-- TO CONTROL MANUALLY!

JUST BECAUSE YOU'D BEATEN ME IN THE PAST, YOU THOUGHT YOU COULD DO SO AGAIN!

I WANTED YOU TO THINK SO! I WANTED YOU TO BE OVER-CONFIDENT

AND PROFESSOR SMYTHE ALWAYS GETS WHAT HE WANTS! ALWAYS!

"THE FIRST TIME WE FOUGHT, I ALLOWED THAT ADDLE-BRAINED JAMESON TO CONTROL MY ROBOT--"

WHY DON'T YOU ANSWER ME, WEB-HEAD? GO AHEAD-- SAY SOMETHING!

"BUT YOU EASILY OUT-FOXED HIM--WITH A STUFFED AND DECOYED COSTUME!"*

IT'S EMPTY! HE-- HE TRICKED ME!

*FROM SPIDEY #25-- AS IF YOU'D EVER FORGET! --S.

I JUST WANTED TO *APOLOGIZE*--FOR THE WAY I *ACTED* YESTERDAY--WHEN YOU AND *PARKER* CAME TO SEE ME*

IT'S ALL RIGHT, FLASH! YOU DON'T *HAVE* TO--

I *DO* HAVE TO! I *WANT* TO!

*YOU *GUESSED* IT: LAST ISH!--S.

AFTER ALL, GWEN--YOU KNOW HOW I *FEEL* ABOUT YOU--

I FEEL THE SAME *WAY*, FLASH. WE'RE *FRIENDS*--I WANT US TO *STAY* THAT WAY.

THAT'S--NOT WHAT I *MEAN*! YOU'RE *MORE* TO ME--THAN JUST A *FRIEND*,

WHAT--ARE YOU TRYING TO *SAY*?

NO--DON'T ANSWER! JUST *LISTEN*

YOU KNOW HOW PETER AND I *FEEL* ABOUT EACH OTHER! IT'S FOR *REAL*, FLASH!

BUT, I'VE A FEELING THERE'S SOMETHING *ELSE*--

THERE'S SOMETHING YOU'RE NOT *TELLING* ME!

I *CAN'T*, GWEN! I *WANT* TO, BUT I *CAN'T* TELL YOU-- CAN'T TELL *ANYONE*!

IF YOU'RE IN *TROUBLE*--IF THERE'S ANY WAY PETER AND CAN *HELP*

PETER AND YOU! PETER AND YOU!

WOW--IF ONLY IT WERE THAT *SIMPLE*!

*B*UT, SPEAKING OF *TROUBLE*, LET'S RETURN TO THE GUY WHO WROTE THE *BOOK*--

THE HOODS HAVE *LEFT*! SMYTHE IS *ALONE*, WORKING THE SPY SCANNER CONTROLS!

HE SET THE ROBO ON *AUTOMATIC*-- TO *ATTACK* ME I TRY TO STRUGGL FREE!

AND HE MADE SURE THAT *I'LL* BE OUT OF ACTION!

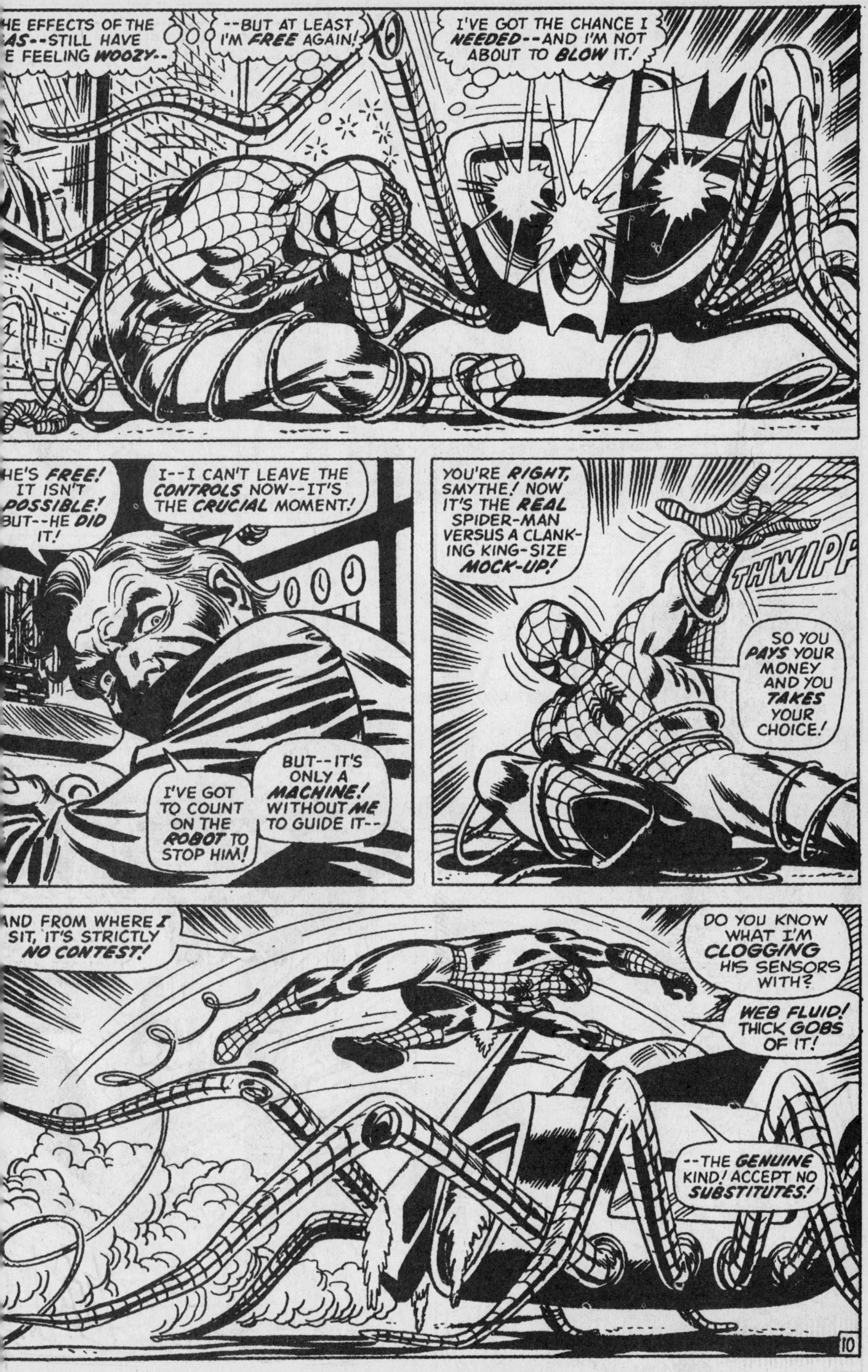
HE EFFECTS OF THE
AS--STILL HAVE
E FEELING WOOZY--
--BUT AT LEAST I'M FREE AGAIN!
I'VE GOT THE CHANCE I NEEDED--AND I'M NOT ABOUT TO BLOW IT!
HE'S FREE! IT ISN'T POSSIBLE! BUT--HE DID IT!
I--I CAN'T LEAVE THE CONTROLS NOW--IT'S THE CRUCIAL MOMENT!
BUT--IT'S ONLY A MACHINE! WITHOUT ME TO GUIDE IT--
I'VE GOT TO COUNT ON THE ROBOT TO STOP HIM!
YOU'RE RIGHT, SMYTHE! NOW IT'S THE REAL SPIDER-MAN VERSUS A CLANKING KING-SIZE MOCK-UP!
THWIPP
SO YOU PAYS YOUR MONEY AND YOU TAKES YOUR CHOICE!
AND FROM WHERE I SIT, IT'S STRICTLY NO CONTEST!
DO YOU KNOW WHAT I'M CLOGGING HIS SENSORS WITH?
WEB FLUID! THICK GOBS OF IT!
--THE GENUINE KIND! ACCEPT NO SUBSTITUTES!

NOW PAY **ATTENTION,** KIDDIES--

THERE MAY BE A **TEST** LATER ON!

WAPP!

BOK!

THWNK!

I'D LIKE TO STAY **LONGER,** BOYS--

BUT PLAYTIME'S **OVER** NOW!

SO I'LL HAVE TO **SPLIT** FOR JUST A WHILE!

PING!

SPONG!

WOW! NOT A SECOND TOO **SOON!**

LUCKY I NOTICED THOSE **POLICE CARS** PULLING UP!

ZPOP!

PTAKN!

I DON'T **GET** IT! WHY WOULD **SPIDER-MAN** WEB UP HIS OWN **ACCOMPLICES** AND CUT **OUT** ON THEM LIKE THAT?

CROOKS! WHO CAN FIGGER 'EM OUT?

THOSE FOUR JOKERS WERE ONLY *SMALL FRY!*

SMYTHE'S THE ONE I'M *REALLY* AFTER!

GOOD! THE STEEL PANELS ARE *OPEN*-- SO I CAN GO *AFTER* HIM!

WHOA! MY *SPIDEY SENSE* IS TINGLING! IT MEANS--

IT MEANS *THIS* TIME I'VE *GOT* YOU!

I *KNEW* YOU'D BE BACK, YOU *FOOL!*

YOU WERE *WAITING* FOR ME--WAITING TO *TRAP* ME!

NATURALLY! YOUR INTERFERENCE COST ME *MILLIONS*-- MILLIONS!

WON'T YOU *EVER* LEARN? YOU'RE A *LOSER,* SMYTHE-- YOU ALWAYS *WILL* BE!

AND FOR *THAT* YOU'LL *PAY*-- WITH YOUR *LIFE!*

MY ROBOT'S OUT OF *CONTROL!* ITS *SYSTEMS* ARE ALL *FOULED UP!*

BUT--IT *CAN'T* BE! I DESIGNED EVERY PART *MYSELF!* IT'S *PERFECT! PERFECT!*

18

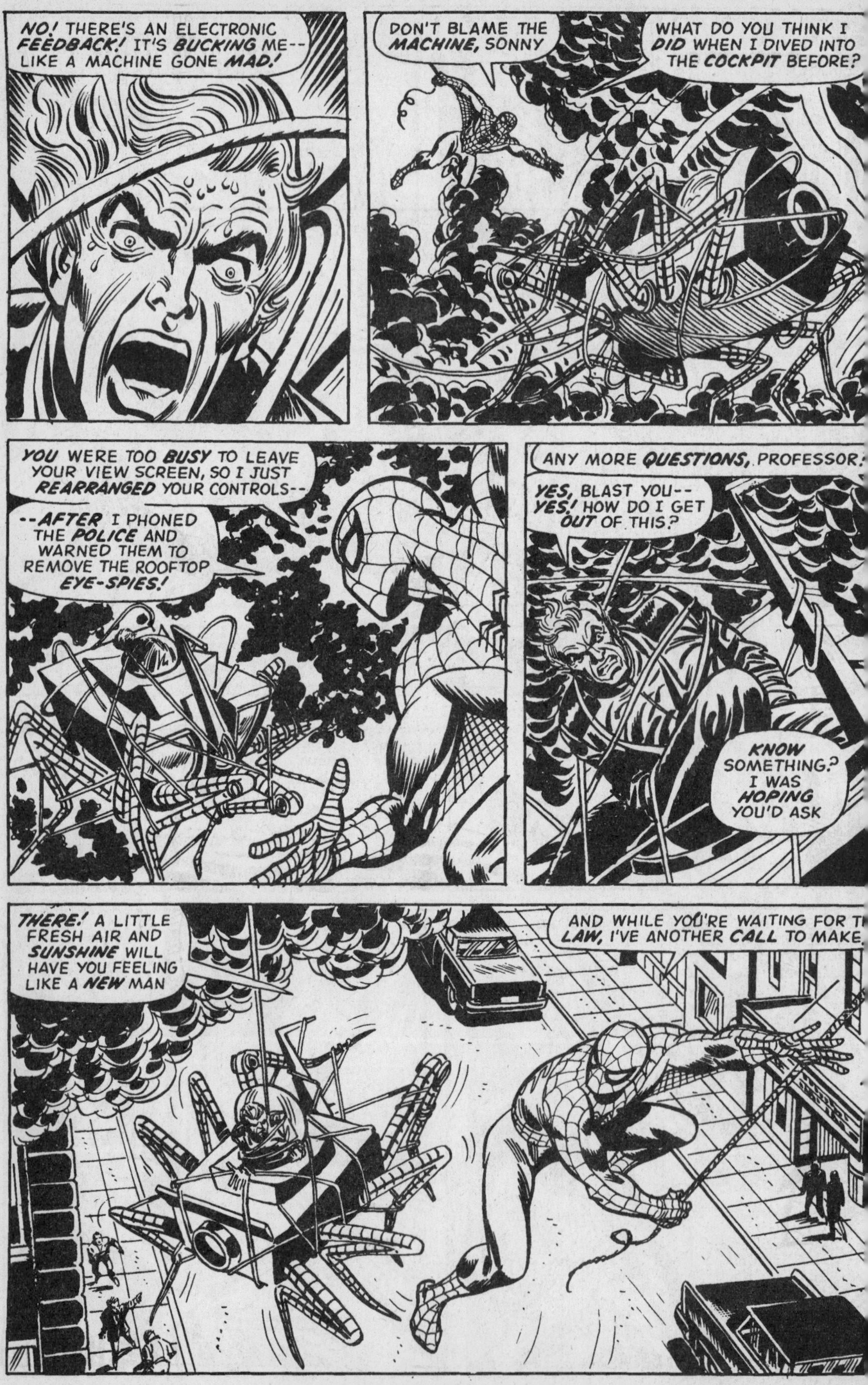

NO! THERE'S AN ELECTRONIC FEEDBACK! IT'S BUCKING ME-- LIKE A MACHINE GONE MAD!
DON'T BLAME THE MACHINE, SONNY
WHAT DO YOU THINK I DID WHEN I DIVED INTO THE COCKPIT BEFORE?
YOU WERE TOO BUSY TO LEAVE YOUR VIEW SCREEN, SO I JUST REARRANGED YOUR CONTROLS--
--AFTER I PHONED THE POLICE AND WARNED THEM TO REMOVE THE ROOFTOP EYE-SPIES!
ANY MORE QUESTIONS, PROFESSOR?
YES, BLAST YOU-- YES! HOW DO I GET OUT OF THIS?
KNOW SOMETHING? I WAS HOPING YOU'D ASK
THERE! A LITTLE FRESH AIR AND SUNSHINE WILL HAVE YOU FEELING LIKE A NEW MAN
AND WHILE YOU'RE WAITING FOR THE LAW, I'VE ANOTHER CALL TO MAKE

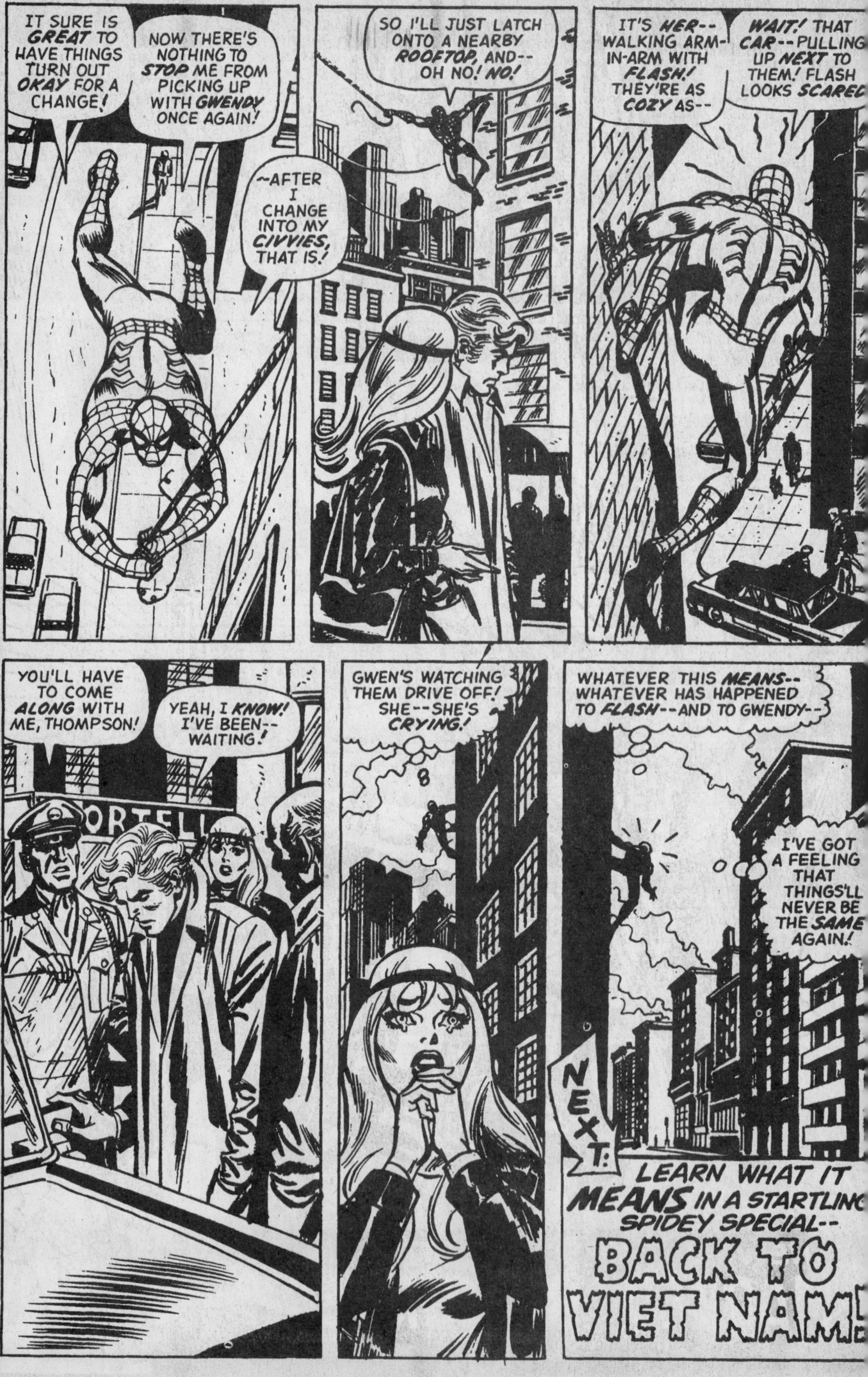
IT SURE IS GREAT TO HAVE THINGS TURN OUT OKAY FOR A CHANGE!
NOW THERE'S NOTHING TO STOP ME FROM PICKING UP WITH GWENDY ONCE AGAIN!
~AFTER I CHANGE INTO MY CIVVIES, THAT IS!
SO I'LL JUST LATCH ONTO A NEARBY ROOFTOP, AND-- OH NO! NO!
IT'S HER-- WALKING ARM-IN-ARM WITH FLASH! THEY'RE AS COZY AS--
WAIT! THAT CAR--PULLING UP NEXT TO THEM! FLASH LOOKS SCARED
YOU'LL HAVE TO COME ALONG WITH ME, THOMPSON!
YEAH, I KNOW! I'VE BEEN--WAITING!
GWEN'S WATCHING THEM DRIVE OFF! SHE--SHE'S CRYING!
WHATEVER THIS MEANS--WHATEVER HAS HAPPENED TO FLASH--AND TO GWENDY--
I'VE GOT A FEELING THAT THINGS'LL NEVER BE THE SAME AGAIN!
NEXT:
LEARN WHAT IT MEANS IN A STARTLING SPIDEY SPECIAL--
BACK TO VIET NAM!

SPIDER-MAN
MARVEL COMICS GROUP
20¢
108
MAY
02457
APPROVED BY THE COMICS CODE AUTHORITY
the AMAZING SPIDER-MAN
SPIDEY! GWEN! FLASH! WHAT STRANGE SECRET THREATENS THEM ALL?
ROMITA
NEW! UNEXPECTED! STARTLING!
MARKED FOR MURDER!

2

THEY ALL LOOKED LIKE REFUGEES FROM FU MANCHU!

WHY WOULD A BAND OF *ORIENTALS* BE ATTACKING THE CAR THAT *FLASH* IS IN?

FLASH! I WONDER IF HE'S *OKAY?*

HEY, *THOMPSON!* YOU STILL *IN* THERE? ARE YOU *ALL RIGHT?*

THWIPP!

WH-WHO'S *THAT?* WHO *ARE* YOU?

RELAX, FELLA-- EVERYTHING'S COOL!

IT'S JUST YOUR *FRIENDLY NEIGHBORHOOD SPIDER-MAN!*

I WAS JUST SWINGING BY, AND FIGURED I'D JOIN THE *PARTY!*

MAN! AS MANY ENEMIES AS *YOU* SEEM TO HAVE-- YOU MUST WORK *OVERTIME* AT IT!

SPIDER-MAN! I DON'T KNOW WHAT YOUR *GAME* IS, BUT YOU'RE NOT GETTING *THOMPSON!*

DON'T! IT'S *OKAY!* I *KNOW* HIM!

I DON'T KNOW WHAT MAKES HIM SO *POPULAR,* BUT SINCE HE'S UP FOR *GRABS--*

AND SINCE *I* KNEW HIM BEFORE *YOU* DID--

THIS'LL GIVE YOU SOME-THING TO *RAP* ABOUT WHEN YOU'RE BACK AT THE *PX!*

ZAP!

6

WHAT ARE YOU *DOING?* WHERE ARE YOU *TAKING* ME?

I FIGURED WHAT'S A NICE KID LIKE *YOU* DOING IN A PLACE LIKE *THIS?*

DON'T SHOOT! YOU MIGHT HIT *THOMPSON!*

THAT'S WHAT I *HOPED* THEY'D SAY!

I'VE *GOT* TO LEARN WHAT IT'S ALL ABOUT--

--ESPECIALLY AFTER SEEING FLASH TOGETHER WITH *GWENDY* WHEN THEY *NABBED* HIM!

NOW, SUPPOSE YOU *TELL* YOUR LOCAL SPIDER-MAN WHY THOSE NASTY OL' *MP'S* WERE TRYING TO HAUL YOU AWAY!

OKAY, *GOLDEN BOY*-- END OF THE LINE!

YOU--YOU DON'T *UNDER-STAND*--

THEY WEREN'T *HAULING* ME AWAY--

THEY WERE TRYING TO-- *PROTECT* ME!

PROTECT YOU? YOU MEAN FROM THE *CHINESE* IN THE GAS MASKS?

WHO *WERE* THEY? WHAT WERE THEY *AFTER?*

THEY *WEREN'T* CHINESE! THEY WERE-- I--I'D BETTER START AT THE *BEGINNING*--

NOW *THERE'S* A BRIGHT THOUGHT!

"FINALLY--"

VENERABLE ONE, I MUST SAY FAREWELL.

MY PLACE IS IN THE OUTSIDE WORLD.

A MAN MUST GO WHERE FATE DECREES.

I'LL NEVER FORGET YOU --NEVER FORGET-- WHAT YOU'VE DONE FOR ME!

THOUGH WE SHALL NOT MEET AGAIN, MY HEART WILL HOLD YOU EVER.

"AND SO I LEFT THAT HIDDEN SHANGRI-LA--THAT TINY OASIS OF PEACE IN A WORLD OF ENDLESS WAR!"

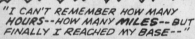

"I CAN'T REMEMBER HOW MANY HOURS--HOW MANY MILES--BUT FINALLY I REACHED MY BASE--"

REPORT TO THE INFIRMARY, SOLDIER! THE MEDICS WILL CHECK YOU OUT!

WE'RE READY TO BEGIN SHELLING, COLONEL.

WHICH TARGET HAS DIVISION ORDERED THIS TIME?

SECTOR "B", SIR! WE'RE TO LEVEL THE AREA TO PREVENT ENEMY INFILTRATION!

VERY WELL-- THE SHELLING WILL BEGIN AT 1800 HOURS!

SECTOR "B"! NO! NO!

9

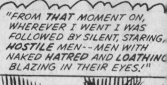

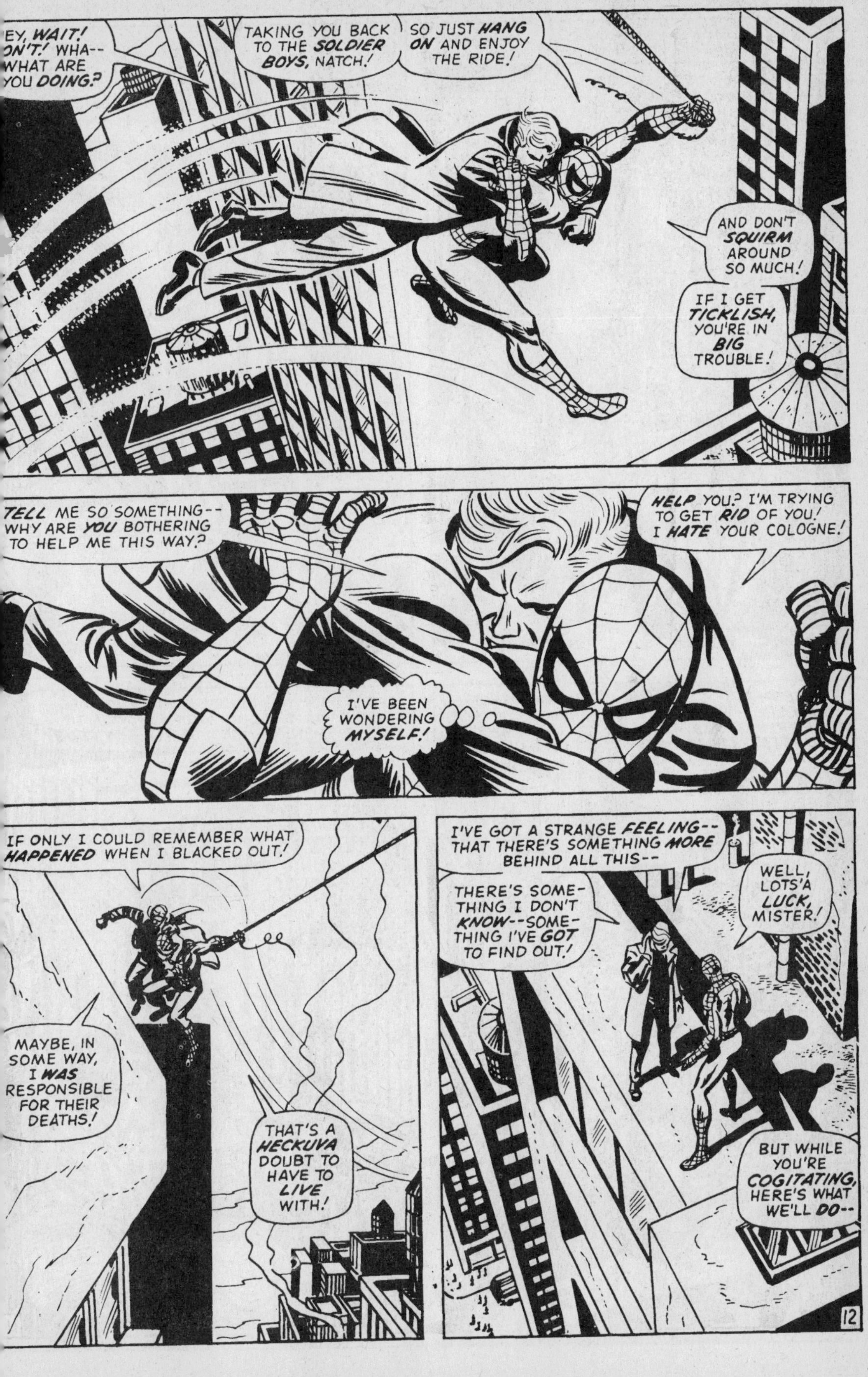

EY, WAIT! ON'T! WHA-- WHAT ARE YOU DOING?
TAKING YOU BACK TO THE SOLDIER BOYS, NATCH!
SO JUST HANG ON AND ENJOY THE RIDE!
AND DON'T SQUIRM AROUND SO MUCH!
IF I GET TICKLISH, YOU'RE IN BIG TROUBLE!
TELL ME SO SOMETHING-- WHY ARE YOU BOTHERING TO HELP ME THIS WAY?
HELP YOU? I'M TRYING TO GET RID OF YOU! I HATE YOUR COLOGNE!
I'VE BEEN WONDERING MYSELF!
IF ONLY I COULD REMEMBER WHAT HAPPENED WHEN I BLACKED OUT!
MAYBE, IN SOME WAY, I WAS RESPONSIBLE FOR THEIR DEATHS!
THAT'S A HECKUVA DOUBT TO HAVE TO LIVE WITH!
I'VE GOT A STRANGE FEELING-- THAT THERE'S SOMETHING MORE BEHIND ALL THIS--
THERE'S SOMETHING I DON'T KNOW--SOMETHING I'VE GOT TO FIND OUT!
WELL, LOTS'A LUCK, MISTER!
BUT WHILE YOU'RE COGITATING, HERE'S WHAT WE'LL DO--
12

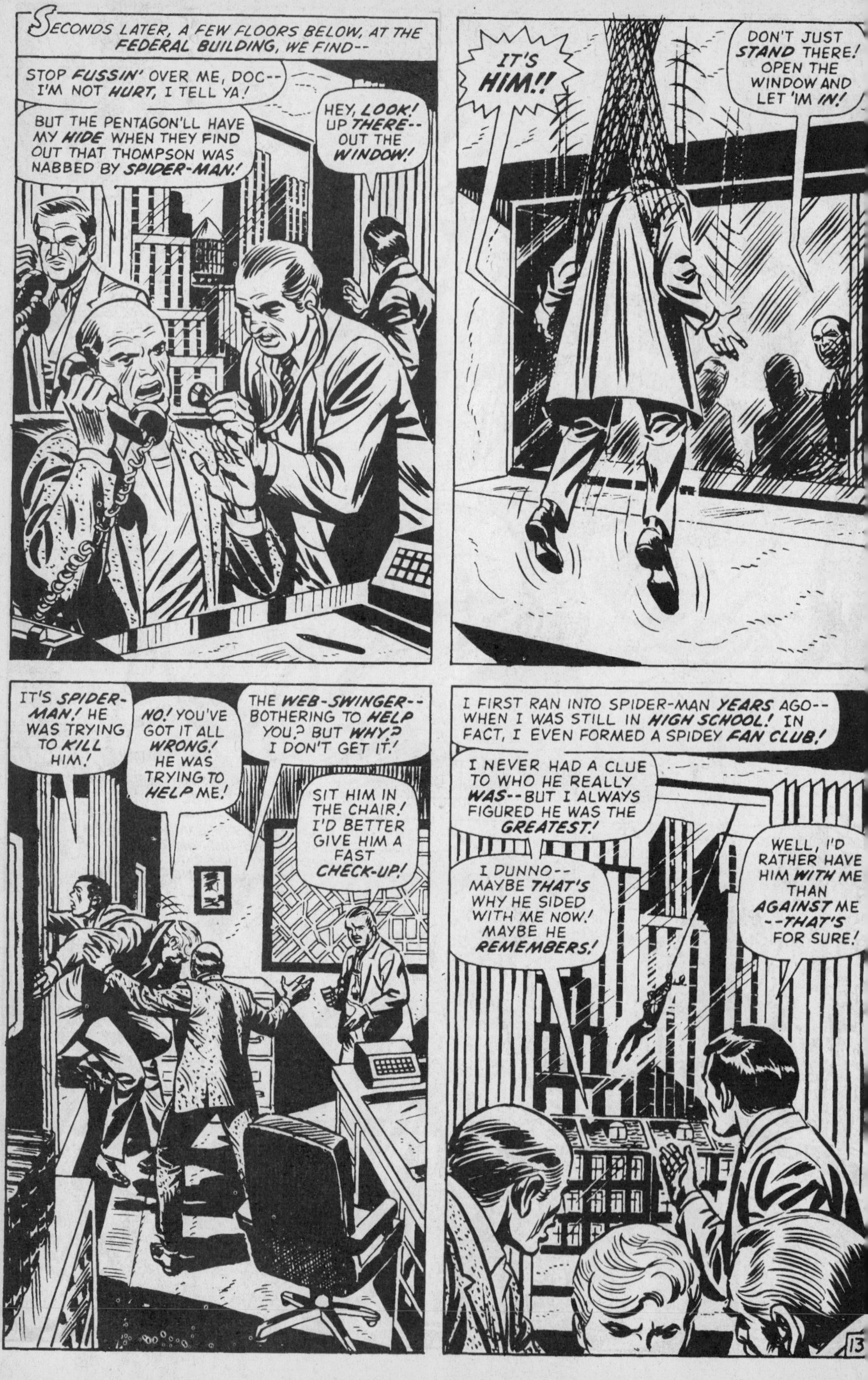
SECONDS LATER, A FEW FLOORS BELOW, AT THE FEDERAL BUILDING, WE FIND--
STOP FUSSIN' OVER ME, DOC-- I'M NOT HURT, I TELL YA!
BUT THE PENTAGON'LL HAVE MY HIDE WHEN THEY FIND OUT THAT THOMPSON WAS NABBED BY SPIDER-MAN!
HEY, LOOK! UP THERE-- OUT THE WINDOW!
IT'S HIM!!
DON'T JUST STAND THERE! OPEN THE WINDOW AND LET 'IM IN!
IT'S SPIDER-MAN! HE WAS TRYING TO KILL HIM!
NO! YOU'VE GOT IT ALL WRONG! HE WAS TRYING TO HELP ME!
THE WEB-SWINGER-- BOTHERING TO HELP YOU? BUT WHY? I DON'T GET IT!
SIT HIM IN THE CHAIR! I'D BETTER GIVE HIM A FAST CHECK-UP!
I FIRST RAN INTO SPIDER-MAN YEARS AGO-- WHEN I WAS STILL IN HIGH SCHOOL! IN FACT, I EVEN FORMED A SPIDEY FAN CLUB!
I NEVER HAD A CLUE TO WHO HE REALLY WAS--BUT I ALWAYS FIGURED HE WAS THE GREATEST!
I DUNNO-- MAYBE THAT'S WHY HE SIDED WITH ME NOW! MAYBE HE REMEMBERS!
WELL, I'D RATHER HAVE HIM WITH ME THAN AGAINST ME --THAT'S FOR SURE!
13

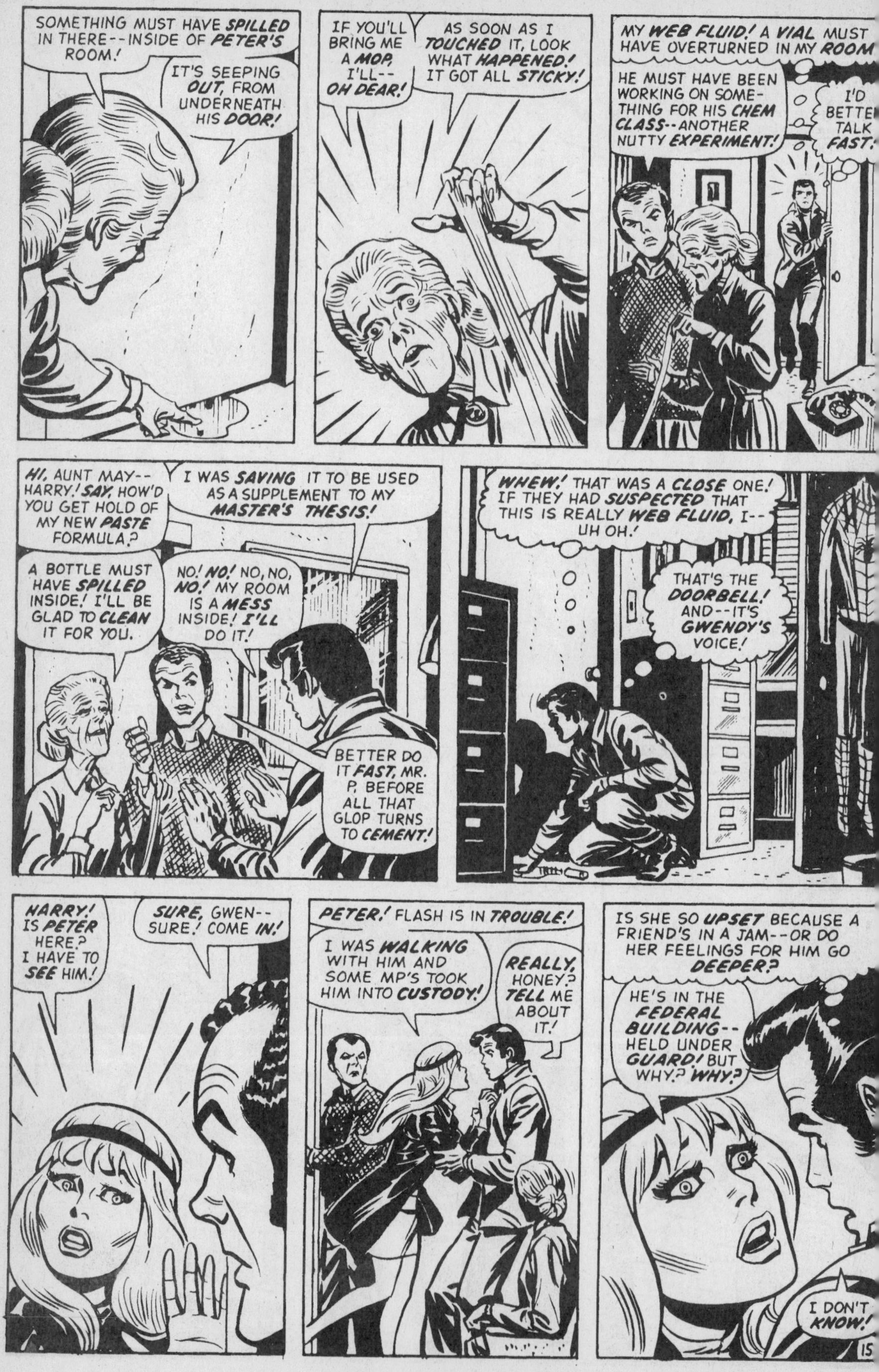

SOMETHING MUST HAVE SPILLED IN THERE--INSIDE OF PETER'S ROOM!
IT'S SEEPING OUT, FROM UNDERNEATH HIS DOOR!
IF YOU'LL BRING ME A MOP, I'LL-- OH DEAR!
AS SOON AS I TOUCHED IT, LOOK WHAT HAPPENED! IT GOT ALL STICKY!
MY WEB FLUID! A VIAL MUST HAVE OVERTURNED IN MY ROOM
HE MUST HAVE BEEN WORKING ON SOMETHING FOR HIS CHEM CLASS--ANOTHER NUTTY EXPERIMENT!
I'D BETTE TALK FAST!
HI, AUNT MAY-- HARRY! SAY, HOW'D YOU GET HOLD OF MY NEW PASTE FORMULA?
I WAS SAVING IT TO BE USED AS A SUPPLEMENT TO MY MASTER'S THESIS!
A BOTTLE MUST HAVE SPILLED INSIDE! I'LL BE GLAD TO CLEAN IT FOR YOU.
NO! NO! NO, NO, NO! MY ROOM IS A MESS INSIDE! I'LL DO IT!
BETTER DO IT FAST, MR. P, BEFORE ALL THAT GLOP TURNS TO CEMENT!
WHEW! THAT WAS A CLOSE ONE! IF THEY HAD SUSPECTED THAT THIS IS REALLY WEB FLUID, I-- UH OH!
THAT'S THE DOORBELL! AND--IT'S GWENDY'S VOICE!
HARRY! IS PETER HERE? I HAVE TO SEE HIM!
SURE, GWEN-- SURE! COME IN!
PETER! FLASH IS IN TROUBLE!
I WAS WALKING WITH HIM AND SOME MP'S TOOK HIM INTO CUSTODY!
REALLY, HONEY? TELL ME ABOUT IT!
IS SHE SO UPSET BECAUSE A FRIEND'S IN A JAM--OR DO HER FEELINGS FOR HIM GO DEEPER?
HE'S IN THE FEDERAL BUILDING-- HELD UNDER GUARD! BUT WHY? WHY?
I DON'T KNOW!

17

20

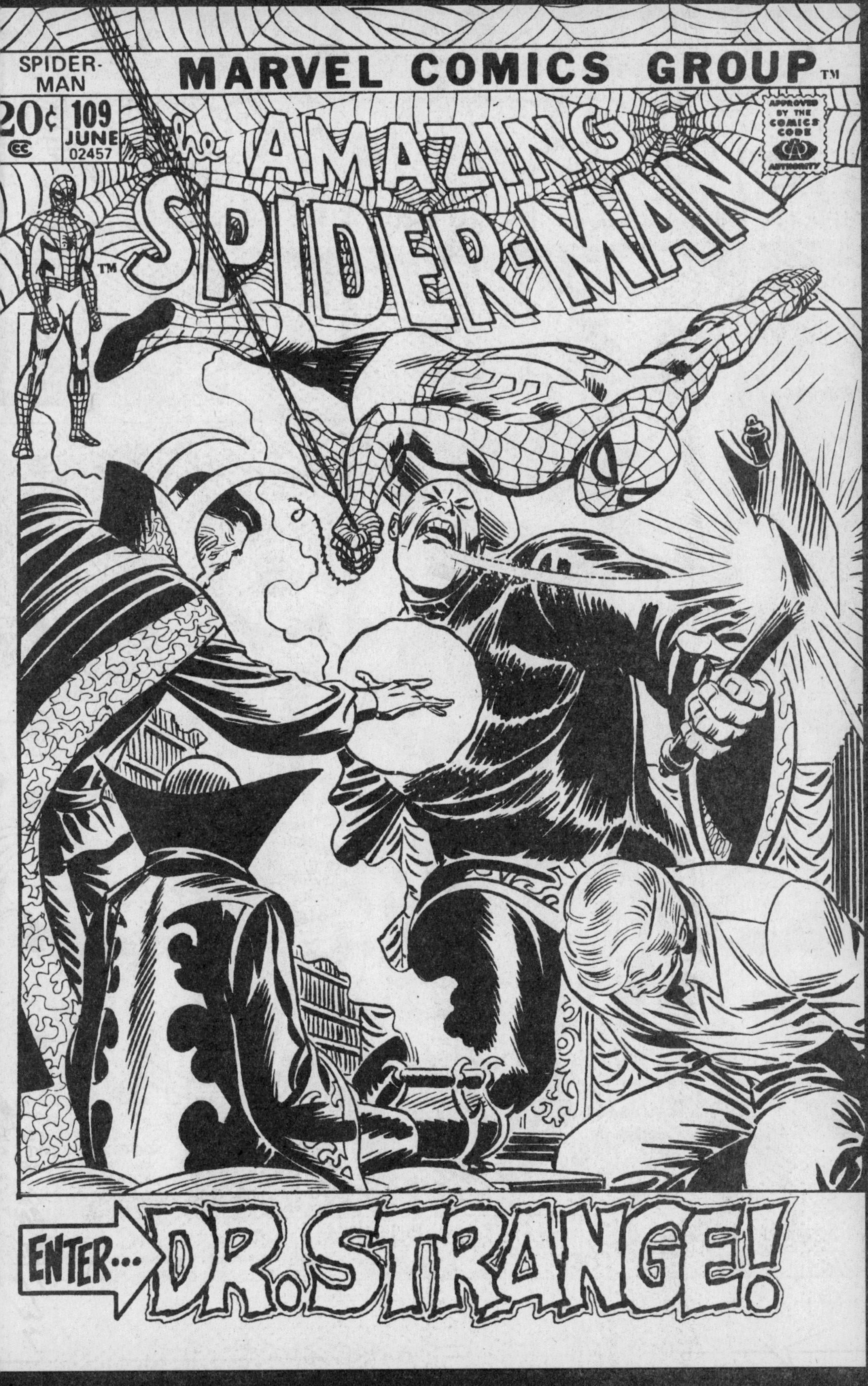
SPIDER-MAN
MARVEL COMICS GROUP
20¢ 109 JUNE 02457
APPROVED BY THE COMICS CODE AUTHORITY
The AMAZING SPIDER-MAN
ENTER... DR. STRANGE!

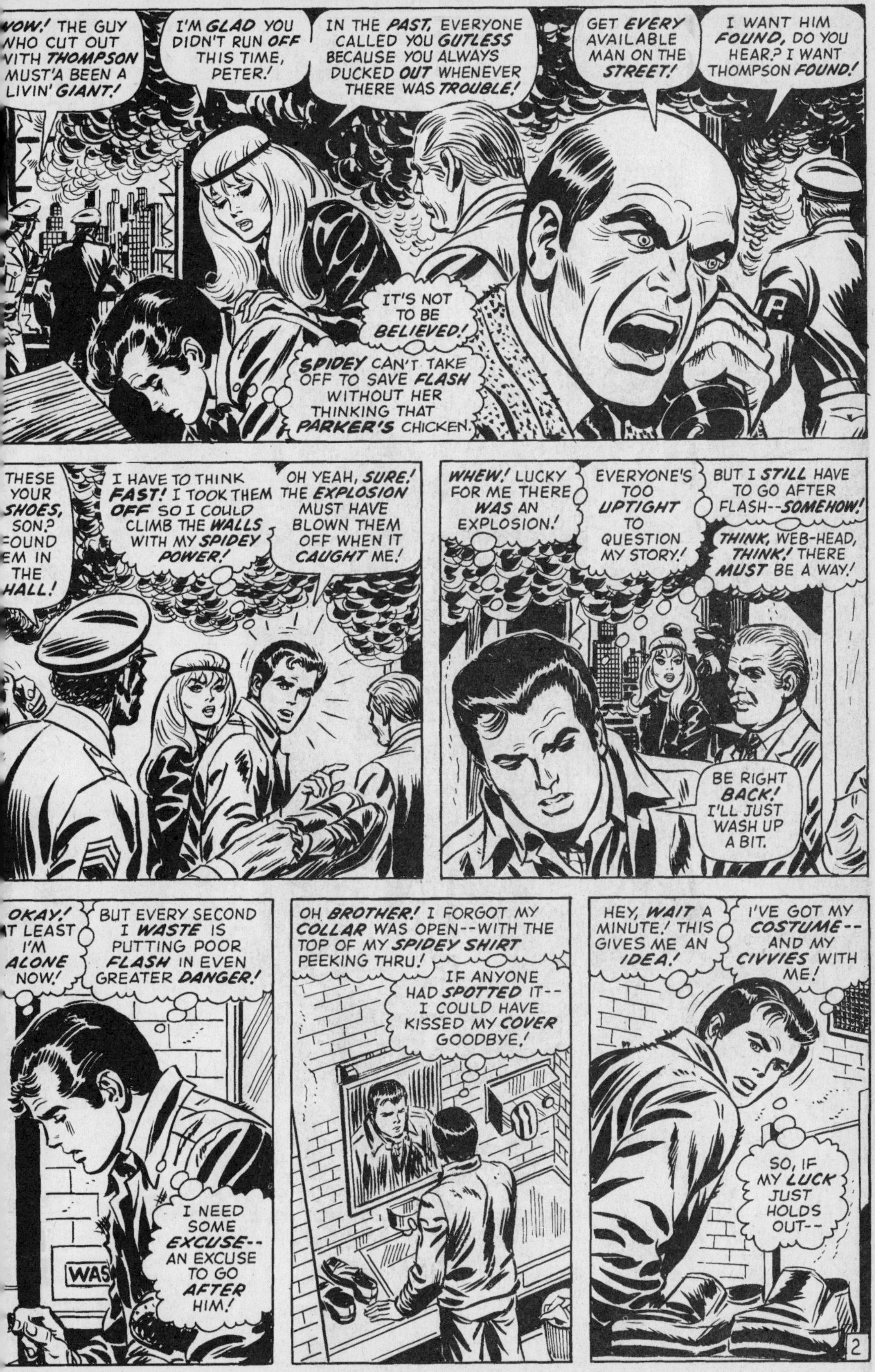
NOW! THE GUY WHO CUT OUT WITH THOMPSON MUST'A BEEN A LIVIN' GIANT!
I'M GLAD YOU DIDN'T RUN OFF THIS TIME, PETER!
IN THE PAST, EVERYONE CALLED YOU GUTLESS BECAUSE YOU ALWAYS DUCKED OUT WHENEVER THERE WAS TROUBLE!
GET EVERY AVAILABLE MAN ON THE STREET!
I WANT HIM FOUND, DO YOU HEAR? I WANT THOMPSON FOUND!
IT'S NOT TO BE BELIEVED!
SPIDEY CAN'T TAKE OFF TO SAVE FLASH WITHOUT HER THINKING THAT PARKER'S CHICKEN.
THESE YOUR SHOES, SON? FOUND 'EM IN THE HALL!
I HAVE TO THINK FAST! I TOOK THEM OFF SO I COULD CLIMB THE WALLS WITH MY SPIDEY POWER!
OH YEAH, SURE! THE EXPLOSION MUST HAVE BLOWN THEM OFF WHEN IT CAUGHT ME!
WHEW! LUCKY FOR ME THERE WAS AN EXPLOSION!
EVERYONE'S TOO UPTIGHT TO QUESTION MY STORY!
BUT I STILL HAVE TO GO AFTER FLASH--SOMEHOW!
THINK, WEB-HEAD, THINK! THERE MUST BE A WAY!
BE RIGHT BACK! I'LL JUST WASH UP A BIT.
OKAY! AT LEAST I'M ALONE NOW!
BUT EVERY SECOND I WASTE IS PUTTING POOR FLASH IN EVEN GREATER DANGER!
I NEED SOME EXCUSE-- AN EXCUSE TO GO AFTER HIM!
WAS
OH BROTHER! I FORGOT MY COLLAR WAS OPEN--WITH THE TOP OF MY SPIDEY SHIRT PEEKING THRU!
IF ANYONE HAD SPOTTED IT-- I COULD HAVE KISSED MY COVER GOODBYE!
HEY, WAIT A MINUTE! THIS GIVES ME AN IDEA!
I'VE GOT MY COSTUME-- AND MY CIVVIES WITH ME!
SO, IF MY LUCK JUST HOLDS OUT--
2

JUST A FEW SECONDS LATER--

LISTEN! WHAT'S THAT COMMOTION IN THE WASHROOM?

IT SOUNDS LIKE A FIGHT! SOMETHING MUST BE HAPPENING TO PARKER!

MAYBE ONE OF THOSE KILLERS STAYED BEHIND! IF THEY KNOW THAT PETER IS FLASH'S FRIEND--!

LET'S GET IN THERE! WE HAVE TO HELP HIM!

NO! LOOK-- LOOK! OUT THE WINDOW--

IT'S SPIDER-MAN! HE'S MAKING OFF WITH PARKER!

RELAX! I'M NOT GONNA HURT THIS CLOWN!

OH MY GOD! NOT AGAIN! NOT AGAIN!*

I JUST WANNA ASK 'IM A FEW QUESTIONS!

*YOU GUESSED IT! THIS ISN'T THE FIRST TIME SPIDEY PULLED THIS STUNT! --SLY STAN.

IT'S A GOOD THING MY VOICE GETS MUFFLED, AND UNRECOGNIZABLE UNDER MY MASK!

WATCH IT! DON'T DROP HIM!

IT--IT'S MY FAULT! IF I HADN'T INSISTED THAT PETER STAY HERE-- IF I HAD LET HIM GO--

DROPPING THAT HUNK OF ROLLED-UP WEBBING WOULDN'T HURT ANYTHING--

--BUT I'M NOT ABOUT TO TELL THAT TO THEM!

NOW, ALL I'VE GOT TO DO IS FIND FLASH!

YEAH, THAT'S ALL!

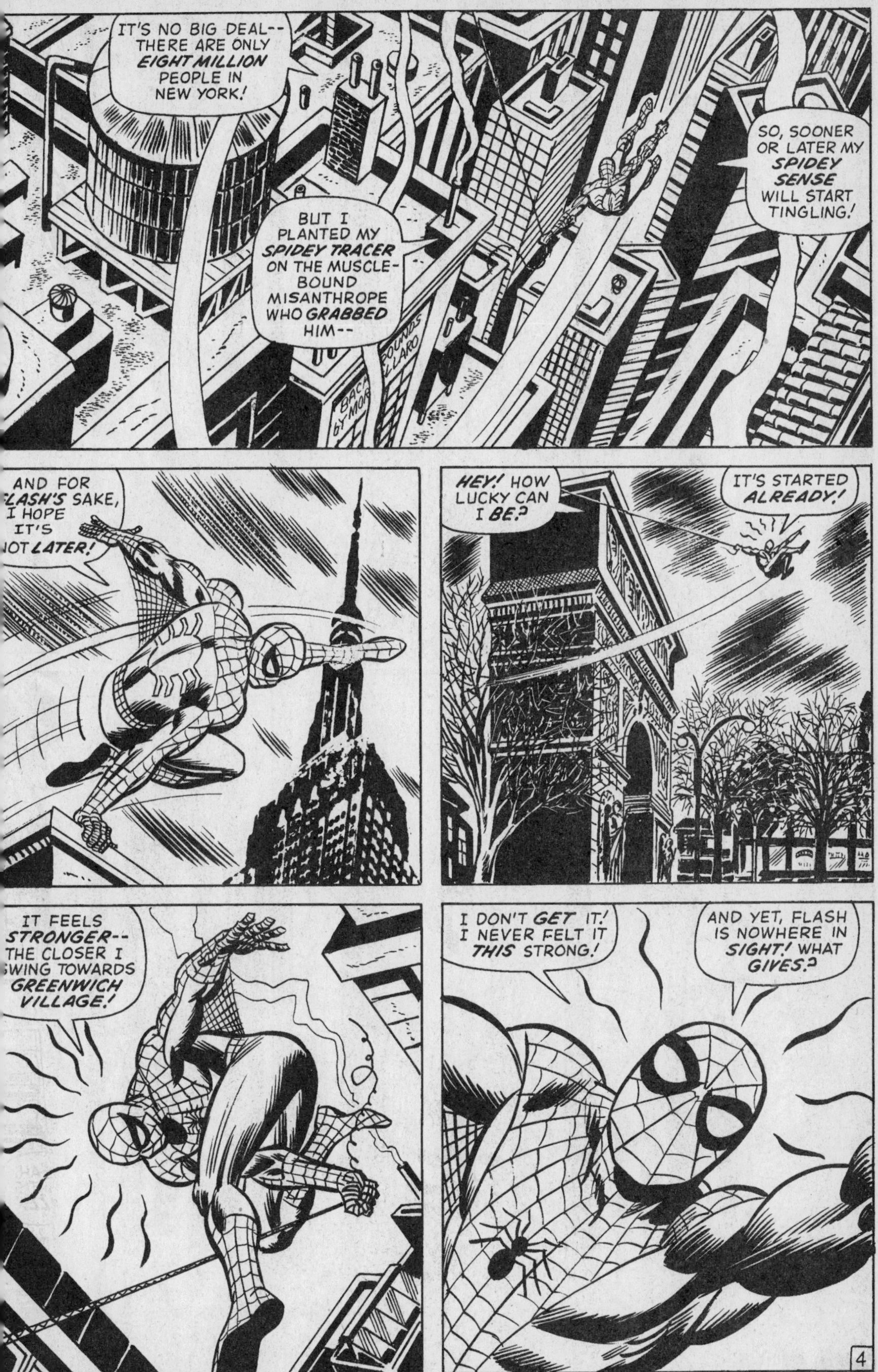
IT'S NO BIG DEAL-- THERE ARE ONLY EIGHT MILLION PEOPLE IN NEW YORK!
BUT I PLANTED MY SPIDEY TRACER ON THE MUSCLE-BOUND MISANTHROPE WHO GRABBED HIM--
SO, SOONER OR LATER MY SPIDEY SENSE WILL START TINGLING!
AND FOR FLASH'S SAKE, I HOPE IT'S NOT LATER!
HEY! HOW LUCKY CAN I BE?
IT'S STARTED ALREADY!
IT FEELS STRONGER-- THE CLOSER I SWING TOWARDS GREENWICH VILLAGE!
I DON'T GET IT! I NEVER FELT IT THIS STRONG!
AND YET, FLASH IS NOWHERE IN SIGHT! WHAT GIVES?
4

OH *NO!* SOMETHING'S *HAPPEN-ING!* SOMETHING'S *WRONG!*

THE SENSATION'S SO *STRONG,* I--I CAN HARDLY *BEAR* IT!

IT'S--NEVER *HAPPENED--* TO ME-- *BEFORE!*

DO NOT BE *ALARMED!* I WAS *FORCED* TO RESORT TO SO *EXTREME* AN EXPEDIENT IN ORDER TO *CONTACT* YOU!

A *VOICE!* JUST A *FEW FEET AWAY!*

BUT--BUT THERE'S *NO ONE THERE!*

I AM *HERE!* BUT WHILE IN *MY ASTRAL* FORM, I AM *INVISIBLE* TO YOUR EYES!

ASTRAL FORM?!! THAT CAN *ONLY* MEAN--

OF *COURSE!* AND NOW, YOU MUST *FOLLOW* ME!

FOLLOW YOU? I CAN'T EVEN SEE -- HEY!

THE *TINGLING!* IT'S NARROWED OUT -- LIKE A *BEACON!*

SOMETHING IS *FORCING* ME TO HEAD FURTHER *DOWNTOWN* -- INTO THE HEART OF THE *VILLAGE!*

IT IS BUT A SIMPLE MYSTIC *SPELL* -- FOR I MUST NOT *LOSE* YOU!

-- FEEL LIKE A *PUPPET* -- FORCED TO RESPOND TO -- SOMEONE *ELSE'S* WILL!

THE SENSATION WILL *PASS,* WHEN WE HAVE REACHED OUR *DESTINATION!*

THAT *BUILDING* -- DOWN BELOW --

I *KNOW* IT -- I'VE SEEN IT *BEFORE!* IT'S THE *HOME* OF --

DOCTOR STRANGE!

6

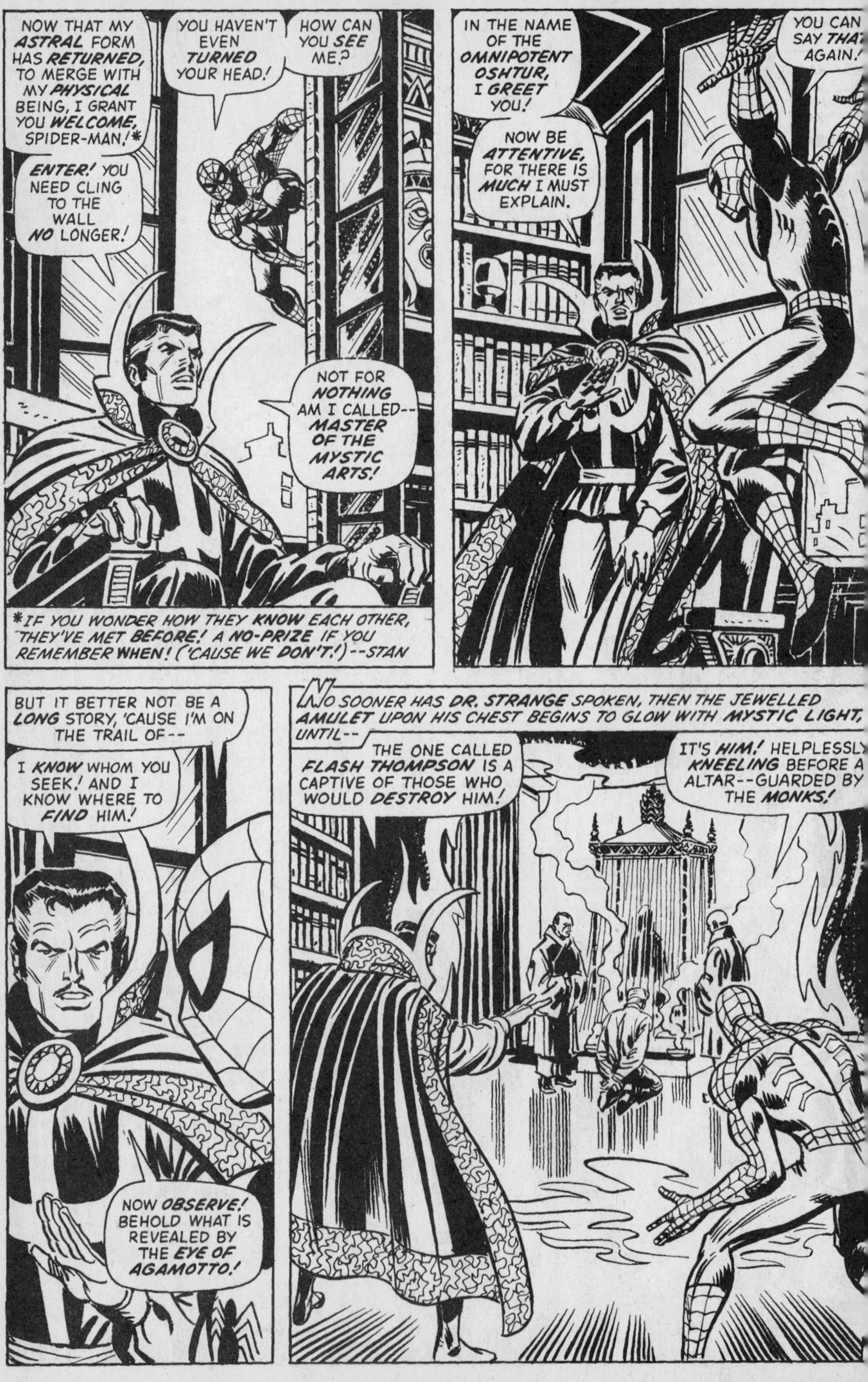
NOW THAT MY ASTRAL FORM HAS RETURNED, TO MERGE WITH MY PHYSICAL BEING, I GRANT YOU WELCOME, SPIDER-MAN!*
ENTER! YOU NEED CLING TO THE WALL NO LONGER!
YOU HAVEN'T EVEN TURNED YOUR HEAD!
HOW CAN YOU SEE ME?
NOT FOR NOTHING AM I CALLED-- MASTER OF THE MYSTIC ARTS!
*IF YOU WONDER HOW THEY KNOW EACH OTHER, THEY'VE MET BEFORE! A NO-PRIZE IF YOU REMEMBER WHEN! ('CAUSE WE DON'T!) --STAN
IN THE NAME OF THE OMNIPOTENT OSHTUR, I GREET YOU!
YOU CAN SAY THAT AGAIN!
NOW BE ATTENTIVE, FOR THERE IS MUCH I MUST EXPLAIN.
BUT IT BETTER NOT BE A LONG STORY, 'CAUSE I'M ON THE TRAIL OF--
I KNOW WHOM YOU SEEK! AND I KNOW WHERE TO FIND HIM!
NOW OBSERVE! BEHOLD WHAT IS REVEALED BY THE EYE OF AGAMOTTO!
NO SOONER HAS DR. STRANGE SPOKEN, THEN THE JEWELLED AMULET UPON HIS CHEST BEGINS TO GLOW WITH MYSTIC LIGHT, UNTIL--
THE ONE CALLED FLASH THOMPSON IS A CAPTIVE OF THOSE WHO WOULD DESTROY HIM!
IT'S HIM! HELPLESSLY KNEELING BEFORE A ALTAR--GUARDED BY THE MONKS!

QUICK! TELL ME WHERE THEY *ARE!* I'VE GOT TO *GET* THERE-- BEFORE IT'S TOO *LATE!*

NO! HASTE WILL AVAIL YOU *NOTHING!*

LET THE SOUNDS OF THEIR *SPEECH* BE *HEARD!*

LIFT UP YOUR EYES AND *SEE!*

WHY? WHY MUST I LOOK AT AN *IDOL?*

IDOL? YOU THINK IT IS MERELY AN *IDOL?* THEN LOOK *HARDER,* INFIDEL!

LOOK! AND BE *APPALLED* AT THE SIGHT!

THE STATUE IN THE MIST IS GETTING *CLEARER-- CLEARER--*

NO! IT-- IT *ISN'T* A STATUE! IT'S--

IT'S THE HIGH PRIEST!

BUT-- HE'S *DEAD!* YOU TOLD ME HE WAS *DEAD!*

8

DEAD? WHO TRULY *KNOWS* THE MEANING OF DEATH?

HE IS *ENTRANCED!* HE SLEEPS THE SLEEP WHICH HAS *NO* WAKENING--

NAUGHT CAN WAKEN HIM--EXCEPT THE *DEATH* OF THE ONE WHO *MADE* HIM SO!

BUT I *DIDN'T!* I TRIED TO *HELP* HIM-- TO *SAVE* HIM!

SILENCE! IT HAS BEEN *DECREED!*

YOU HAVE *CAPTURED* HIS *SPIRIT* BY YOUR *MURDEROUS* ACT! ONLY YOUR *DEATH* CAN *RELEASE* IT!

WHEN THE *HOLY HOUR* DRAWS NEAR, YO WILL BE *SACRIFICED* THE ALTAR OF THE *MOS HIGH!* WHEN THE *LIFE* HAS LEFT *YOUR* BODY, IT WILL ENTER *HIS!*

THEN WILL HE *LIVE* AGAIN?

WHO NOW *INTRUDES*

IT IS I--*SHA SHAN*-- HUMBLE *DAUGHTER* OF HIM WHO IS ONCE AND DEPARTED!

YES, *I*--WHO HAVE LOST *FATHER* AND SAGE--EVEN AS *YE* HAVE LOST A *PRIEST* MOST EXALTED!

GENTLE ONE, ENTER!

SHA SHAN! THE GIRL WHO *BEFRIENDED* ME!

YOU KNOW I HAD *NOTHING* TO DO WITH THE *SHELLING!* I CAME TO YOUR VILLAGE TO *WARN* YOU--TO HELP YOU *ESCAPE!*

TELL THEM, SHA SHAN! YOU MUST MAKE THEM *BELIEVE!*

IT IS NOT FOR *ME* TO DISPUTE THE WORDS OF THOSE WHO SERVE MY *FATHER!*

10

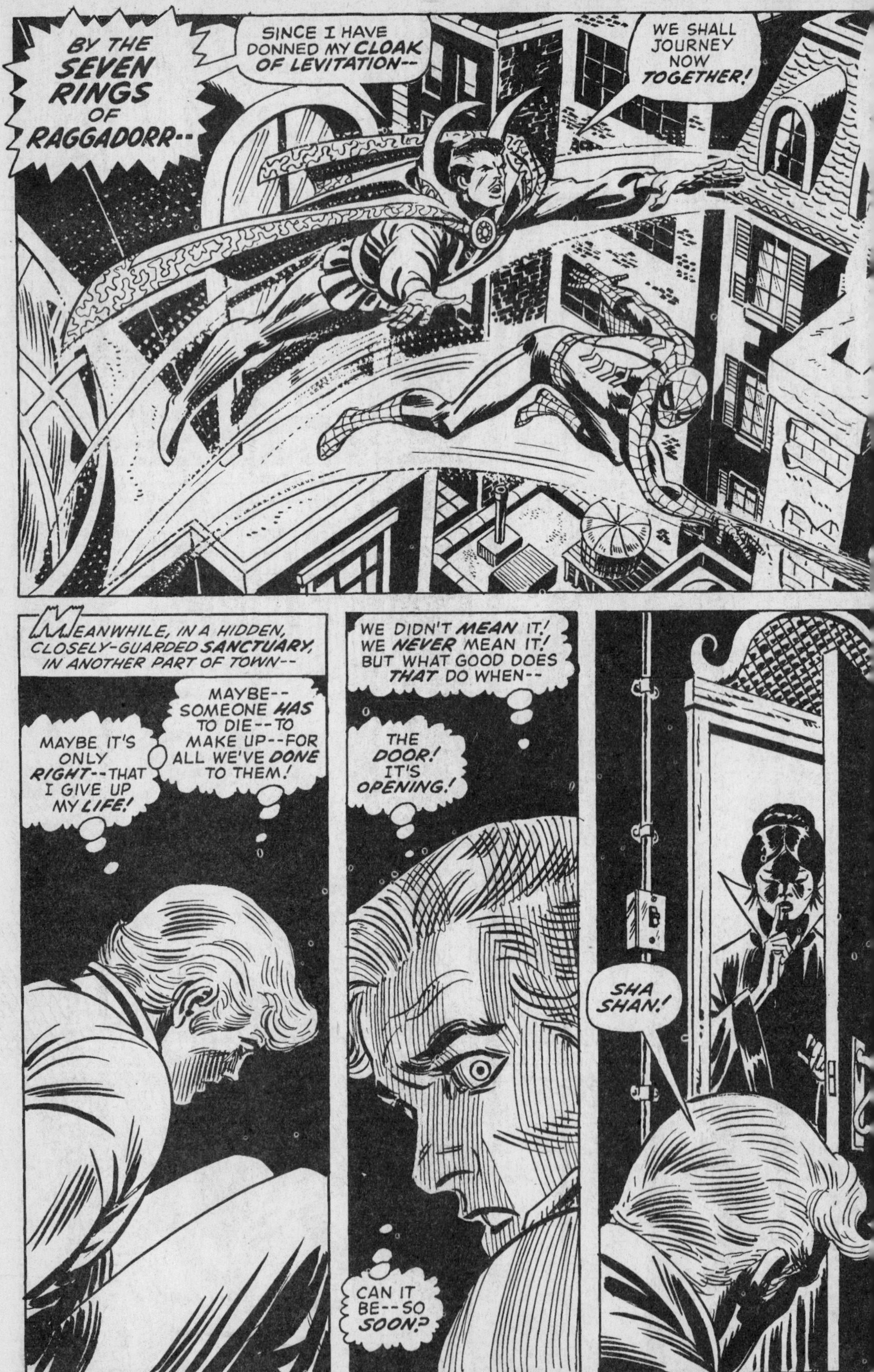
BY THE SEVEN RINGS OF RAGGADORR--
SINCE I HAVE DONNED MY CLOAK OF LEVITATION--
WE SHALL JOURNEY NOW TOGETHER!
MEANWHILE, IN A HIDDEN, CLOSELY-GUARDED SANCTUARY, IN ANOTHER PART OF TOWN--
MAYBE IT'S ONLY RIGHT--THAT I GIVE UP MY LIFE!
MAYBE--SOMEONE HAS TO DIE--TO MAKE UP--FOR ALL WE'VE DONE TO THEM!
WE DIDN'T MEAN IT! WE NEVER MEAN IT! BUT WHAT GOOD DOES THAT DO WHEN--
THE DOOR! IT'S OPENING!
CAN IT BE--SO SOON?
SHA SHAN!

YOU MUST BE *SILENT!* THEY MUST NOT *FIND* ME HERE! NOW HEED THE *WORDS* I SPEAK--

YOU-- YOU'VE COME TO *HELP* ME!

IS IT NOT *FITTING?* AM I NOT MY FATHER'S *CHILD?*

THEN *WHY?* WHY DIDN'T YOU SPEAK IN MY *BEHALF?*

SO *STRONGLY* DO THEY THIRST FOR *VENGEANCE--* THEY WOULD NOT *BELIEVE!*

UT SHA SHAN *EMEMBERS!*

YOU CAME TO THE TEMPLE, TO *WARN* US OF THE SHELLING!

YOU WOULD NOT SEEK *SAFETY* FOR YOURSELF, THOUGH WE PAID YOU NO *HEED!*

AND SO, YOU *TOO* WERE FELLED BY FALLING BOMBS!

"WHILE *OTHERS* FOUGHT THE DEADLY FLAMES, SHA SHAN GUIDED YOU TO SAFETY!"

HOLD IT, SERGEANT! THAT'S ONE OF OUR MEN!

WHAT'S HE *DOIN'* HERE?

WHAT'S THE *DIFFERENCE?* LET'S *GET* 'IM!

"MY HEART *REJOICED* THAT YOU HAD BEEN *FOUND!* BUT, WHEN I RETURNED TO THE TEMPLE RUINS--"

THEY *GRIEVE--* FOR MY *FATHER!* HE HAS BEEN *TAKEN* FROM US!

THIS LOSS MUST BE *AVENGED,* MY BROTHER!

12.

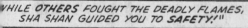

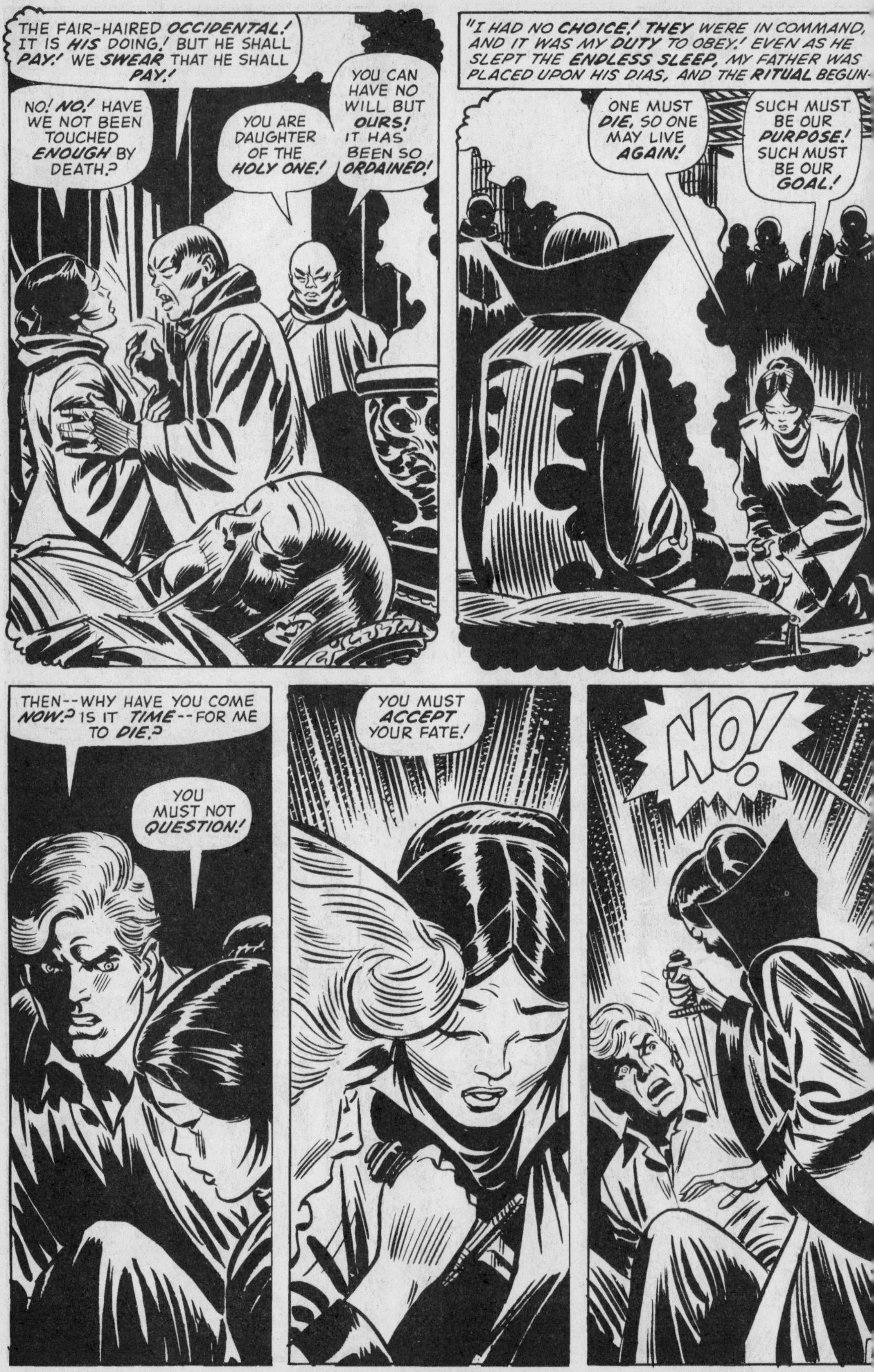
THE FAIR-HAIRED OCCIDENTAL! IT IS HIS DOING! BUT HE SHALL PAY! WE SWEAR THAT HE SHALL PAY!
NO! NO! HAVE WE NOT BEEN TOUCHED ENOUGH BY DEATH?
YOU ARE DAUGHTER OF THE HOLY ONE!
YOU CAN HAVE NO WILL BUT OURS! IT HAS BEEN SO ORDAINED!
"I HAD NO CHOICE! THEY WERE IN COMMAND, AND IT WAS MY DUTY TO OBEY! EVEN AS HE SLEPT THE ENDLESS SLEEP, MY FATHER WAS PLACED UPON HIS DIAS, AND THE RITUAL BEGUN-
ONE MUST DIE, SO ONE MAY LIVE AGAIN!
SUCH MUST BE OUR PURPOSE! SUCH MUST BE OUR GOAL!
THEN--WHY HAVE YOU COME NOW? IS IT TIME--FOR ME TO DIE?
YOU MUST NOT QUESTION!
YOU MUST ACCEPT YOUR FATE!
NO!

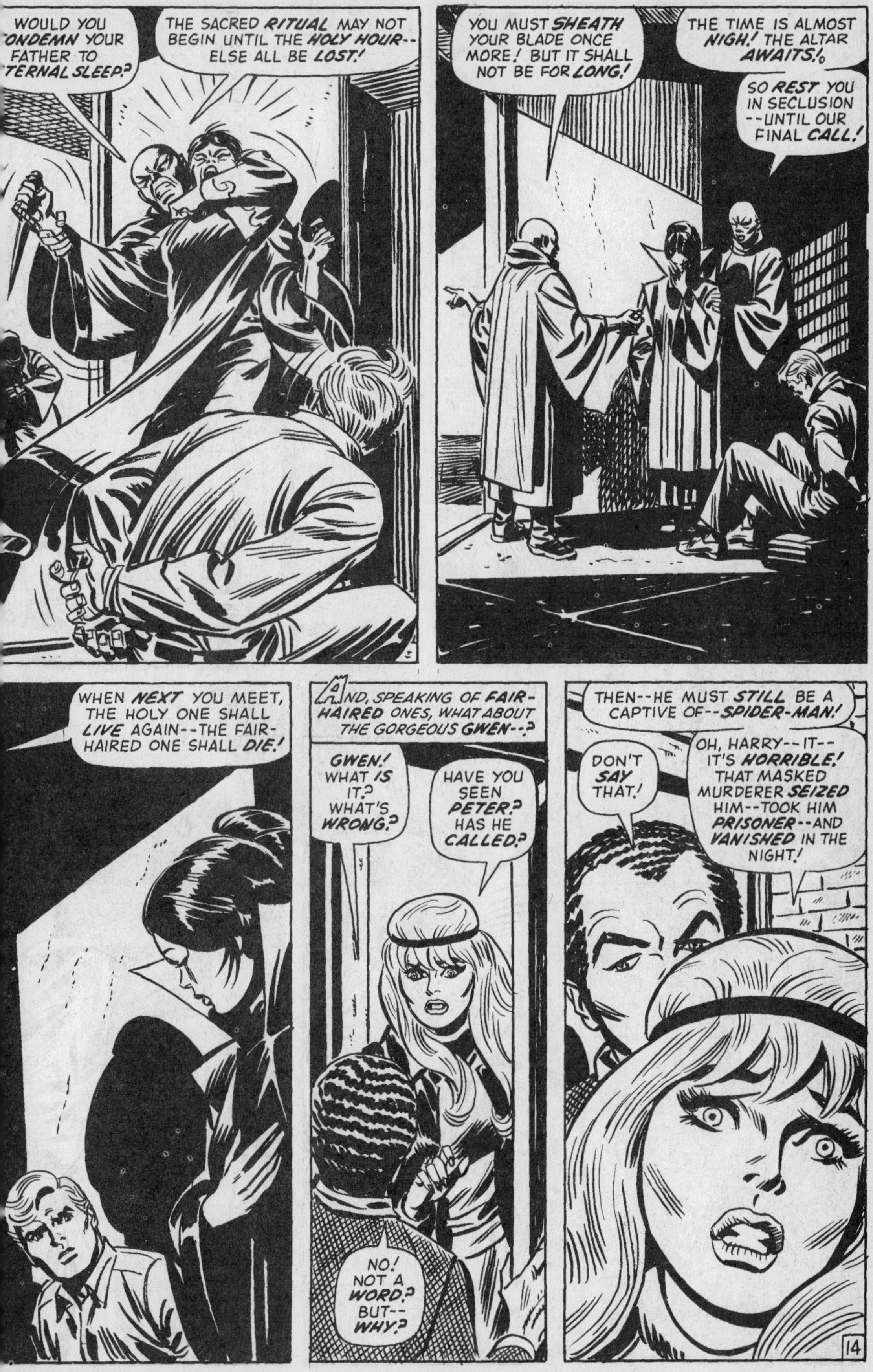
WOULD YOU
ONDEMN YOUR FATHER TO
TERNAL SLEEP?
THE SACRED RITUAL MAY NOT BEGIN UNTIL THE HOLY HOUR--ELSE ALL BE LOST!
YOU MUST SHEATH YOUR BLADE ONCE MORE! BUT IT SHALL NOT BE FOR LONG!
THE TIME IS ALMOST NIGH! THE ALTAR AWAITS!
SO REST YOU IN SECLUSION --UNTIL OUR FINAL CALL!
WHEN NEXT YOU MEET, THE HOLY ONE SHALL LIVE AGAIN--THE FAIR-HAIRED ONE SHALL DIE!
AND, SPEAKING OF FAIR-HAIRED ONES, WHAT ABOUT THE GORGEOUS GWEN--?
GWEN! WHAT IS IT? WHAT'S WRONG?
HAVE YOU SEEN PETER? HAS HE CALLED?
NO! NOT A WORD? BUT--WHY?
THEN--HE MUST STILL BE A CAPTIVE OF--SPIDER-MAN!
DON'T SAY THAT!
OH, HARRY--IT--IT'S HORRIBLE! THAT MASKED MURDERER SEIZED HIM--TOOK HIM PRISONER--AND VANISHED IN THE NIGHT!
14

WELL, IT DOESN'T *MATTER* NOW! IT'S TOO *LATE!* SHE-- *HEARD* YOU!

MRS. *PARKER!* I--I *DIDN'T* KNOW YOU WERE *HERE!*

I WAS WAITING FOR *PETER!* BUT-- WHAT *HAPPENED* TO HIM? WHAT HAPPENED TO MY POOR, DEAR *BOY?*

HE'S *NOT* A BOY! HE'S *NOT!* HE'S A *MAN!*

I *KNOW* HE'S YOUR *NEPHEW!* I *KNOW* HOW YOU *LOVE* HIM-- BECAUSE *I* LOVE HIM *TOO!*

BUT IT'S PETER PARKER, THE *MAN,* THAT I LOVE!

WHEN WILL YOU LET HIM *GO?* WHEN WILL YOU--?

OH! I--I'M *SORRY!* I SHOULDN'T HAVE *SPOKEN* TO YOU THAT WAY! I HAVE-- NO *RIGHT!*

DON'T-- DON'T SAY IT, MY *CHILD!*

YOU HAVE *EVERY* RIGHT! YOU BOTH *LOVE* EACH OTHER--AND THAT *GIVES* YOU THE RIGHT!

PERHAPS YOU'VE *SAID* SOMETHING THAT--THAT SHOULD HAVE BEEN SAID *BEFORE!*

PERHAPS--A FOOLISH OLD LADY--LONELY, AND UNTHINKING--CAN SMOTHER A PERSON--WITH LOVE...

*O*KAY, SOAP-OPERA FREAKS, YOU'VE *HAD* YOUR MOMENT! AND NOW, BACK TO THE *MERRIMENT--*

THE TIME OF *DEATH* IS NIGH!

IT IS THE *HOLY HOUR!*

BRING FORTH THE *SACRIFICE!*

ALL IS *READY!*

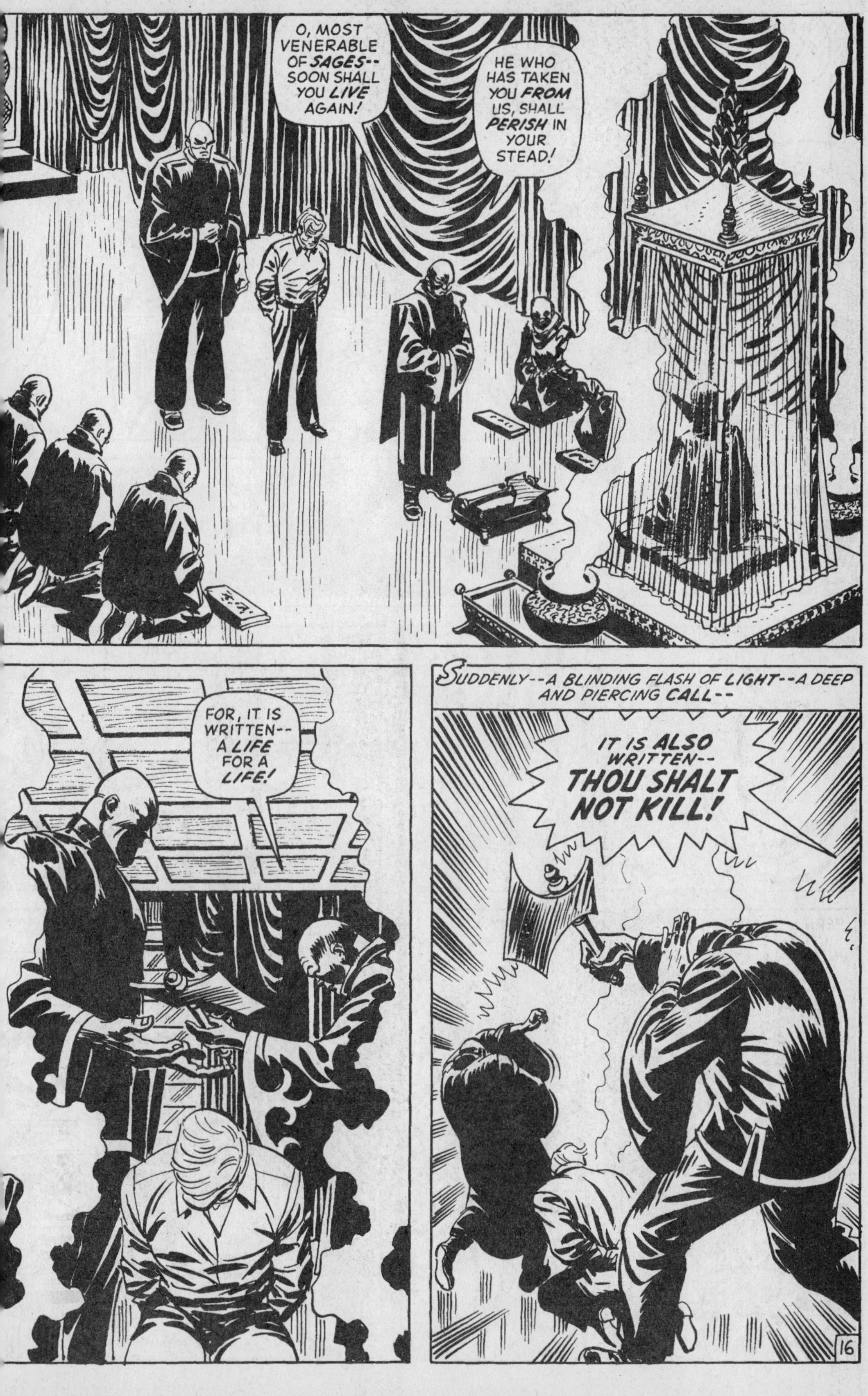
O, MOST VENERABLE OF SAGES-- SOON SHALL YOU LIVE AGAIN!
HE WHO HAS TAKEN YOU FROM US, SHALL PERISH IN YOUR STEAD!
FOR, IT IS WRITTEN-- A LIFE FOR A LIFE!
SUDDENLY--A BLINDING FLASH OF LIGHT--A DEEP AND PIERCING CALL--
IT IS ALSO WRITTEN-- THOU SHALT NOT KILL!
16

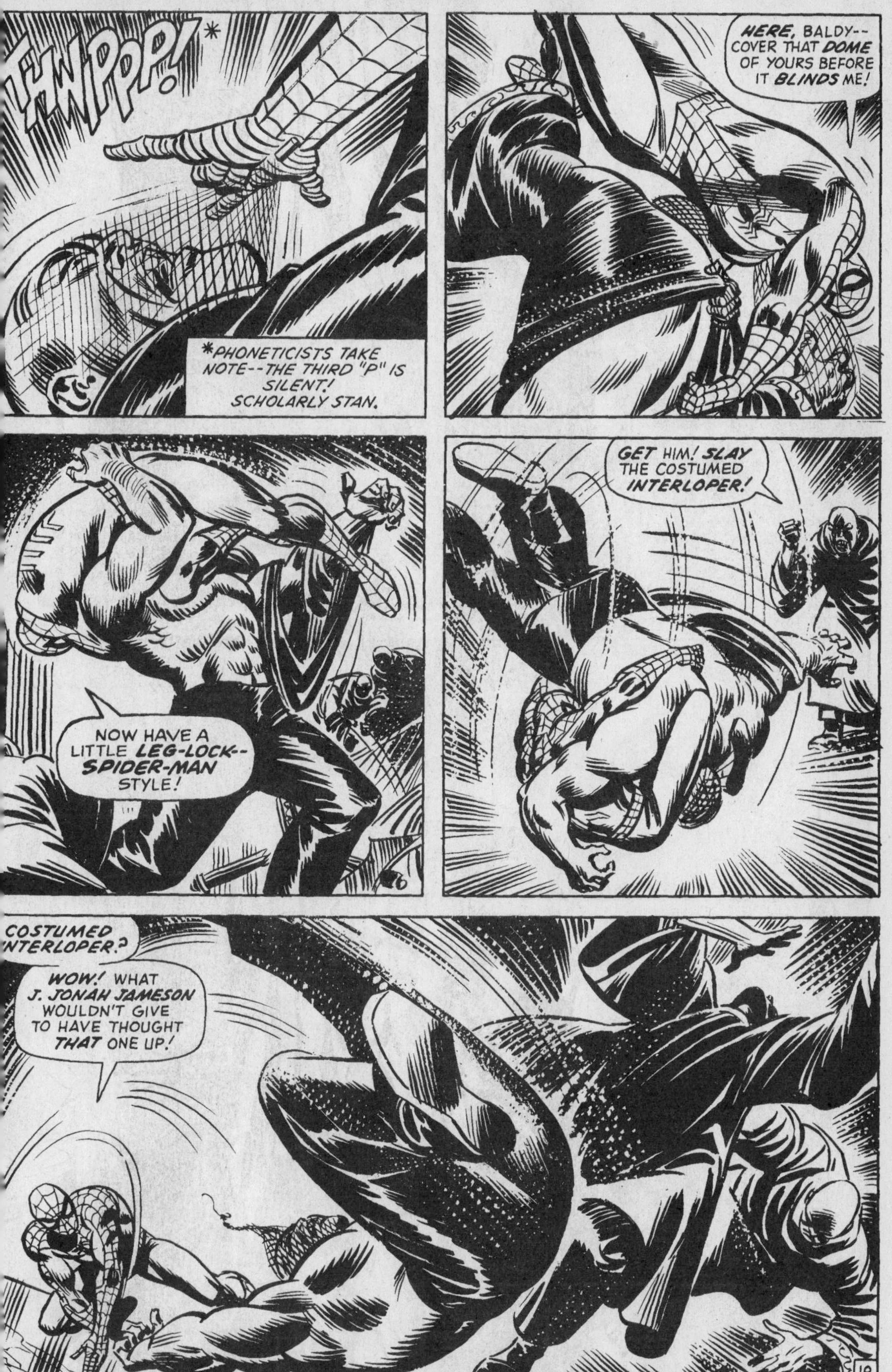
THWPPP!*
*PHONETICISTS TAKE NOTE--THE THIRD "P" IS SILENT! SCHOLARLY STAN.
HERE, BALDY-- COVER THAT DOME OF YOURS BEFORE IT BLINDS ME!
NOW HAVE A LITTLE LEG-LOCK-- SPIDER-MAN STYLE!
GET HIM! SLAY THE COSTUMED INTERLOPER!
COSTUMED INTERLOPER?
WOW! WHAT J. JONAH JAMESON WOULDN'T GIVE TO HAVE THOUGHT THAT ONE UP!
18

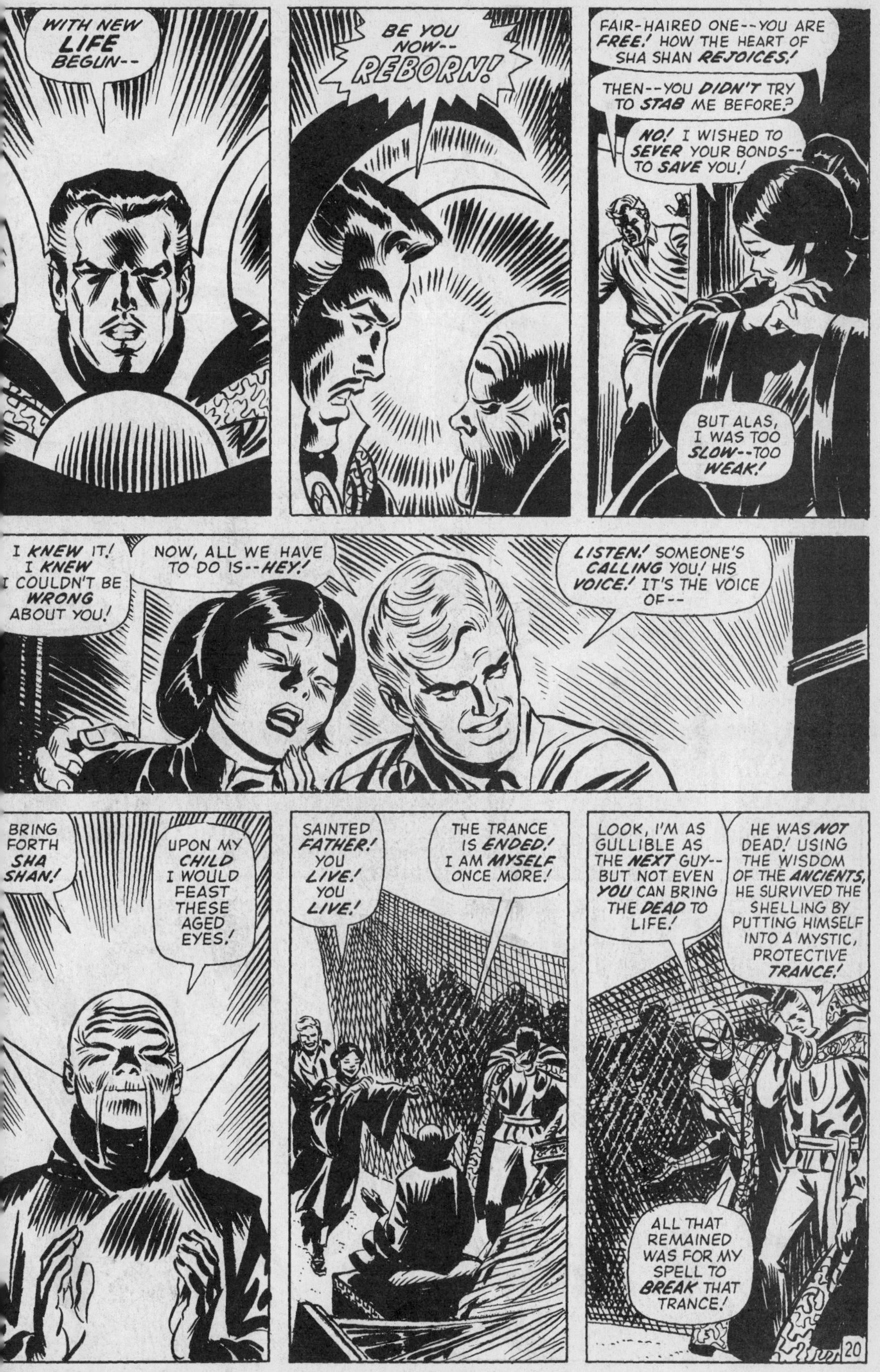
WITH NEW LIFE BEGUN--
BE YOU NOW-- REBORN!
FAIR-HAIRED ONE--YOU ARE FREE! HOW THE HEART OF SHA SHAN REJOICES!
THEN--YOU DIDN'T TRY TO STAB ME BEFORE?
NO! I WISHED TO SEVER YOUR BONDS--TO SAVE YOU!
BUT ALAS, I WAS TOO SLOW--TOO WEAK!
I KNEW IT! I KNEW I COULDN'T BE WRONG ABOUT YOU!
NOW, ALL WE HAVE TO DO IS--HEY!
LISTEN! SOMEONE'S CALLING YOU! HIS VOICE! IT'S THE VOICE OF--
BRING FORTH SHA SHAN!
UPON MY CHILD I WOULD FEAST THESE AGED EYES!
SAINTED FATHER! YOU LIVE! YOU LIVE!
THE TRANCE IS ENDED! I AM MYSELF ONCE MORE!
LOOK, I'M AS GULLIBLE AS THE NEXT GUY--BUT NOT EVEN YOU CAN BRING THE DEAD TO LIFE!
HE WAS NOT DEAD! USING THE WISDOM OF THE ANCIENTS, HE SURVIVED THE SHELLING BY PUTTING HIMSELF INTO A MYSTIC, PROTECTIVE TRANCE!
ALL THAT REMAINED WAS FOR MY SPELL TO BREAK THAT TRANCE!
20

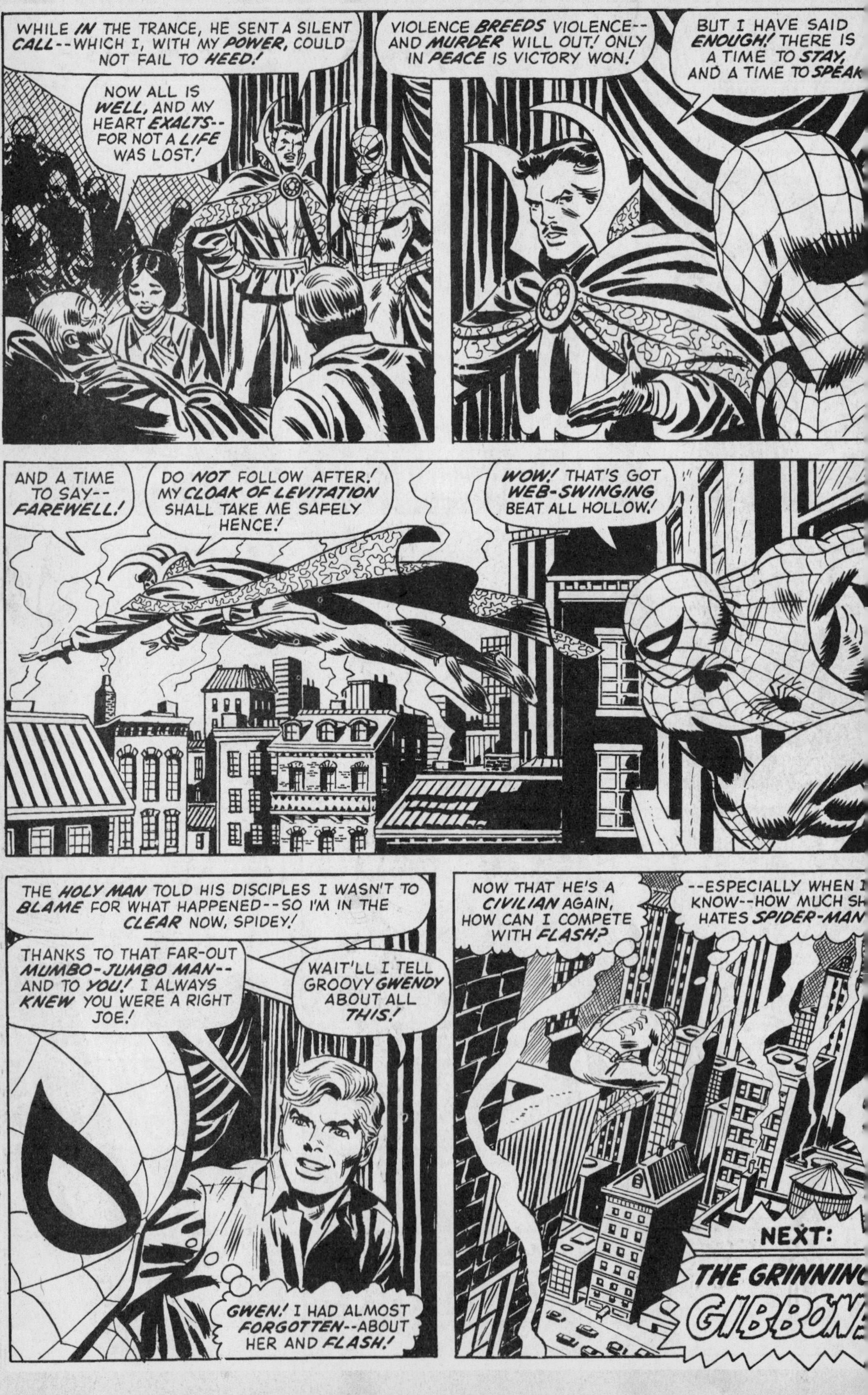

WHILE IN THE TRANCE, HE SENT A SILENT CALL--WHICH I, WITH MY POWER, COULD NOT FAIL TO HEED!
NOW ALL IS WELL, AND MY HEART EXALTS--FOR NOT A LIFE WAS LOST!
VIOLENCE BREEDS VIOLENCE--AND MURDER WILL OUT! ONLY IN PEACE IS VICTORY WON!
BUT I HAVE SAID ENOUGH! THERE IS A TIME TO STAY, AND A TIME TO SPEAK
AND A TIME TO SAY--FAREWELL!
DO NOT FOLLOW AFTER! MY CLOAK OF LEVITATION SHALL TAKE ME SAFELY HENCE!
WOW! THAT'S GOT WEB-SWINGING BEAT ALL HOLLOW!
THE HOLY MAN TOLD HIS DISCIPLES I WASN'T TO BLAME FOR WHAT HAPPENED--SO I'M IN THE CLEAR NOW, SPIDEY!
THANKS TO THAT FAR-OUT MUMBO-JUMBO MAN--AND TO YOU! I ALWAYS KNEW YOU WERE A RIGHT JOE!
WAIT'LL I TELL GROOVY GWENDY ABOUT ALL THIS!
GWEN! I HAD ALMOST FORGOTTEN--ABOUT HER AND FLASH!
NOW THAT HE'S A CIVILIAN AGAIN, HOW CAN I COMPETE WITH FLASH?
--ESPECIALLY WHEN I KNOW--HOW MUCH SH HATES SPIDER-MAN
NEXT:
THE GRINNING GIBBON

SPIDER-MAN
MARVEL COMICS GROUP
20¢ 110 JULY 02457
the AMAZING SPIDER-MAN
APPROVED BY THE COMICS CODE AUTHORITY
INTRODUCING: THE NEWEST MARVEL SUPER-STAR!
THE BIRTH OF THE GIBBON!

2

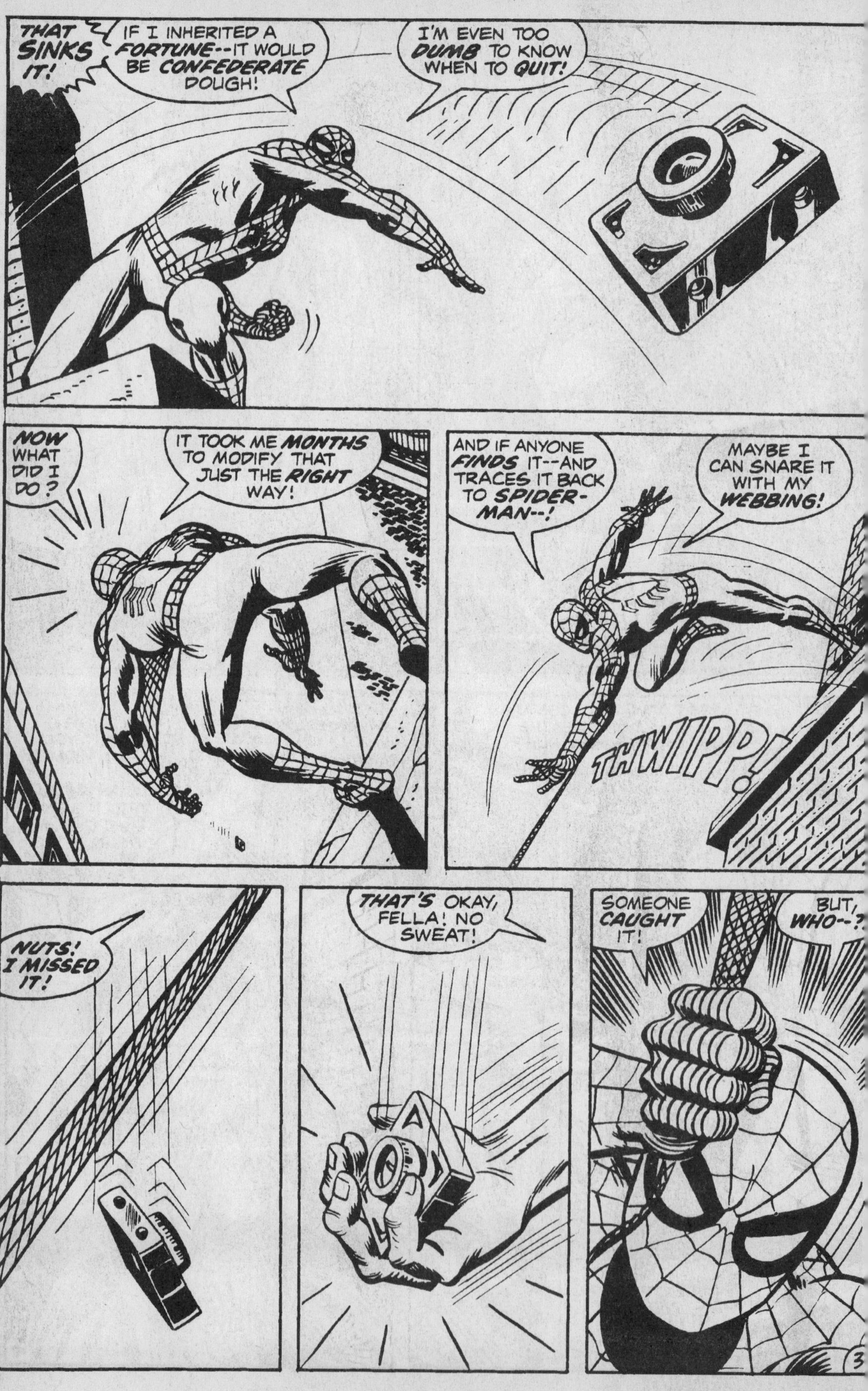
THAT SINKS IT!
IF I INHERITED A FORTUNE--IT WOULD BE CONFEDERATE DOUGH!
I'M EVEN TOO DUMB TO KNOW WHEN TO QUIT!
NOW WHAT DID I DO?
IT TOOK ME MONTHS TO MODIFY THAT JUST THE RIGHT WAY!
AND IF ANYONE FINDS IT--AND TRACES IT BACK TO SPIDER-MAN--!
MAYBE I CAN SNARE IT WITH MY WEBBING!
THWIPP!
NUTS! I MISSED IT!
THAT'S OKAY, FELLA! NO SWEAT!
SOMEONE CAUGHT IT!
BUT, WHO--?
3

STAY WHERE YOU *ARE*, PAL-- I'LL BE RIGHT *UP* THERE!

HE-- HE'S AS AGILE AS *I* AM!

MAYBE EVEN *MORE* SO!

HEY! I'D KNOW THAT COSTUME *ANYWHERE!* YOU'RE THE REAL *SPIDER-MAN*, HUH?

THE NAME'S *MARTIN BLANK*-- BUT IT WOULDN'T MEAN ANYTHING TO *YOU!*

I'VE BEEN *READING* ABOUT YOU FOR *YEARS!*

HOW *ABOUT* THAT? EVEN A FREAK LIKE *ME* CAN HELP THE HIGH 'N MIGHTY *SPIDER-MAN!*

YOU'VE GOT THE ADVANTAGE OVER *ME*, MISTER! WHO ARE *YOU?*

4

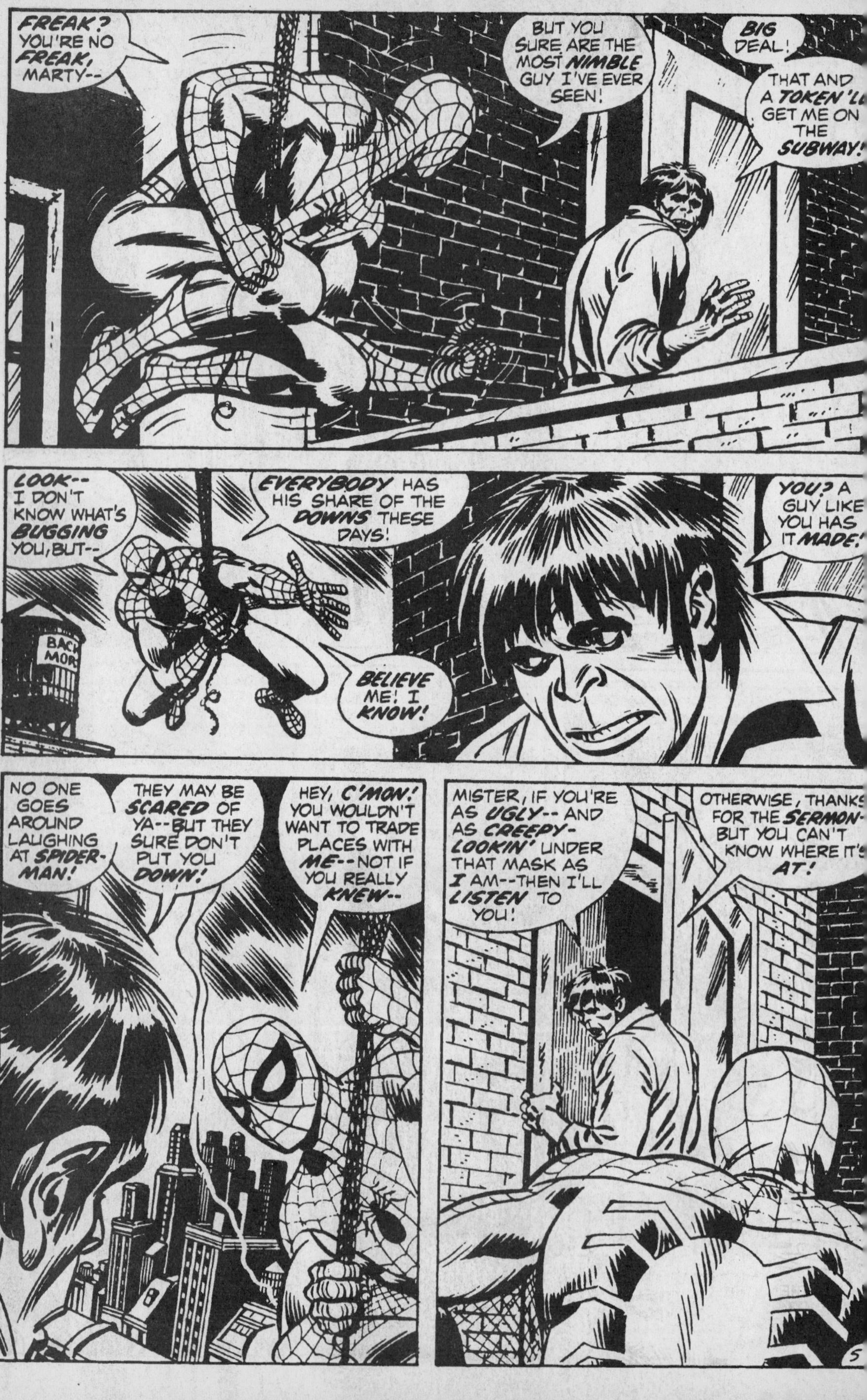
FREAK? YOU'RE NO FREAK, MARTY--
BUT YOU SURE ARE THE MOST NIMBLE GUY I'VE EVER SEEN!
BIG DEAL!
THAT AND A TOKEN'LL GET ME ON THE SUBWAY!
LOOK-- I DON'T KNOW WHAT'S BUGGING YOU, BUT--
EVERYBODY HAS HIS SHARE OF THE DOWNS THESE DAYS!
BELIEVE ME! I KNOW!
YOU? A GUY LIKE YOU HAS IT MADE!
NO ONE GOES AROUND LAUGHING AT SPIDER-MAN!
THEY MAY BE SCARED OF YA--BUT THEY SURE DON'T PUT YOU DOWN!
HEY, C'MON! YOU WOULDN'T WANT TO TRADE PLACES WITH ME--NOT IF YOU REALLY KNEW--
MISTER, IF YOU'RE AS UGLY-- AND AS CREEPY-LOOKIN' UNDER THAT MASK AS I AM--THEN I'LL LISTEN TO YOU!
OTHERWISE, THANKS FOR THE SERMON-- BUT YOU CAN'T KNOW WHERE IT'S AT!
5

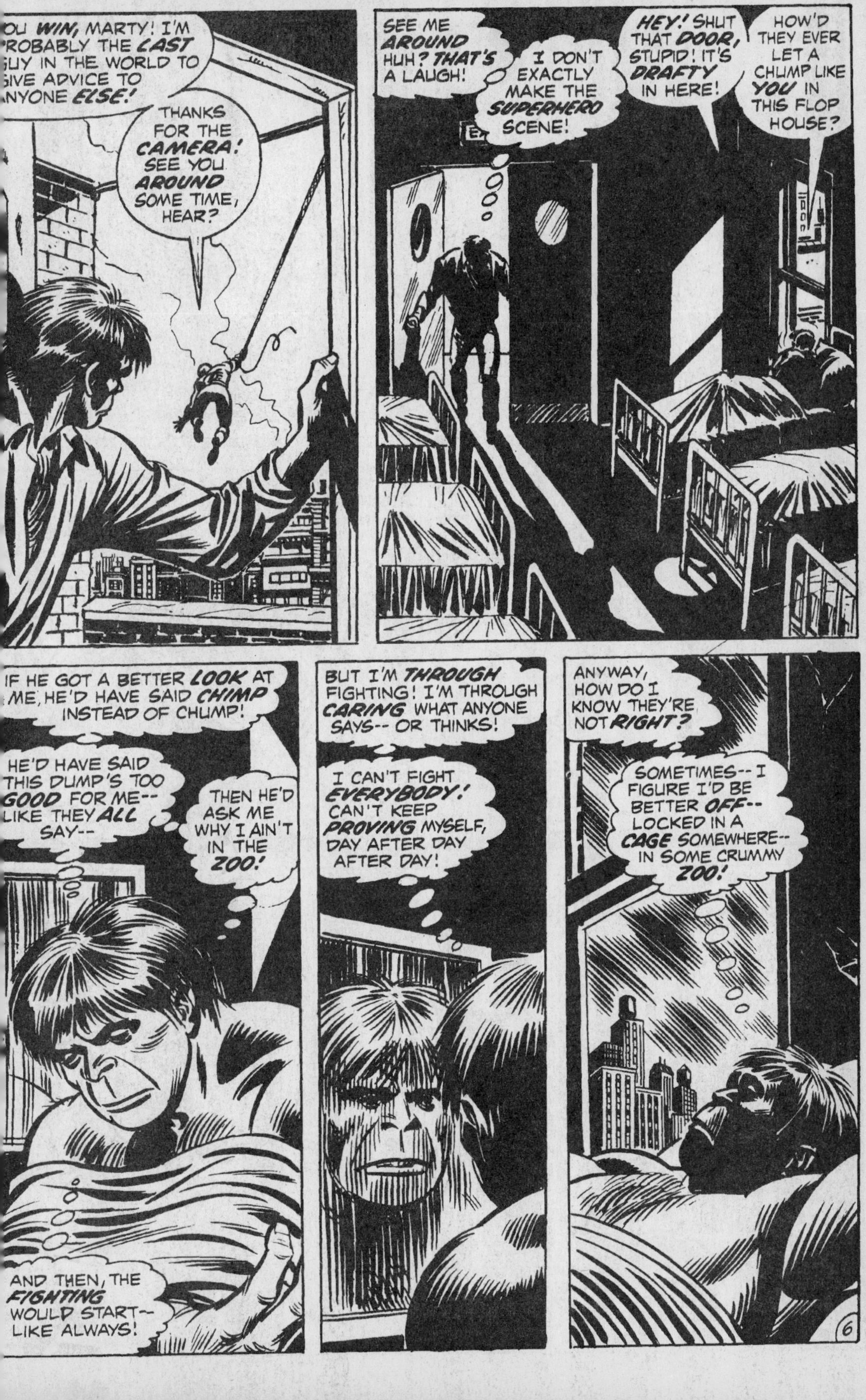

OU WIN, MARTY! I'M ROBABLY THE LAST GUY IN THE WORLD TO GIVE ADVICE TO NYONE ELSE!
THANKS FOR THE CAMERA! SEE YOU AROUND SOME TIME, HEAR?
SEE ME AROUND HUH? THAT'S A LAUGH!
I DON'T EXACTLY MAKE THE SUPERHERO SCENE!
HEY! SHUT THAT DOOR, STUPID! IT'S DRAFTY IN HERE!
HOW'D THEY EVER LET A CHUMP LIKE YOU IN THIS FLOP HOUSE?
IF HE GOT A BETTER LOOK AT ME, HE'D HAVE SAID CHIMP INSTEAD OF CHUMP!
HE'D HAVE SAID THIS DUMP'S TOO GOOD FOR ME-- LIKE THEY ALL SAY--
THEN HE'D ASK ME WHY I AIN'T IN THE ZOO!
AND THEN, THE FIGHTING WOULD START-- LIKE ALWAYS!
BUT I'M THROUGH FIGHTING! I'M THROUGH CARING WHAT ANYONE SAYS-- OR THINKS!
I CAN'T FIGHT EVERYBODY! CAN'T KEEP PROVING MYSELF, DAY AFTER DAY AFTER DAY!
ANYWAY, HOW DO I KNOW THEY'RE NOT RIGHT?
SOMETIMES-- I FIGURE I'D BE BETTER OFF-- LOCKED IN A CAGE SOMEWHERE-- IN SOME CRUMMY ZOO!
6

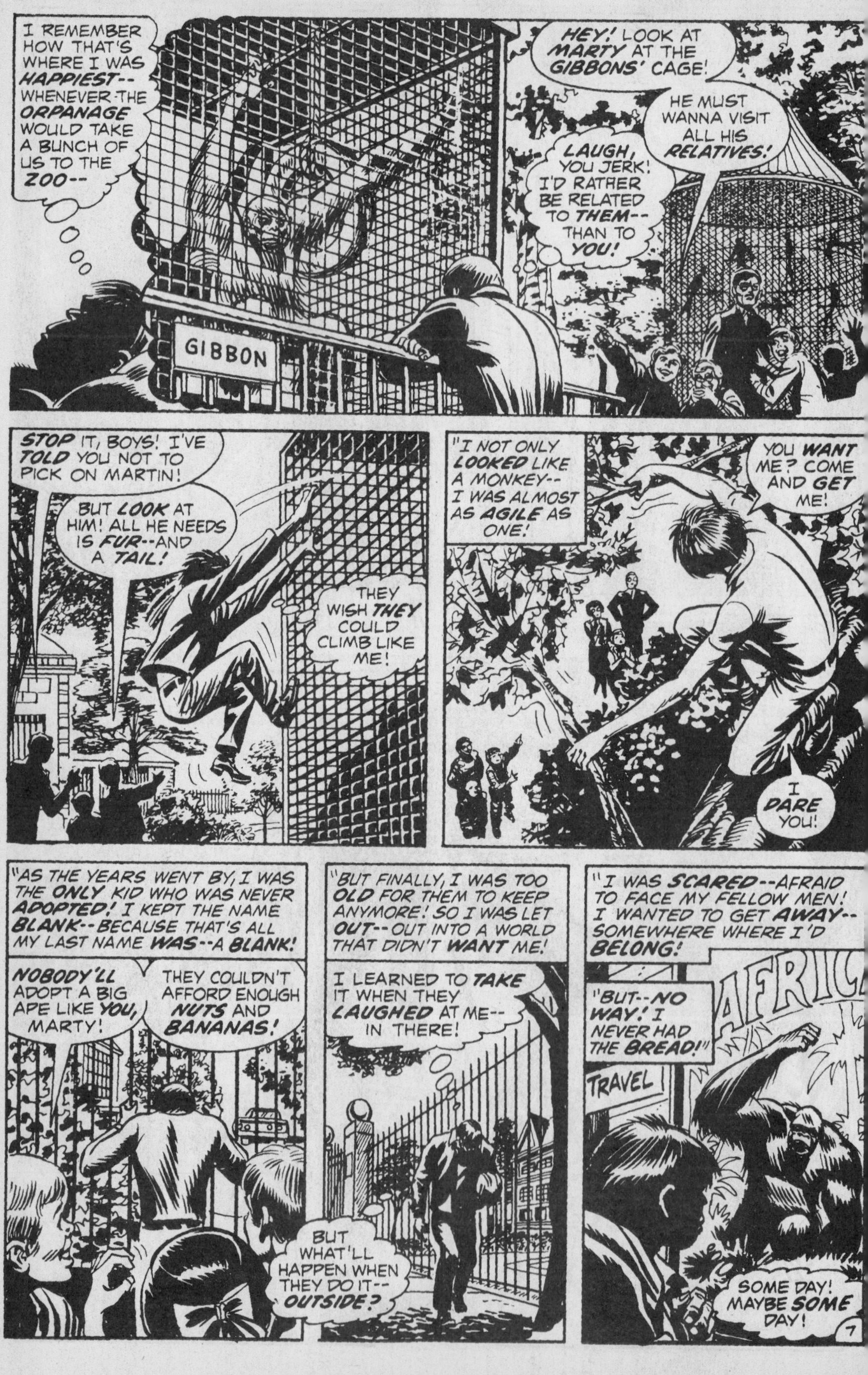
I REMEMBER HOW THAT'S WHERE I WAS HAPPIEST-- WHENEVER THE ORPANAGE WOULD TAKE A BUNCH OF US TO THE ZOO--
GIBBON
HEY! LOOK AT MARTY AT THE GIBBONS' CAGE!
HE MUST WANNA VISIT ALL HIS RELATIVES!
LAUGH, YOU JERK! I'D RATHER BE RELATED TO THEM-- THAN TO YOU!
STOP IT, BOYS! I'VE TOLD YOU NOT TO PICK ON MARTIN!
BUT LOOK AT HIM! ALL HE NEEDS IS FUR--AND A TAIL!
THEY WISH THEY COULD CLIMB LIKE ME!
"I NOT ONLY LOOKED LIKE A MONKEY-- I WAS ALMOST AS AGILE AS ONE!
YOU WANT ME? COME AND GET ME!
I DARE YOU!
"AS THE YEARS WENT BY, I WAS THE ONLY KID WHO WAS NEVER ADOPTED! I KEPT THE NAME BLANK--BECAUSE THAT'S ALL MY LAST NAME WAS--A BLANK!
NOBODY'LL ADOPT A BIG APE LIKE YOU, MARTY!
THEY COULDN'T AFFORD ENOUGH NUTS AND BANANAS!
"BUT FINALLY, I WAS TOO OLD FOR THEM TO KEEP ANYMORE! SO I WAS LET OUT--OUT INTO A WORLD THAT DIDN'T WANT ME!
I LEARNED TO TAKE IT WHEN THEY LAUGHED AT ME-- IN THERE!
BUT WHAT'LL HAPPEN WHEN THEY DO IT-- OUTSIDE?
"I WAS SCARED--AFRAID TO FACE MY FELLOW MEN! I WANTED TO GET AWAY-- SOMEWHERE WHERE I'D BELONG!
"BUT--NO WAY! I NEVER HAD THE BREAD!"
AFRICA
TRAVEL
SOME DAY! MAYBE SOME DAY!

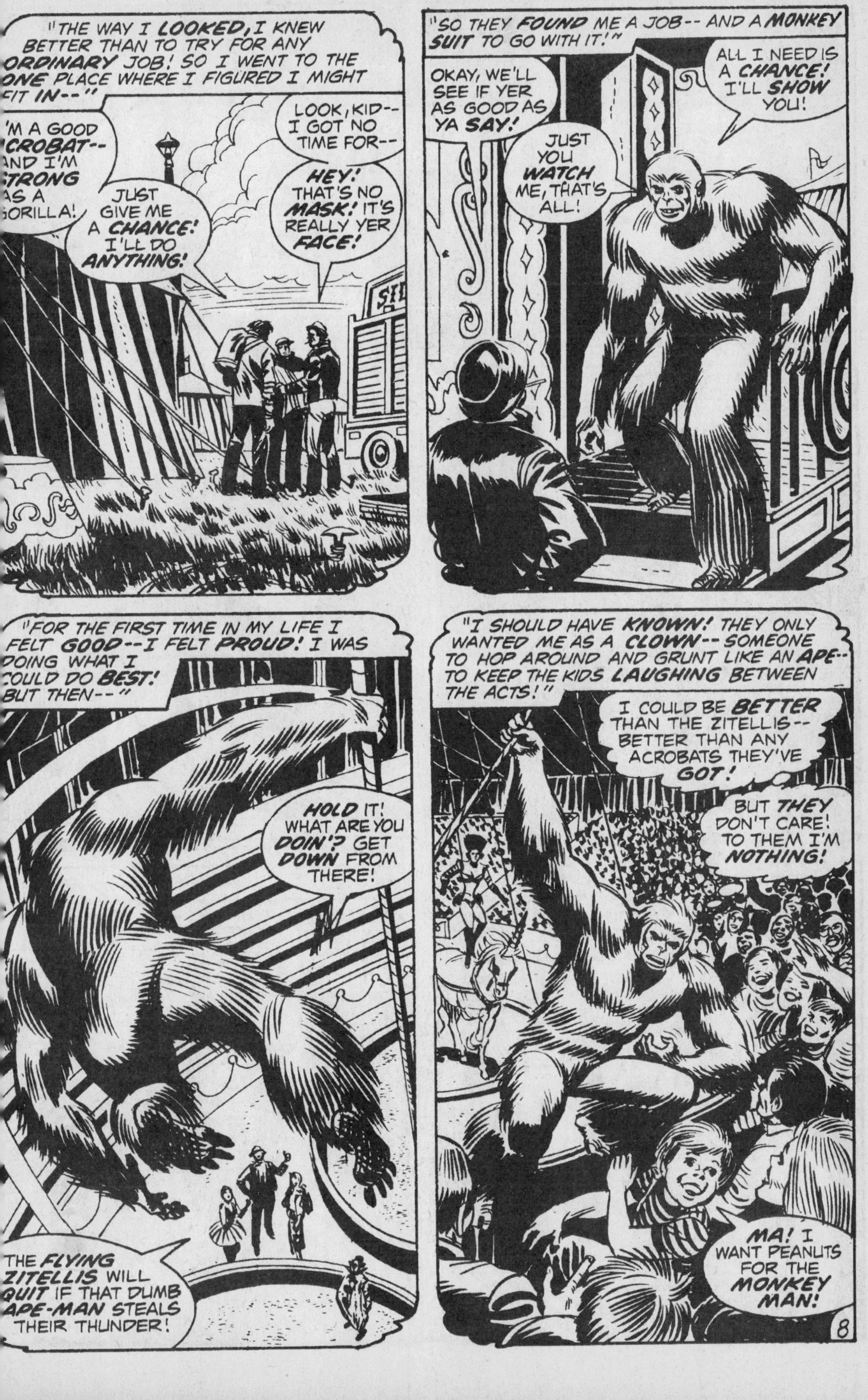
"THE WAY I LOOKED, I KNEW BETTER THAN TO TRY FOR ANY ORDINARY JOB! SO I WENT TO THE ONE PLACE WHERE I FIGURED I MIGHT FIT IN--"
I'M A GOOD ACROBAT-- AND I'M STRONG AS A GORILLA!
JUST GIVE ME A CHANCE! I'LL DO ANYTHING!
LOOK, KID-- I GOT NO TIME FOR--
HEY! THAT'S NO MASK! IT'S REALLY YER FACE!
"SO THEY FOUND ME A JOB-- AND A MONKEY SUIT TO GO WITH IT!"
OKAY, WE'LL SEE IF YER AS GOOD AS YA SAY!
ALL I NEED IS A CHANCE! I'LL SHOW YOU!
JUST YOU WATCH ME, THAT'S ALL!
"FOR THE FIRST TIME IN MY LIFE I FELT GOOD--I FELT PROUD! I WAS DOING WHAT I COULD DO BEST! BUT THEN--"
HOLD IT! WHAT ARE YOU DOIN'? GET DOWN FROM THERE!
THE FLYING ZITELLIS WILL QUIT IF THAT DUMB APE-MAN STEALS THEIR THUNDER!
"I SHOULD HAVE KNOWN! THEY ONLY WANTED ME AS A CLOWN-- SOMEONE TO HOP AROUND AND GRUNT LIKE AN APE-- TO KEEP THE KIDS LAUGHING BETWEEN THE ACTS!"
I COULD BE BETTER THAN THE ZITELLIS-- BETTER THAN ANY ACROBATS THEY'VE GOT!
BUT THEY DON'T CARE! TO THEM I'M NOTHING!
MA! I WANT PEANUTS FOR THE MONKEY MAN!
8

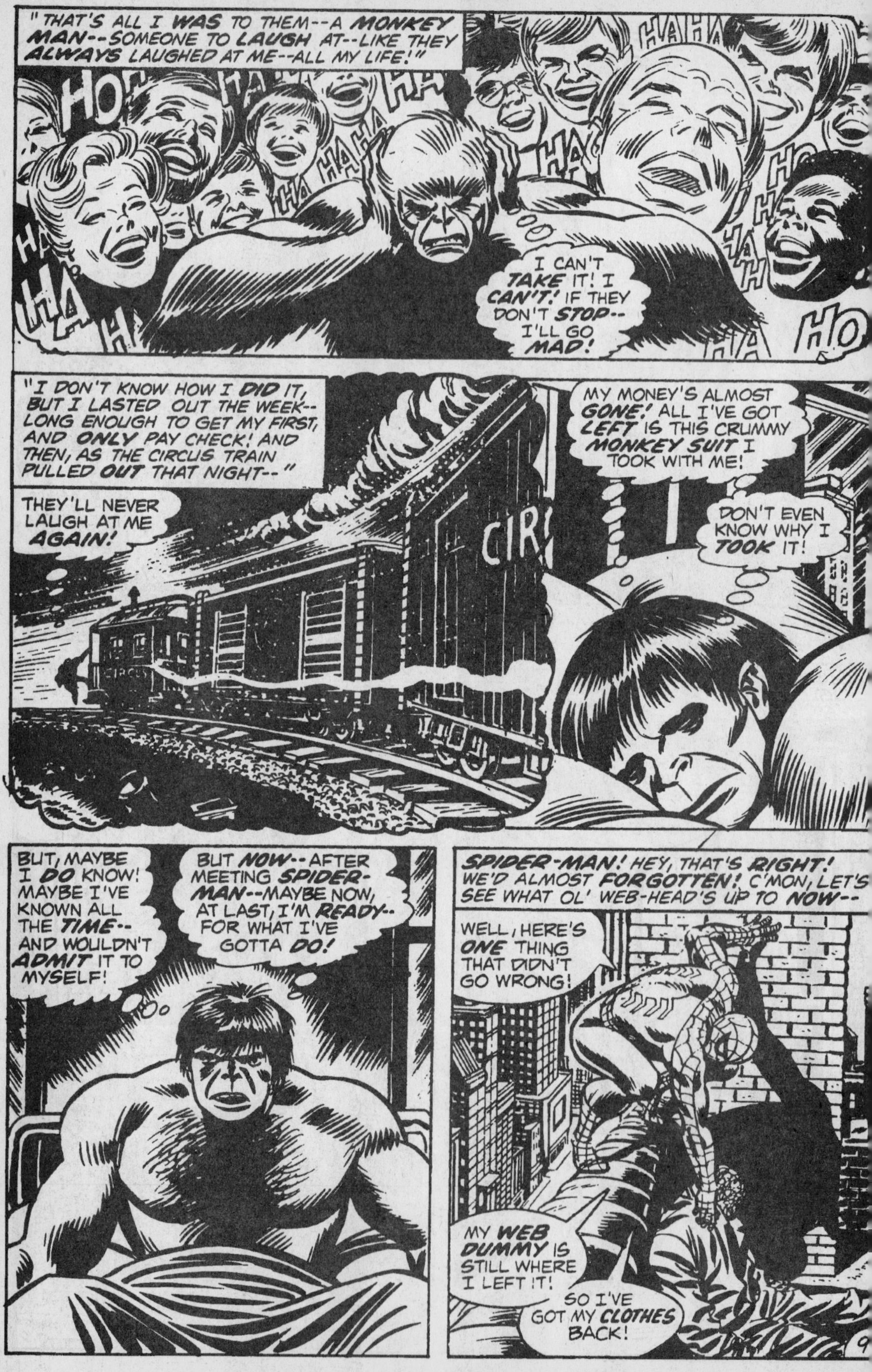
"THAT'S ALL I WAS TO THEM--A MONKEY MAN--SOMEONE TO LAUGH AT--LIKE THEY ALWAYS LAUGHED AT ME--ALL MY LIFE!"
HO
HA HA
I CAN'T TAKE IT! I CAN'T! IF THEY DON'T STOP-- I'LL GO MAD!
"I DON'T KNOW HOW I DID IT, BUT I LASTED OUT THE WEEK-- LONG ENOUGH TO GET MY FIRST, AND ONLY PAY CHECK! AND THEN, AS THE CIRCUS TRAIN PULLED OUT THAT NIGHT--"
THEY'LL NEVER LAUGH AT ME AGAIN!
MY MONEY'S ALMOST GONE! ALL I'VE GOT LEFT IS THIS CRUMMY MONKEY SUIT I TOOK WITH ME!
DON'T EVEN KNOW WHY I TOOK IT!
BUT, MAYBE I DO KNOW! MAYBE I'VE KNOWN ALL THE TIME-- AND WOULDN'T ADMIT IT TO MYSELF!
BUT NOW--AFTER MEETING SPIDER-MAN--MAYBE NOW, AT LAST, I'M READY-- FOR WHAT I'VE GOTTA DO!
SPIDER-MAN! HEY, THAT'S RIGHT! WE'D ALMOST FORGOTTEN! C'MON, LET'S SEE WHAT OL' WEB-HEAD'S UP TO NOW--
WELL, HERE'S ONE THING THAT DIDN'T GO WRONG!
MY WEB DUMMY IS STILL WHERE I LEFT IT!
SO I'VE GOT MY CLOTHES BACK!
9

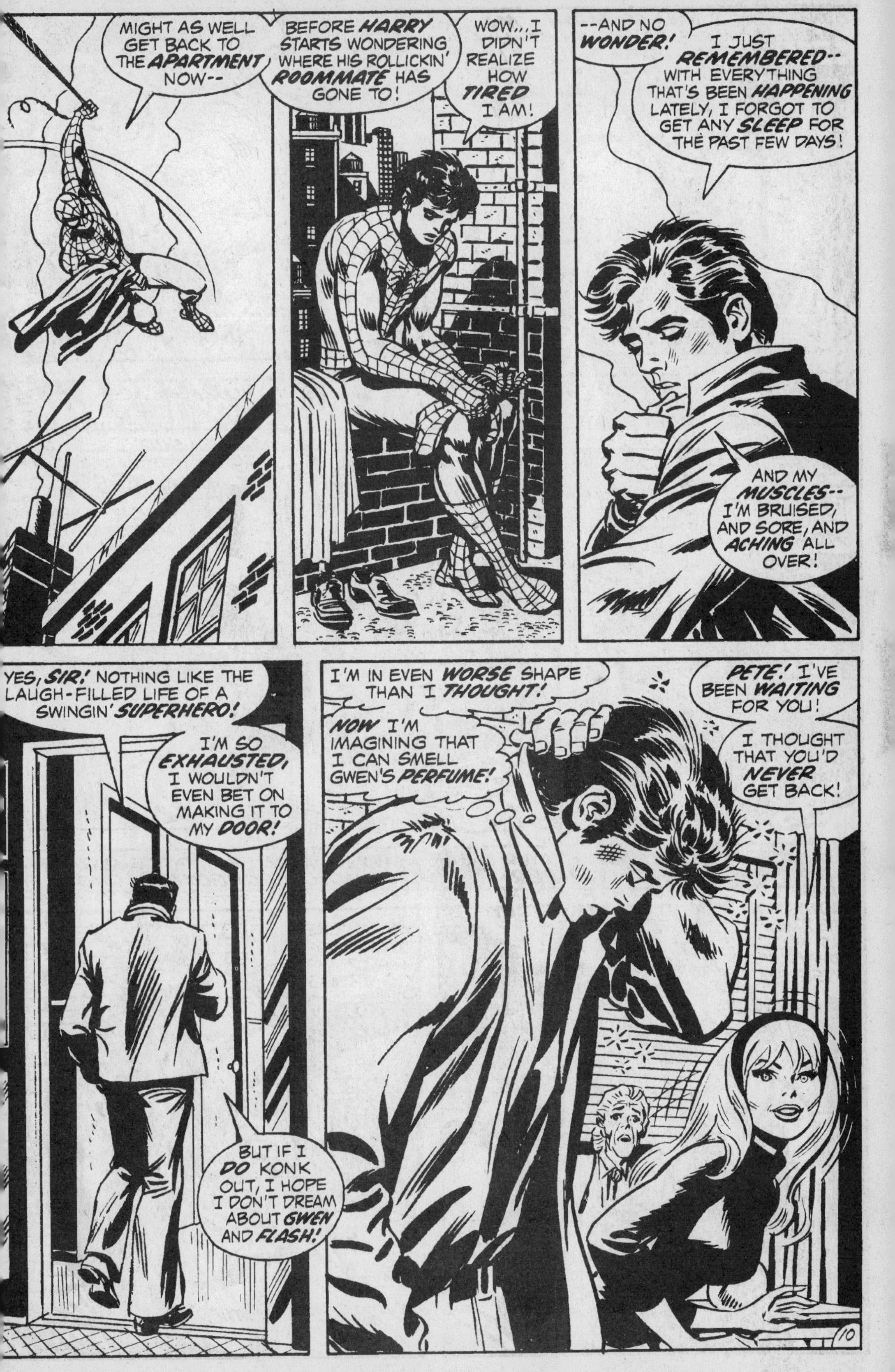
MIGHT AS WELL GET BACK TO THE APARTMENT NOW--
BEFORE HARRY STARTS WONDERING WHERE HIS ROLLICKIN' ROOMMATE HAS GONE TO!
WOW... I DIDN'T REALIZE HOW TIRED I AM!
--AND NO WONDER!
I JUST REMEMBERED-- WITH EVERYTHING THAT'S BEEN HAPPENING LATELY, I FORGOT TO GET ANY SLEEP FOR THE PAST FEW DAYS!
AND MY MUSCLES-- I'M BRUISED, AND SORE, AND ACHING ALL OVER!
YES, SIR! NOTHING LIKE THE LAUGH-FILLED LIFE OF A SWINGIN' SUPERHERO!
I'M SO EXHAUSTED, I WOULDN'T EVEN BET ON MAKING IT TO MY DOOR!
BUT IF I DO KONK OUT, I HOPE I DON'T DREAM ABOUT GWEN AND FLASH!
I'M IN EVEN WORSE SHAPE THAN I THOUGHT!
NOW I'M IMAGINING THAT I CAN SMELL GWEN'S PERFUME!
PETE! I'VE BEEN WAITING FOR YOU!
I THOUGHT THAT YOU'D NEVER GET BACK!
10

GWENDY! I THOUGHT YOU'D BE WITH-- I MEAN, I DIDN'T EXPECT TO FIND--

I GUESS FLASH HASN'T HAD A CHANCE TO CALL HER YET!

YOU WERE GONE SO LONG! WE WERE SO WORRIED ABOUT YOU!

YOU POOR BOY! I'VE NEVER SEEN YOU LOOKING SO TIRED BEFORE!

YOUR CLOTHES ARE SO WRINKLED --AND ALL THOSE BRUISES ON YOU FAC

IT'S THAT HORRIBLE SPIDER-MAN, ISN'T IT?

I HEARD HOW HE ATTACKED YOU! BUT WHY? WHY, PETER?

IT WAS THE ONLY WAY I COULD SET IT UP-- SO NO ONE WOULD SUSPECT THAT WE'RE BOTH THE SAME ONE! BUT HOW DO I TELL THAT TO POOR AUNT MAY?

MRS. PARKER-- YOU PROMISED!

DON'T YOU REMEMBER? YOU PROMISED TO STOP TREATING PETER LIKE A CHILD--TO STOP BABYING HIM!

OH, DEAR! I DID IT AGAIN! AND-- I TRIED NOT TO!

AW, THAT'S OKAY, AUNT MAY!

NO, PETER DEAR--IT'S NOT OKAY!

I--DON'T KNOW WHAT THEY'RE TALKING ABOUT! AND MY HEAD--IT'S ACHING SO THAT I CAN'T EVEN THINK!

GWENDOLYN I RIGHT! I'VE BE TO MATERNAL--TOO POSSESSIVE ALL THESE YEARS!

GWENDY, WHAT IS IT? WHAT'S HAPPENED TO AUNT MAY?

IT'S MY FAULT, PETER! I TOLD HER SHE SHOULDN'T TRY TO CODDLE YOU SO MUCH--

BUT I DIDN'T MEAN TO HURT HER--TO MAKE HER FEEL GUILTY!

I JUST DID IT FOR YOUR SAKE, BECAUSE--

PETE! WHAT IS IT? WHAT'S WRONG?

IT'S--ALL RIGHT, GWEN--I'M JUST--TIRED!

CAN'T KEEP MY EYES OPEN-- ANY LONGER!

PETE!

Panel 1:
'I SHOULD HAVE *KNOWN!* THE STRAIN OF BEING THREATENED BY *SPIDER-MAN--* IT WAS BOUND TO *GET* TO YOU!

MRS. PARKER! WE HAVE TO GET HIM TO *BED!* HE'S *EXHAUSTED!*

NO *ANSWER!* SHE MUST HAVE *LEFT!*

DON'T *WORRY,* DARLING! *I'LL* LOOK AFTER YOU!

Panel 2:
OH, PETER-- *PETER!* IT BREAKS MY *HEART* TO SEE YOU LIKE THIS!

CLICK

I *LOVE* YOU SO MUCH-- SO *VERY* MUCH!

THE *DOOR!* SOMEONE'S *COMING!*

Panel 3:
HI, GWEN! WE PASSED *MRS. PARKER* IN THE HALL, AND-- *HEY!* WHAT *GIVES?*

HARRY! FLASH! I'M SO GLAD YOU'RE *HERE!*

PETER JUST ARRIVED! HE ISN'T *HURT* OR ANYTHING-- BUT HE WAS SO *TIRED* HE COULDN'T STAY *AWAKE!*

Panel 4:
ANY CLOWN WHO CAN'T STAY AWAKE WHEN *YOU'RE* AROUND, HONEY--!

STOP IT, FLASH! IT'S NOTHING TO *JOKE* ABOUT!

MAYBE HE *ISN'T* A BIG, STRONG, RUGGED *WAR HERO* LIKE *YOU,* BUT--

WHOA! EASY, GWEN! FLASH WAS JUST *KIDDING!*

Panel 5:

WOW! I'VE HEARD OF *TIGRESSES* FIGHTING FOR THEIR MATES-- BUT THEY'VE GOT NOTHING ON *YOU,* LADY!

I DON'T MEAN TO GO GETTING ALL *UPTIGHT,* BUT--

I JUST CAN'T *BEAR* IT WHEN I HEAR PEOPLE PUTTING POOR PETER *DOWN!*

MAYBE HE'S NOT *YOUR* CUP OF TEA-- BUT HE'S ALL THE MAN *I'LL* EVER WANT!

Panel 6:

LOOK, WHY NOT LET FLASH TAKE YOU *HOME? I'LL* STAY HERE WITH PETE! ALL HE NEEDS NOW IS *REST!*

I HATE TO *LEAVE* HIM-- BUT I GUESS YOU'RE *RIGHT!*

HE'S A *LUCKY* GUY TO HAVE A CHICK LIKE *YOU,* GWEN!

12

I'M *LOSING* HER! I *KNOW* IT! I *KNOW* IT! AND I CAN'T GET HER *BACK!*

JUST AS I'M LOSING *AUNT MAY!*

WHY MUST I *HURT* ALL THOSE I *LOVE*-- OR HAVE THEM HURT *ME?*

WHY? WHY? WHY? WHY?

PETER! WAKE *UP!* EVERYTHING'S *OKAY!* C'MON, FELLA-- SNAP *OUT* OF IT!

THE *WEB!* IT'S *GONE!* I--I CAN *MOVE* AGAIN!

I--I'M *FREE!*

MAN! YOU MUST HAVE JUST HAD THE *GRAND-DADDY* OF ALL *NIGHTMARES!*

I DON'T KNOW WHAT YOU WERE *YELLING* ABOUT, BUT YOU COULD PROBABLY *SELL* IT TO ALFRED HITCHCOCK!

A *NIGHTMARE?* YOU MEAN-- I WAS JUST-- *DREAMING?*

WHAT WOULD *YOU* CALL IT WHEN A GUY ROLLS AND TURNS AND MUMBLES FOR ALMOST *TWELVE HOURS*-- BETWEEN *SNORES*, THAT IS-- WITH HIS *EYES* TIGHTLY CLOSED?

TWELVE HOURS? IT FEELS LIKE I *JUST* HIT THE COUCH!

BOY, I *MUST* HAVE BEEN TIRED!

FEELING *OKAY* NOW?

OH *GREAT!* CONSIDERING I JUST LOST MY GIRL!

14

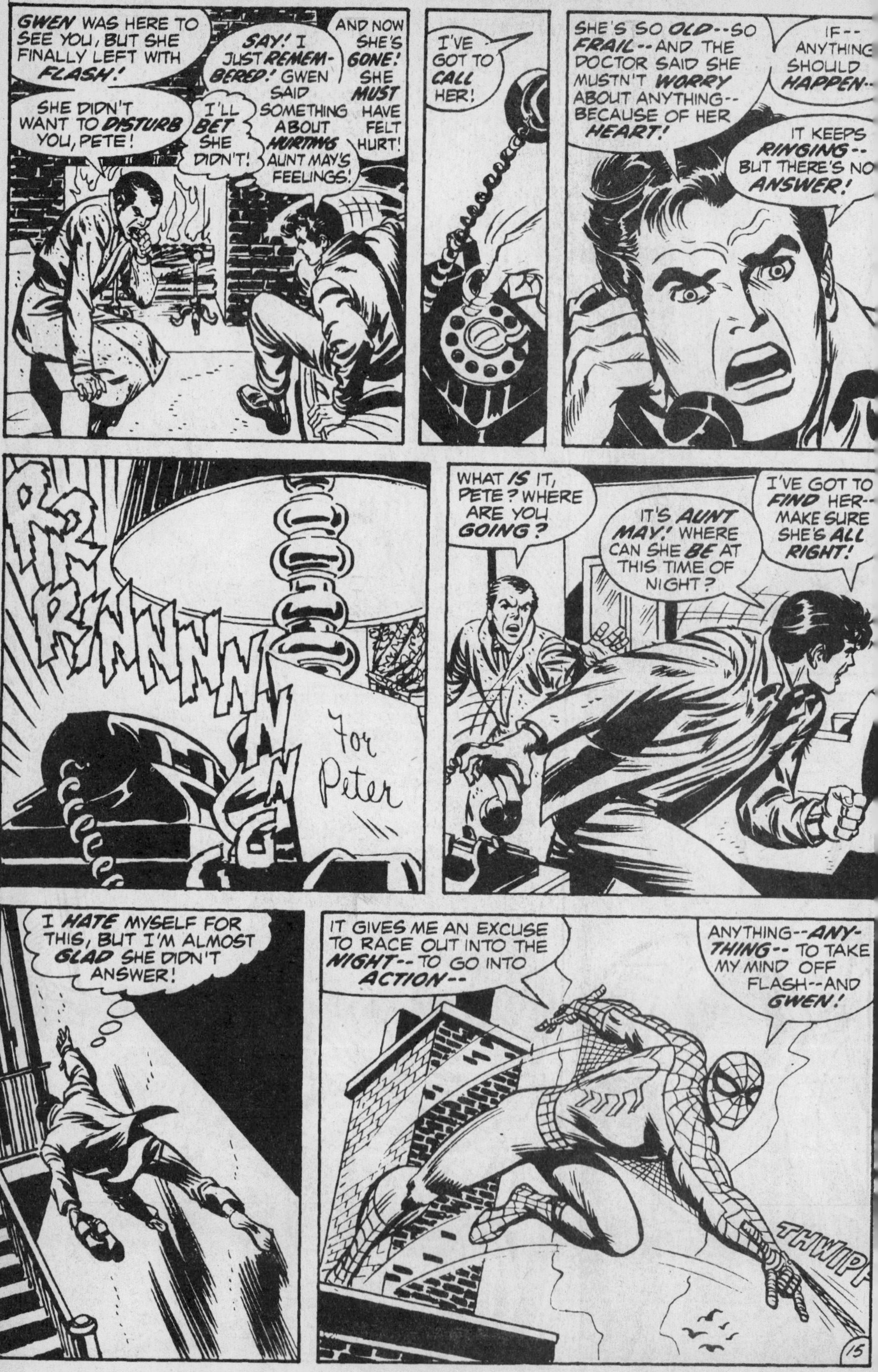
GWEN WAS HERE TO SEE YOU, BUT SHE FINALLY LEFT WITH FLASH!
SHE DIDN'T WANT TO DISTURB YOU, PETE!
SAY! I JUST REMEMBERED! GWEN SAID SOMETHING ABOUT HURTING AUNT MAY'S FEELINGS!
I'LL BET SHE DIDN'T!
AND NOW SHE'S GONE! SHE MUST HAVE FELT HURT!
I'VE GOT TO CALL HER!
SHE'S SO OLD--SO FRAIL--AND THE DOCTOR SAID SHE MUSTN'T WORRY ABOUT ANYTHING--BECAUSE OF HER HEART!
IF--ANYTHING SHOULD HAPPEN--
IT KEEPS RINGING--BUT THERE'S NO ANSWER!
RRRINNNNNNNG
For Peter
WHAT IS IT, PETE? WHERE ARE YOU GOING?
IT'S AUNT MAY! WHERE CAN SHE BE AT THIS TIME OF NIGHT?
I'VE GOT TO FIND HER--MAKE SURE SHE'S ALL RIGHT!
I HATE MYSELF FOR THIS, BUT I'M ALMOST GLAD SHE DIDN'T ANSWER!
IT GIVES ME AN EXCUSE TO RACE OUT INTO THE NIGHT--TO GO INTO ACTION--
ANYTHING--ANYTHING--TO TAKE MY MIND OFF FLASH--AND GWEN!
THWIP!
15

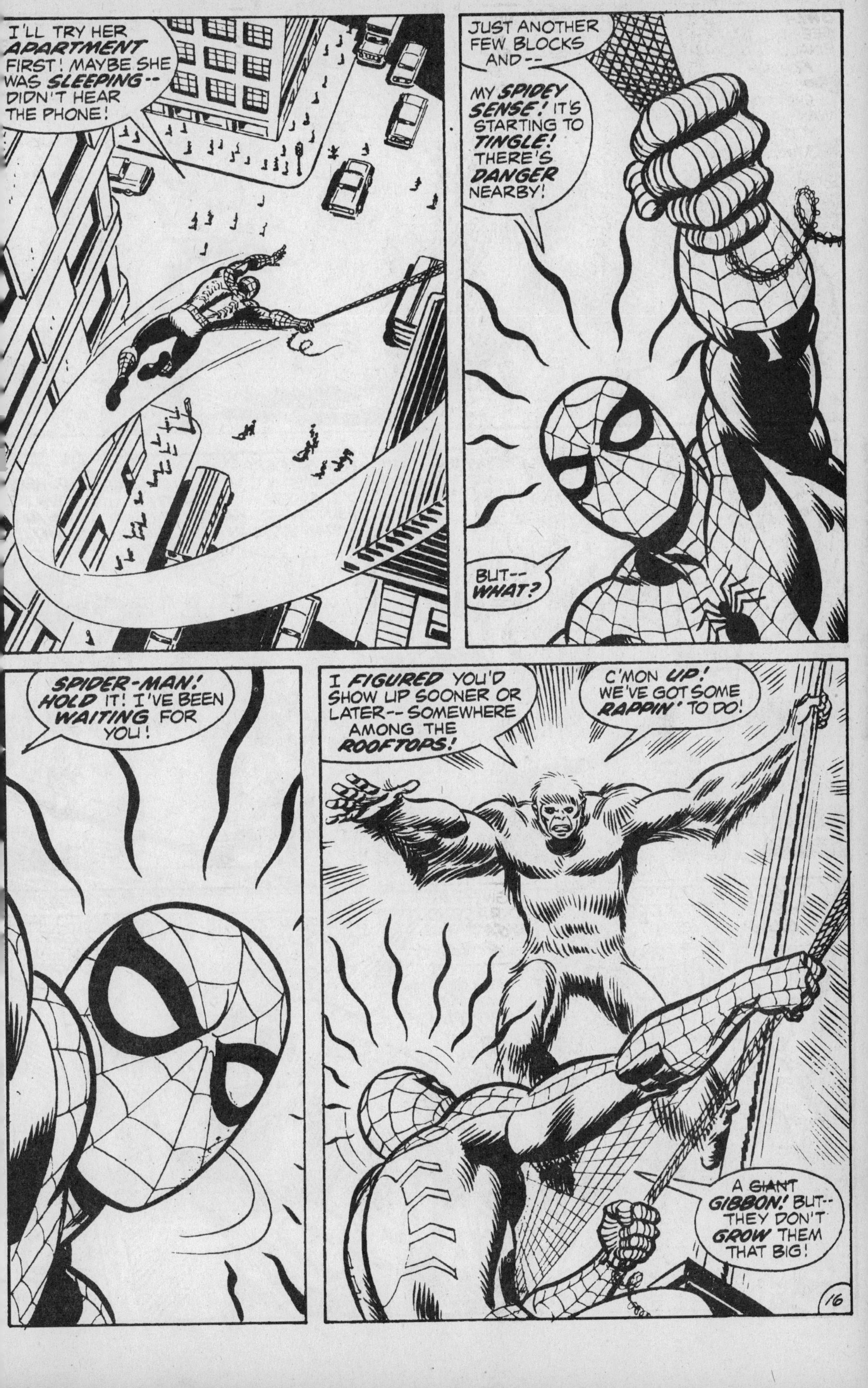
I'LL TRY HER APARTMENT FIRST! MAYBE SHE WAS SLEEPING-- DIDN'T HEAR THE PHONE!
JUST ANOTHER FEW BLOCKS AND--
MY SPIDEY SENSE! IT'S STARTING TO TINGLE! THERE'S DANGER NEARBY!
BUT-- WHAT?
SPIDER-MAN! HOLD IT! I'VE BEEN WAITING FOR YOU!
I FIGURED YOU'D SHOW UP SOONER OR LATER-- SOMEWHERE AMONG THE ROOFTOPS!
C'MON UP! WE'VE GOT SOME RAPPIN' TO DO!
A GIANT GIBBON! BUT-- THEY DON'T GROW THEM THAT BIG!
16

17

18

LOOK, I *HATE* TO BE A PARTY POOP, BUT YOU'RE NOT MY IDEA OF A *FUN* PERSON!

COME *BACK!* COME *BACK!* MY PLANS *DEPEND* ON YOU!

YOU WERE MY LAST *CHANCE*-- MY LAST *HOPE*-- TO *BE* SOMEONE!

NOW IT'S TOO *LATE!* I'M *ALONE* AGAIN! ALONE! *ALONE!*

BUT, ALAS FOR US *ALL*, THE MAN IN THE *GIBBON* SUIT IS NOT QUITE AS *ALONE* AS HE *THINKS* HE IS--

I'VE *FOUND* HIM AT *LAST!*

HE HAS THE *HATRED*-- THE *ANGER*--THE UNTRAINED *ENERGY* OF A SAVAGE *BEAST!*

I WILL *HARNESS* HIS ENERGY-- *NUTURE* HIS HATRED--AND GIVE HIM *POWER* BEYOND HIS WILDEST *DREAMS!*

HE SHALL BECOME-- THE *GIBBON!*

HE'S THE *TOOL* I SHALL FASHION-- TO CAUSE THE *DEATH* OF-- *SPIDER-MAN!*

NEXT: **THE APE AND THE ARACHNID!**

FEATURING THE SHOCKING RETURN OF THE SUPER-VILLAIN YOU HAVE MOST REQUESTED!

20

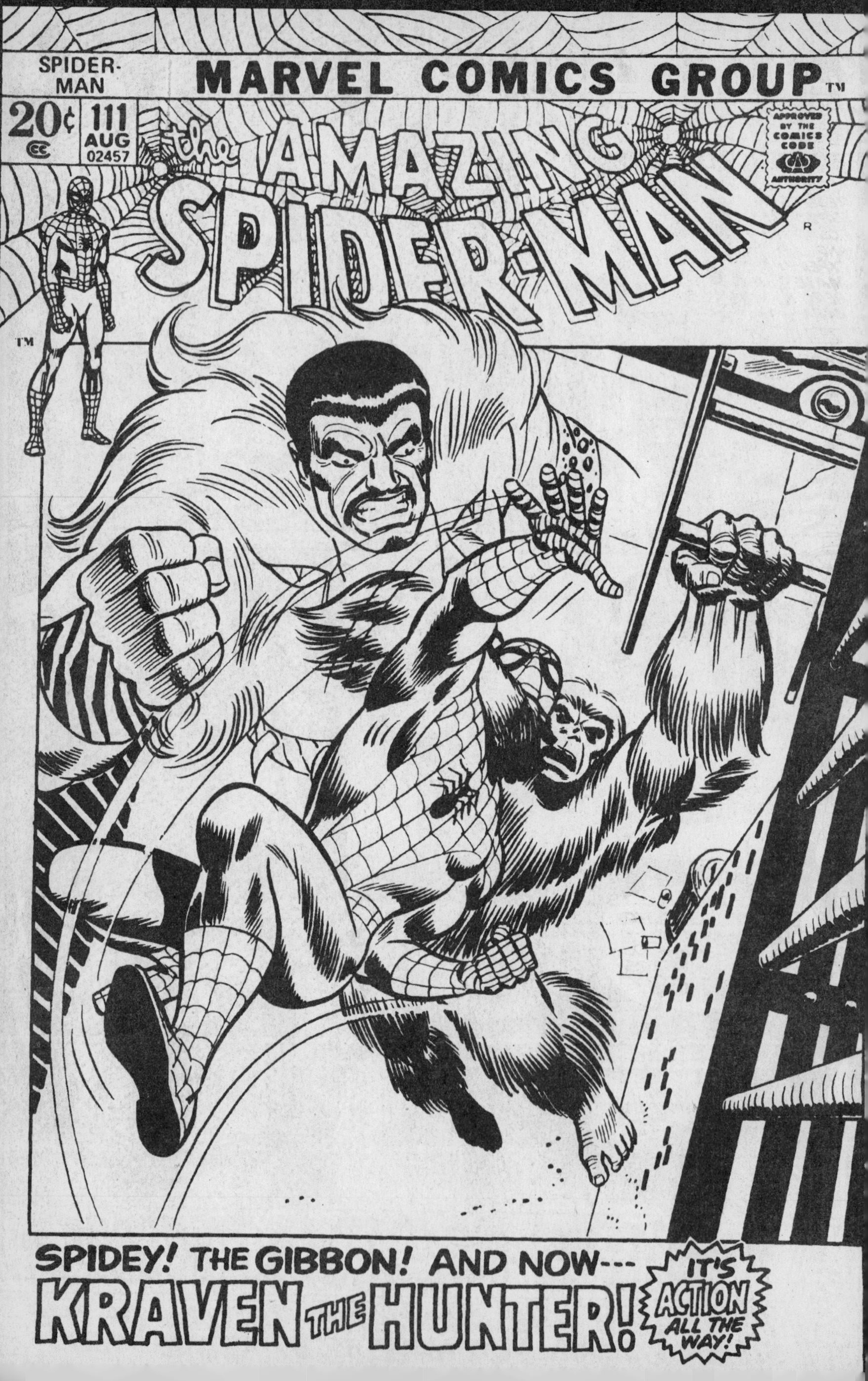
SPIDER-MAN
MARVEL COMICS GROUP
20¢
111
AUG
02457
APPROVED BY THE COMICS CODE AUTHORITY
the AMAZING SPIDER-MAN
SPIDEY! THE GIBBON! AND NOW---
KRAVEN THE HUNTER!
IT'S ACTION ALL THE WAY!

"AS FOR MYSELF, IT DID *INDEED* SEEM AS THOUGH I'D *DIE*--

"FOR WHEN THE JUNGLE LORD CALLED *KA-ZAR* KNOCKED ME BACK IN THE MIDST OF OUR *BATTLE*--*

* SPIDEY #104. --STAN.

"--I FELL FROM THE EDGE OF A PLUMMET-ING *CLIFF*--TOWARDS *DEATH!*

"I *WOULD* HAVE DIED THEN, AS ANY NORMAL MAN MIGHT--

"--BUT A NORMAL MAN WOULD NOT BE *KRAVEN*--

"--NOR WOULD HE POSSESS THE UNCANNY *INSTINCTS* WHICH ALLOWED ME TO SLOW MY DESCENT--

"--TO LUNGE OUT, AGAIN AND AGAIN--TO GRASP PASSING *BRANCHES*-- AND IN *THIS* WAY--

"--TURN AN OTHERWISE *FATAL* PLUNGE-- INTO MERELY A BONE-SHATTERING *FALL*."

3

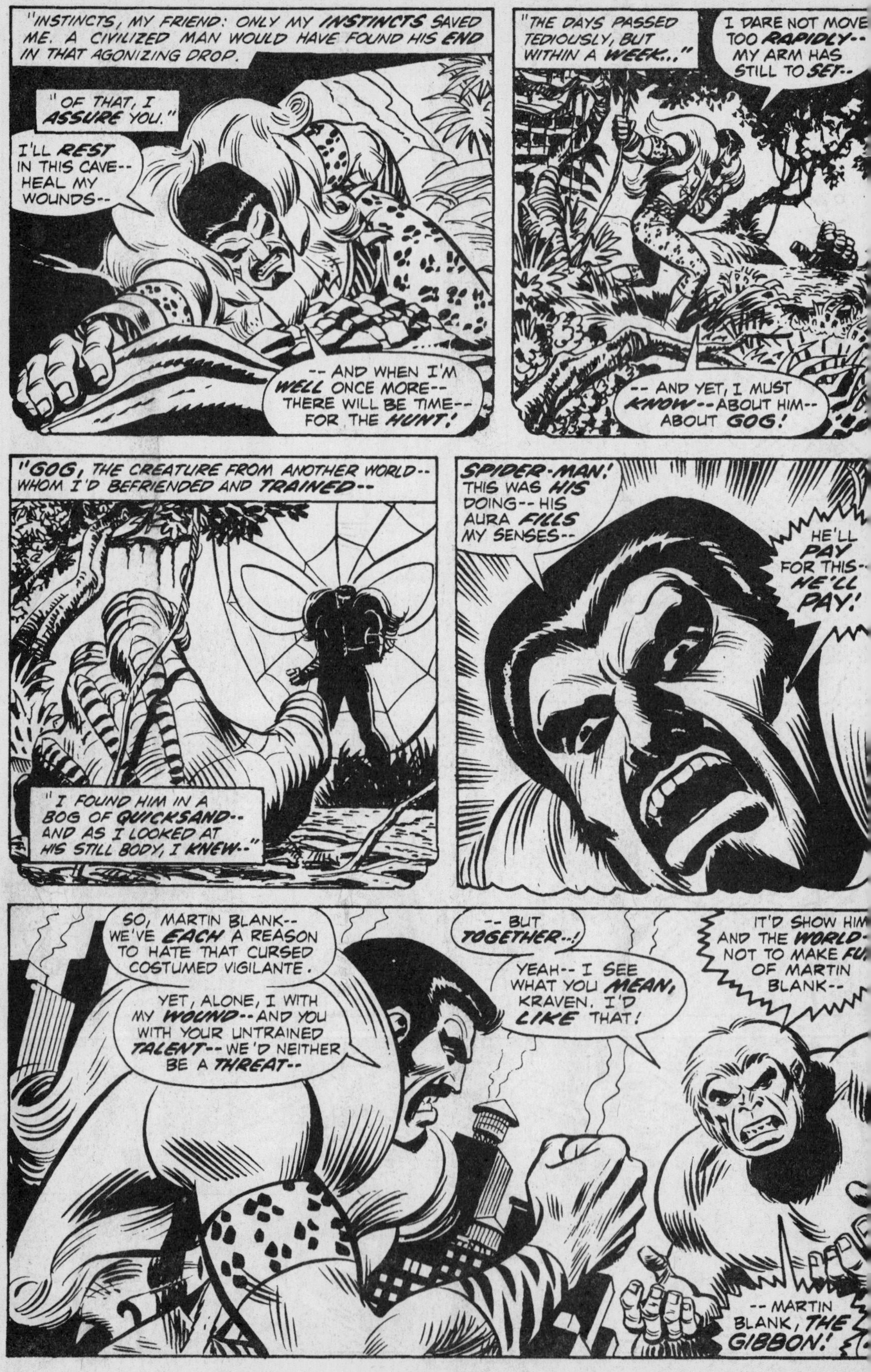
"INSTINCTS, MY FRIEND: ONLY MY INSTINCTS SAVED ME. A CIVILIZED MAN WOULD HAVE FOUND HIS END IN THAT AGONIZING DROP.
"OF THAT, I ASSURE YOU."
I'LL REST IN THIS CAVE-- HEAL MY WOUNDS--
-- AND WHEN I'M WELL ONCE MORE-- THERE WILL BE TIME-- FOR THE HUNT!
"THE DAYS PASSED TEDIOUSLY, BUT WITHIN A WEEK..."
I DARE NOT MOVE TOO RAPIDLY-- MY ARM HAS STILL TO SET--
-- AND YET, I MUST KNOW-- ABOUT HIM-- ABOUT GOG!
"GOG, THE CREATURE FROM ANOTHER WORLD-- WHOM I'D BEFRIENDED AND TRAINED--
"I FOUND HIM IN A BOG OF QUICKSAND-- AND AS I LOOKED AT HIS STILL BODY, I KNEW--"
SPIDER-MAN! THIS WAS HIS DOING-- HIS AURA FILLS MY SENSES--
HE'LL PAY FOR THIS-- HE'LL PAY!
SO, MARTIN BLANK-- WE'VE EACH A REASON TO HATE THAT CURSED COSTUMED VIGILANTE.
YET, ALONE, I WITH MY WOUND-- AND YOU WITH YOUR UNTRAINED TALENT-- WE'D NEITHER BE A THREAT--
-- BUT TOGETHER--!
YEAH-- I SEE WHAT YOU MEAN, KRAVEN. I'D LIKE THAT!
IT'D SHOW HIM AND THE WORLD-- NOT TO MAKE FU OF MARTIN BLANK--
-- MARTIN BLANK, THE GIBBON!

GWEN MENTIONED SOMETHING ABOUT HOW SHE'D *HURT* AUNT MAY'S FEELINGS--

--TOLD HER SHE'D BEEN TOO *POSSESSIVE* WITH ME--

--TOO *MATERNAL.* BUT GWEN DOESN'T UNDERSTAND--

--AUNT MAY'S SO *OLD.* SHE TAKES THINGS TOO *HARD.*

SURE SHE'S GOTTEN ON MY NERVES AT TIMES--

--BUT I STILL *LOVE* HER. NOTHING CHANGES *THAT.*

IF SHE'S--! OH, *NO!*

Dear Peter, I am going for a whi... in it all of us do n... wr...

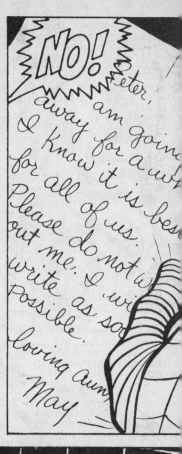

NO!

...eter, am going away for a whi... I know it is best for all of us. Please do not w... out me. I wri... write as soon... possible.

loving Aun... May

FOR AN INSTANT HE STANDS *STUNNED*-- HIS MIND AFIRE WITH THOUGHTS OF GUILT-- AND *FEAR*--

WHERE COULD SHE GO-- WHO COULD SHE *STAY* WITH?

SHE CAN'T HACK IT OUTSIDE-- SHE'LL BE *LOST*--

--AND IT'S MY FAULT-- *MY FAULT!*

BUT BEFORE THOSE THOUGHTS CAN GO ANY *FURTHER,* THEY'RE SHATTERED-- BY AN ABRUPT AND UNEXPECTED *INTRUSION!*

OKAY, SPIDER-MAN-- OPEN THIS *DOOR*--

--WE KNOW YOU'RE *IN* THERE, MISTER-- AND THIS TIME-- *YOU DON'T ESCAPE!*

SOMEDAY YOU BOYS IN BLUE WILL *LEARN*--

THERE'S A GREAT BIG *DIFFERENCE* BETWEEN WHAT YOU *SEE*-- AND WHAT YOU *GET!*

6

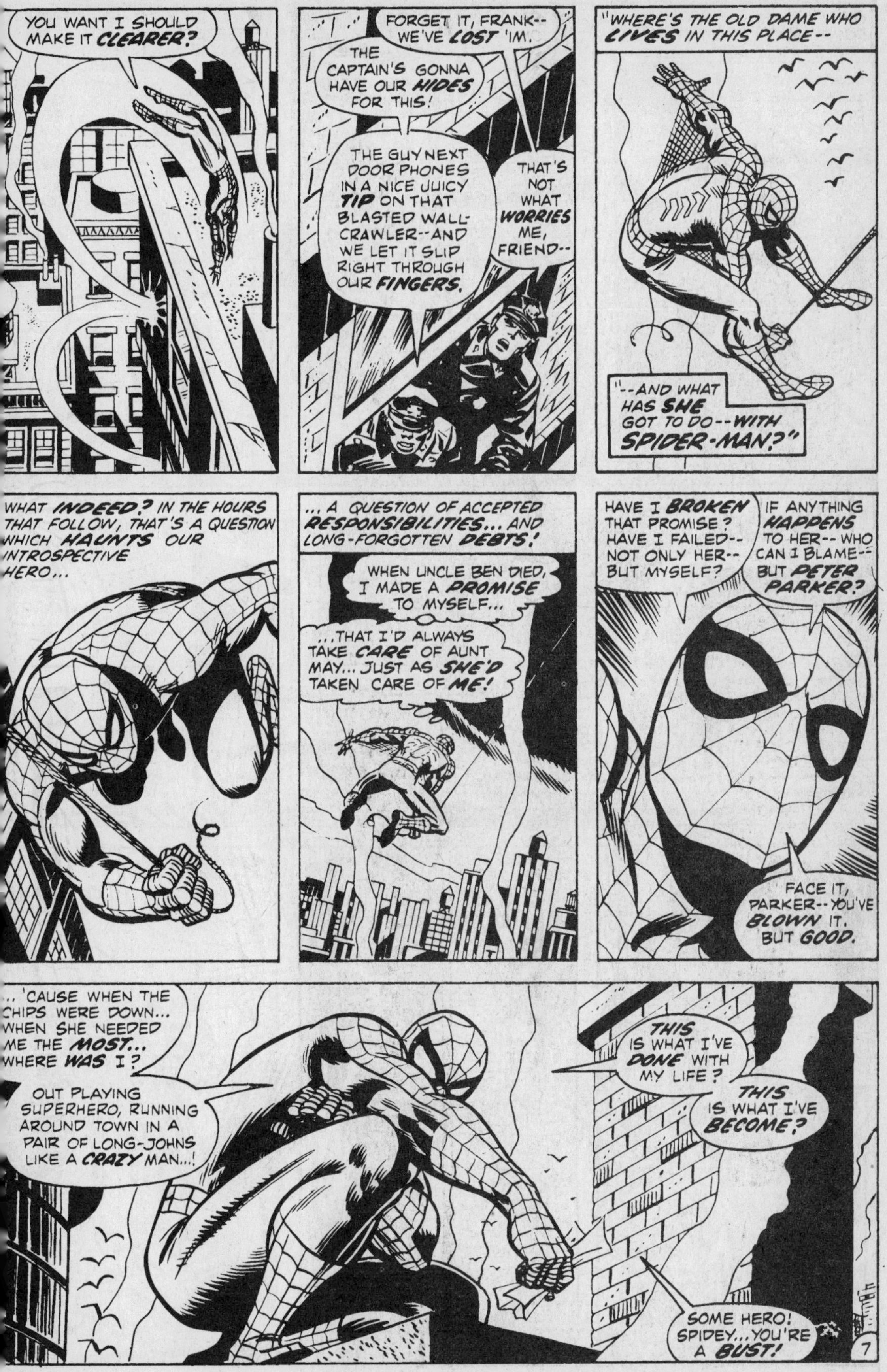
YOU WANT I SHOULD MAKE IT CLEARER?
FORGET IT, FRANK-- WE'VE LOST 'IM.
THE CAPTAIN'S GONNA HAVE OUR HIDES FOR THIS!
THE GUY NEXT DOOR PHONES IN A NICE JUICY TIP ON THAT BLASTED WALL-CRAWLER--AND WE LET IT SLIP RIGHT THROUGH OUR FINGERS.
THAT'S NOT WHAT WORRIES ME, FRIEND--
"WHERE'S THE OLD DAME WHO LIVES IN THIS PLACE--
"--AND WHAT HAS SHE GOT TO DO--WITH SPIDER-MAN?"
WHAT INDEED? IN THE HOURS THAT FOLLOW, THAT'S A QUESTION WHICH HAUNTS OUR INTROSPECTIVE HERO...
...A QUESTION OF ACCEPTED RESPONSIBILITIES... AND LONG-FORGOTTEN DEBTS!
WHEN UNCLE BEN DIED, I MADE A PROMISE TO MYSELF...
...THAT I'D ALWAYS TAKE CARE OF AUNT MAY... JUST AS SHE'D TAKEN CARE OF ME!
HAVE I BROKEN THAT PROMISE? HAVE I FAILED-- NOT ONLY HER-- BUT MYSELF?
IF ANYTHING HAPPENS TO HER-- WHO CAN I BLAME-- BUT PETER PARKER?
FACE IT, PARKER--YOU'VE BLOWN IT. BUT GOOD.
...'CAUSE WHEN THE CHIPS WERE DOWN... WHEN SHE NEEDED ME THE MOST... WHERE WAS I?
OUT PLAYING SUPERHERO, RUNNING AROUND TOWN IN A PAIR OF LONG-JOHNS LIKE A CRAZY MAN...!
THIS IS WHAT I'VE DONE WITH MY LIFE?
THIS IS WHAT I'VE BECOME?
SOME HERO! SPIDEY... YOU'RE A BUST!
7

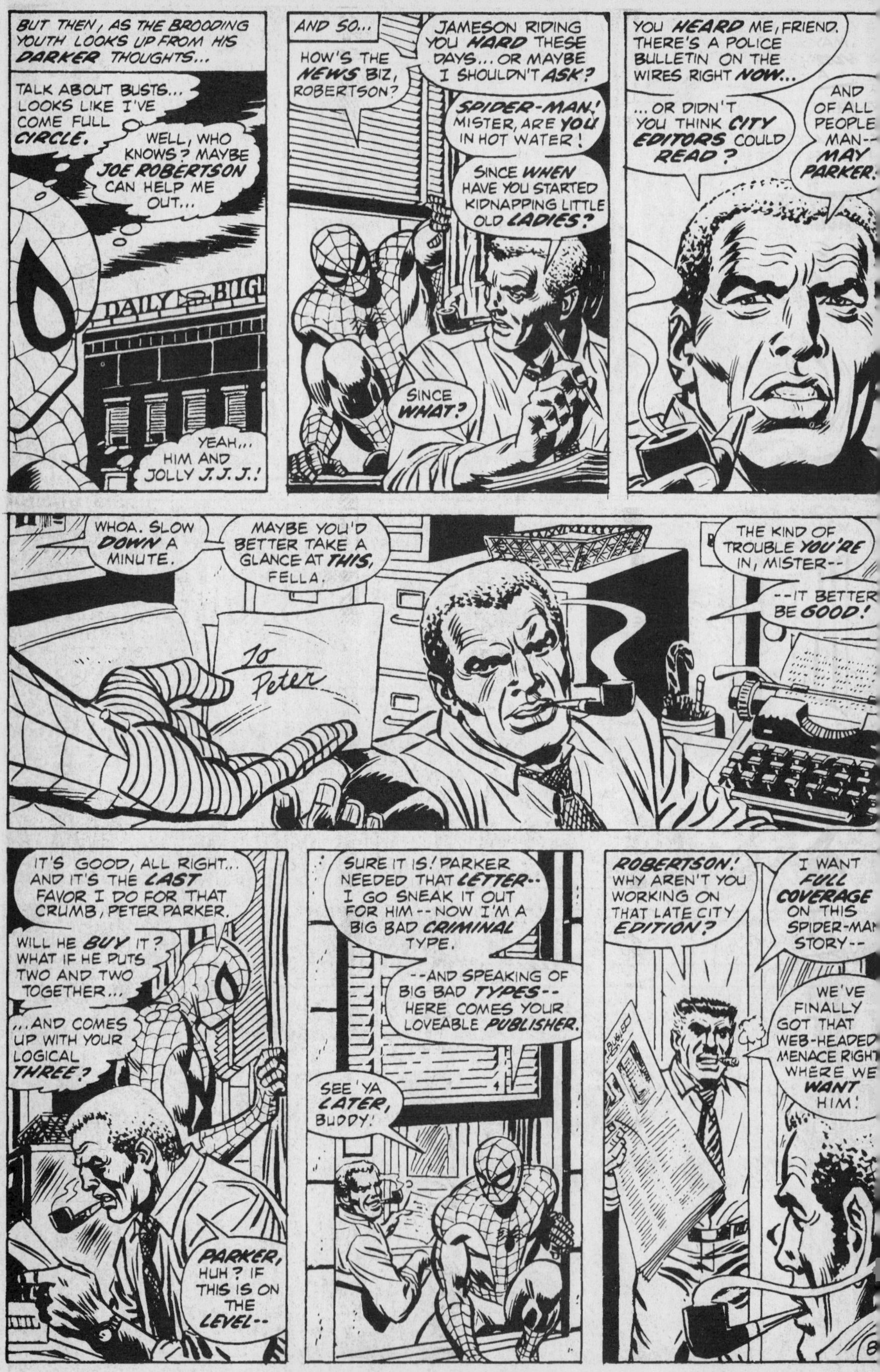

BUT THEN, AS THE BROODING YOUTH LOOKS UP FROM HIS DARKER THOUGHTS...
TALK ABOUT BUSTS... LOOKS LIKE I'VE COME FULL CIRCLE.
WELL, WHO KNOWS? MAYBE JOE ROBERTSON CAN HELP ME OUT...
DAILY BUGL
YEAH,.. HIM AND JOLLY J.J.J.!
AND SO...
HOW'S THE NEWS BIZ, ROBERTSON?
JAMESON RIDING YOU HARD THESE DAYS... OR MAYBE I SHOULDN'T ASK?
SPIDER-MAN! MISTER, ARE YOU IN HOT WATER!
SINCE WHEN HAVE YOU STARTED KIDNAPPING LITTLE OLD LADIES?
SINCE WHAT?
YOU HEARD ME, FRIEND. THERE'S A POLICE BULLETIN ON THE WIRES RIGHT NOW...
...OR DIDN'T YOU THINK CITY EDITORS COULD READ?
AND OF ALL PEOPLE MAN-- MAY PARKER.
WHOA. SLOW DOWN A MINUTE.
MAYBE YOU'D BETTER TAKE A GLANCE AT THIS, FELLA.
To Peter
THE KIND OF TROUBLE YOU'RE IN, MISTER--
--IT BETTER BE GOOD!
IT'S GOOD, ALL RIGHT... AND IT'S THE LAST FAVOR I DO FOR THAT CRUMB, PETER PARKER.
WILL HE BUY IT? WHAT IF HE PUTS TWO AND TWO TOGETHER...
...AND COMES UP WITH YOUR LOGICAL THREE?
PARKER, HUH? IF THIS IS ON THE LEVEL--
SURE IT IS! PARKER NEEDED THAT LETTER-- I GO SNEAK IT OUT FOR HIM -- NOW I'M A BIG BAD CRIMINAL TYPE.
--AND SPEAKING OF BIG BAD TYPES-- HERE COMES YOUR LOVEABLE PUBLISHER.
SEE 'YA LATER, BUDDY!
ROBERTSON! WHY AREN'T YOU WORKING ON THAT LATE CITY EDITION?
I WANT FULL COVERAGE ON THIS SPIDER-MA STORY--
WE'VE FINALLY GOT THAT WEB-HEADED MENACE RIGHT WHERE WE WANT HIM!
8

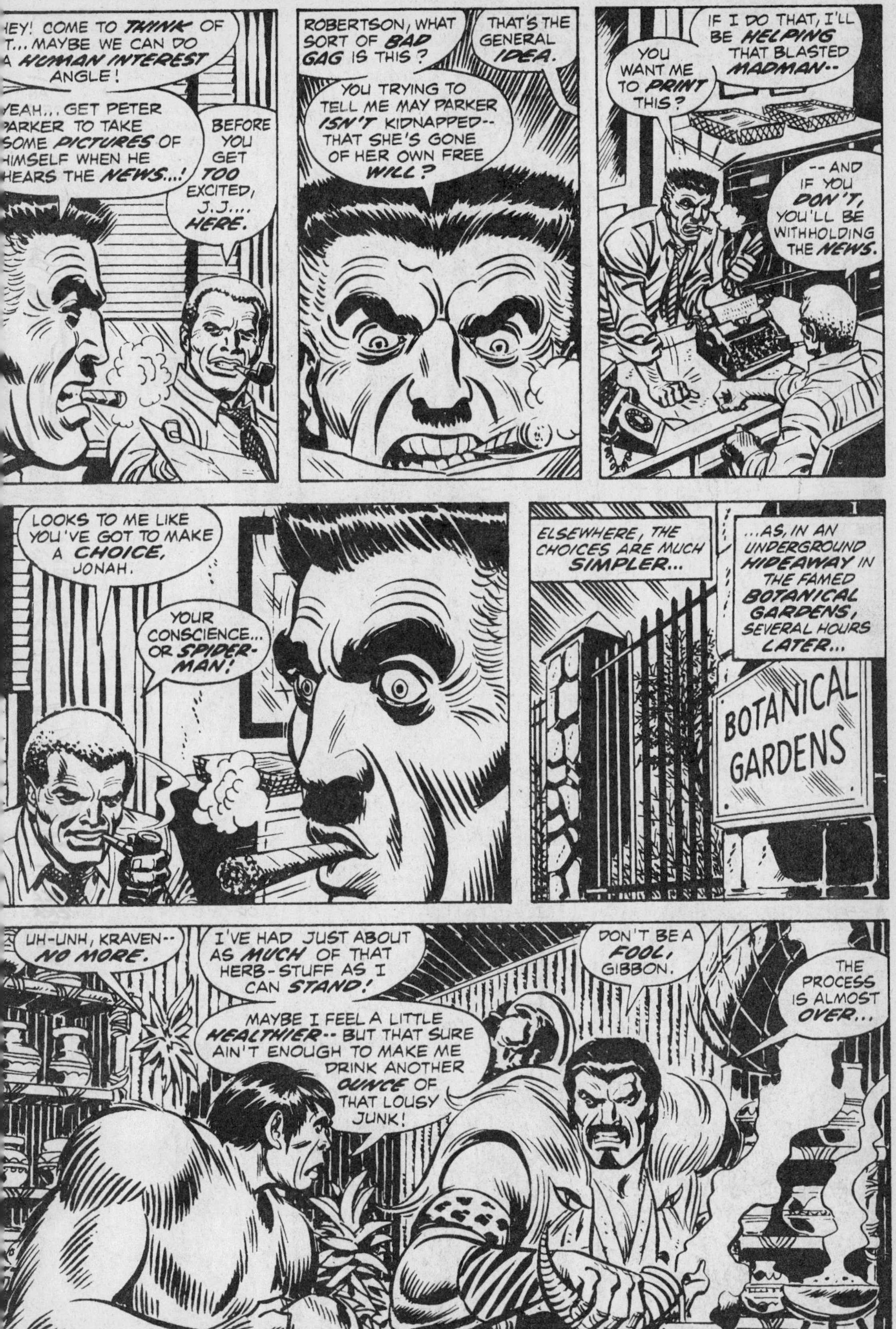
HEY! COME TO THINK OF IT... MAYBE WE CAN DO A HUMAN INTEREST ANGLE!
YEAH... GET PETER PARKER TO TAKE SOME PICTURES OF HIMSELF WHEN HE HEARS THE NEWS...!
BEFORE YOU GET TOO EXCITED, J.J.... HERE.
ROBERTSON, WHAT SORT OF BAD GAG IS THIS?
THAT'S THE GENERAL IDEA.
YOU TRYING TO TELL ME MAY PARKER ISN'T KIDNAPPED-- THAT SHE'S GONE OF HER OWN FREE WILL?
YOU WANT ME TO PRINT THIS?
IF I DO THAT, I'LL BE HELPING THAT BLASTED MADMAN--
--AND IF YOU DON'T, YOU'LL BE WITHHOLDING THE NEWS.
LOOKS TO ME LIKE YOU'VE GOT TO MAKE A CHOICE, JONAH.
YOUR CONSCIENCE... OR SPIDER-MAN!
ELSEWHERE, THE CHOICES ARE MUCH SIMPLER...
...AS, IN AN UNDERGROUND HIDEAWAY IN THE FAMED BOTANICAL GARDENS, SEVERAL HOURS LATER...
BOTANICAL GARDENS
UH-UNH, KRAVEN-- NO MORE.
I'VE HAD JUST ABOUT AS MUCH OF THAT HERB-STUFF AS I CAN STAND!
MAYBE I FEEL A LITTLE HEALTHIER-- BUT THAT SURE AIN'T ENOUGH TO MAKE ME DRINK ANOTHER OUNCE OF THAT LOUSY JUNK!
DON'T BE A FOOL, GIBBON.
THE PROCESS IS ALMOST OVER...
9

...WITH THE INGESTION OF THIS *FINAL* DRAUGHT, THE CELLULAR INTERACTIONS WILL *BEGIN*...

IN A MATTER OF *MOMENTS,* YOU'LL BE TRANSFORMED. THAT, COUPLED WITH THE *TRAINING* I'VE GIVEN YOU--

LOOK, I'VE *HAD* IT.

EVERY TIME YOU TALK LIKE THAT, YOU MAKE ME FEEL LIKE SOME KIND'A *ANIMAL*--

LIKE A DOG YOU CAN TEACH *TRICKS* TO. SURE, I'VE *LEARNED* STUFF--

--BUT I'M JUST *SICK* OF BEING TREATED LIKE-- LIKE SOMETHING THAT AIN'T *HUMAN.*

MARTIN BLANK, BELIEVE ME-- I *UNDER-STAND* YOUR TROUBLES.

I'VE GOT *FEELINGS,* Y'KNOW?

PLEASE, MY FRIEND. *TRUST* ME. DRINK THE *POTION.*

HE HESITATES--BUT THE *DECISION* HAS ALREADY BEEN MADE--AND SO, WITH TREMBLING HANDS, MARTIN BLANK *ACCEPTS* THE STEAMING HERB BROTH--

--ACCEPTS IT AND *DRINKS,* AS A GLOATING *KRAVEN* LOOKS ON!

WHAT'S *HAPPENING*-- TO ME? IT'S NOT-- NOT LIKE THE *OTHER* TIMES--

WHAT'D YOU *DO* TO ME--WHAT-- WHAT DID YOU *DO*--?

EVERYTHING'S *SPINNING*-- GETTIN' ALL DARK AND *HAZY*--

AAAAARGHH

MY HEAD-- IT'S BREAKING *APART!*

STOP IT! *STOP* IT! *STOP* IT!

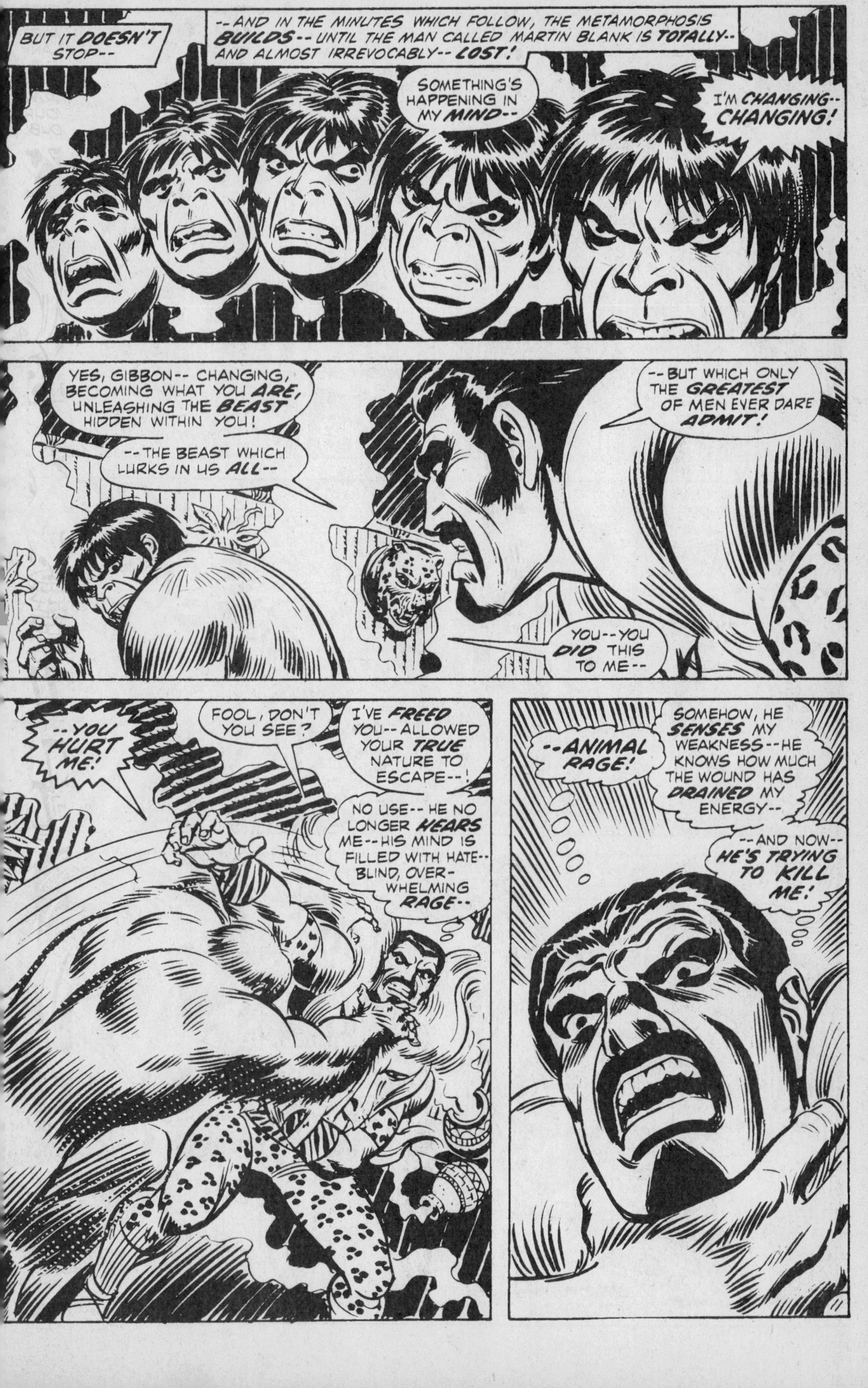
BUT IT DOESN'T STOP--
--AND IN THE MINUTES WHICH FOLLOW, THE METAMORPHOSIS BUILDS-- UNTIL THE MAN CALLED MARTIN BLANK IS TOTALLY-- AND ALMOST IRREVOCABLY-- LOST!
SOMETHING'S HAPPENING IN MY MIND--
I'M CHANGING-- CHANGING!
YES, GIBBON-- CHANGING, BECOMING WHAT YOU ARE, UNLEASHING THE BEAST HIDDEN WITHIN YOU!
--THE BEAST WHICH LURKS IN US ALL--
--BUT WHICH ONLY THE GREATEST OF MEN EVER DARE ADMIT!
YOU--YOU DID THIS TO ME--
--YOU HURT ME!
FOOL, DON'T YOU SEE?
I'VE FREED YOU--ALLOWED YOUR TRUE NATURE TO ESCAPE--!
NO USE-- HE NO LONGER HEARS ME--HIS MIND IS FILLED WITH HATE-- BLIND, OVER-WHELMING RAGE--
--ANIMAL RAGE!
SOMEHOW, HE SENSES MY WEAKNESS--HE KNOWS HOW MUCH THE WOUND HAS DRAINED MY ENERGY--
--AND NOW-- HE'S TRYING TO KILL ME!
11

YEAH? WELL, I'M MARTIN BLANK-- I AIN'T *GOT* NO FANCY LAST NAME--

--THEY NEVER *GAVE* ME ONE AT THE ORPHANAGE-- JUST A SPACE-- JUST A *BLANK*--

BUT THINGS ARE GONNA BE DIFFER-ENT-- I'M GONNA *MAKE* ME A NAME--

--AND I'M GONNA DO IT--*BY SMASHIN' YOU!*

AND SO IT BEGINS! MADDENED BY THE CHEMICALS COURSING THROUGH HIS VEINS, THE GIBBON *LEAPS* ON A SEEMINGLY-HELPLESS HUNTER--

--AND DISCOVERS THAT KRAVEN IS *NEVER* HELPLESS-- NEVER *HARMLESS!*

YOUR *KNEE*-- YOU CAUGHT MY HAND-- HOLDIN' IT *DOWN*--!

WHICH MAKES IT SOMEWHAT *FAIRER*, WOULDN'T YOU SAY, MY FRIEND?

BUT YOU'RE STILL *WEAK*-- STILL AIN'T AS STRONG AS *ME*--

THAT HERB BREW *DID* THINGS TO ME--

I'M STRONGER'N YOU-- *STRONGER'N ANYONE!*

13

LOCKED IN MORTAL COMBAT, THEY *STRAIN*--

ABOUT THEM, THE *AIR* SEEMS TO SEETHE WITH TENSE *POWER*-- WITH THE MINGLING OF ANIMAL *AURAS*, HUMAN SENSES HEIGHTENED BY THE HERBS OF WHICH THEY HAVE *BOTH* PARTAKEN--

AND AS THEY STRAIN, SOMETHING *STRANGE* OCCURS--

--AND GRADUALLY, INEXORAB-- *ONE* WILL PROVES DOMINANT

--AS THE GIBBON *RELEASES* HIS DEADLY HOLD.

GOOD, MARTIN-- *GOOD.*

IT APPEARS WE'VE ESTABLISHED-- A *LINK.*

...SOME FORM OF TELEPATHIC *BOND*... A *MINDLOCK*, OF SORTS.

AS THE *COBRA* HYPNOTIZES THE HAPLESS BIRD... *ENTRANCES* IT WITH HIS OWN BESTIAL ENERGY...

...I...HAVE TAKEN CONTROL...OF *YOU.*

I *EXPECTED* AS MUCH...BUT NEVER DID I DREAM IT WOUL BE SO *COMPLETE!*

YOU...YOU *WANTED* THIS?

OF *COURSE.*

YOU THINK ME A WITLESS *FOOL?* I'VE PLANNED IT FROM THE *BEGINNING.*

MY MIND WILL BE *YOUR* MIND...MY SPIRIT, *YOUR* SPIRIT!

ONLY *THUS* CAN WE TRIUMPH OVER THE ACCURSED SPIDER-MAN!

YEAH...*YEAH*, I GUESS I SEE...WHAT YOU *MEAN.*

EXCELLENT. I SHALL *FORGET* OUR LITTLE... ALTERCATION.

YOU'RE READY AT LAST-- YOU'VE *PROVEN* THAT.

NOW GO-- FOR KRAVEN GOES *WITH* YOU.

MY HEAD STILL *HURTS*-- BUT MAYBE--

--MAYBE YOU' *RIGHT.* YEAH MAYBE YOU *AR*

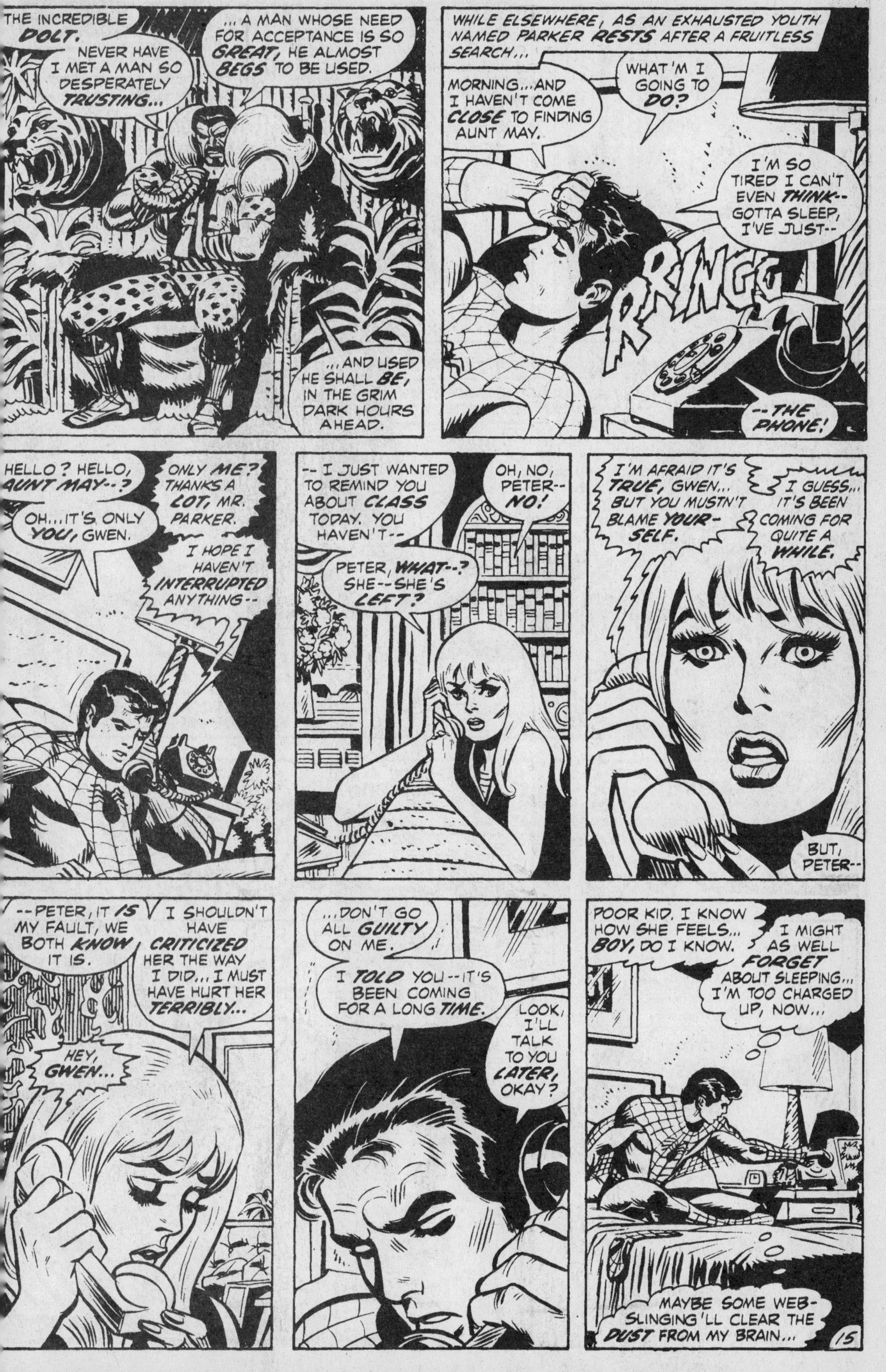

THE INCREDIBLE DOLT.
NEVER HAVE I MET A MAN SO DESPERATELY TRUSTING...
... A MAN WHOSE NEED FOR ACCEPTANCE IS SO GREAT, HE ALMOST BEGS TO BE USED.
... AND USED HE SHALL BE, IN THE GRIM DARK HOURS AHEAD.
WHILE ELSEWHERE, AS AN EXHAUSTED YOUTH NAMED PARKER RESTS AFTER A FRUITLESS SEARCH...
MORNING... AND I HAVEN'T COME CLOSE TO FINDING AUNT MAY.
WHAT'M I GOING TO DO?
I'M SO TIRED I CAN'T EVEN THINK-- GOTTA SLEEP, I'VE JUST--
RRINGG
--THE PHONE!
HELLO? HELLO, AUNT MAY--?
ONLY ME? THANKS A LOT, MR. PARKER.
OH... IT'S ONLY YOU, GWEN.
I HOPE I HAVEN'T INTERRUPTED ANYTHING--
-- I JUST WANTED TO REMIND YOU ABOUT CLASS TODAY. YOU HAVEN'T--
OH, NO, PETER-- NO!
PETER, WHAT--? SHE--SHE'S LEFT?
I'M AFRAID IT'S TRUE, GWEN... BUT YOU MUSTN'T BLAME YOURSELF.
I GUESS... IT'S BEEN COMING FOR QUITE A WHILE.
BUT, PETER--
--PETER, IT IS MY FAULT, WE BOTH KNOW IT IS.
I SHOULDN'T HAVE CRITICIZED HER THE WAY I DID... I MUST HAVE HURT HER TERRIBLY...
HEY, GWEN...
...DON'T GO ALL GUILTY ON ME.
I TOLD YOU--IT'S BEEN COMING FOR A LONG TIME.
LOOK, I'LL TALK TO YOU LATER, OKAY?
POOR KID. I KNOW HOW SHE FEELS... BOY, DO I KNOW.
I MIGHT AS WELL FORGET ABOUT SLEEPING... I'M TOO CHARGED UP, NOW...
MAYBE SOME WEB-SLINGING'LL CLEAR THE DUST FROM MY BRAIN...
15

...MAN, I **HOPE SO.**

WITHIN MOMENTS, A SLEEK COSTUMED FIGURE DARTS FROM AN UPPER-EAST-SIDE **WINDOW**--

HE KNOWS THE SEARCH WILL BE A **LONG** ONE--

--PROBABLY A **FUTILE** ONE--

--BUT IT'S A SEARCH THAT **MUST** BE MADE.

MAYBE IF I GO OVER ALL THE GROUND SHE NORMALLY **COVERS**--

IF I TRY THE BUSES-- THE STREETS-- THE **SUPER-MARKETS**--

MAYBE I'LL FIND HER **THIS** TIME-- I'VE GOT TO--

--I'VE **GOT** TO!

MOMMY, LOOK--IT'S **SPIDER-MAN!**

BLAST. IT'S ALWAYS THE **SAME**--PEOPLE HATING, PEOPLE **AFRAID!**

ONLY-- **THIS** TIME, IT HURTS EVEN MORE THAN IT USUALLY DOES--

--'CAUSE ONE OF THOSE PEOPLE **COULD** KNOW AUNT MAY-- KNOW WHERE SHE **IS**--

--BUT THEY'RE ALL TOO BUSY **RUNNING** TO TELL ME.

GOTTA GET **OUT** OF HERE-- GET SOME FRESH AIR, CLEAR MY **HEAD**--

UH-OH-- **HOLD** IT, SPIDEY--

MY SPIDER-SENSE IS TINGLING LIKE **MAD**--

THERE'S SOMETHING UP **AHEAD**--

--AND IT'S **DANGER!**

16

17

AND EVEN AS SPIDEY *SLUMPS,* STUNNED, AND THE GIBBON'S MASSIVE FINGERS CLOSE AROUND HIS VICTIM'S COSTUMED *NECK*-- IN A ROOM DOZENS OF BLOCKS AWAY, A HERB-ENTRANCED KRAVEN *GLOATS*--AND HURLS HIS SILENT *COMMANDS*--!

NOW, GIBBON-- FINISH HIM *NOW*--

THAT'S RIGHT-- *KILL* HIM--

GIBBON-- FINISH HIM KILL

KILL KILL

KILL KILL

YET--HOW DO YOU *BURY* A MAN? HOW DO YOU *STIFLE* ALL THAT HE'S EVER LEARNED--

KILL-- KILL!!

--ALL THAT MAKES HIM A *PART* OF THE HUMAN RACE?

WHY DO YOU HESITATE?

HOW DO YOU MAKE HIM-- SOMETHING THAT HE'S *NOT*--

SOMETHING--INHUMAN-- SOMETHING THAT'S *TRULY* --AN *ANIMAL*--?

MARTIN-- DON'T-- DON'T *DO* IT, MARTIN--!

FINISH HIM! DON'T FAIL NOW, YOU FOOL! KILL! KILL!

NO! MY HEAD-- SPLITTING-- *THROBBING*--!

FORCING ME--NO-- I *WON'T* BE FORCED--

I *WON'T!*

I *WON'T!*

18

FOR AN INSTANT, THE GIBBON *FREEZES*-- AND IN THAT INSTANT, SPIDER-MAN *ACTS*--

FOOL!

MINDLESS FOOOOOOLL

--MUSCLES TENSE AND *THRUST*-- THE GIBBON SPINS, TWISTING--

--AND *FALLS*, UNHEEDING OF KRAVEN'S FADING *CRIES*--!

NO!

I WASN'T THINKING-- DIDN'T *REALIZE* HOW CLOSE WE WERE TO THE LEDGE--

HE'LL BE *KILLED!*

HEAD STILL *RINGING*--

BUT I'VE GOTTA TRY-- I'VE *GOT* TO!

DID IT!

HE'S OUT-- FEELS LIKE A SACK OF LOOSE *SAND*--

WHAT-EVER WAS HOLDING HIM TOGETHER-- IS *GONE*, NOW.

FUNNY, I *KNOW* I SHOULD BE ANGRY...

...MAYBE EVEN *BURNING* WITH MAD... YET SOMEHOW...

19

...SOMEHOW, I *KNOW* MARTIN WASN'T RESPONSIBLE FOR WHAT HE TRIED TO DO.

...BUT I FEEL THERE WAS SOMEONE *ELSE* BEHIND ALL THIS...

...SOMEONE TERRIBLY FAMILIAR... SOMEONE TERRIBLY *CLOSE.*

CALL IT INTUITION... OR MAYBE MY *SPIDER-SENSE...*

FOOL! FOOL!

WEEKS OF DELICATE *PLANNING* -- OF SEARCHING FOR THE PROPER HUMAN *TOOL* -- ALL OF IT, ALL, *ALL WASTED!*

I SHOULD HAVE *WAITED,* AND DONE THE JOB *MYSELF--*

BUT *NO--* I WANTED IT *NOW--* WANTED THE TASTE OF REVENGE *NOW!*

CHUNK

--AND *INSTEAD,* ALL I HAVE -- IS THE TASTE OF ASHES.

20

NEXT: **SPIDEY COPS OUT!**

SPIDER-MAN
MARVEL COMICS GROUP
20¢ 112 SEPT 02457
the AMAZING SPIDER-MAN
APPROVED BY THE COMICS CODE AUTHORITY
GO ON, WORLD!
HURT EACH OTHER--KILL EACH OTHER--DO ANYTHING YOU WANT!
I JUST DON'T CARE ANY MORE!
ROMITA
SPIDEY COPS OUT!

THE AMAZING SPIDER-MAN!
SPIDEY COPS OUT!
B-BUT YOU SHOULD HAVE TAKEN HIM THROUGH ADMITTANCE! TH-THERE ARE PROCEDURES-- CERTAIN FORMS THAT HAVE TO BE FILLED OUT!
Y-YOU CAN'T JUST DROP HIM IN A BED --AN-AND TELL ME TO CALL A DOCTOR! I DON'T EVEN KNOW HIS NAME-- WHERE HE COMES FROM--
HIS NAME'S MARTIN BLANK.
WHEN HE COMES AROUND, TELL HIM SPIDEY SAYS HI--AND NO HARD FEELINGS.
B-BUT WHAT ABOUT TH-THIS? WHAT AM I SUPPOSED TO DO WITH THIS-- THIS COSTUME?
LADY... BURN IT!
STAN LEE PRESENTS: JOHN ROMITA, ARTIST GERRY CONWAY, SCRIPTOR ARTIE SIMEK, LETTERER ROY THOMAS, EDITOR

THAT *SEDAN!* IT'S TEARING IN FRONT OF THAT OTHER CAR, CUTTING IT *OFF!*

THEY JUST BARELY MISSED THOSE *PEOPLE*--

BUH KOOM

BUT FROM THE *LOOKS* OF THINGS, SOMEHOW I DON'T THINK THESE ARE THE TYPE OF GUYS WHO'D *CARE!*

AND SINCE THE *OTHER* BRAVE MEMBERS OF THE COMMUNITY AREN'T EXACTLY LEAPING TO THE *RESCUE*--

--IT SEEMS LIKE YOUR FRIENDLY-NEIGHBOR-HOOD WEB-SLINGER IS SUMMARILY *ELECTED!*

OKAY, JACKIE-- YOU HAD YOUR FUN, YOU MADE YOUR *BETS*--

--NOW YOU'RE EITHER GONNA PAY *CASH*--

--OR *HIDE!*

HOLD 'IM NICE 'N *STILL*, BENNY.

WAITASECOND! WHAT AM I *DOING?*

MY AUNT'S DISAPPEARED-- AND I'M GONNA MESS WITH SOME FIFTH-RATE GANGLAND *MUGGING?*

AM I *CRAZY*, OR SOMETHING.

LISSEN, SO I MISSED A FEW *IOUs*--ISSIT A *CRIME?*

I'VE MADE GOOD BEFORE-- I WON'T *STIFF* YOU GUYS!

HEY, LISSEN-- *DON'T*-- :MRRRRRMMPH!:

DO US ALL A *FAVOR*, PAL. JUST SHUT YOUR TRAP AND *TAKE* IT, HUH?

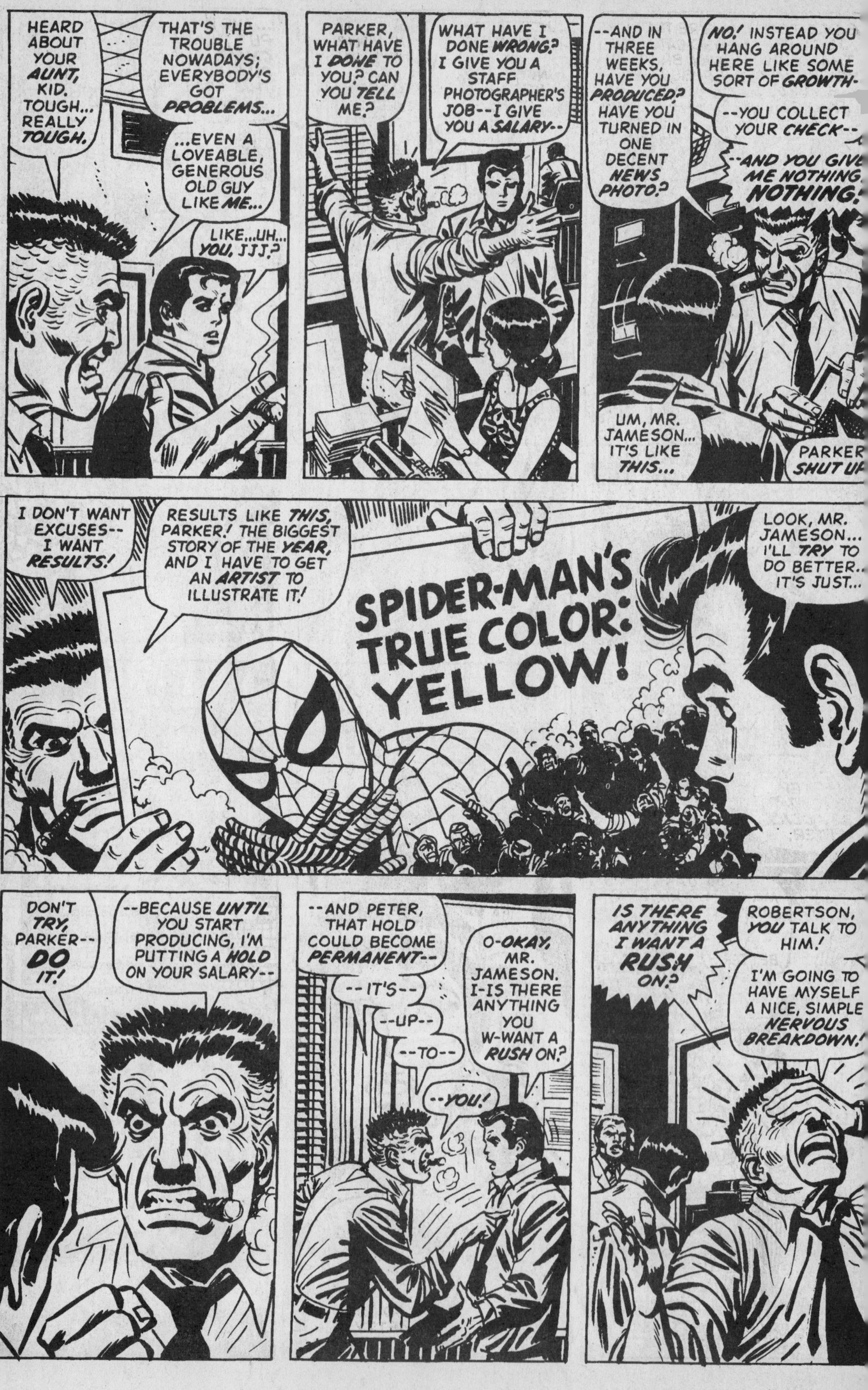

HEARD ABOUT YOUR AUNT, KID. TOUGH... REALLY TOUGH.
THAT'S THE TROUBLE NOWADAYS; EVERYBODY'S GOT PROBLEMS...
...EVEN A LOVEABLE, GENEROUS OLD GUY LIKE ME...
LIKE...UH... YOU, JJJ?
PARKER, WHAT HAVE I DONE TO YOU? CAN YOU TELL ME?
WHAT HAVE I DONE WRONG? I GIVE YOU A STAFF PHOTOGRAPHER'S JOB--I GIVE YOU A SALARY--
--AND IN THREE WEEKS, HAVE YOU PRODUCED? HAVE YOU TURNED IN ONE DECENT NEWS PHOTO?
NO! INSTEAD YOU HANG AROUND HERE LIKE SOME SORT OF GROWTH-
--YOU COLLECT YOUR CHECK--
--AND YOU GIVE ME NOTHING. NOTHING!
UM, MR. JAMESON... IT'S LIKE THIS...
PARKER SHUT UP
I DON'T WANT EXCUSES-- I WANT RESULTS!
RESULTS LIKE THIS, PARKER! THE BIGGEST STORY OF THE YEAR, AND I HAVE TO GET AN ARTIST TO ILLUSTRATE IT!
SPIDER-MAN'S TRUE COLOR: YELLOW!
LOOK, MR. JAMESON... I'LL TRY TO DO BETTER... IT'S JUST...
DON'T TRY, PARKER-- DO IT!
--BECAUSE UNTIL YOU START PRODUCING, I'M PUTTING A HOLD ON YOUR SALARY--
--AND PETER, THAT HOLD COULD BECOME PERMANENT--
--IT'S--
--UP--
--TO--
--YOU!
O-OKAY, MR. JAMESON. I-IS THERE ANYTHING YOU W-WANT A RUSH ON?
IS THERE ANYTHING I WANT A RUSH ON?
ROBERTSON, YOU TALK TO HIM!
I'M GOING TO HAVE MYSELF A NICE, SIMPLE NERVOUS BREAKDOWN!

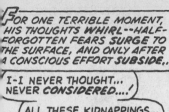

FOR ONE TERRIBLE MOMENT, HIS THOUGHTS *WHIRL*--HALF-FORGOTTEN FEARS *SURGE* TO THE SURFACE, AND ONLY AFTER A CONSCIOUS EFFORT *SUBSIDE*,...

I-I NEVER THOUGHT... NEVER *CONSIDERED*....!

ALL THESE KIDNAPPINGS... CRIMES...COULD THEY BE *CONNECTED* IN SOME WAY?

YOU *ARE* A REPORTER, PETER...OF A SORT...

WHOA, FELLA...

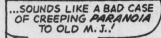

...SOUNDS LIKE A BAD CASE OF CREEPING *PARANOIA* TO OLD M.J.!

NOBODY'S OUT TO GET YOU THROUGH YOUR *AUNT*, MR. PARKER...SHE'S PROBABLY JUST OUT DIGGING A WHOLE NEW *SCENE*, THAT'S ALL!

...IT'S NOT AS THOUGH YOU HAD *ENEMIES*, Y'KNOW, HANDSOME?

G-GUESS YOU'RE *RIGHT*, MARY JANE--

--MAYBE I'LL SEE YOU *LATER*.

I'VE GOT TO GET A *HANDLE* ON MYSELF--PULL MY MIND *TOGETHER*!

WHAT MRS. WATSON *SAID* JUST NOW --SUPPOSE SOMEONE *WERE* TRYING TO GET TO *ME*--?

--ONLY IT'S NOT INNOCENT NEWS PHOTOG *PARKER* WHO'S THE GOAL--

--IT'S A WEB-SLINGING VIGILANTE CALLED *SPIDER-MAN!*

IF THAT'S *TRUE*--

--IT MEANS EVERYTHING I'VE EVER FEARED--HAS *HAPPENED!*

SOMEHOW, SOMEBODY MAY HAVE DISCOVERED SPIDEY'S *ALTER-EGO*...

...AND WITH IT, A GENTLE OLD LADY HE CALLS *AUNT MAY!*

ONLY ONE THING TO *DO*--

THERE WE GO-- ...ICE AND ...RIVATE.

I *HATE* INTERRUPTIONS DURING A FRIENDLY CHAT, DON'T *YOU*, PAL?

WH-WHAT DO YOU *WANT?* WHAT'S GOIN' *ON?*

FUNNY--THAT'S *JUST* WHAT I WAS GOING TO ASK *YOU*, SNOOKUMS.

I DON'T KNOW *NUTHIN'*--I JUST FOLLOW *ORDERS*, Y'KNOW?

SORRY, NO *DICE*--

--YOU'RE GONNA HAVE TO DO A LOT *BETTER* BEFORE WE GO HOME!

WHA-WHAT'DYA *MEAN?*

SIMPLE: EITHER YOU TALK-- OR YOU *STAY.*

OKAY--*OKAY.* ALL I KNOW IS THE *MONEY*--

I GET ORDERS OVER THE *PHONE*--HIT THIS GUY, HIT *THAT* GUY--

I SWEAR, THAT'S *ALL!*

--AND THE *CURRENT CRIME WAVE?*

IT'S THE *WAR*-- 'TWEEN THE BOSS AN' SOME *OTHER* DUDE--!

WHAT OTHER DUDE? C'MON, FRIEND-- *SPILL.*

I TELL YA, I *DON'T KNOW!*

YOU *KNOW* SOMETHING, BRIGHT EYES--

--MAYBE I'M JUST A *SUCKER* FOR A *PRETTY FACE*--

--BUT I *BELIEVE YOU*--

--AND, MISTER --IT MAKES ME *SICK.*

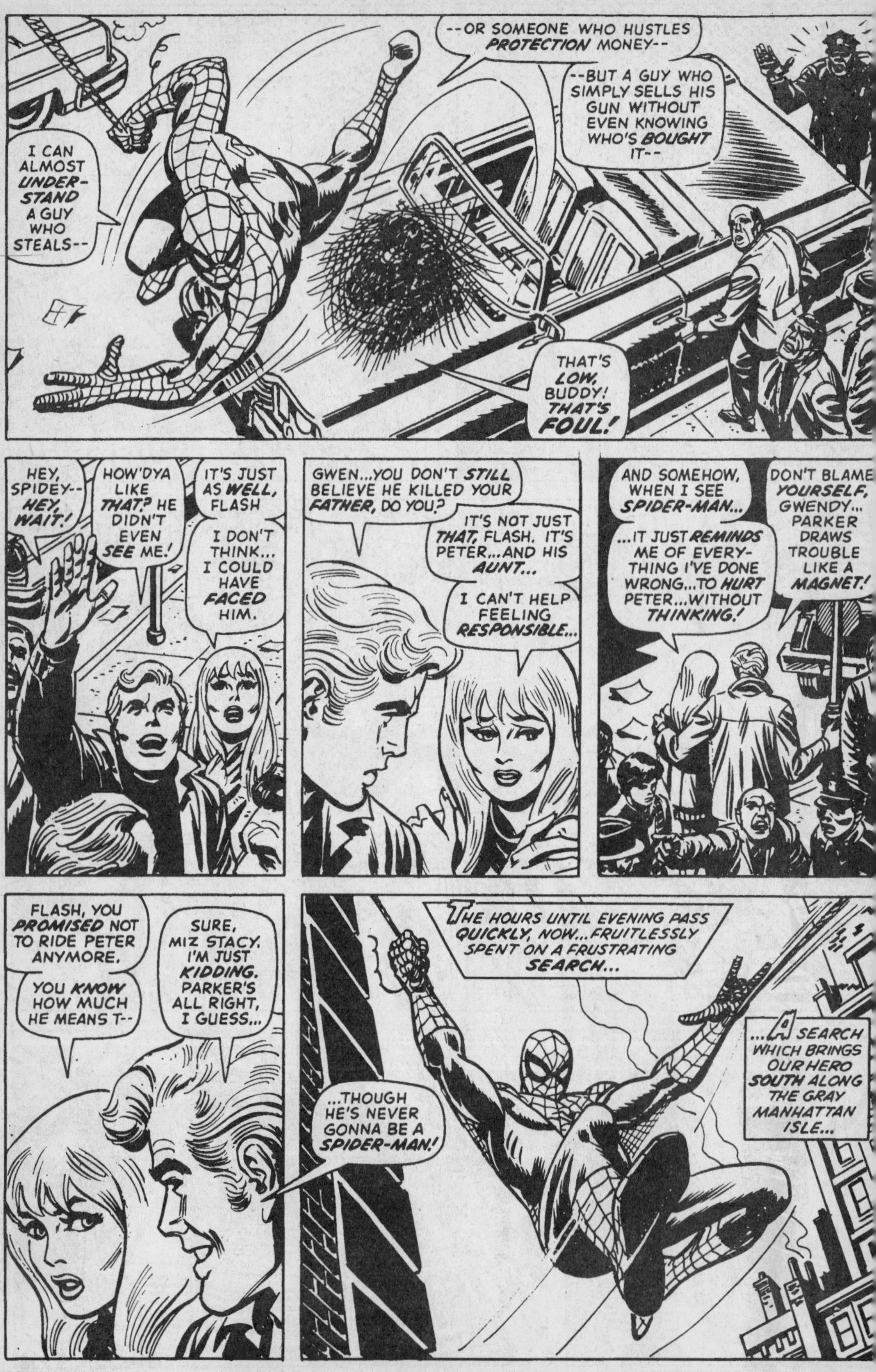
I CAN ALMOST UNDER-STAND A GUY WHO STEALS--
--OR SOMEONE WHO HUSTLES PROTECTION MONEY--
--BUT A GUY WHO SIMPLY SELLS HIS GUN WITHOUT EVEN KNOWING WHO'S BOUGHT IT--
THAT'S LOW, BUDDY! THAT'S FOUL!
HEY, SPIDEY-- HEY, WAIT!
HOW'DYA LIKE THAT? HE DIDN'T EVEN SEE ME!
IT'S JUST AS WELL, FLASH
I DON'T THINK... I COULD HAVE FACED HIM.
GWEN...YOU DON'T STILL BELIEVE HE KILLED YOUR FATHER, DO YOU?
IT'S NOT JUST THAT, FLASH. IT'S PETER...AND HIS AUNT...
I CAN'T HELP FEELING RESPONSIBLE...
AND SOMEHOW, WHEN I SEE SPIDER-MAN...
...IT JUST REMINDS ME OF EVERY-THING I'VE DONE WRONG...TO HURT PETER...WITHOUT THINKING!
DON'T BLAME YOURSELF, GWENDY... PARKER DRAWS TROUBLE LIKE A MAGNET!
FLASH, YOU PROMISED NOT TO RIDE PETER ANYMORE.
YOU KNOW HOW MUCH HE MEANS T--
SURE, MIZ STACY. I'M JUST KIDDING. PARKER'S ALL RIGHT, I GUESS...
...THOUGH HE'S NEVER GONNA BE A SPIDER-MAN!
THE HOURS UNTIL EVENING PASS QUICKLY, NOW...FRUITLESSLY SPENT ON A FRUSTRATING SEARCH...
...A SEARCH WHICH BRINGS OUR HERO SOUTH ALONG THE GRAY MANHATTAN ISLE...

--TOLD US HOW TO *HANDLE* YOU--

SAID YOU WOULDN'T BE *EXPECTING* US TO BE SO *STRONG*--

SAID WE COULD USE THAT *AGAINST* YOU--

KUNK! --LIKE *THIS!*

HE'S MOVING SO *QUICKLY*-- I CAN'T *FOLLOW* HIM--CAN'T *DUCKKKKKK!*

*C*ONSCIOUSNESS SPINS LIKE A SPRUNG *FLY-WHEEL*--AND AS THE ESCAPING CROOKS RUN--

--*S*PIDEY'S HAND *CATCHES* ON SOMETHING CLOTH-LIKE AND SOMETHING MORE--

*F*OR LONG MOMENTS, HE *SWAYS* IN THE STRAINED DARKNESS OF HIS MIND, AND THEN--

MY HEAD--FEELS LIKE A TON OF *MUD*--

GOT TO CLEAR IT-- DRAG MYSELF *TOGETHER*--!

HANG *IN* THERE, HERO... ONCE YOU CATCH YOUR *BREATH*, YOU CAN....HM?

SOME SORT OF *HARNESS*...COMPLETE WITH AN AMPLIFYING *POWER-PACK!* I MUST HAVE PULLED IT OFF THAT *TALL GUY*....!

BUT... HOW DOES IT FIT IN... IF IT *DOES*?

NO SIGN OF LAUGHING BOY AND HIS *PALS*...

LOOKS LIKE I'LL HAVE TO PIECE THINGS TOGETHER ON MY *OWN*...

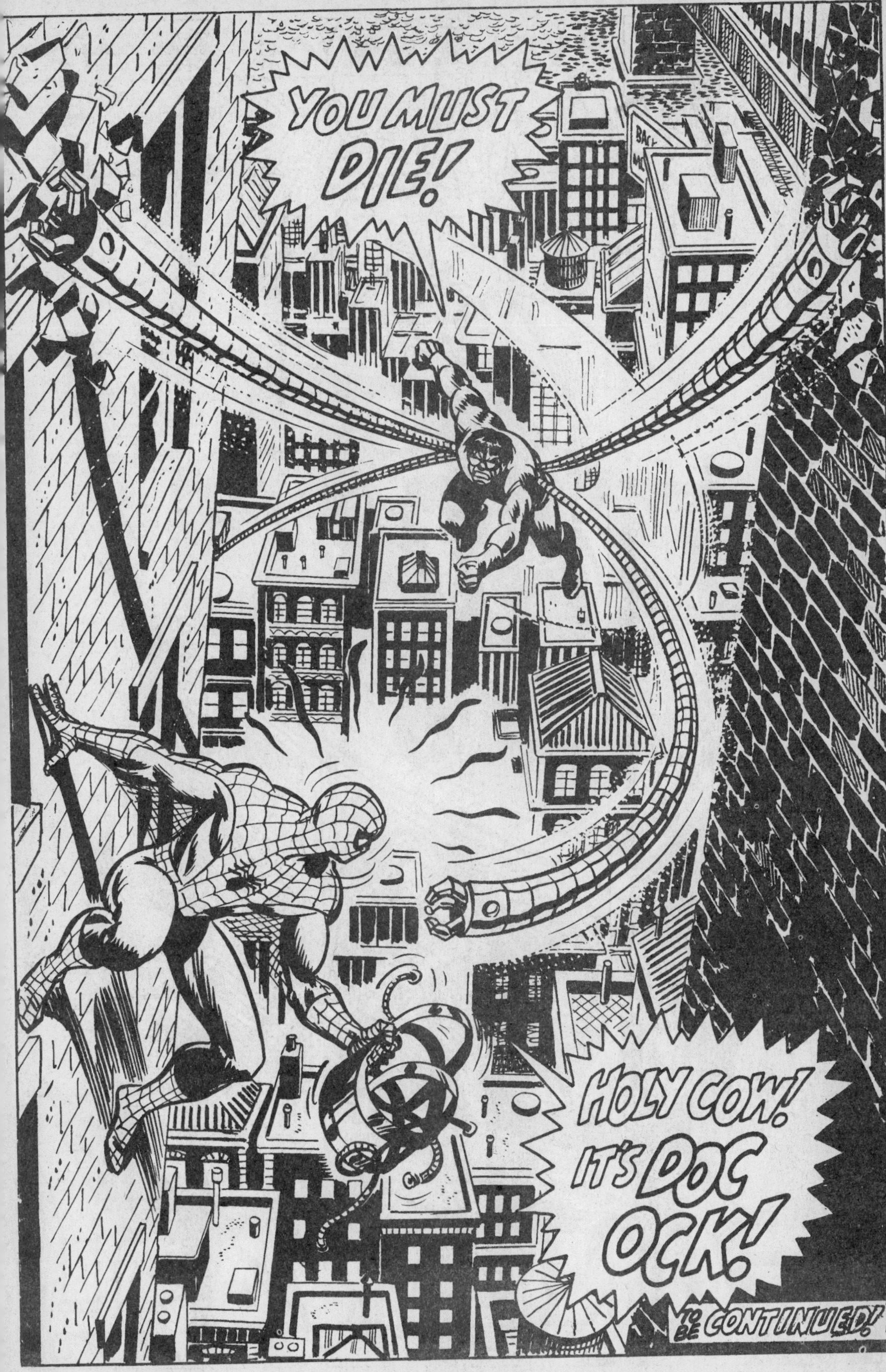

YOU MUST DIE!
HOLY COW! IT'S DOC OCK!
TO BE CONTINUED!

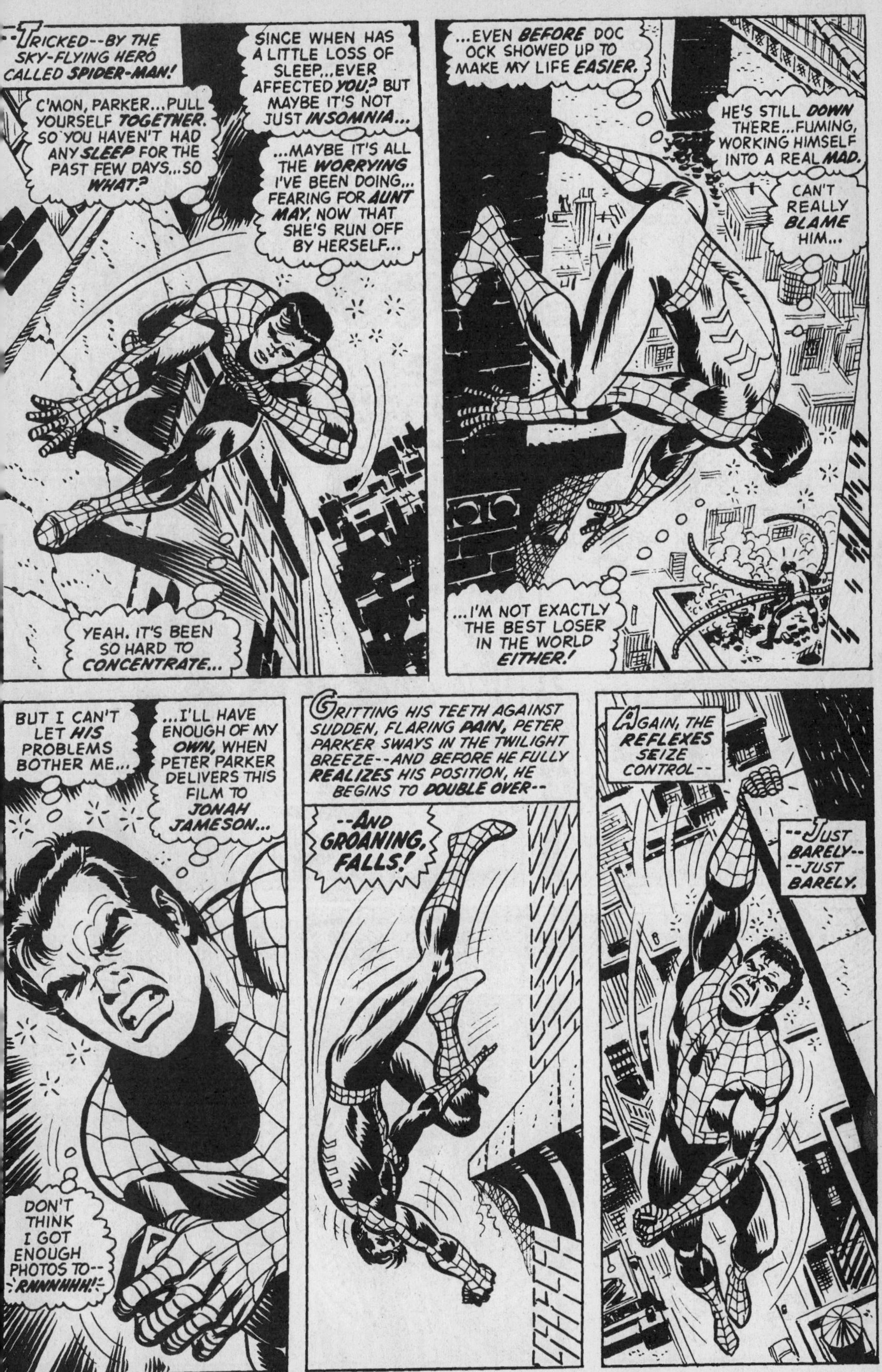
--TRICKED--BY THE SKY-FLYING HERO CALLED SPIDER-MAN!
C'MON, PARKER...PULL YOURSELF TOGETHER. SO YOU HAVEN'T HAD ANY SLEEP FOR THE PAST FEW DAYS...SO WHAT?
SINCE WHEN HAS A LITTLE LOSS OF SLEEP...EVER AFFECTED YOU? BUT MAYBE IT'S NOT JUST INSOMNIA...
...MAYBE IT'S ALL THE WORRYING I'VE BEEN DOING... FEARING FOR AUNT MAY, NOW THAT SHE'S RUN OFF BY HERSELF...
YEAH. IT'S BEEN SO HARD TO CONCENTRATE...
...EVEN BEFORE DOC OCK SHOWED UP TO MAKE MY LIFE EASIER.
HE'S STILL DOWN THERE...FUMING, WORKING HIMSELF INTO A REAL MAD.
CAN'T REALLY BLAME HIM...
...I'M NOT EXACTLY THE BEST LOSER IN THE WORLD EITHER!
BUT I CAN'T LET HIS PROBLEMS BOTHER ME...
...I'LL HAVE ENOUGH OF MY OWN, WHEN PETER PARKER DELIVERS THIS FILM TO JONAH JAMESON...
DON'T THINK I GOT ENOUGH PHOTOS TO-- RNNNHHH!
GRITTING HIS TEETH AGAINST SUDDEN, FLARING PAIN, PETER PARKER SWAYS IN THE TWILIGHT BREEZE--AND BEFORE HE FULLY REALIZES HIS POSITION, HE BEGINS TO DOUBLE OVER--
--AND GROANING, FALLS!
AGAIN, THE REFLEXES SEIZE CONTROL--
--JUST BARELY-- --JUST BARELY.

GENTLY, WALL-CRAWLER... TAKE IT NICE 'N *EASY.*

PAIN'S TEARING UP MY *GUTS...* WRENCHING ME AROUND INSIDE LIKE A TWISTING *FIST...*

...MAYBE I BETTER...GET SOMETHING *SOLID* UNDER ME...AND *SOON!*

MADE IT!

‡UMMPH!‡ SOME CRAZY KINDA... *CRAMPS...*

ALMOST AS BAD AS THAT ENZYMIC *REACTION* I HAD A FEW DAYS AGO...BEFORE THE X-MEN PULLED MY FAT OUT OF THE *FIRE* *...

*MARVEL TEAM-UP #4, FOOTNOTE FOLLOWERS. --ROY

...BUT THAT'S *OVER...* I'M SUPPOSED TO BE *WELL,* NOW...

...SO HOWCUM I FEEL...LIKE SOMETHING RUN OVER BY A *TRUCK?*

THAT'S ONE QUESTION WE CAN'T *ANSWER* JUST YET-- 'CAUSE IT'S TIME WE TEMPORARILY *RETURNED* TO A CERTAIN SPECTACLED SPIDER-*HATER*--

TRICKED!

OTTO OCTAVIUS-- VIRTUALLY *MOCKED* BY A COSTUMED *IMBECILE--*

--YET, NONETHELESS, AN UNCANNILY *FORTUNATE* IMBECILE--

--SAVED SOLELY BY MINDLESS *CHANCE--*

--CHANCE, WHICH REQUIRES MY IMMEDIATE *RETURN* TO MATTERS OF MORE *PRESSING* CONCERN!

YES, KARL-- WHAT *IS* IT?

EXCELLENT. KEEP IN CONTACT-- I'LL BE THERE AS SOON AS *POSSIBLE!*

IT'S BERNIE, DOC...HE SAYS HE FOUND THE SECRET HQ!

*M*INUTES LATER, AS THE SHADOWS *LENGTHEN* AND THE SUMMER AIR COOLS, FATE TAKES A HAND IN THE PROCEEDINGS...

...IN THE FORM OF ONE *RANDY ROBERTSON,* SON OF ROBBY ROBERTSON...

...*R*OBBY ROBERTSON...CITY EDITOR OF THE *DAILY BUGLE...* AND LONG-TIME FRIEND TO A BELEAGUERED *SPIDER-MAN...*

...HEY, LADY... KNOW A GUY BY THE NAME OF *ROBERTSON?*

IF HE'S IN...YOU MIGHT TELL HIM HIS SON *RANDY'S* DROPPED BY TO *SEE* HIM.

NOTHING *SPECIAL,* Y'KNOW... JUST A FRIENDLY *CHAT.*

HE'S IN THE *LIVING ROOM,* RANDY.

TERRIFIC. HEY-- AM I *LATE* FOR *DINNER?*

NOT REALLY, RANDY. WE'RE HAVING *ROAST BEEF*...JUST THE WAY YOU LIKE IT.

MOM, YOU'RE *OKAY*.

ANYBODY TELL YOU YOU'VE GOT YOURSELF A *GOOD LADY*, DAD

I DO, SON... EVERY *DAY*.

YEAH. I *BELIEVE* IT.

IF YOU'VE GOT A SECOND, TAKE A LOOKIT *THIS*...

...AND TELL ME... *AM* I CRAZY...OR IS THIS FOR *REAL*?

*A*LL *QUITE REAL*, RANDY...AS ONE VERY *WEAK* PETER PARKER WOULD BE ALL TOO *HAPPY* TO *TESTIFY*...

CAN'T STAY UP HERE ALL *NIGHT*...BUT I CAN HARDLY *MOVE*...

...THESE... *SPASMS*...THEY KEEP RETURNING, JUST WHEN I THINK THEY'RE *GONE*...

GOTTA DRAG MYSELF TOGETHER... TRY CRAWLING, TAKING MY *TIME*...

...MAYBE IF I GET HOME...GET SOME *SLEEP*...I'LL FEEL BETTER IN THE MORNING...

...'CAUSE IF I *DON'T*...

...THIS COULD MEAN... *THE END OF SPIDER-MAN!*

*E*LSEWHERE ON THE LOWER EAST SIDE, IN THE FORMER HEAD-QUARTERS OF THE CURRENTLY INCARCERATED *KINGPIN*, OTHER MINDS CONTEMPLATE SOMEWHAT *SIMILAR* THOUGHTS...

PATIENCE...*PATIENCE*. I MUSTN'T ALLOW MY EAGER-NESS TO *CRUSH* THAT AGGRAVATING ANACHRID TO INTERFERE WITH MORE *CRUCIAL* OPERATIONS...

I'VE PLANNED THIS TAKE-OVER TOO LONG....AND TOO *WELL*... TO FUMBLE IT *NOW*.

SPEAK UP, YOU FOOL...I CAN BARELY *HEAR* YOU!

WHAT'S THIS ABOUT A *NIGHTCLUB*?

SORRY, BOSS... DIDN'T MEAN TO *WHISPER*. GUESS IT'S JUST MY *NERVES*.

YEAH, IT'S A *NIGHTCLUB*... REAL SPIFFY JOINT OVER ON *SIXTIETH*...

I TRACED HIM WITH THAT *GADGET* YOU GAVE ME... AND HE'S *HERE*, ALL RIGHT.

I THINK WE'VE *GOT* 'IM THIS TIME, BOSS!

YOU'VE DONE *WELL*, BERNIE. THERE SHALL BE AN EXTRA *BONUS* IN THIS FOR YOU...

...I *PROMISE* YOU THAT, MY FRIEND.

THIS IS OCTOPUS... OVER... AND *OUT*.

YOU DID REAL *NICE*, BERNIE.

MISTER H IS GONNA BE REAL *HAPPY* TO HEAR HOW NICE YA DID...

I--I DID WHAT YOU *ASKED* ME TO--

WANNA *BET?*

Y-YOU CAN'T JUST--JUST *SHOOT* ME!

KRAK

Club Four

4

IT'S ALL *SET*, RUFFIO. THE PIGEON JUST SPILLED WHAT WE *WANTED* HIM TO SPILL.

YOU TELL *MISTER H*... I'LL COVER THE *DOOR*.

YEAH, *RUFFIO*...?

HE TOOK THE *BAIT?* GREAT... THAT'S JUST *GREAT*.

SURE...YOU TELL TONY I'M REAL PROUD'A THE WAY HE *HANDLED* THINGS...

AFTER THE WAY THAT *OCTOPUS* CREEP SHOT UP OUR NUMBERS PEOPLE ON EIGHTH STREET, HE'S GONNA *DESERVE* THE LITTLE SURPRISE WE GOT READY FOR HIM...

LIKE THEY SAY, THERE AINT ROOM FOR *BOTH* OF US IN THIS TOWN...

LATER THAT MORNING, AS DAWN LIFTS QUESTING FINGERS OVER THE GRAY MANHATTAN SKYLINE, A VERY ILL GENT NAMED PETER PARKER MANAGES THE LAST FEW TREMBLING STEPS HOME...

...WHERE, DIZZILY, HE TRIES TO STRAIGHTEN, ONLY DISTANTLY AWARE OF THE VOICES MUTTERING IN THE ADJOINING ROOM...

ALMOST, HE GAINS CONTROL OF HIM-SELF...

...AND THEN THE AGONY KNIFING THROUGH HIS MIDDLE BECOMES TOO GREAT...

...AND PETER PARKER... PASSES OUT!

HIS DREAMS, WHEN THEY COME, ARE TORTURED...NIGHT-MARES BORN OUT OF FEVER AND FEAR, AND A ROOTED CONCERN FOR THE OLD WOMAN CALLED AUNT MAY...

...AUNT MAY, WHO DISAPPEARED TWO SHORT DAYS AGO, HURT AND CONFUSED...

...AUNT MAY, NAIVE AND IMPRACTICAL...WHO EVEN NOW MIGHT BE DYING, ALONE...

...ALONE...WHILE PETER PARKER PLAYS AT BEING THE HEROIC SPIDER-MAN!

NO, AUNT MAY-- NO!

WON'T--LET IT BE THAT WAY--WON'T LET IT HAPPEN--

PROMISE YOU-- PROMISE YOU--

--I'LL FIND YOU--NO MATTER WHAT--I'LL--FIND--YOU--

PETER, WAKE UP-- PLEASE, PETER--

--YOU'VE BEEN HAVING A NIGHTMARE-- AND IT'S OVER, NOW.

WHEN WE HEARD YOU MOANING, HARRY AND I REALIZED YOU WERE BACK--

ARE YOU ALL RIGHT?

GWENDY... YOU....?

I'VE BEEN WAITING HOURS FOR YOU, PETER... I WAS SO WORRIED ABOUT YOU, AUNT...

OH! HARRY ...YOU DID GET A DOCTOR....!

I LOOKED IN PETE'S PHONE DIRECTORY, AND--

DOCTOR BROMWELL!

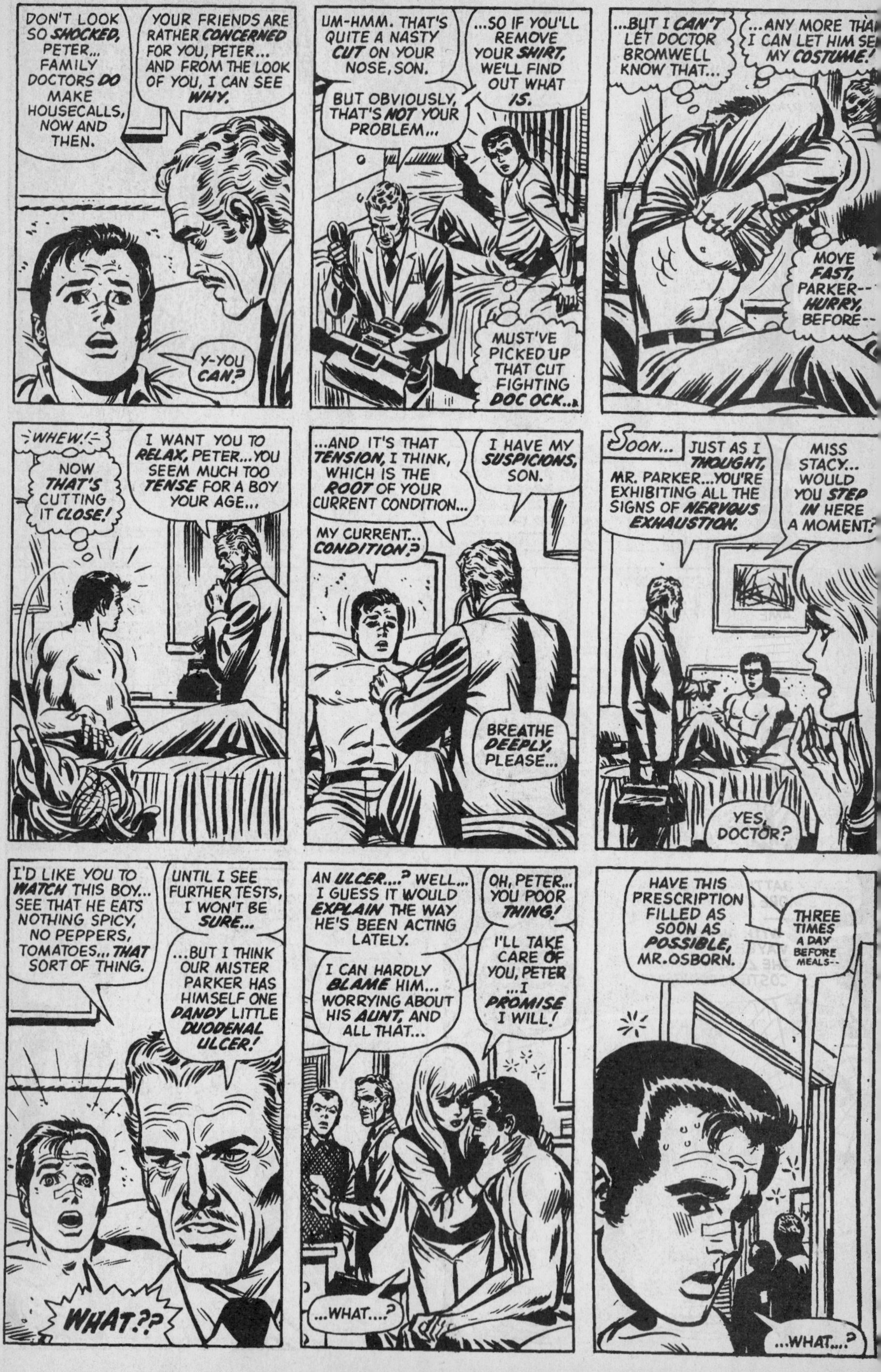
DON'T LOOK SO SHOCKED, PETER... FAMILY DOCTORS DO MAKE HOUSECALLS, NOW AND THEN.
YOUR FRIENDS ARE RATHER CONCERNED FOR YOU, PETER... AND FROM THE LOOK OF YOU, I CAN SEE WHY.
Y-YOU CAN?
UM-HMM. THAT'S QUITE A NASTY CUT ON YOUR NOSE, SON.
BUT OBVIOUSLY, THAT'S NOT YOUR PROBLEM...
...SO IF YOU'LL REMOVE YOUR SHIRT, WE'LL FIND OUT WHAT IS.
MUST'VE PICKED UP THAT CUT FIGHTING DOC OCK...
...BUT I CAN'T LET DOCTOR BROMWELL KNOW THAT...
...ANY MORE THAN I CAN LET HIM SEE MY COSTUME!
MOVE FAST, PARKER-- HURRY, BEFORE--
WHEW!
NOW THAT'S CUTTING IT CLOSE!
I WANT YOU TO RELAX, PETER... YOU SEEM MUCH TOO TENSE FOR A BOY YOUR AGE...
...AND IT'S THAT TENSION, I THINK, WHICH IS THE ROOT OF YOUR CURRENT CONDITION...
I HAVE MY SUSPICIONS, SON.
MY CURRENT... CONDITION?
BREATHE DEEPLY, PLEASE...
SOON...
JUST AS I THOUGHT, MR. PARKER... YOU'RE EXHIBITING ALL THE SIGNS OF NERVOUS EXHAUSTION.
MISS STACY... WOULD YOU STEP IN HERE A MOMENT?
YES, DOCTOR?
I'D LIKE YOU TO WATCH THIS BOY... SEE THAT HE EATS NOTHING SPICY, NO PEPPERS, TOMATOES... THAT SORT OF THING.
UNTIL I SEE FURTHER TESTS, I WON'T BE SURE...
...BUT I THINK OUR MISTER PARKER HAS HIMSELF ONE DANDY LITTLE DUODENAL ULCER!
WHAT??
AN ULCER...? WELL... I GUESS IT WOULD EXPLAIN THE WAY HE'S BEEN ACTING LATELY.
I CAN HARDLY BLAME HIM... WORRYING ABOUT HIS AUNT, AND ALL THAT...
OH, PETER... YOU POOR THING!
I'LL TAKE CARE OF YOU, PETER ...I PROMISE I WILL!
...WHAT...?
HAVE THIS PRESCRIPTION FILLED AS SOON AS POSSIBLE, MR. OSBORN.
THREE TIMES A DAY BEFORE MEALS--
...WHAT...?

MAYBE IF I JUST CLOSE MY *EYES*...?

NO GOOD. WHO AM I *KIDDING*, ANYWAY? IT HAD TO HAPPEN, *SOONER* OR *LATER*...

YOUR BODY CAN ONLY TAKE SO MUCH *PRESSURE*...

...AND THEN SOMETHING *SNAPS*...AND *BAM*...

...YOU'RE ON A *MILK AND TOAST* DIET FOR THE REST OF YOUR TENSION-TORN *LIFE!*

GREAT. SO NOW I'M A *BASKET-CASE*, RIGHT...?

WRONG. MUCH AS I'D LIKE THE REST, I CAN'T STOP *NOW*...

...FIRST I DELIVER THESE *PHOTOS* OF SPIDEY AND DOC OCK TO THE BUGLE'S DARLING *PUBLISHER*...

AND THEN I KEEP *SEARCHING* FOR *AUNT MAY!*

DAILY BUGLE

...DID THE BEST I *COULD*, MR. JAMESON...THE OTHERS CAME OUT *OVER-EXPOSED*.

I DON'T PAY YOU FOR *MIGHT-BE'S*, PARKER.

IF ALL YOU CAN GIVE ME ARE SHOTS OF THAT CONCEITED WALL-CRAWLER BATTLING A TRIO OF *PUNKS*--

WAITASECOND--

SPIDEY BATTLING *DOC OCK*-- THAT'S MORE *LIKE* IT, PARKER!

WITH ANY *LUCK*-- MAYBE WE'VE SEEN THE *LAST* OF THAT COSTUMED *MENACE!*

THE *LAST*...?

WHAT'S *WRONG* WITH YOU, PARKER? DON'T YOU READ THE *EARLY EDITIONS*?

ROBERTSON'S *KID* FOUND THIS LATE LAST NIGHT--

--AND UNLESS THESE THINGS ARE MAKING MARKED WITH *BLOOD*--

--THAT, M'BOY, IS THE *REAL McCOY!*

MY *MASK*--! OH, NO... *NO!*

I'D HOPED TO *RETRIEVE* IT, SOMEHOW... I HAVEN'T GOT *TIME* TO SEW ANOTHER ONE...

MAYBE IF I--

SAY, PARKER..? BETTY TOLD ME ABOUT YOUR *AUNT--*

PARKER--?

NED WANTS TO *HELP* YOU, PETER...

PLEASE LISTEN TO HIM!

NO OFFENSE MEANT, NED... BUT I'M KINDA *TIRED*...

MAYBE IF WE TALKED LATER... *TOMORROW...?*

THAT'S UP TO *YOU*, PETE--

--BUT FRANKLY, I THOUGHT YOU'D BE INTERESTED IN THIS *LEAD* I PICKED UP--

A *LEAD?*

THAT'S RIGHT, PETE! A DOMESTIC *EMPLOYMENT* AGENCY...

WHERE, LEEDS-- YOU'VE GOT TO TELL ME *WHERE--!*

TAKE IT *EASY*, PARKER.

IT'S ON THE *LOWER EAST SIDE*...

THANKS, NED... I WISH I COULD STAY, MAYBE EVEN *EXPLAIN*...

...BUT THERE'S NO *TIME*... NO TIME AT *ALL!*

WHAT'S *WITH* PARKER THESE DAYS, HONEY?

I DON'T *KNOW*, NED...

...PETER'S *ALWAYS* BEEN HIGH-STRUNG, EVER SINCE *HIGH-SCHOOL*...

SOMETIMES... I *WORRY* FOR HIM.

SOMETIMES... HE SEEMS SO... SO *VULNERABLE* ...HE MAKES ME *AFRAID*.

*W*HAT WOULD BETTY LEEDS SAY, IF SHE SAW PETER PARKER NOW...? WOULD SHE *RECOGNIZE* THE BLUE AND SCARLET FORM SWING-ING HIGH OVER MANHATTAN'S MIDTOWN AREA....?

*O*R WOULD SHE TURN AWAY... AND CLOSE HER EYES TO THE LOOK OF GRIM *DETERMINATION* MARING PETER'S YOUTHFUL FEATURES...

...*D*ETERMINATION WHICH LEADS HIM TO A *DARKENED COSTUME SHOP*...

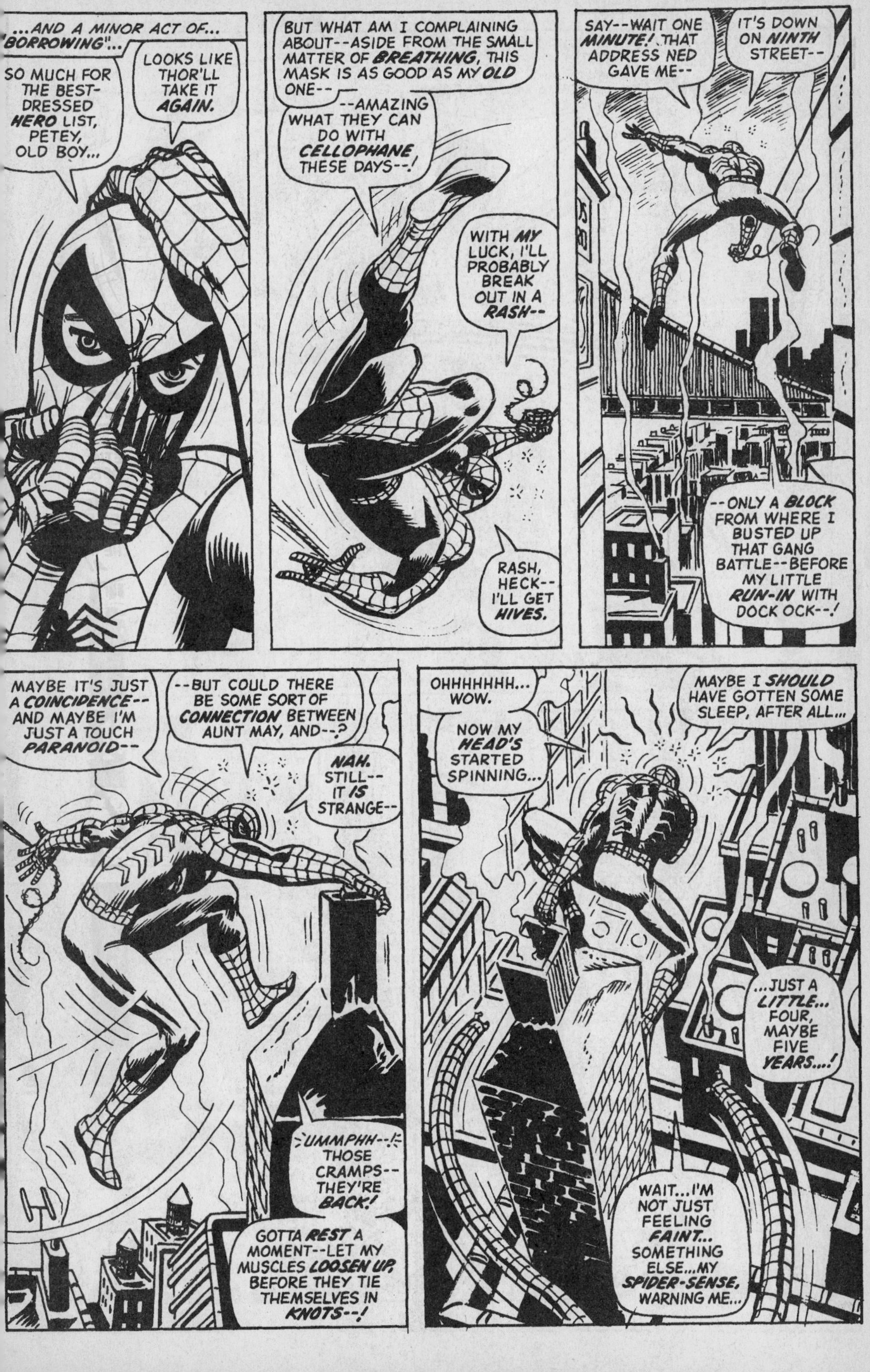
...AND A MINOR ACT OF... "BORROWING"...
SO MUCH FOR THE BEST-DRESSED HERO LIST, PETEY, OLD BOY...
LOOKS LIKE THOR'LL TAKE IT AGAIN.
BUT WHAT AM I COMPLAINING ABOUT--ASIDE FROM THE SMALL MATTER OF BREATHING, THIS MASK IS AS GOOD AS MY OLD ONE--
--AMAZING WHAT THEY CAN DO WITH CELLOPHANE THESE DAYS--!
WITH MY LUCK, I'LL PROBABLY BREAK OUT IN A RASH--
RASH, HECK--I'LL GET HIVES.
SAY--WAIT ONE MINUTE! THAT ADDRESS NED GAVE ME--
IT'S DOWN ON NINTH STREET--
--ONLY A BLOCK FROM WHERE I BUSTED UP THAT GANG BATTLE--BEFORE MY LITTLE RUN-IN WITH DOCK OCK--!
MAYBE IT'S JUST A COINCIDENCE--AND MAYBE I'M JUST A TOUCH PARANOID--
--BUT COULD THERE BE SOME SORT OF CONNECTION BETWEEN AUNT MAY, AND--?
NAH. STILL--IT IS STRANGE--
UMMPHH--! THOSE CRAMPS--THEY'RE BACK!
GOTTA REST A MOMENT--LET MY MUSCLES LOOSEN UP, BEFORE THEY TIE THEMSELVES IN KNOTS--!
OHHHHHHH... WOW.
NOW MY HEAD'S STARTED SPINNING...
MAYBE I SHOULD HAVE GOTTEN SOME SLEEP, AFTER ALL...
...JUST A LITTLE... FOUR, MAYBE FIVE YEARS...!
WAIT...I'M NOT JUST FEELING FAINT... SOMETHING ELSE...MY SPIDER-SENSE, WARNING ME...

HE DOESN'T REALIZE HOW WEAK I AM...

...EH?

THAT LAST *BLOW* OF HIS ALMOST WIPED ME *OUT*...

...SO MAYBE IT'S TIME FOR SPIDEY TO USE HIS FABLED *SENSE*...

...AND TRY FOR A BIT OF *BRAIN* OVER *BRAWN!*

GONE....? I WOULDN'T HAVE CREDITED THAT IDIOT WITH ENOUGH *INTELLIGENCE* FOR A TIMELY RETREAT...

...UNLESS...

OF *COURSE!* OUR PREVIOUS BATTLE MUST HAVE *INJURED* HIM IN SOME WAY--

SO NOW-- IT ONLY REMAINS-- *TO FINISH HIM OFF!*

YOU'VE *GOT* IT, OCKIE--

--JUST DON'T PAT YOURSELF *TOO* HARD--

I'M WEAK FROM A LATENT *ULCER*--THREE NIGHTS WITHOUT *SLEEP*--

--FROM THE TANGLE WE HAD *LAST NIGHT!*

FUNNY-- IT'S--A BIT-- *IRONIC*--

--AND MAYBE-- *ONLY MAYBE*--

--BUT *THAT* FIGHT-- IS JUST WHAT'S GONNA--HELP ME WIN *THIS* ONE--

--IF I DON'T LOSE --MY BLASTED *GRIP* FIRST!

HANG-- --IN-- --THERE-- --HERO!

YOU'RE A GREATER FOOL THAN I'D *IMAGINED*, SPIDER-MAN...

...ONLY A *TOTAL CRETIN* WOULD PLAY GAMES OF *HIDE AND SEEK*...

...ESPECIALLY IN A MATTER OF *LIFE* AND--

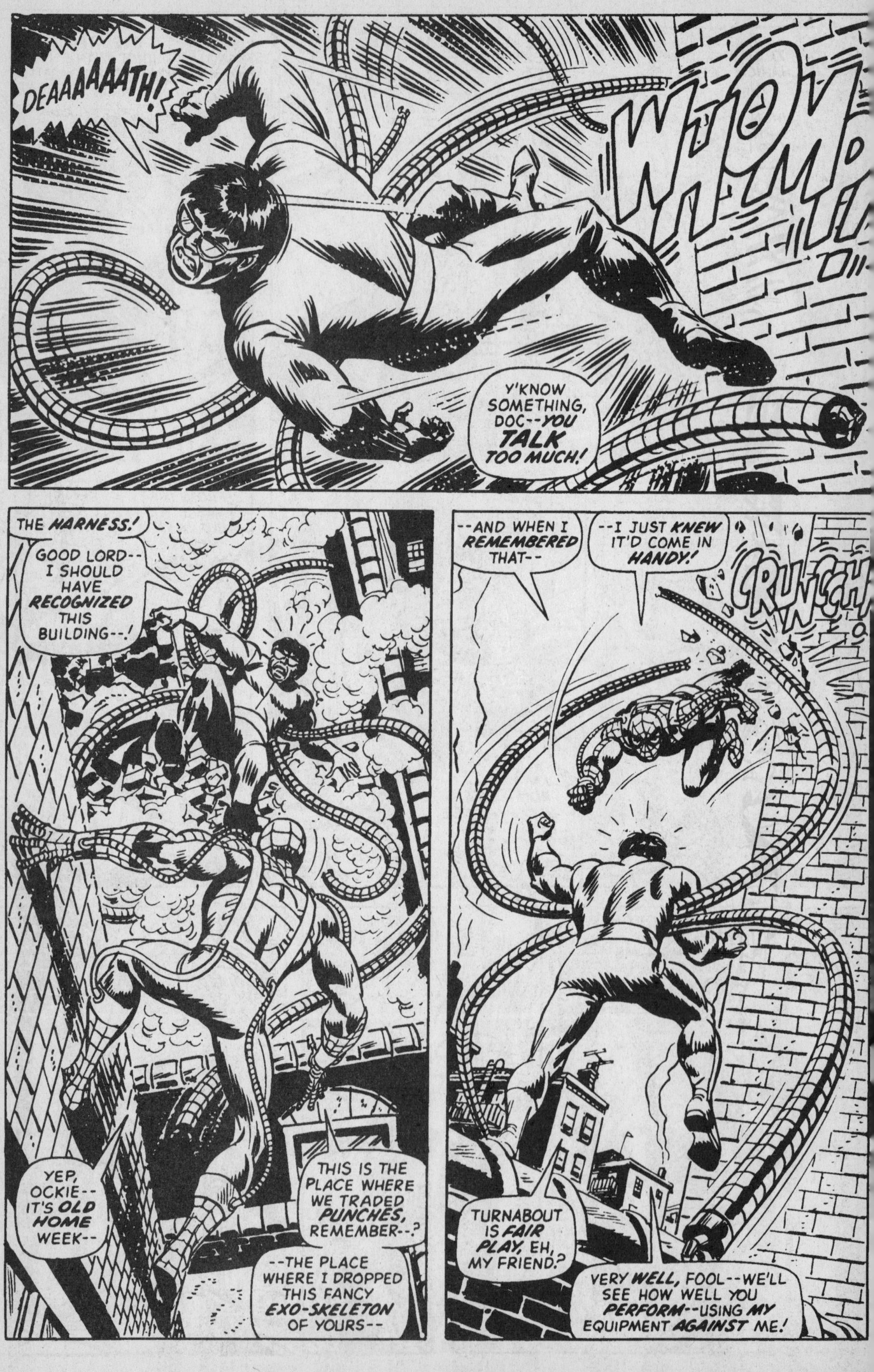
DEAAAAAATH!
WHOM
Y'KNOW SOMETHING, DOC--YOU TALK TOO MUCH!
THE HARNESS!
GOOD LORD--I SHOULD HAVE RECOGNIZED THIS BUILDING--!
YEP, OCKIE--IT'S OLD HOME WEEK--
THIS IS THE PLACE WHERE WE TRADED PUNCHES, REMEMBER--?
--THE PLACE WHERE I DROPPED THIS FANCY EXO-SKELETON OF YOURS--
--AND WHEN I REMEMBERED THAT--
--I JUST KNEW IT'D COME IN HANDY!
CRUNCCH
TURNABOUT IS FAIR PLAY, EH, MY FRIEND?
VERY WELL, FOOL--WE'LL SEE HOW WELL YOU PERFORM--USING MY EQUIPMENT AGAINST ME!

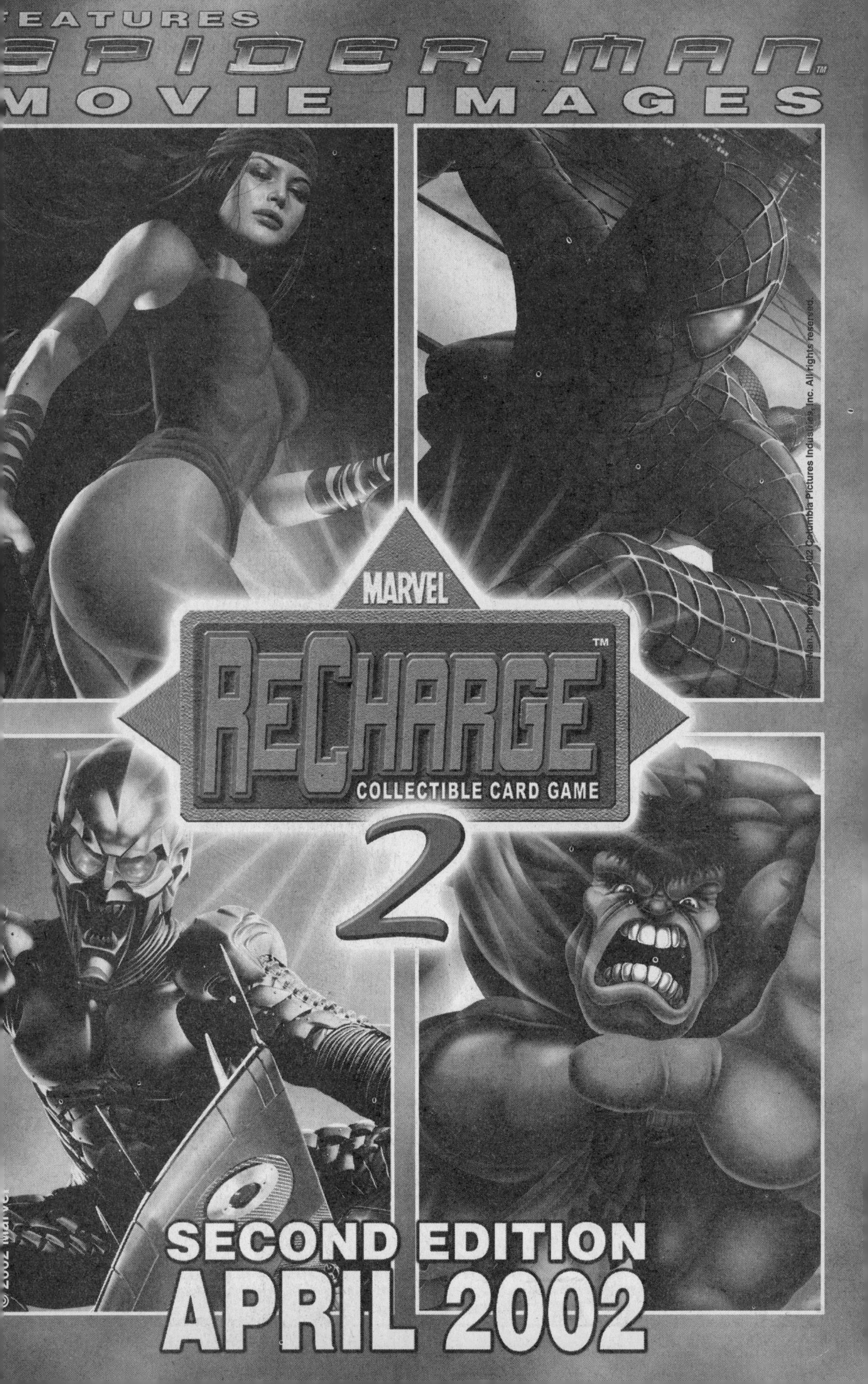

FEATURES
SPIDER-MAN™
MOVIE IMAGES
MARVEL
RECHARGE™
COLLECTIBLE CARD GAME
2
SECOND EDITION
APRIL 2002
Spider-Man, the movie: © 2002 Columbia Pictures Industries, Inc. All rights reserved.
© 2002 Marvel